T0368677

Baseball, Golf, Wars, Women & Puppies

An Autobiography
by Buck Peden

authorHOUSE®

AuthorHouse™
1663 Liberty Drive
Bloomington, IN 47403
www.authorhouse.com
Phone: 1-800-839-8640

First published by AuthorHouse 8/5/2011

ISBN: 978-1-4567-5843-1 (e)
ISBN: 978-1-4567-5844-8 (sc)

Library of Congress Control Number: 2011910519

Printed in the United States of America

This book is printed on acid-free paper.

Note:

Some of the names herein have been changed to protect the guilty.

Preface

If you're reading this preface, there's a good chance you read the beginning of the first chapter and decided it might be worth wading through the whole thing. That's the way I always selected my books. Some people, strangely enough, also go to the last page for an opinion. This first page was supposed to be a "grabber" for those whose interests in "wars" and "puppies" were aroused by the book's title, _**Baseball, Golf, Wars, Women, & Puppies**_.

I originally planned to continue with my three trips to the Vietnam and Korean Wars, including my injury and sad losses of shipmates and friends. Then, go to my childhood, parenthood, many exciting careers, etc., etc., etc. However, it didn't take too long for me to decide the categories overlap in too many places. Hence, the chronological format of a life of a "river rat" born _somewhat infamously_ in 1932 on the banks of Memphis. A few years later Elvis Presley arrived on the planet and eventually became _internationally famous_ there.

Memphis, long known as the "Home of the Blues," was to become also famous as the home of the "King of Rock 'n' Roll." My first high school, Whitehaven, is only a few blocks from Elvis' Graceland. And, my Southside High "bride" and I began training our dancing shoes to the big bands of the 40s and peaked with the rocking and twisting of the 50s and 60s.

Although only a senior-to-be in high school, the Korean War found me an early enlistee. Why? Because I was a youngster almost entering teenage during World War II. Everything was thrilling about the "big one" for a boy that age. All the toys were guns, tanks, jeeps, warplanes, etc. The war movies were always exciting and, in most cases, the hero ended up with the female star. As I was a young budding teenager, females were becoming of <u>more</u> interest in my life. I have never met any male whose sex life began earlier than mine (older girls are great teachers). Also, the U.S. Navy aircraft pilots were my idols. Landing airplanes on a sea-going vessel was my kind of challenge. I was so "hooked" that I joined the Navy to become a fighter pilot. The recruiter was surprised at how I could identify all aircraft of nations involved in WWII. I even memorized the horsepower of power plant(s), plus the cruising and maximum speed, of each airplane. My favorite was our Corsair's F4U, a gull-winged propeller fighter. It never occurred to me until this moment, recalling this tidbit, but one of these planes almost killed me.

However, the "moonlighting" (working a civilian job at night) on shore duty between these wars helped prepare me for my career highlight era in Major League Baseball. There is no doubt about it, my "leash of life" is anchored to the sportsworld. My youth was playing or inventing sports orientated things. It gave me a second glance by people in the sportswriting and sportscasting fields. This all led to sports columnist and sports editor jobs in the newspaper business. This, along with learning the print business, was not only a challenge — which I always relished — but was mucho fun. The many hours and stress involved led to more and more alcohol. Which definitely made a "honky tonk man" out of me where there is plenty of wine, women, and song. The latter threesomes were like a personal little cloud that follows me throughout most of this autobiography.

I wasn't able to attend college fulltime until I finished my 20 years in the U.S. Navy. Finishing "With Honors" gave my mother extreme pride after her total education was a small (12 total students) high school in sticks of Mississippi. I had almost completed my Masters Degree and CA Lifetime Teachers Credential when I got into Major League Baseball and went to Chicago.

It has all this covered, along with many of my photographs — including those of Chicago White

Sox and Cubs personnel while heading public relations and/or promotions/marketing with them — and a little of my artwork. All my experience enabled me to form and head three companies: Shutterbug Fotos Co., Lance Communication, Inc., and T4U T-Shirts & Things. While achieving all my goals and enjoying my work with relish, I would be remiss if I didn't admit I regretted the time it, and the wars, took me away from my wife Carolyn and our children Bob, Debra, David, and Jeff.

Finally, Bob's knowledge of computers and its reproduction of the many photographs within this book was extremely helpful to me. I am very appreciative of the many hours he contributed in its preparation.

I hope you enjoy.

Contents

BGWW&P Times

July 1966-February 1967   *Vol. 1, No. 1*   *Subic Bay, Phillipine Islands*

Author Saved From Shame
He And Top Officer Barely Make Ship's Sailing To States After Vietnam Tour

It was *w e t* . . .

There it was again.

It was definitely **wet** and on my left hand. Things were very vague, dark, and obscure as I awakening from a night of partying. But, I was concentrating more each micro-second and things were beginning to clear.

Then.............. I saw it!

A PUPPY was licking my hand!

The next few moments I spent trying to comprehend the existing situation. I remembered I was on a destroyer in the Navy and we were on deployment in the Vietnam War. But, there was no way there would be a puppy on board. Therefore, I must be ashore.

Finally, it hit me hard and fast. I was wakening from sleep and my ship, the USS PERKINS (DD 877), was scheduled to depart the U.S. Naval Station at Subic Bay, Philippine Islands, at 0600 (6 a.m.) that morning. Glancing around the room while I petted the young, brown and white puppy, things came back to me.

I had ended my final liberty at my favorite hangouts in Subic after approximately nine months operating in the war zone off Vietnam, I thought I had enough and started walking towards the nearby base gates. A glance at my watch and hearing a few rhythmic twangs of a favorite country western tune, convinced me I should have a nightcap as the base entrance was only a couple first-down markers away. Plus, the ship was moored only a short jog away. Normally, since injured in the gun battle we had with the North Vietnamese, I wouldn't be up to ANY kind of jog. However, at the moment, I was feeling no pain in my knee or any other place.

The joint was almost empty as liberty for enlisted men expired in about 40 minutes, but the three-piece band was still playing for the few dancers. Music and the nightcap were enough for me.

"Hey, chief," came a voice

from a small dark table in the back of the room. I squinted to confirm my identification. "Come on, join me," he continued as he pulled out a chair at his empty table.

As I had guessed, it was Lieutenant Commander Michael Smith. He was an important officer on the PERKINS, but I must plead the fifth on his position and other identifying facts. I explained before I started this little literary jewel that I don't want to give any hit men a job or a divorce lawyer a suit.

"I'll buy you a drink, chief. What'll you have?" he asked as a Filipino waiter approached.

"Thanks commander. I'll take a Chivas on the rocks with a dash of water," I said putting my white chief's hat on an empty chair. He looked cool in his flowered short sleeve civilian shirt and light blue short pants.

We were joined by his girl friend, who had chosen "Trudy" as her American moniker while working at the bar. She had a nice smile and, surprisingly for a Filipino, had breasts comparable to American female her age which I estimated about 30. All-in-all, she ranked among sailor ratings as "a good looker."

Although I was having a good time with the jokes and small talk, I drank quickly as I knew my liberty was up at midnight.

"Trudy, commander," I said sliding my empty glass toward the center of the table as I stood. "I enjoyed the drink and the company, but I gotta git. 'Tis almost midnight."

"Chief, what ship are you on?" Smith asked roughly.

I smiled and knew what was coming. Finally, I answered to go along with his little game for Trudy's benefit.

"Your ship, the PERKINS, sir," I answered.

"Then your liberty is hereby extended 'cause it's your turn to buy," he jested with a salute towards me with his drink, which he emptied immediately. I laughed heartily as I motioned for the waiter and dropped my party anchor once again. We had one more round and then left the closing joint. Trudy played hostess after that at her small house nearby. She poured us a drink, but I was more interested in her little six-month old puppy.

I had always been extremely fond of dogs. I've had so many puppies in my lifetime that I can't remember when I got my first one. It was if I had been born with one. And, the pups always were fond of me

for some reason. I guess it was the way I tussled them around when they were in a lively mood and softy massaged their little backs and necks, or scratched their bellies, when they were ready to relax.

Anyway, a couple of drinks while playing with the "Little Guy" was enough for me. Trudy and the commander had just retired to her only bedroom, so I stretched out my injured leg on the couch and relaxed. The last thing I remember of that night was raising up my head far enough to slide a sofa pillow under it. In fact, I don't even remember feeling the pillow. Evidently, I streaked into slumberland before I felt the scotch-saturated noggin touch.

The Rude Arousal By The "Little Guy"

Believe me, "scotch-saturated noggins" do not dream either. The next feeling I <u>felt</u> was wet. The next thing I <u>saw</u> was the puppy and its grinning eyes (yes, puppies can grin with their eyes, believe me and all the other puppy lovers). A zillion questionable thoughts might have gone by as I panned the room, but I couldn't deduce anything until I saw the clock on the television. It read three minutes after five o'clock. **The PERKINS would be departing for the United States in 57 minutes.**

I almost tripped over the "Little Guy," as I stumbled toward the bedroom.

" C O M M A N D E R ! COMMANDER!" I hollered as I shook him. "It's almost zero six hundred!"

I never saw a human being awake with such vigor as he did. From a lifeless form in deep, alcohol-influenced slumber, he was wide awake in an instant. Barely balancing his glasses on his nose, he pulled on his pants, without any skivvies, with one hand while grabbing his shirt and socks with the other. I grabbed his shoes and a sock, along with my hat, as he handed Trudy some bills from the billfold she had picked up for him off the floor. I was waving toward the taxis driving by as we exited onto the street.

We were too busy completing our dressing in the cab to talk. Finally, I broke the silence.

"I think you forgot to kiss her goodbye, commander."

"Shut up, Peden," he said staring at me with his jutting jaw.

Then, as the cab pulled in front of the ship's brow with about 10 minutes to spare, his expression — after seeing the gangplank was still extended to the pier — changed briefly to a small smile.

"She wouldn't have enjoyed it even if I had the time. I had a sock in my mouth until we got in the cab."

I followed close behind LCDR Smith and 'twas a wonderful feeling giving the national ensign on the stern, and the PERKINS' officer of the deck on the quarterdeck,

Marine Co. Photo
USS PERKINS (DD-877)

my final boarding salute in foreign waters that trip.

I had already made about 50 ship sailings and would make about 26 more before I retired. The pup had ensured I would make them all on time protecting my spotless 20-year military conduct record. Then, a few steps off the quarterdeck, I turned toward Subic and gave one more salute.

"That's for you Little Guy," I said aloud and with heartfelt sincerity.

A few more feet forward on the port side, about amidships, I entered my work space, the ship's office.

"Chief, we were worried about you," Jim Wynn, a seaman personnelman striker, said. "What happened to you."

"Commander Smith and I were on a secret Naval Intelligence assignment and it took all night," I lied trying to keep a straight face. They smiled knowingly.

"Did the sailing list get put ashore?" I was all business now. It was my responsibility to ensure this list of everyone on board when the ship put to sea.

Normally, ship's call a muster on the quarterdeck. Division chiefs, or senior petty officers, call the roll and report the results to their respective division officer. The division officers report same to the executive officer.

At abnormal departure times, the muster is not called. Instead, the division chiefs/senior POs make a physical check of the bunks instead of the roll call. The rest of the procedure is the same.

If anyone is not aboard, they are recorded in the ship's log and listed on the ship's personnel diary, which my office prepares and delivers to the officer of the deck at the brow. Immediately prior to removal of the gangplank, when moored at a pier, the

sailing list is turned over to port officials. Anchored in the bay, port officials receive it by the last boat going ashore.

Any shipmember missing the sailing of his ship is subject to disciplinary action. As many individuals have duties vital to a ship operating successfully, missing its sailing is usually a court-martial offense.

"I finished it, but haven't taken it to the exec[1] to sign yet," Wynn said picking it up off the desk. "I didn't know what to do about it with you gone."

No shipmate had missed sailing since I assigned him the diary duty. He had no reason to have that knowledge.

The phone interrupted my thoughts.

"Ship's Office, Chief Peden," I answered noticing my throat was beginning to dry from all the excitement.

"Well,...welcome aboard, chief" was the mild salutation of the PERKINS' Executive Officer, Lieutenant Commander John Johnston. The tone of his voice with that greeting told me he was not angry. Apparently he was aware of why I was late getting aboard.

"Where's the sailing list?" he continued with sterness this time.

"It's finished," I answered shooing Wynn out the door. "In fact, Wynn's on his way with it.

He should be there any second, sir."

---

1   Short for executive officer.

"Very well," the exec said hanging up.

Finally, the sailing list was ashore and the last line released for the Subic Bay mooring.

We were underway.

"California Here We Come"...Second Verse

It seemed like forever until we finally felt the PERKINS quiver slightly as the engines bumped up its speed to a higher knotage. The 21-year-old vessel cut through the morning Philippine Sea as smooth as the l945 day she was launched.

This increase in speed told us we were in **full speed ahead.** As all the "old salts" were expecting, the ship's captain — Commander William A. Teasley — had the quartermaster play an instrumental arrangement of *"California Here We Come."* Naturally, her crew provided the words ("...right back where we started from..." etc.).

It was second time I had sung it. The first was in l953 returning from a deployment in the Korean War on board the USS ORISKANY (CVA-34). The third and, last time as a militaryman, would come in 1968 aboard the USS IWO JIMA (LPH-2).

With World War II included, the joyful song has cheered millions of Americans headed back to their homes and loved ones.

It always switched my mode to a reminiscent one. The site I invariably chose was one of the gun tubs which hang over the side of the ship. They were usually vacant under normal operating conditions. Of course, on the destroyer there were no gun "tubs," so I would sit upon the depth charges on the fantail while watching the wake form.

This PERKINS, DD 877, was the third U.S. Naval warship to form wakes under that name. She was originally commissioned as a DDR when launched on December 7, 1945. Participating in the final stages of WW II, she was present in Tokyo Bay when the formal surrender document was signed.

During the Korean War in 1951, she received a hit from shore batteries which riddled her superstructure, killing one man and injuring l7 others. It was one of several times the PERKINS sustained shore battery shelling, but in each engagement the enemy was silenced. In one month alone, PERKINS' gunners fired 9,000 rounds at the enemy. Three battle stars were earned.

A FRAM II overhaul in l962, she underwent a change in configuration from a DDR to a DD. Two WestPac cruises followed with the last one part of the newly formed "Yankee Team" in the Gulf of Tonkin during the Vietnam War. She performed anti-submarine warfare screening and pilot rescue duties for my ole Korean War craft, the USS ORISKANY (CVA 34), and carriers USS MIDWAY (CVA 41) and USS BONHOMME RICHARD (CVA 31).

I recalled my first meeting with the PERKINS' executive officer after reporting aboard for duty in June 1966. LCDR Johnston, was a grad of the U.S. Naval Academy, class of '53. His office was small. A standard metal desk, his chair, a visitor's chair, a file cabinet, and a few books shelves were its ingredients. To say your elbows bumped both sides of its bulkheads was an exaggeration, but not much. However, it was the administrative heart of the ship. He had reported on board as XO and Navigator with four previous ships and several major shore administrative assignments on his personal navy log. He knew he was going to be busy.

Cruise Book Photo
LCDR Johnston

"Our personnel allotment rated us with a chief yeoman. Instead, we were provided by the powers that be with a first class," he frowned with a knotted brow, which I would learn always appeared when he was dissatisfied or annoyed.

"So," he continued, "I kept bugging them until I got you."

I had a tour of sea duty aboard the ORISKANY during my first hitch, but it was as a member of a fighter squadron. The squadron was a member of the air group on board for a specific deployment and not part of the ship's company.

"I've been in over 15 years, Commander. But, most of it has been in the TAR (Training and Administration of Reserves) Program. I'm afraid I'm going to be a little rusty in regular navy procedure for awhile," I told him hoping he wouldn't detect the worry I was harboring.

Actually, the past 12 years had been shore duty during which I maintained an exciting separate career in journalism while moonlighting. Major U.S. Navy publications, personnel service records, regulations, etc., issued by SECNAV[2], BUPERS[3], and JAG[4] were the same. However, COMSERVPAC[5], COMSEVENTHFLT[6], 11ND[7], etc. publications and instructions were all unknown to me.

---

2   Secretary of the Navy
3   Bureau of Naval Personnel
4   Judge Advocate General
5   Commander, Service Forces Pacific Fleet
6   Commander, Seventh Fleet
7   ELEVENTH Naval District

"I will shape up soon, sir. Your patience will not be wasted," I promised with sincerity.

His response was quick.

"I have no doubt about that. You've been instructing reservists in the Navy's latest forms and publications utilized by the regulars, so that stuff will all come easily to you," he said.

"Plus — with the executive officer having to do the administrative and personnel officer duties on destroyers — believe me, a hard-hat enlisted man is a big asset."

Then he hesitated a moment, and started smiling as he said, "Also, I found out quite a bit about you personally. You should have smooth sailing making the transition."

To this day, I never learned what the "quite a bit" was that he had found.

The rest of the day I met with each one of the yeomen, personnelmen, or respective strikers thereof. Two Californians: Richard Brobst of Imperial Beach, a first class yeoman; and D.M. Throp, a third class, were the only petty officers in the crew. The three seaman strikers were Michael Clement of Des Moines, Iowa; D.V. Jones of Santa Monica, California; and Jim Wynn of Vidalia, Georgia.

Brobst and Thorp were both transferred later so I spent most of my time aboard the PERKINS with those three seaman and another addition later named Pertuka. "Perk,"

as I called him, wasn't in the PERKINS' 1966-67 cruise book , Odyssey.

Since the Odyssey came up, it should be injected that is was well enjoyed by the crew members. It not only had the posed, head photographs and short career blurb of the ship's crew (Pertuka and a few others excepted), but was full of candids of personnel performing their duties, and having fun while on liberty in Hawaii, Japan, Taiwan, and the Philippine Islands as well.

The editor was not listed, but I think he was good and bad to your author. He didn't have a single shot of me on liberty (that's good), but he left me out of the toiling candids as well (that's bad). Then, when posting the ship's mug shots for each division, he switched mine. He had my smiling face opposite Chief Radioman Norm Christman's career synopsis. It didn't bother me, but I felt sorry for Norm and his San Diego family.

Despite not locating the commanding officers during the deployment — Commander William A. Teasley (May 1966-January 1967), CDR Frank P. Wells (January-completion February 1967) — and X0 until page 30 and an upside down map on the inside back cover, the editor did a fairly good job. The cartoons were entertaining, whoever drew them, and the comments under a movie starlet's visit were cool.

Jennifer Jones Pays Morale-Boosting Visit

Phyllis Flora Isley was her given name when she was born in 1919 at Tulsa, Oklahoma. She might have enjoyed the swinging ride in a basket seat over a high line from a freighter to a destroyer while underway in the South China Sea at that age. But, as a 47-year-old, Jennifer Jones didn't appear to be very pleased with it. Her cheerful smile gave the illusion she was, but her eyes showed the apprehension she must have been experiencing with wakes of the two vessels clashing beneath her dangling body chair.

Cruise Book Photo

JENNIFER JONES with her escort Chief Frank Redman while visiting aboard the PERKINS.

—————

When I got to meet her in the chiefs quarters, I was tempted to ask her if the organizers of her goodwill trip to visit the troops in Vietnam had pre-informed her of the ship to ship transfer she would experience. But I didn't. I did ask her, since she was from Tulsa, if she knew Donald Mountain. He was a steaming mate in my first hitch.

She didn't take very long in answering, but in that slight delay I had time to wonder how she looked so much younger than she was. Since then, I have learned a lot about women's makeup magic.

"No, I'm afraid I don't," she said and now I had another item to tell my grandchildren. I think I'll phrase it: "Yeah, kid. I got real close to Jennifer Jones (well, it was about 20 inches and that's close). I asked her a mind searching question, as a matter of fact. But, of course, she softly said no (well, she always spoke softly, in my opinion)."

Seriously, this trip she made was a super morale booster for our little ship. One trip to the line kept us at sea 43 straight days. Even though the 220 men aboard had plenty of camaraderie, almost a month-and-a-half without seeing a woman is tough. One will understand why I felt that way a lot better as one progresses through this book.

Hope Unparalleled; All Were Appreciated

Anyway, not enough can be written how much servicemen appreciated these celebrities taking time out of their busy schedules to entertain or visit in war zones. The late Bob Hope was unparalleled in these much-appreciated trips. Although I never got the opportunity to see one of his wartime shows, I read and saw enough on television to highly respect the comedian for his obvious warmth for his fellow man.

I finally got to meet Hope and it was an emotional event for me. However, that story and the exciting meeting of one of my ships by Debbie Reynolds are down the line when we (you and I) shift the gears of this non-fiction thing into chronological order.

Back to Jennifer's visit, my golfing opponent Frank Redman was the chief petty officer they chose to escort her around the ship. Why they went down into the bottom of the ship and picked a senior chief boiler technician, I'll never know. These guys operated and repaired all types of marine boilers and fire room machinery below decks. They seldom got above the main deck, so how could they escort someone around ship. Plus, the sun would probably blind them if they got out of the superstructure. Just kidding, of course, and all the fellow chiefs did plenty of that afterwards in our quarters.

Taiwan Golf For DD-877 Foursome

Naturally, the *Odyssey* editor had him in several of the pictures with Jennifer. I harbored this jealousy of Frank for months. Finally, we had a liberty in Kaohsiung, Taiwan. Frank, with the captain as his partner, and I, with the exec as mine, played a round of golf during our short rest and relaxation (R&R) visit there.

It was a nice, regulation-sized course with plenty of hills, forests and other vegetation. I had a five dollar bet on the side with Redman. He was a good golfer and carried Captain Teasley most of the way as we were playing the team match play game of best ball of the team wins the hole.

He knew I was unhappy being overlooked as an escort for Jennifer, thus we razzed each other throughout the game. I had more experience playing the game, thus the XO and I were two holes ahead after winning the 17th with a lousy bogey. Therefore, their team had lost the original bet as there was only one hole left to play.

"I press[8] your ass, Peden," Redman said stepping up on the raised tee mound beside me.

"Jennifer would advise you against that, Frank," I ribbed and started washing my ball. Then, continued:

"I accept and since it's really a new bet starting, we'll give you and the captain honors. Is that alright with you, commander?"

The two officers were enjoying the playful bickering between the two of us.

8   Play for double or nothing.

"Sure. Tee 'em up cap'n," Johnston said smiling.

Our CO smiled, too. But, while he had no bet on the side with his XO, he looked serious when he guided the ball a good 230 yards down the middle of the fairway. Redman followed with a 250-yarder, also in the fairway.

They were in excellent position on the par five, listed at 510 yards. While the fairway was long and downhill, it was flanked on both sides with weeds 2-3 feet high in the rough. On the left side, there were three water buffaloes chewing their cuds.

Lucky Bank Shot Provides Satisfaction

Unfortunately, my partner sliced a badly hit shot into the right rough. This really put the pressure on me as I wanted to win that press bet and definitely didn't want Redman to get even for the match. So, I had serious intentions of drilling one past Redman. I crunched it, but got too much right hand in it. I knew I had hit it well, but it was hooking toward the rough. Still on a straight trajectory, the ball hit the massive head of horns on a buffalo at a glancing angle and streaked back down unto the fairway. With topspin already on the sphere from the clubhead, the carom added even more sending my golf ball approximately 360 yards down the middle of the fairway.

The buffalo? It didn't blink an eye or miss a chomp on the cud.

To shorten this tale of truth, I had only a seven iron to the green. I stuck the ball two feet from the hole and tapped in an easy victory on the hole. As I reached down to pull the eagle putt out of the cup, I couldn't resist saying:

"Thanks, Jonesy," kissing ball while looking at Redman. Then holding the ball high toward the water buffalo, added, "And you too, Ferdinand."

Redman playfully threw his putter at me and said, "You lucky stiff!"

Naturally, I got much satisfaction out of the double triumph. However, as the tradition goes, "Winner buys the drinks," I sprung for a couple or rounds. Then, as sober protocol would have it, we went to our favorite Kaoshiung dives and the CO and exec went to theirs. That's when Redman and I really got into what R&R is all about to sailors after a month or so on the line.

An Unhappy Ending After Fun Night Out

On another night at the bars there, some other chiefs and I were coming back on the liberty boat (we had to anchor in the bay) slightly intoxicated. I noticed Chief Elmer Hanson's face was twisted in agony while everyone else was laughing and joking around.

"What's the matter, chief?" I

asked. "You look like you're in pain."

"It's my goddamn ulcers. They're bleeding again," he grimmaced.

He was a machinist mate and had made 12 deployments to the Korean and Vietnam Wars during his 20 years. He was scheduled to transfer to the U.S. Fleet Reserve on our return to the states in February 1967.

"Man you shouldn't be drinking that hard stuff with bleeding ulcers. That can kill you," I said.

Now I knew why the likeable guy was so skinny. I had noticed he was a picky eater at the mess table.

"I'll make it," he reasoned as he took another swig of the half pint of whisky he had. "I'll drink some milk when I get aboard. That always eases it."

"Buck's right," my pal Lint Moeller interjected. "He had a bout or two with ulcers."

Mine were chronic doudenal ulcers and had me highlined to the USS CORAL SEA (CVA-43) for a few weeks treatment. Later, the late summer after we returned to the U.S., an esophageal hiatal hernia and the ulcer problem would be corrected. But, it was not bleeding ulcers like Hanson said he had.

Both Lint, a chief petty officer and also master-at-arms of the ship, and I kept a close check on Hanson. As, of course, did Jim Jones, a senior chief sonar technician and top

ranking enlisted man on the PERKINS.

Marine Co. Photo
USS CORAL SEA (CVA-43)

Despite our worry, Hanson performed his duties without mishap. He was still drinking his milk when we said farewell as he left for the separation activity to be processed for the Fleet Reserve. Whether he he made it back to his hometown at Grand Junction, Colo., we never learned. As some sailors do, he never wrote back.

"They (medical officials at the separation facility) probably got him fixed up before they let him out," Moeller said one day when Hanson's name came up in the chiefs quarters.

Nodding, I noted again how Moeller always liked things proper, smooth, and without complications. I had initially learned it on one of the first liberties we made together. It was in Yokosuka, Japan, as we stopped for supplies, etc., enroute to Vietnam.

"Where you wanna go, Gunner[9]?" I asked him as we

walked down the pier towards the naval base gate. I had been to Yokosuka before, but it was over a decade ago. He had been over many times mostly aboard amphibs and destroyers.

"I'm gonna see my gal, June." he smiled. "She's special. Come with me and meet her."

Eureka! A ★ ★ ★ ★ "Old Salt" Technique

I did and was a little surprised at his technique. She met us just outside the gate with a taxi, so I figured this wiry bachelor must have written her we were coming. After the preliminary kissing and hugging, he introduced me. Then, inside the cab, he pulls out his billfold and gutted it. We had just received

9   Common nickname for the Gunner's Mate rating.

a month's pay in military script and I knew he had drawn it all. I had left some on the books, but he must have had a wad totaling over $700. With a big smile, and a little twinkle in her eyes, she opened her purse and he stuffed it inside.

"Shut your mouth, Buck. There are flies in Japan too you know," he said chuckling. Apparently I had dropped my jaw, while staring at the happening, leaving my mouth open.

Now, I was well aware that sailors had favorite prostitutes in different ports around the world. After all, the age-old cliché (i.e. "a sailor has a girl in every port") must be maintained. And, of course, swabbies are usually these gals' favorite customers due to the generosity of "old salts" like Moeller.

But, a month's pay? Surely, he was just giving it to her to keep for him in case — as has known to happen more than once in a seagoing man's port visit — he got drunk.

"Now I can fucking relax and enjoy myself," he sighed smiling. "Junesan'll take care of me."

(Note: Japanese add "san," pronounced "saun," to all first names.)

I wasn't sold on his method of operation at first, but when we left port I gave it a four-star rating. She paid all the cab fees, bought all the groceries, booze, and beer. When we went to a night club, she paid the bar tab and tipped everyone who

deserved it. Our purchases of anything were always at the native prices. As usual in most countries, the occupying military personnel are charged a higher rate for most items purchased from nightclubs, bars, or individuals on the street.

If a foreign military man entered a local bar, a quart of Japanese beer would cost him 200 yen. However, a Japanese patron would only have to cough up 100 yen for the same beverage. Although not relative, the U.S. dollar exchanged for 360 yen in those days. Therefore, June saved us plenty of loot while we were there.

I paid my share of the tabs when we were out cruising the hot spots, and we certainly did a lot of cruising. I particularly enjoyed the joints that had dancing. She was very fond of the American style of dancing and was adept in waltzing, two-step, jitterbug, twisting, and could even do the cha-cha. Moeller would slow dance, but he didn't appear to like the fast stuff. When she'd ask him to dance to one, he'd shuffle her off to me when we hit our first night club of the evening.

"That machine gun stuff is not my caliber," Gunner would say. "Dance with the ole pencil pusher[10] here (thumbing towards me)."

I was usually obliging. Therefore, the first hour or so June and I danced to most

10 Common nickname for the Yeoman rating.

of the top U.S. songs played. She was a pretty gal and fit my short frame of 5' 7", 158 pounds, with her 5-2 /110 very nicely for the slow ones. She picked up my strange style of "glide/stop/sway-in-place/glide" at once.

The two of us would definitely be enjoying ourselves on the dance floor when Moeller's alcoholic gauge would reach his *"You Are High"* mark. That's when he'd decide to get into action to those great fast songs of the era ("What'd I Say," "Scenic Cruise," "Rockin' Robin," etc.). He had a strange routine with his feet, but he kept good time with the beat of those classics. June obviously loved it. She always displayed a cute smile when she jitterbugged with me, but with Moeller it broadened considerably. Although we obviously were exhausting the 30-year-old chick, she never refused an invitation to dance. Without a doubt, she enjoyed our many cabaret nights with much delight.

The morning after, of course, was quite a chore for us all. But, she not only woke us with her pleasant smile, she had Bloody Mary drinks in her hands.

"Reveille! Reveille, sailors!" she chirped.

"Damn Lint," I mumbled accepting with relish the liquid known for many years to quell my hangovers. "What part of heaven did you find this angel of mercy?"

"Between two fluffy clouds," he growled and took a long

drink of the BM before continuing.

"That's the reason she's so good between two sheets," he said smiling as he patted her buttocks clearly visible through her thin nightgown.

"Lintsan, be nice," she reprimanded with a fake pouting expression while handing me a kimono similar to Moeller's.

Then we sat down around her sunken hibachi pot to get warm. The hibachi was at the end of the living room near her small sunken kitchen. The whole living/dining room was only about 10 feet wide and 18 feet long. Its door at the end opposite the kitchen was the hut's only entrance/exit.

There was a 4x5-foot toilet behind a curtain off the kitchen end of the living room. A hole in the floor, surrounded by a plastic trim and bamboo mats, was for everything. There was a disposable bag underneath to catch the body waste. Waste collectors picked up the bag every few days.

Males had learn to urinate while squatting over the hole to ensure the mats are not soiled. No running water was available, only a pitcher of water and six-inch tissue paper squares for wiping. If one desired soap, it was available for use in the kitchen.

Actually, June's toilet was very clean and the refresher sprayed eliminated any bad odors. The only problem men would have was the embarrassing sound of a fart,

usually emitted when they strain to urinate and almost always when dumping a load. Curtains, per se, are not sound proof.

The only other compartment in the hut (as I called it) was the only bedroom. It was separated from the living room with sliding partitions. June had a chifforobe in one end of the room with a miniature dresser in the corner beside it. Her bed was thick pads of quilting laid on the floor mats.

There was a linen closet at the other end of the bedroom and one in the front corner of the living room next to the front door (only entrance) for coats. All other off-season and inactive items (such as the portable tub for bathing, clothes washing, etc.) were stored overhand on her bamboo rafters.

I never took the time to examine the walls and the roof, but I always had the feeling a big wind would blow her complete estate into the next block. I experienced this feeling every night when I undressed to retire in my skivvies[11].

All Occasion Table Is Center Of Attention

Near the hibachi end of the room was a 12-inch high, four-legged table. Its 2x3-foot top had a colorfully designed ceramic covering of a wooden bridge spanning a

11   Navy nickname for undershirt & shorts.

small stream. Fully blossomed cherry trees bordered both sides of the water.

We had to sit on the matted floor with our legs crossed to eat, play cards, write, etc. at the table of multiple usage. I would learn later that this was the last time I would be able to cross my legs.

While meals were probably the most popular occasions to use the table, card playing was the most frequent. Poker with matchsticks as chips was known by all three of us, therefore, if was the most dealt.

I taught them how to play cut-throat hearts, which was probably the most fun. Mainly because we would be drinking as we played and June's cute little squeal when someone gave her the "*old maid*" (queen of spades) would roll us over laughing. A card of the hearts suit would count only one point against a player, but the spade queen, "*bitch*" as we also called her in the Navy, counted 13 big points. However, if a player captured all 13 of the hearts AND the bitch, he would record zero points against himself and all his opponents would sustain 26 points. The lowest scorer, when any player reaches 100, wins the game. It's best played with four players and, along with gin rummy, became my two favorite card games.

I even taught June how to play gin rummy during my visits with them. It all started when I had her buy some gin alcohol, dry vermouth, olives, and cocktail onions. I usually drank manhattans before dinner, but occasionally I would crave a martini. June had trouble finding the onions and was curious how the drink tasted. I always prided myself in the way I mixed my martinis, so I made her one.

"Oooo, Bucksan!" she frowned at her first sip. "I don't see why you proud of this."

"Don't drink it if you don't like it. Lint'll drink it. Won't cha, Lint?"

"I ain't drinking that fancy shit," he said holding his drink up. "JD and I are doing just fine." If he drank the hard stuff, it was always Jack Daniels on the rocks or with a splash. Most of the time, both of us stuck to Asahi beer.

Anyway, she wanted to keep drinking her martini, so I started teaching her gin rummy while I was playing Moeller for penny a point. She was a quick learner and acted thrilled when Moeller would gin a hand and catch me with a big load.

"Way to go, Lintsan!" she would cheer trying to mimic the western girl while giving him a big kiss on the cheek.

It made me think of how the famous geisha girls would have handled it. They probably would have patted Miller on his hand and said, "Magnificently done, Lintsan."

"There's no doubt about it," I thought. "These prostitutes are a lot more fun to be with than those geisha gals."

June was definitely fun to be with and the more of the martini she drank the more fun she became.

"Bucksan, I apologize," she said smiling. "Da more I drink this martuni, the better it tastes. Wouldya mix Junesan another?"

"Sure," I laughed at her thickening tongue pronunciation. "But, after this next one, I think I better start keeping score."

She had a thing about wanting to keep score in every game. Apparently, she was superb in math and liked to show it. I used this quirk just before we left port to have fun and satisfy my good conscience at the same time.

I had tried several times to give them money for the meals I had eaten at her place, but they refused to accept it.

"You pay for most the bottle booze at EM (Enlisted Men's) Club, Bucksan," June explained. "I enjoy cook for you."

"Yeah," Moeller chipped in, "and you eat like a damn fish...a nibble here and a nibble there."

I had been called a lot of things — stupid, idiot, sucker, snake, city slicker, hillbilly, pussy eater, and a lot of other things — but that was the first time I had ever been compared to a "*damn fish*."

Finally, one day I was there alone with June as Moeller had a day of duty on the ship. June had gotten fairly efficient at the game and relished

every hand she won. With a streak of three straight "*no brainers,*[12]" she finally won a game and skunked me to boot. Wiggling with joy, she figured up the score, doubled because I hadn't scored a single point.

"If we (had of) played for penny point like you and Lintsan do, you owe (would have lost to) me almost ten dollars," she beamed with a big smile, wide eyes, and raised eyebrows.

Then it registered!

"Okay, Junesan. You now play gin rummy just like a professional," I said baiting the abnormal trap I was setting. "Let's play this next game for serious money...a penny a point."

She was still mentally wallowing in her glory of the whitewash moments earlier.

"You gotta bet, Bucksan," she said cheerfully. "You mixum cards and I open you beer."

I had played many thousands of games of gin rummy in my lifetime. I played it as a child, before taps in boot camp, after golf games, at my clubs (Moose, Elk, American Legion, &VFW), on trains, buses, airplanes, and in my home with family and friends. I had been called a master player by many of my friends, but I disagree with that. I can remember all the cards that are played, but occasionally my selection of maneuverability lacks the gift possessed by a true master player.

---

12 Hand dealt which requires no strategy to gin rummy.

Therefore, it was very easy — although sometimes it boggled my mind — to let June win. This way I would be able to repay my portion of all the groceries I had eaten. Plus, her companionship, cooking my meals and dancing with me was very much appreciated. And, although I was not the gold winner of her talents as a prostitute, I was enjoying much of her.

I would get just as big a kick out of her ginning as she did when I discarded the specific card that I had deduced would do it.

If I let her skunk me too often or threw her a card of the same number I had discarded earlier, she would have detected my mission immediately. Therefore, I failed to score only in a couple games, but there were numerous that I would wait until I knew she was very low and then knock. Occasionally, in executing this method, she would undercut me to sock me with a 25-point penalty. This would really excite her. A couple of times I thought she was going to have an orgasm.

"Ahah! You so smart, you dumb," she yelled one time rolling on the mat in laughter. "I smart. I no knock so I be under you."

36,000 Yen Profit in One Day's Play

We played all afternoon and after dinner. She ended up with almost 36,000 yen[13] (almost $100) which I felt was adequate room and board for the seven days spent there. We both were happily content and well satisfied with ourselves: June with her card playing and me with my devious manipulation of the hands dealt to ensure she would win a wide margin of the time. With the two of us reveling in our satisfactions, plus plenty of booze throughout the whole affair, we seemed bound for a peaceful night of slumber.

It had turned rather cold, so I really wasn't too surprised when she said, "You sleep my bed, Bucksan. We keep each other warm."

She said it "matter-of-factly" and no thoughts of "hanky-panky" entered my mind. She was Moeller's lay and it didn't matter if she screwed 50 guys a day some other time, but while she was with us she was Moeller's and Moeller's alone. That's just the way it was with us guys at the time. You didn't mess with another guy's whore and he didn't mess with yours. Physically, or sexually, that is to say. Naturally, one would playfully jest, kiss, hug, etc., but not fondle, titillate, caress, etc. One didn't think of one's wife, or anything like that, you were just a male being a gentleman with your friend's gal.

So, it was still cold as I was getting down to my skivvies

13   Currency exchange rate was 360 yen per one U.S. dollar in 1966 per one U.S. dollar in 1966.

and thinking of those warm blankets. Then, June started undressing and all of the aforementioned flashed before me. I had admired her body while she was shimmering, twisting, spinning, and otherwise manipulating her torso to the beat of the music, but I had not imagined it in the nude. Although she was turned away from me and obviously not trying to tantalize, the clothes she was removing seem to cling ever-so-much to her perfectly smooth skin before dropping to the floor. Her thin waist accentuated her firm, shapely buttocks. This was my favorite part of the female anatomy. Some men are boob worshipers and the others are butt admirers like me.

"Hell," I told myself, "I'm not doing anything wrong behind Lint's back. Maybe she's so used to doing it in front of guys, she doesn't think anything about it."

"Come on, Bucksan," she said shivering between the sheets of her floor-bed. "Get in and get me warm."

Well now, that invitation snapped me right back to reality. Despite the alcoholic anti-freeze I had ingested, I was feeling the coldness of the area although it was only about 12 feet from the hibachi pot. I crawled under the covers up next to her backside. With a small frame peaking slightly under five feet, she was able to cuddle her body in somewhat of a curled fetus position. I hugged her up against me and moments later we were comfortably warm. However, I was feeling the beginning of an erection

"Where's that Scotch," I yelped sitting up. "I can't get to sleep."

"I get it, Bucksan," June responded rolling out of bed and turning on the lamp. She was back in a flash with the quart and a glass. "You want ice?"

"No, thanks. I don't even need the glass," I answered grabbing the bottle while making sure my cover still covered my erection. I took two long swigs and set it down beside the bed.

"Let's try it again," I said laying down facing the other side. "This time you keep my back warm."

"Oaky, doaky," she agreed as she turned out the light and scooted up against my back. She gave no obvious indication that she was aware of my problems. But, I noticed she made no sexual mannerisms on me either. This time it worked, the raw Scotch finally hit me, and I slipped into slumber.

Sufferance Medal Should Be Awarded

I should have been awarded a medal of sufferance. If there isn't such a medal they should make one for people who have had to go through what I did. In fact, the more I thought of it the next morning the more I believed thus. When Lint got

there and we had breakfast, I told him so, explaining in detail what had happened. He agreed and laughed robustly, especially when I told him about the problems sustained in keeping June unaware of the erection.

Then he turned to June, who had been giggling all thru my description or our night in bed, and asked, "How come you didn't crawl on him and take the poor guy out of his misery?"

"I know he want (to have sex)," she said seriously. "His breath warm on back of my neck, but he no kiss me." Then, after a slight hesitation, looking at me she added, "I no touch him. I KNOW Bucksan. He may be thinking of wifesan."

Turning to Moeller, she concluded with a kiss on his cheek, "So I go to sleep and save myself today for Lintsan."

We all had a good laugh over the bit and I came up with the opinion that June was the *sweetest little whore* I had every met. That afternoon, enroute to a nightclub, we stopped at a beauty parlor at June's request. She came out with an envelope and a huge smile.

"Last month's pay," she said to my surprise. I had wondered why she was a brunette and had so many curls in her hair contrary to the common black and straight haired Orientals. She was a beautician. Apparently, I had misjudged her as being a prostitute. At most, she was only a part-time one but took

on the occupation full time when Moeller and other "old salts" visited.

That night, our last in Yokosuka, we had a blast. The band was great and Moeller was at his best with his one liners to keep us laughing. One of them was following a sexy slow dance in which June and I danced very close.

"You need to adjust your shorts again Buck, 'cause I think your erection is showing."

June, of course, told Moeller about beating me out of more yen yesterday than she made last month working in the beauty shop.

"Really," he said . "You must have used your marked deck to beat old Buckaroo that bad."

Except for my interpretation of his sly smile in my direction, no one would have known he was aware. I'm sure he knew what I did and the reason for it.

We laughed, danced, and drank until wee hours of the morning. Naturally, those two had a noisy farewell party of their own in the bedroom, while I turned up the volume on the record player to smother their moans of joy while I slid into slumberland. June prepared a good ole American ham and egg breakfast, then went with us to the base gate for goodbyes. The taxi drivers must have hated to transport us when she was along as she tipped at a much lower rate than we did. I was glad though as I got a good, solid farewell kiss before Moeller got his at the gate.

We started walking the few blocks to the pier where the Viet Nam bound PERKINS was moored, Moeller barbed me with another one of his jewels.

"You shoulda brushed your teeth this morning," he said with a straight face.

It caught me like a high, hard, fastball under the chin.

"Why'd you say that, Gunner?"

"'Cause I could taste your Scotch when I kissed June goodbye."

It was our last laugh in Yokosuka as we left a few hours later for the objective of the trip: to participate in another war to stop communist aggression. However, all things considered, I always remember this stop as one of my favorite fun liberties…definitely, on my top ten list, thanks to Lintsan and Junesan.

Remainder Was Task Force 77 Business

Other liberties on this tour to Nam were all in the Phillipines Islands, which had a small mountaintop CPO Club with a magnificent view of its entire Subic Bay. However, none were as much fun for me as Yokosuka.

Therefore, the conclusion of this chapter will be about operation at sea in the Gulf of Tonkin and South China Sea as part of Task Force 77. All was aboard the PERKINS except

for a couple weeks temporary duty for treatment aboard the USS CORAL SEA (CVA 43). Most of our assignments were escorting her, providing anti-sub warfare (ASW) screening and pilot rescue duties. But, sometimes we came in close and furnished gun support for our marines ashore.

One of the latter came on November 4, 1966, during "Operation Traffic Cop." For two straight days we had been steaming only a few thousand yards from the beach the North Vietnam Coast with the USS BRAINE (DD 630), another destroyer, laying shells from our 5" mounts ashore for support for U.S. Marine Corps in the area fighting the Viet Cong.

We received no return fire from the VC until the third day. It was just before noon so I was in the CPO quarters located on the second deck in the bow of the ship. General quarters (GQ) was sounded which meant I had to be at my station as captain's talker on the bridge immediately. I was bounding aft through the port (left) passageways (men going forward use the starboard ones) and up the ladders as fast as I could. Young (34) and in excellent physical condition, I made the main deck in seconds. It was wet from waves splashing over the side during the quick turns the ship was making to avoid the gunfire. The ship lurched while I was running and leaping for the steep ladder leading up to

the first superstructure deck. When my dripping shoe hit the wet medal portion of the ladder rung for which I had leaped for, it slipped off causing my knee to slam into the knife edge of another rung. It collided just below my kneecap. Needless to say, the pain was excruciating.

Individual GQ stations are all very important, especially when a ship is in combat. Mine was manning a sound-powered telephone for the captain of the vessel. Wherever he went on the bridge, I followed with my long telephone cord. On the other ends of my line were all the ship's heads of departments and all major functional points of the vessel. As the telephone operates on the vibration of one's voice on its diaphragm over a rubber-coated wire, no battery or electricity are needed. This permits intercommunications even if there is a power failure.

I literally drug my injured leg to my station and strapped the phone set in its operable position (breastplate with mouthpiece on my chest and the earphones on my head). This left my hands to keep its cord rolled up and out of bridge personnel's way.

The captain had too many major problems to notice my grimacing and limping. Believe it or not, when we moved outside of the bridge in the starboard gangway and saw the incoming fire, I virtually ignored the pain.

The guns shooting at us,

Moeller told me later, were portable 75 millimeters they had moved in during the night. They were located in the jungle brush, but we could easily spot the location. We saw a ball of flame with black smoke coming out of the brush with each round. Of course, we couldn't see the projectile, but we could hear it whistling thought the air.

The first one I saw splashed amidships about 100 yards short of us and the next soared over us about the same distance. Naturally, any hunter or military man would adjust their aim to shoot the next round in between those two marks. Therefore, when the next flash emerged, my past started racing through my mind. I had heard this happens when death is imminent, but this was the first of my several death-facing situations in which I had experienced it.

Almost Tonkin Gulf Beach Sitting Ducks

"Capt'n, I've lost steering," the helmsman yelled from inside the wheelhouse, which halted my mind's rewinding mode and brought me to the drastic situation at hand.

Apparently, one of the shells must have hit the rudder, or near enough to it, causing us to lose steering with the wheel. The helmsman would spin the wheel with no response whatsoever from the rudder. He had been zigzagging the ship, as per Captain Teasley's orders, but now the bow was slowly turning towards the beach. The rudder was turned to the right and immobile. At its present course, the PERKINS would eventually go aground in a few moments and be a sitting duck for the Viet Cong guns.

"After steering take control!" Captain Teasley commanded. "Hard left rudder!"

I repeated the orders over my phones immediately and the men at the after steering post could tell it was damn serious from the urgency in my voice. But, just to make sure, I added: "We have lost steering in the wheelhouse."

"After steering, aye. We have control," was their instant acknowledgement.

They had to manually move the rudder, but in seconds the bow started coming around. In a few moments they confirmed the position had been reached, which I immediately repeated to the CO: "Rudder hard left, sir."

"Very well. Hard right rudder!" Captain Teasley ordered, then seconds later commanded "hard left," "hard right," etc. until we snaked our way completely out of the range of the enemy's firepower. The enginemen and boilermen kept us at full speed (about 25 knots) throughout the whole episode.

The BRAINE did the same thing, with hostile fire also falling all around her. Fortunately, both vessels escaped the barrage without any damage and returned plenty of ours.

Manpower on the two ships obviously did their jobs well. Damage control restored our steering and the gunners in the second division, under young Ensign Michael Moecker (fire control computer officer) and Chief Moeller, were magnificent in their retaliation fire. The ship's office staff was busy for days afterwards submitting letters of commendation and medal

Cruise Book Photo

RETURNING FIRE — Perkins 5" guns firing back at Viet Cong.

recommendations, but all in all, it was a team effort in which everyone did their job.

Captain Setzer, commodore of our destroyer squadron who was aboard the PERKINS during the fracas, included the following in his message to our crew afterwards:

"...*The fall of the enemy's shot was too close for comfort today, but I couldn't have felt more secure and better equipped to fight back on any other ship. Your professional reaction to the entire battle situation could hardly be improved upon. CIC, radio, guns, director, phone talkers, engineering, damage control, and bridge personnel were all conspicuous in their extremely competent performance under heavy enemy fire."*

We also received a citation later from Vice Admiral John Hyland, Commander of the Seventh Fleet, which read in part:

"FOR OUTSTANDING PERFORMANCE IN ACTION OFF THE COAST OF NORTH VIETNAM… COMING UNDER HEAVY FIRE FROM ENEMY SHORE BATTERIES. THROUGHOUT THE OPERATION, PERKINS PERFORMED WITH SKILL AND AGGRESSIVENESS AND IN SUCH A MANNER AS TO INFLICT MAXIMUM DAMAGE ON ENEMY TARGETS WHILE HERSELF AVOIDING DAMAGE. HER PROFESSIONAL PERFORMANCE, RESOURCEFULNESS AND INDOMITABLE SPIRIT WERE IN LARGE PART RESPONSIBLE FOR THE SUCCESSFUL ACCOMPLISHMENT OF THE TASK UNIT'S MISSION AND IN KEEPING WITH THE HIGHEST TRADITIONS OF THE UNITED STATES NAVY."

The rest of the deployment was primarily ASW screening and pilot rescue duties. However, one night refueling in heavy seas with 45 knot winds, two crewmen of the USS PHILIPS (DD 498) that were swept overboard were successfully rescued by the PERKINS.

Much of all this reminiscing was contained in the *Odyssey*. Plus, it contained a shot of one of the shells splashing in front of the BRAINE. I don't know how the editor got that, as there are no photographers assigned to destroyers.

He ended the publication with an imitation cartoon drawing of Charles M. Schulz's *"Peanuts"* character "Snoopy" lying on his doghouse with the following summary in its balloon:

"Whew! After steaming 53,560.6 nautical miles between 28 July 1966 and 3 February 1967, using 3,652,759 gallons of fuel......not to mention 49 underway refueling, 2 vertical replenishments, 5 underway reprovisionings, 4 underway rearming…118 helo details, 119,408 cups of coffee, and 2,026 rolls of Scott's No. 510.........Home at last!…."

We got home the first week of February and they finally operated on my knee to remove the damaged bone and spurs that had formed. During the rehabilitation every morning afterwards, I was really suffering and feeling sorry for myself until a severely burned sailor arrived. He had third degree burns all over his body and had to be submerged in churning medicated water inside a huge stainless steel tub. I was told this kept scabs from forming until his skin reformed from inside. His screaming during this ritual was understandable, but it was nerve fraying on the rest of us in the rehab room. Needless to say, I no longer felt sorry for myself.

That's about it for my first trip to Vietnam. The second one started less than a year later, but it'll be properly positioned in the chronological portion of this autobiography that follows.

BGWW&P Times

January 12, 1932-36   Vol. 1, No. 2   Memphis, Tennessee

In Fort Pickering

Another "River Rat" Is Born
Third Child Lives Following Two Deaths

This was the greatest day in my life! It was Tuesday, January 12, 1932.

I was out of the basket of conceivement and my cord had been cut!

I was on my own!

I was there, but just like any other infant, I didn't remember any of it. They tell me I got my first whooping (a spank by the doctor on my fanny) and sucked my first tit. I will never know if the move to the big city, with its updated medical attention, was the reason I survived. I do know that the first two born to our parents did not.

My father, Roy Givens Peden (born 5/5/1905), married my mother, Ruby Jane Tutor (12/16/1908), on September 5, 1927. They bought some acreage from her parents, Johnny Morris and Dannie Bell (Mc Gregor) Tutor, and built a one bedroom shack across the dirt Fooshee Bend Road. It was in the sticks of Mississippi, about three miles from a bump in the road called the City of Randolph.

My grandfather owned over 250 acres, most of it flat country with a river running through the middle of it. He was a successful farmer. He was well liked and respected by his neighbors which earned him a berth as a Pontotoc County Supervisor. The family called him "Popa" and my grandmother "Maw."

My dad only finished the eighth grade in school, but my mother had a high school education of which she was very proud. They attempted to farm raising cotton, but I am told he was not made to be a farmer. Popa and his nine children helped the newly weds in their attempts at farming as they began raising their family.

They had two children Thomas David (12/16/1928) was their first born and I'm sure my Christian mother thought him to be God sent as he was born on her 20th birthday. He died 46 days later. Betty Jean (2/22/1930) was born a little more than a

year later. She lived only three months, succumbing on May 22.

Not long after her death, my parents moved to, what was to us, the BIG city of Memphis. We lived only about the length of five football fields east of the Mississippi River and about three of Tiger Woods' mighty tee shots south of the Memphis-Arkansas Bridge. The community was called Fort Pickering and anyone who lived their was called a River Rat." Reason for the nickname was because most of the adult males who lived there worked on the towboats that pushed the huge river barges to other river ports, most down to New Orleans.

So, whatever community or whatever nickname I was to have, I was born this day in the Memphis General Hospital. By the time this is printed, I probably will have passed the 77-year mark. Whether it was the more advanced medical practices that kept me alive longer than my predecessors,

History of Fort Pickering

*The Chickasaw Indians were the original human inhabitants of the area latitude 35° 8",
longitude 90°. A great river the Indians called Mississippi, which meant in their language "The
Father of Waters." History books state the first European to view the river was the Spaniard
explorer Hernando de Soto, who reportedly was searching for the "Fountain of Youth." He
supposedly observed it in 1541 from one of the four bluffs on the east side of the river's bend.
De Soto eventually died of fever while still living in the area. His body was interned in the
river to keep mistreatment of the body by hostile Indians.*

*Several forts were built by the French explorers in the area during the next century with the
Indians, Spaniards, French, and English settlers coexisting until Tennessee became a U.S.
territory in 1790 and a state in 1796. Although the land legally belonged to the Chickasaw
Indians by treaty, the Indians eventually (1818) relinquished their northern territory.*

*The largest settlement of the era was near the first lower bluff where de Soto supposedly
first sighted the Mississippi River. It was prosperous with its cotton and pulp wood trade to
northern river ports and New Orleans for external shipping. In 1798, a garrison was erected
and named Fort Pickering in honor of Colonel Timothy R. Pickering former Secretary of War
(1795) and Secretary of State (1795-1800) in the cabinet of President George Washington.
Consequently, the businesses and residences around it become known as Fort Pickering,
Tennessee.*

*The U.S. War Department established an Indian Factory at the fort in 1802 and Fort
Pickering was no longer one of the guards or the national border after the Louisiana Purchase
in 1803. In 1815, the U.S. Army pulled out of the fort leaving only the factory and adjoining
squatters.*

*A few minutes north, on the fourth bluff, was a settlement at the time referred to as the
"squabing" city of Memphis. It was only four streets wide and was separated by a forest from
the much larger Fort Pickering. Failure of the latter's railway company and other problems,
however, had businesses relocating in Memphis. As more settlers and businesses arrived in
Memphis, it finally spread. The Fort Pickering residents changed the name of their site by
incorporating as Chickasaw City in 1868, but a couple years later it was encompassed in its
entirety into the city limits of Memphis.*

*The city made the historic first bluff area, with appropriate markings of de Soto's river
sighting, into DeSoto Park. The park included two Chisca Mounds named after a Chickasaw
Indian Chief, but later renamed Jackson Mounds. The whole site was renamed Chickasaw
Heritage Park at the turn into this century.*

I'll never know. I do know there was a few things I did during my life to speed up the end of it.

I shall never forget a phrase I read in a book as a youngster that fit my upcoming lifestyle to a "T." It was something like: "I'm gonna live fast, die young, and have a good-looking corpse." I even started it in the cradle, my parents told me.

"You kicked your feet so fast that you wore your heels raw. The nurses put tape on them to keep you from making blisters," my father related.

My mother added, "It was usually when you were getting hungry."

Groceries, Hairs, And My First Pet

My father opened a community grocery store on Delaware Street at the west end of DeSoto Street. We lived in the back of the building for a year or so and then in a one bedroom house a half block north on Delaware.

Eventually, we had to move to 295 W. Desoto Street when the block on Delaware between Peden's Grocery and the U.S. Marine Hospital was cleared to become the frontage of DeSoto Park.

My mother, being the oldest child in her family, had gained plenty of experience setting, rolling, combing, brushing, and designing hair of her four younger sisters (Mossie, Berline, Eva, and Tiny Rose). Therefore, she was very accommodating to the neighborhood women with her skills. Finally, my enterprising young parents bought a large hair dryer and permanent machine on rollers, added a large dresser and mirror, and made the front of the two-bedroom rental house into a beauty shop.

Both businesses did well. My father, despite his lack of education, had a good business head on his shoulders and was extremely swift and accurate with mathematical figures. He hired Morris, my grandparents oldest son, Wayne, & John Paul Tutor, and later Mossie's husband, Fred Tankersly. Profits were so good, my dad started buying four small wooden frame houses immediately south of the 40'x 100' brick store. He used them for rental property.

Berline joined Mother in her shop and added a tremendous boost to the business. She was not only a beautiful young lady, but had a fine female figure, plus a large head of lustrous

black hair. All the Tutor women were very becoming, possessed beaming smiles, and pleasant personalities. All five of them would give the Memphis rebel boys a thrill with their appearance during their lifetime. Mossie was already becoming a nurse and Eva would join Ruby and Berline in the beauty business. They did so well that father added a beauty shop to the north side of the store for the three sisters.

Roy, Ruby, & Bobby Peden

———

Naturally, going to the grocery store anytime the maid would go was a threat. I would grab me an orange, apple, piece of candy — or whatever I desired — without any resistance from the employees. My favorite, and it got to be a ritual, was a small (six ounces, I think) bottle of chocolate milk. I would go with my dad to open the store in the morning and the Forest

Hill Dairy delivery truck would arrive shortly thereafter. The driver would always have my bottle ready before he filled dad's coolers. They took a picture one morning, but I remember it clearly, although I was only three years old.

In fact, the first thing I can remember was in May of 1935 when I was only 40 months old. It was dark, but mother was holding an infant and dad was holding a kerosene lamp for light.

"This is your new little sister," my mother said. I don't remember what I said or anything else about the happening, but I'm sure of it. I've found very few people that believe me.

I also remember my first pet at about three years of age. It was a hen that someone had given me. I kept some corn in my pocket and was taught to drop a kernel now and then for the chicken to eat. It not only followed me everywhere I walked, but I would put it on the handlebar of my tricycle and it would ride there.

I had it for months and it disappeared. We had fried chicken that night and I always suspected our maid Tilly had cooked it, but despite all my crying and accusations, my folks swore 'twas not so.

It roosted out back on a mop rack by the door at night. My father explained that a fox probably got it that night and ate it. But, he assured me, its spirit would be going to heaven and I could regain its companionship when I got there. Of course, this was provided I was a good boy and minded my parents before that glorious day occurred. I finally believed them, but just to make me forget the chicken, they bought me a turtle and a glass bowl to keep it.

When Berline and Eva learned about the happenings, they would really pump me with questions about the turtle to help mend my little broken heart.

"What did you name it?"

"Aren't you afraid it'll bite you?"

"What does it eat?"

"Do you feed it all be yourself?"

"When are you going to celebrate its first birthdate?"

Etc., etc., etc. I can recall it clearly. Their thought-provoking questions had me shyly looking down at the floor of the shop and twisting locks of customers' cut hair with my bare toes. That hair on the floor always fascinated me. Once when they were shampooing a curly haired redhead and had not yet swept up the droppings, I scooped up several hands full of the hair and stuffed it in my pocket. It looked so soft that I took it home and made a bed with it for my turtle. I sat the little green creature on its new bed and felt so good about it.

Mother and Berline came home for lunch and saw the picturesque bed of red curls, which the turtle had already scattered with his movement.

"Son," I think she admonished. "That turtle will just scatter that hair all over that bowl. You should've asked me before doing that."

I was beginning to pout when Berline came to my rescue with a one-liner that I've heard and read many times since:

Famous One-Liner For Male Species

"Awww, don't get on him, Ruby. You know 'Boys Will Be Boys'," she chimed so sweetly as she hugged me. I fell a little more deeply in love.

My goddess aunt has been gone since 1992, but for the rest of my life when I heard **"Boys Will Be Boys"** I always thought of Berline. If I use it hereafter herein (*bet I tied your tongue with that one*), and I suspect I will, then I'll abbreviate (**BWBB**).

All the neighborhood boys my age loved her. J.W. & Kenneth Gipson, Raymond Sanders, and Major Hayes were a few I remember. We would all gather and wait for her arrival each morning when the shop was still in the front room of our house. We'd duck down below the hedge separating our house from the next door neighbors when we saw her coming down the street. As she turned and walked up the sidewalk to the front door, we would pop up with a "Good morning" in fairly close unison. She would always act startled with an open mouth and wide eyes, then a heart-tingling smile.

"Oh! Ya'll scared me," or "Wow! What a surprise," or some similar greeting that was different every day. I think we knew she was cognizant we were there every day, but it was so much fun we kept it up for weeks.

One spring day, with Fort Pickering's flowers in full bloom, I saw a beautiful red rose in a neighbor's bed. I tried to break its stem, but it only bent. I had trouble bending it with its thorns, but I was determined to get it. I was afraid of even trying to sneak a knife out of the kitchen, but I had the next best thing…my teeth. I gnawed the stem in-two despite a thorn prick in my hand. Naturally, she really displayed true joy as I knew she would. I had heard her idolizing the composition of a bouquet at Mossie's wedding, particularly the red roses. After she accepted the rose, she leaned down and kissed me.

Well, needless to say, my buddies went ape. The next day everyone of them had a flower of some sort. This came to a abrupt ending immediately thereafter. A mother had spotted her youngster going out the door with some scissors and, as mothers tend to do, she peeped on the young lumberjack as he clipped his flower stem. She spread the word to the other mothers and any inspirations any one of us may have had to become horticulturists went up in smoke. The local flower beds were saved.

Berline apologized to each of the mothers as she saw them, but understandably they didn't hold it against her. I don't remember if they did, but they probably just thought **BWBB**.

My Aunt "Ber," as she was often called by family and friends, married Aubrey Hall, a Choctaw Indian, and they had two cute kids: Judy Bell (middle name after Berline's mother) and Ronald Keith. They both had the smooth attractive ruddy complexion and black hair of the Hall family.

Meanwhile, I had come to cherish our visits to see my Grandmother Dannie Bell Tutor (Maw) down on the farm. She would cook the most delicious big, soft, fluffy biscuits which I learned to relish with their fresh country butter and the great sorghum molasses Popa made from his fields of sugar cane. It was made even more tasty because I had watched them cut the cane, load it on a wagon and bring it up near the house where wood mashing wheels were located. One had a long pole attached to it with the other end attached to a mule's collar. It would be led around in a circle causing the wheel to roll against the other wheel on a stationary axel. They would put two or three canes between the two wheels and they would mash the juice out of the canes. It would be

cooked with most of the solids floating to the top.

Imagine the odor of it. This wonderful juice of these wonderful canes sending its sweet, unique smell into the fresh country air. Air that is void of automobile exhausts, second-hand tobacco smoke, factory emissions, etc. It was just plain sanctity for true flatland Mississippians.

Popa and his boys, and he had plenty of help as there were four of them (Morris, Wayne, Keister, and John Paul), would strain the molasses into gallon jugs. Tutor molasses and its delicious taste were well known in the area so he did share some with close neighbors and his Memphis off spring. However, most of it was consumed there on their 256 acres.

They would let me stuff a few of the stalks into the masher, which of course was quite a thrill for a 3.5-year-old. But my most fun was going to the barn. It was about 100 feet wide with a center thoroughfare running the 150-foot length. It was covered by a tin roof with a hay loft over the passageway and six large stalls for horses.

Popa had over thirty head of milk cows, therefore there was plenty of milking going on in the six smaller outdoor stalls. They would fill out two or three 5-gallon metal cans each morning. They would be put out on the edge of the little dirt road for the milk truck to pick up for the pasteurizing plant about 12 miles away in

Pontotoc. Looking back on it, this was an amazing amount for four (John Paul was too young) hand milkers. This was 1935, so the motorized sucking machines had been invented several decades before, but the average farmer couldn't afford them.

While they were being milked, the cow's calf was put outside the stall. This was my greatest treat at that age, riding the back of a real live animal. How exciting it was and frightening when I felt myself falling to the side.

Calf Riders Gotta Lock Those Legs

"Lock those legs, boy," Keister would yell at me. I didn't know what he meant until he straddled a wooden horse and locked his feet underneath. Once I saw that, I would tightened my legs on both sides of the calf and dig in with my heels. It worked and, with holding on to the loose skin on the top of its neck, I stayed on pretty good. It was just the first of hundreds of things I would learn from this patient and understanding uncle. He was 11 years my senior and, except of course my father, became the most influential male in my life.

Unfortunately, this advice stuck in my young head so well that, a few months later, it would be detrimental to this lad. My father had this brilliant idea of buying a bicycle to offer free delivery of groceries to customers' homes. Naturally, he also had to purchase a luggage carrier for both wheels. I remember watching him put them both on the bicycle, I didn't quite understand what it was all about. However, when he said, "Now, before I wire the bushel baskets to the luggage carriers I'm gonna take Bobby for a ride on back," I got excited. I knew what a "ride" meant.

He placed me on the back carrier, telling me to hold on to the seat and keep my feet out. We proceeded down the sidewalk south of the store and it was exhilarating. We were passing the last of my parents four rental houses and going down a slope before going over the edge of a ravine that would become my personal little jungle in later years. Suddenly, when we hit a small bump, I began feeling myself leaning to one side. Habitually, I pulled in my heels to "lock those legs." The spokes crushed my left ankle against the steel luggage carrier brace.

Naturally, it broke my ankle in three places, but — as I was just under four years old — it healed fast and without any ill effects. It was the first time I had suffered severe pain, so I remembered it well.

I particularly remember experiencing another emotion, but it was the opposite of pain. But first, I must establish the setting with the proper situation. The mood was a normal one for me at that age (i.e. happy go lucky, fun-loving, etc.). The site was under

our house on Desoto Street. It was a frame house with a front porch the entire width of its 40 feet. Its depth was about 80 feet. As virtually all the houses in the area, it was built on brick pillars about three feet high to permit access to the house plumbing. Naturally, it was a favorite place for the neighborhood kids to play. It was always dry, so a fella could make roads for his little hand cars and trucks and not worry about it getting washed away by the rain. One could even build little service stations, doll houses, cities here, and cities there. It was fun.

Then someone showed me where they had made a play house with pasteboard boxes under their house. NOW THAT WAS REAL FUN. I couldn't wait to ask my dad if I could have some boxes. He took me out back of the store by the garbage cans and told me to take my pick of all I wanted. There were over eight boxes of all sizes to pick from. The large ones were toilet paper and cereal boxes. Tilly got one of them for me and put several slightly smaller ones inside it. From that day on, I would get a box practically every time we went to the store.

In a week or so, I had one of the best "under-the-house" playhouse in the area. The word of same spread and hot summer days found a half dozen kids in the neighborhood playing house. The girls had their dolls and play dishes for their role as the mother and the boys would come in from their road runs

or marble playing and crawl in one of their favorite boxes. Most of the time we cut doors in the boxes so we could lay on the pasteboard instead of the dirt. I had seen that girl babies had different things between their legs than boys. But, I always wanted to know more as the little girls' panties would sometimes be hand-me-downs a little too large and reveal their split. **BWBB.** Then one day a new girl moved into the neighborhood and I learned a *bunch* about all that stuff. I call it: **"My Enlightenment."**

That's What It's Called & Here's Where It Goes

Her name was Lori and she was a pretty little lass. She was several years my senior. On second thought, I guess the best way to succinctly describe her would be as a six-year-old "nymphet."

After she had introduced herself, asked my name, and seen my playhouse, she said, "I'll be right back, Bobby, and we'll play house together."

She returned, not only with her doll and a box of dishes, but with an opened bottle of cola. Then gave me my first of many surprises that day. Turning to the two or three other kids there, she said sweetly, "Ya'll will have to go now. Bobby and I are gonna play mommy and daddy by ourselves."

From there, as they were leaving, she started her charade of being the mommy. She was like a director or a bossy wife.

"This is Bonny, our kid. She'll

sit here in her highchair (make believe, of course) at the table and you sit there at the head of the table," she instructed as she began taking the dishes out of her shoe box. They were small colorful tin plates along with a little cup and plastic eating instruments which she placed quite properly and poured some cola into the cups.

After we faked cutting up and eating our meat, "It's roast beef tonight, Honey," we drank our cola and made up table talk imitating things we had heard our parents say at the table.

"While I clear the table, why don't you get undressed for the bed, Sweetheart," she said shooting a cute smile at me.

I knew how to get undressed of course, but I was still faking it. After I had played like I was undressing and putting on my pajamas, I turned to her to ask where the bed was to be. She was taking off her panties. I was really getting confused now. I had never played house where you *really* take off your clothes.

"You haven't taken off anything. Here, let me help you, Silly," she said and began pulling down my short pants and underwear. "But, let me get in bed first."

It was definitely my period of enlightenment about sex between boys and girls. She was excellent teacher for a first grader.

"You better not tell anybody we did this, especially your mommy and daddy. My mommy told me how to do that, but she said if I ever did it to a boy before I got grown up and my daddy found out, he'd chop off both our heads."

She looked very serious when she said it, and goodness knows, after absorbing everything she had told me thus far as being the "gospel truth," I wasn't about to disbelieve that threat. Those headless chickens I had seen hanging in my father's butcher shop meat cooler flashed through my mind.

"I won't," I gulped.

*And would you believe, **until now**, I never did.*

What A Difference 12 Years Make

Lori had her seventh birthday a few weeks later, then her family — who had been renting from my parents — moved out of town. The two of us were only able to play our mom and pop roles a few more time because she lived over a block away. Most of the time parents kept a tight rein on their kids in those days. But, when we did get together I learned that Lori had originally seen her folks having sex by cracking open their bedroom door. Her mother found out and was liberal enough to think it was time to tell Lori about the "birds and the bees."

It was a dozen years later before I saw her again. I was a knowledgeable 16 by then. I was a master at masturbating (**BWBB**) and had sexual intercourse with a multitude of young gals my age.

I had been driving since I was 12, had a learner's permit at 15, and currently possessed a full-fledged driver's license. Dad now had a pickup truck, which I drove to deliver groceries after school and on Saturdays. When I saw her it was one of the latter, which were always heavy shopping days as most men got paid every Friday. She was standing beside an older woman who was talking to my father. I didn't recognize Lori, but my **BWBB** really surfaced when I saw that beautiful female with such a gorgeous body. She was too old for me, I could see that, but I thought how much I would like to lay that woman down. I grabbed a bushel basket of groceries and hauled it to the truck out front. Dad called me over to them.

"Bobby, this is Mrs. Dawson who used to live in our third house down the street, and her daughter, Lori. You used to play together, didn't you?" he asked innocently. I felt myself turning white as a sheet and I could see her face flushing as she squirmed in her high heels. Gosh, she was a beautiful brunette even while being embarrassed. I truly felt sorry for her.

"Yes, I think we did play in the park together once or twice. Good to see you again, Bobby," she said offering her hand. In those days, I had been taught not to shake hands with a lady unless she offers her hand first. I shook it softly and slowly. It was my last touch of her, *ever*, unfortunately.

BGWW&P Times

1937-44 | *Vol. 1, No. 3* | *Memphis, Tennessee*

The Riverside Adolescents
Puppies And Schooling Came Into Existence

The puppies started coming first, then the schooling. I think people in other neighborhoods would keep their puppies until they were weaned. Then, they would drop them on different blocks in Fort Pickering. They knew the residents would take care of them. They were right as far as the kids were concerned. I'd have one follow me home and by the time we got there, I was adored the friendly little thing.

"Can I keep him, Tilly?" I asked with the first one, a fuzzy mongrel about a month old.

"Massah Bobby, ya gotta ask yo momma 'bout that." She was frowning and shaking her head as she said it so I interpreted it was probably going to be negative. Then when she added, "That thing's gonna mess on the flo'r. She ain't gonna like that."

Later, I begged mother enthusiastically, and, after her initial refusal brought tears, she relented. She included provisions that it would stay in the backyard and that I would take care of it. I did pretty good

providing it water and scraps, and — of course — I played with it all day long. The back yard was fenced separately from the front yard and I made him a bed of rags in a small box on the back porch. Everything was hunky dory during the day. But he whined himself to sleep every night, to our dismay.

After several days of this, would you believe that puppy slipped through a hole in the fence and went back to his family. He was homesick was the reason he whined nights, so my parents told me. I was sad, but my dad reasoned that I would whine too if I couldn't see my mommy and daddy. That made sense.

Then, when I started walking the four blocks to Riverside Grammar School, I would run into older puppies to take home. Strange, they too would get homesick and leave even though they didn't whine at night and we fed them well.

My mother confessed after I got old enough to handle it mentally. She had been taking them to a more influential

neighborhood and dropping them. Apparently, that was a common thing for mothers who didn't want a dog under their busy feet. She was a very busy woman and I did bring the puppies in the house occasionally. And, I was soon to learn, they made the world their toilet.

Bruce Was Legendary To County Cattlemen

Popa's farm dogs never came in the house. They had acres and acres of toilets. But, I couldn't even get them to come in the house. I even tried coaxing them with a fried chicken leg, which they dearly loved to eat, but without success.

My favorite of their dogs was a big black and white German Shepard named Bruce. I think he bought him as a pup from a well known cattle dog breeder about 20 miles southwest in Bruce, Miss. He definitely was from good stock and sired many fine litters in his day. I've been down there many times when cattle men in the county would bring their bitch in heat for Bruce to breed.

Bruce's quality attributes were numerous. For example, if popa saw a certain milk cow he wanted in the barn out in a certain pasture area, he'd simply pick up Bruce, point toward the animal and command, "Bring Elsie to the barn." He would never fail. I couldn't get over how he knew the cows by their name, but he did. Popa and my uncles would always talk to the cows when they were moving the ladies into their respective stall and as they fed and milked them (e.g. "Get in there Betsy," "There's your breakfast Betsy," "Back that leg there Betsy," etc.).

For the evening milking, Bruce would sense it was coming as the sun was nearing the horizon, but he waited for the command. One could see he was getting antsy as he would follow popa every step and turn he'd make.

Finally, "Go get the cows, Bruce." He was off in a happy sprint.

Usually, the 30-35 horde would be loosely scattered over the huge pasture hillside, but they normally were grazing slowly towards the barn. Once they heard Bruce's barking behind them, they would graze much faster in that direction. If a cow refused to move in the designated direction, Bruce would nip it on its back leg. Of course, he eventually lost most of his teeth from brave young heifers kicking back. This was very infrequent, however as

his timing of the nip was as the foot was going forward. Unbelievable timing!

He had help from off-springs later on, but none of them ever was quite as adept at controlling cattle as Bruce.

Watching them function in their roles was just many of the endless things that kept drawing me to popa's farm.

Another was the "swimming holes," as we called them in the 1930s. The Yocona River was a one we frequented most as it ran through the middle of the large farm. The maps listed it as a river, but the Tutors called it a creek because it only averaged 10-30 yards wide across the farm.

My Uncle Keister would throw John Paul and me into it from a eight-foot bank. The thrill was flying through the air, but it was followed by fear. It was over our head in depth and I couldn't swim at age four when he first started doing it to me. Keister would jump in immediately after tossing me, but he would wait to grab me until I had panicky paddled upward to the top, gasping for air.

"Hey boy, I didn't know you could swim. Why, you paddled right up to the top. You don't have to be afraid any more," he cleverly said, trying to build up my confidence. Better yet, get rid of my fear of water, which I definitely had for the few seconds that my head was completely submerged. Strangely enough, it worked. I really never was afraid of

going under water after that. Of course, I would never jump into water over my head unless I knew Keister was coming in after me.

John Paul could swim a little. He was a year older and also very influential in my boyhood days. He showed me in the shallow watering pool behind the barn how to mud-paddle. Some called it mud-crawl. If close enough to the bank, one could reach the bottom of the pool with their hands. Kicking their feet on top of the water with the legs straight while pulling backwards in the mud with alternating hands in the prone position propelled one fairly well.

This was my "swimming mode" for about a year. DeSoto Park had a super nice circular concrete wading pool of about 50 feet wide. It went from about six inches deep on the outer perimeter to about 20 inches deep in the center around its 10' wide island in the center. I could kick around its deepest portion with great pride while showing off for the girls. **BWBB.**

The maid would take my sister JoAnn and me to the pool an hour or so every day. We thoroughly enjoyed it during the hot, humid summer months that exceed 100° many days. The island had seating all around the concrete island with a five-foot wide circular roof about six feet high. On very hot days, the park attendants would turn on a huge sprinkler that was a permanent fixture on top of the roof. The cool fresh water from the famous local artesian wells in Memphis would spray the entire pool.

The thing that has always stuck in my mind about the great wading pool was the day they had a beauty contest for all the little participants. In was packed that Saturday afternoon, I didn't win in the boys category but JoAnn won the girl's and my folks got a large photo made of her in her swim suit.

Finally, we were back down visiting the Tutors and nearby kin. I was doing my thing in a cousin's big swimming hole with my parents sitting on the bank watching from the shade. It was a Sunday afternoon so nobody was working that day and a bunch of the kids were swimming out in the deep portion and diving off a raft. The bottom wasn't too muddy, but I was moving along pretty good with my mud-paddling in the strange big pool.

My Unforgettable Erroneous Crawl

"Mother, look at me," I yelled while kicking and crawling away. "I'm swimming."

Then it happened. I came to a drop-off in the pond. The bottom was several feet deeper, therefore my hands touched nothing. I kept grabbing and kicking.

Nothing.

Another grab, another, another, etc...always nothing

but water. I was panicking for a few moments and then I realized my head was still above water and I was moving.

I WAS SWIMMING!

I started reaching with my grabs to the left and I began turning in that direction. Then to the right. It worked in that direction too. I was IMMEDIATELY confident that I was swimming. I learned later the stroke was called dog-paddle.

I got so cocky I turned to the deep water, paddling and kicking with fast, steady motions. Twenty feet or so into the area everyone knew was over my head I yelled again. This time loud and with enthusiasm.

"Look Mother, I'm swimming."

That was it. I would jump into Yocona after that without fear. The wading pool at Desoto Park was no longer fun to me. I was a five-year-old that could swim.

It wasn't long after that I began holding my breath and swimming underwater followed by overhead strokes as is the normal free style of swimming. I was fascinated by this new element of movement. There have been several good things happen from this devotion to the sport, but a few undesirable ones.

It's A Root...Heck No, It's A Snake!

One was at the farm swimming in my favorite

"hole" in the creek. As all creeks do, it had curves and bends to conform to the terrain. One spot I enjoyed was just south of the wagon bridge leading to what they called the "new ground" of the farm. I think it was because it was the last section popa and maw had acquired. 'Twas many decades ago but they still called it new.

Anyway, there was this stretch between bends that permitted one about 30 yards of good, deep swimming water. I liked running and then diving off the bank when I was about age six or seven. This one particular day I was attempting to see how far I could go underwater. I made a slight mistake in pushing off the bank while executing the running dive and entered the water crooked. So, instead of going down the creek underwater, I went across it and starting hitting the roots of trees on the other side of the creek. I quickly surfaced and it was almost completely dark. Apparently, the creek had washed out the terra firma underneath the bank leaving the ends of tree and bush roots bare. It was scary as hell.

I started toward the light — my feet were touching the bottom there — moving the roots out of my face when I felt a severe sting on my right index finger. I jerked it, then felt and saw it was a _SNAKE_.

It was my first experience with a snake, but instinct told me to get my hand loose, which I did and I have no conception what happened to the varmint. I got out as quick as I could and hollered for my Uncle Keister.

He didn't see the snake but the creek had plenty of poisonous water moccasins, so when I told him what happened and described the varmint, he sliced my finger a little deeper. Then he began sucking and spitting the blood from the wound. I was a frightened little kid, but all that happened afterwards was a swollen hand and a scar which I have till this day. It healed in the shape of a chicken's wishbone.

"You probably woke the old guy up from his afternoon nap and it made him mad," Keister explained to me afterwards. "They usually just bite fish, birds, and mice."

I believed him, as usual. However, it should be noted, I never dove in crooked again, either.

My outdoors mentor supreme had no fear of the varmits and consequently, his pupil became the same. With garden snakes and other non-poisonous legless reptiles, I became so quick I could grab them by the neck from behind before they could turn and bit me. However, the brazen way Keister had dealing with a water moccasin found on the ground was too much for me until I reached the teens. He would grab the snake by the end of its tail and sling it around his head with such strength that the snake couldn't reach back and bite him because of the centrifugal force. Then, after four or five big circles, he would snap its head. If this didn't kill it, he would stomp its withering head.

I would come down for a few weeks visit ever summer and help them farm, primarily hoeing to thin corn and cotton sprouts which always came up densely populated in the rows. We'd run into plenty of snakes then, so at age 10 and up I got pretty good at it. I impressed many of the city boys when we'd find an infrequent snake in DeSoto Park and many times in the nearby woody Riverside Park.

Several Riversides Influential In My Life

Not only did I live a few blocks from the actual east side of the muddy Mississippi River most of my boyhood days, but I spent eight and a half years at the Riverside Grammar School. After we moved from DeSoto Street near DeSoto Park, we lived on Burdock Street two blocks from the large Riverside Park, which was also adjacent to the river. The new house was still within the school's jurisdiction, however.

I don't remember the first grade teacher, but when I was in the fifth grade I remember her getting me to draw a map of the world on two of her blackboards. Apparently, I must have been the top artist in the school at the time. It was very pleasing to me to have been asked.

Besides bringing puppies home and playing under the house, the only thing I remember about the first grade era after getting home was playing marbles. We all had our marble bags and we'd draw a circle about four foot wide in some bare ground without any grass. Then, the leader, or oldest of the participants, would drop five marbles from each of us all at the same time in the center of the circle. They would scatter, of course, and if one rolled outside the circle, it was redropped in the center.

Next, we would draw a lagging line a few feet away from the circle. Shooting our "toy," our favorite marble used to hit the other marbles out of the circle, we would lag for the line. Closest toy to the line would shoot first, next closest second, etc.

We shot the toy by holding it within the inner circle of one's index finger against the nail knuckle thumb of the hand used to shoot. With the other fingers of the hand laying on the ground, one would propel the toy off the index finger with the thumb. The object of the game was to knock the marbles out of the circle with one's toy. If successful, one kept shooting until one missed.

All marbles hit out of the circle became the property of the shooter. When the toy remained inside the circle, its owner shot his next shot from there. If the toy knocked a marble and itself out of the circle, the shooter could propel his next shot from any position around the outside of the circle.

If the shot was unsuccessful in bumping another marble outside the circle and the toy stayed inside, then it became free game. This was a definite "no-no." Everyone loved his toy. Some liked theirs simply because of its design, others because of its weight, or size. Huge ones were called "bollies." A metal ball bearing the size of a regular marble was called a "steely." You couldn't buy steelies. Boys had to know a machinist to get one.

I tried to trade a pocket knife, a superb boy's object, for a steely without success. Finally, one unlucky lad's steely didn't make it out of the circle on a missed shot. It was only an inch from the line. It was my shot and I almost wet my pants lining up this master triumph. I got it and my bag of marbles was never emptied after that.

No shooting allowed at school, but the word spread that the Peden kid now had a steely his toy. Now a boy seven or eight years of age wants a lap top computer. Then before the computer age, it was definitely a steely.

The second grade teacher was Miss McKissack (have no idea how she spelled her name, nor could I find any records of it). She always wore her straight red hair in a bun. It looked like a wig, it was always

identically combed. I liked her and she must have thought the same about me as I remember her meeting the eighth grade teacher, Miss Maude Griffin, in the auditorium and introducing her to me.

"This is Bobby, the young man I was telling you about," she told the large, fat lady. I never did know what she had been telling her, but later Miss Griffin would have me as a teacher's pet.

Only thing I remember about the third grade was the rope that the Miss Roseman used. If a student got up out of their seat without permission, she'd make them sit back down and loosely tie the rope once around the chair and the student. One could have easily taken it off in the event of a fire as the rope was not knotted. It was simply to embarrass the student, but it didn't work that way to me. I enjoyed the attention I was getting.

Grapevine Swinging Starts At Age Nine

When I was nine years old, my friends and I would spend hours after school swinging on a grapevine in the ravine that ran from Delaware Street, along the south side of DeSoto Park to the river. We had cut it at the bottom and get a running jump holding the vine while swinging over the ditch sewer at the bottom of the ravine.

One day, several 12-year-olds came down and were running

us off the vine to take over when one of them said to the leader, "Say Dude," pointing to me, "that's Bobby Peden. His father owes the grocery store up at the corner. Maybe he could swipe us a pack of Bull Durham."

The crafty leader said, "Naw, he looks too chicken to me."

The sacks of Bull Durhan were right next to the candy underneath my father's checkout counter. Often, I had reached in and got me a piece of candy while Dad was checking out a customer.

"I'm not chicken," I blurted back at him with my jaw jutted.

"Oh yeah," he says. "Kid, if you bring us some Bull Durham, we'll not only let you swing with us, but we'll roll a cigarette for you."

"I'll be right back," I said glancing proudly toward my peers as I trotted up the ravine trail.

It was a snap. I just timed my dad's movements when he moved an item down the counter and then turned to the cash register to ring it up. This put his back to me, permitting a quick snatch followed by a disappearing act.

Sure enough, they rolled me my first cigarette. I choked and puffed the whole thing as my buddies watched in awe. The also gave me some tremendous shoves out over the ditch on the grapevine. Needless to say, I got very sick that day, but I thought I was "hot stuff" smoking like the big guys.

In fact, I stole tobacco periodically for three years and was addicted by age 12. It will be 33 years before I would kick the habit.

The Big Bully Becomes A Buddy?

The fourth grade was taught by Miss Podesta. She had one male student that had failed twice, so he was two years older than the other 10-year-olds in the class. He also was large for his age and a real bully. I finally lost my temper one day during recess on the playground. He had pushed a little girl down on the ground during an argument and I hit him hard in the plexus. It doubled him up and he lost his breath for a few moments.

I suddenly remembered he was much stronger than I; therefore, I was wide-eyed and ready to get whooped. However, to everyone's surprise, he started crying and backed away. From than on, he stuck to me like glue. Everywhere I'd go, he'd follow. If I was in line at the lunchroom, he'd jump ahead of everyone to be next to me. I think he failed again that year, because I don't remember him being in the fifth grade.

The only thing that I recall of the fifth year was a fart. Some guy passed a loud one and most of the class snickered. The teacher (can not recall her name) gave us a long rendition of how that is a normal body function, etc., not a laughing matter, etc.

I would recall this about two decades later when, following an operation on me for ulcers, I could not eat solid foods until I passed gas.

The sixth grade was a catastrophe. All us boys, and probably all the girls, had long known how to accomplish a personal orgasm through masturbation. Its broadness was not discussed publicly until the Kinsey Report. When things got dull, these ole Fort Pickering boys would find a spot (under the bed blankets, in the bathroom, in the garage, in the attic, etc.) to masturbate. **BWBB.**

Miss Mormon, the sixth grade teacher had a mean paddle, virtually all school teachers of that day had paddles, but her's was _mean_. Therefore, her classes were without interruption by the students. She was the lousiest _teacher_ at Riverside. She had all of us buy composition books at the beginning of the year. Then, after roll call, she would break out HER composition book of her school days. Slowly, and with great penmanship, she would write the notes for us to write in OUR composition books about the subject of the class period.

Things Never Stayed Boring In The 6th

It would cover four full blackboards. Then, she would erase the first blackboard and use it again for continuation of her notes. She wrote slowly, to ensure her penmanship was perfect. I would scribble my notes so fast I had tons of time on my hand. Boring as hell. So what did several of us oversexed boys do for fun during this dull time? We masturbated.

Using our composition book as a cover, and sitting in the back of the room, we were never detected "pounding their meat," as we called it. There was not enough note taking done, consequently. Naturally, I ended up joining other rowdy boys like Eddie Fink and Jimmy "Steamboat" Stafford failing the class. I enjoyed being with the "in crowd" of the rough boys. I didn't mind failing at all, but it hurt my mother.

She was always so proud of "having graduated from" high school. I think there was 12 in the whole school "at which she was graduated." Her letters to me were always warm, loving, and cheerful, but full of misspelled words and a multitude of grammatical errors. While her education was not up to high standards, she still valued that "sheepskin" as they called the diploma in those day. She was always afraid I would not finish high school.

When I obtained my Bachelor of Science degree _With Honors_ almost 30 years later, she was there beaming with pride. I never told her that I put forth an extra effort to acquire that little bold face font on my diploma especially for her. She saw it in my eyes as I stroked by finger over it on the diploma to call it to her attention to it following the ceremony in Pomona, California.

But this is really jumping ahead in the chronology portion of this autobiography. Back to the learning portion of "me life" (my forefathers/mothers are originally Scotch/Irish).

However, those where the days when sex, orgasms, and further enlightenment about the world and it's belongings were important. When we lived on Burdock Street, between Swift and Arkansas Streets, I used to have the new house to my control most of the time. We had maids, and even a white governess for a short time, but many days my parents would leave me in charge of my sister JoAnn, brother John Lee — who was born Aril 17, 1937 — and Aunt Tiny Rose Tutor.

Tiny Rose is my mother's sister, born April 16, 1932. In other words, she is about three months younger than me. When maw died (Sept. 1937), my mother — being the oldest of the Tutor family — and father took Tiny Rose to raise.

Becoming Hooked On Edgar Burroughs

When we lived on Burdock St., mother would keep her days receipts in a large black trunk in her bedroom. Dad would keep his in the store safe and deposit it the next day in the bank. So, with a little manipulation with a pair of scissors, I learned to pick the lock on the trunk for my rights to her money. I thought family money was also mine.

She would have hundreds of dollars, mostly in $5, $10, and $20 bills. Usually, I would just take $5 every week or so, but once I got fascinated with the comic books it was more. I learned that the nearby drug store received its weekly supply of magazines on a certain day of each week. I was there waiting on that day for the next issue of Superman, Batman, Flash Gordon, Captain Marvel, etc. The old gent who owned the store had me a chair set up in front of the magazine rack on that day.

He saw how much I liked to read, that he suggested I read a book he had just finished by Edgar Rice Burroughs called *Tarzan of the Apes*. He leant it to me, but I accepted it only to be nice. Reading a book without pictures would be like studying in school, which I never did at that time. It was raining heavily the next publication delivery date and I had nothing else to do, so I started reading it.

I don't care if you are a slow or fast reader, in-depth or scanner, realist or fantasizer, moodiest or serious interpreter, the author will capture your imagination with that book.

At that age, I was enthralled with a human infant being raised in the jungles of Africa by a female ape that had lost her first born, swapping its carcass for the crying tot in a tree house crib.

I bought, with OUR earnings, and later with my salary from delivering groceries for my father, every book that the great author wrote. Naturally, Burroughs became famous all over the world with his great conception of the super strong human learned what the "bugs" on the pages meant while being reared in a jungle atmosphere. It was engulfed by publishers everywhere, and of course, movie producers.

I enjoyed the great Olympic swimmers, so I had seen several of the Tarzan movies featuring the great Johnny Weissmuller. The producers had him grunting short sentences like: "You Jane. Me Tarzan." He had a chimpanzee as a pet. Tarzan was actually Lord Greystroke from England whose parents were killed while he was an infant. But, while being raised by the apes, found the books in the parents tree house and taught himself to read. Of course, he could not speak English, only the ape gruntal sounds when he first discovered Jane Clayton.

After becoming civilized, and learning the language, plus his true identity and wealth, he changed his way of life while searching for Jane in America. Later, he returned to the jungle and resumed his role as "Lord of the Jungle." The books were so interesting that I saved all the Tarzan series and even Burroughs succeeding Venus and Mars books. I even collected a few of his earlier western novels.

If I had all my work done at dad's store (I bagged groceries, delivered groceries on the bicycle, stocked shelves, etc.), I'd read my books. Then, when the store became so successful after the great depression we had to start delivering in a pickup truck. I would read at every other stop while my Afro-American co-worker, Tony, was taking his turn unloading. So, I just kept reading and buying books.

I didn't search for first editions, just anything written by Burroughs. I understand he proceeded to form his own printing company and founded Tarzana, Calif. As his books were all censored, no sex or vulgarity that I can remember, I kept them for our kids and grandchildren.

"Darit, King Of The Mound" Monikers

Always was a daredevil-type kid. I loved to climb trees, leaping from one limb to the next (*yep, Tarzan influence &* **BWBB**). Most normal boys like to show off, especially in front of girls. But I would get a swing in the park going higher than my peers and jump out. I would hang by my legs from the chinning bar and drop

down, barely landing on my feet instead of my head.

Delivering bushel baskets of groceries, fore-and-aft on the one speed store bicycle, up and down hills in Fort Pickering had made me very strong, particularly in the hands, arms, and legs. We would frequently play "King of the Mound" in DeSoto Park. With my strength from working, along with my innate quickness, when we had a small number playing, I was usually the "King." However, most of the time we chose up teams with the biggest and best being captains.

Most often we competed on the 50'x75' flattop Chisca Mound, only a sand wedge shot from the back of the store. The other one at the far west end of the park had replica cannons with their 4" diameter balls in concrete facing the river to protect Fort Pickering being attacked from river boats. Its rectangular center was cut out with large bushes planted down inside it. Sometimes, an older boy and girl would disappear under the bushes for awhile. They definitely didn't want to be disturbed by us younger boys. Later on it became one of my favorite places to teach young girls about sex.

Anyway, one team would try to throw, sling, toss, tumble — or even kick — the opposing players off the mound. Losing players would have to buy the winners a Pepsi at Munn's Café a block south on Delaware.

Most fun was down in the

muddy Mississippi. When the river was low and the huge wooden moorings to which barges are secured were 30-40 feet above the waterline, A few of us brave ones would climb up a rope and dive off the top. One day while we were swimming there, in the nude of course, my friend Kenneth "Gip" Gipson dared me to do a flip off one of them. I was scared but didn't want anyone to call me "chicken," so, with considerable reluctance I did it.

They started calling me "Darit" after that until one of the most frightening experience of my young life occurred on the Mighty Mississippi.

The Human Submarine That Almost Wasn't

One of the impressive dares I took, when I was about 11 or 12 years old, was to swim across the Mississippi River to Arkansas. I had been swimming in the river for many years by then, therefore, I was pretty confident that I would do it. However, it would to be my longest distance effort to date.

I got about half way and began to tire, so I stopped my freestyle swimming and treaded water to see whether I could make it or head back. I calculated that I had passed the point of no return regardless of my fatigue.

Then, I spotted a buoy about

ten yards ahead. It must have been one of those marking a sandbar formed as the river split going around President's Island a quarter of a mile south. Much relieved, I dog-paddled to it and hung on for a short rest. Then, finished the swim using backstrokes and breaststrokes to alternate with the freestyle. After waving triumphantly back to my pals from the Arkansas shoreline, I laid down and rested for the return trip.

Using the buoy stop again, the return trip was uneventful except for a startling happening. A small branch was floating downstream, almost completely submerged, and it collided with my naked body. Almost scared the shit outa me, but it only scratched a little.

Steamboat was one of the most impressed.

"Ole Darit did it again," he said.

It was the next to last one I would accept. I had always swam a lot underwater and had very good breath control. At the Shelby Forest Camp one summer I remember swimming underway the entire length its regulation pool and almost back. Therefore, when I was dared to swim under a barge moored in the river, I accepted the challenge without hesitation. After all it was only about 60 feet wide, but it was about 120 feet long and there was another barge secured to the end of it. I was going to swim under the width (only 60') of it and come out on the other side, but I wasn't smart enough to take the flow of the current into consideration.

I was only worried about getting halfway and running into a sandbar and having to come back when I dove under the massive hunk of steel. About two minutes later, I judged I should surely be completely under to the other side. Of course, the river is always too muddy to see, so I tried to surface and my head bumped the barge bottom.

I still had oxygen in my lungs, so I didn't panic yet, thinking — of course — I only had a few more feet to go. But, the current had turned me towards the stern of the barge, which meant I was going to have to swim about 220 feet to clear the length of both barges.

Again, I tried to surface as my lungs were beginning to burn. Contact this time brought terror to my mind. Adrenaline began shooting through my body now as all glands were called to their emergency peak. I swam hard and fast until I could no longer go without replenishment of oxygen. My lungs were virtually searing in pain, so I exhaled which gave me a brief more time. I started panicing, knowing if I didn't surface and get air, my lungs were going to uncontrollably inhale water.

I knew death was imminent!

I made what I knew was my last attempt to surface.

The beautiful sunlight and air was suddenly there. I gasped and gasped until I had enough for a scream. I was so full of adrenaline, I was shaking as I swam to the shore, almost 100 yards downstream from my friends.

They had heard my scream and when they saw how pale I was and how I was breathing, they didn't kid me about the situation as **BWBB** usually do.

They didn't even laugh when I said, "That's it. No more Darit shit."

And do you know, *there wasn't*. After the word of the incident spread, no one every dared me again.

BGWW&P Times

1938-46   Vol. 1, No. 4   Memphis, Tennessee

The Little Round Ball With Stitches
Next To Girls, My World Revolved Around Balls

I put love for the opposite sex foremost in my world as a young lad before and after reaching puberty. What red-blooded human male didn't? Some will deny it publicly, but if they can clear their mind of any outside influence (e.g. religion, etc.) their ranking will be the same. I'm sure the gals have the same feelings for us guys.

I did begin to realize I was going to play ball when I used that steely (a steel ball bearing) which kept my marble bag bulging with winnings. I'm sure I had a rubber ball in my crib or play pen, but the ball bearing is the first sphere that stuck in my recall bin. There are also footballs, handballs, basketballs, cork balls, ping pong balls, tennis balls, golf balls, bowling balls, pinball machine balls, volley balls, soccer balls, and even goofballs.

I played with them all, and probably a few more, but the one most influential in my life was a small sphere covered in horsehide with an unending, curving, loop of stitches. Baseball? Aww, ya guessed

it. It is definitely our nation's most popular game.

I became enthralled with it early, but later than some kids my age. The first time I remember catching that hard ball with a glove was quite a skill, I thought. The boy teaching me lobbed it underhanded at first. Then, when he saw I might handle it, he threw over handed. I took my bumps and bruises all over, but I finally learned to catch just about every one thrown to me in a few weeks of daily playing catch. Throw it in the dirt in front of me was a disaster for all of us kids on our street. We missed it so often and took so many contusions on our skinny legs that it was pitiful.

Then, one day a new kid from a block north came over to the vacant field on the corner of the Indiana Street block east of my house. He was Malcolm Adams, Jr., the son of an editor at the *Memphis Press-Scimitar.* We called him "Wimpy," because he was slew-footed. However, Wimpy had a first baseman's mitt with which he scooped up virtually every ball thrown in the dirt to him. J.W.,

who lived in the second house west of us, and I were amazed. We learned later he had been coached while playing Little League in a community where they had it.

After a few days of playing catch, he brought over a baseball bat. It was the first one I had ever seen. It was fairly light to me as I had learned to chop wood at popa's with his axe, which was much heavier.

"Let's play some left field ball," Wimpy said. "Now that we got a bat."

"We'd have to go over to the (DeSoto) park to do that, stupid," J.W. said. "And, we can't do that 'cause the old boys are playing on the field."

"What's left field ball (LFB)?" I asked.

J.W. explained it thoroughly. He was always the brains in our little bunch around DeSoto Street. In fact, all the Gipsons were smart. Daddy "Gip," a river boatman; mother, Pearl; oldest, Martha; my favorite, Kenneth; and the blonde Deloris.

LFB, sometimes called Memphis Ball by visitors from out of town, may be played with as little as four players, two per side. A teammate pitches underhanded to another at the designated "home plate." As there is no catcher in a four-player game, the batter would catch a bad pitch thrown by his pitcher. One pitches from any position the batter desires as the latter must hit safely between the designated left and center field foul lines. In other words, the left hand hitters would prefer the ball being pitched from some point along the LF foul line whereas the right hand hitters took his offerings from the normal pitching mound in the hypothetical CF foul line. These positions permitted both type hitters to "pull" the ball with power between the foul lines (FL).

One missed or fouled pitch and the batter is out. With only four players, a grounder is out. A ball hit safely in the air over a designated short distance (usually the baseline between second and third bases, if being played on a baseball diamond...otherwise, about 90 feet from the plate) is called a "single" or a "one base hit." A farther designated line (about 20 more feet away) is a "double" or "two base hit," another 20 more feet a "triple," and the last, 20 more feet, the "home run."

The "designated lines" were just two permanent fixtures on either side of the two foul lines, which also had to be designated if not played on a field so marked with chalk. For example, a telephone pole down the LFFL and a cherry bush line down the CFFL could be a single, an oak tree and a player's parked bicycle handlebars could be a double, a fig tree and a water hydrant a triple, and the street a home run.

The batter does not run to a base, but there is vocally established but it is a "man on first" following a single. A succeeding double would put "men on second and third base," etc. A player continues batting until he makes an out. If there are still hypothetical men on base when that batter retires, his teammate had the opportunity to drive them home. One good hitter can drive in four or five runs in one at bat, although this is unusual with large group of players.

More players allows each team a shortstop, third baseman, left fielder, center fielder, and a rover or mid outfielder. Also, if enough, the defense provides the pitcher and the catcher. In large teams such as this, a grounder that gets through the pitcher and infielders, or is fumbled, is also a single.

The main reason the game was so much fun to us was because you (if captain) could choose your best buddy, and other favorites, to be on your team. Also, you didn't have to run the bases after getting a hit. But, biggest plus to the game was everyone got a bat every inning. A large turnout game had typical scores of a football game such as 21-20, 32-25, etc.

The Alley Was Our Home Run Mark

I had no idea whether I would hit the first ball pitched to me, so I was a little dubious. I can't remember where it went, but just that I hit it was enough for me at the time. We had drummed up a game of LFB on "our field," the vacant lot. The whole lot was a half block long and about 100 feet wide. It faced DeSoto Street towards the north, so the sun was never directly in our eyes when catching fly balls.

The distance of the designated hit lines (worn out auto tire & small pasteboard box a single, etc.) were not as great as the older boys played at the park. But to hit the ball all the way to the alley was quite a chore for us eight and nine year olds. J.W. told me it was named Bean's Alley, but none of us ever knew why.

I don't remember all the kids who played. I know Wimpy, Pat Ryan (who years later married Deloris), Eddie Fink, Marvin "Kirk" Kirkpatrick, Earl Carter, J.W. and Kenneth were regulars. Marvin, J.W. and Pat hit well, I think. J.W. could hit legs superbly. He got into an argument, which J.W. did frequently, with "Kirk" and took a few cuts at Marvin's legs while he was advancing to do some whooping. No damage was done, but J.W. had learned new weaponry. He carried a bat around with him all the time thereafter. A few non-player ruffians suffered his wrath with it.

Wimpy was by far the best gloveman with his big mitt. From observing him, I learned to push my glove forward to meet the ball instead of pulling it back and getting my leg out of its line of flight. I guess it was a few weeks watching those with experience swing the bat before I began rapping the ball. When I finally got it all together, I was reaching the alley for home runs every once in awhile.

WHATA THRILL THAT WAS!

We played there a good summer and got halfway through the next, but then we had to reestablish our LFB site. Marvin and I started pounding them OVER the alley off a black family's shack. They never complained, but we knew it was going to come sooner or later. We started looking at the park for a good playing area.

In between LFB games, we were always looking for new spots along the river bank from which to swim. One day three or four of us were walking down Riverside Drive to play in another large ravine that was practically unused by humans. It ended at the river and we would then do our "skinny dipping," as we called it.

We started cutting across a large field along a barbed wire fence, when this boy — about our age, I guessed — stuck his head out the front door of the only little house around.

"Get off our property or I'll shoot," he yelled as he stuck a rifle out the door. "Ya'll are trespassing." We all stopped and my pal, Jackie Golden, propped one of his shoes up on the bottom wire of the fence and yelled back, "We ain't trespassing, we're just crossing over to that ravine yonder."

"I said you are. Now git."

Never Ate Pickle Grass Again

I was ready to "git" myself and leaned down to pick some of the pickle grass in abundant there when Jackie said, "Why can't we…"

That's all he got out before I felt a whiff of wind of the bullet passing my temple enroute to entering my pal's lower leg. Then the sound came. It was a .22 caliber. I didn't know the whiff was the bullet until we analyzed it later. It was a deadly calm day and the angle from the house to Golden's leg passed just in front of my forehead.

We carried him back to the road and flagged a car which drove us to the nearest clinic. The police got the report and we learned it was a boy named Haywood Watts that fired the gun.

I never knew what happened to that case, because Jackie moved out of town and I never knew who to ask about what happened. I never got contacted again by the police. I was scared to tell my parents. That happened outside Fort Pickering, where I was not allowed without permission.

Would I ever again see this skinny Watts boy who almost killed me? Stay tuned…err, keep reading.

Joneses Addition Was Neighborhood Plus

When the Joneses arrived in Fort Pickering, there was not a skinny one in the bunch, except maybe Henry, the father. Maxine (Yelvington) was the sweet mother whose great cooking kept Oliver, Richard, Donald, Joyce, Tommy and Carolyn happy and in good shape. The family was well liked by everyone in the neighborhood. Later, I became very close to that family.

They moved into the first house on NW California Street next to a professional football player, Bob Gude, and his brother Carl. Bob was twice an All-Southeastern Conference (SEC) and a 1941 All-American his senior year at the center position for Vanderbilt. He was drafted and played with the Chicago Bears until going into the military during World War II. Afterwards, he played for the Philadelphia Eagles.

He was big and tough, to put it mildly. Little brother Carl got into a brawl at Munn's Café (& pub) two blocks away on Delaware Street. Someone ran to Bob and told him Carl was losing a fight with three brothers at Munn's. Naturally, Bob galloped down there and joined in the fracas.

There were plenty of witnesses, so it must be true, but I was too young to have been there that night. Bob was slashed across the abdomen with a knife, but he held his intestines in with one hand and whipped all three of them with his other hand.

Another California Street resident a few houses east from the Joneses that made it "big time" was Kathleen O'Conner. She danced for many years with the famous Rockettes at Radio City Hall in New York.

Freddy McCollum lived a few houses east of the Joneses, too. He was a year or two ahead of me, but one of the best all-round coordinated young athlete I ever saw. I hear he played some minor league baseball, but he didn't even play prep ball during my three years in high school. Apparently, he just didn't have the desire to take advantage of his natural athletic skills.

When we played LFB, and later fast-pitch softball, in the park, I don't ever remember seeing him miss a ground ball. Hitting, he was superb in fast-pitch. Thank goodness he didn't play much LFB with us or the game would have lost its luster to us. With his power, his team would always have won by such a large margin that it would have become boring.

Plus, he was an excellent football player, all phases (i.e. run, tackle, pass, & catch). In our sandlot tackle games, he was tough to defense because he could throw on the run or just run with it. He would do the latter frequently and I enjoyed applying my "shin

bone" tackles on him. Then, he found out he couldn't get around me, so he started passing over me. Finally, I started playing defense back until he crossed the line of scrimmage, then I would nail him (maybe 50% of the time).

The results were we became football buddies, playing usually against each other all football season. I'll never forget the day he informed me of my incorrect grip on the ball when I threw it. I was gripping it in the center across the laces and he moved my hand about two inches closer to the end. The ball we had was so old a panel of artificial leather had been torn off, but with his adaptation, my usual wobbling pass spiraled. It is still spiraling. With my experience leading birds flying and rabbits running under Uncle Keister's tutelage, I became an adequate passer.

There's not a doubt in my mind that McCullom would have been an outstanding tailback in the single wing or a quarterback in the straight T-formation football. Why he did not surface in Memphis prep football, I don't know. Lazy maybe, lack of desire probably, and — oh yeah — Freddy was a handsome dude with a fine physique. It could be he was too occupied with the girls. I never saw him with one, so I never thought of that until this day.

I have seen him with Mary Helen Schmidt and her brother Charles that lived between California and DeSoto on

Kansas Street. But, I never thought of them messing around together. For one thing, they never held hands, or anything we saw. They would talk together, but we always figured it was about sports. She was an extra ordinary female athlete. Helen was a pretty, tanned, dark-haired girl that had not yet fully blossomed. She was mentally sharp and by far the best girl baseball and softball player I have ever seen. She'd always win in a "burn-out" (i.e. playing catch as hard as each can throw) game with boys our age.

Another Home, Another Park, Same Old Mississippi

When we moved into the new two-bedroom house on Burdock Street, Berline and Aubrey moved next door. It was only about nine blocks from Fort Pickering down Riverside Drive. It was between Swift and Arkansas Streets, only a couple of blocks from Riverside Park. Naturally, with the Tarzan books coming out my ears, I was at that park every chance I got.

We cut many hanging grape vines for swings. I preferred them over ditches to add more excitement to the movement. One we cut was extremely thrilling. The launching edge of the ditch dropped sharply down to the bottom, about 50 feet deep. The width of the ditch was about 70 feet. Except for one 20-foot sapling about eight feet out from the jumping area, the steep banks had no foliage and the bottom

By Ruby Peden

XMAS DAY - Tiny Rose, Me, JoAnn, & John Lee on 1942 Christmas Day.

was full of big rocks.

I got Tiny Rose, JoAnn, and one of the neighbor boys to take a turn on it after we drug the vine to the edge. It normally hung out over the ditch about 10 from the edge. We found a long stick to drag it to us when we first got there each time. On each of the return swings, one of us would catch the swinger and hold onto the vine for the next person's turn.

This was around 1942, as we moved there in the late 30s. John Lee was only five years old at the time, but I was always trying to "make a man" out of my little brother. So I gave him the vine, which he accepted reluctantly, and said, "Now run and jump just like your daredevil sister did."

His "run and jump" was very weakly done. I knew immediately that he would never swing all the way back to the edge. I ran to the edge wishing I had given him a running push start.

Sure enough, he didn't come near enough for me to grab him. Panic-struck, I jumped over the edge for the top of the young sapling. Sure enough, he finally stopped swinging back and forth even with the slender tree. He was screaming and crying loudly with fear:

"I can't hold on. I'm gonna fall."

I scampered up the tree to its top and reached out for him, "Hold on John, I'll get up."

But I couldn't reach him. He was about 10 feet from the tree and I could only lean and reach out a little over four feet.

"Lock your legs around the vine and hold on. I'm almost there," I yelled as I leaned all my weight in the opposite direction. The tree came with me a few feet. Then I swung my body to its other side and leaned suddenly and heavily as I could in his direction, then back to the other side, then toward John Lee. This only took a few seconds as I was full of adrenaline, but it seemed like minutes.

Finally, I was able to grab his shirt and jerk him to my body. He let go of the vine and grabbed around my neck as I hugged him with tears in my eyes. I thought my brother was going to fall and break his leg or crack his head open on one of the rocks.

There Was No Doubt, He Must Do It Again

I climbed down using the small twig size branches for footholds. I was barefooted, but hadn't noticed them hurting my feet going up. Now I did, however, but the feeling of relief from the danger John Lee had experienced overcame the pain.

We crawled up the steep bank to the rest of the gang. They were all jubilant and hugging the pale kid. He was always fair-skinned but not as white as he was then. Slowly, he began to get over the shock and even smiled as Tiny Rose and JoAnn hugged him.

While catching my breath, I was thinking. The first time Uncle Keister had thrown me in the creek, I was severely frightened. I would never have jumped into any water, over my head in depth, again. Consequently, I probably would never have become the adept swimmer that I became. But, he kept throwing me in, I kept coming to the top, and he was always there for me. I lost my complete absolute fear of water even before I learned how to swim. This made good sense, I reasoned.

"Get the vine," I commanded to the neighbor boy (his name eludes me). "John going to swing again."

"No I'm not," he retorted quickly, jutting his bottom lip forward as he did when he was very serious.

"Yes you are. You held on good, but you just didn't get a good enough running start when you jumped to swing back. I'm going to run you out harder and you'll come back like you're supposed to. If you don't hold on to the vine when I throw you, then you'll fall down on the rocks," I explained.

I held him up and he took the vine, reluctantly, but he knew from the past when I said I was going to do something, I did it. Plus, I had never steered him wrong. So, with his eyes as big as silver dollars and whining away, I ran to the edge with him towards the deep little gorge. Hurling him out, I yelled:

"Hold tight and lock your legs!"

I was a regular church-going Christian at that time, so a murmured a quick prayer as he sailed through the air away from me. Needless to say, I grabbed him tightly when he returned.

"Now, wasn't that fun?" I lied.

"No!" he answered almost before my last syllable left my mouth.

That Sunday, I walked down the isle and joined the Baptist church at which our parents were members. They were very devout (my father became a deacon) in the Christian religion and took us to every Wednesday prayer meeting; and every Sunday's morning and evening services. We Peden kids, and Aunt Tiny Rose, were well indoctrinated in the Holy Bible and the Protestant interpretation. Therefore, I thought sure it was my faith in God and my little prayer that made John Lee's last swing a very successful one.

It wasn't his last one though as he let me sling him off a few months and finally he started doing it successfully on his own. I was proud of him and much relieved over decision I had made to make him continue the exciting play with the vines.

White Horses Were Popular, But Roy Rogers Trigger No. 1

Practically every Saturday, the busiest day of the week for both our parents, I would tell Tilly we were going to play in the woods at Riverside Park. She didn't mind as she thought Tiny Rose and I were very responsible for 10-year-olds. She also knew Jo Ann and John Lee would mind me. But, we didn't always go to the park. Sometimes I would take them to the DeSoto Theater on Arkansas Street in Fort Pickering for movie.

It was almost always a western (black and white, of course). Tex Ritter, Hopalong Cassidy, Bob Steele, Ken Maynard, Johnny Mack Brown, Buster Crabbe, and John Wayne, followed — of course — by the singing cowboys Gene Autry and Roy Rogers. Most of them had white horses (e.g. Cassidy's *White Flash*, Maynard's *Tarzan)* that were well known. Cassidy and *Tarzan* became famous internationally. Of course, with the advent of color movies and television, Rogers' *Trigger* — a beautiful palomino — is the overall No. 1 horse in the history of film land.

Also, along with the featured movie (sometimes, even double-features), on Saturdays they always had the week's news, serial, and a cartoon. I led them across large railroad yards, through huge pipes stacked in storage fields, down and up a big ravine, and over six blocks of residential territory.

It was fun as we all rode our personal stick horses. The sticks were branches trimmed of their twigs and cut to about a foot longer than the individual rider was tall. I would notch a shallow circle around the neck of the stick for the bridle of common white string. Some would like theirs pintos, so I would strip off pieces of bark to give it that effect. Mine? Natch, it was made white by stripping all the bark. Jo Ann's I stripped and painted black liquid shoe polish in large spots on it to make a black and white pinto. I used the same polish on my white string bridle ever other inch to make it look fancy like in the movies.

Rainy days when we couldn't get out I came up with a fun western game with the clothes pins. In those days, housewives and maids used two kinds of wooden clothes pins to hang the clothes and bed linen on lines (three or four of small rope or wire) stretched taut between two T-shaped posts. One kind was round (about one half inch diameter) with a knob at one end and sawed up the middle about two-thirds of its five-inch length. The other was two four-inch by 5/16-inch strips pinched together by a metal spring.

The round one (no longer used) applied pressure between the clothes pin and the wire to the (usually) sheets hanging on the lines. The spring pin (still in use today) pinches closed on the garment and line. I used the round pins as my horses, even looping thread under the knob for a bridle. The spring pins were my cowboys.

Naturally, with the many liquid shoe polish colors available, I could create a different look for my different characters. For example, "Wild Bill" might have a brown stripe painted halfway down its left side with two smaller dabs on the right side. How to tell which way it's facing? The two small black dots up at the pinching portion of the pin with the long brown stripe on the left was its eyes. Of course, "Wild Bill" would be standing on his head when one pinched him onto the back of his solid black stallion, but a little more deviation in one's imagination took care of that.

I made cowboys for all of us kids in the house, or supervised their painting. Hardwood floors allow one to wipe up a mistake, if one was quick enough with the wet rag. Needless to say, we all had bags of personal clothes pins. We probably had more than in the laundry clothes pin bag.

We broke our routine at Christmas time, however. We had REAL toys and I got one that I really wanted more than anything else in the world at that time. The USA was in World War II and I was getting more and more fascinated with flying. Santa Claus (alias my parents) knew it, so they gave me a pilot's cockpit game. It had all the instruments (printed on pasteboard with tin needles) which one could adjust to any reading.

My favorite playmate from the neighborhood had become Margaret Bray from the next block south. She helped me turn all the dinning room chairs on their sides and shaped a fuselage with my cockpit game in front. Then we got a couple bed spreads and covered everything. It was real cozy and I remember us kissing, but nothing more. She had told me about her older sister, Mildred, laying on her bed with a boy friend that may have been a hint for us to try it. But, I can't remember why I didn't pursue it. I remember these was a few years of shyness of sex that I went through during that period.

I definitely was very fond of Margaret and remember having my first fight over her. Tito Wheeler, who lived on Colorado Street a half block from Riverside School, and I got into fisticuffs after school one day because he had been phoning her. I told him to stop doing it that she was my girl.

"Make me," he said, and we starting a scrap that was more wrestling that anything.

What got "my goat" was his mother, a hefty woman, who came through the small crowd that had gathered and asked what the fight was about to a bystander. When she found out, she didn't stop us. She just said something like:

"Well, when you get through whipping him, Tito, come on home. Supper's almost ready."

I was on top and there

was no way he had the best of me rolling in the school playground cinders. He would grow to become the toughest hombre in Fort Pickering, replacing Dude Wheeler (no kin), and could probably have wiped the sidewalks with me then. Tito and I got along fine after that, however, and as far as I know he stopped calling my girl friend.

Tiger Tang, My Life-Saving Bitch

The only other interesting thing I can remember about Burdock years is Tiger Tang[14] saving my life or saving me from serious injury. She was a little rat terrier bitch I had at the time (I always had a pup of one sex or the other). She seemed to ignore the mid-sized chow dog next door, but would frequently leave her droppings next to the field fenced backyard which contained the boisterous, rusty colored neighbor.

When we would roll a ball from over unfenced backyard up against that fence, I would go to pick it up and the chow would come streaking out of his house, barking fiercely and bang up against the fence. It would always scare me reaching for the ball. I would get even with him later that evening as we slept in a bedroom with a window facing his direction.

Punching a large enough hole through the window screen by my bed with a pencil, I would drill him with a few B-Bs from my Red Ryder air rifle.

I think it knew where the sting came from the sound of the rifle. Over the many weeks of scaring hell outa me and sustaining stings from my window, he finally had the opportunity for revenge. One Sunday morning, he escaped, or his owners let him out. He was across the street sniffing around in a flower bed there, but I didn't see him when I came out to walk Tiger Tang. As it was summer time, I was all dressed for Sunday school in a short sleeve shirt.

When he spotted me, he started running towards me, growling with his hair bristling. I yelled for my father and started for the screened front door, but I could see I'd never make it. Tiger Tang barked and charged him, deterring his mission . He was domestic, but he was of a carnivorous breed and he wanted **ME!**.

The slight determent by Tiger had allowed me to move closer to the front door of the house and a few more moments of screaming for my father. I turned back facing the chow, raising my left forearm to block his sharp teeth which were headed for my throat. He was chewing on it as the force of his reared body toppled me backwards to the ground. Tiger was biting fruitlessly on his large back legs, but if my

father hadn't burst out of the screen door yelling at the top of his lungs, I think he would have ripped my neck open.

Dad had pulled out and opened his pocket knife while jumping down the steps, but he never was able to stab the dog. Dad's larger body bounding towards us, along with the adult voice yelling, was enough to scare the chow off of me. As the assailant ran towards his home, dad threw his knife and the handle hit the chow, but not the blade.

The lacerations I sustained were not as deep as my parents feared and there was no bone damage so it healed in time for a scheduled tonsillectomy and removable of my adenoids. Tiny had it done at the same time. It was a common thing to do in those days, although the medical profession learned to save tonsils in later years.

The war was going full speed and President Franklin D. Roosevelt had long since got the nation out of its depression. Women were no longer just housewives and office workers. Black maids were relatively inexpensive and the war factories paid the white females well. Consequently, mother's beauty shop had a booming busy.

Back To The Fort And Another Chow Dog

We moved back to Fort Pickering, this time on Iowa Street. Mossie and Fred — producing Sandra, Freddy

---

14 I have no idea where I got that name, but the fact I can remember it over 65 years later indicates my fondness of the dog.

Lynn, and Brenda — lived four blocks west of us at the southwest corner of Delaware and Iowa. Their backyard overlooked the Mississippi River and the nearby Harahan Bridge.

Mother opened a new beauty shop across the street in the same block of the two-story physician's house we bought. Ruby's Beauty Shop, it was named and she had eight operators. Eva joined them shortly thereafter while marrying big Beauford Layne (he preferred Layne) and subsequently giving birth to their two boys, Larry and Ricky.

Across the street from the shop was a hardware store. Why do I mention that? Because, the owner kept his miniature pet chow dog inside the store. Every time I was sent there for some nails, screws, etc., I had to face that animal coming up to me, sniffing, quietly growling, and staring me in the eye. My later education and experience with animals, that use smell of another's odor to detect mood, taught me that one's exocrine glands become extremely strong under the armpits when frightened.

I couldn't help but think of those fangs of the Burdock chow whenever I saw the hardware dog. I suspect my scent was one of "battle readiness" to him and he was watching my every move. I was very happy when I befriended an untagged German police

dog with a piece of my food and he followed me home. We got him a collar and leash and dad drove a clothesline wire at both ends into the ground along one side of the backyard. Then he fixed a snap on the lease to the wire so "Wolf" could run up and down the wire with his leash. If you guessed that I would take Wolf with me when I had to go to the hardware store, you're right. The chow sniffed Wolf from then on, ignoring me.

We built a nice doghouse at the far end of the wire underneath the overhang of the workshop/coal shed at the back of our lot. The overhang also gave him a nice shade during the hot, humid summers. I used the workshop and the alley behind it to sneak my cigarettes. Ready rolls had made the scene by then, so I usually smoked the Camels brand. They were free to me anyway as I snuck then out of the store; therefore, Bull Durham and Prince Albert roll-your-own became a thing of the past. I never, not once, took a package of anything out of my dad's store for my friends. To me, that would be *stealing*. For me, that was just sharing the family wealth. Naturally, I gave them smokes and cookies from my pack.

John Lee and I slept in the west upstairs bedroom and the girls the east. The spaces must have been a sun room for the doctor's patients as the outer walls were all windows (eight in my room). Each room had a closest and that was it.

Dad gave us boys a dark colored gallon jug to keep in our closet to use for urinating purposes. The girls had to make the long hike downstairs to the ground floor and use the only toilet in the house. The small stairway was between our bedrooms.

I enjoyed the privacy and additional space that John and I had. I laid on the bed and read comic books most nights. We didn't have television yet, but we had seen it in closed circuit operation at the County Fair. But, the radio, comic books, newscasts at the theaters kept fueling my desire to be a pilot when I matured. I began building airplanes by cutting out printed structures from thin balsa wood panels with pointed, single edge, razorblade pens. Then, gluing fuselages, empennages, and wings together with a propeller out front on a thick rubber band stretched inside the former. Then adding a thin tissue paper covering with mucilage followed by a coat or two of model airplane paint.

One could wind up the rubber band by twisting the propeller and, in a calm day, it would fly. Obviously, as balsa wood is so soft, it was a very fragile project. Consequently, I kept most of them hanging from the ceiling of my bedroom along with the solid balsa wood planes I would whittle into the shape of a certain type airplane, be it American, English, German, Russian, or Japanese. I made almost 35 all total.

Then It Was Back To The Kissless Stuff

All of this stuff was squeezed in between my numbers one and two priorities, sex and baseball, on rainy or other bad weather days. When it was nice, I was outside doing my thing. For example, our new church was only a half block west of us on Louisiana Street adjacent to the same alley that ran behind out house. It was on three-foot brick columns, as usual, and down the alley were several Negro shacks. I kept noticing when I would go to church I would see this cute little black girl about my age. She would always look at me and smile.

Finally, I was with a pal that had lived near there all his life and I called his attention to her. He grinned at me and said, "That's Janie. She'll go under the church with ya for a quarter."

"No shit?" I responded and kept on walking, but I remembered it. The next time I went on an errand to the hardware store I left Wolf at home. Walking in the alley, I came to Louisiana, but didn't turn north. I moped around, kicking a tin can around, watching in Janie's direction. Finally, she appeared and saw me immediately.

I reached in my pocket, pulled out a quarter, and held it up between my index finger and thumb. She glanced both ways down the empty alley and then crawled under the church. I was nervous as hell,

but I relished the excitement of getting in a black gal's panties. The thought of doing that had never entered my mind.

I walked casually to the same spot, quick-checked the personal traffic, and then snuck under the place of worship to practice a little stuff of what I thought heaven was surely all about. **BWBB.**

While recalling this one-time event with Janie, I remember everything very clearly. I left first. I got to the edge of the church, peeped both ways, then ran like my pants were on fire to the hardware store. But, I don't remember kissing her. Then I thought about the white girl with whom I was making whoopee regularly in a old coal shed on a vacant lot behind and east of our alley gate. I never remember kissing her either, nor any other childhood sex act I committed. I was about 10 or 11 years old when this happened.

I wanted to make out with Tiny Rose's friend, Margaret Sullivan, but she was a couple years older than I. She would come over and play for hours on our new piano and let me sit with her. She would show me how to play some cord or two. Then, when I messed it up, she'd grab me around the neck with one arm and ruffle my hair with her other hand. The smell of her feminine body aroma and the touch of her breasts against my cheeks would get me very excited. Invariably, I would have to go masturbate in the bathroom after she left.

I don't think she ever knew how she turned me on. Naturally, I flirted openly, but I always thought she took it that way. Now, I'm not too sure. I've found some women, a good majority of them, purposely arouse young boys nearing puberty. Whether it's to tease them, or because they obtain a little dampness out of it, I have never learned for sure. Chances are, I never will. Maybe, **GWBG,** too.

I remember having a crush on one girl at Riverside School in the sixth or seventh grade. I think her name was Helen Warner. She had matured early in her carriage. She was as tall, or an inch taller, than I and her adult female body was well on its way to perfection. Having shed all of her little girl plumpness that most of them went through, she would walk home after school carrying a book or two five blocks to the northern part of Fort Pickering . I was strangely in awe of the girl, so I would follow her home with a reluctant buddy from the other side of the street.

Even now, I can not interpret my brief idolization of a member of the opposite sex the same age as I. When I would make my unpolished, boyish flirtations to her, she would always react and speak with such maturity that I felt amateurish. Not that she was rude or demeaning, but so "grown up." I never got the nerve to make a serious pass at her, because I felt so inadequate.

Fortunately, this never happened to me again. I was usually very confident dealing with girls, wherever our ages crossed. However, I was noticing around ages 12 and 13, the skinny ones were adding weigh and the fat ones were losing it. Naturally, the breasts began protruding and the glutei (especially the gluteus maximus) enlarging, Puberty was arriving. Dolls were passé, boys (older, more mature ones) were vogue.

Christine Wray was a good example. She was not as sexy looking to me as Helen, but she was also in my second year of the sixth grade. We had a male teacher for quite some time and he chose detention instead of the paddle. One day, Christine and I were detained for some reason or the other. Us boys had to stop the masturbating with his frontal style of teaching, so I wasn't detained for that reason.

It was a chatting session to me, except they were doing the chatting and I was doing the listening.

"How many beaus you got, Christine?" this 30ish teacher asks. "Probably, a ton of them as pretty as you are."

"I only got one," she said cooingly.

I had known Christine for a year or so and I had never heard her talk sexy like that to her boyfriend, Steamboat. This went on for entire fifteen minutes of detention. Then, the teacher left with us to walk down the stairs with Margaret and even opened the door for her exiting the building.

"Let me get that door for you, dear," he said giving me an urge of nausea.

"Thank you, kind sir," she syrupped. Auuugggghhh.

A few minutes later as Christine and I walked towards home together, I said, "Man, wait 'til I tell Steamboat about you and whatshisname. He probably would have asked you for a date if I hadn't been there."

Then she brushed back her long, black curls and asked poutingly, "Bobby, you wouldn't do that to ME, would ya?"

I wasn't going to tell anyway, but the little squeeze on my arm when she said it sent my threat to the dead file.

Steamboat With A Quick Jab Or Two

Steamboat never learned of the incident, but they had an unassociated arguement shortly after that and broke up. She subsequently accepted a movie date at the DeSoto Theater with Alex Hess. He lived south across the big ravine in the Meacham community.

The word of the date spread through the neighborhood like wildfire. Christine and Jimmy Stafford had been dating for a long time. Everyone expected them to marry when they got old enough, and they did. So, everyone had taken the breakup as a "cooling off" separation by the two lovers.

Someone dating Christine!

No way. Steamboat was too tough for anyone to muster guts enough to date his simmering girl friend. We had all seen him stop a sandlot football game or stop pitching (he was good) in a fast pitch softball game, to trot over and beat up a stranger walking in the park It got to where some of the players would argue about whose turn it was to challenge the park visitor. It used to burn my tail. I would always try to talk them out of it and continue our game, but most of the time I was unsuccessful.

Another thing Steamboat did that I detested was spitting on black males. He had this uncanny ability to roll up a small ball of saliva with his tongue and blow it out the side of his mouth. He would do it while walking past them going in the opposite direction on the sidewalks; usually downtown where it was crowded. As he kept his head straight toward the direction he was walking, the victim would have no idea from where the small dropt of moisture came. He would stop, wiping it off his face, and invariably look up in search of the source. I'm sure most of them contributed it to a drop of rain, although most of the time there was not a cloud in the sky.

Occasionally, he would "baptize" (as he called his sick "sport") one of us, but he only did me once. I chased him, tackled him, and blew a big ugly wad of mine in his face. **BWWB.**

Bill E. Burk, in his "Good Evening" column in the now defunct *Memphis Press-Scimitar*, in l980 quoted Stafford (with Burk's editorial comments in parentheses on the subject) before Steamboat passed away decades later:

"I never drank. I never got arrested (Ed. Note: He never got caught). *Oh, I got in a few fights. You had to grow up tough over there in a way. Fort Pickering was the type of place if a stranger walked in there and looked like he was looking for trouble, he could find it; but if he looked halfway friendly* (smiled and/or tipped his cap), *he could make friends. I always ran from* (ran to) *violence if I could. I seemed to get along with everybody. I could outrun most of the bad guys* (he couldn't outrun anybody, so he never ran) *and there were always bullies around."*

"We were too poor to go anywhere, so we spent many an hour playing corkball and softball at DeSoto Park. It was like a small town over there...."

We also saw Steamboat box in many gold glove and prep matches as a 135-pound beanpole. We had never seen Hess fight, but he was about 20 pounds heavier and much stockier; therefore, there was a small crowd waiting near Steamboat at the entrance to the theater that night.

When they emerged with the rest of the movie goers, Steamboat walked a few feet behind them for a half block.

We couldn't hear them talking, but when Hess stopped and faced him with his fists raised, we knew the time for bruising had arrived.

Steamboat danced around Alex, throwing his left jabs through Hess' unsuccessful blocking attempts. Hess would swing wildly with much power, but Stafford stayed a distance far enough to dodge them all. All the time, he would counter with quick, left-right combinations. Alex's nose began bleeding profusely, but he kept on trying to box Steamboat.

Jimmy was always slapping us around with light jabs and faked punches. Learning I couldn't compete with him in that fashion, I would duck underneath and throw him to the ground. Then, fake a punch while holding him down by the throat. Why Alex, who obviously was a much stronger youngster, didn't do that I don't have a clue.

Finally, with blood all over his shirt, Christine jumped in between them and held Steamboat's arms while begging them to stop. They finally shook hands and parted, but it was thoroughly settled that Steamboat didn't want anybody dating Christine. As far as I know, nobody ever did after that. J.W. informed me they had kids and had a happy marriage until Steamboat succumbed. He was loved by many, including yours truly.

J.W., along with Howard Ingram and Richard Jones,

also fought in Golden Gloves matches. In fact, J.W. won the North Memphis Light-heavyweight Championship with two victories. He had signed up too late to get entrance in the south division. Then he lost the city finals to the powerful Cotton Miller in :20 seconds of the first round.

"They said afterwards he hit me with a left and right, but I replied, 'He didn't need that right. He could have left it at home.' After the left landed, I didn't wake up until the next fight had started," he remembered.

Richard, who was to become my closest buddy, lost his first flyweight prep bout to George Francis. Then, he won three fights before losing the bantamweight title the next year in the GG.

My "near" fight of notoriety in the neighborhood at that age was neither in the GG nor over a female. It was to "save face," as the Japanese used to say. I had just started learning to drink beer and cheap wine as a budding teenager, so a few beers one night had my buddy Jackie and I feeling no pain. We went to the railroad tracks just north of Virginia Street to hop the freight cars for thrills. The train would slow just before getting on the Harahan Bridge leading to Arkansas. The tracks split the center of the two crude road lanes on the bridge.

We would run alongside the moving train and jump up on a freight car as it started picking up speed. Then we would ride for a block or two and leap off into the soft weeds in a accompanying ditch before the car reached the bridge. Sometimes, when the train was long enough, we could run back and catch another quickie. All the time we were doing this, we were voicing our fun yells in a loud manner.

Staggering back for another ride this late night, we heard a loud yell from the backyard of one of the Virginia Street houses.

"Hey you stupid drunks! Shut up that shit and get the hell outa here. If you don't, I'm gonna come out there and beat your fucking ass," he threatened.

"That's Kevin," Jackie said. "He's mean. I didn't know he was out of jail. We better go."

I didn't like Kevin's attitude, but tripping over one of the tracks, I knew it was time to quit. I was having trouble even walking after all the exercise on top of the booze.

"Sorry," I yelled with an obvious slur. "We're gone."

"You damn right you are. And if ya'll ever come back around here, your ass is mine."

We hustled off and called it a night. I analyzed it the next day and we were out of line because it was late at night. But, the train was making as much noise as we were and I had never had any boy talk to me like that before. I was going to forget it though, until it leaked

out. My buddies started asking me if it had "really happened," and if "I had been run off the tracks, etc."

Finally, I admitted we were drunk, but Kevin "better not show his ass in DeSoto Park." Actually, I was not too sure I wanted that to happen. I did not know the guy. I had no idea how tough he was. He could have been six feet tall and 15 or 16 years old. Then it happened. He came to the park and a kid came to dad's store to let me know.

We didn't have any deliveries to make at the moment, so I told Tony that Kevin had finally showed up at the park. I had already told him about situation.

"Make sure you keep your arms up like I told you and don't take your eyes off him, Bobby," Tony reminded me. He had been coaching me a little on street fighting and a lot on baseball. He was about 30 years old and a shortstop for the Memphis Red Sox professional baseball team in the Negro League. I respected his advice tremendously.

"Make sure you call him 'boy'," Tony said as I was leaving. "He won't know how to handle that."

Time Has Come, "Let's Go, Boy"

When I walked to the park I saw him laying on the ground with one of his pals and four or five park regulars. I walked in front of them toward the

nearby wading pool. I stopped and lit up a cigarette. It was a ready-roll type which I had been smoking since dad said he'd rather I smoke in front of him and mother instead of sneaking around doing it. Then, I sat down and slowly took off my shoes, socks and rolled up the legs of my pants. They were watching in silence as I stepped in and out of the pool.

I picked up my shoes and socks and walked to a wide grassy area about 20 feet in front of them. Taking slow drags on the cigarette between everything, I sat the footwear down and carefully removed my sports shirt, folding it neatly on top of the shoes. Then, I thumped the cigarette away and turned facing my adversary.

"Let's go, boy!"

He didn't move a muscle.

"Whatsa matter, you chicken?" I asked suddenly feeling my "oats" as the adrenalin flowed. I noticed he didn't look a bit bigger nor older than I.

"I'm out on parole from juvenile court. I'll be thrown back in if I get in a fight," he informed us.

"You were ready the other night when I had been drinking."

"It was dark. No cops around."

"Don't let me catch you around here when it's dark," I advised picking up my attire.

"Yes sir," he answered blandly.

I knew he was being sarcastic, but I didn't care. I figured I had "saved face" without getting it bashed. I felt vindicated to those who had witnessed the affair. Plus, I knew the happening would be spread throughout the neighborhood.

Tony relished it all. Especially, the way I used "boy." When we were playing catch later in another work lull, he showed me a few baseball tricks to reward me for using his recommendations. He was probably the most influential baseball mentor in my entire life. He designed my batting stance and distribution of my weight at the plate and I never changed it. Watching the pitched ball all the way into the catcher's mitt was a method he recommended. It kept me from taking my eye off the ball when I would swing at it. My strikeouts were usually the lowest on any team I played and my batting average, baseball and fast-pitch softball, was usually well above the .300 mark.

I tried passing what I had learned about hitting and fielding grounders to my two best friends at Riverside School, Jimmy Miles and Tommy Sherrill, but they were more interested in talking about girls. Tommy was a tough youngster of the lower middle class, but Jimmy was the son of a physician, or dentist, who lived on Wisconsin Street a few blocks west of the school. We were like the three musketeers on the playground and no one tried to bully us because we were so close.

Jimmy had a younger sister and both had been told about the "birds and the bees" by their parents. Apparently, the Miles parents were very liberal for most Fort Pickering natives. I guess my dad presumed I knew it as he never had a father-son talk with me. Jimmy's knowledge was shared about that sperm stuff during ejaculation causing gals to get pregnant. I got Tony to buy me condoms after that.

I could afford them as they were only 25 cents for a package of three and I was making $5 a week after school and on Saturdays helping Tony deliver groceries. He was making $39 a week full time, so he occasionally bought me a pack. Naturally, I shared them with Jimmy and Tommy every once in awhile.

I never will forget Sherrill's theory of "How to get along in Fort Pickering: Keep your head cool, feet warm, mouth and bowels open. Drink plenty of water and eat lots of greens. Walk softly, speak a few kind words, and tote a pistol."

Unfortunately, Tommy broke some laws down the line and spent some time in the pokey. We drifted apart after we moved to Shelby Drive and U.S. Highway 61, just above the Tennessee-Mississippi line.

Riverside School Conclusion Was Sad

I do not remember one thing about the seventh grade, not even the teacher. But the eighth grade was great until we moved Christmas. Miss Maude Griffin was a lovely person. Overweight, but a firm, excellent teacher; sweet; and had a great heart. She spoiled me, so I guess I was her pet. She had me practicing for a month for a big PTA musical she was directing. I had sung in several school holiday shows in the lower grades and had an excellent tenor voice at the time I was rehearsing the lead song I was to sing, "If You Were The Only Girl In The World And I Was The Only Boy."

Miss Griffin had called a voice teacher to hear one of our rehearsals and the lady gave a one-year free scholarship at her studios. I had been going downtown Memphis to take them each week when a natural occurrence in a boy's life happened to me.

Suddenly, my voice start breaking and it was awful. It finally settled first baritone, but too late for the show. Miss Griffin had to use a substitute for me that made me feel so sad after all the training she had given me. None of the other classmates teased me except maybe my buddies Miles and Sherrill, but theirs was attempts to cheer me up and get me outa my doldrums.

BGWW&P Times

December 1947 - January 1949   *Vol. 1, No. 5*   *Memphis & Shelby County, TN*

Two-Year Jaunt To The County

Levi Grammar And Whitehaven High Schools Provide Many New Friends

Both parents were making good money, so they bought a beautiful, three-bedroom brick house less than two miles from the Mississippi border. It was on a four-acre lot a few hundred yards southeast of Shelby Drive and U.S. Highway 61 intersection. It had a concrete driveway curving up its hill to a two-car garage/workshop which had one of the recently invented electric doors.

The garage/workshop was connected to the house by an elevated breezeway. We seldom used the front door entrance which had an open walkway past a huge sunken living room and a coat closet to the large kitchen entrance and hallway. The latter led to the three bedrooms and our nice bathroom, which had our first shower. The kitchen not only had a breakfast table but an eating ledge around one side of a floating counter in the kitchen center. The spacious kitchen exited to a big dinning room and also the back yard.

The last thing I did at the two-story house on Iowa Street was set fire one at a time to my model airplanes and sailed them flaming from my upstairs window to the backyard below. I had been told I wouldn't be able to hang them in our boy's room at the new residence, so I thought it would be a fun spectacle. Several of my friends watched it.

Naturally, I did it while mother and father were at work. My father would have probably punished me had he found out about the use of fire with the performance. He wouldn't have spanked me, though. I had already received my last beating.

The Final Whipping

It was among several things embedded in my mind about the Iowa Street era. I had just got a set of boxing gloves for my birthday, or something, on a Saturday night. I went to Sunday school at our church as usual and took a seat in the back of the auditorium for the main service. Tommy Sherrill and I both detested the preaching portion of the Sunday services. Most of it was above our head; therefore, very boring.

It was comprehendible to my father, but — as always — he would doze away. It was understandable as he worked from 7 a.m. until 8 p.m. Monday through Friday and 7 a.m. to 10 p.m. on Saturdays. A Sunday morning bath and shave, followed by a hearty breakfast, made a doze on a church pew during a serious discourse almost a necessity. Although, I must admit, my superactive mother never succumbed. She would elbow him awake often.

Tommy and I timed one of dad's dozes and snuck out the back door. Less than a block away down the alley and we were in the back yard whamming each other with my new mitts. We were having so much fun, we didn't notice the time. Suddenly, the back gate flew open and there came my fuming father. Tommy stripped off his gloves and hightailed it.

"Nobody gave you permission to skip the church service. Git on the back porch," he ordered with sparks coming from his eyes.

There, just outside the bathroom door, hung his 2" wide leather straps with which he used to sharpen his straight razor and to punish us kids. Mother usually used a switch for her instrument of pain infliction.

Dad grabbed my left arm and was beating me across the back with the two-foot long, double-stripped, razor straps. The pain was excruciating, of course, causing me to twist and turn in his grasp. I was 12 years old at the time, and a strong lad from handling heavy boxes of canned food and delivering 24-bottle, wooden cases of 12-ounce Pepsi and Royal Crown to customers.

With all my jerking body movement, he inadvertently whacked me across my mouth. The blood spurted out on his hand and shirt.

He stopped immediately.

I covered my mouth and ran to the bathroom sink to wash off the blood. Mother came home and saw my injury. Naturally, she showed motherly emotion, but sent me to my room. A few minutes later, dad called me downstairs. By now, my lips were badly swollen and I know I must have looked terrible to my parents. I actually felt much grief for _him_ as my father spoke.

"Son, I'm sorry that I accidentally hit you in the mouth. I will never whip you again. If you disobey, or do something for which you should be punished, we will take away a privilege, restrict you, or something like that," he said with obvious sadness in his voice. Then, he hugged me and repeated his promise, "I will never hit you again."

It was one of the few times I could remember him hugging me. He was not a demonstrative person. I'm not either (but definitely flirty, passionate, and over-sexed). None of the Pedens were, while the Tutors all were warm, affectionate people. However, I knew he did not deserve the sorrow he was feeling. Needless to write, I never skipped a church service again while being a member of my parents household. In fact, except for some **BWBB** stuff, I can't remember ever breaking one of their parental rules again.

"There They Were, Naked As Jaybirds"

My parents always let me go to popa's a few weeks in the summer months and a week during the Christmas holidays. I had gotten proficient enough and large enough to handle a single blade plow behind a mule. "Blackjack" was my favorite and was experienced enough to walk dead center between rows with very few "gees" (move right) or "haws" (move left) commands from

the human. This was when we were "splitting the middles" to turn the dirt smothering most of the grass and weeds which sucked a lot of the moisture from the young corn or cotton seedlings.

Early one day we had finishing the milking and were loading the wagon with three plows. Popa had backed his mule up to the wagon's left single tree. He was hitching the mule's harness without mishap. The mule was calm and everything was going smooth. Then Keister came out of a stall with a younger mule and both the animals got fidgety. I had learned that Uncle Keister had a short fuse with the animals, especially in the early mornings. If they didn't move left when he said "haw" a couple of times in a firm voice, he would bury his fist in their side, jerking the left rein while yelling, "I said HAW!"

Consequently, when the soft-spoken popa was shoving the plow in the ground behind them, they were placid. Keister in charge, they were definitely edgy to say the least. After we loaded our water jugs, we headed for two big fields north of Yocona. They hitched the young mule on the right side of the wagon tongue to let it pull alongside Popa's old timer. This allowed me to bareback ride Blackjack.

Popa plowed the lower field while Keister and I worked the higher ground. Everything was going great in the early hours, but by midday it was very hot. We had all shed our shirts, leaving only our overalls, straw hat, and clodhoppers. Finally, Keister and I took off everything. Popa's mule spotted us during a turn and balked causing Popa to stop and look up the hill to see what had startled it.

"There they were, naked as jaybirds," he would say when telling of the sight he saw up the hill. He was so fond of telling the story that every time I was in his company with a newcomer present, he'd tell it again. He told it with glee until he died in 1956. Maw died of asthma when I was five years old.

My Sexy Uncle Paul

John Paul was their youngest son. He was even more oversexed than I, in my humble opinion. I would bring down a baseball, bat, and a few gloves for Sunday afternoon play. He, like more of the country boys, never had the opportunity to play baseball. Randolph School probably had only 300 students or so at the turn of the 1940s decade. Therefore, the only interschool sports play they had was basketball. That was the only game with which my father was familiar. This would eventually restrict my competition.

Paul, as he was often called, would start pumping me about my sex life as soon as I got off the bus for a visit. He wanted to know all the details. In Fort Pickering, the boys never talked about which girl they had fornicated or any of the details. It didn't seem proper, to me. I guess this was one of my first self-taught feeling of "gentlemanliness." I feel my dad did a good job of teaching me how to be a gentleman, but he never discussed anything about the sex world.

However, I presumed Paul would never see any of them, so we shared experiences openly. That's when I first learned of oral sex with a girl. None of the Fort boys my age ever said anything that method.

"You never eat any pussy?" he asked one time. "Eat" never was the appropriate word to me, but that was the term in my childhood days. After I tried it, I changed it to "kiss" in lieu of "eat." More aptly would be "French kiss" as one uses the tongue as during the passionate caressing of lips between two participants.

Last Of The Bus Traveling Days

I always traveled by bus when leaving Memphis. Traveling inside Memphis travel was on city buses and the old street/trolley cars which was run by a pulley on a pole connecting to an electric power cable running down the center of major streets. Delaware Street was one of these streets and the clanging latter vehicles stopped in front of dad's store.

On one of my early trips to popa's as a youngster, I had to transfer in New Albany, Mississippi. During the long wait for the bus to Ponotoc, then through Randoph headed for Sarepta on a gravel road which would deposit me on a dirt road, with only a one-mile walk to popa's front yard, I had to go "number two." In school those days, maybe is still is thus, a child would raise one finger to request permission to go to the toilet and urinate and two fingers to defecate.

Reaching the stall I learned it took a nickel to open its door. Inside, during my defecation, I read some of the adult graffiti on the side walls. One poet's contribution stuck in my head 'til this very day as I thought it was so clever:

Here I sit broken-hearted
I paid a nickel to shit
And I only farted.

Probably my final trip to the area was in 1944 to spend a week with my father's half-sister Qubelle's relatives. She was married to a cattleman/horseman/farmer and owner of the Pontotoc area, William L. Aaron. Their son Wm. Earl Aaron and Christine had a son named Billy Gordon, who was also a 12-year-old. My paternal family had made the arrangements for this initial visitation for me. I had never met or seen any of them, except Qubelle a couple of time, since I had become of cognizant age.

When the bus arrived in Pontotoc, I walked with my suitcase and sat down on the bench out front waiting for my cousin to arrive. Up walks a young man about my size and asks, "Hi, you Bobby? I'm Billy. You ready to go?"

"Yeah, I'm ready. Where's your father," I replied. We didn't shake hands as youngsters did not usually do it our age.

"He's at home," he answered while putting my bag in a station wagon parked on the street. "Get in, let's go."

I got in the passenger's side of the front seat and was amazed that he got under the wheel and started the car.

"You gonna drive?" I asked in disbelief.

The little guy, probably about 5'1" then, ignored me and backed the vehicle out and motored down the Pontotoc street with confidence. I was completely flabbergasted. He drove us to his home, which was the most impressive residence I had seen at the time. It was surrounded by yards of corrals for their stock Tennessee Walking Horses. The driveway to their entrance of the home was very beautiful. I'm sure it was designed by the exquisite tastes of Christine. She was not only talented in that area, but as a hostess to a youngster from the big city who was learning the basic things of life, she was terrific!

I was amazed at this breed of horses. Popa had horses, but not bloodline horses like these. They had beautiful long manes and flowing tails, which were perky upwards with long flowing ends. Most all I saw were black or extremely dark brown with an occasional white diamond spot on their forehead.

While the Tennessee Walking Horses were fantastic, Billy Gordon's driving was impressed me even more. He could barely see over the dash board (seats didn't adjust then), but he never drove outside the lane or exceeded a turn. I had been watching my father drive for a few years, imitating his shifting of gears with the clutch pedal and braking, but I never thought I could drive.

The Boy Can Drive

It was easy teaching me to drive for Billy. He had hundreds of acres of land with roads void of opposing vehicles. I gained confidence rapidly, after my many dry practices in dad's front seat going to work with him. I went back to Memphis, not only reeling with happiness and enjoyment for the outstanding hospitality of the busy Earl and Christine, but with the knowledge I had learned how to drive. Billy Gordon had taught me everything about the motorized vehicle I felt I needed to know.

The first morning after I got back home, dad and I were going to work at the store from the Iowa Street residence and I asked, "Why don't you let me drive, dad? I learned how while I was at Cousin Earl's."

Surprisingly, he pulled over a few blocks from the store and got out.

"Have at it, son. But, be careful."

I was nervous, of course, but I did everything right and parked it almost perfectly in front of our store. He got me a learner's permit to drive at the age of 15 and I was ecstatic. He had been letting me drive under his observation for several years and I became an excellent driver. Delivering groceries in a three-wheeled motor scooter with a wooden bed between the two front tires and later a pickup truck. This, plus driving back and forth across the states many times in later years, I must have driven over 250,000 miles and I only remember two minor automobile accidents in my lifetime. But, as you will read, I was extremely lucky in my heavy drinking days.

From the automobile experience, I established confidence to my father that I could operate a moving vehicle in traffic. With Levi School, an elementary through the eighth grade, over two miles away and upcoming Whitehaven High over five, he made me a deal. He would buy me a Famous James if I would quit smoking.

I didn't have to think twice about accepting that deal. The Famous James was a popular, chain-driven, miniature motorcycle made in Britain. It had three forward gears and would go over 40 miles per hour on a straightaway.

Naturally, my business-minded father had me sign the agreement and he relinquished me of it when I turned 18.

Loved That Role Of New Kid In School

I had never experience it before, of course, but being the new kid in school was fun as well as challenging. Naturally, when I rode up on my new little motorcycle and parked it with the bicycles, many of the early arriving males came up to examine it (and me). The girls watched from a distance, whispering to one another, and giggling behind their hands. My sweet mother had dressed me in my best "Sunday-go-to-meet'n" clothes, but I took off the tie enroute and stuffed it in my pocket.

The big lady principal, Bertha Forrest, was watching from the school entrance. She had met my parents the day before as they enrolled me in the eighth grade, Tiny in seventh, Jo Ann sixth, and John the third. They all rode the bus. Bertha gave me a little welcome smile, but I could tell she wasn't too happy with me riding my motorcycle to school. It wasn't a week later that she forbade it.

In my grade, with Miss Nelson the teacher, I met many pretty girls and many friendly boys. Some of the latter I remember were Bobby Winchester, Harold Smith, David Ransom, Sonny James, Jerry Collins, Tommy Cooper, Billy Mc Kee, Jue Tong, Jennings Jarrett, Billy Foley and Donald Ransom. The girls were Edwina Arnett, Barbara Jean Collins, Janet Wages, Ernie Lee Foley and Lois Jean Trustee.

The morning session in the classroom was a little rough as several of them kept glancing my way after the teacher had introduced me. The boys' looks in my direction didn't bother me as I was doing the same to everyone in the 35-student classroom. However, the girls all included smiles with theirs, so I had to jerk up a quick grin in return. I was glad when the lunch break came.

It had rained a little during the night so the grass playground was a little wet on my first day at Levi. Despite this fact, most of the male 7th and 8th graders starting playing tackle football after eating. I knew my mother would be mad if I came home with my good clothes dirtied, so I refrained at first. Then, watching from the sidelines, I craved more and more to get in the action. I kept seeing missed tackles and poor blocking. Finally, one boy limped off the field with an injury and some yelled at me.

"Hey, Bobby! Wanna play?" he hollered. It was the first time a fellow student at Levi had said my name. That did it. Enough was enough and I kicked off my shoes and ran onto the field. I knew I had to prove myself to these new friends-to-be.

I had played many, many games of sandlot football at Desoto Park. I had always relished the physically contact of the sport, always tackling below the waist and whenever possible, between the knees and the ankles. I knew I was good at it and the adrenaline induced with my desires to impress my schoolmates made me even better. Playing on the left side of the line, I made every tackle when the runner came that way. On offense, they had a tailback who did all the running and passing, so all I did was block the individuals charging. I wanted to ask for a pass or to throw one, but I didn't want to be a hog on my first day. The bell sounded soon anyway.

I was pleased with myself as I ran for the boy's room to wash my muddy hands. There, I lost all my enthusiasm as I observed my clothes in the mirror. My clothes were filthy, especially at the knees on the pants' legs. I shook it off and hustled to class. My teammates patted me on the back as I passed them enroute to my seat. That made it all worth while.

Then, Miss Nelson spotted me and asked, "My goodness, what happened to you, Bobby?" It was her first time to learn that if she gave me a straight line in class, sometimes I would try to be cute for a classroom chuckle.

"Oh, I fell in a mud puddle and was trying to wipe some of it off," I answered smiling as the chuckles came from the football players and the few girls that watched the play.

She deduced the humor immediately and we had a great student-teacher relationship the rest of the semester.

I rode home with a wonderful warm feeling of being accepted by my classmates as a new kid in their school.

Ransom Worth Weight In Gold

Donald and I became a twosome, inseparable everyone said. We started getting on the same team during the "keep away" game all the boys would play during lunch recess. It was a simple game played with a soccer ball, but not with supervision nor using soccer rules. We kicked it to one another OR threw it. Nobody used their head, as in soccer, and we caught the ball in our hands, rolled it or kicked it to a teammate or ran with it before an opponent tackled or wrestled the ball away. There were no goals, so the winning team was the one with the ball when the bell sounded.

As everyone found out, Donald's cousin David Ransom and I were one-two in the school in speed afoot. He was always a little faster so he probably would have beaten me five yards or more in a 100-yard dash. Therefore, we usually were made captains. Choosing randomly, Donald was always my first choice. He was almost as fast and an extremely strong lad.

He had a used Cushman motor scooter that his father had bought him and fine-tuned it. Mr. Ransom was an electrician for the city for over 30 years and specialized in the electric street cars. He taught Donald how to break the whole engine down, clean and oil up, and put it back together. Donald, who was very adept with engines and understood them much better than I, helped me on many occasions with my little cycle.

The bulky looking scooter had its motor completely covered with formed aluminum and a flat metal runner from the engine under the seat to the steering column and front wheel. It had its brake and gas pedal on that floorboard section. It only had one gear, so I would beat him off at the start with my first and second gears on the left side and the clutch on the right handlebar. But, invariably, he would pass me when I got to third before we had gone 100 yards; grinning like a puppy with an under bite. At first it irritated me something awful, because he would always beep his horn a couple times as he caught up and passed me. But, I finally accepted it and smiled back at him.

He was a handsome young man with light brown hair, bold facial expressions, strong eyebrows, and a firm jaw. While I was outspoken and gregarious, Donald was usually quiet and somewhat laid back. He was very levelheaded and probably could have had any girl he wanted. But the only two I saw him go with was Mary Bonner and a redhead beauty named Betty. He told me of going steady with Edwina Arnet in the 7th grade. She was as a next door neighbor to the Foleys and would become one of my favorite people in my waning years to come.

The Most Handsome Family I Ever Met

My fondest family was definitely the Foleys. Billy was my next best buddy and I spent many hours at his house as the family's guest. I really enjoyed his mother, who was extremely sweet and kind, but I had a definite crush on his sister, Ernie Lee. To me, she was the most beautiful girl at Levi. Already possessing an adult body beneath a magnificent head of long, dark, brunette hair that she wore in large curls tumbling down her shoulders and back. And, her mother Mildred, Billy, and his older brother Nate (then away in the U.S. Navy), Millie, and Iva Mae — who was a model —were all exceptionally good-looking. Their father William worked 3-11 p.m. on the railroad, so I never remember seeing him. But, undoubtedly he contributed his family genes. They were probably the most handsome family I ever met.

They were also talented. Mildred won a national contest with a song she wrote, "My Heart Belongs to America," and it was published. She won an all expenses paid trip to New York City and enjoyed it being sung by Vaughn Monroe on his popular radio show.

I finally asked 14-year-old Ernie Lee for a date, which posed a problem. Her mother had a rule that her daughter couldn't got out with a boy until she was l6. However, Mrs. Foley liked me. Therefore, she permitted Ernie Lee to go if she chaperoned. It was to a Whitehaven High School game, which my learner's permit didn't cover, so my father had to drive us. Mr. Peden and Mrs. Foley sat behind us at the football game.

There was an unwritten code that respectable couples didn't kiss on the first date, so the only sexual contact we had all night was holding hands in the back seat on the way home. Tsk, tsk, tsk…pshaw, pshaw, pshaw.

Billy was a lot of fun. His quips with his impish smile were pleasing. He liked to box and really surprised me the way he handled Donald one day when we were horsing around with the gloves in Bobby Winchester's front yard. Both Billy and Donald outclassed me. Wrestling and street fighting were more my style.

One night when Nate was home on leave, he took Billy and me bowling. I knew how to flirt with women, but not like Nate. He was a real professional at it and I never forgot that night. There were

two nice looking girls bowling on the lane next to ours. One very pretty and Nate set his sights on her.

By unknown professional

DANCING IN LIVING ROOM – I was dancing with Donald Ransom's girl Mary, while he was with my girl Lois Jean far right. Tiny Rose & John Collins handled the middle area.

"Gee, that was nice pickup," he said after she knocked over a simple single for a spare.

"My, my. You really have great form," after she got a strike moments later. "Who taught you how to bowl?"

I could tell she was watching Nate's suave movements at the ball rack as well as on the lane bowling. Before she left, he had not only learned her name but he had her telephone number.

He was about four years older than we were and I made up my mind that night that I

wanted to handle myself just like him when I got to be 20. I never made it, however, as he was tall, dark, and handsome with a few natural waves in his hair. I didn't know it but I had already stopped growing at 5'7" and my hair was straight as a board. The only thing I would have in common with that handsome dude was a ruddy complexion.

Puppy Love Was Never Like This

"Eureka! I have found it," so the Greeks gave us to verbally describe a happening of enlightenment. That's what I thought when I kissed passionately the cute little 7th grader named Lois Jean Trustee for the first time. I had heard of the "puppy love," but — as far as I was concerned — no puppy ever loved as we did.

"Smooching," was the rave for teenagers in the 40s and we got our share of it. Most of the time it was done in cars or movies, but we didn't care where is was as nobody was looking. Even in the class coatroom was a favorite spot. Sometimes there would be two or three couples in there smooching at the same time.

I was so brazen that I'd sit with Lois behind Ms. Forrest running a weekday night movie in the school cafeteria and sneak a few smooches. She would catch us every once in awhile, but would not do anything but shake me. I'd hold off then until she changed reels in the 16MM projector. I knew then she would be watching the machine like a hawk to insure she had treaded it properly.

The most brazen thing I did in class of which schoolmate Jimmy Sheppard reminded me 59 years later at a Whitehaven Class of '51 Reunion at James and Jeffie Dacus' mansion near Arlington, Tenn. On Valentine's Day in February '47 at Levi School I went into the classroom of the 7th graders before their teacher had arrived and gave Lois a big red heart-shaped box of candy. Then pulled her up from her seat and embraced her with a long kiss on the mouth while the rest of the class "awed" or giggled.

Every Sunday afternoon, a bunch of us would ride the county bus to downtown Memphis and watch a movie there. We always sat in the back row of the theater so we could smooch. Some guys even played inside the approving girls panties. The movie? Who cared what it was about. None of us watched it anyway. We just wanted the dark with nobody staring at us.

Parties were plentiful. The one game that was a _must_ on every party's agendum was spinning the bottle. I don't know who invented this game, but it was — and probably still is — a tremendous opportunity for the shy girls and boys of the era: (1) The shy girls that spun the bottle landing on the most attractive male would blush all the way through her kiss, but gain a little boldness from it while shedding a tinge of shyness, (2) The shy boys would envelope the same spinning on the most attractive female, (3) The two shy ones getting bottled

together was usually a fun situation, (4) While the two most desirable would put on a show for the rest with a four-star, memorable, humdinger kiss.

I liked the game, but my favorite was my own game in the back seat of the car. By then I had my license and was permitted to use the family car (1941 Ford four-door sedan). Donald liked to drive and Betty liked to control the music on the radio in the front seat. So, Lois and I usually did our smooching on the back seat.

Later, Donald would start going steady with Mary Bonner, who lived on Shelby Drive a few blocks west of him. He was a tremendous young prospect as a pitcher, but she liked him for other reasons, I am sure. Our Levi School ground baseball play against other schools was fun. I preferred shortstop because I got more balls to field at that position.

However, when Donald pitched, no one could catch his sizzling fastball or vicious curveball, but me. Consequently, when he pitched, I had to catch. This wasn't too tough for me after watching Marvin Kirkpatrick in Fort Pickering catch. Plus, Sidney Moore came on the scene and gave me some helpful advice on the position.

I spent many afternoons at Moore's house on Weaver Road playing a form of left field ball, modified to centerfield ball as his back lot was so designed. His little brother, Johnny joined us and learned from both elders. Sidney was a couple years older and his father was the only parent I remember. Mr. Moore was very devoted to some lodge in Memphis. They had a tiny shed for a milk cow, but they only thing that really stuck in my mind was their chickens. I was invited to eat lunch with them one day and there was a hen that walked on the dinning room table while we ate. The house was very messy, but Sidney was instrumental in me becoming more knowledgeable about the professional game of baseball. He knew everything about the box scores in the newspaper and I became enthralled with it as, inherited from my father, I had a fairly well balanced, mathematical mind.

Memphis Chicks Were My Favorite

This all led to attending the Memphis Chickasaws games in Memphis. I used to ride my motorcyle to the games and one summer I sold Pepsi Colas at the night games. The insulated aluminum cooler strapped over my shoulder was extremely heavy when filled with ice and the 12-ounce glass bottles. Carrying it up and down the stands was very tiring. They sold for 10 cents with all us hawkers getting three cents of it.

When the Chicks — as most fans called them — got Ted Kluszewski, I attended over 90% of the home games and listened to all the road games on the radio. He led the Southern Association (Class AA)[15] with a .377 batting average and in

---

15 The current minor league team is the Memphis Redbirds, an affiliate of the St. Louis Cardinals in the Southern League (AAA).

triples. He was very powerful, I think a tight end in college, and hit the ball up the middle. The centerfield fence was 420 feet with many of his line shots bouncing off it for a triple. I remember one time he hit it so hard and fast that the official jogging out to where the ball hit. His sight was so impaired by his bouncing frame he didn't see it clear the fence, hit the Memphis Steam Laundry building, and bounce back onto the field. Thus, one of his home runs was improperly called a triple.

When he was elevated to the Major Leagues with the Cincinnati Reds in 1947, he started slow and sustaining injuries managed only 74 home runs through the 1952 season. Then, healthy and obviously instructed successfully by some batting coach on how to pull the ball instead of hitting to dead center, he hit 171 homers the next four years (40, 49, 47, & 35). The 1954 total led the National League as did his 141 RBIs (runs batted in).

As in Memphis, the sleeveless home run slugger was the crowd favorite. His biceps were so large, he would

cut the sleeves out of the uniform shirt so it would not restrict his swing. In Memphis his arms were bare, with Cincinnati he wore a red sweatshirt.

"Big Klu," as he was lovingly called by teammates and fans, made a big target to throw to at first base. He was 6'2" tall and weighed 255 pounds. For

five consecutive seasons (1951-55), his fielding average topped all NL first sackers.

Roy Buechen, a slew-footed right fielder, and left fielder Lindsay Deal were two of my favorite outfielders to play for Memphis in that era. Another was Pete Gray, a one-armed outfielder who was to play 77 games in the war-thinned majors in 1945 for the St. Louis Browns of the American League at age 30.

Gray had his prominent right arm amputated leaving only a stub following an auto accident as a teenager. Determined, he learned to catch, quickly place both ball and glove under his stub, withdraw the ball and throw with his left arm. His jump on the ball, his speed, and his quickness enabled it to be executed effectively. Batting left-handed, he got out of the batter's box rapidly for many infield hits in the minor leagues, but he only batted .218 in his year in the big leagues. Had he known what kinesiology studies has taught us (i.e. pulling the bat across the hitting zone with the leading arm is more powerful than pushing with the trailing one), Pete would have batted from the other side of the plate.

My Sub-Freezing Winter Swim

One winter day, must have been a Sunday as I was not working, several of us went duck hunting around a nearby lake. I bought me some #3 shot to use with my 12-guage, single barrel, shotgun I had gotten for Christmas. I already had #6 for rabbits and #8 for quail and dove, but I knew the double load of powder in the #3 would be needed for ducks that usually got airborne along the cedar in the wading surface of the lake.

The lake was seven miles around it, so we parked near the levee and starting walking around it. It was a slow trek as there was still a lot of snow on the ground from two days earlier. We had almost covered a full circle around it, without any luck whatsoever. Then we came to a creek. It was only about 17 feet at its narrowest part, but it was deep and mucho cold. We were well covered in cold weather clothing, but it was below freezing in the water which was substantiated by the thin ice forming on its edges. We walked a little ways looking for some kind of crossing or narrower width, but found nothing as it was running west towards the river. It was getting near sunset and we knew we could never trudge back the way we came. Someone must swim the creek and go get a boat.

Naturally, they all looked at me as I was the best swimmer of the bunch and probably the oldest. I suggested we flip a coin, but they wouldn't even think about it.

"No, Bobby," Donald said. "You know you can swim better than us and that water is so cold it's gonna cramp us."

He wasn't emphatic, in fact it was said in a pleading manner. I couldn't refuse as I knew someone had to do it. So, I started stripping naked.

"We got to throw my clothes over," I chattered through my teeth. "You gotta do it Donald. Don't miss."

I rolled everything up in my thick coat, after taking the belt out of my pants to strap tightly around it. I was shivering as I backed up about 10 feet from the closest edge to the other side. Then, without hesitating, I sprinted as fast as I could. I tried to dive at a low glancing angle such as one would sail a flat rock on top of the water. I knew a deep dive could be disastrous.

The shock of the coldness to my body was excruciating. I probably would have coasted all the way across, but I had to move my limbs; actually jerking them more than swim stroking. I felt the bottom and seemed like five or six seconds before I finally got out of the water, although the whole thing was done in a couple of moments. I was blue and stiff as I readied myself for Donald toss of my clothes.

He was already slinging it around his head to gain momentum for the throw.

"Okay, throw it," I screamed.

And he did. It was going slightly higher than he needed and just barely made it to my side of the bank. It hit just inches over and was falling backward towards the water when I snatched it up. I don't

know what we would have done if my clothes had gotten soaked.

Trembling, I unbuckled the clothes as fast as I could, ignoring the cheers coming from across the creek. After I got dressed, Donald threw my boon dockers one at a time. I caught them both and, after wiping the snow off my feet with my gloved hands, I pulled the socks out of my coat pockets and put on the shoes. Then, following a brief series of exercising my limbs, I started my hike for the car. I left my gun and ammo with them.

Another Stomach Sinking Surprise

Knowing I had less than a mile to reach the car, I was elated as my body warmed with the exercise of walking. Then, before I had gone 200 yards in the woods, I came up on another creek. My stomach felt like it dropped two feet I had such a sickening feeling.

It wasn't as wide as the first one and, fortunately, I walked inland about 150 feet and found a large fallen tree that crossed the entire creek. I started to walk across it, but I decided not to push my good luck. I straddled it and scooted across it.

I ran the rest of the way and borrowed a boat from the closed fishing camp owner. Enroute to picking them up, I passed a duck that had its foot hung on a trotline. We got him on the way back to the car and had mallard for dinner that night.

"All is well that ends well," somebody wrote sometime, somewhere.

Girls Telephoning Boys? Never!

In those days, girls definitely did not telephone boys. That was a no-no, very unladylike to do such a thing. Now it is a normal occurrence, but I had just started eyeballing the cutest lass at Levi (Lois Jean) when Janet Wages and Harold Smith had a spat and broke their steady couple relationship. I didn't know about the break, but was not expecting a call from a girl, regardless, as formerly explained. So, when Tiny Rose answered the phone and heard the female voice ask for me, Tiny's jaw dropped and eyes widened as she covered the mouth of the phone.

"It's for you, Bobby. It's a girl," she whispered, obviously startled, while handing me the phone.

"Hello," I said.

"Hi, Bobby. This is Janet. Harold and I broke up," she opened which was followed by a long silence..

Harold was little strange acting to me in the short period I had known him. For example, he didn't participate in the tackle football or "keep away" soccer games. He looked as if he was several years older than the rest of us and carried himself as if he were. Maybe

he was and didn't want to hurt any of us. Anyway, we all respected him and treated him as the "King of the Hill" as Dude and later Tito Wheeler had been in Fort Pickering. In other words, no one gave him any shit.

Consequently, I definitely did not want to arouse the wrath of this peer I held with respectable esteem. So I small-talked with her, all the time trying to figure out why she had decided to call me. Then I thought of the Minstrel Show we had just completed with great success at Levi. Tommy Cooper was the interlocutor and I was one of the endmen. I had cut up one of daddy's old felt hats to make it jagged at the top and drew a few items on it, so with the blackened face and hat I even looked funny. Being the "ham" that I was born to be, as well as a couple of our kids became, I was told by many that I was the hit of the show. But, the choir that sang in the show was the highlight of the night for most of the packed audience. Janet's lead solo, with Edwina and the others in the background, to *"Kentucky Babe"* was tremendous. 'Tis only natural that Janet and I have a warm feeling toward each other.

Fortunately, they went back together right away. Therefore, I only got the one call (that I can remember), and I continued my pursuit for Lois. She lived a mile north of us behind the Levi Baptist Church. I would telephone

to see if I could visit. I would run up there in the spring and summer in about five minutes. When I got to Whitehaven (Tenn.) High School, I never went out for the track team as its season conflicted with the baseball. As my father was not an athlete, I had nobody in my family from whom I could get advice about competing in sports.

Tiger Sports And Art At Top Of My List

After girls, of course, sports and art headed my list of interests at Whitehaven. The school colors of black and gold was not a pleasing combination to me, but I liked the "Tigers" nickname. First, I played on the frosh football team as a quarterback with David at left halfback and Harold at fullback. Donald and Harold dropped out of school to work and I eventually lost touch with them.

I was always particularly fond of playing linebacker on defense. I remember making my buddy Moore, who was a halfback on the varsity B-team furious in a scrimmage game we played. Sidney was not too swift, so every time they would pitch out to him for an end run I would dart in and tackle him behind the line. He told me I could at least let him get to the line of scrimmage before tackling him, but — even though he was a good friend — I didn't agree at all.

As we practiced every

afternoon, I had to refuse the offer of our homeroom teacher to do the male lead in a school comedy play she was directing in her speech class. I regretted the decision later when she gave it to Harold Snell and he became one of the most popular students in school after his performance. I did work on the sets as stage manager during speech class and during the several productions we made. I was very interested in the girl that had the female lead, but did not date her although Lois had moved across town and was attending Fairview Junior High. Our relationship started waning because of the distance between us. Then, with her personality and charm, she was voted "cutest girl" and eventually started dating the captain of their football team.

There was plenty of cute girls in my art class at Whitehaven. I took two hours a day under a brilliant little dumpy teacher named John Fyfe. I have used so many of the things he taught my about art design and composition in my careers in newspapers and public relations. However, he was a big flirt with the female students. He would glance at my work as he walked around and nod to me, but no specific contribution. One of the cute gals working next to me would receive several instructional comments as he drooled over their shoulder and patted her back.

I made the mistake of whispering some catty remark under my breath, I thought. But, he heard it and slapped me in the face. I didn't squeal to Principal F.S. Elliott, but I told my father. I never complained to my parents when I got spanked, but this was entirely different. My dad didn't report him either, but he went to Fyfe's classroom entrance with me and verbally reprimanded Fyfe for his "undignified behavior." Dad demanded Fyfe give me an apology that instant, which he did.

Understandably, the remainder of that school year there was an atmosphere of coldness between us. But, to my pleasant surprise, he gave me an "A" grade each of the three semesters I had him. This showed me class. While he must have despised me personally, I made outstanding scores on his exams and we both knew I was one of the top artists in the school.

I made fair grades in the other classes, especially speech and chorus, but I no longer was asked to sing the lead in anything. I was definitely a first bass by then, but no girls ever swooned when I sang.

In sports, I decided to try out for the freshman basketball team after football season ended. I was surprised when I made the team even as a substitute. We didn't have a gym at either of my grammar schools. The only experience I had was "choose up" games on the Fort Pickering Catholic school's asphalt court on its playground. My quickness made me handy on defense, but my shooting and rebounding stunk.

The first day of tryouts for the freshman baseball team was very interesting. There were over 50 aspirants, which delighted the coach, but he had only two dozen uniforms available. Competition was obviously going to be stiff. He told us to go to the position we wanted to play. Naturally, I desired shortstop, but about 20 went to that spot. It was the most popular position by a long shot. When I saw only two boys go behind the plate, I didn't have any problem figuring which was the best position for me to compete to make the team.

By the end of the first week, I had won the starting catcher's berth. My arm was not powerful, but Marvin Kirkpatrick at Riverside School had taught me how to snatch the ball out of the mitt, get it up behind my ear, and propel it in a low trajectory to second base. My quickness enabled me to get the ball to my target fast. In the few intra-squad games we had, I threw out all runners that attempted to steal a base.

I also was fairly successful at bat. By the end of the second week, I was very pleased when I got my first baseball uniform. It was the varsity's attire from the previous season, so they were not new ones. I didn't get to wear it in a single frosh inter-school game however as

I was moved up to the varsity team. I was flabbergasted. I had never expected it. To be able to travel on the team bus to compete with other schools was going to be fun, or so I thought. Unfortunately, all they wanted me for was to catch batting practice and warm up pitchers. The first string catcher never missed an inning of play. It was good experience, however. I enjoyed warming up our ace of the pitching staff, Pete Dixon.

Jerry Alsup, a pitcher-outfielder, was another Class of '51 member that made the varsity. He was good enough to get in a few games. In fact, he later played at Memphis State University and signed by the Detroit Tigers to play for the Greenville (Miss.) Buckshots of the Cotton States League (Class C). In 1954, during his nine years as a professional, he played at Crestview (Fla.) with Robert Fulton. Alsup nicknamed Fulton "Steamboat" and Robert still had it when I later met him as a sportswriter in 1960. Alsup became a teacher and finally a principal of several schools in the Memphis area before retiring in Walnut, Miss.

Famous Cowboy Jack And Charlie Pride

Another local that I got to know in that little Shelby County area was a musical genius named Jack Clement. He was born on April 5, 1931, so he was less than a year older than I. His dad was the musical director at the Levi Baptist Church and they lived over the hill, only a couple of John Daly's tee shots south of us on U.S. 61.

We had absolutely nothing in common. He wouldn't give a "chick" a second look, while I wanted to get closer to her just to smell her natural odor. He could play any string instrument, but couldn't begin to hit a fast ball. He had perfect pitch, musically that is, just like his dad. I had my complimentary voice training and a few months of piano instruction — plus choir in school and church — but, while I had projection, my voice was lackadaisical compared to band vocalist & guitarist Herbert Burnett's. Jack could sing on key, of course, but his individual vocals weren't as soothing as Herb's.

Before I got my motorized transportation, I would catch the school bus with Jack almost across the highway from his house. Being the young devils that we were, sometimes we would duck into the woods and let the bus pass. Then go to my vacant house as both my parents had to drive to their businesses in Fort Pickering.

Jack would head for the refrigerator first. Grabbing whatever was in there he liked, then he would go flop down on the sofa without removing his shoes. He wore an expression when he wasn't smiling as being on the stupid side. I always

figured this was to fool people. We would listen to records for entertainment on these hooky days. My parents had the first television, probably a 12" black and white job, in the area, but it only had a test pattern on until the mid afternoon. People from all around the neighborhood would come sit in our living room to watch the new evolution in our sunken living room. The evening crowds got so large that my folks couldn't get through the parked cars leading up to our garage. Dad finally got a huge window shade and mounted it outside the garage door with the words "No TV" printed on it. The neighbors would drive up, read the sign, and make a U-turn exiting. It had really gotten bad as I remember counting 22 people sitting in any available chair, coach, etc., or laying on the hardwood floor while watching the new phenomena.

Dad was letting me use the car more and more for dates and gigs with Jack. Herb played the guitar while Jack played the fiddle, banjo, and ukulele, as well as guitar. I would drive them there and kick back listening to them, but never got involved performing. Jack tried to talk me into learning how to play the bass fiddle, but I was too involved in my sports and girl chasing to commit myself. He was going to teach me and I laughed at him, never guessing this big buddy would eventually make Nashville Songwriters Hall of Fame.

I learned later from Bobby Winchester that, before Clement went into the U.S. Marines as a guard at the White House, Jack fought in the l951 Memphis Golden Gloves. I would never have guessed this finesse musician would don the mitts.

"He was knocked down four times in the first round before they stopped the fight," Winchester told me recently. Bobby won the heavyweight championship that year.

I lost touch with Jack until I came home on leave once from the Navy and found him working at Sun Studios. He had toured with a bluegrass band after his four-year hitch and was working at the mixing board for recording sessions with Roy Orbison, Carl Perkins, Johnny Cash, and Jerry Lee Lewis (including *Whole Lotta Shakin' Goin' On).* Another Sun artist, Elvis Presley, even opened for Clement at the Memphis club "The Eagle's Nest. In those years he wrote two of Cash's most enduring songs, *Ballard of a Teenage Queen* and *Guess Things Happen That Way.* The former song, Jack played and sang for me before Cash recorded it.

After leaving Sun Studios, Clement moved to Nashville to work for Chet Atkins, then relocated to Beaumont, Texas. There, he met George Jones and they cut the song *She Thinks I Still Care.* In 1965, Clement returned to Nashville and financed a demo by an unknown Charley Pride and persuaded Atkins to sign him to RCA. Jack also wrote Pride's first two hits, *Just Between You and Me* and *I Know One*, and produced Pride's first several hundred songs.

Clement launched the solo career of Don Williams through his JMI record label, a project that also introduced Allen Reynolds as a record producer. Reynolds later produced Garth Brooks, Crystal Gayle, Emmylou Harris, Bobby Bare, and Kathy Mattea. In addition, Clement was Townes Van Zandt's first publisher and Bob Mc Dill also wrote for Clement's publishing company. Jack released his own album, *All I Want to Do in Life* in l978 and 25 years later his last one, *Guess Things Happen That Way.*

Beyond country music, Clement produced three tracks for U2's *Rattle and Hum* sessions in Memphis and also produced an albumm for Louis Armstrong. In other ventures, he built four of Nashville's leading studios, produced a cult classic horror film and made perhaps the world's first music video on Don Williams in l972, nine years before MTV was launched.

Jack now operates out of his spacious Nashville home. It has a fully equipped studio upstairs, a pool in the side yard, a hammock out back (in which he lounges, I would guess, with his shoes on), and all the rooms are wired for filming. The last I read about him, he was an executive for the Country Music Hall of Fame and Museum.

Two Front Teeth Lost In Scrimmage Game

My sophomore year at Whitehaven only lasted a half-year as we returned to Fort Pickering. Only a couple highlights are worth mentioning.

With Lois Jean out of my life, I started dating this one female who switched my sex methods. She wouldn't let me get in her panties, but she would get in my jockey shorts. We would park and smooch while she masturbated me. Strangest high school gal I ever dated.

In a scrimmage football game with Southside High, I tackled All-City Fullback Donald Cowan at the shoe tops. He had legs the size of tree trunks like Army's great Doc Blanchard. Churning them out of my grasp, he broke my two front teeth out with his cleats which were hard rubber. Helmets didn't have face masks then.

Ironically, The Chipmunks came out with a song titled *All I Want for Christmas is My Two Front Teeth* about that time. Until the gums healed and I got a partial, my dating girls were held in abeyance.

BGWW&P Times

January 1949 - July 1950   *Vol. 1, No. 6*   *Memphis, TN*

At Southside High

Little Heaven & City Title Found
Hickman Ewing Lays On "Wild Buck"

We moved back to Fort Pickering. This time it was on Delaware Street, a corner house at California Street one block north of Peden Grocery and across the street from DeSoto Park. Our garage faced the Joneses' house so I was able to maintain a close friendship with them, particularly Richard. Oliver, his older brother, had joined the U.S. Air Force by lying about his age of 16. He was caught, but allowed to remain when his parents gave their written permission. I really missed the home run rivalry Ollie (as he is called now) and I had playing left field ball. Plus, he had become a pretty good softball pitcher, hurling a no-hitter.

My father was really curtailing my ball playing as he had taught me every job in the store (e.g. cashier, stockman, etc.). We had a produce manager that had special training in that capacity. He was paid a good salary as was the butcher, Paul. I would help the produce manager

sometimes, but he would go to the market place early in the morning and have most of the fresh food on ice by the time dad and I got there. I would make trips to the wholesaler for dry and canned foods, plus daily trips to the bank to make deposits.

Then one beautiful summer day, he told me he was changing the name of the store to Peden & Sons as I had always been so helpful to him and he expected John Lee to do the same when he was older. He was going to leave the store to us when he retired. Meanwhile, he wanted me to learn to be a butcher.

I always got along well with Paul. He was a big man, about 6' (that was tall in those days) and 230 pounds. But, he was an alcoholic. He never got drunk at work, but he kept a bottle in the market cooler where we hung the beef and pork carcasses. About once, sometimes twice, an hour he would go in and chugalug a shot or two. The cooler had a glass window in front, so I could see him if I desired.

He would chase it with a cold Coca Cola. He never offered me any, of course, and I never mentioned it to dad, although I am sure he was aware of it.

I'm sure dad ignored it because part of Paul's salary was the rental of dad's house next to the store and because Paul was such a good butcher. He was strong enough to manhandle a half a cow. It took me a few times before I could flip it over on the meat block as he did, but I got sufficient enough at it that he would let me do it by myself.

We had a large electric band saw that we used for smaller sections, but cutting the half into quarters and most of the big roasts, we'd cut with the large knives. Dad, as well as Paul himself, insisted on an appealing display of the cuts we had for sale. Keeping the blood cleaned out of the trays and off the glass display cooler was one of my main tasks.

Plus, keeping the dropped meat scraps picked out of the sawdust we kept covering the floor of the butcher shop area was another major chore. We had to dump the sawdust and put down bags of fresh, nice smelling replacements. It was a very clean butcher shop in which I was proud to work.

Not once did I ever cut myself with a knife or cleaver, but one day I was flirting with a pretty customer while slicing baloney with our electric slicing machine. I was holding the almost depleted tube of baloney with my hand instead of the adjustable aluminum holder and sliced off the end of my thumb. It was only the width of a slice, so I grabbed it off the sliced baloney and placed it properly on my bleeding thumb. Paul took over while I rinsed the excess blood off it and wrapped it tight with gauze and tape. Would you believe (1) it grew back on the thumb, and (2) I didn't ever use my hand again when a tube got down to a small size.

I dressed out for baseball practice during its healing process, but wasn't able to throw the ball or bat for almost a week. Hickman Ewing, our coach, used me in a game as a pinch runner during that period and called me a new name. It was the bottom of the ninth and one of our slow players got a base on balls with Central High ahead of our Southside Scrappers, 1-0.

I was sent in to replace him and was very excited as it was my first appearance in a high school game. My adrenalin level was high taking my lead off first base, but when the ball popped out of the catcher's mitt on the next pitch. I didn't hesitate and streaked for second base. The ball only fell a few feet in front of the catcher, so he pounced on it quickly and fired it to the shortstop covering the bag. I made it safely with a picture book hook slide, but it was a very close play.

Ewing was furious. He yelled at the umpire for time and came steaming from the third base with his hat in his hand.

"You wild buck," he sputtered loudly. "You could have taken us out of the game." (Note: My Fort Pickering friend Kenneth Gipson was at the game and heard the coach. The significance of this is in a later chapter).

I was very confused. "But I stole the base, coach. What did I do wrong?"

He took off his cap and rubbed his head grunting, "I'll explain it to you in my office after the game. Don't you dare try to steal third base unless I signal. Understand?"

I understood that alright and afterwards in his office he explained why I should not have taken the chance with Central ahead only one run. Fortunately, I scored on a single by Jimmy Cantrell with Wilbur Conley driving Jimmy in for the victory with a long double. Conley was one of the smoothest centerfielders that I saw play in high school.

Dick Hearn was one of the best third basemen in our circuit and I learned from Alsup that Dick played professionally. I'm not sure whether Conley, our top hitter Billy Russell, or our ace senior pitcher, Billy Joe Emmons, made the pros.

Southside High's Silent Mound Battery

Nor did I learn whether or not Haywood Watts made it to the pros. I was shocked when I learned Watts, the kid that shot my friend Jackie Golden in the leg while almost hitting me in the temple, was on the team. He was gifted with a strong arm, throwing a hopping fastball. In fact, I caught both of them many times and I think Watts' ball was faster then Emmons. However, Billy Joe — a high scoring forward on the All-Memphis Basketball Team — was more accurate.

I never discussed the near deadly accident with him. In fact, I hardly ever spoke to him, even while I was catching him. Someone told me somewhere along the line that he swore he was aiming to the ground to warn us off their "no trespassing" posted land. I tried, but I never believed it.

This silent treatment of Watts, my "wild buck" running on the base paths, and maybe Coach Ewing's opinion was just low on my ability. Whatever the reason, he played a taller, big-boned freshman more than me at the catcher's position. I don't remember the nice kid's name, but I'm sure the coach wanted to develop the young man's talents for the future. He couldn't catch, throw, run, or hit as well as me, so I never understood the coach's reasoning. The kid did have potential and a father in county politics. And Ewing, who became a Tennessee prep HOF football coach, finally became a county clerk (*hmmm, maybe help from the kid's father...no, probably just sour grapes from me*). Tsk, tsk, tsk...pshaw, pshaw, pshaw. Ewing was subsequently jailed for embezzlement.

Most Kin Folks Back From World War II

None of the Pedens participated in World War II. Dad and his older brother Albert were too old or couldn't pass the physical for some health reason. Reid, the youngest, I was told was serving time for manslaughter after shooting a man in a fight across the street from our grocery store. Of course, dad had three kids, Reid two (Walter Leonard "Pete" and Robert Reid) and Albert one (William Albert). That may have kept them from being drafted as well.

From the Tutors and their spouses, John Paul was still in the Army over in Korea before that war developed. But Keister, who participated in the most combat, was back from WWII after participating with the First Army in the famous "Battle of the Bulge" in

December 1944. In a retaliatory attack, they recaptured all the territory in and around the Ardennes Forest gained earlier by the Germans. An estimated 110,00 prisoners were taken and the Germans suffered over 100,000 casualties. They surrendered the following May to end the war.

Aubrey, Berline's husband, was also in the Army while Morris, the oldest male Tutor, returned from the U.S. Air Force. I don't think either of them saw any action. Morris, who had married school teacher Mable Ferguson, became a barber and they had two beautiful healthy kids, Michael and Dannie Sue.

With all his kids gone, widower popa was alone for a while. Then, his daughters found a nice widow lady and talked the two into a marriage of convenience. Popa's sister Layla Hall (no kin to Aubrey) and her family moved into the old place on the south hill. I would still make my annual winter visits to hunt, now with her son David, about one year my senior, and Charles Kenneth, several years plus. Her oldest, Gayland, was in the U.S. Navy, and she had five daughters: Virginia, Jane, Patty Viola, Berline, and Frances. I loved that family dearly.

Layla was an outstanding cook. Her big fluffy biscuits were outstanding with popa's molasses. She was a great story teller, also. We would always get her to tell us tales before we fell asleep laying in our

two big feather beds while watching the big logs burn in the fireplace. The boys would sleep at one end of the bed and some of the girls at the other. One or two would snuggle in Layla's bed.

One story I never forgot and still use it with my grandchildren today. It explains the reason dogs sniff other dogs rear end: *There was once a humongous banquet held for all dogs in the world. To enter, each dog had to hang its tail on nails at the entrance. During the affair, a large fire broke out with all the dogs scampering out the door to escape the fire. In their haste, they had to grab whatever tail they could get. Ever since then, they have been trying to fine their own tail.*

Sneaky Trip Has Sorrowful Ending

I didn't get to visit often with Sidney, Donald, and Billy after moving back to Fort Pickering, but Sidney had talked me into joining the U.S. Naval Reserve with him after I turned 17. Therefore, he and I would see each other every Monday night at the training site near the fairgrounds in Memphis. We both were still following the Memphis Chicks and wanted to see some other baseball fields in the Southern League. I knew my folks would not let me go, but they would let me drive to popa's farm to visit. So, we planned a secret trip one summer to Birmingham

(Barons team), Ala.; Atlanta (Crackers), Ga.; Chattanooga (Lookouts) and Nashville (Volunteers), Tenn. We had it planned so we would arrive in time to see night home games at Atlanta and Nashville and just view the other parks during daylight hours. All of this was to occur in one weekend in my father's car while our parents thought it was to be a trip to my grandfather's farm which had no phone.

Things went according to plans until the last stop. I even got to see the young phenomenon, Eddie Mathews, playing at third base for Atlanta. He would enter my life in the near future.

We made it to Sulphurdale Park in Nashville in time to see the Vols play our Chicks in a Saturday night game.

We saw the infamous short right field, I think only about 225 feet from the plate to its fence. Naturally, the fence had to be high up on a mound. Consequently, what would normally be a high fly out to the right fielder in other parks would be a home run. And, a slammed line drive that would be a home run in any other field would only bounce off the high screen extension for a single. Occasionally, if hit low enough to hit the wooden part of the fence, and the runner was slow, the fielder would fire it to first base and throw out the batsman. Due to this fence, the Vols usually had the circuit's leading home run hitter, which irked true power hitters like Mathews.

When the game ended, the huge crowd started for the exits. As it was a close game, practically everyone stayed until the last out was made. We had been sitting up high in the grandstand behind home plate. Being the stupid daredevil that I was, I decided to jump off the stadium grandstand onto a building on the ground level and then to the ground and beat the crowd. I landed on my feet, but the momentum of the jump forced me forward; therefore, I fell forward at impact. Unfortunately, there was a broken beer bottle that cut a deep slash in the heel part of my right hand. The blood came forth immediately. I jumped down to the ground and went into the rest room and washed it. Then I got paper towels and pressed it against the cut to stop the bleeding.

I met Sidney at the car and he started driving to Memphis, which was over 200 miles away. I had crawled onto the back seat to sleep until it was my turn to drive.

Then it happened. Sidney went to sleep in a curve and the car glanced off the side of a blunt hill and slid 20 feet or so down a drainage ditch. Neither of us were injured, so he must not have been going full speed when he fell asleep. I observed that if the car had gone off the road 30 yards farther, it would have tumbled down a 200-foot cliff. We were lucky to be alive.

The first car that came by stopped and drove us to the

nearest auto repair shop he knew well. The owner was very kind and an extremely knowledgeable mechanic. He towed the car to his shop and examined it immediately. He told us what he could replace from his shop but the bent wheel would have to be purchased Monday when the parts store would be open. We had nothing to do but sleep in the car and wait.

Monday finally came after a miserable day of nothing for us. Sidney was really depressed while my feelings were of the shame I knew I was going to suffer when my parents learned I had deceived them. The kind mechanic had not only fixed the car, but his wife had fed us three full meals. I called my father and explained everything to him, then I gave the phone to the mechanic as directed. He told my father that the complete bill would be $78 and he could just mail it. That was a lot of money in those days. After I got home that night with the mechanic's bill and address, dad — learning of the mechanic's hospitality — sent him a $100 check.

We got home late Monday afternoon. Sidney begged me to take him home first as he didn't want to face my father. He promised to pay half the damages as he found work. I paid my half from my savings. My parents were very understanding about the whole thing (the bloody hand helped), but were very disappointed in me lying to them. I knew

I would never get permission to make a weekend trip in the family car again. So, except for the shame I was experiencing, there was no punishment, but that was enough. The cut took 15 stitches.

Art From One Extreme To Another

Although I never lied to my parents again, I was far from being a good kid. I had to ride the city buses to and from Southside High, which was rather boring. It gave me an opportunity sometimes to do some of my homework required by the art teacher which was to do 20 sketches of local scenes. This was required to be turned in each Friday by Mrs. Cornelia Wolfe, our instructor

She was just the opposite of Fyfe at Whitehaven. He taught theory and concepts that one could use in postgraduate jobs in life. For example, if one needed a straight line drawn, but didn't have a ruler handy for the sketch, you simply line the paper up with a table or desktop edge and hold it with one hand. Then, take a pencil and place it in the other hand with the point at the mark the line was desired. Using the last three finger to hold the pencil against the thumb. Then, with the index finger straightened and serving as a guide along the table, the pencil would be pulled making a straight line.

Mrs. Wolfe was more into "arts & crafts" things. I couldn't believe it when we painted eggs in class. Some of the things were good, of course, but the A&C stuff was not what I wanted to learn and she detected it.

She would get so disgusted when she had given us a project to complete she was expecting to keep us busy for the rest of the period and I did it in 10 or 15 minutes. I had been painting prices of specials on my father's glass windows for years, so drawing something in ink and brushing on tempera colors on show cards was a "piece of cake" for me. When I would turn it in to her, she would give me a hard look. Also, when she would return our sketch books on Monday, she once asked me if I had observed the subjects and not made them up in my head. I lied and said that I saw every object.

Sometimes I wouldn't get the 20 completed until Friday morning before the first bell. I would go to the lunch room and draw there. Usually, some of the interested students would gather around watching me and sometimes suggesting subjects. They seemed amazed at me doing it, but it is just a gift I possessed as some people have perfect pitch musical ears and some are born with arm strength to throw a baseball 95-100 miles per hour. All the attention pleased me, of course, and I noticed several cute girls watching. Unfortunately, I couldn't chat as I had to beat the first bell.

One boy in the group asked me if I could draw a girl in a bathing suit. I made the mistake of satisfying him with a well endowed adult female doing a swam dive. Mrs. Wolfe reprimanded me in front of the class the following Monday.

"Now I got you," she said with a devilish smile. "This is January and there are no pools open. Where did you see this diver?"

"I saw it on television. They were having a contest or something in Florida," I finally murmured. I suspected she didn't believe me and when I saw the "D" on my report card she gave me, I knew it. There was no way I deserved that grade, but I didn't contest it. It was the only one I made, but there were no "A's" either; Just "B's" and "C's." I didn't care. All I was interested in were girls and sports.

A Matt Greenhorn With Quick Moves

I didn't even try to make the basketball team, because I knew I'd never make it. Southside had Billy Joe Emmons, our baseball pitching ace, as high scorer. He was an All-Memphis forward and Richard Hearn was tops in the league as an All-Memphian and league high scorer next season.

Several of my friends urged me to go out for the wrestling team, most of them had been participants in our "King of the Mound" games in DeSoto

Park. I don't remember the coach's name, but he had only been graduated from Southside a few years past. He had Jerry Crum returning after winning the city welterweight championship in 1948. I was at 150 pounds, three over the welterweight limit. So, I didn't know where I would fit on the team, middle or welterweight.

The coach had Jerry and I wrestle practice against each other. Jerry knew many more moves than I, but with my innate quickness and strength from bicycling and handling heavy loads at the store, it was clear that I would beat him in a heads-up match. Also, his natural weight was 145, so the coach had him lose down to lightweight and instructed me to get below 147. The workouts did that; therefore I became a full-fledged welterweight.

I had a great season, winning all eight of my matches and all but one were by pinning my opponent. When I told my father that I was going to wrestle for the Memphis High School Wrestling Championship Saturday afternoon, he was very happy. Professional wrestling was the only sport he would watch on television and he was extremely fond of it. His favorite was Farmer Jones. He was a big fat pro with a beard and dressed in overalls with the two-strap bibs and all. He had a pet pig he always brought with him during his parade around the matt to warm up. An attendant kept the pig in his corner while he was wrestling.

Dad would get so excited he worked up to the edge of his seat yelling at Jones' dirty opponent during the match. The opponents would do something like using fake sandpaper and, while Farmer was in his hold, act like he was sandpapering Jones' eyes.

"That's not fair, you dirty scoundrel," dad would yell.

"Dad, that stuff is all fake," I would tell him trying to calm him. "You know that, right?"

"No it's not," he would say. "He's really hurting Farmer Jones' eyes."

I tried many times to explain some of those holds they were faking would break an opponent's neck, arm, etc. He never believed me and I understood why. He had never wrestled in his life, even as a kid. So, I wasn't too disappointed on our way home from the city championship matches. It was the first match he had taken off work to see and it was a dull one to him. My opponent was extremely proficient and I was on the defense most of the match. He finally became tiring as I forced him to use so much of his strength to keep me in his grasp after his takedown. My last takedown, I put him in a cradle lock and applied all my power in a tight hold almost forcing his knee into his face. I won the decision by only one point. I felt sorry for my opponent, as I believed he was the more knowledgeable wrestler. I had won only because I had more stamina.

But, I was very happy. Before then, I didn't ever remember being as happy as I was at that moment.

I hadn't even thought about college, but I started thinking after the matches were all over when a man came over and congratulated me introducing himself as the wrestling coach at the University of Tennessee. He said he'd be watching me next year as his permanent residence was in Memphis.

"How did you like the matches, dad?" I asked on the way home.

"Oh, they were all right, but kinda dull compared to the pros," he said seriously.

I knew he meant it. I understood.

"You're right, dad."

Other Classes, Then One Choir Class

Some days I had a few bucks of change in my pocket and felt like playing the pinball machine a block away instead of attending class. It was easy to cut some classes. One of those was typing. Once introduced to the method of typing with the touch system utilizing the basic keyboard without looking at the keys was a challenge to me. As any other challenge for me at that age, I relished it. My parents had purchased me a used portable Underwood typewriter, so I mastered it in a couple of weeks mostly at home. In class, the teacher would assign three typing tests after our warm up drills. Then all she would do was start the five-minute timer for each test. At the end of the class, students would turn in their three tests. After a few weeks of this I was getting about 30 words per minute with less than five errors. It then became boring to me.

A cute lass sitting next to me was a whiz. She could do 60 or 65 WPM easily. We got to be pretty good buddies, so we worked out a scheme for a big Christmas gift. Instead of going into the classroom, I'd meet her in the hallway and motion toward the school exit with my thumb. She would smile and do my three tests for me instead of doing her warm-up drills. Then she would do hers during the teacher-timed tests. As the teacher never called role, using the turned in speed tests as proof of attendance. It was a cold, all business, class.

Meanwhile, I was down at the ice cream shop playing pinball with the other derelicts. I also played the juke box frequently as we gambled a dime on each of the pinball games. Both the pinball and juke box took a nickel to play. I remember my favorite was Nat King Cole. I thought he was real "groovy."

Another class I cut every once in while was literature. It was so much fun doing it that I caught myself chuckling as I wrote about it. The teacher, Mrs. Allensworth, would go to the glass door holding it open with the inside door knob as the second bell rang signifying the start of the next period.

When they bell stopped, she would slam the door shut and would not permit another student to enter.

If I wanted to skip the class and go play pinball with the guys, I would walk slowly down the hall until the bell started ringing. Then, I would run for the door. If I wanted the class I would run fast enough, otherwise I would not and watch her sneer at me inside the slammed door. I would kneel, put my palms together begging, to no avail. The other kids loved it. I was a show-off clown all the way during my Southside High era.

I enjoyed algebra as math was always easy for me and the Reserve Officers Training Corps (ROTC) was intriguing to me. Sergeant Charles Farris taught us map reading that I never forgot. It was very helpful to me in the Navy and invaluable during my many motoring trips across the states. Chorus was a treat for me as I liked to belt out those musical ovals from the first base section.

One particular class in chorus, the teacher, Mrs. Loula Mallory, had a trio of girls from another period sing a special for us. The girls — Jean Watkins, Carolyn Esrey, and Dean Sanders — had sung the song on a church television show the weekend before. As they sang, Carolyn had the lead while Jean sang alto and Dean tenor. It was an excellent performance and I was particularly impressed with the

beautiful lead singer. Her body was so well shaped and she had the tiniest waist and the most perfect shaped behind. I found out then, observing women I was definitely a "buttman" as opposed to a "boobman".

"Man! I'd like to make out with that lead singer," I said punching a tenor named Johnny Jones sitting next to me.

"Well, you better not try," he said with a very serious look on his face. "That's my steady."

"Ooops, sorry there Johnny," I responded quickly, but I still entertained those initial thoughts. Then I remembered, she was one of those students that would crowd around my lunchroom table when I did my sketches on Friday mornings. Then, and I hadn't noticed before as I usually read or did sketches, I found out she was one of the monitors in the huge study hall period that I had.

The next few months, there was a lot of reasons I needed one of the monitors. Thinking back on it, some of the quirks I used to spend a few moments with her were corny, to say the least. But, we were slowly got to know each other just with the moments in study hall and Friday morning comments between sketches. I even threw a little green snake on her once during lunch recess on the school campus front lawn. She never really forgave me for that, I don't think, although I told her it was harmless.

Finally, it happened. Johnny

and Carolyn broke up. I never asked why, but I was first in line to ask for a date. It was February 1950 and the St. Valentine's Day Sox Dance was going to be held at the high school gym. I asked her to go with me and we arranged for a blind date with her best friend, Billie Frances Roberts, and my best friend, Richard Jones. It was all set and I picked up everyone in my parents four door sedan.

I got off to a successful start with Carolyn's mother, Lillian Esrey. She answered the door and I said, "Oh, I didn't know Carolyn had an older sister." She smiled and probably thought it was a line of gaff I used, but I was dead serious. The looks definitely told me they were related and, to me, she looked younger than her age.

It Was Heaven With All Its Trimmings

We all sat nervously in the stands waiting for the music to start. Billie Frances and Richard were making small talk as they were getting to know each other. Carolyn and I were very attentive to their conversation until I took her hand in mind. She glanced at me with her eyes and gave me a soft smile. Blood started tingling in me.

Then, the music began. It was a slow dance, so I escorted my date to the gym floor. I took her into my arms and reality slowly disappeared. I felt like

I was floating in soft white clouds. *I had never experienced the feeling that I had during that dance. It was passionate.* **It was love!** I was floating in what I imaged heaven to feel like. It was a feeling I would never experience again.

Carolyn was an exceptionally good dancer. Consequently, she was a popular partner to the males. I didn't give them an opportunity to dance up close to her as I danced every slow tune that was played by the band. Unfortunately, I had never jitterbugged in my life. To me, that dance was "showing off." So I had to sit and watch as she entertained her dance partner, and others watching as I, with her perfect timing while twirling, stopping, restarting, and shuffling to the beat of the music. She always danced with a pretty smile on her face for her leader in the dance. I experienced the feeling of *jealousy* for the first time in my life. I swore to myself then: "*You are going to learn to do that stuff.*"

Finally, the night of floating on clouds and smothering jealousness ended and we walked to the car. I never will forget the dumb-founded expression on Richard's face when we got to the car and I handed him the keys.

"You don't mind driving do you, buddy?" I asked opening the back door for Carolyn.

It was a bold move toward advancing a brand new romance into its second gear. There was a moment of frozen

stillness among the four of us. Then, Carolyn entered and it quick-thawed us and we all got in. In those days, couples definitely did not kiss on the first date, sometimes not until the third or fourth. I wanted it **NOW!**

Apparently, so did Carolyn. We embraced and our lips met even before Richard got the car started. The kiss was titanic. It made me feel even more passionate, if that were possible. We must have smooched over a 100 times that night.

After that night, we dated as frequent as we could. Much of it was movies or bowling as we both enjoyed the sport. Whatever we did, we always stopped at Kay's Bar-Be-Que drive-in. Leonard's was closer to her house, but I didn't like their food as well. Plus, the car hops that waited on us at Kay's would bring Richard and I beers, never checking our ages. Whatever we did, it was usually with Richard and Billy Frances who had also started going steady.

With so much talk about me between Carolyn and her mother, her father, Virgil, once asked at the dinner table when Carolyn would say "Bobby did this" and "Bobby did that," if I had a last name.

"Sure, Bobby Peden (emphasizing PEE-den)," Carolyn answered.

"Peed in what?" he joked and she left the table crying. He was sorry that he had upset her as she was his only daughter and they were very close. I came to be very fond and respectful of him the following years. I didn't learn of this kidding about my last name until a few years ago. Tiny Rose used to kid me, Jo Ann, and John Lee with the same question. It got to be old stuff. One Peden cousin pronounced it PED-n on his radio show.

Love Me Enough To... Whoops!

After several months of numerous dates, we were falling more and more in love. One night we were parked on a levee overlooking the Mississippi River south of Memphis doing our necking before I took her home that night. We couldn't smooch on her front porch swing as her mother was laying on the bed by the bedroom window listening and probably watching us. So we'd park and smooch before her 11 p.m. curfew.

We got into a silly lovers playful argument as to who loves each other the most. Something like: "You don't love me as much as you love banana puddin" or "you don't love me enough to jump off the Golden Gate Bridge" or "you don't love me enough to give up jitterbugging." Of course the answers were "I'd burn all the banana plants in the world for you" and "I'd jump and parachute right into your arms" and "I'd tie my legs together and walk with crutches for you instead of jitterbugging."

Then, I casually said, "You don't love me enough to marry me."

"Oh Bobby, yes I will! Yes, I do love you that much. Do you mean it," she blurted and started kissing me. I was devastated. I had never thought of matrimony. Suddenly, I had a girl with whom I was deeply in love thinking that I had asked her to marry me. *What should I do?* I kissed her hard and long while I thought of an answer. It wasn't any doubt that I wanted her the rest of my life. She wouldn't let me get into her panties, but that wasn't the reason I decided to made this "little boo-boo" the real thing as she was receiving it. The main reason was I loved puppies and kids. I wanted her to be the mother of my children.

"You know I mean it," finally said. "Not right now, but I want you to marry me."

"Let's go home. I want to tell mama," she said full of joy.

"I should ask your father's permission to marry you before you do anything," I said using 18 years and five months logic over her bubbling 16 years and two months. It was June and we had been dating only four months. Of course, it was a heated affair.

I was extremely nervous asking Mr. Esrey if I could marry his daughter the next afternoon. He had been a party goer in his day. As a foreman at Slumber Products, a huge furniture manufacturing company next to the opening

of Riverside Park off South Parkway Blvd. and Riverside Dr., they would get paid every Friday. Most of the workers would stop by their favorite tavern to drink beer and shoot pool or pinball, sometimes spending much of their payroll. He was no exception. He was an infrequent church attendee until he went to hear his daughter singing a special and changed his lifestyle completely. He eventually joined the Trinity Baptist Church on McLemore Street and never drank alcoholic beverages again.

That occurred long before I had submitted my request to him, but it made me understand why he answered: "We will pray on it."

A few days later, the Esreys gave me their consent. I went to my parents immediately with the news and promised them I would finish school before we got married. I knew I had a fulltime job at Peden & Sons for the rest of my life. But, several months earlier, I had given my mother my entire life savings ($300) to buy one of the first postwar cars that became available. Available metal had all gone to the war effort. The Kaiser Co. was first with a Kaiser and Frazer Models. My mother put up the rest and we bought a four-door, maroon Frazer for $1,700. It even had overdrive, a new automobile innovation. It was in mother's name, but she said it would be all mine when I received my high school diploma. That all was well and good, but I wanted an engagement ring for Carolyn.

"My son, you know I how let people charge groceries sometimes?" he asked when discussed the problem with my father.

"Sure, you sent me yesterday to collect from that colored family that had not paid their bill," I said because I really detested doing that. "I understand credit."

"Well, that's what you're going to have to do. You're going to have to establish credit at a jewelry store and but it on credit," he explained knowing that the jeweler would approve it with a grocery store owner backing it.

Carolyn and I chose one for $150 (wow), dad gave me $70 to pay down and I worked it off immediately. The other $80 I paid $10 a month. Everything was rosy, she showed the ring to all her friends and I boasted of the engagement to my young single friends.

Then it happened!

There was a communist turmoil in a peninsula off Asia called Korea. It would redirect my life.

BGWW&P Times

July 1950-Sept. 1952   Vol. 1, No. 7   Memphis, TN & San Diego, CA

Boot, Taste Of Air, & Fatherhood
Marriage Will Not Wait, War Or Whatever

Suddenly, the United States is extremely concerned with the communists-ruled North Korea rejecting by force South Korea's effort to unify the country. This aggression occurred on June 25, 1950, and was against the charter of the United Nations, which had formed by major nations of the world following World War II in l945. The United State was a strong member of the UN, therefore rushed great numbers of troops and supplies to aid the South Koreans.

I was a happy lad when 51 charter members formed the United Nations. I thought these countries would come to the aid of any major fracas in the world. I thought UN forces would quickly subdue any group who took up arms against a democratic nation. I was gladly ready to go do my part in this belief and finally talked my friend Richard Jones into joining the regular U.S. Navy with me on July 20.

Naturally, I wanted to be a pilot with all the studying I had done during WWII of the USN fighter pilots. I told this to the recruiter that had administered us the entrance exam. He told me that I had scored very high on the test, so I should not have any trouble passing the examination to becoming a USN pilot. However, he said I would have to take a General Development Test (GED) to get an equivalency certificate for a high school education. All applicant's were required to have same, he explained, but swore I should have no trouble with the high score I made on the entrance test.

So, Richard and I made the long train ride to the Naval Training Center in San Diego. We were among hundreds of volunteers pouring into the place. We faced a physical examination first thing and the burr headed haircut came next. There were so many that we would all have to strip in a huge gym and line up for what the corpsmen called a "short arm" inspection. Actually, the physicians checked your whole body, but the nickname for the inspection was because they also checked everyone's penis and had us turn, bend over and pull our "cheeks" (glutei) apart to observe our rectums.

They had separated us into alphabetical order by the first letter of our last name. I was dressed and assigned to a Company Commander (CC), a chief petty officer with a gold rating badge and three hash marks.[16] Richard had been detained by one of the physicians and was assigned to a separate company. Our CC was a handsome, well-tanned dude, about six feet tall, and in his early thirties. He told us we would receive a "little trim" at the barbershop, march to receive our military tuxedoes and then to the barracks especially reserved for Company 228. Then, he asked if there were any important questions. I shot up my hand from the second rank immediately. He acknowledged and I said:

"I joined with a buddy in Memphis and he's not here. What could of happened to him? Won't he be in this company with me?" I asked.

"They must have found <u>something to hold</u> him up. If

---

16 Each red hash mark indicates four years of service & gold ones indicate good conduct during that period.

he passes his physical, he'll be assigned to the next company being formed. Unless you have a signed agreement with your recruiting officer that he guaranteed boot training together, there's nothing you can do. We're full to the brim, so there's no chance he will be assigned to Company 228," he explained and then went to the next question. Richard and I had not thought of this happening. He was assigned to a later company and I finally found him three weeks later.

My First Look At San Diego And Tijuana

I got my firsthand knowledge for sure that I was short. I had not grown an inch or gained a pound since I was a regular sized youngster in the ninth grade. I was still 5'6.5" tall and weighed 150 pounds. As they started assigning us to one of the three squads in our company first platoon, they started with the shortest and worked up to the tallest. I was next to the smallest in our first squad. Jimmy Clements, who became my best pal in boot camp, was the smallest of the seven-squad members.

The CC appointed James (I think) Brewer as the Recruit CC. I nicknamed him "Rooster" and the rest of the company picked it up. Great guy. Everyone liked him.

Tony Harrison and James Haynes were my two other good friends. We usually pulled liberty together. It was the third week before we got liberty and our company section got it Saturday and the other section Sunday. It started at 9 a.m. and ended at midnight each day. We just walked around the main drag downtown San Diego the first liberty. It was one of the cleanest big city I had ever seen. Naturally, in August, everyone was in short sleeve tops and most in short pants. Being on the coast, it was sunny but cool enough with the ocean breeze. We found all the favorite places such as the movie theaters and the bowling alley. One week we spent almost the whole day at the famous San Diego Zoo. The rest of the time we spent at Mission Beach, except for the trip to Tijuana. Everyone said we had to go there and check out the whores.

We did and I was shocked at their method of operation and open talk. We would go in a place that appeared to be a bar and grill. It would be full of senoritas, some of them very nice looking. They would hang back a little until the sailor had looked them all over and if his eyes came back to one twice she would make her move.

"Hi, sailor. Buy me a drink?" they would usually say and move in close to the target. Some would rub a guy's crotch, as she got close. We were really flabbergasted, as we had never seen whores operate before. In fact, it was the first time any of us (Clement, Harrison, Haynes and I) had ever been out of the country before. Haynes and Clement were city boys but Harrison was a farmer's son and had never been out of his county in Tennessee. Fortunately, they didn't check our age or their wasn't any restriction of drinking alcoholic beverages. So, a few beers and we were all at ease in this strange environment.

The place was packed with sailors and marines from the states. When the guy was ready for sex, the girls would take them out back to four or five motel rooms. I noticed the prostitutes took a roll of toilet paper on the back porch while exiting. The guys told me they had some kind of lubricant, like Vaseline, stuffed inside the roll. It was very unromantic to me, plus I had seen enough V-D films at the base to take any chances with these prostitutes who had worn trails through the grass in the backyard.

I was feeling no pain when we returned to the base, but I was in better shape than the others. Haynes probably had never drank that much and necessitated a little help along the way. All in all, the dirty little Tijuana trip was a learning experience of what sailors might experience visiting other foreign cities near U.S. military installations.

Number One Mail Recipient Of 228

Another thing I experienced for the first time was getting mail. I was without a doubt the number one mail recipient in our company. Rooster, who got a lot of mail too but shy of my daily receipts, would call "Peden" for the first letter on a heavy Monday mail call, especially after a holiday lengthened weekend. From then on, he would jokingly grunt "unh" with the rest of my letters and sail them to me among the gathered group. Most of my letters would be from Carolyn, of course, as we both wrote virtually every day. The rest came from mother, JoAnn, Tiny Rose, and Sidney Moore, who had also joined the USN. Dad's and John Lee's were very infrequent.

Slowly, as the days apart mellowed some of the passionate loving we had, we began to think about holding off our marriage until after the conflict was over in Korea. We only expected a few more months of it and I wouldn't want to leave her any kids without a father if something happened to me.

I had started calling her "Gertie," a short for her (and her mother's) middle name of Gertrude. She went along with it, but wasn't overjoyed. She didn't protest as long as I didn't use it on my mail envelopes.

In almost all my letters, I drew a cartoon in the return address portion of the envelope. They were often with a sailor flirting in form, fashion, or method with a pretty girl or girls, but not always. I even drew a couple to Sidney, but they were usually baseball oriented. Carolyn wrote me that her postman told her he always looked forward to delivering my mail to her because of the cartoons.

Sidney, four Fort Pickeringites, and I all got together one liberty at Mission Beach. My ole FP buddies, all seaman recruits at Diego, were Tito Wheeler; Frank, Charles, and Howard Ingram. We got some great candids of the six of us. Richard had duty that day and couldn't join us.

My First Fight With Gloves Was Exciting

I had quite a hangover from the beer we drank the day before, so I was glad that day was Sunday, a day of rest. But I couldn't sleep in because of the company bully. I can't remember his name because I never had anything to do with him. He found out who the weaker ones were in the company and he would bully them. My upper bunkmate was one of those.

This particular day I was trying to sleep off the hangover and he kept hollering at Billy about something, and then pushed him vigorously. I saw it as I was raising up to tell them to take it outside. Billy fell onto my legs on my lower bunk. I was already irritated at the hollering and when that happened, I lost my temper. The bully was a little larger and heavier than I, but he was walking away when I sprung out of my bunk, jerked him around by the shirt collar, and popped him dead center in his nose. Falling backwards to the floor from the blow, his nose squirted blood all over the front of his torso.

"Leave him alone," I ordered standing over him with my fists clinched.

"Okay, okay," he muttered through his hand holding his still bleeding nose. I helped Billy off my rack, crawled back into it, and appeared to roll over to sleep.

Naturally, I was faking. I had no idea what the bully would do after he stopped the bleeding at the washbasins. He may come challenge me for hitting him without warning, so I just lay there taking slow and deep breaths as if I was asleep. He never came, however, and stayed away from me from then on. He not only ever pushed Billy around any more, but I never saw him bully anybody any more.

That happening, although only witnessed by a few company members, must have spread through the ranks. Because, two weeks later the battalion had companies compete in a boxing tournament. I had never fought in the ring, so I had no desire to volunteer when they were forming the representatives by weight classes. The marching we had and exercises with the .30 caliber rifles had given us plenty of exercise and created great appetites. That, followed by big, healthy meals from the gallery, had us all over our normal weight. My platoon buddies all pushed me into representing Company 228 as its middleweight.

I was quite nervous, wishing it was wrestling instead. However, I had seen Richard, J.W., the Ingrams, and especially Steamboat box in prep and golden gloves. With this knowledge, my fight plan was to box and win by a decision. My opponent had a body a little like a weight lifter. I figured his muscles would be tight like Alex's were when he fought Steamboat. With that in mind I shook hands planning to show the huge gymnasium filled crowd of several companies how fighters from Fort Pickering box.

I danced around throwing little left jabs and he was doing the same. Then, I thought I saw and opening for a right cross and tried it. He leaned back slightly to dodge it, then he hooked me with his left on my temple. I staggered back and went down to my knees. It had stunned me, but my head was clear.

"So he wants to play like that," I thought as the referee wiped my gloves.

I waited a few seconds after I got up to see if he would try to finish the job and sure enough, he came on with both hands flailing. I met him with the same and caught him with a overhand right that literally slammed him to the matt. He shook his head while getting to his hands and knees, but got back up immediately. The rest of the round was the same, he'd knock me down and I'd knock him down.

The second round, we must have both decided to box instead of slug. Suddenly, I caught him with a left hook that sent him spinning into the ropes. Then, he'd retaliate and stagger me with a blow. This kept up the entire second round and all of the final third round. At the waning seconds of the bout, we both were exhausted. Neither of us clinched the other during the fight, making it a full fledged free for all with plenty of knockdowns by both during the entire nine minutes.

The applause was great when the final bell sounded, but when the referee motioned us to the center of the ring for the decision there was complete silence. Then, he took an arm from each of us and raised them indicating a draw and there was a tremendous roar from the crowd which came to their feet and gave us a standing ovation. We shook hands, then hugged briefly. I had never experienced such physical acclaim by a crowd before and, I found out later from my opponent afterwards in the locker room, neither had he. Unfortunately, I never saw him again and can't recall his name, but I know he'll remember it if he reads this. From the short post fight conversation we had, I found him to be a fine young man that had never fought in the ring either. We both will remember that event as long as we live.

Short Visit To San Francisco For A Ship

Two non-military events I remember during boot camp was watching Eddie Mathews work out with the NTC baseball team and a filming session involving Dean Martin and Jerry Lewis. Mathews had enlisted for four years, but was given an early discharge when his father died and he was the family's main provider. I wanted to talk baseball with him as one infielder to another, but never got the chance. I would talk with him often in later years. Martin and Lewis had filmed a scene with our company and they clowned around with the guys in rank. I always liked Martin, but he disappointed me when their limousine arrived to pick up the two of them and two of the female actresses. He opened the door and climbed in ahead of the women. Ungentlemanly, I thought.

The rest of boot camp was hard military stuff that taught us ship nomenclature and naval terminology. I didn't understand why we had to march around with rifles all the time. However, I did enjoy the rifle range. I scored well there, but then I should have as much hunting that I had done at popa's.

Finally, in October 1950, I left for the U.S. Naval Station at San Francisco for further

AIRCRAFT of VC-61
From top to bottom they are PB4Y-2 Liberator, SNB Beechcraft, F4U Corsair, F6F Hellcat, F8F Bearcat, and F9F-5P Panther.

transfer to the USS BOXER (CVA-21). I finally got to see the famous Golden Gate Bridge, but just barely. It was foggy and overcast almost the entire two weeks I was there. They changed my orders and sent me back to the San Diego area to Composite Squadron SIXTY-ONE at the Naval Auxiliary Air Station, Miramar, Calif. It's located about five minutes east of the Linda Vista Community, which was the last residential section of any San Diego suburb at the time. The base, which was surrounded by barren plains with scattered brush off U.S. Highway 395, would soon have its landing fields extended and improved to become a full Naval Air Station. About the only thing that lived off the base and Quonset huts were prairie dogs, ground squirrels, rabbits, snakes, hawks, and buzzards.

I had volunteered for the air department during my classification testing and interview period prior to the conclusion of our boot training; therefore, I left NTC as an airman apprentice. Pay grades E-l through E-3 uniform insignias were white for all regular ship ratings (plus medical, dental, and stewards); red for engineering and hull ratings; light blue for construction; and green for aviation. Therefore, I reported as an airman apprentice (E-2) with two green diagonal stripes.

The department head interviewed each of the new green stripers and put me in the ordnance division. I didn't mind it as I knew it had something to do with the fire power in an aircraft. However, when he asked me for which rating I wanted to strike, I told him I was going to become a pilot as soon as I could take the GED test and get the equivalence of a diploma. He smiled and wished me good luck. He said I should see the education office to apply for the test, but in the meantime, I was to become an ordnanceman striker.

I soon found out the purpose of the squadron was to train pilots to take aerial photographs of prospective bombing and strafing targets of the enemy. We had six different types of aircraft in our squadron: several four-engine PB4Y-2 Liberators; a two-engine SNB Beechcraft; several F4U Corsairs, F6F Hellcats, and F8F Bearcats; and several dozen F9F-2P & F9F-5P Panthers. The latter had a powerful camera in their nose section as it was a jet. The other fighter aircraft were single engine, propeller driven planes using smaller camera in their wings.

I didn't mind the hard workload, but it got a little uncomfortable during the windy evening on the landing strip aircraft parking area. So, when our department head asked if there was anyone in the division that could type, I volunteered. It was easy work and gave me extra time to study for the GED test.

A Surprise Christmas With Wedding Bells

I studied guides suggested for passing the GED test and wrote Carolyn all about it. I didn't write her about the surprise opportunity I had to go on leave. One of the Liberators had a scheduled hop to Pensacola, Fla., with a stopover in Corpus Christi, Tex. I was drinking beer with one of the operations office personnel at the Enlisted Men's Club (EMC) and they told me about it. It was leaving in two days. I rushed a chit through the channels for a week's leave and got it approved.

We left for Corpus Christi at 0430 and ran into a storm over Arizona. We had to get up to 19,000 feet to clear the roughest part of it, but there was a problem with availability of oxygen. There was only one line available for the after fuselage section and

there were three of us. The plane's member there removed the oxygen mask and us two passengers shared it with him at 15-second intervals. It was working alright at first, then the PB4Y starting hitting large vacuum pocket in the atmosphere. When it did so, it would make approximately 10- or 20-foot drops. It was like suddenly zooming downward in an elevator and suddenly soaring back upwards. Needless to say, the other passenger and I got airsick. The member gave us both paper bags in which to heave, but mine were all dry heaves as I had eaten no breakfast and the beer had been passed. My first "taste" of flying.

As soon as I exited the vehicle, I literally dropped to the landing strip and kissed it. I had never been that nauseated before in my life. I swore I'd never fly again without consistent oxygen availability.

Hitchhiking in uniform, with my overnight case I had borrowed, was a cinch. I never had to wait over five minutes until the patriotic Texans pickup me up. One nearly drove me nuts. A young man gave me a lift in the cab of his old truck that had been used for hauling cotton. The cab had a hole in its floor and the draft blew dried pieces of cotton husks all over my wool blue uniform. I wanted to tell him to let me out, but I had already told him I was headed for Memphis and he was going

75 miles in that direction. Needless to write, I was very happy to get out of the kind young farmer's truck.

My last ride let me off just over the Memphis-Arkansas Bridge, which of course was Fort Pickering. I walked the four blocks south to my Delaware home and startled my mother who had added a small shop on the front of the house with a picture window view of DeSoto Park. After many hugs and kisses, I trotted down the block to Peden and Sons to surprise dad and borrow his automobile. *I wanted to see Carolyn Gertrude Esrey and hold her in my arms again.*

I gave my future mother-in-law a well-meant greeting and took off after Carolyn who had just left walking the three blocks to church to rehearse with Dean and Jean, the rest of their trio. I pulled up slowly beside her and gave the usual "wolf whistle" for a good-looking girl.

She ignored it and kept walking straight ahead which, of course, pleased me. Then, I said out the open window while still driving along:

"Hey, Gertie! You sweet thing."

She took one more step then "Gertie" registered. She had to turn and look after that. *"Nobody knew her middle name but me!"* she reasoned.

I parked.

She ran.

The car door was barely shut and I was in heaven again. We embraced and kissed for at least several minutes. The absence had actually made our relationship more solid. I had learned that there was another instinct given humans in addition to the desire to have sex with a particular member of the opposite sex. I felt a desire to protect this woman for the rest of my life. It was a distinct feeling with which I shared with her, but I still held that I would not want to leave a child fatherless because of a military action.

Now I know this will sound very admirably reasonable to you, the reader — but believe it or not, after a day holding, kissing, and feeling this soft, young, tender, flesh I loved — these thoughts began to whither slightly. The second day of being with her made me divulge to her that I was questioning thoughts about my postponement of our marriage. She, in the passionate mood we were in all the time now, agreed.

The third day, December 21, 1950, we motored south of the border to the State of Mississippi. There in the city of Hernando couples could get married at our ages (18 & 16) with parents consent. We had a small family contingent of Ruby & Roy Peden, my sister JoAnn, Lillian & Virgil Esrey, her brother Tommy, and cousin Cooper "Tiny" Mc Daniel (who would become very instrumental in **MY** future). We had it done by a local Baptist minister, Rev. W.C. Whitten. It was not very

ceremonial, but it was legal and done. That was all I cared about at the time being. I only had four more days to get back to my duty station and, now that I was married, I wanted to make the most of it.

By Vi rgil Esrey

LAST TWO DAYS as singles before we tied the knot on Dec. 2l, 1950. Only a 16-year-old, she was beautiful and with only a 22" waist.

"Aaaaah," An Old Four-Poster Bed

My father had once again come to the top in the churning process of blending my life into a happy one. I remember briefly

being with his mother Maggie Peachy, I don't remember his father Given Davis Peden who died in l941. Qubelle, 57, was my dad's half sister and had married with the successful William Earl Aron and had a nice big house in Pontotoc, Miss. She had a magnificent dinner made for us and gave us their guest room available to us for our wedding night.

It not only had a fireplace, but a four-poster bed that was as delicately decorated as any Carolyn and I had seen in any movie. She was ecstatic over the setting, but **BWBB** I had one thing on mind. The rest of the night is **TOP SECRET & STRICTLY CENSORED!**

Believe it or not, the next morning I drove the remaining 10 miles or so to popa's to show off my new bride and take her squirrel hunting with me. I shot one only a few hundred yards in the woods behind the house and let her help me dissect it by holding its front paws while I gutted its innards. I learned years later that she detested doing that for me. Come to think of it now, that was pretty gross for a 16 year-old girls on his first hunting trip.

She enjoyed the walks around the farm with the stories I told her about hoeing in the fields, plowing, the mules, swimming escapades with Keister and John Paul, etc. She also was fond of mom and popa and relished his tales after dinner around his large fireplace as were warmed to the fire burning one of the logs she sawed.

She had never slept on a feather bed before, so it was quite an experience to her. The only heat in the house, of course, was in the combination master bedroom/living room. Therefore, it was freezing in the room in which we semi-retired. We stripped and dove under the many quilts and on sheets filled with bushels of goose feathers, which was the bed's mattress. It swallowed our young bodies, which was good in that it maintained our body heat under the quilts but was not conducive to the excited love-making of two newly weds.

The two days and nights at my childhood pity-patter and stomping grounds with the girl (excuse me!)...**Woman** of my life was divinely exquisite. When she felt of the bark of a sapling that I knew three or four years earlier because of its unique shape and location, I would kiss her fingers that had touched it.

"That was one of my favorites, too," I would say. I was so much in love with her that even when she grabbed me while startled by a common garden or grass snake, I would embrace her to ensure protection and then search for her lips as a reward. She probably got a little annoyed by all that stuff. But, would you believe, she never told me stop.

All good things must come to an end, I had been told, and our three nights and two days

honeymoon did also. I drove back to Memphis, found a classified advertisement of a guy driving to San Diego and wanting three riders to share expenses, and left the next day. He was a nice guy and the other two riders were readers and sleepers, so the drive back to Diego was uneventful. I drove a few legs (150-mile jaunts) on the trip while the main driver napped. It cost me $20 in gas contributions, plus my few hamburgers and Pepsis along the way.

All in all, the week of leave (actually nine days as the day of departure and day of return did not count as leave dates) cost me less than $150 (including a $10 wedding in Hernando). I paid that much for a dinner night (parking attendant, pre-dinner cocktails, wine, after dinner cocktails, tips, etc.) my "bride" and I had in Hawaii during our 50th anniversary.

"Sylvester The SP" Popular Comic Strip

Everything was going rosy for me for a while. My successful GED results came and I obtained my high school diploma from Southside. The '47 Frazer was mine. All I had to do was pick it up. That was a big problem, but not quite as bad as it was since I now was making $82.50 a month base pay as an airman apprentice and received $45 a month dependent's allotment for Carolyn. I started saving most of that as she was still living

with her parents without charge. In March, I took the test for advancement to pay grade E-3. By April I would be making almost $145 a month. WOW!

All the time I was trying to figure out a way to get home and get Carolyn, who had already quit school and was ready to join me while I had shore duty. I had applied for an article in the *Jet Journal,* the NAAS Miramar's new monthly paper, requesting an artist to do a comic strip in each edition. I submitted a drawing of a skinny sailor on Shore Patrol. He was so lazy his eyes were always closed and he had to have his night stick dragging with a little four-wheeling cart followed by a small cloud of dust. Around his head, I had a bug circling. I named the script "Sylvester The SP."

By Buck Peden
SYLVESTER the SP

The editor chose me from the applicants, thus my career in journalism began as a comic strip artist. Whitehaven High School's Fyfe would have agreed with the editor, but I'm not too sure about Southside's Mrs. Wolfe. With the little notoriety I got from it as a member of VC-61, I made a lot of friends within the squadron. One seaman was a personnelman striker in the Personnel Office where they maintained all the enlisted service records. He told me of an opening that was available in the Administrative Office typing the Plan of the Day. After hearing all the fringe benefits of being a yeoman I applied. I was given a typing test and interviewed by the chief yeoman. The change was made, after approval of the two division officers involved.

I then began studying for the seaman test to change from airman and passed it easily. In the meantime, I received quite a shock.

Sad Definition Of "Marital Status"

After receiving the HS diploma, I started filling out the application form to take the exam to become a pilot when I came to a block that was titled "Marital Status." I didn't know what that meant, so I asked the administrator what I should enter in that block.

"That's to let them know whether you are 'married' or 'single,'" he answered.

"Oh, I just got married last month," I said proudly.

"Really? Then you are not eligible for the Navy's flight school. Only single guys are accepted," he explained bluntly.

I was devastated! I had to be shown in writing. No one had ever told me of that restriction. It was the last time that I ever failed to be thoroughly cognizant of any detailed requirements concerning an application for anything else throughout the rest of my 20-year career. I finally got over it, but I was really in the "dumps" for several days.

I told the editor of the *Jet Journal* about my disappointment of being ineligible because of my marriage. He was a family man and had a long talk with me that helped tremendously. Basically, he made me see that my love for Carolyn and being with her was much more important than being a pilot. He even put a note in the March edition asking if any sailor was driving back east in April that would consider a gas-sharing passenger for me. With the inquiry, I connected with an airman transferring to NAS Millington, Tenn., a few miles north of Memphis, for a navy school.

Mid-April I was in Memphis and had already passed my seaman exam. So I drove my young bride (she couldn't drive yet) to California with three seaman stripes on my dress uniform. She had never been out of Tennessee, except for brief trips over the Arkansas and Mississippi line to visit kin, plus our marriage and honeymoon. I took a route through the former and Oklahoma to Colorado to drive over the famous Pike's Peak. She was enjoying the sights until we were almost at the crest of PP. Then we ran into a snowstorm. The wind was blowing the thick snow so hard that the Frazier's wipers wouldn't clear the windshield enough to see. I tried cracking the door and looking out it, as we were only moving about 5-10 miles per hour, but it was blinding.

Finally, having trouble seeing in that blizzard where the two-lane highway's outward side dropped off into a deep canyon, we decided to give it up and turn around. There was no other traffic and hadn't been for miles. Ever so slowly, I turned the car toward the cliff for a few feet, then cut the wheels starboard and backed a few feet. I kept repeating this until I slowly got the car facing downhill on what we thought was the right lane of the highway. We weren't sure as the roadway was already completely covered in snow. We both could have bitten 10-penny nails in two we were so scared.

Coors Beer Drinker For Ever & Ever

Then, what one might call a miracle happened. A huge 18-wheel diesel truck came chugging up the road. It's powerful lights were clearly visible through their large windshield wipers. It was moving straight into the blizzard at about 10 MPH and leaving big tracks in the snow.

I quickly made a decision to turn back around and follow in its wake. I knew we were only five or six miles from the peak and the same distance on its other side should be clear. Using the truck's truck as an easy guide, I reversed our course more quickly and soon caught up to within a car length behind its huge body. Naturally, it blocked the blizzard off our windshield so we had a clear view of the owner's name of our savior truck. It read "Coors Beer." It was April 16, 1951, with Carolyn celebrating her 17th birthday as I swore that Coors Beer would be my brew for the rest of my life.

It's been over 58 years now, *AND I STILL MAINTAIN THAT OATH.*

Sure enough, it was clear on the downside of Pike's Peak and we had no more problems. We ate at a real restaurant instead of our normal fast food place as it was Gertie's birthday. As a friend in the Personnel Office made a mistake retyping my new military identification card and it showed me being over 21, I was able to celebrate her birthday and our close call with my first Coors Beer. To my surprise, it was a fine tasting drink.

Gertie had never drank, although I had given her a sip of a Tom Collins my knowledgeable friend J.W. had mixed at my parents house one day while they were working. He put a shot of gin in it, but it almost taste like lemonade as he filled the glass with ice, Seven-up, a teaspoon of sugar, and a HALF of a lemon. So, after we got to the San Diego area, she finally had a one of those when we went to hear Nat King Cole sing at a local night club.

When we first got to California, we slept on a sleeper couch for a month at a Boatswain's Mate friend's house in Escondido, Calif. But the couch squeaked so much while we were having sex that we moved in a month.

We rented a bedroom and shared a kitchen with a elderly widow lady in La Jolla. She said we could use the living room also, but the first time I sat in her big recliner I found her big dog sitting in front and staring at me. When I asked her why he was doing that, she said, "Because you're sitting in his chair." We loved the beach there, but the $50 a month rent and 20-mile roundtrip to the base was too expensive.

Then we found a two-story, two-bedroom house for rent on 30th Street in Diego which we shared with Tom and Cherie Gilliand, also two Memphian newly-weds. It was a very sociable arrangement. We all got along well with each other with their bedroom on the ground floor and ours upstairs.

Gertie's parents, Virgil & Lillian, even came out for a few days visit. They taught us the card game of Hearts, which we enjoyed immensely and passed it on to our kids and grandchildren. Mr. Esrey was a "dirty" player — as some called it — when he would include the queen of spades in the three cards passed before each hand and then lead the recipient out of the queen. Catching that spade (we called "old lady" in family play, and the "bitch" in games with my shipmates) was 13 points against the player (13 hearts cards each were the other minus points in a hand of play). If one captured all 26 points, it was called "running the deck" or "shooting the moon" which gave the "moon shooter" zero points for the hand and all other players 26. The first poor player to get a total of 150 points would end the game and the participant with the lowest total who win the game.

Carolyn would usually be the game loser as he particularly relished passing the queen to her. He bought her an ironing board (she had been putting a flannel blanket on the dinner table and ironing there) before they left and I always kidded him as doing that to try to nurse her heart wounds. That was in 1951 and she finally sold it in a yard sale in 2004. I always had the best pressed dress blues at all our squadron personnel inspections.

Champion Fastpitch Softball Team

I joined the tryouts for the VC-6l Softball Team formed by Ensign Marv Warner, the squadron's athletic officer whose athletic equipment room was handled by Seaman Russell Goetz. Ensign Warner named Chief Robert Hein as manager and Hein had me playing third base. Goetz, with whom I became very fond, played centerfield. He wasn't fast, like most middle outfielders, but he was a super ball hawk. He played in close and was so tall and gangly he could reach balls well over his head. He always got a super jump on the ball as if he knew where it was going as the batter swung. At bat, Goetz would sometimes clout balls well out of the strike zone as Yogi Berra of the New York Yankees used to do. So, I hung a nickname of "Yogi" on him which he liked and we still use to this day.

We had been practicing only a week or so and had an intrasquad game. My little buddy from Fort Pickering, Kenneth Gipson, was visiting us that weekend on a liberty from NTC recruit training. He was at the game cheering me from the sidelines. He used Southside Coach Ewing's phrase "Wild Buck" every time I would bat and urge me to steal. Some examples: "Give us a hit, Wild Buck" and "Pilfer one, Wild Buck."

None of the team understood the "Wild" part, but they knew he was a friend. I knew how to run the bases correctly now, so my teammates just picked up the "Buck" part as we were learning each other's first names and/or nicknames. I liked it also. I have used it later as a pen name ever since that occurrence.

We had an outstanding infield with Jack Harrison, an Atlanta lawyer in civilian life, at shortstop; Quinton positions were Beryl Yates, Eddie Flack, Ray Riale, and E.J. Miller. In 1952, we won the Fleet Air Detachment (FAD) Miramar and the ELEVENTH Naval District Championship. Moore's fastball was the key along with the great defense we possessed. Harrison (.405) was our top batsman in l951 and I (.347) was runner-up. Bane led in l952 (.338) while I fell to a lousy .253. I massed

U.S. Navy Photo
VC-61 11ND SOFTBALL CHAMPS
Standing (L-R): Quinton Johnson, Bill Keyser, Buck Peden, Coach R.A. Hein, Bill Smith, Beryl Yates & Ray Riale. Seated: Jack Harrison, Russ Goetz, Ed Miller, Chuck Bane, Andy Moore & Paul McAuliffe.

"Johnny" Johnson at second base; and Paul Mc Auliffe at first. Andy Moore, an Indian from Yazoo City, Miss., was our ace pitcher with Chuck Bane, a power hitter, as his battery mate. Bill Keyser was another hurler.

Playing the other two outfield 101 assists (team high) and 94 putouts during the 50 games I played both seasons to do my part defensively.

We also played in SD's top night league in 1952 with an overall 35-15 record. I'm sure our team was one of the top three positions as Andy's fastball appeared even faster at night.

I never will forget a one-night game at a diamond that wasn't well lit. Usually, unless I know it is a powerful pull hitter batting, I played even with third base to ensure I was able to successfully field any surprise punts or slow rollers. I was this night when one of the opposing batters nailed one of Moore's best fastballs. It was a line drive hit straight at my chest. My past starting shooting through my mind as I jerked my glove up for protection. I thought I was a goner, but the glove sustained most of the blow. It knocked me off my feet, but instinctively, I leaned over and picked up the ball. Throwing while still on my knees, I still got the runner at first base by several feet. It all happened so fast, the runner hardly was out of the batter's box while I was picking up the ball. I had the wind knocked out of me, so I didn't breathe until 30 or 40 seconds afterwards.

Kevin Huffstetter, who was attached to VC-61 but assigned to the station barbershop as he was a Ship's Serviceman with a haircutter's job code, played in five games that season. He cut my hair, but I don't remember him being on the team. He was to become my best friend during my Chicago era.

School Bells Chime Once Again For Me

I may have missed a game or two at the end of '51 as I was sent to the Yeoman Class "A" School at NTC, San Diego on August 27 for two months school. It was the first time I had studied hard to excel. I wanted to be tops in the class of YNSN rating designation. With Gertie drilling me with questions every night, I led the class every single week of the school.

We would not see the weekly standings until Mondays, as the weekly typing exams taken each Friday had not been computed. The five minute exams counted 10% of our grade. I was usually very accurate, averaging about 50 words per minute with only one or no errors. Two other students, both from the fleet with most of the class straight out of boot camp, were always right on my tail with the second and third best marks.

Then it happened. The final written test we all three aced, but the final typing test was only one 5-minute exam whereas they usually gave us three and chose the best. I didn't choke, but I made three typographical mistakes which shot me down to a third place finish overall. Needless to write, I was very disappointed and felt sorry for Gertie. She had spent so much of her time and wanted her gob to be No. 1 almost as much as I did.

I tried to perk her up with news that I got back at the NAS Miramar Dental Office. The dentist had finally decided to pull all my remaining upper teeth and all but the front eight of the bottom ones. I disliked the way my mouth looked ever since a tall basketball player had jerked down a rebound and jammed my partial in between the two adjacent teeth. The space caused was not pleasing to me at all.

It wasn't too bad until he got to several impacted jaw teeth. They required surgery for extraction and subsequent root canal. The pain from that filing conclusion was terrific despite the medication.

Then, I had to wait three months while the surgery healed and the gums shrunk before they could cast the mold. Gertie and I both got tired my eating soft meals only. Then to top it all off, I decided not to tell her the date I was getting my teeth. I was going to greet her at the front door with a kiss as usual and then disengage backward a little, smiling to show her my new shinny white teeth. Baaaam! Three months of kissing without teeth was a different meeting place between our lips. Not thinking of that, I ended up with a busted lip when the two sets of buckteeth clashed at the different place.

I didn't care though. I was so happy with the teeth that I spent half the night walking past mirrors and smiling to myself.

Became A Teenage Father By One Day

We were very excited when Gertie missed her third period in July. The Naval Hospital would not examine dependent wives until they missed their period three times, so we knew for sure she was pregnant then. We had a celebration party at the Enlisted Men's Club on the base with most of the softball team, and their wives if married, attending such as Jack and Shirley Harrison. She was such a flirt that all us guys loved her.

Others were Tom & Cherie, Howard (stationed in the area) & Billie Ingram of Memphis, and our good Georgian friends Jack & Bernice Hornsby. As most of the ball players were not married, the wives got plenty of dance time at the party. I probably celebrated the most as I remember drinking the hard stuff mixed with cola. Usually, all I drank was Coors Beer.

Shortly after that our application finally came to the top of the waiting list for a two-bedroom Quonset hut located just outside the main gate at our base. Their $37.50 rental was a nice improvement over the $100 rent we had been splitting with the Gilliands.

Finally, Gertie was a week overdue in the doctor's opinion. He told us the baby was ready the second week of January 1952.

"It's just waiting on mommy," he told her.

When I told that to my mother when she called on January 10th, she said, "You go buy a small bottle of castor oil and give it to her."

"Mother, you're kidding," I said.

"No. It's an old country method that always works. Now, you do it," she concluded with a very serious tone.

I asked Mrs. Esrey, Gertie's mother, who was visiting to help her daughter during her first child's birth, if she had ever heard of the method my mother had recommended, but she never had. She said she didn't think it would hurt. So I told it to Carolyn and she agreed to try it, she was so uncomfortable. I bought it and gave it to her that night. It cleaned her out and sure enough, she had our first son the next morning after a long period of laboring.

Poor Gertie had to suffer alone as nobody except medical personnel were allowed in the delivery room. Finally, she gave birth and we got to see him from outside the glass enclosure. Boy was he pitiful looking. The doctor had to use forceps during the otherwise normal birth and the 5'1" mother had produced an 8 lb., 2 oz., lad. His head was warped and with the bruises I was sad at first sight, but mom (as I had started calling Lillian) explained that his head would get normal in time and we knew the bruises would heal. I was just a nervous 19-year-old teenage father that could have had my first son born on my 20th birthday (January 12) if I hadn't been so impatient and ignorant about that castor oil.

Parents had no knowledge of the sex prior to birth in those days, but we had agreed I would name it if male and she would name it if female. So before I left the hospital, I gave his name as Robin Roy Peden. But, after I got to the Quonset parking lot and started walking home between the rows of huts late that Friday afternoon, I began having second thoughts. Everyone that knew us was aware she was giving birth as news travels fast when you live in a neighborhood of about 20 huts, 12 feet apart, with a family living in each end. So, as I passed they stopped me to ask how Carolyn was doing and the sex of the child. I would tell them.

"Oh, it's a boy," they would invariably say and then ask, "What did you name it, Buck Junior?"

By the time I got to my hut, which was the last one in the outer row, I had been asked that five or six times by our neighborhood friends. By the next morning, I had made up my mind. When I got to the hospital I had its name changed to Robert Roy Peden, Jr. I was now a proud, happy 20-year-old with a son to carry on my given name, Robert, and my dad's, Roy, Peden.

Mom liked my decision and continued to treat us to her great southern dishes, especially biscuits and corn bread. Carolyn had not been taught to cook and my mother was a believer in three main meals a day, so I had really been missing those big southern meals with which I had been raised. I praised mom continuously for her meals while she was there, which she appreciated, but my remark about the beautiful lining she sewed for the baby's bassinette proved to be one of my many terrible "let-jaw-and-tongue-function-before-putting-mind-in gear" in while becoming a respectful son-in-law. When I saw it finished, I said, "Gee, that's beautiful, it looks just like one of those pretty caskets." I thought casket lining were always so soft and dainty, but it was VASTLY INAPPROPRIATE to use the comparison with a newborn's bed lining. Tsk, tsk, tsk… pshaw, pshaw, pshaw. I don't think mom ever completely accepted my apologies, which I gave immediately after I realized she was hurt by the innocent comment.

Between her mother's visit and later our kind next door neighbor Dorothy's help, Carolyn was slowly becoming a cook. I remember how happy she was when I came home one day and Dorothy taught her a new "trick," as she put it. Dorothy had told her to not cut the root end of the onion and she never had watering eyes again when slicing or chopping onions. She sounded happy as a lark, so I think that was near Gertie's starting blocks to enjoying her meal preparations. Now she has 25 cook books and can prepared just about anything with the best of them.

Dorothy also had a four-year-old daughter named Lynn, so she was very sweet to advise us with things in raising a baby. I had baby-sat many times for Uncle Morris and his school teacher wife, Mabel, with their children Sue & Michael; Aunt Mossie & Fred Tankersly's Sandra, Freddy Lynn, & Brenda; and Aunt Berline & Aubrey Hall's Ronald Keith & Judy.

The other Tutor cousins I saw, some often, but did very little sitting. For example, Uncle Wayne had a son with his first wife, Helen, named Wayne Jr., & Jonathon with the very personable Libby; Eva & Beauford Layne's Larry & Ricky; Keister & Geraldine's Barbara Sue, Kay, Randy, Patty, & Cherlyn; John Paul & Jean's Linda, Tommy Paul, & Kathy; and Tinye & Rev. Tommy's Paulette.

The Peden kids were too old, such as Uncle Albert & Nell's William Albert; and the others, such as Qubelle & William Aron's nine and Uncle Reed & Etheleen's Walter "Pete" Leonard & Robert Reed, lived too far away.

So, I had been around quite a few babies in the area family. At least I knew how to change Bobby's diapers without any instructions. That, plus I would haul most of the wash to our central washers and dryers. That stuff and playing with our son was all I did in the evenings. I tried to teach him things everyday, loving every bit of it. Then, when he got old enough to sit up, we got a high chair and I began teaching him (a little early, probably) how to hold a spoon and carry it to his mouth. Most of the time he would grab for the food with his hands. I grabbed it, patted it a little firm, and with a stern voice said, "No, no!"

"You stop that," Gertie snapped at me.

"Honey, that's the way he learns to stop eating with his hands and use the spoon," I reasoned.

"No it isn't. Don't you do that again," she rebuked obviously angry with me.

I lost my temper and suppressed a brief urge to reach across the little dinette and slap her. Instead, I just threw the small piece of bread crust I had in my hand at her.

"Don't you talk to me like that," I yelled. She left the table crying into our bedroom. That was only time I came close to hitting my wife in the 55-plus years of our marriage. We've had some pretty heated arguments, but never have either of us struck the other.

It had nothing to do with the aforementioned incident, but I decided to join the squadron's wrestling team. I was so far out of shape that the workouts nearly killed me. One night, after overdoing it while rolling with my head and ankles supporting my whole body to strengthen my neck muscles, my head kept flopping to the side. I told Gertie it was necessary to have strong neck muscles so one can keep the shoulders off the match during a pin attempt. I knew it would get better after a night's sleep, and it did. However, I reduced that exercise the next few days.

11ND Championships My Wrestling Finale

I found out a lot of the other sailors were not in top physical condition as we began practice workouts against each other. I started getting Carolyn to fix me a few sandwiches and a small fruit and I'd brown-bag lunch daily at the station pool. Doing this would allow me to swim 30-35 minutes before lunch.

While I was doing this, one day the base recreation department had planned a volunteer swimming, with squadron sailors as well as station personnel. It had been on the pool bulletin board, but I hadn't had the occasion to see it. Anyway, it knocked the few lap swimmers out of the normal workouts as the events took up the entire pool.

Then, they announced the need for one more entrant in the Backstroke Event or they would have to cancel the event. I wanted to swim anyway, and since I had plenty of experience swimming on my back in the Mississippi River, I entered just to qualify the event for the other five entrants. I had no idea I would win, but I did and was presented with a nice First Place blue ribbon. I still have that little prize in our family scrapbook as it was such a surprise.

In the wrestling, I really wanted to succeed and I had some confidence going in with the Memphis Prep Championship experience. Fortunately, I won every match to make it to the FAD 11ND Championships at the North Island Naval Air Station. I was ecstatic when I made it to the finals with three triumphs, all by pins. All three opponents had such muscular-looking bodies that I thought sure I was going to lose each. As in the past, it was my quickness getting to the advantageous point of leverage that won for me.

Therefore, I was very confident going into the finals with a 16-0 career amateur wrestling record. I hadn't seen my opposition in any other matches, but when we met in the middle of the mat to shake hands, my observation of him didn't dent my confidence. Although he was taller, his muscles didn't show the bulges indicative of a weight lifter. Plus, he had on red trunks and black leotard pants. Not very smart I thought. Black pants would not only make a wrestler sweat more profusely, but would make it easier to grip his legs.

The first prick in my huge ego bubble came when we shook hands. His smile was friendly enough, but his large hand, not only engulfed mine, its firmness signaled a definite message: *strength!*

From the moment we touched to begin the match until its end, I was on defense.

He not only had great strength, but was just as quick as I. I tried a knee grab and thought I had grabbed a parking meter pole it was so hard. He got the first takedown, but I escaped. Then I got one, and he escaped with a reversal. His big hands would completely cover the back of my neck, which made me fearful of trying to work inside as I preferred. I knew he was ahead on points as the match was in its final period. I calculated the only was I could win was to get a pin. Then, suddenly it happened. I had him face down on the mat while I held his long left arm under my back.

His right arm I was holding by the wrist bent at the elbow behind the small of his back. Then I leaned back to apply more pressure to his left shoulder toward the mat. My intentions were to quickly roll over to be on top and get credit for a takedown.

BAM!

The referee had ended the match with the signal of slamming his open hand onto the mat. Both of us got up, looking questionably at each other with our jaws hanging and then to the referee. The official grabbed my opponent's hand and raised it in the air announcing the victor. Stunned at first, it suddenly came to me that my shoulders must have both touched the mat, which is a pin by the rules. I knew he was going to win on points anyway, so I didn't feel any resentment at all.

I shook his hand grinning at his dumbfounded look.

"You pinned me, big guy," I told him.

When the ref told him what had happened, he finally laughed along with me. But he was such a nice guy that he didn't feel he should have won with a pin. I couldn't find anything in my notes or album about him, as they didn't give us any programs. We left by bus right away and showered at our gym, but I do remember he said he was a farmer from Minnesota. First time I ever knew they made farmers so slim and strong in The Gopher State.

That was the last time I wrestled in competition. I was proud of the 16-1. I don't remember wrestling with an opponent who wasn't a nice chap. Always wondered what I would have done with that Tennessee University coach.

My First Crow Came On A Birthdate

I wrestled with the kids as they grew up. I would roll Bobby around on the bed for 15-20 minutes every night before he had his last meal. He became a good sleeper early in his life.

Meanwhile, about all Gertie and I did for entertainment in the evening after he went to sleep was play gin rummy or read library books. That is,

By Carolyn Peden

SN RICHARD JONES & I before we got our Third Class "crows."

until the results from the navy wide petty officer examination were released. I was advanced to third class petty officer (E-4) on Carolyn's 18th birthday, April 16. With my naval reserve time prior to entering active service, I then had a base pay with over two year's longevity of $125 a month. That, with the additional $20 to Gertie's allotment, we were

now grossing almost $200 a month.

We decided that was enough to buy a television set. So we did!

We decided that was enough to buy a television set. So we did! We splurged and got a 17" Crosby Console, one of the few in the Quonset complex. We were proud when Richard Jones, John Lee & JoAnn, Kenneth Gipson, and John Paul & Jean Tutor visited us.

We were really enjoying married life, raising a youngster, going to the base movie for 10 cents each, and swimming at the base pool. Occasionally we would drive to our favorite La Jolla Beach, but most of the time enjoyed visiting friends and playing cards with plenty of beer for the men and wine and cocktails for the girls. And of course, us guys had our softball games, day and night times. It was a pleasant summer in '52 until September.

Then, before my new crow, crossed quills rating insignia, and red v-stripe was five months old, **Yeoman Third Class R. R. Peden** was permanently transferred.

BGWW&P Times

September 10, 1952 - May 18, 1953   *Vol. 1, No. 8*   *San Diego, CA; Far East; & Memphis, TN*

Korea Bound Three Days Later

VF-783/122 Aboard USS ORISKANY
Family Returns To Original Turf

Fortunately, we had driven back to Memphis for a month's leave to show off our son in March and April before the orders were received. I had split the driving and the expenses ($35.30 gas for l04.4 gallons over 1,856 miles) with Henry Ingram. It only took us 42 hours driving straight through in shifts. I drove back without stopping in 36 hours taking No-Doze tablets and drinking a Coors or two between meals. On barren stretches of two-lane blacktop highways (there were no four-lane freeways there yet) where the road was straight and level for miles, I would let Gertie scoot over close and take over the wheel and accelerator. Then I would hang my left elbow out the window and lay my head on it to nap for 3-5 minutes. She would holler me awake immediately if she saw an upcoming crossroad sign, an approaching car, or any hill or curve.

I was a nervous wreck when we got home, primarily because of the pills and lack of rest. However, the little three-month old boy made it like a man. Gertie and the car did, too. Fortunately, my Uncle Albert and I put new rings in the six (straight) cylinders, reseated all the valves, and did other tune-up work (new spark plugs, etc.). I did most of the labor, but under his close supervision. All of it cost us only $170 to return the five-year-old vehicle to tip top operating condition. Looking back on the trip, with the old highways we had to use and the many small towns we had to drive through in almost 4,000 miles, we had not one speck of automobile problems, not even a flat tire.

Getting Gertie and Bobby back to Memphis was going to be a problem after we learned of the pending transfer, but we were lucky again. My parents came out for a visit and brought JoAnn and John Lee. They stayed a week and then took my family back with them to stay with Gertie's parents until I returned to the states.

In the meantime, I got a friend to store the TV set in his garage and made plans for a shipmate to take care of the Frazier by driving it a few miles every week while I was gone to keep the engine turned over and the tires rolled a bit. I moved into the VC-6l barracks with a rack under my friend Theodore "Mitch" Mitchell. Most of my off duty time was "hanging out" with him and Donald Mountain, a Tulsa, Okla., native. Mostly shooting pool and playing ping pong at the EM Club, watching base movies, and sipping suds. Sometimes we would go downtown SD, usually after pay day, and tour the taverns. Mitch and Donald were both underage, but with my false ID card we finally found a pub just down from Presidio Park where they would sell a large pitcher to me and they ignored who I let drink it with me.

I began to particularly like the place because it was small, had good music on the juke box, and had a long table shuffleboard game. We got to playing a game of it for a dollar and I won more than I lost. I had seen a real competitive marine shoot one day with both hands. He would use his bottom three fingers along the rail of the board as a guide and, with the puck cupped in between his index finger and thumb, make the puck ride the rail all the way down if desired. With a little lift at the end, he would guide the puck anywhere off the rail he desired. I worked and worked on it until I finally mastered it. From then on I lost very few beers.

My orders came in August to report to Fighter Squadron 783 (VF-783) at NAS Miramar for duty on 10 September 1952. The squadron patch had a revolutionary shooting two pistols while sitting on a short-nosed cannon firing a round which gave them a nickname of "Minute Men." My VC-61 softball teammates kidded me quite a bit that last month, "Buck used to run around the bases in seconds. Now he's a 'Minute Man.'"

One More Trip Down South To Mexico

The weekend before I was to report for duty, I decided one last fling below the border. I was authorized to draw three months advance pay on permanent change of duty orders such as I had. I did so and talked Mc Auliffe, our tall first baseman, and Goetz into joining me as my guest. Secretly, Mc Auliffe and I had

plans to get Yogi, who was still a bachelor, laid by one of the whores. We didn't want to mess with those in Tijuana, so after a few beers there, we got a couple six-packs and headed to Ensenada, about 60 miles down the coast of Baja

USS ORISKANY (CVA-34)

California. It was an asphalt road some of the way, but in the small mountains much of it was gravel in those days.

We stopped at the first bar we came to and drank for a hour or so of their Tecate and Corona Beers. The inhabitants were very friendly and they didn't know we were sailors as we were in civilian clothes. However, there were no "bar flies," as we called them, hanging around as they do in Tijuana. None of the customers or bartenders spoke English. But, using the universal hand maneuvers for women, we finally got it across that we were looking for the species of the opposite sex. Yogi was feeling no pain, we thought, so we took off for the whore house. As we pulled up to the building, which was surrounded by a chain fence about four feet high, several

girls came out to the fence to greet us.

Mac and I were trying to negotiate their prices down a little when, sudden one pulls up her dress and squats down to urinate. None of us appreciated such informality and Yogi couldn't take it.

"Com'on guys. Let's go," he said pulling my shirt with him towards the car.

We went back to the tavern and drank several more beers. I couldn't resist telling the bartender what had happened using pantomime to imitate what the girl had done. I pointed to Mac and Yogi then used my fingers to illustrate how we hustled away. He, and several of the other customers, understood and they rattled it off in Mexican to the others, all having a round of laughter of us naïve boys from the north.

By the time we left, we were near intoxication. We couldn't find a decent motel, therefore we decided to drive back to Tijuana and get one. Mc Auliffe climbed in the back seat of the spacious Frazier and was asleep in minutes. Yogi, who couldn't drive, was wide awake as I was spinning gravel around those mountain curves. I kept drifting off to sleep and he'd grab the wheel to keep the car on the road while he yelled me awake. He told me the next day that he would never go through that again even if he had to walk back.

By some miracle we made it without sliding into a ditch and spent the night in the first motel we saw. Back to the base the next day, I packed my sea bag and reported to VF-783 Wednesday.

1945 Attack Carrier Loads & Steams West

Two days with my new command ashore and we boarded the USS ORISKANY (CVA-34), an 888-footer commissioned in l945. CAG 102 consisted of us and VF-781 with F9F-5s; VF-874 with F4Us; VA-923 with ADs; and Detachments GEORGE of CS-3 with F4U night fighters, VC-11 with radar equipped ADs, VC-35 with night & all-weather ADs, and VC-6l with aerial camera loaded F2H-Ps. All the planes, ammunition, bombs, and related maintenance materials along with administrative and personnel files were all loaded in three days. We were underway for Korea.

We stopped a few days at Pearl Harbor I thoroughly enjoyed the tour of Oahu Island from Honolulu. It was my first stop in a port outside

the continental limits of the United States and I celebrated it heartily with the two other main members of our squadron office, Seamans Al Hiatt and Jack Shaffer. It was the beginning of my drinking of mixed drinks at bars. I never will forget the first one I drink in a bar. I had quickly sat down on my stool after nervously passing the exam at its entrance with my false ID card. The bartender asked for my drink order immediately and I couldn't remember the name of J.W.'s Tom Collins. I was so ignorant of drinking anything except beer and cheap wine that I was momentarily in shock.

Then I heard a customer down the bar ordering from another bartender so I ordered the same, "CC and ginger." I had no idea that it was Canadian Club and ginger ale, but it taste alright to me so I drank it as my bar booze for several years after that. I tried a few of the local Hawaiian drinks, but I always went back to "CC & ginger."

On one liberty with Ed "Governor" Quigley, a wise storekeeper in our squadron, a guy walked in the bar mad as hell. Apparently he had bad day in a court appearance.

"All lawyers are ass holes," he said to anyone who would listen as he sat down next to Ed.

"I resent that remark," the well tanked Quigley fired back.

"Oh, you a lawyer?"

"No, I'm an ass hole," the Governor retorted in a serious tone with a straight face. Even the bartender laughed along with us.

On Line October 1952 Thru April 1953

Except for the trips to the Naval Station in Yokosuka, Japan; a short stop in Nagoya, Japan; and a goodwill trip to Hong Kong, China, we were operating as a member of Task Force SEVENTY SEVEN and ComCarDiv FIVE under the United Nations off the east coast of Korea. Once we steamed far north near Manchuria. We were told that United Nations' aircraft would no longer be required to cease pursuit of the North Korean aircraft when they entered Manchuria space. The rumored revision never came about. Removal of General Douglas Mac Arthur as top honcho in the conflict, which became recognized as a war, had some bearing in it. However, it was all scuttlebutt to us at the bottom of the political ladder.

Most of our service on the line was 30 days or so. However, one period we did touch land for 63 days, if my memory serves me correctly. Naturally, we would replenish once a week or so with oilers, cargo, and ammunition ships bringing us our needed fuel and supplies. The replenish vessels would usually service us using highlines on its port side and a destroyer at the same time on its starboard side. This impressive operation would take place at a uniform speed of 10 knots[17] or so. Very seldom do the skillful Boatswain's Mates, who handle the rigging involved in this treacherous execution, make a mistake or have an accident.

The Air Group, which was changed from CAG 102 to CAG 12 and my squadron from VF-783 to VF-122 in February, published a cruise book for the tour. Some of the following enemy items destroyed/damaged by our pilots during the seven months on the line were listed in its final pages: boats 12/110; factories, shelters, fuel facilities & buildings 881/1,256; road & railroad bridges 5/33; trucks, tanks, & other land vehicles 349/632; locomotives, railroad cars, rail cuts, etc. 77/350; gun emplacements 41/33; aircraft 2/1; troops 224/130; ammo stockpiles, installations 5/25; trenches (in yards) 820/590; and bunkers 43/88.

George Salinas, a third class aviation photographer's mate, and I were members of the Cruise Book Committee. Naturally, he contributed many photographs while I became one of the contributing artists The committee asked me to participate after one of my ex-shipmates in the VC-61 detachment showed then one of my "Sylvester the SP" comic strips.

Some members aboard the ORISKANY failed to make it back. The cruise book listed Ensign A.L. Riker missing in action with Commander J.C. Micheel, Lieutenant G.A. Gaudette Jr., Lieutenant (Junior Grade/LTJG) J.A. Hudson and LTJG Ralph N. Mew killed in action. The latter officer was our squadron personnel/education officer. Tex Wainscott, another yeoman striker, had worked close with LTJG New and probably was most moved by New's death. New was killed when his jet lost its hydraulic boost while being catapulted and plunged into the ocean.

LTJG Roy Taylor was assigned New's duties and, although not listed in the cruise book, was killed while flying Combat Air Patrol (CAP) over the fleet. He sustained a flameout at 12,000 feet which he reported over his radio. Why he kept trying to start it instead of jettisoning the cockpit and parachuteing down, it was never found out as he never spoke again over his radio. His aircraft crashed and sunk. Both VF-122 pilots were in their early 20s of age and had been promoted from ensign to LTJG the first day of the month in which they were killed (Mew 3-22-53 and Taylor 4-13-53).

Unarmed Hung Bomb Disaster

Our sister squadron's (VF-121) administrative staff shared the small (approximately 12x24 feet) office with us.

Personnelman Second Class Dave Lomeli, Seamen Richard "Shorty" Young, and John "Willie Green" Walser were their full-time workers. They shared the outer portion of the office while we (Hait, Shaffer, & I) t.oiled in the inner half. It killed two (Thomas M. Yeager, an aviation electrician's mate (AE) airman, from Columbus, Ohio; and Thomas L. McGraw Jr., a photographic airman from Watertown, N.Y.) and injured 15. The only VF-122 member injured was Bob Brockmayer. He took some shrapnel in an arm and in the stomach.

The pilot, LT Edwin Kummer of Rochester, N.Y., looked in terrible condition as I darted out on the catwalk to find out what was happening. He was being cut loose and removed from the sweltering and smoking cockpit by the hot-suit man, Airman Richard D. Donovan of Emmetsburg, Iowa. He was aided by Airman Michael J. Yox as they carried the pilot, who had miraculously escaped death, to safety. Fortunately, the plane did not explode with its gas tanks, but everyone was expecting it to do so as the ORISKANY firefighters were smothering it.

The blast had gone through the #3 elevator and injured several men on the hanger deck and punctured several of the wing tip fuel tanks. These caused a pool of gasoline on the hanger deck which, if ignited, could have been terrible to our mission over

---

17 A knot is one nautical mile per hour. A nautical mile is 6,080.2 feet, about a sixth longer than a land mile (5,280 feet).

U.S.Navy Photo

F4U LANDS WITH HUNG BOMB
This Corsair tried to land on the USS ORISKANY with supposedly a hung unarmed bomb. The disastrous results are shown in these photographs.

there. The fuel was removed safely by the firefighters and repair crew with no further damage occurring.

The medical department worked through the night and the next day. Hundreds of us lined up to donate blood to help sailors like AE3 Langford W. Henshaw of Odessa, Texas, who sustained a serious injury with a large piece of shrapnel in his back.

I was extremely proud of my shipmates reaction of heroism and maintaining one's line of duty. Special memorial services were held for Mc Graw and

Yeager and the sad feeling of humbleness for those injured was felt by all of us.

Believe it or not, the repair crew had the hole in the elevator repaired the next day and we were able to continue our mission of supporting the United Nations action in Korea.

This was the only trip the "Big O" made to Korea but she made several to Viet Nam. I was on the PERKINS in VN when the ORISKANY lost 44 crew members in October 1966. It had a fire burned through four levels reaching

the officers staterooms where many officers returning from a mission got trapped.

"War is hell" someone once said.

A Religions Fork In My Adult Road

All those deaths brought my religious beliefs to a fork in the road. I had been raised as a child in a Christian world as almost 33% of English speaking nations had. I was taken to a Baptist church every time its doors were opened. I didn't know in my adolescent days that the other 67% consisted of many other religious. These, I learned later, were approximately (with figures rounded off if above .5%) 21% Islam, 14% Hinduism, 18% others (e.g. Buddhism, etc.), with about 16% non religious. All totaled about 4,200 religions[18].

From the first grade until somewhere in high school, I had assumed everything we read in the schoolbooks and the newspapers was a true fact. It never occurred to me to doubt it as it came from people or things I respected. I didn't know the stuff they were teaching us in church came from Hebrew, Aramaic, Greek, and Latin translations centuries before 0001 A.D. The King James version came from the Hebrew and Greek interpretations. But, even it has been revised a few times to

---

18 Information obtained from www.adhents.com on the internet.

make it more understandable by the readers. However, I was always told, its many books were written by authors inspired by God.

My first doubt came at an outdoor party I was attending as a young teenager. We played a game of whispering a joke into the ear of one seated at the end of the circle of attendees around our fire. They would then whisper it to the next person. When it got around the end of the 15-or-so in the circle, they would tell what they heard as the joke. It never was anywhere near the original. I thought about how the happenings of Jesus Christ would be promulgated around fireplaces back in his day when almost no one knew how to write. The miracles he performed became greatly exaggerated, if they even happened.

In boot camp, NAS Miramar, and on board the ORISKANY, I had approached chaplains of the three religions the U.S. Navy provided: Catholic, Protestant, and Jewish. I told them in depth how I was doubting some of my teachings of the *Holy Bible* hoping they would aid me with my problem of doubt. None of them came close to helping me. They all said it boiled down to the same fact: "You must believe."

I was standing in a gun tub leaning on a rail one warm night as we were on our way to Japan for repairs, upkeep, and a few days of liberty. It was a clear spring night with all the stars shinning brilliantly. I started thinking about what they had said, what I had been taught, and what I had read. I knew I should evaluate all of this objectively as my father had always taught me. He told me to take my spiritual mind out of the middle of any problem and consider every element involved without any prejudices. He'd hold up both his hands, as if he had two handfuls of something.

"Weigh all the factors and thoughts fairly and justly," he would say raising one hand while lowering the other, then did it vice versa as if weighing something to decide the lightest or heaviest.

I always did it by thinking as if I was in a space ship from another planet approaching earth. Then, evaluating everything I found about the problem as an honest alien I came to a conclusion. I believe Jesus Christ was a great evangelist in those days like Otto Graham was in our day. Christ influenced many to believe in God, but it was only a handful compared to Graham and his 100,000 audiences did in huge football stadiums, plus the millions Graham touched worldwide over television. I know the devout Christian reading this would argue that the *Holy Bible* books about Christ and his disciples influenced more to turn to God.

While I can't dispute that, and wouldn't, I just don't believe it as 100% true facts.

There are too many revisions and too many translations by too many different people in too many languages. There is no doubt that the book has had millions and millions of readers making it easily the most read publication in the history of mankind. It has helped families raise their children with admirable positive thoughts, with a few exceptions. I do not want to get into details on which passages or verses I believe to be positive or negative. I just believe that Christianity as a whole is good for the human races and do not believe some others are.

I finally resolved that night in the gun tub off the coast of Korea that I did not believe any religious concept but agree they are needed. I am not a atheist. I definitely believe in a supreme being, or beings, but not as any religious publications describe.

Supreme Being(s) Incomprehensible

I don't believe we can __*comprehend*__ *the supreme being(s).* But I strongly believe there is one or some. That a pitiful human being can conceive this super being, I think is ridiculous.

Every day we discover ways to see things more microscopically as well as more telescopically. Medicine has advanced tremendously over the last decade with their minute findings while astronomers are finding our universe is surrounded by unknown other universes. Where does it stop? Nobody knows…nobody.

Does the supreme being(s) regulate every thing that we do. I do not believe that. But I do believe it instilled instincts in every creature born. The most convincing observation I had to solidify my belief that was true was films of new born kangaroos (called joeys). Expelled at birth through the mother's vagina, the fetus instinctively climbs straight up its mother's torso to reach her pocket containing her nipples and the joeys' nourishment. This alone should influence atheists to accept my theological thinking, not that I care.

I feel that all living creatures have the same instincts of their breed when conceived. Influences during gestation (e.g. irregular diet of mother, etc.), during infancy (e.g. sudden loud noises, etc.), and a slight degree while reaching adolescence (e.g. peer influence, etc.) will add to, subtract from, or modify these instincts. I do not believe the supreme being(s) affects any of this maturing. Living creatures react to all things instinctly or in their own-formed opinion of what is best to do. Dealing with other people was always easy and comfortable for me because I always, if possible, follow the "Golden Rule" I learned in the second grade: *Do unto others as you would*

have them do unto you. Some idiots believe when they do something bad, "The devil made me do it."

When a good person is killed by accident, most religions believe it was God's will. Even thousands suffering death through floods, hurricanes, tornadoes, volcano eruptions, and other catastrophes was the will of God. I never understood all that reasoning. "God is good" some believe and reason that those innocent mothers and children succumbing from the aforementioned catastrophes that it is the work of the Devil. Why an all powerful being would allow the existence of a "Devil," is beyond my comprehension.

Enough of that heavy stuff and back to our first and only visit to Nagoya.

The Long Ride To & From Pleasure

It was relatively a small city and located in the Isle Wan, a harbor on the southeast corner of the main island of Japan. The bay was so shallow that we had to anchor so far from the shore that it took us about 30 minutes to get to the beach in a LCM (landing craft, mechanized). The craft was made to haul vehicles such as jeeps or tanks. Therefore, it had no seats but could carry 40 or so sailors standing. We boarded the LCM and returned aboard via a ladder over the port side off the quarterdeck.

Why we stopped there for a

few days, I never found out. I assumed it was part of USA's post WWII occupational plans. All I know is we were glad to get terra firma under our sea legs for a change. Seaman Ken Cunningham, Shaffer, and I toured the town for souvenirs, but most of the time we spent in taverns drinking their local beer. Between the pubs, sometimes one of us would need to urinate. The Japanese thought nothing of urinating in the gutter of the streets. We did not even consider it. I didn't care whether is was the country's custom or not, I preferred to wait until we got to the next beer joint. Even there it was co-ed. I was urinating and a Japanese girl entered the toilet, while ignoring me, squatted over an empty hole in the floor and did her job. They probably laughed at us being so embarrassed about doing a natural body function with a member of the opposite sex.

We ended our liberty near the pier to ensure we caught the last LCM and it was packed. I never forgot the boat full of happy drunks singing a song made up that trip: "Oriskany, Oooooooriskany. Piss on thee Oooooooriskany." I figured several would fall in going up the ladder, but they didn't. On to Yokosuka.

Surprise, Surprise! It's My Ole Buddy

One trip to Yokosuka shocked the dickens out of me. Richard nor I wrote each other that frequently, but I did know he was a gunner's mate aboard the USS IOWA (BB- 61). As we pulled in to our mooring pier, there was the IOWA anchored in the bay. As soon as I got liberty, I boarded one of the liberty launches headed for the IOWA. I learned at the quarterdeck that Richard, now a gunner's mate third class, was assigned to the forward turret of the three 16-inch (406 MM) turrets on board. There I learned he had just taken his division's mail bag down to their sleeping quarters and he was attempting to open the bag with his back towards me when I entered the compartment. I snuck up to him and pushed him aside.

"Move aside there sailor, let a man show you how to do that," I said authoritatively.

He turned toward me with an angrily knotted brow. Then, his mouth dropped as my face catapulted his thoughts into a brief shock.

"Bobby Peden," he blurted while smiling widely. "What in the world are you doing here?"

"I'm on the ORISKANY that just moored a few hours ago," I said hugging my best male friend in the whole wide world. "Get into your liberty togs and let's go ashore."

He had no trouble at all getting an early liberty pass and we soon were bar hopping from his favorite hang outs to all of mine. We spent a couple liberties together reminiscing about old times and sharing pictures of his family (I was very, very fond of all members of his family) and mine. He admitted he had been writing to Billie Frances, but nothing serious yet. I told him then that she'd get him if she so desired.

"Just don't be surprised," I told him. Sure enough it happened after he got discharged but he had no such plans during our great fun liberties in Japan.

On another liberty during one of our sight-seeing trips, Willie Green took me to a spot he knew in Yokohama, between Yokosuka and Tokyo. It featured Hot Sake chased with cold Akadama wine. It tasted great, but after a bottle of the two, I was feeling no pain. Willie's vulgar language used on the packed train up to Yokohama ("They don't know English," he reasoned) didn't bother me a bit on the return trip.

Another R&R trip I really enjoyed was to the base of the famous Mount Fujiyama, a sacred and highest mountain in Japan. There I really put to a test my camera stuff learned from Dale Hayes, a first class parachute rigger I had met on board the ORISKANY. We had become friends when he found out my interest in photography. He let me watch him develop and print still photographs in his dark room setup in the parachute loft where he hung parachutes to be aired. He showed me how to take a picture of Mt. Fuji using the moonlight reflecting its snow by depressing my box camera shutter open for several minutes. I was so thrilled with it that I bought a Japanese twin lens reflex camera (Ricoh, I think) that had adjustable speed adjustments up to 1/200th of a second. His schooling and my subsequent training under his guidance was extremely valuable to me in my later journalistic training. Where ever you be, I will never forget the knowledge of photography that you so kindly bestowed me. Mucho thanks, Dale. You taught me well.

BGWW&P Times

May 1953 - July 1954   *Vol. 1, No. 9*   *San Diego, CA; Memphis, TN; & Huntsville, AL*

Debbie Socked It To Me!
Had To Have A Daughter After That

We finally headed for San Diego, with the usual stopover at Pearl Harbor, with our ship's band playing "California Here We Come" in May. When we left the line off Korea, the pilots of the last few jets flew about bridge high (07th deck in the superstructure) before landing and trailed out a roll of toilet paper from each cockpit to make, in their clever little minds, a festive occasion of the final landing of our mission.

When we steamed into the harbor at Diego, we saw a crowd of about 5,000 standing behind a restraining rope and I even spotted "Ski" Maduska in the front row. He was an injured squadron member of the our maintenance department that had been flown back to the San Diego Naval Hospital for treatment.

Out in front of the crowd nearer the edge of the pier was Debbie Reynolds, who had been overwhelmingly chosen the "Ship's Pin-Up Girl" after her big hit starring with Gene Kelly in the great 1952 musical sensation "Singin' in the Rain."

She was born on April 1, 1932, in El Paso, Texas, a few months after I was born (1/12/32) and hit the big time when she won the Miss Burbank (Calif.) contest when she was only 16. (She was fortunate Carolyn was too young [14] to enter at the time.) Warner Brothers signed Debbie, and a few years later, MGM. She had made numerous "girl next door" movies, but the Kelly-Reynolds movie zoomed her to international fame as at the time it ranked as movieland's greatest musical.

That day in 1953, she was greeting us in her prime as a beautiful 21-year-old 5'2" starlet. Smiling her darling little face to the thousands of ORISKANY sailor lined along the flight deck and all the other decks with open spaces to the starboard side, she threw kisses up and down the pier. I was one of her most ardent fans, even before her '52 hit.. Therefore, I was craving to be near her when I saw the ground crew roll up the huge two-story steps and platform to receive the ship's brow[19]. Once secured, they rolled up a large trash bin and the crew began taking garbage bags ashore and dumping them in the bin…***ONLY 50 FEET OR SO FROM DEBBIE!***

I had my camera hanging around me neck and "Ski" was nearby my object of adoration. Those two certainties was all I needed to give me confidence to make a daring move. As the entire crew was dressed in undress blues (i.e. no pinstripes on the collar, no cuffs, nor neckerchief), I was inconspicuous when I grabbed one of the bags and followed the line of the other garbage bearers. After I dumped my load, I ran to "Ski" and pulled him under the rope. Handing him my camera, I said, "Howdy 'Ski.' You look great. Com'on and take a picture of me and Debbie. Just get us in the center and push this shutter button."

---

19   A large gangplank leading from a ship to a pier or its portable retainer. The gangplank usually has rollers on bottom and hand rails.

"Debbie, I'm on the ORISKANY and just sneaked off to get my buddy, 'Ski" here (motioning towards him), to take a photograph of you and I. Will ya?" I rattled off nervously.

"Sure," she said with the most radiant smile I had ever seen.

She really socked it to me! She kissed me right smack dab in the mouth!

The crew went wild with their cheers, probably all envisioning theirselves down on the dock with Debbie Reynolds in their arms. We kissed for several seconds, which I realize she was just holding it for the enjoyment of the glaring, envious swabbies, but I was enjoying it thoroughly.

Thanking her, I quickly darted to my camerman.

"Did you get it?" I yelled, excited as a humming bird in a bed of orchids.

"No! I pushed the button, but nothing happened."

"You didn't cock the shutter?"

"You didn't say anything about cocking a shutter," he said defensively as, in the excitement of the happening, I had neglected to tell him. My happiness thermometer went from its depressing low. Then,

I shook it off and cocked the shutter.

"I'm sorry, 'Ski.' Here, its cocked now. I'll try to get her to pose again."

Fortunately, she was still close by and was understanding. She had four years experience already in filming scenes in which some had to be retaken. I was hoping for another big hug and kiss, but when I puckered up she put her fingers on my lips with a soothing, "One of those is enough for a lifetime, sailor."

Instead, we just stood arm in arm and (I discovered when seeing the print) with her beside a warning sign that read: "Danger 480 Volts."

Our paths never crossed again, but I shall never forget

meeting her at such a historic occasion for so many U.S. Navy men. It was the ORISKANY's only tour in the Far East during the Korean War, so over 3,000 men remember that day of return and, when they do, they always remember our pin-up girl:

xoxoxoxox xoxoxoxox Debbie Reynolds xoxoxoxox xoxoxoxox

Believe it or not, I jumped back in line with the garbage swabs and returned without

By Ski Maduska
DEB WITHOUT THE KISS – Debbie Reynolds was our mascot and met the ship when we returned from Korea. I snuck ashore and got her first kiss.

mishap. Naturally, Debbie was brought aboard to meet the ORISKANY skipper, Captain Courtney Shands, a WWII Navy Cross recipient who shot down six Japanese planes in 23 minutes.

Also returning on the vessel was Rear Admiral R.F. Hickey, Commander of Carrer Division FIVE and Task Force 77. The commanding officers of the squadrons of Air Group TWELVE returning were Lieutenant Commanders Standley R. Holm (VF-121), James W. Wyrick (our VF-122), M.D. Carmody (VF-124), and A.H. Gunderson (VA-125). LCDR Gunderson had assumed command of that attack squadron on Feb. l, 1953, when its CO, CDR J.C. Micheel, was killed in action.

The news media were following Debbie around while she was meeting those important officers available, but I don't know for sure if she got to meet three hero pilots of our sister squadron VF-121: LT Elmer R. Williams, LTJG David Rowlands, and LTJG J.D. Middleton. The media sought them out as they shot down two MIGs and damaged another in a dogfight with seven aircraft.

My meeting her and the way it was done was the talk of our compartment that night. But those on liberty, or those with family living in the San Diego area, had other things of more personal interest to chat about. It's for sure, not a single one will ever forget OUR pin-up girl.

Back To NAS Miramar & Unpacking Duties

We had to keep many of our files and records open until we were securely docked and most of the married gobs took leave to get their families, some up to 30 days. I finally got another Quonset hut to rent and drove to Memphis to get Carolyn and Bobby in June. I sure was glad to see them and the rest of my family. As dad was an active Mason and mother in its Eastern Star affiliate, Jo Ann had became a member and finally its top officer, the Worthy Advisor, of the Rainbow Girls. She had put on a sock dance at South Side High as each member had to raise $200 and its profits far exceeded her quota. She also completed high school and married a school dropout several months her junior. He was an Arkansas native named Kenneth Long that quickly won the hearts of the Peden Family. He worked for Fruehoff Trucking Company as a welder under his uncle-in-law, Wayne Tutor, who was superintendent. After that he went into truck driving for several cattle hauling companies, then National Food Co. 8.5 years and finally 28.5 years with Roadway Expressway Co.

John Lee was in high school and according to his buddies — James Earl Davis, Charles "Hog Jaw" Pressley, Bob Fink, etc. — John was still the "quiet one" but carried a long stick."

In other words, he had become one of the Fort Pickering laid back, but tough guys. He was working for dad, as I did, at Peden & Sons. Dad told me he was considering an offer by Malone & Hyde Co., a large wholesale food company we had always used, to open one of the new type "supermarket" stores that were becoming popular and killing the small neighborhood grocery businesses. He would wait until my scheduled discharge the next year was firm.

I had been advanced to YN2 the month before we returned to the states, so things were going a little better for my little family when we set up our little hut home outside the base. We renewed our friendship with all the VC-61 friends and I ever got to playing softball games against my old championship squad. A smaller squadron, our team we couldn't come up with a good, fastball pitcher, but we had a 5-2 won-loss record for the short season. I led the team in hitting (.400) and didn't make an error all season while handling 31 chances at the hot corner.

Tex taught me the game of tennis that summer. When I was a kid, we would see adult men playing on the one court we had in DeSoto Park. Some would play in tight short pants like the girls wore. All the Fort Pickering boys thought it was a sissy game like golf. I told Tex about that and he "pshawed" it as hogwash.

"If it's a sissy game, then a tough dude like you should be able to beat me, right?" he reasoned tempting me to try the sport.

The second day we played, I beat him a game to the surprise of both of us. He was about 6'2" with long arms and legs, but my quickness made up for his reach. After he taught me the grip, etc., I had no trouble hitting the ball solid, with top spin, or cutting the ball as I could do easily with the bat in a game of pepper. As neither of us had an "ace" serve, I finally got to where he seldom could beat me. I became very fond of the game.

A Discharge And A Daughter Enroute

I didn't forget about Debbie Reynolds so I kept hoping Gertie would get pregnant again. I wanted a daughter and I was determined to name it after Debbie. It was a new name to society as no one I talked to had ever met anyone with that name. Our daughter was conceived that September and we knew for sure of it by the turn of the year. Of course, we still didn't know whether it was to be another boy or a girl.

I was transferred back to VC-61 in January as VF-122 went back aboard ship and I had my discharge scheduled for July 1954. We decided it best to move to Memphis in later March before Carolyn got too big and uncomfortable. We sold the TV and few pieces of furniture we owned. Her folks offered to let us live with them until we got settled so I left them there after getting her checked in with the Naval Hospital staff at NAS Millington, Tenn., for the upcoming delivery.

Then, I return to duty and began working on my plan for a early discharge. As the Korean War was over, separation activities would discharge any enlisted member they received within three months of the individual's scheduled discharge date. Having an inside pull with the our department chief, I explained that my wife was expecting in mid-May and got them to transfer me to the Naval Receiving Station in San Diego at the end of April. I learned just before my transfer that I had passed the examination for Yeoman First Class (pay grade E-6) and would be adding my third red chevron beneath the white embroidered eagle ("crow" was slang term usually used) and crossed quills (indicating yeoman rating) on June 16th . That was good to have in my files in case I decided to reenlist prior to the three-month deadline following a discharge.

I was discharged on May 4 in plenty of time for Gertie's second child. All this time I thought the mother's egg always determined the sex of the child. It wasn't until my biology class in college that I learned the male's sperm was the mastermind behind this important decision. Therefore, when mom and I learned that the child was a girl I greeted my wife afterwards with many hugs and kisses for giving me a daughter as I wanted. She was a beautiful infant, not bruised with a warped skull as her older brother had sustained coming out as Gertie's womb's first product. She had a little light brown hair and looked even smaller than her seven pounds and six ounces.

When the nurse asked Carolyn the name of her new born, Gertie answered, "It's Debra Lynn Peden, but I'm sure her father is going to call her Debbie."

She was right, I called my little gal Debbie while holding her in my arms or rocking her in the crook of me left leg with it folded across my right knee. The slow, soft bounce of the rock apparently created a satisfying feeling to all my kids as babies. She enjoyed it as much as Bobby had.

She obviously didn't like the night as she repeatedly woke us in the middle of the night crying. It wasn't a painful sound, but rather a unifying crying. She wanted to unite someone with her and in the immediate future. Naturally, I had to work the next day so it was poor Carolyn who did the pacification chores, walking and swaying with the loud mouthed little miss so I could sleep.

Trinity Church & More Softball

With Carolyn's background as a soprano singer of many specials at her family's Trinity Baptist Church on Mc Lemore, a block from now Elvis Presley Blvd., she attended every Sunday with her family. Virgil, her dad, was a forman at Slumber Products where he had lost his left thumb in a mattress-making machine. They were paid every Friday and he would drink with some of the guys a pub on the way home. Lillian had to go get him late at night on several occasions. Finally, they got him to church to hear his daughter Carolyn sing. Her singing, and I'm sure some things the pastor Dr.William Sutton said during his sermon, Virgil joined the church. He never drank booze again.

I went knowing I was being a hypocrite, but it pacified my wife, my in-laws, and my parents. I enjoyed singing the songs with my most-of-the-time adequate bass voice and playing third base on the church fast-pitch softball team. My good buddy Richard, who I had starting calling "Mystro" because of his leadership qualities, played left field on the team. He hit .279 that season while I batted .350. Others were Frank "Fat Back" Love (lB, .383), James Bynum (SS, .286), Russ Medlock (2B, .286), Charles Ferrell (OF, .167), Richard O'Keefe (P, .204), Richard Cargill (C, .304), and Duggan (P, .364).

Love was our best player, but we didn't have enough of him to go around so finished the short season 7-12. I had by far the most total chances (112) but made a horrendous (for me) 14 errors fielding.

Tip Top Came And Went Fast

Dad had his new "supermarket" already opened and doing business a few months ago as the corner building of a small row of establishments on South Bellevue Blvd, or U.S. Highway 51. To put it in perspective for today's Memphis layout with its many street name changes and freeways added, it would be still US51, but now called Presley Blvd. The name of the cross street eludes me, but it was about halfway between South Parkway and Elvis' Graceland in Whitehaven, now a Tennesse Landmark.

It was larger than any grocery store I had ever been in that era. To the best of my memory, it was 100x150 feet and had three checkout counters. The office was in the corner in line with the cash registers and had a large mirror hat we could see through from inside the office. I was the assistant manager and did a little bit of everything. As we had two butchers, a produce manager, a stock boy, a bag boy, a nightly janitor, and two fulltime cashiers, I would spend most of my time helping any where I was needed and filling in as the third cashier

on unexpected busy times. Monthly pay days, and all Friday, Saturday, and Sundays (yep, we were never opened on the Sabbath in the past) we added another cashier.

Dad started turning the bookkeeping over to me and left me in charge of the store most of the time as he went to the bank or met with Malone & Hyde executives on the newspaper advertising we were doing. I interviewed all the prospective employees except the butchers and produce manager, which we never replaced during my tenure. We didn't deliver any more and had a huge parking lot available for our customers. I painted our specials on the windows, as in the past, but my favorite chore was as a part-time cashier. As usual, I enjoyed flirting with the female customers and they seemed to appreciate my little witticisms.

We were making good money and I was enjoying my job until a supermarket chain opened a store only a quarter of a mile south of us on U.S. Highway 51. The area was all residential in back of both of us, but they were determined to put us out of business. For example, they would price everyday commodities, such as milk, half the wholesale price just to get the customers to shop there. Dad tried to compete, but they continued to undercut all of our prices with several other stores in their chain to make up their losses. Finally, foreseeing the inevitable, he told me that if I wanted to reenlist and make a career in the U.S. Navy that I had better do so as the chain was breaking him.

The reenlistment bonus was well over a thousand dollars and I would be making pay grade E-6 salary, plus the Navy had a program called Training and Administration of Reserves (TAR) Program. A billet was available in Huntsville, Ala., for a Ynl after completion of a two-week instructor's training school at the NAVSTA, Charleston, S.C. After a few weeks of studying the program and its total commitment within the SIXTH Naval District (Tenn., Ala., N.C., S.C., Ga., Fla., and Miss.), we went for it. We were not rolling in dough with no debts.

We traded the Frazer in on a new four-door l954 Mercury with automatic transmission. Carolyn had trouble trying to drive the Frazer because of the straight transmission, but she was willing to learn when we got to Huntsville. She gained confidence fast and became an excellent driver.

I drove to Charleston to break in the new two-tone green vehicle. The school was a "piece of cake" for me. Learning lesson plan preparation and properly presenting the subject matter was the main jest of the course. I made a few trips ashore to see the terrain, but limited most of my beer drinking to the Enlisted Man's Club on the base. The seriousness I gave my study after hours paid off as I finished top in the class despite my nervousness in some of the presentation drills we had to make.

Prospective Dancer Said To Take A Hike

One Saturday night I went ashore with William, another TAR student, and stopped at a bar neither one of us knew anything about. We were seated in a booth and had four or five beers while shooting the gab about the program. The place was packed and mostly women. They were dancing with each other, which was common in those days, as there were only a few men in the place.

Someone played "Tennessee Waltz" on the juke box and I always liked to dance to that song so I poked one of the female couples on the shoulder to "cut in" for a dance.

"Take a hike, sailor," one of them told me haughtily.

I didn't feel like taking a hike, but I got the message. I tried another couple and they both stared at me with knotted brows and one jutted her jaw outward shaking her head. I was dumbfounded. I returned to me booth with a puzzled look on my face.

"Queers, huh?" my friend asked.

In those days, the general public called members of the same sex dating and making whoopee together "queer" people. Lesbians and gays terminology had not yet "came out of the closet," as it would be written. This was my first encounter with lesbians, but I had met several men I suspected to be gay. The thoughts of two women having sex together turned me on, but two males were indigestible for my small brain.

William was a storekeeper and headed for the Naval Reserve Training Center (NRTC) in Natchez, Miss. I didn't know it, of course, but that place would become a tremendous influence in my family's life. He was a deacon in his Baptist church in Natchez, but obviously a hypocrite as he was out in a den of iniquity drinking beer which was a "no-no," according to my teachings of that denomination. He makes another entrée herein in a later chapter.

Huntsville, Redstone Arsenal, & New Hope

When we moved to Huntsville, then with a 35,000 population, we rented and moved twice. The NRTC was at the foot of a city pond, which provided a nice relaxing place with its adjacent little park along the south side of the pond. Fishing was allowed to my enjoyment.

Then, my best friend among the station keepers, Storekeeper Second Class Bill Doran, talked me into renting a new two-bedroom house

By Carolyn Peden

BATHING OUR BEAGLES – Bobby and I giving Pottie & Ribbon a bath which they despised.

beside the new one he and his wife, Gertha, were renting. They were located in a pine grove and the only two houses (no phones) on the little dirt road in New Hope, Ala. The only problem was the 20-plus miles to work; however, the rent was so cheap that it was worth it. After all, he just bought a new 1955 Chevrolet and I had the new Mercury. We rotated daily driving to the center so the girls always had a vehicle available.

The U.S. Army had the Redstone Arsenal just outside of Huntsville and it had a military commissary, which saved us quite a bit on groceries. The thing I liked best about the Redstone was its lake. It was not maintained therefore the young saplings and brush encircled it excluding general access. However, with a permit, we could cut our way through it and drag a fishing boat. The fishing was outstanding. We didn't have a freezer yet, but I kept the freezer section of our refrigerator well stocked with fish, mostly bream and catfish.

I also kept Bill's full, especially during hunting season. Most of the time it was squirrels and quail.

Finally I bought a couple of beagle bitch puppies from a neighbor as Gerite and I were both were fond of fried rabbit or rabbit dumplings. Bobby was three years old then and

a real daddy's boy. I let him help me build the dog house and the pen, which was only a three-foot wide chicken wire around four of the close pine trees. Then, I had him name the puppies.

One was a blanket back beagle with its back a solid black like a blanket had been thrown over it, with of course the usual beagle brown trim on the ears and face. The other was a broken back beagle with spots. He named them "wibbon" and "pottie." We didn't learn until much later that he meant "ribbon" for the blanket back which had a white circle around its neck and "spottie" for the broken back's many black spots.

When they got old enough, I started training them and they both learned fast. I would kick up a rabbit and yell, then shoot it. Acting very excited, I ran to the bush from which the rabbit came and put their noses down into it, trail my finger down the patch it had run, and let them smell and examine the carcass. Then, the first few times I shot rabbits in front of them I would gut it and cut a few pieces of raw meat for them to eat. Later, of course, I had to teach them not to eat the game I had shot. They caught on fast that when I approached their pen with my gun we were going hunting.

Eventually, letting them out of the pen was interesting to watch. The both were very happy to see me, jumping up on me for petting, scratching, etc.

Pottie (we maintained Bobby's pronunciation), however, was extremely affectionate. Ribbon (we used his intended name in lieu of "wibbon") was more interested in trailing a rabbit. Therefore, after a few second of greetings, she was off to the nearby cotton fields with Pottie and I in her wake. That became our hunting routine at about six months and continued for a couple of years. Ribbon would hunt about 30 yards out front of use while Pottie usually hunted within 10-15 feet from me. When we were out of sight from Ribbon in the woods, she always governed her range by the sound of me kicking brush and dead tree branch piles along the way. Rabbits in the woods usually hop ahead of the sound unless they were in good cover. This enabled Ribbon to cross its scent trail and start sounding off. Pottie joined her immediately and the two of them would drive the rabbit around in its habitual circle enabling me to get a shot when it came back around. When Pottie or I would "jump" one or kick one out of the brush, Ribbon would join Pottie on her trail. It worked fine and we never were out of rabbits in the freezers of the Pedens and Dorans. I would occasionally take some game to the rest of the station keepers when our freezer became full. All total my diary for 1956 showed 59 wild rabbits killed addition to 22 squirrels, 16 quails, and 8 doves. 'Twas definitely a good year for my single shot

12-gauge shotgun I've had since my 16th birthday. We ate well.

Heavenly Litter Then The Heartbreaks

When they finally went into heat, I mistakenly thought their were safe in their pen as I had never seen any stray dogs around. I was mistaken and work up one morning and found Ribbon locked up with a male semi-shepherd mutt. I had to dump some cold water on them to get them undone from their sexual encounter, but it was too late. Apparently, he had not gotten to Pottie yet, but Ribbon gave birth to five cute puppies. Four of them were of the beagle black coloring with tan & white trim. However, one was reddish like his father.

Debra was about 30 months old by then and she really enjoyed playing with them. We named him Rusty and it also became my favorite. He was the liveliest of the littler. They weren't even six weeks old and they started dieing. I didn't know what it was until I took the last two to a veterinarian and learned they were being eaten internally by worms. The fourth one died that night and the pills the vet had given the last one, which was Rusty, where to late. He was whining and barely had his eyes open. The Tutors were all soft-hearted people and so was I. Watching the little puppy suffer was more than I could take. I got

my gun and put him out of his misery. I cried openly in the forest behind our house. I didn't let either of the kids see the sympathetic execution nor the burial. However, I showed them where they were buried and let them help me make five little crosses to stick in the ground around the graves.

I made sure the two grown bitches were dewormed and the pen completely sterilized. I learned the symptoms to watch for are lack of energy and whitening of gums. The latter is a dead giveaway and afterwards I always made it a habit to check all of future dogs gums frequently.

Another thing I learned was about having a pen out doors under trees. One must be sure to cover their pet's food trough. Beagles, as all hounds, tend to gulp their food. I knew that and, therefore, would not give them pieces of meat with a small bone in it. Bones I gave individually and after stripping most of the meat so they would chew on the bone.

On day after dumping some table leftovers in their troughs, without my knowledge the wind blew a tiny piece of a branch from one of the pine trees into Ribbon's trough. She gulped it down and it punctured her throat. After hunting the next day, I noticed her neck being swollen on one side. The vet diagnosed it as a snake bite and lanced it to let out the pus. Then, he stuffed a 12" strip of gauze he had medicated inside the opening.

He left a little sticking out and said to pull it out the next day and it should heal well. I thought that was crude, but what did I know about doctoring animals? I did as directed.

The swelling went down in a few days and for about a week she showed no problems whatsoever, even hunting a couple times. Then it swelled again and this time the vet suspected a foreign object. He x-rayed it and found the stick. He kept Ribbon overnight saying he would operate the next morning.

She died during the operation...

When the vet called me, I was at work. It shocked me so, I agreed to let him take care of disposition of the remains, before I let it totally register. Then I chokingly excused myself to Doran sitting across from me and went outside and bawled for 10 minutes. I loved that bitch.

(I had to take a break while writing this as I became so choked thinking of her death that I couldn't write.)

I was extremely fond of both dogs as true animal lovers are of their pets. But, I think I was more fond of Ribbon. Pottie was a cute and playful bitch while Ribbon seemed smarter and more businesslike. She would play with Bobby and Debbie along with Pottie, but when see saw my shotgun in my hands, Ribbon was ready to get down to serious stuff.

Pottie was definitely 90%

or so beagle, but her spots wasn't the traditional blanket back design that most hunters expect of that breed. Ribbon had a beautiful face. Had I been a dog, I would have fell for her just because of that. Maybe that's why Rusty's sire selected Ribbon over the two that were both in heat.

Pottie Gave Me Goosebumps

It was a few weeks before I felt like rabbit hunting again. Finally, I put Pottie in the car and drive to a nearby wooded area that we frequented. I let Pottie out and she circled me several times, jumping in joy to be out with me again hunting.

*Then...*she trotted out with her nose to the ground searching for a fresh rabbit trail, exactly as Ribbon always did. I could feel the hair on the back of my neck rising with the goosebumps I was experiencing. The rest of her short life, she hunted out front of me as Ribbon always did. I began to wonder if maybe a supreme being did take an interest in the non-instinctive things, but I would always remember the thousands of innocent kids suffer and die of starvation, wars, floods, etc. Still, it was one of the little smatterings of possibilities that the religious propaganda I had been fed all life might be true.

Consequently, I still went to church in New Hope

with Carolyn. I tried, and I believe is one of my strongest of the few assets I possess, to keep an open mind. The propaganda lost, but I still enjoyed singing. In fact, we formed a male quartette with me singing bass. We weren't very good, but we had fun and nobody ever asked me if I was a hypocrite (probably because many of them fit that role).

One of the members of the quartette heard about our loss of a beagle and showed me an ad in *Sports Afield* for registered beagle pups for only $45, plus shipping. I knew of the reputation about the bloodlines of canines maintained by the American Kennel Club (AKC) so I ordered a male pup. When he arrived at the post office in his wooden crate, he was obviously a nervous wreck from the shuffling around he had experienced in the trip from Oklahoma. Gertie cuddled him all the way home, but he didn't show any response to anything until we put him in the pen with Pottie. She was obviously overjoyed to have another of kind in the pen even it was a four-month old pup. It was several days, however, before it started acting normal instead of cowering. Deb and Bobby spent as much time with him as we would allow. They quickly became his most ardent fans.

He had longer ears and thicker bones than the two half-breed bitches we had raised. He was a blanket back as I had ordered and had a blood line certificate with many generations hence. We were pleased with his appearance and proud that I could boast being an owner of a registered beagle. Down the line, I planned to charge a pup in return for his stud service and gain me a pack of beagles.

Honorable Sir Bogey

In a few weeks, the new addition to our dog pen began to wag his tail when he heard my voice or he smelled my presence. He was finally showing some signs of being a normal dog. He wasn't exuberant in his greeting as Pottie, but the happiness to see me was there. It was just displayed in a more dignified fashion. I joked that it must be his ancestors' hierarchy. As the oldest in his bloodline chart were of England owners, I originally started calling him "Sir Pup." That preliminary title changed when I started training him to hunt.

He would follow close to me and when I would jump a rabbit he did not instinctly react. If I was not able to get a shot, I would show excitement in my movements running to, and pointing at, the track of the rabbit's departure. He could see Pottie's reaction when she was called to that point and got a whiff of the trail. Her barking while trailing the small furry mammal did not impress the confused pup. When I would

shoot my gun, he would creep away from me with his tail pulled under him.

Being an inexperienced dog trainer, I became very disappointed in our purchase of this registered beagle. He had not responded to my training methods as my bitches had. (*I must write the next, because it is true, and all you female readers will smile with a "We know, Buck."*) I took into consideration the fact that it has been long known that the female canines are smarter than the males. So, when I had to send in the registration form with his formal name to AKC, I decided he wasn't quite up to par — but my fondness for his superiority disposition was still there — I kept the "Sir" but changed "Pup" to "Bogey." A bogey in golf is one over par, one stroke over that expected for a player to attain on a hole. All my golfer friends chuckled at my philosophy in determining the name for this inept beagle.

I did all the normal stuff for months with the growing pup such as letting him smell the carcass and watching me gutting and skinning it. I would give him a taste of it raw and scraps after he had eaten it. He finally put two and two together and came up with "for." He must have finally thought: "We smell that thing's trail and bark until my master's stick goes 'boom.'" There was no reasoning as to "why" it happened "when." It

just clicked in the little guy's head one day.

I remember it because I was getting a little wet from a light rain falling one November day and was about to whistle to my four-legged crew and call it a day. Then Pottie sounded her high-pitched yelping indicating she had picked up a trail. Then, to my joyous surprise, there came some beautiful saxophone bass rumbles that had to be the voice of our own Sir Bogey. Needless to write, I was very pleased. From that day on, he produced his great sounds over the countryside while tracking the long-eared furry little creatures.

First Fish Caught Was A Surprise

My parents were very impressed with Sir Bogey's voice during one of their few visits. Berline and her family came one weekend and took us up to Waynesboro, Tenn., with Aubrey footing the meals and $7 motel room cost. We fished in the big lake near the famous Natural Bridge, but only Debra was successful. While wading in one of the shallow streams empting into the lake, she came running out with a minnow in her panties.

We drove to the Tutor farm in May of 1956 to attend popa's funeral. He was a highly respected farmer in Pontotoc County and dearly loved by many, many people. JoAnn and Kenneth were there with their two girls, Connie and

Sharon. She was carrying Gary who would be born in November.

Not long after that, Pottie got out of the pen one night and was run over by a car on the nearby highway. I think she was carrying her first litter sired by Sir Bogey when she was killed. All four of us shed tears when we buried her next to Ribbon's puppies' graves.

The rest of the tour in Huntsville was pleasant working under LCDR J.B. Walker along with the other enlisted men. YN2 Robert Troupe, was a local resident. Tex Bess, a BM2, was a whiz with working on our cars. ET2 Jack Welch taught me the Morse code and helped me build a ham radio. Chief Corpsman S. Mc Cormick kept up well physically and RM2 Joe Mc Donald kept us laughing.

The latter boozer, Doran, and I pulled a first tours of the local bars on occasion. One Saturday night, after dropping Joe off at his home, Doran and I decided we were too drunk to drive that curvy mountain road home so we called the wives and went to the training center to sleep on the couches in the recreation room.

EM1 Phil Oppenheimer had the duty that night and was already asleep in his bunk. Ole Bill and Buck were feeling no pain and still wanted to have fun as we opened another beer.

"Reveille sailor!" Bill yelled

as I turned on the light. "Beer time."

"Go away," Oppenheimer murmured turning over.

"You can't sleep with all this beer here," Bill said shaking the bed cover.

Suddenly, Phil threw back the cover with one hand and came up with our security watch's .45 caliber automatic pistol in the other hand pointed at us.

"Get out of here…NOW!" he ordered, obviously mad as hell.

We were sober enough not to take any chances with some crazy bastard pointing a firearm at us, whether it had a shell in the chamber or not. I knew it wasn't cocked, but I wasn't foolish enough to try anything. We exited quickly, turning out his light. We went outside, both of us fuming. We even talked about jumping him after he went to sleep and beating the shit out of him after getting the gun. Still drinking our six-pack, we finally cooled our temper and decided to drive home.

On the way to work Monday morning, we were still hot under the collar as we discussed how ridiculous Phil had been pointing a loaded pistol at two shipmates. We both thought we saw the ammunition clip in the handle of the weapon, but there was no way of knowing if a shell was in the chamber of its barrel. We decided we would have it out with Oppenheimer in the parking lot before entering the building.

He came early, as we did, and started apologizing immediately. He reasoned that (1) he was tired and sleepy, (2) we were drunk and wouldn't leave him alone, but (3) he should not have pointed the pistol at us. He said he was very sorry and begged us not to tell the episode to any of the crew.

We told him if he ever did that again to ANY shipmate that we would beat the shit out of him, but we finally accepted his apology as he definitely sounded sorry. We had already decided we wouldn't tell any of our shipmates. So, it was settled, but never forgotten.

All three of us had a horrible day handling our routine duties. I always wrote me radio script for my commercials in a Naval Reserve public service show I did once a week and nothing clever would materialize for me. I ended up using some old ones.

"Records Aweigh" and "Talent Time"

My weekly show was called "Records Aweigh" after the old nautical term "Anchors Aweigh." It was over WBHP and the disc jockey that trained me was Jay Hargrove, who — along with his wife Patsy — became close pinochle playing friends. I chose "Lisbon Antigua" as my theme song and chose my favorite poplar hits and occasionally phone-in requested songs. It was only 30 minutes in length, but we were able to advertise Naval Reserve news about the local division's activities and the advantages of becoming a member. I had thought of the show and my OINC liked the idea, especially as the radio station was donating the time as public service.

I even got more energetic in my off hours and produced and directed a competitive musical show on the stage of the local movie theater on Saturday mornings before film time. It was called "Talent Time" and lasted an hour. We had it on the airways also, with the radio station selling commercial time. The theater charged a minimal fee just to cover their expenses, but it was not a packed audience. Most of the attendees were family members, friends, and neighbors of those in competition. I didn't make any money from it, but I had fun and gained some valuable experience.

I also played guard on our basketball team in the winter months. As I was a starter, it indicates we didn't have a highly rated team.

I managed and played third base on the Naval Reserve fast-pitch softball team. Doran was the pitcher and was very successful. I would run into Bill about eight years later at the Millington NAS. He had obtained a commission and looked even more handsome with his tall frame and wavy hair under a hard hat with gold on it.

My brother came down and played a few games with us as I was enlisting him in the USNR. He wanted to go on active duty, but was afraid some misdemeanor arrests in Memphis for fighting would exclude him from enlisting in the regular USN. It probably would have, but knew he'd make a good sailor.

It took a couple of weeks until were received his orders to active duty and then it would be a few years before I would see him again. I never will forget the incident he told about he and a couple shipmates stationed in Panama City went to a strip joint. The naked entertainers would dance around the tables to the juke box, raise one of their legs, and *with her vulva* actually pick up a coin placed half off the edge of the table by the customers.

That was gross enough for me, but then he added that one guy at the table next to them heated the portion of a half-dollar coin hanging off their table with a cigarette lighter. When the unaware dancer tried to do her thing, she screamed from the pain. The idiot laughed out loud as she ran for ice.

John said he was so mad that he grabbed the culprit by the back of his hair and the seat of his pants. With his buddies protecting his back from the others at the torturer's table, John shoved him out the door into the street. The others, although innocent of the act

and having permitted it, were thumbed out by my brother and left without resistance.

I had heard of some bizarre happenings before, but none exceeded the cruelty of that one. It was hard to believe it was an American that did it. John Lee wasn't sure whether he was a native, one of the many U.S. Civil Service workers in the area, or a U.S. military man.

The rest of the tour there was mild, except for that occurrence.

Our Yellow Bobby And Another Child

Bobby coughed most of the weekend and vomited several times Sunday. Monday his skin and the whites of his eyes had a yellow tint to them. We took him to the Huntsville Hospital emergency room and the doctor admitted him immediately with a diagnosis of hepatitis. Mom Esrey and my mother came to help with the vigil we had to maintain in his isolated room for the next 11 days.

When he finally got out and finally was eating normally, I took him fishing in North Salty Lake. I had borrowed an outboard motor so we rented a small boat. I let him steer the boat while fishing and the car driving home, so he had a happy day. He even caught the only two fish we took home that day. He liked going fishing, although — as would be expected of a 4.5-year-old

— he got bored after a long period of idleness between nibles or bites. He particularly enjoyed this day, however, as he could boast that he caught two and daddy none. His descriptions of landing the little bream in the boat were enjoyed by all of us.

Even Debbie, who was now three months shy of being a three years old, was becoming anxious for her younger brother or sister to arrive as Carolyn neared her delivery date. I wanted another boy and told her so many times, as if it would make any difference. Mom Esrey, as for Bobby's and Debra's birth, came for the birth to help take care of the kids and the household chores. No son-in-law was more appreciative of these grandma-type duties than I.

Gertie came through again with my choice. He was born on Feb. 11, l957 and was named him David Thomas after my older brother (Thomas David) and Carolyn's younger brother (Thomas Lee). The kids were thrilled with joy when we brought him home, especially little Deb.

Five months later I was transferred to the Naval Reserve Training Facility in Natchez, Miss., to report July 31. Included was two weeks leave enroute, so we went to Memphis to visit family and old friends

BGWW&P Times

1957-64   Vol. 1, No. 10   Natchez, MS

Fork Time Arriveth

Natchez — Where The Old South Still Lives

We enjoyed showing off our precious new baby to everyone. The Esrey's next door neighbor, Tommy and Carolyn called "Aunt Jo," spent some time with our little tot. She played the piano by ear and was amazingly good at it. Her repertoire of tunes was tremendous. I enjoyed her mucho during the two weeks as the two Esrey kids had done all their lives.

However, we came to despise her yard. It had a quick slope in the middle of it on the side and Bobby fell and broke his left femur (upper leg) bone. It not only necessitated a pin through the bone and the cast. It was a body cast that went up to his chest and down both upper legs. It had an opening to permit natural expelling of feces and urine. It had a bar from one leg to the other to facilitate carrying him. He got to where he could scoot a little with his arms, but he had to be carried from one place to another. It was a clever devise designed by the Memphis Orthopedic Clinic and he had to wear it almost two months.

We were fortunate to find a brand new brick veneer house with three bedrooms in Vidalia, La., across the river from Natchez, Miss. It was only $9,000 and was our first use of the Veteran Administration's home loan service. It enabled us to have a room for Debra and the two boys separately.

It was only five miles from my duty station in Natchez at the U.S. Naval Reserve Training Facility (changed from a facility to a center months later) located in the rear of the beautiful Duncan Park with its picturesque trees containing gray Spanish moss. The road leading to the building cut through the heart of a nine hole public golf course. There was a Babe Ruth League baseball field about 100 yards on the other side of the NRTC driveway. Little did I know that it was a *fork in the road* of my major career. Sportswriting would be the final road to the goal of my life.

On Monday nights, the Naval Reserve Surface Division met at 7 p.m. All of us station keepers

had to be there to instruct the reservists; therefore, I usually didn't go home until after the drill at 10 p.m. We were on tropical working hours (7 a.m. until 1 p.m., no break for lunch) in the summer months. I got in the habit of walking over to watch the boys (ages 13-16) play baseball.

As a boy, I had always kept a scorecard of the Memphis Chickasaw games at Russwood Park and over the radio on road games during the summer. In the winter, I invented a game of baseball with a pair of dice (e.g. "snake eyes" [pair of 1s] was a two-base hit, total of 3 a triple, a pair of 2s a home run, a 1 & 3 was a one-base error hit, any 5 & 10 totals were singles, 4 & 5 was a walk, 6 & 3 was a strike out, any 6 total a ground out, any 7 total a fly out, 8 total was a pop out, 11 was a stolen base, and "boxcars" [pair of 6s] was a sacrifice bunt if player on first or sacrifice fly if player on third base, otherwise the roll was ignored).

I had learned to use my father's ditto machine, so I made sheets identical to baseball score sheets. I made up teams to form an eight-team league and a schedule for a season of play. I would play a game between two teams and afterwards make up a box score identical to the ones published in the newspaper of Southern Association and major league games (i.e. players, position, at bats, runs, hits, etc.). At that time television was not available, therefore radio was the only form of entertainment. I would play the game, make up a box score, and write a little summary of the game in one or two paragraphs. I even kept standings of my make believe teams and figure the batting averages of the hitters, the won-lost records and earned run averages of the pitchers.

Serving As A Pinch Scorer Started It All

With all this background experience, I had no problem accepting the Babe Ruth League scorekeeper's request to take over for him while he was out of town on a vacation for a few weeks. The field had a little press box and a public announcing system where I worked during the game. Towards the end of the game, the sports editor of *The Natchez Times* would stop by and pick up the game results, hitting or pitching stars of the game, etc. He was late a few times so I wrote him a synopsis of the game one time. He read it and liked what I had written. When he asked if he could use

it verbatim in his sports page, I was flattered. Naturally, I consented and began writing him a summary of the game every evening.

The readers response to my write-ups was so positive that Elliot Trimble, editor of that afternoon daily newspaper, hired me as a part time sportswriter. The other paper serving the 35,000 readers was a morning newspaper named *The Natchez Democrat*. The high schools in our circulation area were Natchez, Washington, Fayette, and Catholic Highs in Mississippi; Vidalia, Ferriday, Jonesville, and Sicily Island in Louisiana. During the football season, which was very popular to the readers, I would cover most of the Louisiana games at the beginning, with the sports editor covering Natchez High. The Rebels, as they were nicknamed, was in the tough Mississippi Big Eight Conference. We staffed them even on the road.

I photographed action shots of the games I covered hauling the big, bulky press camera with a its large flash unit and about eight fragile flash bulbs. Staying about 10 yards ahead of the line of scrimmage on the sidelines, I would get some good running shots and receivers reaching for a football pass just inches from there hands. I was really honored at one of the football banquets when James Lambert, owner and publisher of the *Democrat* came over to our table. He

shook my hand and introduced himself to me, complimenting me on my action photographs. Apparently, neither of the two newspapers had a decent action photographer.

It Was An Interesting Block Of People

I developed and printed all my photographs. There was a female that did all the other photographs, including some of her own. I thought she might be offended by my doing it, but when she saw me printing wet negatives on the enlarger and other dark room techniques of which she was unaware, she didn't mind. In fact, she would question me when she was having problems with some of the other writers' jobs. I became her mentor.

A small coincidence at the paper was that one of the perforator operators[20] was Cossie Kyzar, our next door neighbor. Her husband, Charlie, was a seaman in the Naval Reserve and was in my Yeoman Class. His parents, Charles Sr. and Daisy, lived with them in a house immediately east of us. The Wisners, Chases, and Wiggins completed the block the that direction on Murray Drive. West was the Boles.

20 A person who types news copy onto a 1" wide roll of paper with a machine that perforates codes onto the tape which is clipped to the copy and given to the composing room linotype operators who run it on a linotype machine which makes it into lines of type.

Charlie and I became the best of friends playing poker at many of the tavern backrooms, playing golf, and watching sporting events on TV. He would hit some of his drives 300 yards with his 6'5" frame while my best ones were about 25-30 yards shorter with the smaller arc produced by my 5'6.5" height and old clubs. I was more accurate with my short irons and putter, however, so we averaged about the same score when we played. Most of the golfers in Natchez bet on their games and we were no different.

Bill Mc Kinney, the alcoholic golf pro and manager at Duncan Park, gave us free tips on our game and I even broke down and paid him for a couple of lessons with buckets of practice balls at $5 a lesson. Those helped me, but when Carolyn's cousin visited us, I really improved my game. He was an assistant professional at Cherokee Valley Golf Course in Memphis and not only changed my grip but had me comply with the basic standards of the golf swing.

We played several times while he was visiting and I never forgot his instructions. I passed them along to Charlie and we became a solid team with his long game and my short one. Some of the other golfers, such as Paul Byrne who had a nickname for everyone, started calling us "Mutt and Jeff" after the comic script of that era.

All this happened the first year I had joined the NRTC staff basically composed of CDR L.H. Roark, the Officer in Charge; Radioman 2nd Class Al Lusk; and Storekeeper 2nd Class Ray Sellers. All of them would join me in a game of golf occasionally at the Duncan links. Roark was kind enough to let me moonlight as a sportswriter the second year I was aboard. I wasn't making much money in this part-time job, but I gained a lot of experience and enjoyed every minute of it.

Sports Editor & "Down the Middle" Column Of My Own

Suddenly, the sports editor had to leave and I took over temporarily until they could find a replacement. To the publisher's surprise, I was able to write headlines for the Associated Press and United Press sports stories, edit copy, and markup dummy pages for the composing room to follow for the 1.5 or two sports pages we put out daily. They thought all I knew was how to write sports copy and take action photographs. They didn't know I was so inquisitive about all the aspects of production of a newspaper that I queried everyone about their job (e.g. the wire editor about the Associated Press & United Press International teletypes, the backshop headline setter about the different fonts, the linotype operator, the page makeup man, etc.).

As it was an afternoon paper, the deadline was 10 a.m. in the morning. I did all my on-site coverage, writing of copy, headlines, and photo lab work the night before. I would stop by at 6 a.m. the next morning and write heads for the late wire stories. Everything went so smooth the first three days that they offered me the permanent job at $90 a week. The CO okayed it so I accepted.

I was in "hog heaven" seeing 20,000 copies of my work in print every day. As the weeks progressed and it became such an easy chore for me, I began writing a column for Sunday's edition where I usually had three pages to fill. I chose the name "Down the Middle" because it was an applicable phrase for virtually any sport. For example golfers try to hit the ball DTM, fullbacks slammed through the middle of the line for first down chunks, basketball player dribbled DTM for lay-ups, and in baseball batters hit grounders DTM for singles while pitchers try to throw DTM when behind on the count 3-0.

I also would be called on to aid the general news writers with my photography. I remember one vividly:

The wire services are very prompt on national news, but the television station sometimes records the event and show it an hour or so later. That was the case one day when they were holding the

Miss America Contest and we had a Natchez girl, Lynda Lee Meade, representing the State of Mississippi in the contest.

Boom! She won the national title of Miss America so our editorial staff was in a hissy. Trimble, the editor of the paper, sent me to take a pictures of the event that would be on television shortly. As we didn't have a television in the little newspaper offices, I went a couple blocks down the street to the Hale's Bar & Grill which I frequented often after work at night. By the time I got there, the announcer Bert Parks was about to announce the four finalists. With Mrs. Hale's permission I stood on a chair to take my photos. Most of the customers knew me and laughed at my optimism.

"I think she's not only gonna be one of the finalist, but she'll win the contest. In fact, I'll bet $20 she wins cause she's so beautiful," I said with my experienced poker face. I had three takers immediately. Naturally, they wanted Lynda to win. They were simply betting the odds. She had not even made the final four yet at the time of the bet, so the odds were 49-1 against her winning. Plus, Mary Ann Mobley of Brandon, Miss., had won the Miss America crowd in 1959. They didn't ever remember any state gal winning the popular title two years in a row. It would be precedent-setting if Lynda won.

They were so happy when she won they didn't seem to mind

paying me the $60. One said it most aptly for the situation, "I just don't believe that."

"I told ya'll I could pick 'em," I said as I was leaving. "Thanks, fellas."

I waited a few minutes to let them mull over the happening and wonder how I could be so lucky. Then I went back in and gave them their money back. I knew better than to keep it. If I had and they had found out, they would've beat the feces outa me.

Sooner Or Later Everyone Learns

One of my favorite columns included notes I had made of a Natchez City Golf Championship between a 14-year-old phenom named Charles Buccantini and two-time defending champ Cliff Weeks. Charles was so well known for his slow play that Cliff brought a small folding chair to the 36-hole finals. I wished I had thought of that myself as I walked the hilly Natchez Country Club course.

It was paying off for the tall, lanky youngster as he swallowed 10- and 12-footers as if they were a piece of cake. They finished the first 18 tied and had lunch. I moseyed over to Buccantini's father Bill and asked him how Charles got so good at putting.

"He doesn't know yet he can miss one of those," chuckled the proud poppa, who was a Duncan Park Champion himself.

Cliff was a power hitter and a proven scratch golfer, but NCC was a goat hill course of small tricky greens, several atop little steep hills. He never took the lead and twice went to three down in the match play event. Charles was one hole up going into the final hole; therefore, winning or EVEN A TIE, would give him the city title.

Weeks parred the 36th hole, so all Buccantini needed to upend the defending champ was make his remaining 20-inch putt for his par.

I had starting timing Buccantini's pre-putt examinations and study since the beginning of the final round. His longest scrutiny to that point was the 29th hole…a two-foot eagle putt = two minutes and 35 seconds. "He wouldn't take longer than that for a 20-incher with only a slight break to the left, would he?" You're right he did. He took four minutes and 43 seconds walking around in big circles, stopping at points to observe, getting over the ball, then withdrawing and make the trip around again.

Finally, this lad who had been stroking putts firmly all day, "babied" it permitting the break to take command. It rimmed out on the amateur side for a bogey deadlocking the match. Weeks won the sudden death playoff on the second hole.

I started to end that column with "Now he knows he can miss." But, everyone that knows me knew that I couldn't do that to the kid after such a magnificent attempt to wrest the crown from this great, veteran city champ.

Gobble, Wobble, Giggle, & Git

Golf tournament and high school football/basketball banquets were always well attended by the participants and their family. Naturally, the two newspapers had to cover them. I even served as master of ceremonies for a couple minor ones, but a local attorney named Graham Hicks handled most of the big ones. The first one I attended with this colorful spokesman I was accompanied by my new part time sportswriter, Donald Guin. Both of us fit Graham's definition of attending a sports banquet.

"You gobble, wobble, giggle, and git," he explained.

After throwing a few witty puns at notable people on the dais or in the audience, he would pick up a piece of paper and pretend to be reading flowing, highly prestigious, complimentary statements about the guest of honor sitting beside the podium. After capturing the audience's serious and silent admiration, he would then stop...wrinkle his brow at the paper...and then lean over to the guest of honor he had been praising and ask:

"What's this word, coach?"

It produced the loudest laughter and applause of the night. The GOH was usually the athletic director or head coach of the high school events, who would hand out the individual awards to his students athletes. The tournament chairman or golf professional usually presented golf banquet awards. Sometimes they would bring in former PGA members who had the gift of gab. Don and I would publish them all the next day along with a photo or two we took.

After my highlights of the affair, I concluded my column with: "We gobbled, wobbled, giggled, and got."

Guin Gets Democrat's Sportswriting Helm

Don was short, about my height, and was a nice-looking lad in his early 20s. He had black hair and sharp facial features. He had a slight limp as if one of his legs were shorter than the other, but whether he was born with it or had an accident I never knew because I never asked. His personality was so pleasing that all the coaches liked him as much as I. We became very close drinking buddies concluding virtually every night's work at Hale's drinking beer and shooting long table shuffleboard.

He had studied journalism, so he was educated in my position whereas I had none. Therefore, I seldom had to make editorial changes to his copy. He didn't know photography, however, so I taught him how to handle the big press camera and even a smattering of the dark room chores. He was excited about learning it and mastered the chore of taking action shots in less than a month.

The *Times* head honchos put him on full time at my recommendation and we put out a pretty good sports "rag" to the Natchez afternoon readers.

I taught him how to shoot shuffleboard utilizing both hands with fingers as a guide down the board's side rails. We were a tough pair to beat. Then I got a call from Mrs. James Lambert, part owner, publisher, and editor of *The Natchez Democrat*.

"I have an application for employment to fill our upcoming vacancy as sports editor from your Don Guin. I have already talked to Ed Brown (*Times* publisher) for permission to talk to you about Guin. I've read his stuff and I've heard you've spent some time with news photography. Would you mind giving me a reference on the young man before I meet with him. I respect your opinion," he said.

He had called me at the training center during working hours, so I got his number and called him back after I got off duty. I NEVER let my moonlighting jobs interfere with my military duties... EVER.

"Mr. Lambert," I said beaming with pride that HE

would respect my opinion, "he is an excellent writer, I think, and he has learned the many uses of the press camera well. He is very dependable and gets along real well with all the area coaches. I think he'll do a good job for you, although I sure would hate to lose him."

He thanked me and in a few days Don came and told me he was getting the job. I never did tell him about the conversation with Mr. Lambert. So we had another reason to celebrate that night! Yeeeeeaaaaahhh.

I was sad that I would no longer have his talent to help my in my coverage of the local sports, but I was happy for him. I knew it was a great opportunity for him and that he would be making a lot more money.

I wasn't always slaving for my extra loot. Charlie and I would stop by one of the many bars in Natchez that had poker rooms in the back. My poker playing had matured during my first four-year hitch and at the NRTC in Huntsville. I won 65-70% of the time. However, I found that my golf was becoming a source of income with an ever better percentage.

I had been playing with a floppy bag of clubs consisting of a driver, three wood, and 3, 5, 7, 9 irons, and a putter. They were a mixed brand put together by some sailor in California that gave up the game and sold them cheap at a yard sale. I was winning pocket change playing for 25-

cent skins[21] and $1 Nassau[22] as my game was developing while playing opponents close to my average or with a spot of a hole or two. I even entered a few Duncan Park club tournaments and won runner-up fifth flight and consolation fourth flight prizes, but never finished first. I was trying hard because we were not going to buy me a full set until I captured a winner's trophy.

Finally it happened. I was shooting well enough to qualify for the Second Flight of the 1961 Natchez City Golf Tournament. I defeated Ted Mc Allister, Bill Yvelerton, and Scotty Byrne (in that order) to win it. As promised to myself, I went to Mc Kinney the next day and ordered a complete set of Gary Player's signature set with the fiberglass shafts. Of course, I had to buy a big bag with independent holes for each shaft (driver, 2-wood, 3-wood, 2-9 irons, pitching wedge, and a putter).

At first I was slicing everything as the fiberglass was slightly limber compared to the metal shafts I had been using. But, when I learned to time its whip action, I was hitting my drives at 275-280 yards. This was 25-30 farther than I usually hit. With all the clubs having the same shaft and grip, my game improved to such as extent

---

21   Lowest score on hole wins skin from all participants. Tied low extends to next hole, etc.

22   $1 bet on lowest front nine, $1 bet on lowest back nine, $1 best on 18 hole total.

that I was able to qualify for the Championship Flight the rest of my competitive career.

In fact, the International Paper Company's Natipco Country Club was the site of my best nine hole round of golf EVER. At that time it was a fairly new 6,402-yard, par 72, 18-hole course and very flat along the Mississippi River a few miles south of Natchez. I was playing a practice round on August 13, 1962, with Russell Kaiser, Billy Byrne, and Gilbert Savoy. I carded a legitimate **five-under-par 31** on the first nine which club professional John Morgan said was a **Natipco 9-hole record**.

I was still hot on the last nine, paring 10 and birdying 11 to reduce my overall scored to 6-under-par. The next hole was an easy par 5. If one hits his tee shot past the turn on the sharp 90% dogleg left, it would be reachable in two shots permitting a putt for eagle. There were many young trees planted in the out of bounds section of the dogleg and I thought about trying to fly them as I was hitting so fantastic that day. But, I thought better and just decided to hit close to the turn as I could and go for the eagle, which would've put me 8-under-par in 12 holes.

For the first time in ages I hooked my drive out of bounds. That took the wind out of my sails, so I sputtered the rest of the way to finish was a 4-under 68.

Gilbert Savoy Was My Cajun Leprechaun

Gilbert Savoy was a full-blooded Cajun, no doubt about that. He, his wife Margaret, and their five kids lived on the south side of Vidalia while Murray Drive was north. All the "block people" knew the Savoys. In fact, I think Vidalia was less than 3,000 population at that time so just about everyone knew everybody.

He volunteered to help me on game nights at Viking Stadium. He'd keep statistics and he wanted to try his hand with the camera a few times. Most of our time together though, was on the golf course. He was a high handicapper, but he loved to play the game.

I got to wondering if he was my Cajun leprechaun. He was in the foursome when I set the Natipco 9-hole record and was in foursomes when I hit my second and third hole-in-ones.

My first single shot occurred at the San Diego Naval Station's little par three course. It was just after boot camp and I remember it was on the first hole (distance is vague, but I remember I hit an 8 iron). The green was slanted toward the tee, so we saw it coming down straight for the hole, but never saw it hit. We assumed it went over the green.

We looked for it unsuccessfully. The space behind the green was clear and the grass cut, but no ball. Finally, I dropped another ball and chipped up on the green. My fellow golfer started to pull the flag out of the hole and there was the ball. It had hit directly into the hole jamming against the flagstick.

The second one was the number two green at Duncan Park with Gilbert and two others making up a foursome. We had already played 10 holes with 25-cent skins bet. The last seven holes had been tied necessitating carry-overs, so when this red-head (name eludes me) hit his ball that stopped three inches from the hole he was jumping for joy.

"A tap-in birdie gives me $5.25," he chirped. "Yeah!"

Gilbert and the other golfer had already hit and missed the green, but I had yet to stroke my 5 iron on the 167-yard hole. I hadn't been playing too well on the earlier holes, so I was shocked as everyone else when me ball hit on the green and rolled into hole.

"God damn you lucky bastard," he yelled chasing me into the woods. We were all laughing, but I wasn't taking any chances. I knew too many redheads.

Now my third hole-in-one is also noteworthy. I was playing on the same course a week later with the same ball in another foursome that included my leprechaun, Gilbert. It was on number four green, which is also a par 3 but only 120 yards.

Another One With The Same Golf Ball

I already had a hole-in-one, so the second one was not significantly impressive to me. I had told Mc Kinney about hitting it and he wanted to send it in to the manufacturer to get it set in a trophy, which I wasn't too interested. Then when I hit the third one with **THE SAME BALL** a trophy of the happening would have some merit to me.

By Gilbert Savoy

CAJUN WITNESS – My friend Gilbert who had witnessed the two hole-in-one events took this photo of me.

I probably would not have a believer that I hit two hole-in-ones in two different rounds on two different days with the same ball. But everyone knew I was fairly accurate and that over 90% of my tee shots were in the fairways. I lost very few balls back then in my prime golfing days. Knowledge of that information, plus when

Savoy attested that he had seen the Acushnet ball used in both occasions, eliminated all original non-believers.

I was really expecting a fancy trophy from the Acushnet Company, the largest golf ball manufacturer in the world (Titleist, Pinnacle, & later Cobra balls). They ceased making balls with their name on them. But, a month pased and I had heard nothing so I told Mc Kinney.

"Oh, gee Buck. I got it right here in my cabinet, but I forgot to send it off. I'll do it first thing tomorrow," he explained. Too many snorts from the pint of booze he kept there too, I reasoned.

Three months later I questioned him again.

"Buck, that trophy will be here any day now. I did send it off," he promised. I left Natchez before it ever came.

He told the story to the regulars so many times that they became tired of it. He loved to tell golf tales of the past and, I must admit, he was exceptionally good at it. One that he always told, and swears it was true, when the subject of hole-in-ones came up was his mole story.

Bill had been babying his number eight green all season long. Checking it one evening he caught a mole cutting its way through the tasty morsels growing there. Furiously, bill dug up the mole, stomped it dead, and gave it a vicious kick intended to send it off the green. Ironically, a miss-kick

sent the carcass rolling into the hole.

I wrote in my column that readers needed to be there to see Mc Kinney's portrayal of his kick and the flopping of the animal into the hole. "First mole-in-one I've every heard about. How about you?"

Agatha, the 18-year-old daughter of Bill and Liz, came in saw him at the end.

"Daddy, you telling that again?" she asked before we had time to congratulate her for winning the Duncan Park Women's Championship over Robin French, manager of the NCC. Agatha later married Cliff Weeks to give Natchez the prospective birthplace of future city golf champs for years to come.

Hole Winner With Seventeen Strokes

One of the funniest golf holes I saw occurred during the 1964 City Golf Championship which was held at NCC, the goat hill course that was covered with thick vines in the gullies on the sides of the fairways. If you hit in the rough, you usually couldn't find your ball.

I was playing in the foursome with Fred Foster and Bob Foley, with my opponent in the Championship Flight of the match play event. Fred was a colorful former head football coach at Fayette High and now a FB assistant and basketball coach at Vidalia. Bob was an oilman of fine repute, but — as will become apparent — with

a short temper. I think they were competing in the First Flight.

I had already clinched my victory, but they were tied. We were on the second round of the nine hole course playing the seventh hole as the 16th. It was a par four with a narrow fairway with deep gullies on both sides. Foley had the honors (we shot last as our play was irrelevant). He blasted a long hook well into the twines of vines. Disgusted, he started to step down off the elevated tee so Fred could hit.

"It's still your shot according to the rules," Fred said, which was true.

This infuriated Foley even more and he hooked two more into the same area. My opponent and I were choking down laughter as best we could.

Fred was gentleman enough, or afraid enough, to say anything during the last two hit, but I detected a twinkle in his eye as Foley stormed off the tee grunting something like "…two balls was all he was going to lose on this hole." He relinquished the tee.

Foster calmly returned his driver to his bag and pulled out his putter. He teed up, tapped the ball straight down the fairway, at least 25 feet, and nonchalantly strolled off the tee. **BWBB.** Fourteen more putts and he was on the green without coming anywhere near the dreaded vines. Foley was silent during the proceeding down the fairway, but he was so mad his face was flushing. However, I thought his coloring was almost back to normal until Fred two putted the green and said to his opponent, "Mark me down a 17, Bob."

Fred easily won the 17th and consequently the match.

First Time At The Top In City Golf Tourney

I continued my torrid golf in that year's city golf play and reached the finals for the first time. I had to play Leigh Masterson for the Natchez City Golf Championship. I knew he probably would beat me, but I hoped to make him play his best to do so. He was a former member of Rice University's golf team and spotted me two holes per 18 every time we played a $5 Nassau. He usually pocketed my money even with the spot.

It was fun playing in front of a crowd of bystanders, even though it was a small one of 25 or 30. I hit some good shots, but he hit better shots. I think he disposed of me on the 28th hole. I wasn't too sad as it was my first competition for a city golf championship and won me the runner-up award that was bigger than any other trophy I had won. It also looked good beside the two I had won earlier that year against my peer sportswriters.

I had gained the finals berth by defeating Powell Kaiser, Al Graning Jr., and Charles Mascagni in that order. Leigh

had triumphed over George Guido, Henry Eidt, and Paul Klotz, Sr.

Glenvall "Mr. Sports" Estes & "Steamboat"

As both Natchez newspapers had distribution in both states, I was a member of the Mississippi Big Eight Sportswriters Association and the one in Louisiana as well. All the sports editors and sportswriters in each state distributed newspaper were members.

The two associations would meet in early December and select the all-state prep football players. The Mississippi association usually met in Jackson and the Louisiana association in Monroe. We would select first and second teams, back & lineman of the year, plus honorable mentions, in the various classes of the public schools. Then, on pre-set dates, we would announce the selections. This would be of value to the college football coaches. They scouted as much as they could, but occasionally they would miss an outstanding player at some small school. Then after reading our selections, statistics on the player, accolades, etc., they would investigate and sometimes offer a senior a football scholarship that they would not otherwise have received. Far in between did this happen, but once in awhile.

Then, in the summer, usually

July, these large colleges and universities would host a three-day meeting for us. We would have a business meeting to elect officers, etc., but Saturday was our annual golf tournament which also had a coach and celebrity division. The big banquet was held that night with prizes awarded that the hosting association members had gotten donated locally. Then a Sunday breakfast concluded the fun weekend.

I had been driving to the winter and summer meetings with Glenvall Estes, the longtime sports columnist titled "Just Talkin'" for *The Natchez Democrat*. He didn't play golf, but he was a tremendous aid to me during my years in Natchez with his vast knowledge of the local sports scene the past 15 years as a columnist. I always thought of him as "Mr. Natchez Sports." At the summer meetings his lovely wife, Laverne, and my wife Carolyn would accompany us. I had been drifting away from calling her Gertie as me were meeting so many new people. It was my pet nickname and I didn't want to share it with anyone.

I think it was the 1960 summer meeting in Vicksburg, Miss., when I tied for the sportswriter's division with Robert "Steamboat" Fulton. The tall southpaw, I'll estimate at 6'3" or 6'4", wrote for the Jackson *Clarion-Ledger* following a couple years in the Florida minors of Major League Baseball. He had a tremendous tee shot that left me 40 yards behind him, but it was a handicapped tournament so I must have had a higher mark than the popular Jackson writer.

Anyway, the tournament officials had us start on the 10th hole for our sudden death playoff. It was a 500-plus yard par 5 that had the club entrance road running along its left side, which was out-of-bounds. I won the toss and hit first, a 250-yarder down the middle. He uncorked a tremendous clout, but it sliced. For left-handers, that was trouble and it landed OVER the out-of-bounds road. Sustaining the one-stroke penalty, he hit third drive about 290 yards in the fairway. I three-wooded within a wedge of the green, but this anal sphincter not only hit his fourth shot on the green but 12 feet from the hole.

I wedged my third shot to 14 feet north of the hole on the huge green that sloped down toward Steamboat's ball. I missed my putt, but tapped in for my par. With a ball OB, he still could par the hole and send us to another hole if he made his putt. I mentally sent every devious jinx I could think of to make him miss that putt... *and it worked.* He rimmed the cup for a bogey giving me the championship.

He, and his wife Gussie, had a wonderful personalities. Carolyn and I would have many good times with them over the years. I would learn later at a school reunion that one of my Whitehaven '51 class members[23] had given him that moniker as Robert possessed the same given name as the first designer and creator of the first commercially successful river steamboat.

Thom McAn Award Hassle With Guin

The Thom McAn Shoe Co. came out with a novel idea of bronzing one of the football shoes of a player participating sports editors selected. Basically, it was for a team leader whose performance on and off the field was exemplary. I decided to make the selection and planned to make the announcement and presentation details in our upcoming Sunday edition.

Guin and I had been discussing my selection for a few days and he agreed with me. We knew Quarterback Perry Lee Dunn, a starter since he was a freshman, was going to get a multitude of national awards. However, Dunn was considered along with 15 other seniors from Natchez, Washington, and Cathedral High Schools.

Will Warren, guard & defensive signal caller on the NHS team, fit all the criteria the award. The team's defensive unit was called the "Blue Barricade" as it held their 10 opponents to only 26 points

during a 9-0-1 season. He was the 191-pound right guard opening the hole for Dunn's many crunching QB sneaks and made all the kickoffs with outstanding distances. He also lettered in baseball and basketball and was president of the senior class. His popularity was shown when the students elected him "Mr. Natchez High."

Another important factor was his scholastic record. He possessed a straight "A" record in subjects of Mechanical Drawing, Solid Geometry, English, and Physics. Warren was selected Representative to the Boys State.

I had the story all written earlier that Friday night since *The Times* did not publish on Saturday afternoons. We were drinking beer and chatting about it when he dropped the bomb:

"Ole Will aught to be tickled pink when he reads about it in *The Democrat* in the morning," actually smiling as he said it.

I could not believe, as close as we had been the past year as drinking buddies and the things I had taught him about photography, that he would announce the recipient of a *Times* award before we did it.

"You're kidding, right?" I asked, I'm sure with a rapidly flushing face.

"Heck no, we're competitors and I never promised you I wouldn't use it," he said with sincerity.

It only took me a few seconds to retaliate. I had also given it

---

23 See Jerry Alsup in Chapter Five.

to Fred Kimball, the Rebels' outstanding 6'4" tackle that would make All-Big Eight and sign a scholarship agreement with Ole Miss. He had missed some games earlier in his career due to injury, but was a super senior lineman.

"If you break our award story in the morning, I'll give the award to Kimball. I'll make you and *The Democrat* laughing idiots of the year," I said with steaming emphasis.

"You wouldn't."

"I damn sure would, you dirty bastard," I confirmed in my unusual language.

He thought briefly, then relented, "I'll kill it."

I drove him to his paper and insisted he bring the metal lines of type and its headline before I would believe him. He did so and I scrutinized his sports page that morning. It was without any exposure of our Thom McAn Award.

Most Acclaimed Prep Star In United States

The recognition, acclamations, and awards came soaring in from everywhere for Perry Lee. Before I get into them, it would be appropriate to give my description of this prepster. I only saw him his last two years, half the 40 he started, and he was fantastic.

For example in practice, he would run through the running drills such as rapid foot-chops through two rows of tires laid side-by-side slightly ajar as if he were a college running

back. He would slam into the tackle dummy as viciously as any of the Rebel's toughest lineman. He not only threw passes accurately but with power resembling Johnny Unitas of the era.

He played deep safetyman on defense and, when he once while hit the opposing receivers off balance trying to catch a pass, they always had one eye on him while looking for future passes. He jarred the 150-160 pounders with such smashing tackles with his 205-pound, 6'2' frame that they never forgot.

In Furman Bishop's 87 column-inch *Sport Magazine* article titled "The Courtship Of A High School Football Hero" he quoted Jack Davis, NHS head football coach, as saying: "…There is no streak of prima donna in him (Dunn). He plays the defense as hard as he plays offense, a 48-minute man in tough games. In fact, he's often scared me with the way he throws everything he's got into a tackle."

Furman also wrote: "A Vicksburg end hobbled back into huddle last fall in a game against Natchez with a word of warning for his quarterback. 'Don't throw that ball to me again,' the end said. 'If you do I won't catch it. That Dunn's killing me.'"

He was very difficult to tackle with his powerful legs which also made him a state contender in high hurdle tracks events. All total his senior year, he massed 2,609

yards running and passing. He scored 20 touchdowns rushing, unheard of for a high school quarterback, and passed for 14 others. Natchez had such a powerful running attack, he only threw 98 passes and completed 59% of them.

He was unanimous choice for an All-Big Eight berth and as Mississippi Back of the Year. He also was leading choice of the All-Southern prep selections and as a Prep All-American choice. Even *Time* had an article on his achievements and public interest. He was easily the most publicized high school football player in the nation.

He competed as a guard in basketball and third baseman in baseball, but football was the sport that captured the attention of the nation's top college coaches. He was swamped with invitations from New Hampshire to Texas, according to Furham's article. All the Southeastern Conference (SEC) schools wanted him, with the most local influence coming from Mayor Doug Watkins (Ole Miss '48), Dr. Jack Phillips (LSU '46), and a respected insurance man Bill Priester (Miss. State '36).

Ole Miss would give football scholarships to Kimball and center Bobby Dossett while Tulane signed Warren. It gave the NHS team a total of five players inking college pacts including Dunn and Morgan.

Dietzel Severs Duo "Dunn-To-Morgan"

December 7, 1959, five minutes after midnight, Dunn signed with Ole Miss in a Jackson Hotel while his favorite target, end Mike Morgan, signed with LSU Head Coach Paul Dietzel at Dr. Phillips' home in Natchez. My pal Kyzar, who I had talked into writing a weekly SEC column for the *Times*, and I were there. It was a fun night for the two of us as we had chatted with the great man who was in his prime as a head football coach.

Dietzel (LSU l955-62) posted an 11-0 record with his '58 Tigers with the last win a 7-0 victory over Clemson in the Sugar Bowl. Halfback Billy Cannon threw a nine-yard TD pass to win the game. The year gave the team the hypothetical National Title and Dietzel National Coach of the Year honors.

We talked mostly about the l959 SEC contest between Ole Miss at LSU's home stadium in Baton Rouge, La. He had read my column picking the Rebels to win by a score of 3-0 although both teams had an All-Americans in its backfield: Ole Miss quarterback Jack Gibbs and LSU halfback Cannon. He hadn't laughed at my score as virtually all my competitive peer columnists had done. Both teams had been clobbering opponents by 25-40 points a game; therefore, my fellow columnists on

other papers were predicting 38-24, 34-28, 21-20, etc. The victors were usually picked depending for the team within the newspaper's distribution area (i.e. Mississippi writers picked Ole Miss and Louisiana counterparts LSU).

I knew they both had superior defensive teams, so I chose a field goal by the Rebels as the only score. My predictions were so accurate, several times during the second half while ahead 3-0, Ole Miss punted on third down. They did this in case there was a penalty, fumble, etc., then they would have to chances to get off a good punt. This kept the ball deep in the LSU territory almost the entire second half.

Then it happened. Cannon, behind some excellent blocking, returned a Reb punt 89-yards giving the hosts a 7-3 victory. It was one of 46 Dietzel would etch in LSU history books while losing only 21 and tying three. He would leave in three years to coach at West Point for Army and at South Carolina, came back in 1972 as athletic director. However, Vaught and that Ole Miss unit would get one more shot at Paul's brilliant team on neutral turf.

Revenge Was Sweet As Sugar But Scary

John Vaught was one of the most successful football coaches in college history. He was elected to the Coaches

National Football Hall of Fame with a 190-6l-12 wins-losses-ties career record in over 24 years atop University of Mississippi's gridiron staff. He won SEC championships in '54, '55, '60, '62 & '63. A LCDR in the U.S. Navy before his coaching began in l947, he was a wise man in many ways.

Vaught had out-serenaded Dietzel for Dunn, with both flying him for weekend tours of their campuses, as John had done with Gibbs to take the QB helm l958-60. Believe it or not Gibbs, also a College Football Hall of Framer, preferred baseball in which he was also All-SEC and played nine years (1962-71) for the New York Yankees as a catcher. After his professional baseball career, he came back to Ole Miss and coached baseball for 19 years.

Jake (given name was Jerry) was 29-3-l during his three years as quarterback as he spearheaded the Rebs to a 11-0 SEC & share of the National Championship his senior year. The first win that year (1960) was his 21-0 revenge victory over LSU in the Sugar Bowl.

My buddy Kyzar, a NHS grad, had attended Ole Miss in l954 and knew a lot more than I did about the history of the SEC and its teams. To have watched the Tigers victory over such his powerful alma mater was a demoralizing experience for my friend/neighbor/golfing partner. It had been such a great game, the Sugar Bowl officials chose them as opponents for its New

Year's Day in New Orleans. Naturally, Charlie and I drove down for the highly publicized fracas between these two great rivals.

Charlie was deliriously happy with the game. We had sipping suds all the way driving to the game, but drank Old Charter and cola during the game. We were in the upper deck of the Sugar Bowl which was packed. He was loaded by the time the game ended and I was afraid we weren't going to get out of the stadium alive. All the way through the game, he would yell cheers for Ole Miss which was expected of him. However, he chose to use the southern Mississippi natives favorite nickname for Cajuns[24] which was "Coon Asses."

For example, after a long Gibbs pass, a good run, or a touchdown, he would yell, "How do you like that you Coon Asses?" These comments were sobering me somewhat.

Cannon's usual brilliance was stifled by the revenge hungry Rebs as they permitted him only eight yards rushing the whole game. In fact, if my memory's correct, the Tigers never got within Mississippi's 38-yard-line.

Every time they would drop him for a loss, Kyzar would jump up, turn to the huge crowd behind us and bellow, "All-American? That 'Coon Ass' is not a cannon. He's Rebel chewing tobacco now."

---

24 Natives of Louisiana who are descended from the French colonists exiled from Acadia, Canada, in the 18th century.

Or, "That 'Coon Ass' Cannon is too pooped to pop."

He barely could walk down the ramps. He had to hang on me, but kept his "Coon Ass" yells going despite my pleading to "cool it." I was so relieved when I dumped him in the back seat and he went to sleep before we got out of the parking lot. I had fun but I must admit I was glad to get out of there alive. Those Cajuns are good natured people, but one can go too far. Apparently, most of the fans around us were also Ole Miss fans.

Study Time Out To Get The Hard Hat

Later in 1960, I decided to resign from the busy moonlight job as a sports editor to study for the Chief Yeoman's test. I had presented Washington High's James Boyette the next Thom McAn Award and raised several thousand dollars promoting a Mary Lynch Fund to send a 21-year-old black athlete from Sibley, Miss., to the Deaf Olympics in Finland before I quit. I enjoyed doing those things.

We had had to participate in several military burials that year. When a deceased military man's remains were shipped to his family for burial and they desired a military burial, we would get together with the Mississippi National Guard to provide the firing squad, folding the colors, and presenting it to the next of kin with an appropriate verbal military condolence.

Lusk and I had formed a photography company called "Shutterbug Fotos." I did all the dark room work in the room located in the rear of the carport of our new house. It was at 131 Lee St. only a few blocks away, across the highway leading to Ferriday, La. It was a three bedroom made out of white bricks.

I had talked *Times* officials into letting me use (Photo by Shutterbug Fotos) under any photos my shipmate Al and I took. This and a small ad in the telephone book was the only advertising we did. Most of our business was Little and Pony League team photos, high school team photos, and some weddings I took. Debra and especially Bobby were a big help in rinsing the prints and cleaning up afterwards. I would give them money for their assistance.

Bobby was making money running his daily requirements. I would give him 50 cents every time he would beat his record in the mile or in one of the two 100-yard dashes I had him run each day, except Sundays. I was getting real proud doling out those half dollar pieces until he ran a mile in 5:10. I was bragging about it to Coach Chase and he suggested I get my watch fixed or watch him run the entire distance.

"That's way to fast for an eight-year-old," he said.

He was right. The new route he was running was down a new dead end street that had a curve in it precluding me from seeing him all the way to the end and all the way back. We both ran the old mile route along Murray Drive and even I couldn't make it under six minutes and I beat him about 50 yards. That was one of the few times I had to spank him in his life, but — as I always did — it was a good one. Debra and David saw it and Carolyn used the threat of telling me to spank them if they didn't mind her.

Basically, they were good younguns, or so we thought then. After maturing, they told us of some disobedience in our absence. I don't think I ever told my parents any of mine, which were plentiful.

My cramming for advance to pay grade E-7 was successful. I made the grade and was well initiated by the new Officer in Charge, LTJG Fred Grimes, and some of the reserve chiefs. Grimes, a very likeable OINC, started the day of initiation by calling me into his office when I arrived for work in my new hard hat, and dress khakis with the required tie.

"You look sharp, chief. But I thought you told me once that you joined the Navy because you hated to wear ties and sailors wore neckerchiefs with their open jumper," he asked appearing serious.

"Well, I didn't know at the time that I would stay in long enough to make chief petty officer," I said.

"Tish, tish," he said. "Here, we'll take care of that tie."

Then he picked up scissors off his desk and cut my tie in two about halfway down. Then he ordered me to turn my shirt and cap around. Then, with a huge sign around my neck that read "I am a boot chief," everyone took me around to my favorite drinking spots and made me perform humiliating tasks for the proprietor or bar tenders. For example, Mc Kinney at the Duncan Park pro shop made me clean out all the toilet stalls.

My favorite stop was the main bar and restaurant in Vidalia. There Grimes went down the bar pouring a shot into a large glass of every bottle they had lined up on their shelf (I.e. whiskey, gin, vodka, rum, brandy, etc.). Fortunately, they put a few cubes of ice in it. Of course, they were drinking too, but their favorite drink or beer, not a "Zombie" like mind. Then, they made me eat out of a pig's trough they made for the occasion. It was a mixture of all the different dishes they served, plus catsup, mustard, salt, hot peppers, raw oysters, horse radish, etc. Believe it or not, it absorbed a lot of the alcohol enabling me to stay sober enough to make it home for the party Carolyn, Charlie, and Cossie were throwing for me that night. Kyzar's dad had passed away and his mother Daisy, moved to Natchez to be closer to her work at Ulman's, so the two-house fete was attended by mostly 20- and 30-year-olds.

By then I was drinking my normal Old Charter and cola as we danced and partied at both of our houses. I had so much adrenaline that I outlasted everyone. As usual, Charlie went to sleep in his easy chair, but it was after he shocked everyone when he lost his balance falling backwards onto his coffee table. It was so comical as he sat through the thin coffee table top and ended with his legs and arms hanging over the sides of it. The amazing thing about the 6'5" fall was that he had just mixed a full drink and didn't spill a drop of it.

Back To Night Toiling With Larger Rag

Guin left the *Democrat* to accept a position with the newspaper in Columbus, Miss. He would eventually end up with a super sports writing job with publisher in Palm Springs. We remained friends, but we never regained the close bond we had before his ALMOST big blunder. I don't know whether Editor James Lambert every found out about that episode, but I'm sure he would not have approved of Don's attempt to expose a competitor's award in a small town like Natchez.

The *Times* had hired a brilliant young experienced sportswriter named David Carpenter to replace me as their sports editor. So, Jimmy (as everyone called the friendly *Democrat* publisher, president, and editor) felt no qualms about hiring me to head his

By Democrat Photographer

PAGE ONE photo of me the *Natchez Democrat* editor ran announcing my employment with them as Sports Editor.

---

sports department. I was happy about it as that morning "rag" (as we called them) had a larger circulation than the afternoon *Times* and I would be working more closely with Glenvall Estes. Plus, the pay was better.

David would move on to another job, or got the axe, I never knew which. He didn't like the top honcho, Ed Brown. I guess they didn't get along too well. Anyway, Carpenter wrote his final column and brought a galley proof for me to read the night before it was to appear.

"I got even with ole Brownie," he said. "I wrote 'FUCK ED BROWN' in my column. Did you see it?"

"Hell no I didn't see it. It's not in there," I rebutted. "I read it thoroughly and you didn't write such a phrase."

"Check the first letter of the first word of every paragraph," he said raising one eyebrow and knotting the other with a devilish smile.

He had done it and, of course, I didn't tell anyone but Charlie, Cossie and Carolyn. As far as I know it was never known to the public. He wished me well with the *Democrat* before he left and the *Times* ceased publishing not too long afterwards.

Joining the Lambert family's publication also gave me an opportunity to keep up to date on the excellent crop of Natchez High players that would soon be sophomores and eligible to play at their respective colleges. I was particularly interested in how well he would do with Dunn as his quarterback.

While I was still a kid in Memphis watching Ole Miss games, Vaught had his first of many great passers in his initial head coaching season in 1947. Charlie Conerly was calling the signals on the field then with Barney Poole as his main receiver. As tailback in the last year of the Notre Dame system on the Ole Miss campus, Connery set a national record with 133 completions and 18 touchdown passes while Poole also broke the national mark with 52 catches, 44 from Conerly.

Vaught shocked the heck outa me when he played Dunn as a fullback his first two seasons with All-Americans Doug Elmore ('61) and Glynn Griffing ('62). I knew he was a strong runner and a vicious tackler, but I learned he was also an excellent blocker. Then Dunn took over as QB in '63 and led them to a 10-0 record and a second straight SEC Championship.

Other great Rebel signal-callers developed by Vaught were Farley Salmon, Rocky Byrd, Jimmy Lear, Eagle Day, Ray Brown, Bobby Franklin, Jim Weatherly, and finally the great Archie Manning, one of his four Heisman Trophy winners during his brilliant coaching career.

Morgan, who had three great seasons at LSU, and Dunn both played professional football in the NFL. Perry Lee (1964-69) with Dallas, Atlanta, & Baltimore and Mike (1964-70) with Philadelphia, Washington, & New Orleans.

An Unforgettable Experience In "Rolling The Drums"

I was steadily improving my golf game. When the 6ND decided to remove the active duty officer's billet at Natchez and give the OINC responsibilities as collateral duties to the commanding officer of the NRTC in Jackson, Miss., I was the senior enlisted man there until RMC Glen Josey replaced Lusk. LCDR Melvin Hemphill was a local reserve officer given the authority to sign correspondence "By direction" of our Jackson regular officer who came down about once a month. Hemphill trusted me thoroughly and after a few weeks of reading the mail and asking me how I suggested we answer it, he finally just told me to answer it and sign his name. I would always save the copy for him to read at the next Monday night reserve meeting before I filed it. He never disagreed with my answer. He trusted my judgement completely, which made me feel very confident.

We worked out a work schedule with the station keeper having the duty would have to be at the center all day and night. Sellers would always pickup the mail at our post office box and I would open and answer 95%. Supply and Communication mail was very slim. I would open the letter, if an answer was necessary, I simply typed the reply, sign Mr. Hemphill's name "By direction" immediately and staple the file copy as I mailed the original.

We would stop work at 11:30 a.m., shoot eight-ball pool for the drinks, prepare sandwich lunches, and play a card game of hearts with three losers contributing a dollar each for our lunch "pot." Then, if I didn't have the duty, I would go play golf. At first, it was always at Duncan. But, when the Natchez Country Club and Belwood CC offered me honorary memberships and free electric carts so I would write tidbits about their members, I played there to get in on the gambling.

Every day, 16 or so golfers would tee off at each site and most betting $25 Nasaus. At first, I couldn't afford that much of a bet as one could lose $75 if he lost both nines and the 18 overall in match play. One could press (start another bet) if he got two holes down, so the bet sometimes exceeded $100. I was playing so well, many of the competitors would take me for a partner and cover whatever part of it I couldn't afford. At first, I would just take $5 of it. Then, as my gambling winnings increased I took, $10 then $20, and eventually, all of it.

Each foursome usually played skins[25] at $1 a hole and sometimes "roll the drum[26]" in partner play. The latter can get very expensive. My first big taste was against Paul Byrne, an "A" player 0-3 handicapper like me, and his "D" player. My "D" player was Dlynn Braswell's father-in-law, Sidney Hughes. He was in the

_____

25 Lowest score on hole wins skin. One tie, all tie. Next hole is worth two skins, next three, etc., until a golfer wins hole alone.

26 Usually start with $1 a point. Maximum 5 points: 1-longest drive, 1-closest to pin in regulation, 1-birdie, 2-lowest team total. Any partnership losing the previous hole may "roll the drum" which doubles the point value on the remaining holes (e.g. first roll $2 a point, second $4, etc.).

oil business and had plenty of money, so he wanted to roll 'em after any hole we lost.

This would have been great if he had been carrying his end of the load as I was shooting two under par. But, Hughes kept chipping over the little hilly greens at NCC and getting double, triple, and quadruple bogeys. Paul was shooting his usual good game, but was one or two over par. So, with his 4 added to his partner's 5 on a par four hole, they would win two points for the team total and most of the time one point for Paul's longest drive. I would usually win closest to the pin and an occasional birdie. Their sample team score on the hole would be 9 while we were averaging 10s, 11s, etc. This netted them an average of 3 points per hole to our 1 or 2 resulting, with all the drum rolls, in a 17-hole debt of $672 for each of us.

"Let's press 'em, low score for double or nothing," my pathetic partner said on the 18th tee.

I stared at Sidney to see if he was kidding, but he wasn't.

I quickly analyzed the press. As we were not playing drums on the hole, the team scores would not matter. It would be as if Byrne and I were butting heads. I'm sure I started sweating like a pig, but I agreed. They had honors and hit good tee shots down the middle of the fairway of the easy 400-yard hole. My partner hit his out of bounds.

His next one went into the woods.

I couldn't take my normal swing at the ball, because if I sliced it I was out of bounds on the road adjacent to the fairway, or, hooked it I'd be unplayable in the thick woods on the left. Therefore, I shortened my backswing and guided the driver straight through the ball. It went straight down the middle, but not as far as usual.

I was about 150 yards from the small, round green that sloped steeply toward me. I was easy to hold the approach shot because of that.

A Strange Distance To A Familiar Green

I had never hit from there before, but I figured a strong 7-iron shot would put me pin high. I hadn't contemplated the adrenaline that I was possessing with the thoughts of losing the hole and $1,344. I only kept $700 in cash to cover a bad day on the course. Anything I won over that after my bar bill, I gave to Carolyn. I kept up with it one year. I won over $10,000 playing golf and over $3,200 playing gin rummy after the golf while our CPA figured up all the golf team bets. He would put everyone's name horizontally on his large pad and draw vertical lines between each name. Players would give him their scorecards with the bets made against any single or partners of the day. He

would put winnings above the individual's name and losings below. Then, after he had all bets recorded, he would put the net total won (+) or lost (-) in a circle in each individual's column. Naturally, he was supplied free drinks from us as he did this while we were all playing gin rummy.

All of this did not go through my head while I was hitting the 7-iron shot, but the thought that I better not lose the press or be embarrassed did enter my thinking. I hit the shot perfectly, or so I thought as I saw it sailing in direct line with the pin.

Alas! I had so much adrenaline, it completely cleared the green and rolled into the rough on the other side. To make it even worse, BOTH of our opponents hit their second shots on the green for 15- and 20-foot putts for a birdies. Fortunately, I had a decent lie about 20 feet from the back of the raised portion of the green which was taller than me. I couldn't even see the hole from my lie. So, with only 24 feet of down hill green to retain my chip, it was going to require an extremely delicate shot.

I knew the shot I had to execute, but to be able to execute it was another thing. I opened my pitching wedge to its extreme. Played it off my back foot and sliced under it with a rapid and follow-through motion. It popped out beautifully and rolled within four feet of the hole. It had a

sharp break from left to right, but it gave me a definite chance for a par.

Paul and his partner both barely missed their birdie putts for pars. They clinched the original bet. If I missed, my partner and I would lose $672 more.

Needless to write, I was nervous. I lined up the putt, although I knew exactly how it would break, and addressed the ball. I COULD PHYSICALLY SEE MY KNEES SHAKING THROUGH MY PANTS.

I did a "fake insect in the eye" routine and stepped back taking deep slow breaths as I rubbed my eye. Then, addressed the ball, imagined my line of stroke, and putted it. My complete concentration was to stroke straight through the ball and not raise up during the stroke as so many of us amateurs do. Consequently, pressure of knowing I could lose $672 more if it didn't got in made the time it took seem triple until I heard the "clunk" of the ball in the cup.

"Way to go, partner," my friendly D-man said from the fringe of the green. Then when we were in the bar having our post-game drinks while paying our debts, he added, "They got us today, but we'll get 'em next time."

With my gambling kitty almost completely emptied with this "A&D" vs. "A&D" stuff, I had already made a resolution:

"There won't be any next time for me. Those drums

don't beat to my rhythm," and I think he understood. I never matched up with him again. I liked Sid and he was a nice guy. He just didn't play enough golf to compete in this semi-pro racket we had going in Natchez at the time.

Trip To New Orleans With Our "Unitas"

I shot real serious the next few months and got my $700 "cushion," or "kitty" back in tow. One spring, all the sports-minded people, especially the NCC golfers, went to New Orleans to see the Baltimore Colts play some team in an exhibition NFL game. One of our guys had a connection at the Metairie Country Club in nearby Metairie, La. He got us all on that morning for 18 holes prior to the football game.

The course was the most prodigious and well-maintained course on which I had ever played. It was 6,600 yard of perfect condition. The fairways were so plush that one's tee shot was sitting up as if on a 2" tee. It was just waiting to be stroked to the soft, thick greens that were luscious for a stroke-putter as I. I always liked to feel the stroke of my putts, which was not possible on most of the professional fast-putt greens. They usually required a soft tap instead of a sturdy stoke.

Anyway, admiring the long first fairway lined with aged oaks trees down its starboard side, we began our game with the usual bets. My usual favorite partner, Kyzar, wasn't along on the trip, so most of my wages were individual bets. Braswell, probably a "B" or "C" player, and I were one of the few partner bets I made. He was young (25 or so) and hit a long ball with his excellent physique All of the bets were with an automatic, two-hole deficit, press. I could not believe how tempting the balls looked in the lush fairways in which I always landed that day, except the par threes on which I landed all my tee shots on the green. I bogeyed two holes and birdied one, so I carded a 73 to win over $300 for the day. It was enough to pay for our ritzy hotel room, meals, and booze for the weekend for Carolyn and me.

Unitas, the Colts quarterback, was his usual super self as they won the contest. Afterwards, we went into the packed hotel cocktail lounge for a nitecap with Dlynn, his wife Rosemary, and a few other Natchezians. We found stools at the bar for the ladies, but Braswell and I had to stand with our drinks. He was about five inches taller than I, had wide shoulder, and looked like an athlete. Plus, he had a flattop haircut jump like Unitas wore. I noticed people at the nearby tables staring at us and whispering to each other.

"Look Dlynn," I said softly to him. "Those people think you are Johnny Unitas."

"Really. You think so, huh?" he smiled and that brought the first autograph seeker.

"You really played a good game, Mr. Unitas," the fan said shaking Dylnn's hand. "Would you mind signing this menu for my wife over there?"

To my surprise, Braswell set down his drink and took the pen and menu.

"Be happy to do that for your lovely wife," he said smiling. He held his smirky one for us, who were feeling like accomplices to a wrongdoing in that we didn't tell the fan he was only kidding and not really Unitas. But, he obliterated my feelings of guilt when he said:

"You know Buck, that really made me feel good to know I made someone happy thinking they got to meet the famous football star. I just scribbled an undetectable signature, but they'll probably be talking about meeting Unitas to their friends the rest of their lives."

Several more came up as the word started spreading throughout the lounge, so we finished our drinks quickly and got out of there before someone questioned what we thought was a harmless impersonation.

The Moonlit Plane Flight Back Home

I covered many of the SEC football games when they were played in Jackson, Hattiesburg, Starkville, or Baton Rouge. I always used Glenvall's column and the syndicated column that came over the sports wire service written by internationally famous Jim

Murray, when space permitted. He was the best, but there will be more about him later.

I also used many of the photo and news releases provided by the Sports Information Directors (SIDs) at Ole Miss (Billy Gates), Mississippi State (Bob Hartley), Southern Mississippi (Ace Higgins), and LSU. I got to know them all and never will forget the advice given to me by Hartley.

Kyzar and I had hired a local pilot Charlie knew to fly us in a little Piper Cub to a game at Starkville, Miss., between host MSU and UM. At the game, we sat in the press box and made our notes. Hartley's statistian handed out halftime and final stats he had maintained during the game, but Hartley didn't do anything but make a few informative announcements. During the halftime break, I went over and told him how much I appreciated his player photographs, news releases, and weekly notes on his team. I asked him what would be the best way for me to become an SID after I retired from the Navy.

"I'll be honest with you, Buck. I don't think any college will hire an SID applicant without a college education. I enjoy reading your columns, as I'm sure all readers do. You use a lot of sports jargon, clichés, colloquialisms, and slang when a more concise word or phrase may be comprehended by more of your readership. I doubt that you had ever attended any college. Am I right?" he asked.

"I have not. I have taken a few college correspondence courses however, and I plan to take some at Southern Mississippi's Resident Branch opening soon in Natchez," I explained. The direction in my career fork in the road was definitely determined at that moment. I knew my goal. Get that education and became an SID.

I told Charlie about it on the flight back and we also chatted about the game with our pilot. Casually, he pointed to his gas gauge and said, "I better land in Vicksburg and get some gas. We're almost on empty."

Then he radioed to the little private airport there for landing instructions for refueling. Their answer shocked us: "Sorry, they're closed. There's nobody here with the keys to the fuel tanks and he has no phone at his home. The closest gas is at the Natchez airport."

"Dammit!" barked the pilot. "I don't know whether we have enough fuel to make it the 35 air miles to Natchez. Ya'll better keep your eyes on the ground for a smooth pasture in case I have to make an emergency landing. It's a good thing there's a full moon out."

He really looked worried as he eased back the throttle a little to save gas and lowered our altitude for a better view of the terrain.

Charlie, who had a ruddy complexion with all the golf he played, looked almost as white as a sheet. I probably

did also as I searched the land below for an emergency landing site. After three or four minutes of this agony, he started laughing as he pushed a switch overhead.

"Now that we had out little laugh, I guess I better change to the auxiliary tank," and increased the power back to the cruising speed.

We landed a few minutes later and I handed him the $150 we owed him as I smiled with clenched teeth, "That's for the thrilling ride and this is for your little prank," and punched him hard in the stomach. I turned and walked to our car without looking back. I knew Charlie felt the same way and would have intercepted the guy if he tried to catch me and retaliate.

Then we stopped by Hale's and had a few laughs over the scary flight with a couple of double shots and a few beers.

Navy, College, Radio, Newspaper, & Golf

Doing all my Navy work and putting out a couple of sports pages a night would have been enough for the average person, but I was always full of energy from kicking in the cradle to date. I still was able to work in a college course one night a week at USM's Resident Branch and on weekends I got a partime morning job as a disc jockey on KFNV in Ferriday, La., and later with WMIS in Natchez.

The latter was fun as I played

the latest popular music and talked with listeners on the air about any subject they desired. Most of the callers were girls, which was fine with me. I also taped the conversation before I aired them to "beep" anything raunchy or unsuitable for the public. I never mentioned my Navy or sports editor's job on the air as per the manager's suggestion. When someone called that recognized my name and wanted to talk sports, I would do so off the air as I was playing one of the 45RPM records we used in those days.

A few of them I can remember:

"You sound like an old fart, Buck."

"I'm old but farts are manufactured that day, you know."

"Wanna know the world's most popular indoor sport. Ask any dirty old man and he'll tell you."

One sweet young southern lass called about a salesman about to show her a new house: "Now here's a house without a flaw," he said. She slowly asked, "Really? What do ya'll walk on?"

Another related that she had just given his baby his bottle. "I couldn't help but notice he looked just like his father laying there on his back with a bottle in his hands."

One caller had just returned for a cemetery burial where he had been mourning beside an old man. He asked the old man his age. "When the old guy answered 92, I said its hardly worth your going home isn't it."

A Sunday caller in response to my mentioning how I despised the Monday morning blues: "Know how to get rid of them?" he asked. He answered himself, "Don't go to work until Tuesday."

One guy said he was desiring a cigarette while waiting with a woman at a bus stop, but possessed none. "Lady, do you smoke?" he hopefully asked. "I get hot but I don't smoke," she answered.

Blonde jokes were popular, such as: "What a blonde does with her ass hole before sex? She drops him off at the golf course."

Her host asked a blonde after seeing her first football game if she like it. "It was pretty stupid to me," she explained. "They flipped a quarter at the beginning and all they did afterward was yell, "Get the quarter back."

A male caller said he was feeling amorous the night before, so he hinted to his wife, "Let's do something different tonight." Without too much hesitation, she replied devilishly, "Okay. You do the dishes while I watch TV on the couch and fart all night."

I enjoyed the conservation with the listeners, and when there were no calls, I would study the college basic courses I was taking such as geology, modern algebra, and journalism. I only took one course a semester, so I was able to work it in to my busy schedule.

The latter class was full and the instructor was probably in his late 50s. He knew I was the sports editor of the local rag, seemed to enjoy having me read my homework to the class more than the others. He would ridicule some of my choice metaphors, etc., which the class seemed to enjoy. I thought he was just having fun with me until I went to a dinner party at the Windmill Restaurant & Lounge. Sitting next to him at the dinner table, he put his hand on my knee several times along with a little squeeze. He must have been gay and was putting the make on me. Needless to write, I left the party early and didn't appreciate his jokes about my selections of words and phrases in future classes.

I continued my Navy work and instructional duties on reserve meeting nights with Charlie Kyzar advancing from seaman to a third class yeoman's level and William Browning to second class. William's older brother, Lester, was a first class yeoman and headed the unit's administrative and personnel office.

William was a top supervisor at the local lumber company. Like Lester and Charlie, he was a tall slender lad. Turning the large heavy planks to examine and rate them at the mill gave him tremendous power with his huge hands. William's one major fault was that he couldn't swim.

I found that out one day when we went fishing in one of the bayous along the levis of the Mississippi River. I commented on what a nice jacket he was wearing when we loaded the small, wooden fishing boat.

"Yeah, it's brand new. You better be careful steering this boat 'cause I can't swim," he said entering the bow as I attached the small 3.5 horsepower outboard motor to the boat's stern.

I really thought the 35-year-old, powerful man was kidding until a 15 minutes later. We were motoring in the middle of bayou about 50 yards from either bank when the outboard sprung a leak in its gas line. It's spray ignited from the hot engine and was sending a flame of fire towards me and the boat.

I knew from my military fire fighting training that water wouldn't put out the fire, but I tried splashing it on the flame anyway. Then, I started trying to undo the two clamps holding the motor on the boat. It was so hot that it burned my hands, but I kept doing it as frequently as I could stand it with hopes to dunk the little motor in the water to extinguish the flames.

William was panicking. He probably feared the wooden boat catching afire and him drowning.

"Here," he yelled frantically as he jerked off his new jacket handing it to me. "Smother it, smother it!

I covered the motor and hugged it tight with my arms. It was doing the job for a few seconds, then the flames started coming up underneath the jacket.

I used the jacket on the clamps and finally loosened them enough to raise the hot motor off the stern section. However, I was unable to hold it as it hit the water, so it sunk with a little puff of smoke.

"God! Thank you, Buck," William said ecstatically. He paddled us ashore with much enthusiasm.

He related the event with much humor when he and his pretty wife, Myrna, attended our Halloween Party we had later. Always a jokester, he came to the costume affair dressed as a bum with a foot long, thick rope, knotted at its end, hanging like a penis out the zipper of the fly of his pants.

BGWW&P Times

| *1957-64* | *Vol. 1, No. 11* | *Natchez, MS* |

'64 Two States Champion
Lucky Twice In The Same Year

After beating Steamboat for the l960 Mississippi Big Eight Writers Association Golf Championship, I continued to improve in golf. I always had to compete heads up against Paul Byrne, E.L. Larry Tom Armstrong, Billy Hall, and the other low handicap regulars who played in our "semi-pro" gambling group that teed daily at l p.m. on the Natchez Country Club links. Weeks, Buccantini, Charles Moroney and other city champions seldom competed in these high- stake games.

Byrne, Armstrong, and Larry hit long balls, but Larry (we called him by his last name) had trouble hitting and the fairway. We always were happy to see him play as he was well-heeled and liked to gamble. Hall and I were usually shorter on the long holes, but seldom hit into the deep roughs. Armstrong, a bass-talking plantation owner who always captured the ladies' glances whenever he swaggered into a room, had an ideal swing in my opinion. When he was on his game, he was unbeatable

such as 1963 when he beat Larry for NCC title.

Byrne was the toughest competitor of the bunch. He was a good-natured, colorful opponent who loved nicknames and one-liners. I would have more trouble beating him and his partner than the others, but I probably had the slight edge over him in the history of our competition. When I had Charlie as a partner, very few couples ever beat us twice.

Paul was the one that started the "Mutt and Jeff" stuff when Charlie and I arrived together. He sometimes referred to Kyar as the "human 1-iron." When I arrived alone, he would say, "Here comes Augustus." He called me that because he felt I'd win even if I went to Augusta, Ga., and competed in the Masters. Or, maybe he nicknamed me for Augustus Caesar, the ancient Roman Emperor.

He once told me privately as we had a post-game cocktail, "I figured you out, Augustus. You're a damn hustler. You shoot just one shot under what ever your opposition shoots,

or you win just one more hole than your opposition won. Whatever it takes to win, that's all you shoot. You keep 'em coming back."

This took place after I had just birdied the last hole in our match for a 72 to beat him 1-up on our bet and win a bunch of partnership bets. Thinking back to the last competition before that, he had shot a 75 and I came in with a 74.

That is the way a hustler shoots to keep guys playing him and to keep them from asking for strokes (medal play) or a hole(s) (match play), but I never did that. I was never that confident that I could win the next hole so I always went for the next shot with gusto. I never intentionally missed a putt in my life, but at first I thought he really believed I did. Then, on occasion, he would salute, "Oh-oh, the hustler's here. Get your bets ready." The guys would laugh with him, so I guess he was only kidding with that stuff.

The money I won kept us living high on the hog as I only kept about $700 in my wallet to cover a day of losses, which were few. One day in the early l960s, I took a putter instead of the $20 one friend lost to me. He had a lousy day with it and he despised it. It was a Bullseye Putter that I always wanted, but couldn't find in Natchez. I never regretted that as I became an even better puttsman. I shot under par frequently with it.

Belwood CC Hosts '64 Summer Meetings

Estes, Kyzar, Larry Dickinson and I were members of the Big Eight Conference Writers Association; therefore, we had no trouble getting the l964 summer meetings hosted in in Natchez. Naturally, we had to get the local merchants to contribute prizes for the members. Carl Walters, Wayne Thompson, Steamboat and other Jackson *Clarion-Ledger* and *Daily News* sportswriters brought nice gifts also and the affair was well attended.

Ray Poole and Dave "Boo" Ferriss were the two most famous that played in the Celebrities Division. Both are members of the Mississippi Sports Hall of Fame.

Ray, Barney's older brother, was one of five Pooles that had notable careers at Ole Miss and played six years afterwards for the New York Giants in the NFL. He returned as an assistant to coach Vaught, who coached Ray in his senior year ('47).

Dave was the son of a cotton farmer at Shaw, Miss. A strong

Buck Peden Top Winner In Writers Golf Tournament

By LARRY DICKINSON

Buck Peden of Natchez, Ace Higgins of Louisiana State University and Coach Fred Morris of Natchez-Adams High School were the top winners in the annual golf tournament of the Big Eight Conference Writers Association played at Belwood Country Club yesterday.

Peden, a sportswriter for the Natchez Democrat, took the championship honors in the writers' division 18-hole handicap flight with a net score of 72. Peden also captured low gross score honors in the tourney with a hot 78 over the Belwood links.

Peden edged out Eddie Dean Dispatch for the championship honors by one stroke. Dean gained a net score of 73 with his 92 gross play.

Wayne Thompson of the Jackson Clarion-Ledger captured place in the flight with a net 75. Thompson was the tourney's defending champion, having won the title last year on a Jackson course.

Carl Walters and Claude Sutherland of the Clarion-Ledger tied for fourth place in the flight with net 76's.

Higgins, sports publicity director at Louisiana State University, won first place in the 9-hole "duffer's division" with a 59.

Second-place finisher in the division was Larry Dickinson of the Natchez Democrat with a 59 and third place was won by Floyd Johnson of the Yazoo City Herald with a 59.

Morris shot a net 74 in the 18-hole "celebrity division" to gain top honors in his flight.

Charlie Kyzar of Natchez carded a net 79 for second place in the division and Billy Gates and Ray Poole of Ole Miss tied for third with 76's.

Thirty-one sportswriters and guests vied for prizes donated by businessmen of Natchez and the surrounding area in the tourney, which kicked off the second day of activities in the Association's annual summer fun and fellowship weekend.

Prizes in the tourney were awarded at a luncheon sponsored by International Paper Company at Belwood Country Club following the tournament play.

The festivities continued Saturday night at Natchez Country Club with a fellowship hour followed by a steak supper, which was hosted by the City of Natchez and Adams County.

The sports scribes and their wives and guests will be hosts of the Natchez Democrat at a farewell breakfast to be held at 9 a.m. today at the Holiday Inn, which is serving as headquarters for the meeting.

7. Perry Nations, 79	
8. Billy Rainey, 84	
9. Wallace Dabbs, 85	
10. Glenvall Estes, 89	

CELEBRITY DIVISION
1. Fred Morris, 74
2. Charlie Kyzar, 75
3. Billy Gates, 76
3. Ray Poole, 76
5. Butch Kempinska, 77
6. John Correro, 77
7. Herman Moore, 79
8. Jack Berkshire, 79
9. Dick Smith, 80
10. B. O. Van Hook, 8
11. Dave "Boo" Ferriss 85
12. Paul Davis, 86

DUFFERS DIVISION
1. Ace Higgins, 53
2. Larry Dickinson, 58
3. Floyd Johnson, 59
4. Wayne Easterling, 60
5. Billy Ray, 70
6. Lewis Lord, 70
7. Ken Ernst, 74
8. James Saggus, 81
9. Bill Ross, 84
10. Bob Hartley, 85

NEW BIG EIGHT

Buck Peden of Natchez (second from right) i Writer Association golf champion after dow from left), Clarion-Ledger Sports Editor and football coach Fred Morris won in the celebrit (left) of the Natchez Democrat was host and the winner's trophy, while Thompson has the Perry Nations.

NEW BIG EIGHT CHAMPION

Buck Peden of Natchez (second from right) is the 1964 Big Eight Conference Writer Association golf champion after downing Wayne Thompson (second from left), Clarion-Ledger Sports Editor and defending titlist. New Natchez football coach Fred Morris won in the celebrities division, while Glenvall Estes (left) of the Natchez Democrat was host and master of ceremonies. Estes holds the winner's trophy, while Thompson has the perpetual trophy. — Photo by Perry Nations.

and extremely talented young man, he pitched for MSU before signing with the Boston Red Sox. As a minor leaguer in a Texas professional league, he pitched right-handed and played first base left-handed. He was such a good hitter he won the league batting crown that season with a .417 over future MLB Hall of Famer Enos Slaughter's .414.

"Boo" got his nickname when he was a babe larning to talk and mumbled "brother" that came out "boom" and the family thought it was so cute they started calling HIM "Boo" and it stuck.

He still had it when he became the rave of Boxton. "Ruggedly handsome," as one writer described the amazing right-hander that could throw any pitch he wanted precisely to the spot he aimd. Arriving in l945, he started his major league career with 22 consecutive scoreless innings and caught the attention of the American League by posting an impressive 20-10 rookie season record in the big leagues. This was with a 7th place team behind him.

Then, in his second year, he handcuffed the opposition so well that Boston won the American League pennant with his 25-6 mound performance. His .806 won-lost percentage was tops in the loop, but Hal Newhouser and Bob Feller had one more victory to cut Ferriss out of the running for the AL Cy Young Award. Then, next season, something popped in

his arm in a game and he never regained his masterful control of the plate nor his normal velocity. Sadly, they treated it with heat in those days while now it is with ice.

He only had a career record of 65-30 in the majors, but just a few years ago the "apple of Boston's eye" was named to the Red Sox Hall of Fame. Ferriss was well liked wherever he went and ended his career as a very successful pitching coach and athletic director at Delta State.

I would learn most of this about Boston's love for "Boo" in my later years, but in this tournament I was deadly serious in winning on my home turf. I had a 2 handicap at the time, so when I shot a 74 gross, my net was a winning 72. Eddie Dean of the Columbus *Dispatch* was runner-up with a 73 and 1963 defending champion Wayne Thompson a 75. Steamboat, who probably had celebrated too much the night before, was way back at an unusual 6th rung. Fred Morris, the new NHS football coach succeeding the departing Van Stewart, won the Celebrities Division with a 74.

The wives and non-golfing members were given a tour of the beautiful antebellum homes in the Natchez area, courtesy of the Natchez-Adams County Chamber of Commerce. Edna Carroll guided them through the Parsonage, D'Evereux, Connelly's Tavern, and Stanton Hall.

This event was held on July 11 and I reveled in my victory that night at the BCC banquet. Also, the next day when Dickinson, who manned the sports editor's desk that night, wrote about it.

Another State, Another Tournament

Then, my next big event would be only two weeks later in New Orleans at the Louisiana Sports Writers Association's annual summer meetings. It was my first one to attend so I drove down Friday with my buddy sportswriter from the Monroe *Morning World*, Stuart Hill, to give me some background on my new association. He had been our houseguest after covering prep football games in Ferriday or the nearby area. I had learned then he was quite a boozer, so I let him drive before we got there. We shared a room at the huge, fancy hosting hotel, unpacked, freshened up with a few highballs and then joined the other members at the cocktail party preceding the dinner.

While I was there, I learned Bill Carter, sport editor of the Alexandria *Town Talk*, was not only president of the organization, but was the player I would most likely have to beat to win the tournament tomorrow. He had shared championship last year with John Ferguson, sports director of WBRZ-TV in Baton Rouge, but Carter had won outright the previous five years.

I watched my intake of alcohol as I wanted to win very much, but I still got around to meeting all the sports editors to whom I had been sending Louisiana District 3-B's weekly news. I had been compiling results, standings and other new information about the circuit for several years. Most Louisiana NE area newspapers published it. Stuart, however, was not a golfer and had no connections with the other papers. He enjoyed the camaraderie, however, and tried to have one of the free drinks with each of them. He was feeling no pain when we left the party.

I undressed and hit the sack, but he slipped on his swimming trunks saying he was going to take a midnight dip in the pool.

"There's no lifeguard down there and the pool's closed," I said trying to talk him out of the idea.

"The pool lights r'on, an' I was a diver on my school's swimming team. I don't need any frigin' life guard," he reasoned with a thick tongue.

I also had had enough to not want to argue with him and went to sleep immediately. I was awakened later by knocking at the door. Going to the door, I noticed his bed hadn't been touched, so I presumed it was him with no key. I jerked open the door, ready to chew him out for awakening me, and was aghast to see him covered with blood from the top of his head down to his feet.

"I did a one-and-a-half off the low board and missed the pool," he groggily mumbled.

I examined the gash in the side of his head and it was barely bleeding at that stage. So, I got him in the shower as I kept a compress on his head, we dried him off, dressed him and took him to the nearest emergency room for treatment. Several stitches, a head bandage and medication, and we were back in our room asleep about 4 a.m.

I made the tee time, but I was feeling rotten. Fortunately, many of the players were hung over from the great cocktail party the night before. Therefore, it wasn't exactly a bright and bushy-tailed group that teed off at 8 a.m. the next morning on the tough, 7,130-yard layout at Timberlane Country Club. The celebrities division, composed mostly of Tulane and LSU coaches, were able to avoid the 17 ponds of water prevalent on 15 of the holes and the 80 sand bunkers scattered on the highly rated

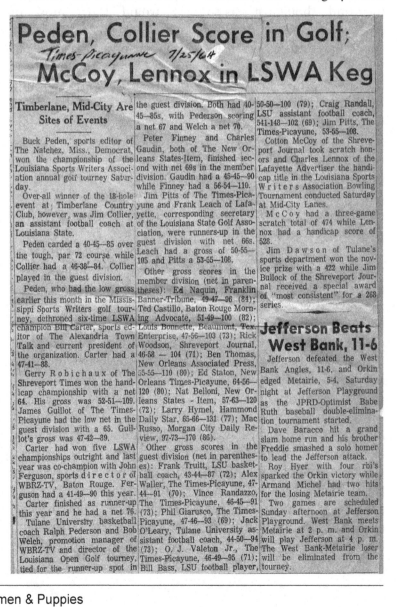

Peden, Collier Score in Golf;
Times-Picayune 7/25/64
McCoy, Lennox in LSWA Keg

Timberlane, Mid-City Are Sites of Events

Buck Peden, sports editor of The Natchez, Miss., Democrat, won the championship of the Louisiana Sports Writers Association annual golf tourney Saturday.

Over-all winner of the 18-hole event at Timberlane Country Club, however, was Jim Collier, an assistant football coach at Louisiana State.

Peden carded a 40-45—85 over the tough, par 72 course while Collier had a 46-38—84. Collier played in the guest division.

Peden, who had the low gross earlier this month in the Mississippi Sports Writers golf tourney, dethroned six-time LSWA champion Bill Carter, sports editor of The Alexandria Town Talk and current president of the organization. Carter had a 47-41—88.

Gerry Robichaux of The Shreveport Times won the handicap championship with a net 64. His gross was 52-51—109. James Guillot of The Times-Picayune had the low net in the guest division with a 65. Guillot's gross was 47-42—89.

Carter had won five LSWA championships outright and last year was co-champion with John Ferguson, sports director of WBRZ-TV, Baton Rouge. Ferguson had a 41-49—90 this year.

Carter finished as runner-up this year and he had a net 76.

Tulane University basketball coach Ralph Pederson and Bob Welch, promotion manager of WBRZ-TV and director of the Louisiana Open Golf tourney, tied for the runner-up spot in the guest division. Both had 40-45—85s, with Pederson scoring a net 67 and Welch a net 70.

Peter Finney and Charles Gaudin, both of The New Orleans States-Item, finished second with net 69s in the member division. Gaudin had a 45-45—90 while Finney had a 56-54—110.

Jim Pitts of The Times-Picayune and Frank Leach of Lafayette, corresponding secretary of the Louisiana State Golf Association, were runners-up in the guest division with net 66s. Leach had a gross of 50-55—105 and Pitts a 53-55—108.

Other gross scores in the member division (net in parentheses): Ed Naquin, Franklin Banner-Tribune, 49-47—96 (84); Ted Castillo, Baton Rouge Morning Advocate, 51-49—100 (82); Louis Bonnette, Beaumont, Tex. Enterprise, 47-56—103 (73); Rick Woodson, Shreveport Journal, 46-58 — 104 (71); Ben Thomas, New Orleans Associated Press, 55-55—110 (80); Ed Staton, New Orleans Times-Picayune, 64-56—120 (80); Nat Belloni, New Orleans States - Item, 57-63—120 (72); Larry Hymel, Hammond Daily Star, 65-66—131 (77); Mac Russo, Morgan City Daily Review, 97-73—170 (86).

Other gross scores in the guest division (net in parentheses): Frank Truitt, LSU basketball coach, 43-44—87 (72); Alex Waller, The Times-Picayune, 47-44—91 (70); Vince Randazzo, The Times-Picayune, 46-45—91 (73); Phil Giarusco, The Times-Picayune, 47-46—93 (69); Jack O'Leary, Tulane University assistant football coach, 44-50—94 (73); O. J. Valeton Jr., The Times-Picayune, 46-49—95 (71); Bill Bass, LSU football player, 50-50—100 (79); Craig Randall, LSU assistant football coach, 541-148—102 (69); Jim Pitts, The Times-Picayune, 53-55—108.

Cotton McCoy of the Shreveport Journal took scratch honors and Charles Lennox of the Lafayette Advertiser the handicap title in the Louisiana Sports Writers Association Bowling Tournament conducted Saturday at Mid-City Lanes.

McCoy had a three-game scratch total of 474 while Lennox had a handicap score of 528.

Jim Dawson of Tulane's sports department won the novice prize with a 422 while Jim Bullock of the Shreveport Journal received a special award of "most consistent" for a 268 series.

Jefferson Beats West Bank, 11-6

Jefferson defeated the West Bank Angles, 11-6, and Orkin edged Metairie, 5-4, Saturday night at Jefferson Playground as the JPRD-Optimist Babe Ruth baseball double-elimination tournament started.

Dave Baracco hit a grand slam home run and his brother Freddie smashed a solo homer to lead the Jefferson attack.

Roy Hyer with four rbi's sparked the Orkin victory while Armand Michel had two hits for the losing Metairie team.

Two games are scheduled Sunday afternoon at Jefferson Playground. West Bank meets Metairie at 2 p. m. and Orkin will play Jefferson at 4 p. m. The West Bank-Metairie loser will be eliminated from the tourney.

par 72 course. However, as most sportswriters are sports-loving, but frustrated athletes, they were unable to do so.

Never playing the course before, I was extremely happy to post a 40 on the first nine. I stumbled into a few ponds on the back side, but still managed a humble gross 85. However, of the entire entourage, only Jim Collier, an assistant football coach at Louisiana State, posted a lower gross on the tough links with an 84.

My triumph for the LSWA crown gave me the first, according to old timers in both organizations, two-state championship between the two closely rivaled states. I was very proud when I saw my picture holding the LSWA trophy and seeing my name in headlines in the famous New Orleans *Times-Picayunne*.

Carter's 47-41-88 for runner-up in the membership division with Ralph Pederson, Tulane's basketball coach, and Bob Welch, promotion manager of WBRZ-TV & director of the Louisiana Open Gold Tournament, the second place finishers in the celeb division.

Stuart was feeling better by the time the awards banquet was held that night so he helped me celebrate my victory. In fact, as usual he celebrated more than me even though he didn't play. However, I insured he didn't have any intentions of swimming in the pool when we retired for bed. It was a good thing I had planned to drive us home.

Naturally, our best friends and next door neighbors, Charlie & Cossie Kyzar, had a welcome home party for me that Sunday night. Others I remember attending were Ray & Ruby Sellers, Dan & Lilly Chase, "Crutch" & Nadine Chruchfield, and J.C. & Yvonne Roberson.

Rosy Life For Pedens

Things were going great for our family in those days. I was burning my busy life at both ends, but we were making a good living and enjoying it. Bobby and I went fishing often during the spring and summer weekend mornings followed by Debra and David during the last few years of my tour in Natchez. I taught them all to swim early as we frequently took picnic fishing and swimming trips to the many recreational lakes in the Miss-Lou area.

Carolyn could swim 15 or 20 yards before getting tired, but she could float on her back for hours. Even with this experience in the water, one time I pushed her off the rowboat we were in and she panicked. She sunk flapping her arms uncontrollably instead of swimming. I had to dive in and pull her up to the surface and to the boat. I asked her why she didn't swim or float and she just didn't know why she panicked. I never did that again and I started watching her, like I did the kids, any time she was in water over her head.

We usually went with Charlie and Cossie, born Mary Elizabeth Smith in Mc Call Creek. I couldn't wait until they had children so I could pull tricks on them as Charlie did us. When David was still in his play pen at these outings, he showed the youngster a loose rail and how to raise it up slightly and take it out of its holes. Then, he pulled him through the opening that had been created. David responded immediately and took it out himself when it, and him, were returned to the pen. We were in the water when he taught the little rascal. When we returned to the camp site, Charlie had him out playing with him. Then he put David back in the pen while saying he was headed for the rest rooms. But, he ducked behind a tree to peek through the bushes as David did his thing with the rail. We were shocked to see the kid so deftly remove it, turn sideways, and waddle out.

As we ran to get David, Charlie started laughing loudly with his deep bass voice and came back to enjoy our startled expressions. He loved doing things like that to get "our goats."

Charlie and I had many fun times together. One was day after a very successful day playing golf and gin rummy afterwards at Belwood Country Club. We had both won several hundred dollars and another $50 or so playing cards. Charlie, a bookkeeper at the huge International Paper (IP) Company eventually for 30 years, was an excellent card player. This particular day an ex-Ole Miss student with Kyzar in 1954 was in town on IP business. He was feeling no pains when we finished as he drank while cheering Charlie to victory in his golf and cards. He was horny as hell and wanted "a quick pop or two."

We stopped downtown Natchez at the Sportsman, which was a bar & grill only a block away from the *Democrat*. They drank and chatted with "Spot" the bartender and local bookie while I went in and put my Tuesday morning, one-page, sports edition to bed. All I had to do was write headlines on wire copy, dummy them onto my page, and I was finished. I had gotten so efficient at selecting the correct font to clash with other headlines in the article's next column that it had become a snap judgment for me.

They were still going strong when I returned, but we left immediately. Charlie was taking him to a place he knew near the levy south of Vidalia. His friend, I'll call him Josh as I can't remember it for sure, was still wanting his "pop or two." I followed Charlie in my '61 Oldsmobile Cutlass as I hadn't ever been there and knew home would be my next stop.

The place was well into the uninhabited wooded area by the levy. It had no neon sign and looked like a large house

except for its gravel parking lot out front. The front room had a small bar, a juke box, and several tables. We sat at the latter and drank beer while Josh looked over the barmaid and the several female waitresses. They were all prostitutes.

He finally chose one and settled on a $50 for an hour of sex in the back bedrooms. Charlie and I drank beer, played the juke box, and chatted with the gals while we waited. Josh came out an hour later rubbing his eyes and mumbling.

"She gave me a great blow job on the bed and we both fell asleep the rest of the time. Then the bouncer came in and told us the time was up. I was mad at her, but what could I do?" he explained. We understood completely as he was well under the influence. Charlie drove him to his motel room and I went home.

F-F-Frank & I Tour Town Bars

With the complimentary NCC membership, Bobby started playing golf and Debra loved the swimming pool. She even placed at the top in the 7-through-9-year-olds events in one of the swimming and diving contests. Carolyn would bring them out and eat lunch by the pool. Food and beverages were the only charges we had so they would just eat, drink, and be merry by initialing the check.

They would usually ride home with Cossie or some other neighbor Carolyn had brought as a guest. I would usually play gin rummy after my golf for an hour or so. One day during the period I was studying for chief, I had a break between games and went to the bar to get a refill.

"Give me another Old Charter and coke," I told the bartender as I sat down beside Frank Byrne. He was a treat to be around as he enjoyed telling and hearing jokes. He would bet on anything, although he was a little overweight and toted a pretty hefty handicap. He always tried to make his golf bets more one-sided in his favor by getting a spot of a couple holes from most opponents.

"B-B-Buck, you're w-w-wasting your money on that expensive call whiskey," he stuttered to me. "You c-c-can't tell the difference between t-t-that and the b-b-brand in the well."

"Sure I can, Frank," I said and I could. At that period in my life, although I was smoking a pack of cigarettes a day, I had very acute olfactory nerves. One's tongue only tastes four flavors (sweet, sour, salt, & bitter). The olfactory system determines the odor to send the brain an identification of the flavor in one's mouth.

"I-I-I'll bet you $20 t-t-to $10 you can't p-p-pick Old Charter o-o-out of four drinks," he offered, which didn't surprise me nor the bartender. The guy just loved to gamble, and, most of the time, he would win.

The bartender, expecting a good tip I'm sure, mixed four small glasses of cola with different whiskies in the other three while I left the room. The deal was, one HAD to have Old Charter and the others NOT.

I sipped them and selected the correct drink as OC. He did it again and again, even tried subbing water and Seven-Up, to no avail. I won every time until he had lost $100.

"C-C-Come on Buck. W-w-we're going d-d-down town. W-w-we're gonna m-m-make some money," he said all excited.

I went along with him and we went from bar to bar with him betting bartender's 2-1 that I could pick OC. Not one bartender refused the bet. He won several hundred dollars and I got drunker than "Cooter Brown" free.

Guido Prediction By Kyzar Excellent One

Frank and Paul were only two of the many Byrnes that lived in the area. The other two that I remember that played golf were Scott and Bill. All the Byrnes were well liked by the local population. Another family that had a golfer that I gambled with was the Guidoes. George was a likeable guy until he got on the greens. Then, you had to watch him like a hawk.

When someone else was putting, he would stand near the hole. If the person putted within the leather, we gave the next putt automatically so George would tap it back to the individual. One game I remember there were five carryovers (i.e. one tie on the hole & everyone ties with the bet carried over until someone wins a hole outright) in our skin game. My putt for a birdie to win the hole rolled up to a stop teetering on the lip.

Quickly, Guido taps the "gimme" back to me with congratulations on getting a par and tying another hole. The ball could have fallen in by the time I walked up to examine it, but he didn't give it a chance. I never forgave him for that one.

Marking his ball in someone's line of putt was his most masterful deception of cheating (he thought). We all knew he did it, but I guess we felt sorry for him. He first appeared to be lining his putter blade and his ball with a tree in the background and then moving his ball to the heel of putt face. This would always be several inches closer to the hole, which is alright if one returns his ball back at the same angle. Then he would spot his ball with a coin, usually an inch under the ball towards the hole.

After the person behind him had putted, he would reverse this procedure. However, he would place his ball on the green an inch or so in front of the coin. Then, using his mythical alignment tree, he would angle his putter face a few more inches closer to the hole, and move his ball to its SUPPOSEDLY original spot. In all, he would gain 6-8 inches nearer the hole. Bad boys will be bad boys, I guess.

Kyzar once said after a game with Guido, "George will probably have to hire pallbearers for his funeral."

Mighty Joe Fortunato

We liked playing with Joe Fortunato. He was just the opposite of our friend George. Everything was by the book. He was an outstanding 6'1", 225-pound lineman at Mississippi State who was drafted by the Chicago Bears in the 7th round of 1952. As a professional (1955-66), he made the All-NFL Defensive Team as an outside linebacker five times.

I always wrote a feature story on him each year when he left for Chicago. We became friends and I always got pleasure out-driving him on the links. He had such massive gridiron muscles they not only restricted his back swing but his follow through as well.

I used him as a reference years later in my post graduate resumes.

Commissioner, Ump, Coach And Player

I formed a Naval Reserve team in the city fast-pitch softball league and we played night games on the Duncan Park field. Sellers played the outfield, Kyzar caught and played first base, and I played third. We only had a fair team as we were playing against teams that had superior athletes such as Premo Stallone and the three Bradley Brothers: Jim, Milton, and Lamar.

Stallone is the only batter in the league that made me line up on defense behind third base. He was an extremely powerful slugger who pulled every pitch he hit. It only took a few one hoppers slammed off my chest to learn to position myself back on the edge of the outfield grass when he came to bat. He was such a big guy and swung so hard that it took him almost two seconds to recover from his swing and get out of the batter's box. I always had plenty of time to throw him out at first base.

The Bradleys were all good hitters, but not as powerful as Premo. They were also assests afield; Jim at shortstop, Lamar at third, and Milton at second. All were fast with the lighter, smaller Milton probably having a slight edge. A right-handed batter, I always had to play him in close as he bunted frequently and outran it for a hit.

I was eventually made commissioner and hired interested parties to help me umpire. They were usually players also and we never umpired the night our team was playing.

I also started a touch football league consisting of seven-player teams sponsored by local businesses. We played on Sunday afternoons at the NHS Stadium several seasons and CHS field one season. The latter season Milton and I played on the same team along with Billy Yvelverton for a couple games.

Yvelverton played at Jackson (Miss.) HS and Ole Miss. He was drafted in the NFL's 18th ground in 1956, but only played in 10 games (due to injuries) as a defensive end for Denver. His one highlight was intercepting a pass and returning it 20 yards for a touchdown. He was very, very fast.

The teams could have a center, two interior linemen (only players ineligible for passes), two ends, and two backfield men. I received the snap from center as the tailback in a short punt formation with Milton flanked on either side. Most of my passes were to him or Sammy Eidt, but my longest was a TD aerial to the racing Yelverton that covered 50 yards in the air. It was my longest EVER and I have no idea from where it came. Lefty Andrew Eidt and Jim Bradley were the strong arms in the loop that year. Lamar Bradley was another good passer as well as a rusher, receiver, and PAT kicker.

We named the loop the Honor Touch Football League as we decided in its organization meeting that we would have just one official who would keep up with first down mark which was the second 10-yard marker from the orginal line of scrimmage. In other words, a team would have at least 11 yards — and at most 19 yards — for a first down. The ball carrier would feel when he was touched by an opponent and would stop running and the official marked the new line of scrimmage. If the defender touched only the runners loose clothing, shoe, etc., and the ball carrier didn't feel it, then the official would take the word of the defender and mark it at that spot.

We emphatically made it clear to all the team coaches that if an official clearly saw that the defender lied and not have touched the runner then the defender would be not only ejected from the game but expelled from the league. And, believe it or not, in all the years we played there was not one disputed touch. It was truly a touch football league of honor sportsmanship.

And serious injuries were zilch as one could not leave one's feet in making a block and hands were used only to ward off an opposing blocker. This was unbelievable when players like Jerry Brewer and Ray Sellers collided. Brewer was a stout, hard charging defensive lineman. On our Naval Reserve Blue Barons team, I used Ray as a halfback about five yards to the side I was going to scramble before passing. I had plays inked on 2"x2" cards which I would pull out of my pocket and hold the play selected up over my head as I kneeled on one knee in front of them in our huddle. At the snap of the ball, I would stay in my position briefly to draw the rugged rushers, such as Brewer and Sammy Eidt, towards me. Then, I would cut to my planned route as Sellers slammed his shoulder block into the first rusher. This would always give me plenty of time for our receivers to run their scheduled routes.

No one wore pads, but when Brewer and Sellers clashed into one another, it sure sounded like they were needed. I don't know where Jerry played in school, but Ray had told me he was an all-conference guard in his Florida home town. No body ever doubted it. So, he was an important clog on our team as a blocker and defensive lineman. We would occasionally pass to him, but he was not adept at catching passes.

Most of my passes were to center Milton Bradley, ends Charles Mingee and Robert Ogden. Robert was so quick and fast that he was almost always in the open. He was a young seaman in the reserve unit and made us proud by leading the small four-team league in scoring and the two of them made me top scoring passer in the one season we beat Holsom Bread, Rex Sporting Goods, and Sports Center. Unfortunately, Milton's season was cut short to attend college.

My Final Ring Appearance In 1960

On top of all this, Sonny Finn — a first class signalman in the reserve unit — in l960 wanted me to help him publicize the Natchez Golden Gloves Boxing Club he was trying to get started in the city. I made the mistake of telling him about my first ring encounter in boot camp and a couple of others I had won at NAS Miramar. He begged me to join his group and fight in an event he had scheduled later in the month. A relentless Irishman, he stayed after me until I finally consented and started out under his supervision.

I frequented a small bar called George's Corner that was owned by George Vallas. He was a professional heavyweight contender in his younger days, so I got a few tips from him while working sipping a few suds at his place. George recommended that I box in a crouch and counter punch instead of leading.

I stopped smoking and trained for a few weeks hitting a sea bag I stuffed with sawdust and hung in the machine shop of the NRTC. Naturally, I was still not in a top fighting condition by the time of our matches against the Jonesville (La.) golden glovers at the Natchez Auditorium. However, I did get down to 145 pounds to make my high school welterweight wrestling division over 10 years ago.

I had written several articles about the formation of the club which had John Callon as general manager, Finn as head trainer assisted by Charlie Goddard and Don Marvin. Even Yvelerton stopped by to inspire the first aspirants and was in one of several photographs I took promoting the event. He was the l952 Mid-South Heavyweight Champion representing Mississippi. But, despite all the publicity and the meager prices ($1.50 for ringside seats, $1 for others, and $.50 for children), there was only a few hundred people that attended the non-profit making event.

By Sonny Finn
MY PRE-FIGHT PHOTO

———————

Jonesville was favored as they had previous fights under

their belts while almost all of us were first timers. Mickey Finn, Sonny's 12-year-old kid, won the opening 70-80-pound match, but Don Wiley and Gale White won the next two for Jonesville. Natchez Ralph Spring won the lightweight division with a technical knockout in the second round with teammate Ed Bolyer and Jonesville's Robert Beach battling to a draw in the fifth match.

So, the team tallies were 2-2-1 when I walked down the aisle to face the 19-year-old Jerry Wilbanks. I heard one customer say to another, "Here's the match I have been waiting for."

I didn't know whether he disliked my columns and wanted to see me get my butt beat or liked them and was pulling for me. I heard no boos when I was introduced; therefore, I assumed the latter.

We were halfway through the three-minute first round and I floored him. He had missed with a soaring hay-maker with his right hand and I countered quickly with a hook coming back from a dodge leaning to my right. It caught him square on his jaw, but he got up and we slugged wildly the rest of the round.

I had taken a few good ones, but kept my feet. So I plopped down on the stool, winded but in good spirits. I was ready for the second round and determined to box instead of that damn slugging exhibition we had put on the first round. He had other thoughts, I guess, as he came after me with that wild overhand right. I just started waiting for it and hooked him with a counter punch as he tried to recover from the big swing. I knocked him down four times in all, but he kept getting up on the count of eight.

When the round ended, blood was streaming down from my nose and I was exhausted.

"Now you got him," Finn said doctoring my nose.

"He's about got me," I in his towel, indicating "no contest" giving me a TKO.

The *Democrat* writer covering the event wrote: "Buck Peden…was the winner over Jerry Wilbanks…in one of the fastest and best fights on last night's card."

But the *Times* writer Wayne Knabb wasn't as complimentary: "Blood flowed for one Natchez man in the sixth event. Buck Peden, although winning his fight, suffered a bloody nose, a scratch over the left cheek, and a scratched back."

Leroy Spring out decisioned Jonesville's Wade Purvis to

By Democrat photographer

FOURTH KNOCKDOWN – I floored Jonesville's Jerry Wilbanks four times in the second room, but he got back up each time. His coach threw in the towel later.

muttered. "Why doesn't he stay down?" I don't remember when I have been so tired.

Then when the bell sounded to start the final round, I saw something that thrilled me tremendously. His coach threw clinch it for Natchez as their light-heavyweight Hulan Walker and Jonesville's J.C. Goetzman fought so aggressively they fell through the ring injuring Walker. However, the fans got a treat in the finale as two Natchezians, Joe Hardy and Boone Richard, fought an exhibition contest. Hardy had him so outclassed, they had to stop the fight in the first round.

Hardy Outstanding Novice In State

It was the first look that the city had seen of the super light-heavyweights, but would not be the last. He and Ralph Spring would make it all the way to the finals of the Mississippi State Golden Gloves Tournament. Ralph would get decisioned by Buddy Miles of Hattiesburg in a close match, but Hardy edged Greenville's Joe Couccoli in the most exciting bout of the Jackson hosted event.

Naturally, I retired from my Golden Gloves career so I was able to attend the tournament as a writer. About 2,000 fans watched the event in February of 1961. I was sports editor of *The Natchez Times* at that time and wired back my story: "The crowd applauded vigorously at the end of the Joe Hardy Joe Couccoli title bout. Not only for Hardy's blinding speed of delivery, but for Couccoli's ability to withstand the beating of the Natchezian's hooks to the head and mid-section. Although the stout 170-pound Couccoli… outweighed Hardy by eight pounds, he failed to find this weight to his advantage. He registered several stiff jabs through the open-style

defense of Hardy, but with little success. Hardy stayed on the offense throughout the fight, compiling a high total of points, but toward the end of the third round he tired considerably and ceased his weaving and bobbing to become an easy target…This was the only round in which the loser scored any points."

The tourney officials satisfied the large crowd by picking Hardy to receive their "Outstanding Novice Trophy." I followed him to Memphis and covered him in the Mid-South GGBT. It brought back memories of the times dad and I went to the Memphis Auditorium to watch professional wrestling. Lou Thez was the world's champion in those days and his wrestling was not rigged nor a farce. At least, I couldn't tell if it was.

My buddy Steamboat Fulton was there at the ringside representing his Jackson newspaper so I had fun telling him about Fort Pickering and my youthful escapades there in Memphis.

Hardy made it to the semi-finals before he lost a questionable split decision to William Duke, a Memphian. Finn had told him he should hold his guard higher. But Joe had not lost a fight in five contests, therefore he kept on holding his mitts about waist high so he could bop opponents with his vicious

hooks coming from down below. In my article I wrote:

"Duke, a local 270-pounder, had his victory call booed heartily by the Memphis fans….Hardy stalked the Memphis opponent all around the ring, but Duke backed well out of reach of the soaring kangaroo hook of his stocky opponent. This was the first back-tracking counter puncher Hardy has met in his young career with the Golden Gloves.

"He was the aggressor in the slow moving fight but according to the judges decision the taller Memphian collected the majority of points with his short quick jabs which had little steam. Neither fighter suffered any shaking blows although Hardy jarred the head of Duke with several hard hooks."

Trixie And "These Boots Are Made…"

I stopped by George's Corner the next night and had to describe Hardy's loss blow by blow to George and Donnie Beard, my favorite of his bar maids. Both had seen Joe and I fight in Natchez before I "hung up my gloves." George and Donnie made the Corner a fun place to go and shoot the bowling machine.

George even sponsored a bowling team in the Merchant's League at Rebel Lanes. I had plenty of experience bowling while Carolyn and I were dating back in the '40s. It came back to me fast. I used a short hook that had a lot of spin producing frequent 1-3 pin strikes. Once, I got seven in a row before missing , but only managed a 278 out of the game for a 622 set. My average was a 174, which led our four-man team made up of Malcolm Mitchell, Chuck Bass, Barton Swinny, Bill Sybille (movie actor Aldo Ray look alike), and I (shortest on the team). I think we finished third for the season, but we had lots of fun with plenty of beer.

On one occasion, I had finished my sports pages for the night, I made the mistake of stopping at a cocktail lounge. It was located a half block from the By-Pass U.S. Highways 65, 84, & 98 on what was then Homochitto Street. It was convenient for me as all I had to do was hop on the By-Pass and within a mile I was over the Natchez-Vidalia Bridge and home in another mile.

The mistake was I met a few golfing buddies and started drinking mixed drinks with them. I had only planned to have a few as I had already drank several beers. But, there was a waitress named Trixie, if I remember correctly. She was a pretty thing about 25 years old with long, wavy blond hair. As it was late, there were only one other table being used and only one drunk at the bar. She must have had a good tip night as she kept playing the juke

box with her own money. She would get one of the guys at the other table to dance with her when I first got there.

Nancy Sinatra had just came out with her recording of "These Boots Are Made For Walking." It had started playing on the box when Trixie asked, as she rocked side to side, the guys at our table if they wanted to dance. One said he didn't dance, another that he couldn't jitterbug, and the third one pointed to me and said, "Get Buck up. He's a good dancer."

That was my downfall as she took my hand and started pulling me up out of my chair towards the empty dance floor.

"I'm Trixie," she said with a captivating smile above her low cut blouse that barely covered her boobs. "I just luvvvv this song."

Her slur told me she had been drinking with her customers, which was common practice for waitresses in Natchez drinking establishments. However, it was not enough booze to affect her dancing. She was outstanding and followed me immediately. When I spun her under my arm and in a twirl, her short skirt would almost spin upwards enough to see her panties, which made the by-standers smile with glee. They even applauded us when we finished dancing.

That was all it took. She would dance with the other

guys in the lounge, but when a fast one came on, she would come to get me. We all started giving her quarters for the juke box and, invariably, she would include her Sinatra favorite in the set. I enjoy dancing very much, so I didn't mind. However, I was staying very thirsty. The Old Charter was going down like water.

Finally, everyone left but me and the bartender. I moved up to the bar and had a finale drink with him. I bought him one and he returned the favor. It was 3 a.m. and, as I started leaving, he asked if I was sober enough to drive. They didn't distribute Coors Beer that far east in those days.

"Sure I am," I said seriously. I had drank a lot, but all the dancing I did, I only felt tired. I honestly thought, as I guess all drunks do, that I was sober enough to drive. It was only a half of a block to the stop sign, then a right turn, and then practically a straight shot over the bridge and then home.

After warming the motor a minute, I backed out onto the street, which at that time of the night had no traffic whatsoever. But, I fell asleep heading for the by-pass and smacked head-on into the stop sign. I couldn't have been going fast, but when I looked up after the jar, the stop sign was bent towards me only inches from my windshield. It dented the hood a little with the bumper taking most of the damage.

My motor was still running and there was nobody in sight at the intersection, which was Lower Woodville Road on the other side of the by-pass. Without thinking about it twice, I backed up, pulled around the bent stop sign and drove home. I don't remember getting there, but Carolyn told me later it was about 4 a.m. She had to wake me for Navy work in three hours.

She couldn't get me awake after calling and shaking me several times. She was mad as a hornet, anyway, so she dampened a wash cloth with cold water and put it in the freezer. Five minutes or so later, she threw the icy rag on my face. Believe me, that will wake one. I sat up quickly, and as I sleep in the nude, the cold rag fell on my knees. I jumped up and was finally awake, but furious as I started for her. She started screaming and ran into the bathroom, locking the door after her.

I was so mad, I would have slapped the shit out of her had I caught her. It was the first time I had a desire to hit the one I loved most in the world since I threw the crust of bread at her for loudly reprimanding me as I was trying to teach Bobby to eat with a fork instead of his hands in the Quonset hut at NAS Miramar. These were the only two instances for me, but I know she swallowed desires to hit me many times during our lengthy marriage.

Naturally, I cooled off after I dressed and ate breakfast. I apologized before I left for work, so it was hunky-dory after that, especially when I gave her the $50 I won the next night playing shuffleboard at Hale's.

Charlie and I teamed as partner's in the fine, long-table shuffleboard Hale's possessed. We were tough to beat as we shot with both hands down the rail or freehanded if needed. Charlie, who virtually everyone agreed was the best male dancer in the city, and I both lagged well displaying a soft touch. Over 90% of the time, I could lag the hammer (last puck of a turn) for a three or, the higher singular scoring puck, a hanger (partially over the end of the board surface).

Everyone always wagered a beer or drink and sometimes for $5. I think I was probably recognized, along with a hair dresser that came in every night about 9 p.m., as the best two shooters among the regulars. Charlie was not quite as accurate and also wasn't able to play as much after Cossie gave birth to her daughter, Kay Ellen. As soon as Kay got old enough to walk, I taught her to go over and hit her dad on his leg. Charlie would always sit in his easy chair with his legs propped on a foot stool and usually was asleep within an hour of seating. The little bop would always startle him awake with the rest of us laughing at him. He never did learn why his sweet little daughter started doing it.

The reason I rated myself so high on the board was that Mrs. Hale, or one of her bartenders, would call me at the NRTC when a shuffleboard hustler came to town. I would take the afternoon off and wander into Hale's and challenge the board as one must do to compete against the winner. As is almost always the case, the board had certain breaks in it which I knew very well. The hustler would eventually learn that I not only as good as he was, but I knew the breaks too well for him to compete equally. After dropping a mallard ($100) or so, they would usually quit. Naturally, I shared about 10% of my winnings with the lady bartender that had called me. I lost very infrequently and never large amounts that I sometimes suffered on the golf course or playing poker.

Final Dance For Trixie And Me

I like to play poker as much as Charlie and he was good. We both were mathematically minded, and he had an edge as he was a bookkeeper at International Paper Company (eventually over 30 years). A bar and dance spot between Vidalia and Ferriday was owned by a scar-faced guy that had a poker table just inside the entrance. We would go play there often.

One night there was no poker as they had a three-piece band. Charlie and I got a booth to watch the customers dance. The band was good so it was crowded on the dance floor. As it happened, we had sat down on the band's last song of that segment. True dance lovers will play the juke box to continue their dancy night and this group was not any different. There was a crowd around the juke box, but it was so dimly lit at that end of the room that I didn't recognize anyone.

Then the music came on and it was "These Boots Are Made For Walking." Sure enough, a girl came out of the bunch and headed straight at me.

It was Trixie!

"Charlie, this is Trixie," I said getting up to take her extended hand.

"Hi, Charlie. Com'on let's dance. Where have you been?" she rattled and pulled me off before Charlie could speak.

"I've been working late at night for a Natchez newspaper. You know, this will be the first time I've danced to this song since that night at your place," I said starting her off with a one-two tap of the back foot and then sending her on her way. She loved to twirl and shake her shoulders in another low-cut blouse. She was showing off her wares to the non-dancers in great fashion

when, suddenly, another female exhibitionist bumped into her with equal energy.

There was no break in her steps, but she gave the other girl a hard look. The bumper completely ignored Trixie, kept on dancing also, and even started singing along with Nancy Sinatra. I guided her away, but they bumped again moments later and Trixie stopped.

"You do that again and I'll blow your ass off," she yelled

By Frank Bryne

THE FUN FOURSOME
Cossie & I in the foreground cart with Carolyn & Charlie in the background one.

drawing a derringer-sized pistol out of her brassiere and pointing it at the bumper.

I was shocked, but I grabbed her hand with the gun and pointed it to the ceiling. Her yell had been loud enough that the scarfaced owner and his bouncer grabbed her from me, took the gun out of her

hand, and scuttled her off the dance floor. They took her in the back room and I never saw her again. Charlie was laughing his butt off.

"Do you know who that girl is?" he asked.

"All I know is she's a waitress I just met at that bar on Homochitto a few weeks ago," I answered, still slightly in shock with the happening.

"Somebody told me one time that she was the mistress of the president of the Mississippi

Klu Klux Klan," he informed me with wide eyes and raised eyebrows. "You shouldn't be messing with her if you want a full life."

Needless to write, I didn't go back to the Homochitto bar until I heard she was gone. My dancing after that included our block group gals and nearby friends such Cossie, Yvonne, Nadine, Lilly, Donnie, and Shirley. There were others at parties, such as a French guest of Shirley's, who was mucho fun for a while. I enjoyed dancing with all of them with Yvonne ranking a close second to Carolyn in smoothness. However, Cossie was the most fun to dance or be with at the outings we attended or parties we held.

Cossie was always my partner in golf outings and Carolyn Charlie's. Those two argued too much when they were partners. We enjoyed the Mixed Scotch Foursome[27] Tournaments at NCC. We would carry a cooler of ice on one of the mechanized golf carts with Old Charter and everyone's favorite chaser. We had a ball boy ahead of us to keep up with the location of our balls and hold the flag on the green. I was so loaded one tournament, when I leaned over my putt and looked at the hole I was swaying.

---

27 Male and female partners would both hit drives, choose the best; then both hit from that spot, choose the best; etc. until ball is sunk.

"Keep that hole still, boy," I joked at the young lad.

He had no idea what I was talking about, but he grabbed the pole with both hands and quickly responded, "Yes suh."

We all laughed and he got a large tip for being so good-natured.

BGWW&P Times

1958-66   *Vol. 1, No. 12*   *Natchez, MS & Vidalia, LA.*

Chase Puts Vidalia On Map
1961 Finale Gave Vikings 11-0 District 3-B Mark

When they made Coach Walter Stampley principal of Vidalia High, the little tiny school was located a block from the Mississippi River and a Tiger Woods' 9-iron from the Natchez-Vidalia Bridge. It was the first time I got that close to a football coach when they gave Dan Chase the head reins of the Viking unit with Mike Brabham his assistant in 1958. I had played freshmen quarterback and linebacker for the staff at Whitehaven High, but never got on a first name basis to the coaches at that big school. It had about 2,500 students, which was probably more people than the entire city of Vidalia at that time.

Everyone in the state at that time probably thought of Vidalia as a little suburb of Natchez or a last stop before leaving Louisiana and entering Mississippi. Other than that, it was not very well known in the South. In a couple of years Chase changed that as the population of the city expanded to almost 5,000. He had a large enough roster to have scrimmage practice whereas Stampley had problems getting enough students that wanted to play the rough game. It should be injected that Stampley became an outstanding principal and still is one of the most respected citizens of Vidalia.

Over half a decade covering the close area sports of the Natchez Rebels, Washington Pirates, Cathedral Green Wave, and Vikings I got to know some of the coaches real well. Don Alonzo and later Jim Eidt at Cathedral, also later Van Stewart who took over at NHS. But, Dan, because he was so close by, received most of my attention. Fred Foster, who later became his assistant (1962-63) and VHS's basketball coach, was a pleasure to cover as he was so colorful. Part of it was a little devil gene which much have existed in his body. His pretty tennis-star wife, Billie Ann, put up with his devilment for many years before she finally gave up.

Dan's wife, Lilly, was pretty too and always had a smile on her face. I learned after she had her daughters Marty and Lisa that they all had hearing problems. When Lilly wasn't sure what one said but could detect the pleasantry on one's face, she would smile. In my later years, I started missing some people's conversation and caught myself doing the same. Unfortunately, a stupid TV repairman mistook Lilly's for a "come-on" and made a grab for her. Lilly ran to our house down the street screaming to Carolyn and Cossie. The guy was arrested and it was settled in the courts.

Whatever the guy got for making the error, he was lucky. If Dan had been there, the guy would have been one of Chase's taxidermy samples. As a part time hobby, the deer-hunting enthusiast learned taxidermy and started mounting deer heads in a shop he built in his back yard.

On the football field, Chase was all professional. He charged up his kids with a rough, aggressive tone. When he said to do a certain block, tackle, or run pattern a certain way, it was with definite authority.

I particularly remember the kid that lived in the house between the Chases and the Kyzars, Eddie Wisner.

Eddie was a big lad, but was "mild mannered" as the famous Superman comic books described Clark Kent. Dan wanted to make Eddie more aggressive as his vicious right tackle, Jerry Richardson. He kept making Wisner pound the hand held pad until he understood. Then, he made him use it against a teammate. Eddie did not like throwing an elbow into his teammate, but Chase was breathing down his neck with commands to "hit him, hit him, harder, harder, etc." I couldn't believe it several years later when he graduated that LSU signed him to a full football scholarship and had made the Tigers starting team. Whata coach!

Richardson was an All-Louisiana tackle and one of the reasons the Vikings went undefeated in ten games. His rugged play was recalled when I first saw Dick Butkus, the all-time great NFL linebacker for Chicago. I was told after we moved from the area, Richardson played four years with Ole Miss and was captain of his teams. Sadly, I also learned that later working for a Texas cattle company, he was killed in a train crash.

End Maurice Greer and guard Wayne Holloway were two other defensive standouts, along with injured players Cliff Feduccia and Wally Wallace. George Franklin (Yvonne's younger brother) and Jesse Wilson were Vidalia's halfbacks and did most of the ball carrying in their wing-T offense with QB Jimmy Stringer doing the passing.

Soft-speaking Roy Peace, probably the most-winning high school coach in Louisiana history, used the old Notre Dame box during his 40-year career at Sicily Island. His Tigers this season were led by tailback Albert Krause and fullback Jerry Hinton on offense. Defensive standouts were guard Carey Fairbanks, tackle Ken Byrd, and center Joe Peace. They held five teams scoreless while pasting their 10-0 record. La Salle's points (27-14 loss) were the most scored by one team in their other five victories.

Neutral Site Ferriday Hosts Championship

Ferriday was chosen as a neutral site for a Wednesday night playoff game between these two powerhouses. Its high school stadium was large (5,000 seating capacity, I think) and was only 19 miles southeast of SIHS and nine miles northwest of VHS.

I'm sure Chase had good feelings about the location as his Vikings had beaten the Ferriday Bulldogs, a much larger school and higher ranked football district, 13-7 during the season. With Clyde Thompson (1960-61) as his new assistant, it was the first time Vidalia had ever beaten Ferriday in a football game.

Also, only two other schools (St. Francisville 7-13 and Newellton 7-27) had managed to score the powerful VHS defensive unit. Whitewashing St. Joseph (27-0), Block (41-0), Wisner (7-0), Crowville (65-0), Waterproof (13-0), Woodville (73-0), and Natchez Cathedral (27-0), the Vikings scored a total of 306 points while permitting only 21. For you stat nuts, that an average of 30.6 to 2.l.

Unfortunately, a tremendous storm blew into Ferriday Wednesday and it poured down rain onto the field all day requiring the game to be postponed until Thursday night. The field was still soaked but they played as the winner had to compete in the first round of the state playoffs at Plain Dealing Saturday night.

Most expected the Islanders to win their fourth District 3-B Championship under Peace while the Vikings had never come close in their budding existence. Plus, it had a coach who had only three years experience as head coach until that season.

In their first experience facing the Notre Dame box, the proud Vidalia unit won handily, 32-6, surprising many area football fans. However, it was a tougher game than the score indicated. Plus a tremendous blow to the team morale, Richardson was injured and would not be able to perform at his awesome capability in the Louisiana State Class B Championship

Game, if at all. All of Vidalia's injuries, and the fact they only had one day to prepare, resulted in a disheartening 13-7 lost to Plain Dealing in the last few minutes of the game.

Carolyn rode with me to the game and, after I dictated the results to my staff back in Natchez, we spent the night there in a motel. She had brought a midnight snack and I brought a fifth of Old Charter so we partied, just the two of us, until wee hours in the morning. We had almost been married 11 years, but it was like a second honeymoon.

She was only 5'1" and 105 pounds when we got married. A decade later, she still was only 115 pounds after giving birth to three children. I was still trim with my softball, football, and golf activities. So, the two of us could still "cut the mustard," as they used to say, in the sex department. Neither of us wanted any more kids, so she always took care somehow to ensure that didn't happen (this was before *the pill*). If she hadn't, that night's activities certainly would have produced another. Maybe even twins, or triplets. It was a wonderful night.

My First Attempt As A Publicist

I went to several of the District 3-B coaches meetings and established an unofficial relationship as their publicist. I got all their phone numbers and addresses. Then, I established a contact with all the newspapers that had circulation within the district (primarily *Monroe Morning World, Alexandria Town Talk, & Shreveport Times*) to be a correspondent. They would call me after a game, or I would call them the next day, and publish a news release on the results, district standings, leading scorers, and upcoming games of the next week. I would mail it on Sunday and the newspapers would get it on Mondays or Tuesdays. This gave the papers plenty of time to publish it before the next Friday's games. The coaches appreciated their copies of the releases and the newspaper would pay me a nominal correspondent's fee. It wasn't much, but it paid for the paper, envelopes, and stamps with enough left over for some pocket change for a beer or two on the golf course.

Naturally, with all this bookwork on the district, I became knowledgeable of the District 3-B top offensive players. As I witnessed games, I became fairly knowledgeable of the best defensive players on each team. Sometimes, the team's best defensive lad was injured when I viewed the team in action. Therefore, I was definitely not an expert. I did see some game films in Chase's office as the area coaches would swap films of teams they had played with teams meeting that opponent the next week. In most cases, it was a reciprocal agreement between coaches.

Everything was going great in Vidalia football. A new school was built at the end of Murray Drive with a football and track stadium behind it. Franklin, Robert Forester, and Jimmy Hibbs — in that order — were the ball-carrying crowd pleasers and record setters on the Viking teams in the early 60s. In addition to Stringer, Butch Wiggins and his brother Billy, were the quarterbacks during that era.

Franklin was a shifty runner and smart. I remember in one game the opposition had punted a little short, so George let it roll dead a few feet in front of him as several defenders were there to down the ball. When they hesitated for a second as they ceased their approachment, Franklin suddenly scooped up the ball and returned it for a touchdown.

Hibbs was the smartest prep runner I ever saw. He not only followed his blockers perfectly, but he used them advantageously. At slightly reduced speed during a run, he would take a few steps towards one direction (behind his blocker) forcing the defender to step in the same direction. Then, with a sudden burst of speed, he would shoot forward at an angle in the other direction putting the defender in a vulnerable position for the blocker. He was so good at this, even a soccer coach would admire his moves.

Chase couldn't teach that, of course, as he was a guard during his playing days without any experience as a runner. Besides, it was an instinctive thing, not something teachable. But, he knew so much more about building an athlete's body than most high school coaches. Lifting and working with weights was the normal method of increasing a youngster's strength (and still is in most strength building programs). Dan used isometrics[28] to the "...enth" degree.

I wouldn't know the full significance of this until I was working on my master's degree in kinesiology in college. The weights add strength to one's body, but also creates bulk. Isometrics increases strength but does not add the bulk. It permit's the normal range of motion (NRM) as the weight work does not. The latter produces shapely muscles for some to admire at Mr. Universe contests, etc., and adds protection to one's bones, but it inhibits quickness and NRM.

Of course, all this stuff was kicked around by our block group after the Friday night football games. Charlie and I would drive to the plant and write our coverage of area home games while I took correspondents call-in reports on the out-of-town games as my film was developing of the

---

28 An exercise where muscles push against a fixed, immoveable object, to strengthen them.

game I staffed. Originally, I would walk the sidelines, take pictures, and keep statistics at the same time by myself. Later years, Gilbert Savoy and J.C. Roberson wanted to take the pictures for me, so I taught them. It eased my workload during the games, but I still had to do all of the developing and printing, plus scan the photo onto a plastic half-tone machine for the plate makers in the back shop.

I would write the call-in games as they reported. Wearing a headset ear phones and microphone, I would ask the caller the basic journalistic information for the beginning of a news report (i.e. who, what, when, & where). Then I would ask the touchdown, PAT information — as it occurred — composing and typing the article on my typewriter as I went. The headline for it always came easy to me.

Naturally, all this along with the film, half tones, headlines for the wire copy, cutlines for the photos, totaling stats for my game staffed, and dummying everything onto my usual two sports pages, was extremely hectic. I had cigarettes lit continuously those few hours. Most of them burned up in the ashtray, but it was always there for a quick drag whenever I got the chance.

Fun After The Event

Finally, I would flop into the habitual post game party at the Chases. Dan was always there in his recliner with a

huge tea glass of booze and some kind of chaser (I would learn latter, it was not too much chaser). Lilly was "the hostess with the mostest," as we all loved her dearly. Charlie, Cossie, Carolyn, and I were always there. Others — such as the Savoys, Robersons, Fosters, and Wiggins — were infrequent attendees. We always, especially the men, had fun talking about the game, or games, that were played that night.

Sometimes it was laughable stuff. For example, Dan had a partial upper denture. In one game, he got so excited and upset with something that happened on the field that his partial came flying out of his mouth onto the turf along the sidelines. The game was so exhilarating; he couldn't stop walking down the line to look for it.

However, after the team dressed and left following another exciting victory, he had the light turned back on and finally found them. I saw him searching from the press box, but I had no idea of the reason until later that night at the post game party.

Another time, he pulled off a touchdown with a touchdown play I didn't comprehend. The quarterback and the rest of both teams were flowing to the right when all of a sudden the right end scampered around to the left sidelines for a 35-yard touchdown to win the game.

Chase, it seems, had a sneaky play for just the right

time. It was so tricky that he discussed it with the officials before they started the game. Running from a wing-T with the flanker positioned outside the right end, the quarterback took the snap from the center and, hunched over to hide the ball, started running to the right side along with the only other two backs behind him. With all this starboard action, the opposing defensive team also flowed in that direction.

The quarterback, however, had indiscreetly laid the ball in between the back legs of the right guard. It was a free ball in that the guard didn't touch it with his hands and only protected it with his body. It was to be treated as the same as a fumble. With the QB brushing with the halfback enroute at full speed towards the right, the defense thought one of those two humped over runners had the ball. Meanwhile, the right end ran behind the blocking line, picked up the ball, and dashed for the TD and another VHS victory.

I never wrote about it in a later column for fear of it causing some red neck father on the losing team to come after my coach friend with vengeance. It looks like us southerners would have learned after losing the Civil War, but we still have not. We hate to lose.

Missed Meeting & My All District Team

Dan's teams never lost. In fact, in his six years (1958-63) as head coach he won 44 while losing only 13 and tying 5. He made one big mistake, however. He missed a post-season meeting of the District 3-B coaches at which they named the All District 3-B Teams. Whatever the reason, it must have been personal, so I never asked.

His fellow opponent coaches placed a few of his players on the first and second teams, but Chase was devastated. I decided to select a *Natchez Democrat* all-district team of my own. I was the sports editor and had reported on all of Vidalia's games; therefore, I felt I had the right to use my "freedom of the press." I did ask Dan's opinion in some instances to assist me, but I was satisfied with my choices.

All kinds of mail came pouring in to the "Letters to the Editors" refuting my choices and questioning my ability to judge talent. Lambert printed most of them (it gained readership in the Louisiana area) all week long. Charlie wrote one in retaliation that bonded our friendship even more. In summation, he wrote to the irate mother that I had written over 106,000 inches of column covering local sports and hers was the first negative letter the newspaper had ever received.

It finally blew over, but it definitely caused a ripple in the small community sports circles in the area.

Chase's Biggest Dream Fulfilled

Dan then went to Arkansas University and with his master's degree (MD) in Education Administration, the start of his doctorate. Then the Chases moved to Baton Rouge to enable their daughters Marty and Lisa to get special education for their hearing with Lisa attending a school for deaf boarding school. Marty was graduated at SE La. State (3.5 GPA) and obtained a MD at NW State and Lisa at LSU (3.7 GPA) followed by her MD at Mc Daniel College in Maryland. Both are now teachers.

"They fulfilled our biggest dream," Dan said recently.

While they were doing all of that, Dan was working for Exxon in the evenings while working on his taxidermy hobby which finally grew into a very lucrative business. In 1971, he discovered how to make manikins out of plastic polyurethane of deer heads in different positions and of other animals the public usually want to mount. Naturally, his biggest customers were small taxidermy shops all over the United States.

Lilly kept the books and was a vital clog in the Dan Chase Taxidermy and Supply Co. as it was growing into a multi-million dollar business near Baton Rouge. Dan was drinking alcohol more frequently and heavier. She got him into the hospital seven times before the physicians finally correctly diagnosed his problem. It was manic depression and bipolar disorder. Through all those trips, some I'm sure had a dramatic effect on their marriage as well as much mental pain on him, she was able to maintain their national business.

Now he is sustaining a cancerous brain tumor in a state of remission. His other problems are also inactive as he has not tasted an alcoholic drink in 26 years. *I have always felt that one could put a good man down but there is no way one could keep him down.* He is healthy otherwise and in good spirits.

I always expected him to return to coaching and become a winning college coach that someday make Vaught, Bear Bryant, and Frank Broyles move over a seat to make room for him in their high SEC coaching plateau.

Foster Was Also A Winner At Vidalia

Foster hadn't joined VHS coaching staff yet, but probably flipped a few cartwheels when he heard Dan's trick play. He was the backfield coach for Dan, but foremost was the basketball coach at Vidalia. He stayed on the officials' backs during his cage games.

Clarence Bowlin, manager of a sporting goods store (Sports Center) in Natchez, was one of the officials that had to take Fred's abuse. Clarence told Fred and me of a happening to a coach who had exceeded his authority during a game in a Baton Rouge City Basketball League:

"The referee called a technical foul on a coach for 'mouthing off' at him. Moments later, while the ball was still in play, the same coach walked out on the court and tapped the official on the shoulder. The shocked ref immediately stopped play, called two technical fouls on the arrogant coach for being out on the court during play, and added one for each step it took the coach to return to his seat. A total of ten free throws later, the coach was burning in his seat where he remained quietly the rest of the game."

Foster laughed along with me after hearing it, but he didn't change his fiery style of yelling at the refs. However, I never saw him go on the court during play after that little story.

He was a very successful coach, but some times would rave too highly on his team prospects for the upcoming season. One preseason interview (1965, I think), he was slobbering all over himself talking about a 5'10" guard he would have that year. Another one of Fred's white lies, I assumed. I was wrong.

Bill Holland was amazingly accurate with his one hand jump shots and very elusive with his driving lay-ups.

Against the Ferriday Bulldogs, he broke the VHS record with 48 points. The record of 38 had been shared by Fred Falkenheimer (1958) and Mike Pool (1961). Holland surpassed the 40 mark many times during his playing career for the Vikings. He kept the hometown gym packed with cheering fans at all home games.

Sir Bogey Shines Before Local Owners

My sister JoAnn and Kenneth brought their family down for a visit with us. They had been popping out the kids since their marriage starting with Connie Marie followed by Sharon Ann, Gary Eugene, and Stoy Kenneth Jr., who they called Kenny. Connie loved her pony and everyone loved Sharon, who would die in a tragic automobile accident before she reached the age of 21. In those young days, little Kenny was quite brat.

Gary was a good kid and only seven months older than David, so we kept him with us for a few weeks in Vidalia one summer. I took them fishing several times, which he enjoyed. He also really got a kick out of playing with Sir Bogey, who we usually kept attached to a wire laid on the ground. Bogey's lease permitted him to run the width of the entire back yard ending in his dog house. When he was playing with the kids and the Boles' twins, I would let Sir Bogie run loose.

Bobby still tells the tale of 1957 when he first saw the next door twins: "I was still in my semi-body cast. Dad had placed me on two dining room chairs in the driveway so I'd be out of the way (while we were moving furniture into the house). The neighborhood kids gathered around me in wonderment. I, on the other hand, laid there looking up in astonishment at two shirtless twin boys, Ronnie and Donnie. I had never seen twins before. I'm not sure which of us was more amazed. Of course, my cast came off and I was the fastest kid in the neighborhood and they stayed the same, so I guess I got the last laugh."

I wasn't able to hunt near as much as I had while stationed in Huntsville, but I would take Bobby on my rabbit hunting around the Louisiana bayous. Sir Bogey was running well now in his adult life.

One winter day I joined a group of guys in Adam County who hunted together with their beagles. It was quite a thrilling day for me. Sir Bogey, who had been a slow learner as Pottie's prodigy, made me proud.

Each one of the five of us had brought a dog. Some of them owned kennels, but only one animal each was allowed in the planned hunt.

The dogs hadn't been turned loose five minutes when one found a rabbit track. Barking distinctly, we knew it was fresh by the excitement in the delivery. A hunter named Big John pulled out a half pint of whiskey from his jacket, opened it, held it in the air smiling broadly with pride.

"That's my Bess," he boasted before taking a swig.

Another yapping joined Bess, which meant it had found the trail also.

"No doubt about it. That's my ole Biscuit. He's got it," chuckled the bald-headed owner, Jim, reaching for a celebration nip from Big John's bottle.

A third one found it and was immediately identified by its happy owner. He had his own bottle. I was very impressed with these guys recognizing the sound of their hounds. Then it happened.

"Aaaaaaah-RUUUUEEEE," came the deep-throated sound of a beagle with royalty. All the hunters halted in their tracks. It was silent for a moment as they waited to insure they had heard what they had heard.

"Aaaaaaah-RUUUUEEEE," sailed through the woods and over the dale once again.

"Who the hell is that?" asked Big John.

Proud as a peacock, as I reached for his bottle, I answered, "That gentlemen is Sir Bogey."

I have never seen guys so fascinated by the bugling sound of a dog. Their dogs were all beagles, born from and bred to, other beagles in the area. Same as Ribbon and Pottie had been in Alabama. But, none of their dogs were AKC (American Kennel Club) registered nor had a blood line such as Sir Bogey. Before the day was over, I was offered $150 in cash by one hunter and three of his best bitches by another. I wouldn't accept any of their offers.

Apparently, the word spread about my superbly voiced blanket-back beagle. Some lousy bastard stole him within a month.

Earl Bufkin Of Sligo Plantation

While I had gained an experience raising and training beagles, I was ignorant of another wonderful breed of canines in the outdoors sports world, the bird dogs. With the fifth running of the Natchez Field Trial Association scheduled at Springfield Plantation near Natchez, I needed to learn all about it. Naturally, when I found out the field marshal was going to be Earl Bufkin of Sligo Plantation nearby, I contacted him and requested an interview.

He had been training bird dogs over 30 years. He invited managing editor Larry Dickinson and I out to his immaculately maintained breeding grounds which currently had 56 bird dogs of many breeds and all ages. He also raised quail and chukars with over 8,000 in his hatchery. We got an excellent tour and one of his top workers took us bird hunting in a truck with several dogs and a cage full of game birds.

I learned how they stocked

bush with game. Before they let the dogs loose, our escort would carry a cage of birds to a bush, taking them out one at a time, then spinning them around with his hand before placing them in the bush. This would make the bird dizzy; therefore, it would not leave the bush until it was flushed in fear of its life..

Then the dogs, who had not seen the operation, were released to do their thing. Amazingly, they would obtain the scent of the bird, point in its direction and hold their frozen position until the command to flush was given.

One would think that Dickinson and I would have been very successful with all of this knowledge of when the game would surface from what site, but we weren't. We took 50 shots from his 20-gauge shotgun and my 12-gauge to bag 16 birds.

I knew that was bad, but Dickinson had the gall to ask Bufkin if we were the worst shooters he had ever seen. I figured we had been, but I didn't want to hear it.

"Ya'll were pretty lousy, but you weren't the worst," Bufkin said laughing. I actually felt relieved to hear that I was just "lousy" and not the "worst."

We had cocktails with his charming wife, Mae, serving us a delicious meal with some of the our game. They were tremendous hosts and I complimented them with a full column on the affair. Naturally, with the knowledge

of bird hunting I had learned from the interview with Earl, I wrote many pre-trial articles on the upcoming annual trials. It had a record of 86 entrants and was a very successful event.

I'm sure Earl was happy with my successor as sports editor of the *Democrat*. He was Al Strickland, a true outdoorsman. He did a tremendous job on providing our area with that type of reporting on sporting activities such as field trials and especially fishing which was so popular in the area.

His brother (Steve, I think) was a Duncan Park expert. He knew every inch of that small (2,857 yards), nine-hole (par 35) course. His quirk was to play you match play with only one club, a 7-iron. If you would spot him two holes on two rounds (18 holes total), he would bet you $5 he could beat you.

I lost a few times to this weirdo as did many other people until they found how efficient he was with that one club. He was a very strong man, so when he closed the club face on his 7-iron it was almost as if he were hitting a 2-iron. His drives would go about 230 yards. Then, opening the clubface slightly, he would hit it as a 5-iron, etc. His grip and forearms were so strong, he usually accomplished his shot. Putting with it was no problem.

My Biggest Boo-Boo

In the l963 City Tournament qualifying, my best friend Charlie outdid himself. He shot a 68 to win the medalist honors. It was the lowest qualifying round Kyzar had ever shot, and the only time he had ever parred NCC, so naturally he was extremely proud. I hurried to get the story written for our Sunday edition in hopes of joining Charlie to celebrate with him before he got smashed.

The runner-ups to him were John Tyler and Howard Magee who shot 74s. Naturally, I wrote it up with a six- column main headline ("Kyzar Outshoots City Golfers"); a two-column sub-head ("78 City Golfers Begin Play Today"); and a two-column, 10-point, two paragraph lead followed by 11 more inches of regular one-column type.

I usually stayed until the composing room made me a proof of my pages as they sometimes made a mistake in getting the correct article under the wrong headline. However, I wanted to join him and left early. He was already feeling no pain when I bragged about how happy he was going to be when he saw the paper the next morning.

Alas! The damn back shop makeup man left off the two 10-point lead graphs. All the who/what/when/where information — as well as all my accolades — were missing. It was just terrible and bothered me for months.

By Buck Peden

FUN IN THE LAKE – Of the hundreds of candids I took of Carolyn and the kids, this one was my favorite. Deb is on her mother's shoulders and David on Bobby's.

Naturally I showed it to Mr. Lambert, our head honcho editor and publisher. I never had any mistakes in my pages since that date, but it didn't help the deep regret for the boo-boo I made of leaving the plant before I had approved the proofs.

Fun On A Houseboat

A lot of changes in personnel occurred during the NRTC Natchez tour. Lusk was replaced by RMC Glenn Josey and the OINC Grimmes by LT C.E. McIntosh, plus we were added HM1 Clifton Thompson. He was not only challenger to William Browning and me on our ping pong tournaments, but was a good Heart game player as well. LT McIntosh came up with the brilliant idea to build a houseboat. Sellers was hot for the idea and I chipped in my affirmative assent and contributed to the effort with my cash and physical effort.

The lieutenant designed it so we bought eight empty 50-gallon metal drums for the buoyancy elements, four on each side. Sellers ensured the previous ingredients of the barrels would not ignite while he was welding them together in columns of four each by spraying CO_2 inside and sealing them closed. We cut circular notches in the bottom of the four 2"x12" cross beams that were 10 feet wide, then to the barrels. This gave us a main deck of 10' wide and 20' long as we extended the length of the deck a few feet fore and aft of the barrels.

Our stern contained a loading plank for an outboard motor with waterproof cables for steering running underneath its deck. We put a steering mount and wheel on the main deck forward on the starboard side, and a few feet forward, of the superstructure that we added last. McIntosh designed the latter to be 10' high in its front and 9.5' in the rear so the rain would flow aft or to the side and not on the sun deck area. It was 7' x 12' with two side windows and a front door and was center on both sides. This left a sun deck positioned two feet from the on with which to lean our poles stern which gave an 18" walkway on both sides. This left a sun deck on which to lean our poles when we anchored and fished.

We sealed the planks covering The roof and painted the whole houseboat, but we decided to get some of the waterproof coated material from Armstrong Tire Company's scraps to ensure it wouldn't leak. We built a ladder on the front port side of the structure so anyone could sun bathe on it. Also, the girls would sometimes relieve themselves off the rear to avoid having to climb down the ladder to use the bucket we had for that purpose. The men, naturally, just went the bow of six feet, which we encircled with a three-foot high latticed fence. It gave us enough room for lounge chairs and a rail off the stern of the main deck.

Very seldom did we spend the night on board, but if we had we had to bring a sleeping bag or pallet-making materials. We partied on it many, many weekends the first

expect, the boat was an easy moveable object. I tried to turn us into the wind which would make us a smaller target, but we had lost steerage. The rudder, which was the outboard motor's long shaft containing its propeller at the bottom, was not responding to the steering wheel. We finally were blown against the young willow trees that grew out 50 feet or so from the shore.

he did it without a whimper and successfully rehooked the cable.

Another problem, and one that happened more than once, was hitting an underwater stick or log. When the propeller blade hit something immoveable it would sever a small pin in its mechanism to keep from stripping a gear. I would have do that underwater. Sticking a new pin in my mouth and sticking the wrenches I needed in my swimming trunks, I would go under and could work almost three minutes before coming up for air. I had to take the prop off, replace the pin, and rebolt the prop. It usually only took me seven or eight minutes for the whole job.

Unfortunately, the one station keeper that didn't help build the houseboat, nor did he contribute to its expenses, was able to buy it from us cheap. We wanted to keep it in the NRTC family, so when a "plank owner" of the houseboat got transferred those PO left owned it and when the last one left, the non-contributor was able to buy it. What a lucky guy.

By Bobby Peden

OUR HOUSEBOAT we kept moored in a nearby Louisiana lake.

year, rotating turns to use it. We docked in a space at a pier we rented by the night and all winter. The kids really enjoyed it with Bobby even finding enough nerve to dive off the roof with me.

We caught a lot of fish, but our anchor was not too efficient. One day an unexpected breeze came up and, as one might

Bobby, 12, was aboard and was an excellent swimmer. I diagnosed the steering cable had came loose and sent him under the boat, with a screwdriver hanging around his neck, to correct the problem. He told me later it wasn't fun doing it because of the snakes we frequently saw near the banks. However,

Little Tessie — My Kind Of Doggie

John Lee Moore relieved transferred Ray & Ruby Sellers, who had been my favorite pal of all the station keepers during the almost nine years at Natchez. Moore was short like me. And he liked golf. He had a little white and black spotted terrier bitch that was amazingly smart. Tessie was her name and she loved her master. He would bring her to work with him and even take her on the golf course with him.

She would find a ball in the rough and bring it to John Lee. You would think she would get one of our balls hit down the fairway or into the rough, but she never did. She must have learned to avoid touching a golf ball with a fresh scent on it.

One day I got him to empty his cloth sack of balls she had found and took a picture of him, her, and the pile of several hundred balls. It was well received by readers. I didn't know there were so many terrier lovers in Natchez.

She was a housedog, naturally. I should say trailerdog as John & wife Lou lived in a trailer. I was invited over one afternoon to watch the professional football games and drink beer. When Moore turned on the TV I learned how prejudiced he was racially. He would not watch a game if one of the teams had a black player on it.

In those days, there weren't many as most of the owners were still racially prejudiced. Now, of course, John Lee

THE GREAT FOURSOME of me, Carolyn, Cossie & Charlie posing for the final photograph at our Farewell Party the city held at the Belwood CC.

might as well leave his TV off on Sunday afternoons as the pro teams all. have a black majority.

Whata Farewell Party

I got my orders to report to the USS PERKINS (DD-877) on June 15, 1966, as the Viet Nam War was underway. The *Democrat* threw us a farewell party at Belwood Country Club that Carolyn and I will never forget. Somehow they got a small replica made of the PERKINS and invited all our friends and business

associates. The Lamberts (Jimmie, Grace, & Johnny) were there along with coaches Van Stewart, Don Alonzo, Fred Foster, and my pal Dan, plus their spouses or dates. These topped a list of over 100 attendees. We thoroughly enjoyed the great sendoff the Natchez and Vidalia people gave us that night.

BGWW&P Times

July 1966-June 1968   *Vol. 1, No. 13*   *San Diego & Far East*

In my life

Iwo Jima Takes A Page
Marines Were The Weapon Of This Warship

Chapter one fits here in chronology of these memoirs. It was primarily of my first tour to Viet Nam on board the USS PERKINS. When we returned and I completed the operation on removing the bone spurs under my right patella (knee cap) I was hospitalized for a three-fold operation: Agronomy & pyloroplasty, hiatal hernioplasty, and gastrostomy. In other words I had an upper hernia near my esophagus and a chronic duodenal ulcer. They cut the vagus nerve leading to my stomach and enlarged the exit leading to the duodenum. The vagus nerve grew back, but I never again have suffered from acid pains in my abdomen area.

From the Naval Hospital there in San Diego, I reported aboard the USS IWO JIMA (LPH-2) for duty on August 1, 1967. When most people my age think of Iwo Jima they recall the famous photographs of the U.S. military forces implanting the American Flag on that island. Significantly,

during World War II, it was the first time a foreign flag had ever flown over a Japanese territory.

Captain F.X. Timmes was the commanding officer when I went aboard and Commander R.S. Vermilya (a great guy) was the executive officer. LTJG H.R. Parnell was the X Division Officer and I was the division's senior enlisted man. The 27-man unit was made of personnel from the following offices: Administrative, Personnel, Printing, Chaplin's and Postal. Therefore, we had ratings of yeomen, personnelmen, lithographers, draftsmen, postal clerks, and 10 non-designated seaman.

The ship's armament was very meager with only two 3"(75MM) 50 caliber anti-aircraft guns, eight cell sea sparrow launchers and two phalanx anti-missile systems. The major weapon of this warship was its 25 helicopters and its battalion of U.S. Marines.

Its length was small (592 feet) after serving on the USS

CORAL SEA (CVA-43) (968 feet) and the USS ORISKANY (CVA-34) (904 feet). But, my administrative office had plenty of room to hold my desk and six folding typist desks. It was on the first deck below the flight deck and only a few compartments forward of the captain's cabin where I spent a lot of my time as the captain's writer.

Richard And His Little Sexy Tassel

We rented a nice three-bedroom Naval house in a community north of San Diego. Carolyn's cousin Richard Le Verne, civil service computer expert, lived in Imperial Beach south of San Diego, Chula Vista, and National City. He had a beautiful house on a high hill overlooking the Pacific Ocean where he lived with his wife Irene and his step-daughter Nancy. We became very close, spending a lot of time at this nice house which had a wonderful little swimming pool in the backyard surrounded by exquisite small desert cacti and flowery plants in a sandy terra firma. He had a small bar that led onto the large patio and swimming area. It was just a magnificent home and kept immaculate by the very strict hostess, Irene. She loved to drink with Richard, Carolyn and me, but everything had to be so-so according to her specifications. Even the full-blooded schnauzer they owned watched his P&Qs when she was around. To say that Richard was hen-pecked would be putting it mildly.

Richard and I became close as brothers. Carolyn told me he was a accomplished pianist before he went into the Air Force. I believed it because all the rest of his family were talented musicians of some sort. I asked Richard why they didn't even have a piano if he was so talented. He shrugged his shoulders and said he had lost interest in it. He liked golf instead.

I always felt that Irene had something to do with it, but I let it slide and didn't pursue my questioning. Besides, I had a golfing buddy and we played every weekend. I improved his game immensely and he was very thankful for it. One day we had played the Balboa Golf Course in San Diego, and as usual, we drank beer as we played. This particular day we both had shot well and I felt like celebrating on the way home. I suggested we stop at this topless joint I knew in downtown San Diego. At first, he declined as our wives always expected us to come home and have cocktails before dinner with them in his little bar. Whenever I wanted him to break Irene's rules and he was reluctant, I would go "puck-puck-puck" in a tenor range that sounded like a chicken. THEN he would do it just to prove he was no chicken.

The dancers were outstanding. Richard had never been to a topless bar before, so he spent the whole time there with his mouth open staring at the gals dancing on the bar right in front of him. One only wore one garment: a small brief that only had a covering over her vagina and had small colorful tassels hanging from the top of it. As he had seen other patrons do to other dancers, Richard held up a $5 bill and she squatted, doing her gyrations inches from his face. He was going ape. I was afraid he was going to grab her, but he just slid the folded bill into her scant costume. She returned the favor by pulling one of the green tassels out of his panties closest to her pussy, kissing it, and dropping it in his hands.

I thought I was never going to get him out of that place. We had been drinking mixed drinks, so we both were not feeling any pain. He was in heaven on the way home. Fortunately, we were in my vehicle, so I drove as he smelled the tassel all the way home, even asking me once if I wanted a sniff.

Naturally, there was no mention of the topless joint. We were late because a golfing friend had hit a hole-in-one and bought a keg of beer for us all. It had been fun and I didn't think about it again until we visited again a few weeks later. I had already had a few dives off the board and played around with the kids when he asked me if I was ready for a toddy. He motioned me into his bar with a sheepish little smile letting me know he was up to something of a mischievous nature.

Standing behind the bar with his massive mirror behind him, he said, "You see it?"

At first I was dumbfounded, but the evil look on his face was a hell of a clue. He was talking about that tassel the dancer had given him. I looked over his body then to the intricate carvings of the mirror's frame. It was thick dark brown filigree sprinkled with gold and black.

"Nope," I finally said.

He reached behind him to the far corner of the mirror and pulled it out of one of its crevices. Satan himself would have been envious of the devilish smile on Richard's face at that moment.

Eleven Years Later It Happened Again

My mother and Aunt Berline surprised us with a visit that September and we took them to Disneyland. They enjoyed it immensely and were very tired from all the walking as they were 59 and 52, respectively. I bought a few quarts of good wine to celebrate their visit and the four of us had a little party in our living room. It was the first time I had ever seen my mother tipsy. They only spent a few days, but the kids loved it as much as we adults.

The last week in September following their visit, the IWO JIMA had a ship's sailing dance. We were to leave for Viet Nam October 2nd. They had over $5,000 in the ship's recreation fund and they must have spent it all on this party. They rented a huge stage and dance hall at one of the fancy hotels on the coast. It was a large orchestra of the Glenn Miller era that played from the stage with a large dance floor below them. We all had tables at the side surrounded by six temporary bars.

Carolyn still was not much of a drinker, still sipping two or three Tom Collins was usually her limit. Tonight, it was such a gala occasion I talked her into having martinis with me as they were free. Well, the orchestra was fantastic, best we had ever heard in person. And, as we both loved to dance, we were on the dance floor almost constantly. We danced waltz, two-step, jitterbug, twist, samba, cha-cha-cha, and rumba.

We were so thirsty that we were drinking the martinis as if they were water. We would drink at dances. Needless to write, we were slightly inebriated when the dance ended. I should have known something would happen that night when, as we passed a little goldfish pond in the hotel lobby, she stopped, leaned over and poured the rest of her last martini in the water.

"L'ttle fishy wants a drank too," she cooed hanging onto my arm.

Now, I'm sure most readers would expect a 35-year-old male and a 33-year-old female that had been married 17 years to go straight to sleep after all that dancing and drinking, right? Wrong. We had sex and I went to sleep. She had always taken care of not getting pregnant after we partook in that heavenly bliss. Whether it was a douche or whatever, she didn't do it that night.

Three months later off the coast of Viet Nam I get this letter that she is pregnant. Neither of us would even consider an abortion. I always loved kids so it wasn't too bad a shock at the time, but she added a post script at the end of her letter: "P.S. Get yourself fixed." She had heard other wives telling her how their husbands had got vasectomies in far east for peanuts and she was right. I asked around with my shipmates in the large chief's mess (eating area for E-7s through E-9) and they knew of a bar owner in Subic Bay that was Filipino male nurse at the Naval Base during week days. He only charged $20 to do the operation at his establishment. I made up my mind to get it done next time we were in port.

The first time we were in for rest and recreation at Subic Bay, the IWO JIMA's recreation committee, of which I was a member, held a one day, 18-hole, tournament on the Naval Base Golf Course. One of the officers on the committee came up with the Peoria Handicap System for the tournament. I had never heard of it before, but have seen it played in various parts of the United States with various titles.

Basically, if the course has a 72 par for 18 holes, then strokes were given thusly: (1) if you shot a 72-75 or better you were given no strokes, (2) 76-79 got minus ½ your worst hole, (3) 80-83 got minus your worst hole, (4) 84-87 got minus your worst hole and ½ your next worst hole, (5) 88-91 got minus your two worst holes, (6) 92-95 minus two and ½, etc.

In other words, if you shot a 75 that was your score. If you shot a 79 and your worst hole was an eight you would net a 75 (79-4 which was half your worst hole). If you shot a 91 and your two worst holes were an eight and a seven (91-15) you would net a 76. Surprisingly, most finish with a net score in the 70s. The player that shot consistently steady golf near par on most holes and then zoomed his score with one lousy hole, would usually win the tournament. I was the lucky one in the our first tournament and just barely beat Captain John Shepherd who had taken over command of the ship from Captain Timmes in December.

The Bam-Bam-Boom Popular Folk Dance

Captain Shepherd liked the way we ran the tournament and the handicap system we used. But he would kid me frequently about his getting revenge the next time we were in port. He put me in charge of setting up the next tournament.

I would always open the ship's official mail and put routing slips on correspondence which needed routing. If it would require answer, sometimes the skipper would just jot a note to me on the routing slip: "Chief, write 'em I agree with their proposal." Then I would type up a double-spaced rough letter in the proper formal language expected from a commanding officer. Usually it suited Captain Shepherd to a "T" and then I'd smooth it up for his signature. We had a very good rapport.

Finally a month later, we steamed into Subic again for R&R and supplies. I headed for the golf course and set up our golf tournament for the third day and then went ashore on my overnight pass to set up my vasectomy. The owner of the night club that worked on the base medical corps was not there yet, but his manager reached him by phone. Fortunately, he said for me to be there at 1800(6

p.m.) hours and he would do it that day. I was surprised to get it arranged so easily. But, everyone that I talked to that had the operation said it was a simple local anesthesia, a couple small incisions, and a few clamps was all it was to it.

Cruise Book Photo
Captain John Shepherd

I went to back to the naval base CPO Club and started guzzling the booze to aid the anesthesia and was waiting for my surgeon in his office at 1800. It didn't take him 10 minutes and I was on my way to my favorite night club. A couple of my shipmates were already there enjoying the dance band. I had bought a quart of bourbon as I had planned to get a room ashore for the night, so all I had to buy was the chasers.

As the night progressed, I was feeling no pain whatsoever from my testicles so I danced frequently and every time the band played their folk song that has two people holding

bamboo poles in each hand on the dance floor about three feet apart. The song starts out slow with three or four couples dancing with each beat. The holder would click the hollow poles on the floor at each of the first two beats and them slam the two poles together on the third beat. If you get hit by the poles you are out of the dance competition. If you didn't get hit you hop back in when the poles open immediately for the next to floor beats. As the music progressed, it slowly gets faster and faster. Naturally, the last remainder pair to do a complete "step in, step in, hop out" without getting hit by the poles is the winning couple. The establishment owners reward them with a free drink.

The unattached girls would run to get me as a partner as I usually won the dance. I was always very quick so made a good partner. Needless to write, the girls wanting me was good for my ego and the free drinks kept our table well stocked. I really got smashed that night dancing so much and quenching my thirst with bourbon and water or coke. I don't remember getting a motel room, but I woke up the next day in a bed.

I was cold when I awoke, but I was so weak I couldn't pull up the quilt and sheet laying at my waist. I was trembling and started moaning. I actually thought I was dieing. We had been at sea almost 40 days without any alcohol whatsoever in our system. Then, come in port and drink a over a quart in six or seven hours was just too much for one's system, even if I was only 35 years old.

A Filipino woman appeared and realized my predicament as she saw my pale skin coloring and my trembling. She pulled up the cover and added another quilt and tucked it tightly around me. I dozed a little and woke up very thirsty. She must have handled hung-over sailors before as she gave me some water and then mixed me a bloody Mary cocktail (tomato juice, shot of Worcestershire sauce, couple shake of salt, and a shot of vodka over ice).

After a few of those, I felt a little better and was able to eat some bacon and eggs she prepared. It was already after noon and I finally felt as if I *might* live. I gave the nice woman who had taken me to her house, put me to bed, and taken care of me that morning twenty dollars for which she seemed very thankful. I stopped by the CPO Club and had a few drinks with a couple chiefs off the IWO. Then I went aboard, showered, and hit the sack to try to get enough strength to play in the golf tournament the next day.

A Happy Champion With Bloody Balls

We sent off the senior officers first and I teed off with the final group with a couple of the other committee members that had helped me with the arrangements. I not only was feeling terrible from the hangover, but my testicles didn't feel too good and the incisions looked a little red. I guessed it was because of all the sweating I had done down there while dancing into the wee hours.

The course wasn't too long, but it was built on rugged terrain. We had pull carts, but there were no motorized carts to ride. I suffered all the way around and once hit into a grove of bamboo where I received the shock of my life. I searched for my ball and knowing that I couldn't hit it out of the thicket I called it an unplayable lie. It was beside a bamboo stem, I thought, but, when I reached down to pick it up, the damn thing wiggled away. It was six or seven foot (I sure didn't try to measure it) and was told it probably was a reticulate python. It sure got my adrenaline going as I birdied the last two holes to win the tournament again. I didn't stick around to celebrate as I found a little blood on my testicles and they appeared larger.

I was lucky Dick Beckstead, the ship's Chief Hospital Corpsman, was on board. He examined me in privacy and said they were definitely infected. He gave me some medicine and had me soak in a small tub of some kind of mixture in hot water. He had me soaking them every day for a couple of weeks and they must have been bad as I could see pus coming out the incisions. His treatment definitely saved me from becoming a soprano.

I was still able to perform my regular duties. I just didn't walk very gingerly. I even published a ship's monthly newspaper, but guess I never kept a copy of it. I think it was named *Jumpin' Jima* or *Jima Journal*. With the lithographers and draftsmen available in the X Division, it was a neat little publication with photographs and well as various type fonts.

Gin Rummy In Chief Petty Officer Mess

During off hours, we played a lot of card games in the large CPO mess compartment. It had long tables and benches to seat 10 for a meal. Occasionally we would get up a game of poker, but most of the time it was just heads up gin rummy for a half cent or a penny a point. Most of the time we played the Hollywood style which would go to three games at once. However, you didn't get into a game until you scored once, the second game until you scored twice, and the third time you scored you got into the third game. Scores were added to every game in which you had scored.

As one might suspect, there would be times one player never got in the second or third game before his opponent reached 150 points. This resulted in a skunk game in which all the points were doubled. Half cent games usually ranged in the $5-$10 area while penny a point games average between $10 and $20 dollars.

For seven months of the cruise the IWO JIMA was the flagship for Commodore T.C. Harbert, Commander Amphibious Squadron THREE. His signalman was Dave Graham. Graham was one of my favorite opponents. He was a suave Senior Chief Signalman that not only was tall, handsome with wavy hair, but possessed a polite and charming personality. Everyone liked ole Dave and when he retired years later he was the founder and chairman of American Battleship Association and founder of USS IDAHO (BB-42) Association.

He was an enjoyable opponent as one could ask. He even lost to me many more times than he won, so what more could a pasteboard adversary want.

Then one day the ship's Chief Quartermaster, John "Sully" Sullivan, became an interested bystander.

"So that's how gin rummy is played, huh?" he asked as I computed my winnings of a single game we had played.

"Yep," I answered and then said, "Dave, I had 80 more points than you and I get 150 for winning plus 25 points each for the three more boxes I had, so at a penny a point you owe me $3.05."

"Shit, I can handle that. How about me playing a game," Sully asked excitingly.

"You got him, Sully. I'm weighing anchor. Ole Buck is just too tough for me," Graham said scooting over and picking up a book to read.

"You wanna just play for fun for a few games until you're sure you're familiar with its method of play?" I asked knowing how cocky he was that he would refuse.

"Hell no! I've watched you two guys play several times now and it's a simple game. You gotta just be lucky enough to get the right cards. Let's go. Penny a point," he said smiling broadly. I liked the guy and we went on liberty together several times, but "gotta just be lucky" will enable one to win a few games of rummy. A lucky soul may even win a game or two, but in the long run, the more knowledgeable and intelligent player will always win most of the games. I had played GR every day after playing golf in Natchez the last seven years against a few of the masters of the game. I would estimate over 300 games a years or 2,100 games for money. I never classified myself as a master, but the year I kept a record of my won-loss at over $3,000 won told me I ranked in the top echelon of gin player standings.

Sully scored only twice so he never got in the third game. When I ginned to go out the last hand and clinch the skunk for double money, he threw

his hand up in the air cursing loudly.

"**Gin?!!** You lucky bastard. I never seen anybody so goddamn lucky."

I just made myself busy with the score pad. He acted so mad I was afraid to kid him a little for fear of him hitting me. But, big Dave couldn't choke it back. He had been sneaking glances at Sully's hand and method of card retention, so he took his pipe out of his mouth, chuckled and asked Sully:

"Man, that Buck is really a go-getter in that game, huh Sully? When he picked up that three of clubs early in the game, I never figured he had a little run in clubs 'til you threw that six (of clubs, which ginned me)."

"Fuck you old man." Then started picking up his cards and said to me, "Deal the damn cards. You can't do that again."

I evaluated it as I was collecting cards: I knew he would be a sore loser so I considered clipping competition with him in the bud. But then, I felt he would be a *frequent* competitor as well as a *frequent* loser. I decided I could put up with his bitching for the money I could win from him. He had no dependents, that I knew, so he had plenty of money to spare. My pregnant bride liked it also as I sent half of my winning to her at home.

I even captured the next Hollywood set, but he won one of the games (no, I don't believe in throwing card games, he won on his own). The next time I ginned to skunk him, I got up and walked about six feet from my seat before I threw my discharge card face down meaning I was knocking or ginning. Then I would meekly whisper, "Gin, by golly."

That got a roar from bystanders who would sometimes watch us play. However, a few days later when I got up to do it again, he jumped up and pointed to my seat.

"Sit your ass back down if you're gonna play cards or this hand's a misdeal."

I promptly sat back down and said — with no hesitation — in one sentence, "Yes sir, gin."

He torqued his face into a grimacing look in preparation to yell at me again when I interrupted.

"Simmer down now or I'll give the next prostitute you patronize an apple to eat."

He burst into laughing along with me. He had to tell the surrounding listeners what we were laughing about.

"Buck was talking about how he had got so used to that destroyer he was on firing their heavy armament that he became accustomed enough to sleep with that loud boom going on. He asked me what was the loudest sound I had ever heard and I told him. I was fucking this Jap whore and just reaching my climax when I heard this tremendous noise. **CRACK!**...right beside my left

ear. I jerked up to see what it was. The goddamn little shit had taken a bite out of an apple while I was having an orgasm," he explained frowning as if it had just happened.

"I don't have to tell you, I was so shook up, I couldn't fuck no more. She didn't get paid either," he concluded. The listeners enjoyed it.

Sully got a little better playing gin as I would point out any obvious mistake he made after the hand was over. He still occupied the most pages in my receipt book with Graham, my most enjoyable opponent, a page or two back in second place. I even got a few challenges from the top sergeants in the Marine battalion on board.

The Private Was Reluctant Twice

The sergeant major (senior enlisted man) of the battalion was the most successful one of them, although he didn't play that often. He was a very smart man and I enjoyed chatting with him between games, etc. I had seen a black private refusing physically to get on the helicopter in their last attack against the Viet Cong. I asked the SM what it was all about.

"He refused to fulfill his duties. His squad had to function without him covering its left flank. That was his squadron obligation," he explained.

"So, what happened to him?

I saw them take him off the flight deck."

"He was put in the brig," the SM explained.

I always felt sad every time a company or two was 'coptered ashore as they always came back shy a marine or two and others with serious injuries. One time it was extremely excruciating when they were ashore several days in fierce battle. The returning helicopters had so many casualties that the bodies had to be laid on the hanger deck until the medical department , headed by LT R.A. Coulon, MC, could attend to them. As Chief Hospital Corpsman Dick Beckstead and his crew were moving them to be cleaned, I noticed some of the bodies had weeds and dirt stuffed in their mouths by the VC.

It wasn't long after that I heard that they released the reluctant private from the brig and he again tried to refuse getting aboard the helicopter, but this time was unsuccessful. During evening chow, I asked the SM if it was true.

"Yes it is, chief. He finally was boarded but, believe it or not, that private jumped out of that helicopter from 2,000 feet," he said with a very serious look on his face.

I searched his face for a "... and that's the way marines take care of marines for not carrying their load" grin, but there was none. He took another bite of his food and we never mentioned it again. I'm sure that the rest of the battalion never mentioned it again either. It was a dead issue but a living message.

Before we were relieved in Subic Bay by USS PRINCETON in late May 1968, other members of the battalion lost their lives in this Viet Nam War. One was the IWO JIMA's sergeant major.

Kaohsiung, Yokosuka, Pearl, & Then Home

We stopped a few days in Kaohsiung, Taiwan, and eight days in Yokosuka, Japan. It was beautiful in Japan the middle of June, so I managed to play a beautiful golf course in nearby Yokohama. What I had heard about it did not do it justice. It started with a beautiful 310-yard par four initial hole that was straight downhill. I really got lucky and blasted one down the middle with the wind. It gained "oooohs" and "aaaahs" for the Japanese golfers and their female caddies (all caddies were women) along the tee area.

It rolled up on the green about six feet from the pin. I'm sure the slope, wind, and thin atmosphere of the mountainous terrain was the reason for the long distance. I had never before (nor would since) hit a ball that far.

And to impress me even more, I made the putt for my first eagle on a par four hole. The next hole gave me another little surprise. It was a long par five built along side of the mountain. I hit the ball near the edge of the right rough which dropped far downward. My caddy was very loudy hollering, "OoooooBeeeee, OoooooBeeeee"

"What the heck is she saying?" I asked anyone. A fellow sailor playing with us had played there before knew.

"She's saying you hit out of bounds (OB)," he explained.

I didn't care. I was still on cloud nine from the first hole.

Finally, we got to the highest point of the course which had its 10' square tee (can't remember the hole number) elevated atop the peak of the small mountain. The fairway dropped almost straight down before it turned into a fairway leading upward. When I stood on the tee, I had my first feeling of a fear of heights. Now, even on my rooftop gives me that fear.

It was a magnificent hole and beautiful view of the green valleys below us. I would advise any golf lover going to Japan that he/she put Yokohama Golf Course (?) on their must play list. I hated to leave, but I wanted to get home an see my new son, Jeffrey Lance, who was born on April 30.

A one day stop in Pearl Harbor, and we made it to San Diego on June 28, 1968.

BGWW&P Times

July 1968–September 1971   *Vol. 1, No. 14*   *Chino, Pomona, & Walnut, CA*

Final Assignment & Few Degrees
Transferred NROTC Unit At USC For ADCOP Duty

The IWO JIMA already had received my orders to shore duty at the Naval Reserve Officers Training Corps (NROTC) Unit at the University of Southern California (USC) in connection with administration of the Associate Degree Program (ADCOP) at Mt. San Antonio College (MSAC) in Walnut, Calif. Therefore, a month after we returned, I was transferred with 30 days delay in reporting authorized. I said my farewells, picked up my orders, and departed July 28, 1968.

I had no idea why they chose me to be the administrative assistant at this junior college for the Navy's new ADCOP. It would require maintenance of personnel records, all administrative tasks, along with respectable relations and liaison with college officials. I was very honored that I was chosen for the assignment and super pleased when I learned the college was providing me with a secretary. It softened the irritation I had against the Navy bureaucracy in not promoting me to senior chief (E-8) nor warrant officer, even

though I had tremendous recommendations from my COs and always passed the written exams. 'Twas always below the number of quotas available, I guess.

Before reporting and meeting my secretary, I took a months leave back to Memphis to show our families the new addition. He weighed seven pounds and had red hair at birth. My bride would have been in deep trouble having a son from me with red hair if it hadn't been for the time I grew my red beard in Huntsville during the city's sesquicentennial in the mid-50s. Neither of us had any red heads, of which we were cognizant anyway, in our family background.

She chose the name Jeffrey and I got her to okay Lance for the middle moniker after my favorite football receiver, Lance Alworth. An All-American Running Back at the University of Arkansas, where he ran the 100-yard dash in 9.6 seconds in track, he made the College Football Hall of Fame. Then, with San Diego (1962-70) and Dallas (1971-72) he made the Professional Football HOF.

Made a wide receiver in the pro ranks, he way awesome with his quick cuts, speed, and graceful leaps high into the air to catch passes. He set records for most consecutive games with receptions (96), most games with 200 or more yards receiving (5), and the only receiver with three consecutive seasons (1964-66) with 100 yards or more receptions in games.

None of our families were sports enthusiasts; therefore, had never heard of Alworth so we used "Jeff" as a primary beckoning name after the visit to Memphis. It was our easiest 4,000-mile round trip as Carolyn could take turns driving and Bobby took over in open stretches on the way by across Texas, New Mexico, and Arizona. We skipped Carlsbad Caverns and the Grand Canyon this time as Jeff was too young to appreciate and the other three had seen them on a previous trip.

Bobby, who had turned 16 in January, had not had too much driving experience while I was gone, but he had done an excellent job as "man of the house" while I was gone. Of course, he had a lot of help with best friend Jim Lawler. They were almost inseparable sophomore buddies at Kearney High after meeting in Montgomery Junior High. Bob was at Whitehaven High School in Memphis as a freshmen, but had to go to a JHS as Kearney was only l0 thru 12 grades. He still uses the woodcraft knowledge he learned at WHS. He also gained some valuable knowledge in the Performing Arts at the Federal Conservatory in San Diego.

Just before we moved north, my favorite striker while I was on board the USS PERKINS, Jim Wynn, visited us for a weekend. Debra, now a pretty 14-year-old 8th grader at Montgomery, developed a crush on the dark-eyed lad. It was the first time I noticed she was in the early stages of womanhood.

David was 12 and had finally outgrown his desire to throw rocks at things. He we thought he did no wrong during that era until he got grown and laughed with us about some of the little sneaky things that he did (**BWBB**) behind our back. For example, we thought he was going to the local park to play, but he spent most of his time playing in the gorge located behind our house. It was full of brush and known territory for rattlesnakes; therefore, we excluded it from his permitted play areas. David and his friends respected the poisonous reptiles, but were not afraid of them. We learned later that they actually made a game out of hunting and killing them.

I was always afraid one would slither through our chain-link fence some day and strike Carolyn when she was hanging the wash on the clothesline in the back yard. Fortunately, her cousin Cooper Mc Daniel had found a three bedroom house for sale at 14949 Sandalwood Lane, unbelievably located across the street from him and his family in Chino, Calif.

Orbited To Mt. San Antonio College

I drove to the NROTC Unit at USC on August 2 reporting for duty to CAPT Garrison Brown, the CO. I spent several days of orientation on my function as the Navy's administrative liaison with the ADCOP unit. CDR John Jones, the XO, met me at the flag pole in the middle of Mt. San Antonio College and then introduced me (jokingly as NROTC's satellite) to the vice president with whom I would be dealing while administering the ADCO Program at his college. I worked with him the entire 25 months I was there and he was extremely cooperative in every facet of our dealings. I think his name was Allen Burns, but remember, this is a 7th decade "senior citizen recall attempt." We never corresponded, except for an insignificant unsaved memo or a note . The payment to the college for the men in the program came direct from the Chief of Naval Personnel in Washington; therefore, our transactions were virtually all verbal.

The Navy and Marines made this two-year associate degree program to its pay grade E-5 and above enlisted men of any rating provided they extended their enlistment four years. Approximately 40 sailors and four Marines had been selected for this highly competitive program at MSAC, one of the large community colleges in California and one of the finest academically in the U.S. It was named after Mount San Antonio (more commonly called Mt. Baldy for its snow-capped peak) which was visible in the background of MSAC's 421 acres approximately 22 miles directly east of Los Angeles in Walnut, Calif.

At our ADCOP office I met my secretary, a lovely blonde lady that I estimated in her late forties. She had short hair, which she always kept neatly arranged to compliment her fair skin that provided the perfect background for her soft, but colorful, facial makeup. With her radiant smile and slim body, bumped in the right places, Mrs. Jeanette Martens was a definite plus to the 15'x20' office.

The admin building was new; therefore, our office had never been used. It had a tall vertical window for natural lighting, which overlooked a huge field for the physical education department. Jeanette's desk in front of the window had a slide-out electric typewriter and the only telephone. My work area was a large conference table in front of her desk. I did not mind not having a desk for the first time since I got into the administrative and clerical field which allowed me plenty of work space. Beside the office entrance, the closets also contained the filing cabinets with which I was to utilize while working on the participants' records and a bookcase with college references publications, etc.

The men started arriving the following week, so I barely had time to get to know my secretary before I was bogged down with work. We clicked professionally, but I could tell she had never been around anyone like me. She had been accustomed to working for education executives that took their business very seriously. She had never been around a sailor who had traveled half the globe numerous times; dealt with numerous thousands of individuals from all over the Pacific, Far East, and USA; plus, never ever met a "River Rat" from Fort Pickering.

I had to learn shorthand as a yeoman in those days to handle the court recording chores in military court-martials. But, I had never wrote for Captain Sheppard, I would rough it out on my manual typewriter. Words would come easy to me there as if my fingers knew the words I was going to originate. However, looking at her beautiful crossed legs below a shorthand pad in hand, there were many problems at first. The nouns were usually correct and came out all right, but the verbs, adverbs, and adjectives sometimes were non-intended humor. She never embarrassed me by laughing out loud, but the little smile and erecting eyebrows told me when I had made a "boo-boo."

One's Kissing Method May Give One Away

I took her to lunch several times, usually in her new Mustang, and got to meet her husband, Bob, who was in the real estate business. We eventually became very close with Carolyn and I partying together with them on many occasions during my tour. Jeanette and I originally greeted one another casually, at first. Then, we hugged. A peck on the cheek, with the hug came next. Finally, in the last year I was there, it was a kiss on the lips. It was like leaving one female I loved dearly, and was the mother of my children; then greeting another with similar symbolic affection. Jeanette wouldn't turn her head, as all couples I had seen would do when kissing on the their mouths. It was a simple maneuver to avoid bumping noses.

One day I had overslept and skipped shaving that morning. When I kissed Jeanette that day, she noticed it.

"Aah ha, you forget to shave this morning," she said rubbing her chin which was already turning a little pink from the abrasion of my short stubble. I apologized and took my electric shaver out of my briefcase and went directly to the head[29] and shaved.

We became very busy when all the men reported from their two-year participation in their ADCOP courses towards acquiring an Associate Degree. Helping them find local residences for them and their families was the initial objectives in which Jeanette was a tremendous aid as she had lived in the area for many years. The guys were extremely pleased with her smiling face and pleasant disposition. She also was very helpful to them in selecting instructors in their required curricula.

For example, some professors had quirks she felt most military men would find unpleasant, obnoxious, etc. She diagnosed the personalities of our members very rapidly. It was one of her best assets. In fact, she was very friendly and helpful to all of them. I noticed one tall good-looking chief would spending a lot of his between class study time at our conference table instead of frequenting the library as most his shipmates did. Therefore, it came as no surprise to me when Mrs. Martens told me the chief was taking her to lunch in nearby Pomona, Calif., and asked if it would be

29   U.S. Navy term for toilet.

alright if she was a little late returning.

I consented, of course, but was a little surprised when she took almost three hours for the meal. Then I figured it out real fast when I noticed her heavy powder on her chin. It was thick, but unable to cover the pink chin. That observation, plus my knowledge that the chief's wife hadn't moved out yet from her home back east. The temporary bachelor had obviously been kissing my secretary and had neglected to shave very close that morning.

I gave her a sly smile as I accepted with **BWWB** understanding as she blushingly apologized for being so late in returning to work. We never discussed it, but I'm sure she knew I suspected.

Dudes So Sharp Four Make Warrant Officer

These guys were so intelligent, I think they all made the Dean's List every quarter. Glenn Martin, a master chief machinist mate, was the senior Navy enlisted and Rick Budd, a gunnery sergeant, was the top Marine. However, Al Edmonson and Francis Thomson, Jr. were enlisted men recently appointed to Warrant Officer with Richard Horne and Alberto Betancourt receiving their selections to WO1 while they were completing the ADCOP. I am sure many of

the others were chosen to the officer ranks after completing their Associate Degrees.

I was allowed to take one course a quarter during normal working hours and usually took two courses a week in the night program at MSAC. I had completed 12 Navy courses, seven USAFI[30], and 16 night courses in Natchez at the U. of S. Mississippi Resident Branch; therefore, I was given commensurate credit by the MSAC evaluators. I majored in journalism and minored in physical education.

We formed a flag football team to play in the college's intra-league competition. Practicing on Saturday's at a park in Pomona, we began playing a sandlot game against a team made up mostly of beer drinking employees off work from a large local factory. We didn't have the flag belts as the college used so we played touch below the waist.

We all played different positions on our team until we decided who was best at which. I had the slight edge in the passing department and Duane Harris, a very gregarious senior chief aviation electrician's mate (E-8), was by far the best pass receiver. He made quick cuts to get into the open and was very fast. We usually beat the workers with Harris snagging most of my passes. His favorite was the "bomb." I had drawn diagrams of plays on palm-sized cards

30 United States Armed Forces Institute.

as I had done quarterbacking in the Natchez Honor Touch Football League. We would use it successfully several times in these sandlot games. Even with my bum knee, I could evade these middle-aged rushers on Saturday.

Things were different in the MSAC intra-mural play. Our opposing teams were mostly fraternities made up of former high school players that weren't quite good enough to make the college grid team. They were usually in the 19-20 age group with plenty of speed. Our overweight, out of shape, beer-drinking ADCOP linemen had a tough time blocking for my passes. Consequently, we went through the entire season with short runs and quick passes resulting with no victories against the young lads.

Harris had pleaded for the long "bomb" during every game, but our offensive line and blocking back could never give me enough time for him to run the pattern. It called for a slant to the middle, a quick fake button-hook, followed by an all-out sprint towards the deep right flat. Finally, in the last game I called it in the huddle with a slight deviation. The blocking back would take over for me at tailback. As the ball is centered to him, I drifted behind him towards the right flat. Then, as the defenders are almost to him, he fires me a lateral. This should give me plenty of time to throw the "bomb" to our loveable Harris.

It worked like a charm, with Duane breaking into the clear at full speed with my aerial sailing through the air in a perfect arch towards him. He was behind the safety man and would surely score a touchdown. It would have been only one of a few our team had scored the entire season.

ALAS!!!!! The ball bounced off the top of his head and beyond his extended arms.

The poor guy was razed (e.g. trying to catch a football with his head, etc.) about it by his shipmates the rest of his time there at MSAC, but it was all in fun and he absorbed it thusly.

Become A Statistician & Stringer For MSAC

I didn't have any courses on Saturdays so I volunteered to help the coaching staff by keeping the football team's statistics. I would give a copy to Fred Claire, a sportswriter for a local valley newspaper that covered sports at MSAC. Occasionally, when he had a conflicting event to attend, I would be his stringer and telephone him the results, scoring, etc.

Fred would later be hired by the Los Angeles Dodgers as public relations director and eventually elevated to executive director and general manager. He was not only an intelligent and knowledgeable man of the sports world, but he was highly respected among his peers. The latter is a quality I have always held in high esteem.

I don't recall getting any stringer pay as I did for the Mississippi and Louisiana newspapers as I was doing it now simply because I enjoyed it. Money was not a problem as Carolyn had gotten a job in MSAC's mailroom and a few months later an administrative assistant's position in one of the VP's office.

Also, except for a internal blockage I sustained during an astronomy class one night, everything was hunky-dory in my work, school, and at home. The pain in my abdomen, during the three hours they had ambulanced to the Pomona Hospital and then to the Naval Hospital in Long Beach including many internal tests, was the most severe I have ever had before or since. It gave Carolyn and the kids quite a scare. I was too occupied yelling for drugs for the pain (which would have masked the test results) to worry about succumbing.

Bobby was busy setting distant track records at Chino High School and charming the female students with the male lead in the two school plays, "Bye, Bye Birdie" and "Blithe and Spirit," before being graduated in 1970. He would attend nearby Chaffey Community College a year before and joining the Navy.

Debra was 16-plus and a huge help to Carolyn in the kitchen, housework, and baby-sitting Jeffrey when not in school. When not, Jo Ann Mc Daniel kept him across the street

along with her three: Michael, Jimmy, and Mary Ann. Deb had already filled out and become a woman already as he mother had when I married her at 16. The older boys were already flocking at our door for her attention.

Gertie (I still called her that when she was mischievous) found Debra'a diary opened, or opened it as virtually all mothers have a tendency to do, and read where Debra wrote "making out" with some lad in our enclosed garage. Carolyn told me about it, obviously very upset. When we were teenagers, "making out" was having sex. We learned from Debra that to the late 60s teens, it meant what we called smooching.

David was 12-plus and was still running daily. He had a nice tree-shaded bridle trail in which to run. It was on the outside of the beautiful stone wall that encircled the entire neighborhood. Much of the valley south of Pomona and Chino consisted of pastureland inside white fences, most of which contained many of the beautiful racehorses owned by Rex Ellsworth, owner of the multiple national champion Swaps (1952-72), a HOFamer.

Our back yard abutted the five-foot stone wall so that we could sometime see the horses in the pasture on the other side of the outside road. Most of the time, the damn smog was so bad one could not see that far. I swore to Carolyn many times that I was going to get us out of there after I finished my graduate and post-graduate education.

Although we didn't get to play often was we would like, Cooper and I would pound the little golf pill on the spacious Los Serranos Golf and Country Club only a few miles east of us off U.S. Highway 71. Bobby joined us a time or two, but the rest of the kids were too young for that course.

Graduation Party Had Sour Ending

I was able to complete my associate degree at the same time the ADCOP students were graduated so we threw one hell of a party in the back yard of one of the member's house. We ate, drank, danced and was merry until wee hours on the morning. Unfortunately, Glenn and Dorothy Martin had an argument as the party was breaking up. Glenn and I had stopped by our favorite bars after work hours many times, but I never saw him as intoxicated as he was as they were driving to go home.

We left only minutes later in our brand new station wagon, a beautiful yellow one and the biggest made by Ford in 1969. There was Dorothy walking down the street by herself. Their argument had gotten hotter and she made him let her out. Knowing his temper, I knew he would oblique. We drove her home and his vehicle wasn't. I promised to find him and see that he got home safely.

The local taverns stayed open all night and I was sure I knew the ones he would attend.

I drove Carolyn home and, to her dismay, insisted I was sober enough to keep my promise. Actually, I had been drinking the hard stuff all night, but felt clear-headed as they had plenty of ham, chicken, and potato salad to eat throughout the festivities.

I thought it was safe to have a beer at each of the places I stopped while waiting for him to show. Finally, after the third one and noting the sun was up, I gave up and headed home. I was driving fine and well within the speed limit, but the soft car seats and warm interior was too much for my carcass which had a lavish workout earlier that night on the patio dance floor.

I had just checked on the distance of my vehicle from the one in front of me. I knew we were approaching a stop sign; therefore, I wanted to make sure I had plenty of room to brake behind them. Then, I panned down to check my speed and went sound to sleep.

WHAM! It was the shortest nap I ever had before or since. I had my seat-belt across my waist, as they were made in those days, so my head crashed against my right thumb on the steering wheel and broke it. I was only going about 20 MPH, but the victim had stopped completely. No one was hurt in their vehicle, but their rear end and our new jewel was

well dented. Our insurance paid for everything.

Needless to write, Gertie was mad as a wet hen. I told her I wasn't drunk, I just fell asleep. It had been a long day and night (about 26 hours) almost all of it with the graduates on their feet before, during, and after the long ceremony.

"Holy guacamole,[31]" I told her. "Be thankful I didn't fall asleep meeting an 18-wheeler when I got on U.S. 71."

Would you believe, it didn't change her mood one iota. **GWBG.**

Did Junior Year At CSC Fullerton

California must have the most educational institutions of any state in the union. I finished my AA degree in Walnut and planned to go over the hill to California State Polytechnic College (latter changed to University) in Pomona. However, as they had no night courses, I acquired the courses needed for my junior year in college by driving only about 20 miles-or-so to California State College at Fullerton. This means I had every establishment I needed to complete my higher learning within a 20-mile radius. I shall always be thankful for this happening luckily available to me by my country and the U.S. Navy.

The only problem with CSF

---

31 My favorite little pet exclamatory remark.

was to reach it I had to drive the narrow Carbon Canyon Road. Although blacktopped, it was a two-lane snake. Sometimes, when I caught up with other vehicle also enroute to Fullerton, it would take me 30 minutes to make the drive.

By Bobby Peden

SWAN MURAL I was painting on the bathroom wall for a break in my college studies.

The three-hour courses started at 7 p.m.; therefore, I had to leave no later than 6:15 and got back at about 10:35 p.m. I would spend the rest of the night studying with instrumental music I had tapped swapping album reels with shipmates while returning from Korea & VN Wars. Naturally I would use ear phones so as not to ever disturb Carolyn or the kids watching TV on those nights or weekends.

Communications department was in a new building and the photography offices, class rooms and modern lab & dark room

on an upper floor. When the department head saw my extensive background in photographic journalism and as a former owner of a photography business, he let me challenge the Com 218A course, Introduction to Photography with a special assignment. He wanted me to take random photographs of the photographic facilities and/ or students involved therein. I took approximately two dozen one day, developing and printing them the next day. He liked them so well that he had me enlarge and mount 10 of them. He placed them artfully on the wall facing the elevator opening to his department. Naturally, I was very proud and pleased. That was in the spring semester of '70, so I'm sure they have been replaced many times by now.

I enjoyed the campus and

chatted many times with the sports information director of CSF. The school had, and still has, an excellent baseball program. With a 45-10 record in 2001, they were seeded #1 of 64 teams by National Collegiate Athletic Association (NCAA), Division I.

At CSF, I made one of the three "C" grades I made at the three California colleges I would attend (rest were "As" & "Bs") . It was awarded by a professor, about my age, in Eng 463, Contemporary Novels. He would assign a chapter in one novel we were studying to read for homework and discuss the next week in class.

"The author writes 'Gilbert slept facing the opposite direction of Jennifer in bed after sex the entire wild weekend escape the pair spent together.' What was the author really conveying to us?" was a typical question he would ask about the novels we were covering.

My first thoughts were he slept on the right side of the bed and she the left. As he, like many of us, preferred sleeping on his right side in lieu of his back or left side, it would result in him facing an opposite direction of her. I knew this was not what the professor wanted to hear. Sure enough, he called on me.

"What was your interpretation, Mr. Peden."

"I think he was conveying Jennifer had bad breath," I answered with a serious face.

The class giggled with

approval and one young lad even gave his agreement out loud, "Yeaaah."

The prof even smiled a little; but, as the semester progressed and I gave him a few more similar witticisms to the delight of the class, he obviously did not appreciate my humor. I got to know many of my classmates during the two short intermissions we took. I still had a lot of my southern drawl at that time so they interrogated me soundly about my childhood in the South and my military background.

Finally, one of females had trouble giving a decent answer.

"I didn't quite get any underlying meaning, but I bet Buck did," she said grinning like a possum.

"I think we've heard enough of Mr. Peden's clever ascriptions of our esteemed author's material," he quickly declared. He thusly censored my "cool quips," as the students called them. From then on I was very serious with any oral comments, but he still gave me that "C."

Hickman Laughs From His Grave

Another interesting class at CSF was Speech 211, Oral Interpretation. However, in this one, I got a twinkling "A" from that instructor. The course was taught only in the spring semester and the subject was required before I obtained my Bachelor's Degree in Communication Arts at Cal Poly. It was critical I get that particular course if I was going to finish all my studies to qualify for the graduation exercises June 12, 1971.

I was one of 62 students that were also qualified and applied for the course. With only 40 desks in the class room, we had 22 hopeful entrants standing along the outer isles when the teacher arrived. He was a little late so he was moving fast when he entered the packed room. Braking with wide eyes and a dropped chin, I knew from the startled expression he had on his face that he was going to be a entertaining tutor and I would enjoy being in his class.

"Whoa," he exclaimed. "I knew I was a popular lecturer, but I didn't anticipate this large of a turnout."

Then, he put his brief case on the desk and stepped to the podium. He gave us a brief history of his life which started as a monk in a monastery after he finished college. After learning it was not for him, he became a professor. He now adores his new profession, but explained that he would have to cut the class down to 40. To determine which students would make this semester's class, he told us to give our name and some statement that would influence him in choosing that individual.

He started from his far right which meant the eighth one to respond would be me. I knew I would have to make a clever statement to get into the class; therefore I was rapidly trying to think of something as the preceding students rattled off theirs.

With all my experience at writing headlines in the newspaper business while being pressed by deadline, one would have thought this would have come easily to me. However, my mind was blank when my turn came. I was so disgusted with myself that I stepped forward and meekly said my name, "Buck Peden."

"I didn't quite get that first name," the instructor said. "What was it?"

Really pissed with myself, I blurted loudly, "**BUCK...you know, it rhymes with...**"

He quickly jumped before I finished, "That's all right. I think we know what it rhymes with."

I quickly concluded, "**... luck, duck, and many other things.**"

The class laughed heartily, as did the professor. "Okay. You're in the class," he said smiling to my great relief.

Coach Hickman Ewing, who gave me the nickname in high school, I am sure joined in the merriment from his grave somewhere back in Shelby County, Tenn.

Also, the little event had a happy ending as I was awarded an "A" from the former monk.

Students Get Revenge On Govenor Reagan

Ronald Reagan, then governor of the state, made a speaking appearance in the CSF auditorium that was interrupted several times by boisterous students letting their disagreements be known to Reagan's subject matter. His body guards finally escorted them outside to their dismay.

They got their revenge at the end of the school year when the beautiful college annuals were printed. It seems some of those dismissed at Reagan's address were members of the editorial staff of the publication. They had gotten together volunteers to pose in the nude scattered around an outdoor swimming pool. All were facing the camera with one hand raised above their heads giving the infamous "Up Yours" sign with their middle finger.

It was printed on the inside of the paper covering the book with its outside printed with respectable information. Hundreds of the publication was distributed before the CSF officials discovered the prank and absconded the rest. For those who got one, it probably became a collector's item. Unfortunately, I saw a few, but did not purchase one as they were expensive. I wasn't in it, but I regret I didn't get one with the cover.

The Carbon Canyon Mystery Solved

All the tiring trips back home to Chino after my night classes were monotonous. It was practically void of any residences or businesses, except for one about halfway. I could see a light in the parking lot of a two-story building. I couldn't see any neon sign on the building, but there was always plenty of cars parked when I drove even though it was usually well after 10 p.m. My curiosity finally got the best of my enroute from my last night course of the semester. I finally drove down the little road to it, parked, and went inside the only front door that was well lit.

Inside, it was a long cocktail bar as I had suspected, but the bartender and one male customer was the only occupant. It was confusing, but I waited until I got my scotch and water before asking where the heck was all the drivers of the 20-25 cars in their lot.

"At tables upstairs," he answered motioning towards a door in the back of the room.

I really was too exhausted to desire any conversation, but I was always a nosey one as was my mother. We gotta know what's going on behind that closed door. Finally, after I got a refill of the expensively priced cocktail, I opened the door and started up the stairs.

I could hear the music immediately and it sounded great for a juke box. Then, reaching the top of the enclosed narrow stairways, I found the crowd. They, men and women, were all seated at small tables in a dimly lit room. All staring in my direction with pleasant expressions on their faces, suddenly I realized that the music was coming from behind me.

Turning around, I not only saw there was a well-lit stage with a naked woman doing the bumps and grinds with her dark pussy almost in my face. (I've been told that they shave those little mounds nowadays.) I don't think I every ducked a high, hard fastball any faster than I stooped down below the five-foot high stage waddling out of the audiences line of sight.

What a stupid place to have the stairs leading into a room, I thought as I sought a stool at the bar in the back of the room. Later, watching the floorshow sipping my drinks (now I knew why they were so highly priced), I saw another poor unknowing soul come up the stairs. It was funny watching him cringe as I had, so I guess they had it designed for the kicks it gave some of the customers. I noticed the gals at the tables got the majority of the chuckles from it. The male sights stayed glued to the entertainment on the stage.

I told Gertie about it, but she didn't think it was as funny as I had. She asked me twice if that was my last class at Fullerton.

"I think that's a good thing now that you found that joint," she philosophized.

Surprise Farewell & Retirement Party

She even got more upset a few weeks later. She had taken Debra to the infirmary at March Air Force Base (about 20 miles east of us) for treatment of a painful crick in her neck. I was critically busy at work preparing orders for the ADCOP grads going back to regular Navy duty assignments and David was baby sitting Jeffrey, now two years old. The little guy stood up in a dinning room chair, leaned back, and tipped it over backwards. The chair mashed about a quarter of an inch of flesh off the end of his middle finger.

David got Jo Ann across the street and she had administered first aid to him. Carolyn got home and then the poor gal had to drive Jeff back for stitches. When I got home and saw it, I knew his finger would be alright, just a little crooked at its end. My first thought was that of a typical baseball-minded father:

"Gosh, if he grows up to be a pitcher that crooked digit would make the baseball move oddly giving him an advantage over the hitters," I said aloud.

Carolyn almost beat me up, but when I told the ADCOP guys about it the next night at a surprise farewell and retirement party they gave me, they thought it was funny. The fellows wanted to show their appreciation for the little extras Jeanette and I had given them during their two years at MSAC. They gave her a nice gift and really surprised me with a small commemorative plaque for my retirement desk or trophy case. It has an engraved brass inscription flanked by two CPO gold collar insignia anchors:

**R.R. "BUCK" PEDEN
CHIEF PETTY OFFICER
UNITED STATES NAVY
1950-1970**

Above the inscription, with a maroon felt background, was the four rows of my medals, commendations, citations and campaign ribbons awarded or authorized during my 20 years active service that would end on Oct. 9, 1970, at the Naval Station in Long Beach:

Medals: *National Defense Service (2nd Award), United Nations Service, Korea Service (w/2 Stars), China Service, Viet Nam Service (w/1 Star), Republic of Viet Nam, Combat Action, Meritorious Unit Commendation, and Good Conduct (5th Award).*

Warrant Officer Dick Horne, whose subsequent destination was to be Fight Squadron TWENTY-FOUR, presented me the plaque at the little farewell party. Afterwards, as any inquisitive yeoman would be, I couldn't figure out how he could have found out all those medals and ribbons I possessed. My current service record would only show those awarded during my current enlistment. I finally asked him after a few farewell drinks.

"Buck, I knew you were going to ask that," he said smiling sheepishly. "You remember those new ribbons you had on your dress blues at the graduation ceremony?"

I nodded.

"Well, that's them, compliments of your sweet obliging wife," he said leading the laugher among those still at the waning party. Obviously, all of them knew about it.

Fulltime Civilian At Cal Poly Alma Mata

I hated to see them go as we had become pretty close friends. I took the rest of the leave time I had on the books in September to enable me to get started fulltime in the senior year of my major in Communication Arts and my minor in Physical Education. Oct. 9th I was transferred to the inactive Fleet Reserve in which 20-year Navy veterans are maintained 10 years drawing retainer pay before they are actually retired with the same pay.

I had a portion of my pay provided by the Veteran's Administration as I was deemed 30% disabled due to the injury to my knee. It would eventually deteriorate so bad 25 years later that the joint would have to be completely replaced which would change it to a 40% disablement. I was able to get an extra educational allowance from the U.S.

Government; therefore, with a part-time job on the weekends at a neighborhood liquor & convenience store in Pomona, we made it financially. Plus, Carolyn had been promoted to an administrative assistant's position at MSAC to round out the family income.

Bobby had our '61 F-85, but with a couple wrecks and a transmission failure it was in our garage most of the time. We got a l963 Volkswagen for me with Carolyn motoring to and from work in the new station wagon.

I enjoyed Cal Poly and the instructors in the Communications Department and even served as vice president of its journalism club, Sigma Delta Phi. It held a national convention at Las Vegas one weekend that all our officers attended. I had planned to get a room at the hosting hotel for myself, but the youngsters insisted I join them in their room. There were six of girls, boys, sharing two beds. Fortunately, some of them brought sleeping bags and slept on the floor.

The night before the convention meeting was a night to have at the casino portion of the hotel. I went with our president, but when I suggested we buy some chips and partake in one of the games she refused.

"I would like to play the slot machines, but I don't have any money," she confessed.

I offered to lend her some unsuccessfully. Then I asked her if she would let me give her $20 of my winnings.

"How do your know you're going to win?" she inquired.

"Come on," I said escorting her to the cashier where I gave them a credit card and got $1,000 in chips. Then, we went to a roulette table. I bet $20 on the red and lost. I bet $40 on it again and it repeated the black. Once again I stayed on the red, this time with $80. Another black. When I laid down the $160 on the red again, I hear her gasp as she put her hand over her mouth.

It finally came up red. I had gotten back all that I had lost, so the next bet was only $20 on the red. The ball dropped in on a red number now giving me a $20 profit. I picked up all my chips and left the table handing her the winning chip.

"That was so cool. How come everyone doesn't do that," she asked smiling ear to ear.

"Because of the two green slots. If I had lost twice more, which would mean a very unusual sequence of five blacks in a row, I would have to wager $640. That would be unusual, but possible. The killer to that system of gambling is that if the ball lands in '0' or '00' the house wins all bets on the board. However, as there are 36 numbered red and black slots, the odds are 36-2 against that happening,"

The trip proved financially successful as she won $75 on the $.25 slots and I netted over $200 throwing dice. She enjoyed telling her communication classmate friends about it when we returned and about the booze we bought for a nightcap in our room. I enjoyed being with the young people and sharing some of my experiences with them.

I also had several professors tell me on conclusion of the course that I had been an asset to the class. They admitted that sometimes they had to research some of the questions I asked with my journalistic/ photographic background.

I wasn't too surprised when I attended a seminar class my final semester and I was the only one that raised their hand when the teacher asked who had kept the same major and minor throughout their college career. Young minds of 18- and 19-year-olds are not usually mature enough to know for sure what they want to pursue.

There Were Proud Mothers In Audience

There were many happy mothers in the audience of the June 12, 1971, graduation ceremonies at Cal Poly, but I think Ruby Jane (Tutor) Peden was the proudest. She had walked a couple miles a day on a small, one lane, dirt road to get to and from her little high school in the flatlands of Mississippi, but she had managed it along with her farm hand chores (hoeing, picking cotton, etc.) until she graduated. She was very proud of that accomplishment although her educational achievement was very limited as there was only one teacher instructing all ages in the one room school back then (early 1900s).

All she ever wanted from her kids were to finish high school. I'll never forget the tears in her eyes when I came off the stage with my "sheepskin" for a Bachelor of Science Degree, *with honors*, in Communication Arts. I had studied extra hard, with plenty of help from my loving spouse, to obtain a final a grade point average over 3.60 to earn the *with honors* tag on the diploma containing the signature of Ronald Reagan, Governor of California and President of the Trustees.

Dad, naturally, was pleased as well, but as usual for him, it was not as obvious. He had only finished the 8th grade, but had been very successful with his community grocery business in Fort Pickering. He not only gave credit to customers and handled all his books himself but he even filled out the federal income tax forms for his less illiterate ones for a small fee.

Learning the background history of Cal Poly interested him considerably as he, and I, had stacked many thousands of Kellogg Corn Flakes on the shelves in the grocery store during our lives. Will Keith Kellogg started his breakfast food company in 1906 in Battle Creek, Mich. In the 1920s, as a child's fondness of pet horses named "Spot," formed an Arabian horse ranch in the Pomona Valley that would eventually be the home of the California State Polytechnic University. Now dad was selling insurance with my brother John Lee's insurance company on U.S. Highway 61.

John and his wife Mary (O'Guin), nor their kids Brad and Kelly (now 10 & 8), could make the trip from Memphis. After his hitch in the Navy, John was a mail carrier before opening Peden's Insurance Company. He eventually moved to Brooks Road after dad retired and it is still going strong in that location with its new owners.

Mother and dad only stayed a few days. I immediately started my postgraduate courses for a Master's Degree and a Lifetime Teacher's Credential. I had enjoyed the physical, biological, and anatomical courses I had completed in my minor of PE. Therefore, as I knew I would enjoy teaching and coaching, I would earn the MD in kinesiology. I had heard Cal Poly had an excellent program in that subject and I found it a correct reputation. Also, my first course included a classmate with international track achievements.

Asian Woman Athlete Of 20th Century

Chi Cheng was generally acknowledged as the greatest Asian Woman Athlete of the Twentieth Century. She sat beside me in the first row of the kinesiology class. She was tall, she was beautiful, and she was *very smart*. But her accomplishments that gained her such recognition was when she set, or tied, eight world records and 23 Asian marks in events ranging from the 50-yard dash to the 200-meter hurdles in one year alone (1970).

She won the 100-meter dash with a :11.0 and a :22.4 in the 200-meter while tying the 100-meter in :12.8. She was the U. S. National Champion with an excellent :10.2 seconds in the 100-yard and :22.4 in the 220. At the popular MSAC Relays, she won the 100-yard with a :10.5, the 100-meter hurdles with a :13.3, and the 220-yard hurdles with a :23.2. This outstanding 1970 performance earned her **World Athlete of the Year Award** from the Associated Press and *Track and Field Magazine* (Pete of Brazil, runner-up). For AP's Female AOY, she compiled 572 points to best swimmer Debbie Meyers (176) and tennis star Margaret Court (154). The great football professional George Blanda was AP's Male AOY in 1970.

She gained the bronze medal in the 1968 Olympics with a :10.51 in the 80-meter hurdles. Unfortunately, an injury kept her from competing in the 1972 Olympics in Munich, Germany, but she attended where the officials had specially composed and dedicated a "Welcome to Chi Cheng" song for her prior to opening of the games. The international press had pet names for her such as "Flying Antelope," "Gazelle of the Orient," and "Yellow Blitz."

She was born in Taiwan in 1944 and married Claremont (Calif.)-Mudd College Coach Vice Reel, who brought her to the States. From 1969-70 while competing in college, she would win 153 or the 154 events (sprints, hurdles, long jump, relays) in which she competed. Naturally, Cal Poly inducted her into its Hall of Fame and she is in the International Scholar-Athlete Hall of Fame.

By Jerry Miles

CHI CHENG and I walking from our Master's Degree class in Kinesiology.

She would return to Taiwan in 1980, after a tour as athletic director at University of Redlands (Calif.), and be

elected congresswoman in her native land for three terms. She would also serve as secretary-general of Taiwan's Track and Field Association and as a member of the Olympic Committee playing a key role within Taiwan for China's successful bid to host the 2008 Olympics.

But back to Pomona and Cal Poly's kinesiology class in 1971 where she was competing with me for top score in the class. We were neck-&-neck on our professor's periodic test scores. With our chair/desks side by side, we kidded about our race to be top at the end. The prof was not only an excellent instructor, he made this class race a fun thing. He would give five points on the next test grade to anyone who could get up at the end of any class and tell a joke that related to kinesiology (the study of the muscles and bones interacting in one's body). For the life of me, I couldn't think of a good one, nor did Chi. Then I got a surprise.

Sports Information Director Finally

The job, that had been my goal since working with the SIDs of the SEC colleges and universities in Mississippi and Louisiana, came available. I had got to know Jerry Miles, sports editor of the *Pomona Progress Bulletin*, plus his lovely wife Elaine and son Craig), while keeping stats in the press box for the MSAC football team.

Apparently, I had impressed him with my background as a photo-journalist. He had recently been hired by Cal Poly's Athletic Director, Don Warhurst as an Assistant AD-Business. They had an opening for a new SID and I took the job, provided I could continue my postgraduate work.

This made me very happy as I had reached my zenith. I would write news releases about the Broncos athletic teams, and take pictures for our press guides. I particularly enjoyed watching Chi practicing her sprints. She is the only racer that I had ever seen that held her head perfectly still while all the muscles are churning rapidly underneath it. He balance was immaculate.

I was telling her, after one of our kines classes, that she would be an outstanding professional golfer with her great athletic ability if she devoted as much time practicing golf as she does running, etc. She seemed to like me until I told my joke in class. After that, I'm not sure.

It went like this: Two doctors met in the hallway and greeting each other started sharing information about the interesting patients they had treated lately. One spoke of the one he had yesterday, "She was like this," he said holding his hands in front of his chest with the fingers wide apart and half closed towards him.

"Oh," the other one speculated. "She had an acute case of arthritis of her phalanges (fingers), eh?"

"No," he said pulling his cupped hands closer to his chest. "Excessive adipose tissue here."

The class enjoyed it immensely, I guess, as they applauded well as was necessitated by the professor to insure he would give the five bonus points. Sure enough, Chi and I both aced the final exam, so those points gave me an edge for the fictitious title of "tops in the class."

"You Are Wrong" Coach Of Century

She had been tops in many of her classes as she had a brilliant mind as well as legs, so I don't really think it tarnished our brief friendship. She knew I was not awed with her, but was fond of her as a classmate.

However, I don't know how John Scolinos felt about me. He was the very successful baseball coach at Cal Poly for many years. I know he approved of my SID coverage on his team, as he told me so. But, his reception of my disagreement with him verbally in class, I never knew for certain, although he gave me a "A" in that Advanced Analysis & Theory.

He proclaimed that a player should play within his range of capabilities and not beyond. I respectfully disagreed and told him that I always had goals which may have exceeded my abilities. Some of the times I failed short, but it was better than most with the same

athletic abilities. In other words, I told him, "If I sought — with all my aggression — a .500 batting average, but fell short and only hit .350, I still would have been a successful asset to the team and therefore felt satisfactory. If I projected my capability to be able to hit, at best, .350 and batted .200, I would not.

My actual happening was a good example. I set my goal to become publicity or public relations director of a professional sports franchise with my experience in sports writing and photography. I fell short thus far, but still reached the next rung down on my desired career ladder and was happy there.

Obviously, he knew more about coaching than I probably would ever learn. John went on to coach for 45 years with a 1198-949 career won-lost record, which included three NCAA Division II National Championships and three National Coach of the Year Awards, including four halls of fame. All of this gained him Collegiate Baseball Coach of the Decade (1970s) and Division II Coach of the Century.

Sneaky Way To Get Desired Information

I wanted to know some confidential information about my final goal (such as salaries), but I knew I couldn't acquire it with direct requests in letters. Therefore, I came

up with a sneaky way to do it. I reproduced a simple questionnaire my senior year explaining that I was completing my final research paper to earn a college degree. The key statement in the opening of the questionnaire was:

"Your name or sports team affiliation is not necessary as my report is a general informative paper on all franchises responding. A self-addressed (no return address necessary), stamped envelope is enclosed for your convenience. A few minutes of your time in answering the five questions below would be sincerely appreciated."

The questions were all very simple (e.g. "What will be the toughest problem in a major sports organization that an inexperienced PR employee will have to face?"). The main one was the salary. Most were kind enough to respond, but even if they mailed it from another city (a different postmark resulting) than the franchise for which they were employed, I knew the organization.

Before I had mailed them to all the teams in the NFL, MLB, and NBA, I laid each 8½" x 10" questionnaire on an 14" x 17" master sheet with all the teams listed approximately ½" apart around the outside border of where the query sheet would fit. Then, one sheet at a time, I would lay in that space and put a very minute, light pencil dot on it adjacent to a organization's name. Hence, when it was returned completed by the team PR director, I could reposition it on the master sheet and tell, from the light dot, the franchise.

Shortly after that, I completed my resumes and mailed them to all professional sports organizations. I was two weeks from completing my Lifetime Teacher's Credential, almost eight months later, when I got **THE** call.

By Buck Peden

16-Year-Old Debra and four-year-old Jeffrey prior to a dip in a nearby Chino pool.

———————

BGWW&P Times

1971-75   *Vol. 1, No. 15*   *Chicago, IL*

The Chicago White Sox Call

Sailor Bob Becomes My Investigator

Bob finished high school and went to nearby Chaffee College for a year and then joined the Navy. I didn't learn until after the turn of the century that he had been ignoring draft notices. He said the second notice had mild threats about the FBI, and three months later the notice was not somild so he joined. He qualified on his entrance exam for any billet he wanted following boot training at USNTC, Great Lakes, Ill. He chose Class "A" Gunner's Mate School, also located at Great Lakes. This was going to prove helpful to me in the very near future.

In early August of 1971, we received a phone call on Saturday at 8 a.m. Carolyn came in the bedroom and woke me saying,"There's a phone call for you from Stu Holcomb."

I staggered to the phone half asleep muttering to myself, "Who the hell is Stu Holcomb?" Being on the west coast almost half of a decade, I had forgotten of his best known accomplishments as head football coach at Purdue

University (1947-55). I didn't know he later became Athletic Director at Northwestern University at Evanston, Ill.

"Good morning, Stu," I answered cheerfully just in case it was someone I had met briefly and forgot.

A nice sounding female voice acknowledged, "Mr. Peden?"

"Yes it is."

"Just a moment for Mr. Holcomb," she said.

With all that formality from what must have been a secretary, my head started clearing a little faster.

"Buck, I hope I didn't wake you. It's 10 o'clock here in Cicago, but I know it's only eight there. Anyway, are you still interested in a job with the White Sox?" he asked.

"I sure am, Stu," I said quickly. He was informal so I kept it thus.

"We're looking for a Publicity Director and you certainly have the experience we want. According to your fine resume. I'll be in Anaheim when the team plays California next weekend. I would like you and your family to join me

for dinner at our hotel near the stadium so that I may interview you and also meet your family. If that's acceptable, my secretary will wire you all the details," he concluded.

Naturally, I accepted and thanked him for the opportunity to be considered for the job. The rest of the weekend I was on needles and pins. I telephoned Fred Claire, who was now the Los Angles Dodger Public Relations Cirector, to ask him who Holcomb was with the White Sox.

"He's their top man, Executive Vice President and General Manager to owner John Allyn. If he's going to interview you for that position, why don't you come to our home game tomorrow afternoon and I'll leave you a press box pass. It son't hurt to see what happens in a major league press box before you meet him," he suggested. I had plenty of experiences in large college press boxes such as Ole Mill, Mississippi State, LSU, etc., but nevery in MLB. I promptly agreed to accepted his find offer and was thankful to have the opportunity.

Then, after checking the schedule in the paper, I had the GM School at Great Lakes page my son, Bob. I told him of my upcoming opportunity and asked him to attend the Sox game at Comiskey Park tomorrow. There, I wanted him to interrogate some employees and/or ushers to find out Holcomb's reputation as an administrator and any personality Quirks he may have.

While Bob was doing his research in Chicago, I was enjoying the hospitality of the Dodgers beautiful stadium. Fred gave me a tour before the game and I sat beside him as he manned the media microphone over which he would alert the radio, television, and print media booths of any noteworthy events in which they would be interested (e.g. pinch hitter John Smith on deck, Bill Jones warming up in bullpen for Dodgers, etc.). I studied his newsy pre-game notes distributed to all press box inhabitants and was able to answer one of my questions in slack moments. It was very educational for me and I let him know how much I appreciated it afterwards.

Bobby was able to accomplish his mission, also, and gave me a glowing report. Holcomb was in the early stages of revamping the organization after Allyn had bought out his brother, Arthur, in 1969 to become sole owner of the famous Chicago American League team. John hired Stu, who was well liked and respected by everyone Bobby contacted. Even the fans he talked to in the stands had praise for the man. His report even added more fuel to my already boiling pot of anticipation.

The rest of the week I did my homework on Holcomb's past so I would be well prepared for the upcoming interview. I learned that he gained his notoriety after coaching football championship teams at Purdue, Miami, and West Point. He also coached in three shrine All-Star Games, twice as head coach. He also coached baseball at Findlay, Muskingum, and West Point to round out 24 years as an athletic mentor which he followed with 11 years as an Athletic Director at Northwestern University. He is a member of the Pennsylvania Sports & Helms Football HOFs.

The First Year, Then The Second

As directed by Stu's secretary, we motored down to Anaheim only about 30 miles southwest, and telephoned Mr. Holcomb's suite from the hotal loffby. H came down immediately and met us. He had to be impressed with my lovely wife, who was very colorfully dressed in a beautiful dress and daughter, who looked gorgeous in a colorful adult dress. Both had "dishwater blonde" hair. Deb was 17 then and definitely a full grown women. I had started calling her "BB" as she had a big/beautiful butt like her mother. Although it became inappropriate after motherhood, I still use it.

David was a typical looking young baseball player. He was running the mile daily, as Bobby had done, and looked in perfect boyhood health. I learned to regret that I had corrected his natural baseball swing that cut down on the ball slightly. I worked steadily with him to make him swing straight through the ball. I'm sure that Mr. Holcomb saw him as an athletic youngster and a well-mannered boy as he answered all of Stu's questions with a "yes, sir" or a "no, sir."

Then he said, "I apologize for not having dinner with you, but I'm on the Rose Bowl Committee and we had a luncheon meeting this noon that just ended a few minutes ago. The rest of the committee is waiting for me in my suite. You lovely people enjoy your meal, compliments of the White Sox, and I'll meet with Mr. Peden in my suite afterwards."

I knew from his words and the sincerity in his voice that my family had given me a lead-off hit for this job interview. Obviously, I had the background experience and education for this job. All I had to do was prove my character to him. I thought about this all the way through the luscious meal we consumed. Then, I went to his suite and knocked on the door, leaving my family in the lobby to look at the many California Angels and Gene Autry souvenirs in the shops.

"Come in," Mr. Holcomb directed as he opened his door. There were three or four elderly gentlemen at his dinning room le. Which he waved off as the rest of the Rose Bowl Committee and told them my name. "We're almost through with our game of cards and I'll be right with you. Just have a seat in the living room."

It wasn't a long wait and, after complimenting me on a fine looking family, he began the interview. I detected the change in senses as he talked. At first, it was a general sense: "The publicity director for the White Sox must deal with all the media and in Chicago it is enormous, etc."

Then, as the intercourse progressed, I noticed it shifted to the future perfect tense: "If we were to hire you, you would be required to prepare our scorebooks and oversee the Sox-O-Grams on the scoreboard, etc."

I'm responding all along the interview, so he must have liked my answers or the way I was answering as he moved into the present tense: "When hired, you would have all expenses paid and during Spring Training in Florida, you would have a rental car at your disposal."

He asked my last salary in the Navy and I told him it was $9,500 a year, plus an allowance for my dependents. Then he asked what the White Sox would have to pay me to work for them.

I'm sure my face was twisted in deep thought, as I knew what and how I answered was very important. Then, I smiled as it came to me:

"I really want this job so how's about I will pay the White Sox the first year, and they can pay me what they think I'm worth the second year."

That cinched it. He got up out of his chair and offered his hand saying, "You're hired. How about the salary of a first year major league player, $13,500, plus all your moving expenses."

We didn't sign a contract, but I've thought many times how nice it would have been to have one stating I would always be paid the minimum salary of a ML rookie. It's well over $200,000 last time I looked.

He went down to the lobby and welcomed Carolyn and the kids into the Chicago White Sox family. We stayed for the game with box seats just behind the White Sox dugout, compliments of Mr. Holcomb, of course. I don't remember who won or anything that happened during the game or on road returning home, I was floating on cloud nine.

Told Me I'm Crazy In Seven Languages

I told Miles and Warhurst the next day giving them the required two weeks notice of departure. Then, I found the professor who was teaching my final class required for obtaining a Lifetime California Teacher's Credential. The succeeding quarter of student teaching in journalism would have been a snap for me with my experience in the newspaper business and my instructor training & teaching at the Naval Reserve Training Centers in Natchez and Huntsville.

I had so many loose ends to accomplish before I reported to the CWS the first of September that there was no way I could attend the final four classes necessary to complete the course. For example, I had to train my successor how to handle the SID chores, close out my records with the VA school financing, buy some clothes (I only had one decent suit with its several matching ties), decide on a new automobile, etc. I tried to explain all this to the professor, but he tried to reason with me.

"But, you are passing the course. If you like, I will give you a special assignment to complete to make up for the final few weeks. You can work on it at home and turn it in to me for approval," was his suggestion. I finally told him I had no time for any of that. My door of opportunity had knocked and I was not going to let anything keep me from answering it with a clear mind. At that time, teaching school was the far most priority in my thoughts.

The senior professor was an elder statesman who could speak in seven different languages.

"You're crazy," he said to me in all of them, one at a time.

His evaluation had some merit. I would, a few times later in my life, wished I had qualified for the credential. The special assignment would not have been difficult and California may have waived my student teaching requirement if I had only proved my years of instructing in the Navy. Tsk, tsk, tsk...pshaw, pshaw, pshaw. 'Tis all academic now.

I needed a car in Chicago and that was a fact. The old VW would never make the long drive, so Debra got it. I shopped to local car dealers and found a '71, 4-door sedan, dark green Fiat that I liked. I called Stu and told him of my feeling and he put me in touch with the Director of Park Operations, Ed Holstein. Holstein knew a Fiat dealer where he lived in Oaklawn, Ill. He told me there would be one waiting there when I arrived.

We threw a farewell party for me at our house. We decided it would be best for me to move there and find a house. I knew I would be smothered with work hours while learning the ropes and setting up my department.

Plus, and it was an important reason for Debra, a delay of moving the family until next summer would permit her to graduate with her friends, particularly her best friend Brenda Galvin. Also, Debra had starred in the school play "The Curious Mrs. Savage" and was a very student at Chino High. Moving to Chicago her senior year would dim the glitter she had gained.

In addition to our family there and the Le Vernes from San Diego, we had my MSAC secretary and the Vescios, Vern & Jody, at the party. Carolyn was working with Jody and we had tipped a few many times at their home in Walnut. We always enjoyed their company.

My Residence: Old Windermere Hotel

I flew in with two new large suitcases and my reel to reel tape player. It also had a slot for eight-track tapes. I brought a few of my favorite musical reels and a couple of the latter tapes, including one just out Bobby had correctly suggested I get, *Close to You* by the Carpenters. I adored it immediately.

Johnny Mc Namara, an employee for the Sox, met me at O'Hare Airport with a company vehicle and drove to the Windermere Hotel on the south side of Chicago, only a block from Lake Michigan on 56th Street. It had been recommended to me by

Holstein as it housed many bachelor players throughout the WS history. In fact, the Sox trainer, Charlie Saad, had been rooming there during baseball season over a decade.

After I checked in my little room (living room/bedroom combination, kitchenette, and a bathroom), Johnny drove me to White Sox Park on West 35th Street at Dan Ryan Expressway (I-94). The first employee I met was the switchboard operator of several decades, Irene Kerwin. Between calls, we talked briefly as she was expecting me to arrive that morning. Then introduced me to Marilyn "Mickey" Yunker coming out of the accounting office. Mickey took me into the office adjoining the huge switchboard Irene controlled. There she introduced me to "Dizzy."

I know I must have appeared dumbstruck when she said his real name was Paul Trout. I had been raised following the Memphis Chickasaws' parent club in the '40s, the Detroit Tigers. They finished second in the American League in '44 & '46 and went all the way in "45 defeating the Cubs in the World Series. They had only lost the pennant to the upstarts St. Louis Browns by one game in '44. Diz won 27 games and led the league with a 2.12 earned run average and 33 complete games. His southpaw teammate Hal Newhouser won 29 that same year and in later years when Virgil Trucks got back from his military service, the media called the three of them TNT (Trucks-Newhouser-Trout) and the public adored it.

WINDEMERE NITECAP by (L-R) Connie Uhrig, me, Margi Menzel, & Marilyn Yunker following Margi's retirement following her many years at White Sox Park.

Trout hit with power, too. He won a few of his own games with his home runs. I was pleased to know I would be working with this big guy who was doing community relations work for the Sox. He would show me around the huge metropolis and nearby towns during the off season. We played in many benefit golf tournaments representing the White Sox organization and he was introducing me to many important contacts.

That first day, he also introduced me to a secretary, who would share her duties between us. She was Antoinette "Tonka" Scalise, a member of the Croatian families that made up the community around 35th Street in those days. She greeted me with sincere warmth that made me like her right away. Then, after showing me my desk, she immediately took me to meet Stu's secretary, Connie Uhrig. She was a slim, small young lady, with lots of makeup around her eyes.

"So you're Buck Peden. I couldn't wait to meet you to find out why Mr. Holcomb had picked you out of a stack of resumes three feet high," she said smiling radiantly and offering her hand.

"Well, I hope ya'll won't be too disappointed," I said taking it and kissing its back.

"Ohhhh, he's a southerner, ya'll," she said mocking me to Tonka. "I love to hear you southerner's drawl."

I laughed along with them, but it threw me a little off balance. I thought I had lost my southerner drawl years ago while sailing the seas with hundreds of non-southerners. But, I was wrong as Connie would let me know about it the instant it got out of my mouth. She completely broke me of saying I'm "fixing" to do something, or, "fixing" to go down town.

We all ate lunch in a dinning area of the famous Comiskey Bard's Room. The male's usually sat together apart from the gossiping females. When I would say something and hear a giggle coming from the girls, I would always glance quickly at Connie. If she glanced at me and smiled, I knew I had said some southern slang word that she thought was funny. It didn't make me angry. In fact, I grew to adore her tremendously.

That first day sitting in her office waiting for Stu's visitor to leave, she answered a lot of my preliminary questions about the employees and the neighborhood, in which she lived with her family near Tonka's home.

Intros & Tour Time

Stu really greeted me enthusiastically . He briefed me about my key mentor, who would be their traveling secretary, Donald Unferth. Don had been with the club over 20 years and had been keeping its history updated annually. Howie Roberts, a retired sportswriter, had been the publicity director for several years, but Stu said Don would be more knowledgeable about the overall picture of the organization. I found this to be true to a huge degree. He would become extensively valuable to my indoctrination into the wide world of the public's consumption of Major League Baseball.

With his background experience and my ideas, we made a good pair with our desks side by side in the publicity office. Stu sent me on the road with the team on their last trip to the west coast that season. It enabled Don and I plenty of time to chat on the plane the Sox chartered.

Before we left I met most of the front officer personnel. Roland Hemond was the Director of Player Personnel and had just been hired at the end of the '70 season along with Field Manager Chuck Tanner. Little Glenn Miller (about 5'1" in height) was the Farm Director along with C.V. Davis, Jr., his assistant and Player Development Director. C.V. and I became immediate friends when we learned we had both worked for the Chickasaws as kids in Memphis. Neither of us remembered meeting back then.

Vice President Leo Breen was the business manager & treasurer and Roy Milostan was his Assistant Treasurer & Accountant. Tom Maloney the Ticket Manager. Millie Johnson and I would work closely in preparation of the scorebooks in her capacity as Promotions Director.

Ernie Carroll was the black Chef of the Bard's Room and the senior employee. He was hired by Charles "Old Roman" Comiskey at age 12 and would work there until he died 66 years later. He always helped churches and children organizations. He was as well known in baseball circles around Chicago as any Hall of Famer.

Stu introduced me to all of them and later took me on a tour of the field where I met the Grounds Superintendent, Gene Bossard. The outfield grass was immaculate. The infield was artificial, which eliminated many rainouts.

Then he showed me through the press box which had the owner's booth, which he and John Allyn — sometimes accompanied by their families — on the far left. The Sox TV booth was next where Jack Drees and Bud Kelly toiled. Ralph Faucher and Harry Caray handled the radio broadcasts in the next booth and the visiting team's radio was in the next one. Both radio booths were very small.

Next was the large, three-row press box for the Public Address announcer, Bob Finnegan, in the left corner of the front row with my station and all my operating equipment in the second row above him. The two wire services, Association Press (Joe Mooshil) and United Press International (Ed Sainsbury) were in the right end of the front row, with their teletype operators up in the third row. The visiting TV booth was down in a auxiliary booth hanging from the roof down the third base line.

The four Chicago Metropolitan newspapers occupied the middle of row one with the rural area papers seated in the second and third rows. Also, to everyone's delight, there were free hot dogs, soda, and beers on the second row as one enters the box.

The press box wasn't near as big as Dodger Stadium's, but it was the largest one in which I had ever worked. Cal Poly and MSAC were 80% smaller.

There was an elevator leading to the upper deck and then to the press box. Instead of walking up the ramps with their portable typewriters and brief cases, all the media personnel used the elevator. Its operator on game days was a black man named Virgil Taylor. He always kept a highball setting on one of the inside rails. Occasionally, he'd come into the Bard's Room with his large cup held about a 12-ounce drink.

"Tighten it up a little, Johnny," he would say to Mc Namara, the bartender. Then, he would break out a wad of greenbacks big enough to choke a horse and tip Johnny a buck or two. The drinks

and beer were free to anyone allowed privilege to the historic room.

The poor guy was found dead at the bottom of the elevator shaft one morning after a night game. The speculation was that he got drunk and accidentally fell down there, but none of us believed it. He was known to lend money to his "brothers" at a tremendous rate of return interest. My guess was one of them that owed him a lot of money bashed him in the head, took all of his money, and then dumped him down the shaft.

My First Home Game

Stu sat beside me in the press box showing me how to correct the scoreboard and use the microphone for announcements through all the media boxes. Bob Finnegan, the public address announcer, was seated in the first row directly below me so I could give him the information I may have received from the dugouts of the managers making player changes. I would always announce it to the media first over my mike before he broadcasted it out to the fans.

I was very nervous with Stu sitting next to me and watching every move I made, but I kept my score sheet as I always did and that was old hand to me. Then, suddenly, everyone in the press box started clapping and cheering. I saw the reason immediately. It was for me. Stu had put a message on the scoreboard that read:

**Welcome to
Buck Peden
New Sox
Publicity Director**

It was the first time I had ever seen my name in lights and definitely the largest ovation I had ever received as the 30,000-or-so fans cheered also. One fan was to be a huge asset to my getting to know Chicago baseball. It was the former member of VC-61 who was a barber at NAS Miramar that always cut my hair, Kevin Huffstetter. When I got his note delivered to me that night in the press box, I remembered him distinctly because of AL umpire Russ Goetz's many letters to his VC-61 teammates over the years. Many things would happen between the Huffstetter and the Peden families the next three-plus decades, but here's what he wrote about that night at WSP (ed. note: 1967-75, Comiskey Park before & since then), which was publicized in some publication after the turn of the 21st century:

"One night at Comiskey Park was not only memorable, but the events of the evening would have a direct bearing on the lives of two families. The events that led to this night began 20 years before when for a brief time (ed. note: five games) I was on the squadron softball team with Russ Goetz and Buck Peden. Russ and I would later play an entire season with the station team at Miramar, but Peden was on a detachment to Korean waters by then (ed. note: Peden had been transferred to VF-783 that embarked on the USS ORISKANY (CVA-34). Buck seemed like a good guy as a teammate but we never became buddies or went on liberty together.

"After the Navy I didn't see nor hear from him, but Russ kept in touch with us both (via Christmas cards & letters). Russ (then an America League umpire) had told me that (White Sox field manager) Chuck Tanner had informed him that Peden was the favorite to be named the White Sox Publicity Director. That is why I was not completely surprised to see…(the welcome message)…flashed on the big screen in center field. I told my companion of that evening, (his son) Steve Huffstetter, that I knew the new Sox employee had played ball with him in the Navy. I had an idea, so Steve and I made our way to the Press Box in the upper deck behind home plate. As soon as the game ended I sent a note up with the attendant at the press box gate reintroducing myself and offering my congratulations. As we awaited a reply I thought to myself how ridiculous I would be in the eyes of my first born if no one showed. Just about the time I was berating myself for my impetuosity, the man himself came bounding down the steps and greeted us more warmly and sincerely than I had any right to expect. And so began the first of many good times shared by these two ex-sailors, their wives, and their families."

Goetz had always written in his letters so positively about "Huff" that I used that nickname when I burst out the door to greet him. There were still fans in abundance around them, but I remembered Kevin's appearance as my barber more than as a ballplayer. We talked briefly and he invited me to his home in a little town in Indiana about 17 miles southwest of South Bend called Walkerton.

The Wonderful Huffstetter Family

I would drive down there for weekend visits many times during that first winter in Chicago. His wife Carol was not only a delightful hostess but a wonderful cook as well. Yorkshire Pudding was her specialty and a new dish for this middle-aged southern lad who had enjoyed many Navy and foreign concoctions, but never that delicious English meal she prepared so tastefully. Her six children and frequent dinner guest Kevin's father Ken, a long-time Walkerton resident approaching 90, all enjoyed it as much as I.

THE LOVEABLE HUFFSTETTER KIDS:
Dan, Anne, Steve, Delia, John, & Mary

Their kids were Stephen, 12; Delia, 10; twins Mary & Anne, 9; John, 8; and Daniel, 6. They had a field next to their small house on which we played softball and other games. A few years later, with Kevin teaching speech in high school and Carol teaching in grammar school, they bought a new larger house with a built on garage, four bedrooms, including one in the basement with another bathroom along with a family room and a little bar. Kevin, a talented ball handler in basketball, also built a cement half-court in their backyard so we added that sport to our fun. I also got to meet Kevin's younger brother Mickey and some of Carol's family: brothers George & Ed and sister Donna Kessel.

All things considered, they were very warm and receptive to my visits and I frequently referred to them as my second family. Later, after my family joined me and we had our

house, they would come up to visit us in Chicago. We spent many fun times together over the 12 years we were there. Kevin was so knowledgeable of the White Sox that, next to Unferth, he was the most helpful source of my acquiring a thorough background of the club's history. Being the public speaker that he was, I eventually got him the title as the WS's Indiana Representative.

We printed him some business cards and at any requests for a WS speaker from organizations in Indiana, he would perform as our We printed him some business cards and at any requests for a WS speaker from organizations in Indiana, he would perform as our rep. While he didn't receive any pay from us, his season pass to any WS home game for him and the seven member of his family was beneficial. Plus, almost all of the organizations requesting a speaker would pay an honorarium. Therefore, we were happy, he and his family were happy, and the organizations were happy.

My First White Sox Trip On The Road

On the plane to the west coast, I finally got to meet Chuck Tanner and his coaches: Luke Appling, Johnny Sain, Joe Lonnett, Al Monchak, Jim Mahoney, and Glen Rosenbaum. Appling and Sain I had read about, but I hadn't heard of the others.

Tanner started his eight year major league career with a bang! In his first at bat in the majors with the Milwaukee Braves on April 12, 1955, he slammed a home run on the first pitch in his first time at bat. He only 20 had more the rest of his tour in the big leagues as an outfielder for Milwaukee, Chicago Cubs, Cleveland Indians, and the California Angels but he finished with a decent .261 batting average.

He started managing for Quad Cities in the Midwest League (Class A) in 1963. From there he moved up to El Paso of Texas (AA), Seattle & finally Hawaii of Pacific Coast (AAA) where they led the southern division. He and Hemond joined the White Sox at the end of its horrendous 56-106 last place season and he inspired the lads enough in his first full year to a 79-83 mark for third place in the western division this year. I enjoyed the last month of it especially

meeting every member of the team.

Wilbur Wood would post his first of four straight 20+ victorious seasons with a 22-13 mark and an ERA (1.91) second only to Cy Young winner Vida Blue's 1.82. Tom Bradley (15-15, 2.96) and Bart Johnson (12-10, 2.93) were the other two Sox pitchers that maintained sub-3.00 ERAs.

While we were in Oakland, Johnson ignited a team fight with their first baseman, Mike Epstein. Bart bunted a teammate over but when Epstein fielded it, Johnson stopped running down the line where Epstein was waiting with the ball to tag him. Then when Mike started for Johnson to tag him out, Bart back-peddled away from him. Epstein, noted for his short temper anyway, slammed Johnson to the ground with the ball in his hand. Both benches emptied and I had my 200 MM lens filming so I caught several good shots of it at ground level.

Breen liked it so much, he got Millie to use it on our 1972 season pocket schedules as "The Fighting White Sox For 1972."

I talked a lot with Tommy John, but he would be a key in a trade at the winter meetings, so that friendship would not get past the budding stage. Luke Appling was a swell talker and I would ensure I sat near him during our motel pool conversation. In all my years in MLB, I never tired

of hearing the old timers talk about their exploits in this great American game.

Appling became so very frustrated with the phenomenon rookie shortstop from LSU. His name was Lee "Bee Bee" Richard and he was a slim black athlete with extreme speed on the base paths and wide range at the shortstop position. He also possessed a rifle arm. His only problems afield were routine ground balls hit straight at him. Luke said he had too much time to think about it is the reason he booted them so frequent. He fielded almost everything in the hole between third and short and well behind second base. He made those look easy.

Luke once said, "Richard was so fast that he could run through hell with gasoline drawers."

I watched Luke lecturing him about what he did wrong and Richard looked him straight in the eyes as Luke talked. But, to me, Lee's eyes looked glazed as if he wasn't paying a bit of attention to the coach's words. Poor lad would get four trips to the majors during his next five years and his ast one in 1976 with the Cardinals. He finished with a .209 batting and a .923 fielding average. Thousands of young players fail to make it, but I never saw one during my 12 years that had the outstanding skills he possessed.

Melton's Exciting Season Finale

Bill Melton, on the other hand, was having another outstanding year with his bat. In 1970, with the lowly Sox, he had hit a total of 33 home runs, a record number in the club's 70-year history books. We returned home with him in the thick of a race for the club's first individual AL Home Run Championship with Detroit's Norm Cash and Oakland's Reggie Jackson.

The latter two would end their regular season tied with

By Buck Peden

BILL MELTON

32 home runs. Melton made it a three-way tie with two home runs in his last regularly scheduled game to the delight of the hometown fans. Luckily, the White Sox had to play one more game to makeup a rained out contest with Milwaukee.

I had a fresh roll of slow color film in my camera with my 200 MM lens attached. I wanted to get a shot of Bill hitting and one of anything he would do if he drilled another four-bagger

afterwards. I caught him in the tunnel of White Sox Park leading

to the Sox dugout before the game. We had become friends on the last road trip, so he stopped to talk to me.

"I got slow film in my camera today and I wanta make sure I'm in focus for anything you might do *when* you hit the big home run. What are your plans?"

I purposely made sure I didn't say "*if*" he hit it to be positive. He reacted the same way.

"Well, I'll probably tip my cap to the fans when I step on home plate, I guess. What did you think I was going to do?" he asked.

"I'll be ready for that. I just wanted to make sure you weren't going to do something unexpected like throwing your cap to the fans for a souvenir. If I wasn't in exact focus, it would burled," I explained.

Sure enough, a dead pull-hitter, he soundly pounded a breaking ball from Bill Parsons for his 33rd home run. I was lucky enough to catch him just at the finish of the swing for a great shot in next year's scorebook and on our '72 media guide. I also stayed in focus at home plate to get his tipping his cap to the fans.

Happy and exciting I advanced my film while watching as he entered the dugout. Then he stopped and **threw his damn cap to the fans!**

I was too exhilarated to be

pissed, but I've had fun telling about it over the years.

Bill's fearlessness at the plate got him hit 11 times (2nd most in league) and his aggressiveness afield got him the second most assists and total chances of any third baseman. His .9682 even earned him a slight better fielding average of the touted hot-sacker at Baltimore Brooks Robinson's .9681.

The team finished with a 79-83 record for third place behind Oakland and Kansas City in the AL Western Division. It was 31 more victories than the horrendous '70 campaign. Tanner had accomplished more than anyone expected.

Busy Off-Season Activities Were Many

I was enjoying my new Fiat and was very glad I had it because of the working the late hours I was putting in at my office reorganization. Many days Dizzy and I would attend benefit golf tournaments as representatives from the White Sox. He would hit tremendous drives with his power, but I would usually outscore him a stroke or two with my soft touch with the wedge and my hot Bull's Eye Putter. This always aggravated him, or so he acted. We became very close and he had me come to his home in South Holland, Ill., to meet his wife Pearl and their 10 kids for several dinners. Pearl was a wonderful cook and a lovely person. Their son Steve would become a major league southpaw pitcher through the Sox system and also played for the Cubs during his 12 years (1978-89).

I would finally get to my room between 9 and 10 p.m., and open a can of soup or something similar while I listened to my recorded music. I must have played the Carpenter's "Close to You" song and the rest of that eight-track 500 times or more that winter. I would go to sleep listening to it and the machine automatically turned off at the conclusion. In subsequent years, I purchased everything Richard & Karen Carpenter recorded. We would even get to see them perform on stage in Chicago. And when Karen died of anorexia, I was so sad that I actually shed tears as I am sure many of her other fans did.

Usually, I was tired by the end of a long busy day and would last less than an hour after I got to my room. One of such nights, I got a phone call that awoke me at 2 a.m. Carolyn, Vern, and Jody were out on the town and had decided to let me verbally get in on their fun. I could tell they were tanked and having a ball, but it was not funny to me as exhausted as I was. When Gertie finally got on the phone, I told her so. She apologized and said she had tried to talk them out of it and promised it wouldn't happen again that late at night. It was only midnight there in the Los Angeles area, so — being a little tipsy — they

probably didn't think of the time difference. However, at least they were thinking of me so I shouldn't have been as rude as I had been. I regretted it afterwards.

I was involved in preparing our media guide for the upcoming season. Also, I had 14"x17" mounted black and white prints of action photographs I had taken the last month of the season placed all around the publicity office and some larger ones in the hallway leading from the offices to the Bard's Room. John Allyn was impressed with my photography, as he was a very knowledgeable photographer himself, and introduced me to the manager of a huge camera store. He told me to buy what equipment I needed for the upcoming season. This enabled me to buy a 500 MM lens and a multiple-frame pack. I could now shoot a sequence with my 35 MM camera (i.e. a batter swinging with maybe six still-frames of the swing in stop action, perfectly focused). I couldn't wait to use it in action.

My Initial MLB Winter Meetings

The first week in December was traditionally when Major League Baseball held its annual Winter Meetings. All club owners, major executives, field managers and major team scouts would attend for meetings in their respective categories of the game. It was

when major internal business took place between owners and the Commissioner of Baseball announced any major business from his lofty office.

The general managers talked trades from the beginning of the meetings until the end. Naturally, the field managers and each club's major scouts were involved in these discussions. We had top scouts Fred Shaffer and Walt Widmayer there to aid Holcomb, Hemond, and Tanner in making decisions in trades.

I flew in by myself at the busy Phoenix Airport and, after getting my suitcase, stood on the curb waiting my turn for a cab to the Scottsdale hotel where the meetings were held. I was next when an elder man tried to get in the cab.

"Hey, this is my cab," I said grabbing the cab's door handle.

"I'm sorry. Are you here to attend baseball's Winter Meetings?" he asked

When I nodded, he smiled and added, "I am too. How's about sharing the cab with me to the Arizona Biltmore and we'll split the fare?"

I agreed and we rode in relative silence. Apparently, he wasn't very friendly and I didn't have anything to say to someone who had tried to jump line on me.

When we got there, he gave me a $1.25 for his half of the fare. I added mine and a 50-cent tip for the driver. A miser, I thought when he didn't tip the cabby. Then, inside he walked straight pass the desk clerk to the elevator with the hotel attendant carrying his bags.

As I checked in I asked the clerk why the guy didn't register as I had noticed he had greeted the man.

"Oh, that's Mr. Del Webb. He's an owner of the hotel," he said softly.

Gee whiz, Del Webb was a multiple millionaire and one of the major owners of the New York Yankees. He split the taxi fare with me and he could have bought the cab. I just shook my head and went to my room. I unpacked the properly numbered ties, shirts, etc. that matched according to my wife's great taste of dress.

I had dinner that night with Holcomb, Hemond, Tanner, and Unferth. The other couple of nights I ate with Unferth and once with Shaffer and Widmayer. After dinner, the teams would have scouts scattered all over the lobby talking to other scouts or general managers. It was trade time for many of the clubs. I stuck pretty close to Unferth and Davis to pump them with questions, usually about who was who.

Several I knew by sight, such as Ted Williams, Stan Musial, and Billy Martin. Ted, who would manage the Texas Rangers in '72 even more poorly (54-100) than he had the last two years at Washington (133-188), was showing some of the other managers how to

properly hold a golf club. I had learned a little differently, but I kept my mouth shut as nobody knew me.

However, C.V. and I stopped in the suite the Hillerich & Bradsby had, which was primarily a small bar with bat samples and sofas/chairs to sit, chat, and have a cool one.

Lefty Gomez, everyone's favorite deviate hurler was there, admitted he never hit the ball very hard. "In fact," the great southpaw said, "I never broke a bat in my life until yesterday when I ran over one backing out of the garage."

He always denied throwing a spitball, "I never threw one but I used to sweat very easily."

Also, Musial was in attendance as their most notable representative. It was so casual, and everyone was so friendly, I found myself feeling at ease. Maybe it was the several cocktails I had consumed. Anyway, I shocked the hell outa C.V.

Told Great Musial He Was Wrong

"Stan," I asked holding a regular baseball bat and a slim fungo bat, "if the fungo bat wouldn't break, with which bat do you think you could hit the ball farther?"

"The thick-barreled bat," the seven times NL Batting Champion with 475 home runs answered without hesitation.

"Wrong," I said to C.V.'s dismay. "The distance of a ball hit is determined by

the velocity of the striking element, which this light fungo bat can be swung with much more velocity than this much heavier thick-barreled one."

While C.V. was having a "hissy" over me telling one of the greatest hitters in baseball history he was wrong about anything that had to do with batting, Musial and the rest of the baseball men in the room didn't argue with me. I could tell they were mulling it over in their minds.

One other time I would get C.V.'s goat that year during lunch at White Sox Park. I had learned from my golf readings and substantiated by my instructions in my kinesiology study for a Master's Degree, that the bottom hand of the grip in golf or baseball is the power hand. The other hand is more of a guiding hand. We were arguing about it when Melton, the new AL home run champion, comes out of a contract meeting with Holcomb.

C.V. grabs him and says, "Tell Buck here which is your power hand on the bat."

"My left hand," he said immediately. "The bottom hand is always the power hand as it slings the bat through the hitting zone with terrific speed. My right arm is stronger, so I woulda hit more homers if I could have batted left-handed."

Fortunately, Davis got over both those incidents, although I know it must have hurt his ego after being player development director for the Sox many years. Back at Scottsdale, we had a nightcap in the hotel bar and enjoyed a private performance of the great former second baseman Billy Martin, now managing the Detroit Tigers, giving his rendition of the comical way second sackers during his era made the double-play execution with opponents coming in with high spikes. It was hilarious. Billy always shone his brightest in the bar room lights. It may have been dim, but after he arrived, it glimmered with fun and mirth.

I attended the public relations meetings and got welcomed from the dais by Chicago Cubs' Chuck Shriver, NL spokesman, and Hal Middlesworth of the Tigers, the AL spokesman. They asked me as a newcomer to their ranks if I had any PR suggestions to contribute to the group. I suggested that MLB strongly move to have highlight film produced each weekend as the NFL does. MLB has nothing I explained. One of the networks had a Saturday afternoon game, and that was it. I told them virtually all clubs have their games televised and there must be a way we could get highlights to a central point and mesh them for a MLB weekly show. It took a few years, but it was accomplished with PR directors making video recordings and sending it, along with a typed play-by-play of the game, overnight to a

new MLB department formed to handle it and other such items, Major League Baseball Promotions Corporation.

About the third day, Stu told me they weren't making any progress with any trades so I might as well get back to Chicago. I must have just got on the plane and they made a deal with the Dodgers. I walked up the stairs to my office and was greeted by the switchboard operator, Irene:

"Well, I wasn't expected you back so soon after the trade."

"What trade?" I shockingly asked.

"We got Richie Allen for Tommy John and (infielder) Steve Huntz. Didn't you know?" Trout answered behind her.

I explained why I left early, but I was very disappointed that I wasn't there to do my duties when the trade was announced. Stu called shortly thereafter and apologized. He said Tanner and Hemond thought it was a good trade, which we would learn later was an understatement. He explained Tanner knew Allen well as a young Pennsylvania lad born in Wampum only 20 miles south of Chuck's home in New Castle, Pa. Holcomb instructed me to use "Dick" not "Richie" as the Phillies had called him after their fine hitting outfielder several decades earlier, Richie Ashburn. Ashburn was their color man on Philadelphia's current broadcast team. Tanner said his name was Richard and

all his friends knew him as Dick. So it was, everything I published emphasized the first name that was new to the U.S. baseball public.

My Infamous Christmas Party

Meanwhile, the Sox had a employee Christmas dinner dance at the top of a downtown hotel. I went alone in my Fiat parking it in the hotel underground lot. The dinner was early with the band playing appropriate music. It was very informal and I was sitting at a table of 10 of the front office executives and their spouses. As I was a new employee, I didn't know anyone too well yet, except my secretary, Trout, Unferth, and Davis. But, when the band started playing dance music I came out of my shell. As I was very fond of dancing, I started asking the females at the table to be my partner. Milostan had the huge bottle of whiskey in front of him sitting next to me. Every time I would finish a dance, he would have me a full glass of whiskey and some kind of chaser. I would drink any kind of chaser in those days, then water, and finally on the rocks with a dash of soda or water.

The band was terrific and played the jitterbug pieces at my favorite tempo. I danced practically every dance and had some of the girls at the other tables coming to ask me to dance. I was in heaven, but the dancing gave me a great thirst, consequently I almost chugalugged my drinks that Milostan kept filled to the brim.

I remember enjoying dancing with Mickey Yunker and Nancy, C.V. Davis' wife, as he didn't dance that I saw. He was having fun pulling his latest "knock-knock" joke on all of the gals in a low-cut dress. He'd have them put their temple up against his and say:

"Knock knock."

"Who's there?" they'd innocently ask.

"Emma."

"Emma who?"

"Emma some nice boobs you got there," he'd climax. He would laugh at his joke as much as the victim. He always had a good sense of humor and loved people. Their children had excellent dispositions, also.

"Walk That Line Straight, Boy!"

When the wonderful night ended, several asked me if I needed a ride home. The top echelon had already left the party so I had really "let my hair down" as the girls say. I really felt great. I had eaten well and was enthusiastic in my informal communicating and dancing with my new "shipmates."

The cold air in the underground parking gave me a jolt and it continued until I got the heater in the car warming me. That, and the soothing sound of the soft music on my car radio, was too much for my tired body.

I started having to fight sleep. The Chicago neighborhood through which I was driving did not look too receptive to an intoxicated Southern white boy, elaborately dressed, in a new Fiat, taking a nap on the side of their street. So, I kept slapping myself on the cheek and trying to stay awake.

It was about 3 a.m. in the morning; therefore, there was virtually no traffic but me. Jerking my head up from a doze, I knew I was not driving perfectly. Then it happened. The Chicago Police flashed me to the curb. They put me through their routine of that era. The main thing was walking a straight line. I didn't do well at all, so they hauled me to jail.

I was given one phone call. It was a tough decision, because my wife in California couldn't help me and I certainly didn't want to call Mr. Holcomb or Mr. Allyn. C.V. would know the predicament I was in and had been with the Sox long enough to "know the ropes." He was there in about an hour and had me out on bond. I went to the lawyer he recommended and he beat the case by telling the judge I was 30% disabled from a injury in combat in Viet Nam which made it difficult to walk a straight line without a cane which had not been available.

It cost me $720 for the lawyer, which was a huge sum in those days, but it kept my record clean. It should have taught me a lesson, but my alcoholic days were just beginning. I would live many lucky days after that, but fortunately I never caused anyone to physically suffer because of it.

As far as I know, C.V. never told Stu or John about my episode in court. It was never mentioned to was 30% disabled from a injury in combat in Viet Nam which made it difficult to walk a straight line without a cane which had not been available.

He didn't even tell my buddy Diz, because he would have kidded me about it had he known.

Trout's Final Performance

Diz was quite a funny guy. Asked to explain his pitching effectiveness while pitching for Detroit, the bespectacled Trout answered, "No body likes to hit a man who wears glasses."

One of his favorite jokes was to ask some fan during cocktails prior to a banquet: "What do you do with an elephant that has three balls?" The fan would give up and Diz would say, "You walk him and pitch to the giraffe."

Another of his favoite jokes was "diplomatic phraseology." He would say my son was reading a book and asked me, "Dad, what is diplomatic phraseology?"

"'Well, I answered after thinking about it for a little

while, 'If you were to say to a homely girl, *Your face would stop a clock* that would be stupidity. **But,** if you would say to her, When I look into your eyes, time stands still, that would be diplomatic phraseology'"

I was shocked one day when he said he was getting a physical examination the next day.

"Feel this knot in my abdomen," he said pointing just below his sternum. I felt and it was hard. I knew it was serious and after the examination he was told it was cancer in its final stages. I was devastated. I had seen plenty of death during my military career, but this was the first time a friend of mine knew he was going to die any day in advance.

In January, the Chicago Baseball Writer's Association held its annual banquet at one of the large hotels in downtown Chicago. Over a thousand attendees packed the audience which ate and drank at tables of 10 below the elevated dais that held the master of ceremonies and about 20 dignitaries, some of whom were being honored or were on the program to speak.

Trout was one of these as it was then known publicly that ole Diz was dieing. The Sox, and the Cubs as well, had four tables for its top echelon and their spouses. Pearl was at our foremost table nearest the dais. When Paul got up to speak, he received a standing ovation from the crowd that adored him. From our second table, I took my camera and went up to the back balcony which also held many tables.

Standing on a chair to get above those seated, I took a time exposure of the entire dais and many of the audience tables. I had Bodhi's Photo Service, who processed all of my film, print a large black and white photograph of Trout speaking. Then, before framing it, I got a photograph of Dizzy pitching while in his prime with Detroit. Off to the right side of the banquet photograph, I painted a dim image in light gray ink of him in a follow through delivery position. It was a ghostly figure, but told a message

him in his young pitching days. I gave it to Pearl at her home without any fanfare a few weeks after Paul died the last day of February in '72.

John Allyn thought it was a terrific memento and so did I.

Spring Training In Sarasota, Florida

My first Spring Training in Sarasota, Fla., was fantastic. I had a rental car and drove the baseball writers to all the exhibition games. I also used it at night to drive one, and his wife if applicable, to cocktails and dinner. Some of them stayed at the same motel as the Sox officials, but some had come for many years and learned of places on the Gulf Coast that they liked better.

I think the regulars from the print media that I got to know well in my first Spring Training were Jerome Holtzman, Dick Dozier, Dave Nightingale, and John Hillyer. We played poker on a few occasions and tilted many cocktails together in the pressroom we had established in the room we had established from that purpose above the motel lobby.

When we started playing exhibition games, me know one of the basic rules about major league baseball press boxes. Melton had belted his first home run of the spring to win a game for the Sox and I let out a cheer and starting clapping.

"Hey Buck, don't your know? There's no cheering in the press box," one of them informed me quickly. I never did that again.

The Chicago newspapers all had a daily story about the Cubs in Scottsdale, Ari., and the Sox in Sarasota ne day we had no exhibition games scheduled. Holtzman, decided to write his daily article about what the field manager, coaches, and club executives did on their day off. He came by me sun bathing beside the motel swimming pool and noticed the 11" scar on my belly. When he asked me the reason for it.

"I was in a couple of wars, you know, and this is where the bullet went entered," I said kidding him. I explain pointing to the small circular scar where the drainage tube had come out of my stomach while it was healing from the ulcer operation to enlarge the exit from my stomach. "And, would you believe this 11-inch vertical scar was how big that had to cut to get all the pieces out."

I thought he knew I was making it up, but he wrote within his article that he stopped by the pool while making his rounds on our off-day and found Buck Peden, new Sox publicity director, sunbathing his bullet-ridden body. I had to explain that to a lot of people. I'm sure he did it to have some fun with me.

Jerome Holtzman[32] was a very clever veteran baseball writer, columnist, and publisher on the side of a beautiful 10-book set of *Sports Classics* written, or ghost-written, by many baseball knowledgeable. Many of the latter composed books in the set were told by old-time diamond stars of the past. If you enjoy baseball memorabilia from the mouths of those who played, you will definitely add this beautiful red, black, and gold hard-bound set to your bookcase.

I saved his first mention of me in one of his columns. Under a subhead "**Peden a Publicity Whiz**" he wrote: "The White Sox have a

miracle worker. He is Robert (Buck) Peden, a rookie publicity man who in the first two weeks of his first spring training camp, did the following: (a) took head shots of all the players, both in black and white and in color; (b) fixed the typewriter of a forlorn Chicago scribe; (c) retrieved and measured Bill Melton's first 1972 home run; (d) won $105 playing poker *(against the baseball writers* Allen, from *in camp)*; and (e) showed a New York writer how to work the free Pepsi-Cola machine in the Fort Lauderdale press box. The only mistake he's made thus far is that he's been caught cheering in the press box. He's promised not to do it again."

Holtzman and all the others were continually after Stu and me about the late arrival of Dick Allen to the camp. Nightingale was the worst. He was the "birddog" of the group. He snooped every avenue available, even questioned the switchboard operator at the motel daily to see if we had received any calls.

Apparently, Allen had learned Stu's private line and told Stu his personal matters had been obliterated and would be in camp the next day.

Stu directed me to prepare a of his arrival and explaining the delay had to do with private personal reasons. But he specifically told me, not to tell anyone until he approved the press release and made the announcement at a press conference he would call.

"Anyone" meant "everyone" to me. I had 20 years of military duty, which included a SECRET security clearance.

When I was hastily walking to my room to type the release, I met Tanner and Unferth on the walkway.

"Hey Buck, where you going so fast?" Chuck asked me.

"I gotta write a news release right away," I said.

"Oh yeah. What's it about?" the big Sox field manager continued with raised eyebrows.

"Mr. Holcomb told me not to tell anyone, so I can't tell you." He didn't like that answer and he let me know as if I was one of his players. With a stiff index finger poking me painfully in the chest, he added, "Listen Buck, I'm the

By Buck Peden

MGR. CHUCK TANNER

———————

manager of this club and I get to know everything up front. You understand?" "I'm sorry Chuck. The man that hired me, and to whom I report, told me not to tell anyone. I'm sure he'll tell you when he wants to do so."

32 Holtzman retired from writing for the Chicago *Sun Times, Tribune.* and *The Sporting News* at the end of 2006 & was immediately hired as MLB's Historian. Among the books this HOFamer wrote was one titled "No Cheering in the Press Box" published in 1974.

Then, I turned and went about my chores. Chuck, I think, eventually thought about it after Stu told him of the announcement he was to make. Tanner seemed to respect me after that. We got to know each other much better with chats in his room with a glass of wine or two. I spoke and wrote many glowing words about him over the next five years. His control of his players was the best of any mentor I ever seen before or since. He never reprimanded one in public, except maybe a stiff index finger-jab-the-chest or two in Spring Training. Otherwise, he kept it within the confines of his office. He even chewed on a few sportswriters in his private domain and rumor has it that he hung one little arrogant media individual on a coat hook in there.

Chuck was a little vain about his looks, but he had a right to be. He was very handsome and kept himself neatly dressed, close shaven, and his wavy hair well groomed. The only reason I had that impression was his inability to pass a mirror, wherever it may be, without glancing in it with several angles to check his appearance. Probably, me and his sweet wife Babs are the only two that entertained that opinion.

Fantastic Individuals Of 1972 Season

Tanner's great field managerial ability and man-handling attributes zoomed to major league surface after the Sox had acquired the Dodgers, Stan Bahnsen, a right-handed starter from the Yankees, and brought up two outstanding pitchers from the Sox minor league system, righty Rich Gossage and lefty Terry Forester. With Sain, an outstanding pitching coach after his successful 12-year major league career (139-116, 3.49 ERA) with the Boston Braves, had reduced the WS 1970 staff ERA from 4.54 to 3.12 with a club record of 976 strike outs. With starters Wilbur Wood (22-13, 1.91), Tom Bradley (15-15, 2.96), and Johnson (12-10, 2.93) returning along with newcomer Bahnsen and the two new rookie relievers, the Sox would post a 87-67 record to finish only 5 ½ behind Oakland in the Western Division. The powerful A's 93 wins were the only other AL team with more victories in the strike shortened season.

Tanner's outstanding success turning the a team at the bottom of the cellar in the league to a definite contender earned him the **American League Manager of the Year Award.** If Melton had not herniated a spinal disc, which limited his performance to only 57 games and only seven home runs after two straight 33 home run seasons, the White Sox probably would have overtaken the A's.

Woody," as his teammates called him, was a tireless moundman starting a total of 49 games. Occasionally, Chuck would use him with only two days rest. His 24-17 record tied Cleveland's Garylord Perry most wins in the loop while his starts, innings pitched (377), most assists (82), total chances (95), and starting double plays (8) were unequaled by league pitchers. All that netted him **AL Pitcher of the Year Award.**

By Buck Peden
WILBUR WOOD

Dick Allen Earns Several Top Awards

Dick Allen was tremendous that year. He paced all AL batsmen in home runs (37), RBIs (113), base on balls (99), on base percentage (.420) and in slugging (.603). He had outstanding speed on the base paths which he demonstrated with his two inside-the-park home runs in one game at Minnesota which tied a ML record.

His .308 batting average was a close third behind Twins' Rod Carew (.318) and

Royals' Lou Piniella (.312). It's possible he could have caught them and won the coveted triple crown (BAVG,

By Buck Peden
DICK ALLEN

RBI, HR leader), but when the Sox were mathematically eliminated from the division race, Tanner permitted him to take off. the rest of the season. Dick accomplished all his totals in only 148 of the 164 games scheduled.

All his achievements earned him the title of the highly coveted **AL Most Valuable Player Award** from the Baseball Writers Association of America, **Player of the Year Award** from the Baseball Digest, and **AL Player of the Year Award** from *The Sporting News*. All these were the first major awards he had received since 1964 when he batted .318 and hit 29 home runs to earn **NL Rookie of the Year** with the Philadelphia Phillies.

Carlos May, who was **AL Rookie of the Year** with a .281 and 18 home runs with the WS in 1969, was the other offensive leader for Tanner in

'72. He hit .3078, which was fourth in the loop behind Allen's .3083. Tanner said May would have been a steady .350 hitter had he not lost most of his right thumb in a mortar accident during training with the U.S. Marine Corps Reserve in 1970.

By Buck Peden
CARLOS MAY

The last of all those awards, which all came to my office first, was the **Major League Executive of the Year Award.** Roland Hemond, our Player Personnel Director had been selected to receive it. I was very enthusiastic as I went through the offices to lunch telling everyone of the news. When I got to the Bards Room dining area, John Allyn and Stu Holcomb were together at a table. I excitingly told them the news of the selection and was shocked to see their reaction. Neither displayed any enthusiasm, but looked at each other blandly.

After getting over the shocked feeling I was sustaining, I started deducing their lack of joy. Holcomb had

hired the personnel that put together the fabulous change in the Chicago White Sox. He probably resented that he, as Executive Vice President and General Manager, had not been selected for the award. My mind flashed back to the banquet in Spring Training that had a huge dais of baseball officials. Before it began, Roland had gone down the entire dais shaking hands with the individuals. Most he knew from his 10-year career background as farm and scouting director for Fred Haney of the Boston/ Milwaukee Braves, but the ones he did not, he introduced himself. He had also married Margo, the colorful daughter of John Quinn from another well known baseball family.

I liked Roland from the beginning and particularly enjoyed his sassy little wife. She was a real live wire. I heard Hemond and Holcomb arguing over our prospective player procurements, usually their salaries. I was very cognizant of Roland's influence in the acquisitions we had made, but the final decision was always made by Stu. He was fair and tolerant with player contracts if they had earned it.

For example, Ed Spiezio — a local lad from Joliet, Ill. — had been acquired from the San Diego Padres as a utility infielder. He did a very adequate job replacing the injured Melton at third base defensively, but was primarily a singles hitter at the plate and batted only .238. When he held out in Spring Training for more money, Holcomb released him.

Allen, on the other hand, was rewarded with a raise in salary to $225,000. In 1973, that was the biggest one-year contract in MLB history. Now, of course, top players are paid in the millions. In fact, I think now the minimum major league salary is as much as Dick's was that year. I often thought about wishing I had told Stu when he said he hired me at the minimum pay a rookie receives that I would like to always receive their same pay as my salary.

Smoke, Smoke That Cigarette Once Again

I hadn't spent much money since joining the Sox, except the cash I paid for the Fiat. And I had quit smoking the last year in the Pomona Valley when I developed asthma from the thick smog in that area. I never had it before in my life, but my mother had it all her life. However, I still drank my share of beer and booze.

Once, when my running mate, Bards Room bartender Johnny Mc Namara, was showing me the dives on Chicago's famous Rush Street, I saw my first set of artificial boobs. I was admiring this dancer's beautiful body, clad only in a G-string, until she laid on the floor during her performance and the breasts stayed straight out instead of

flattening as they normally would have. It was the first I had ever seen, but wouldn't be the last as the operation would become popular among the less endowed showgirls.

The California VA hospital at which I had been treated used scratch tests on my arm and back to determine my allergies. The Chicago VA doctor would treat four or five of us at a time. He would give us a pill and a small absorbent pad. Then, after a determined time, he would prick the lobe of one of our ears with a small blade. We would keep dabbing its blood until it coagulated and completely stopped. We would instantly tell him and he would mark the length of time it would take each of us.

This went on weekly for a month or until the asthma pills he was giving me kept it in control so well I slowly stopped having any attacks. Finally, I quit taking them and was never bothered with asthma again. It had lasted only about two years in all and it never stopped me from my work.

Towards the end of the great season, we were definitely in contention to upend the powerful Oakland unit. If we had done so, we would be in an American League playoff with the Eastern Division winner and in the World Series if we won that playoff. This meant, scorebooks for those speculative events had to be designed, written, and ready to print NOW.

Some of the time I would have to proofread copy I had written, edit, and write headlines, along with captions for the photographs I had chosen, all during a home ball game. This, in addition to keeping the scoreboard accurate as all lettering and numbers on the board had to be punched in by hand from men inside the board — plus, announcing any managerial changes on the field to radio, TV, and print media in the many press box booths — was tremendous pressure on me.

It was very similar to the pressure I used to have on Friday nights as sports editor of *The Natchez Democrat*. I had staffed one high school game myself and took my own action photographs. Then, while the film was developing and I was writing up the game, there would be calls piled up "on hold" waiting to give

me their report of their school's football game. I would smoke one cigarette after the other. Of course, most of them burn up my ash tray as I was so busy talking with my telephone head set while I wrote their game as they reported the facts to me. Then, rushing to the dark room, making prints of my photographs, grabbing wire copy off the AP & UPI telecopy machines on the way back, typing a few headlines on another typewriter, and marking everything on my page layout sheets which would go to the makeup man in the composing room.

I had not desired a cigarette during my last two years, but suddenly — with all this pressure on me in the press box at White Sox Park — I immensely craved one. I bummed cigarettes during the rest of the game and took up win the division, but I kept smoking anyway.

Finally Found Justice

I had plenty of money for the Windermere Hotel, but I had nothing in common with Charlie Saad, the other Sox resident there during the season. Nor did I like the neighborhood. Therefore, I moved to an apartment on the southwest side of Chicago where Mickey Yunker resided and had recommended. She was born and raised in that area; therefore, she became a big asset to me in getting settled and learning that neck of the woods.

She introduced me to a real estate sales lady named Marge Lewis, a White Sox fan who had an even more devout season-ticket-holder fan as a son. Ed was his name and he told her all about me when he learned she was looking for my house. Ed, and his wife Mona, became our friends and he was also, after finishing school, our veterinarian.

Marge was extremely helpful in my search for a house. Finally, shopping while the team was on the road, she found a brand new tri-level house in Justice, Ill. It had three bed rooms upstairs, a built-in bar inside a lower deck family room, and a huge living room, dining room, and kitchen on the ground level. It also had a separate two-car garage with a large driveway we later made into a small outdoor basketball court.

Debra was 18 then and had been driving a couple of years. She helped Carolyn make the long drive in the station wagon. The whole family adored the house, except that the back yard fence was only about 100 yards from U.S. Interstate 294. They thought the sound of the traffic would be overbearing, but the house was so well built that we never noticed it when the doors and windows were shut. We had central air so we very seldom opened them.

One weekend, a school bus of first and second graders on a trip broke down on the freeway. After an hour or so, I noticed the teachers had them out of the bus on the grass. It was obvious they needed a toilet as many of the little girls were crossing their legs. I went out and took a long plank from the garage to the fence. I uprooted two of the fence posts and laid the plank over the loosened chain fence. Then I walked out to the group and told the teachers they were welcome to bring their students in our house to use our two toilets. They accepted immediately releasing the urgency of the situation.

We took them in through the back basement door which led to the family room and its toilet and escorted some of the more urgent-looking kids to the one upstairs. After the emergency situation was subsided, Carolyn and Debra served them some cookies we had on hand and followed with some Kool Aid. I had them take a seat on the family room floor. It was linoleum tile so any crumbs or spilled liquid wouldn't hurt it.

Then, to keep them entertained while we were waiting for their substitute bus, I told them scary tales I made up on the spot. I had learned many years ago that I, and other normal kids like me, enjoyed being scared. It's the release from the scare at the end that is so exhilarating that one enjoys. When they left, many of the kids ran to give me a hug and the teachers were very sincere in their warm words of appreciation for our kindness.

We talked about the happening for quite a while afterwards. All our kids enjoyed it, especially Jeff who was four years old then.

David was a freshman at Argo (Ill.) High School and made the varsity track team with his distance running. Eventually, in November 1974, he would break the school cross country course record in the three-mile run with a 14:46.

Debra Gets Hitched

Debra had totaled the '62 VW we had given her for graduation in a wreck in Chino.

She only got $200 insurance money, but she wanted a car. I dropped her off on the way to work at a used car dealer and she paid down on a '69 VW. She was a very beautiful young lady and the mechanic there noticed her immediately. He talked her into a date and they had several until she went to work.

DEB & ANDY

I got her an interview at the huge Wilson Sporting Goods Company and she went to work there right away. Anxious to meet new friends at work, she asked if the company had a softball team she could join. They told her no, but one of the bowling teams needed a substitute bowler, which she accepted immediately. The first Friday after that she was needed to sub and there she met Andrew John Lengyel. The tall, dark, handsome lad swept her off her feet. About 10 months later they were married.

It was a wonderful church wedding on June 2, 1973, with Carolyn's and my parents in attendance. Her brother Tommy, his third wife Jackie and their two youngsters, Tommy and Melissa were there and my sister JoAnn. Andy's parents John and Sophia, plus his sister Mary and daughter Laura made it, but John Lee couldn't and GMSN Bob was in the Tonkin Gulf aboard the USS CAMDEN (AOE-2).

The reception was extremely nice and well attended. My friends from the White Sox that came were Bob & Connie Uhrig, George & Cee Sobek, Frank & Tonka Scalise, Irene Violante, Irene Kerwin, and Mickey Yunker. We did the whole bit: ate, cut the cake, and danced until the wee hours of the night. It was the type of affair that Gertie had missed marrying a poor sailor on a short leave.

Brenda Galvin, Debra's best friend in Chino, and Amy Whitehead, the same in Vidalia, both came for the wedding. I was taking them on a tour through the press box prior to a night game. I explained some of my chores during a game, including notifying the scoreboard crew to blast off the fireworks when a Sox player hit a home run.

"You ever do it by mistake?" one of them asked. I told them, "No. Not Ever."

Then later that night Allen belted one of his line drives to deep center. The centerfielder raced back to the 400-foot fence and leaped up trying to catch it with his back to the press box. The lights were very poor in deep centerfield; therefore, I couldn't tell whether it went over the fence or not. Then, the outfielder came down from his leap with both arms dangling at his side and his head drooped. I assumed by those indicators he was disgusted that the ball had cleared the fence.

I yelled, "Blow it, blow it" to the scoreboard crew over my direct phone.

By Buck Peden

STUART HOLCOMB observes the new Sox rookies in action with Mgr. Chuck Tanner at Sarasota Spring Training Camp.

Then, as the fireworks were beginning, the centerfielder turned around and held his gloved hand high to show the umpire he had caught the ball. I was humiliated, to say the least. My other phone rang and it was Holcomb.

"That'll cost you $300," he said. But, he never did make

me pay it. From then on, I made sure I saw the umpire's signal before giving the command. That was my first and last mistake I made performing my press box duties in my five years I would spend with the Sox.

Holcomb Retires After '73 Season

Stu had enough after the 1973 season as he retired with his sweet wife Betty. He would succumb in January 1977. His career in sports as a player, coach, and supervisor — in football, basketball, and baseball — was a tremendous one.

During his hall of fame career as a football coach, he had hired Hank Stram as an assistant, who become very successful as a head coach of the Kansas City Chiefs. Stu took me with him to hear

him speak at a banquet honoring Stram. On the way back, Stu confided in me that he was hanging it up after that season.

His other selection of talent in their respective fields that I personally got to know real well was Hemond, Tanner, Caray, and the Sox organist, Nancy Faust.

Nancy was outstanding. She not only had a natural musical ear, but she was very clever. When Bill Melton would come to bat she would play "Will You Marry Me, Bill?" and Dick Allen "Jesus Christ Superstar." The one that would spread all

over the nation was "Na Na Hey Hey Kiss Him Goodbye" after she started playing it when opposing pitcher would get taken out. Later she even played it when the Sox scored and at the end.

By David Peden

NANCY FAUST & I after one of her great performances on the organ at White Sox Park.

Allen Hits One On Comiskey Roof

About the only highlight of record pitching 1973 (77-85 season), came on May 1 when Dick hit one on and over the roof of the left field, double-decked grandstand onto the parking lot. Coincidentally, his uniform number was 15 and he became the 15th player to hit one out of White Sox/ Comiskey Park.

The first one was Babe Ruth in 1927. Others were Jimmy Foxx, Hank Greenberg, Orestes Minoso, Mickey Mantle, Ted Williams, Elston Howard, Boog Powell, Don Mincher, Bubby Bradford, Dave Nicholson, Tom Egan,

and Harmon Killebrew. Allen followed his gigantic blast with another solo blast as the Sox downed Baltimore, 6-5.

During all my research in obtaining this information I got to talk to some of baseball's greatest, some Hall of Famers.

One was Lefty Grove, who amassed a 300-141 won-lost for the Philadelphia Athletics and Boston Red Sox in the '20s & '30s. Williams belted his roof top off him.

"And, believe it or not it was off a changeup. He got all of it."

Hemond, who became a vice-president and general manager after Holcomb's retirement, had recommended the research and had put markers with the last name of the hitters and he always had a great flare for originality. In fact, he liked my idea of getting a tree-trunk and goose costumes made to represent our two great relief pitchers, Terry Forster and Rich Gossage[33] wanted to have the costumed fire on the bullpen roof while the players themselves were warming up in the bullpen in a late-inning close game, but it never got off the ground.

"Sure I remember it," he said when I called him to find out the approximate spot the hit cleared the top edge.

---

33 Gossage would be named *The Sporting News* Fireman of the Year in '75 & '78, and Forster in '74.

By Bob Langer

Tremendous home run by Dick Allen bounces on and over the White Sox Park roof as Bill Melton (14) and batboy watch from the on deck circle. First one to do so was Babe Ruth in 1927.

Wood And Kaat, What A Pair!

Jim Kaat was acquired from the Minnesota Twins early enough to pitch seven games at the end of the '73 campaign for the White one and posted a 21-13 record in 1974 to become the most successful active pitcher in the American League with 215 total victories. Only Bob Gibson of the St. Louis Cardinals of the National League had more (248).

Wilbur Wood etched his fourth straight season of 20 wins or more with a 20-19 mark to go with his 22-13 in '71, 24-17 in '72, and 24-20 in '73. It was the first time any Sox pitcher had won 20 or more games three consecutive seasons since Frank Owen

(1904-06) and Urban "Red" Faber (1920-22). At that time, Wood possessed an incredible lifetime major league 2.87 earned run average.

His "knuckleball" was actually a "finger-nail ball" which he threw with uncanny accuracy towards the plate in only 1½ revolutions. With the normal spin of a thrown ball cutting — with its seams — a vacuum to permit its movement therein, a catcher could follow its movement with a positive amount of calculations and catch it easily. With Wood's ball darting into any vacuum in the air, not only could the batter not hit it solidly, the catcher had quite a chore catching it. Ed Herrmann did a tremendous job catching the

elusive pill with an oversized catcher's mitt.

Wood, who was always the first player to arrive in the clubhouse, was a jovial 33-year-old who looked more like a bartender than a pitcher. His weight and height were listed as 190 pounds, 6'0". But most of his weight was distributed at his midsection. For that reason, all the Chicagoland beer drinkers felt like he was one of them. He was well-liked by all his teammates.

Right fielder Pat Kelly, who was the brother of Cleveland Browns football star Leroy Kelly, was another popular teammate. One of the top ten best dressers in Kansas City, he wore skin tight pants to a game with a bag hanging from his shoulders to his waist containing his billfold and other personal belongings. It got quite a rise out of the rest of the team that night. Kaat razzed Kelly as much as any of the players, but Kaat was very serious out on the mound.

He was the best fielding pitcher in baseball winning the Gold Glove Award 16 straight years. I had him fly in all 16 of the awards, which were replicas of a baseball glove on a stand containing each award's inscription. I had a large horseshoe made of wood with shelves for each of them and had Jim holding his 16th with the other 15 on the horseshoe at home plate. With the famous Bill Veeck's famous exploding scoreboard in the background, it made a great photograph and gave the home crowd quite a thrill that day.

Kaat would not only field anything hit his way, but when the batter would hit a pop foul ball, he would analyze quickly whether the catcher or first baseman should catch the towering ball down the first base line and the same with the third baseman down the third base line. Then, he would go to the opposite one and hold him to eliminate them colliding and dropping the ball. He was a very intelligent ball player even though he did throw with his left hand.

He ended his 25-year ML career with a 283-237 won-loss record in 1983. He was highly respected at all of the five teams with which he played during that time.

Some Of The Players Had Great Humor

THE LONG KNOCKER — Wood was a good fielder, but while Kaat was respected at the plate, Wilbur was a patsy. I think his longest hit was a pop fly just over the first baseman's head. His batter mate, Ed Herrmann was one of the most feared southpaw hitters in the AL (led loop with 19 intentional bases on balls). One day in the clubhouse, Ed was making jokes about Woody's lack of power at the plate. Woody, a real prankster, came by and put Ed down. "Hermy, you might be a long knocker in baseball but I bet you a $100 I can out hit you off the tee in golf."

Ed, who pounds the little golf sphere over 300 yards most of the time, was leery. "There must be some kind of catch to this," he said.

"The only catch is that I select the course, the tee, and the time & date," Woody said. "I'll even give you first shot to put the pressure on me."

They agreed and grabbed me walking by to witness the handshake on the bet. Six months passed and hard winter set in before Woody called Ed and me. He had the contest set for Lakeside CC, the 5th tee, at 1 p.m. We met and they took warm-up shots, Ed three and Woody one, on the long par five hole located alongside Lake Michigan.

Then, with the contest on, Ed smashes a long one down the middle of the snowy fairway. Woody then tees up, takes a practice swing, repositioned himself towards the frozen lake, and slaps a 50-yarder that bounced & skidded, bounced & skidded, and finally bounced & skidded on the frozen lake until it was out of sight.

Woody reached in his pocket and, to add fuel to the fuming Herrmann, pulled out a tap measure.

"Would you like to check 'em?" he asked straight-faced. Luckily, Ed's driver missed Woody as he raced to escape to his car. To this day, I don't know whether Ed ever paid him for that bet.

ADAM'S NATIONALITY — Pat Kelly, an Iranian-American outfielder, and rookie pitcher Dennis O'Toole, an Ireland descendent naturally, were jokingly debating that the first man was "black" or "Irish". Bill Melton walked by and corrected, "You're both wrong. Adam was Polish. who else would stand there eating an apple in front of a naked broad."

GRAVEYARD SHORTCUT — Tanner's success with players is derived from the fact he studies people. He told this tale once from the dais on our winter caravan: "One dark night, when I was a youngster working in the coal mines in Pennsylvania, I decided to cut across a cemetery to get home. A grave had been dug late that afternoon and I fell in it. Naturally, it frightened me, but I couldn't get out despite my jumping and clawing. I finally calmed myself by reasoning it would be easy to get out when the workers arrived the next morning to finish the grave. So, I went to one end of the grave and sat down to wait. Finally the midnight shift started coming home and one of them cut through the graveyard and fell in the same rave. I thought I'd just observe this man's reaction from my dark end. The man panicked, as I had. After watching the fruitless efforts of the man, I finally said, 'Give it up man, you can't get out.' And...he did!"

FAITH — O'Toole told this one. Three nuns ran out of gas driving through a desert. One walked back to a gas station miles away and the only can or container available to hold gasoline was a potty jar to carry it. Finally, while they were pouring it in the tank, an Irish bus driver stopped and saw couldn't get out despite my jumping and clawing. I finally calmed myself by reasoning it would be easy to get out when the workers arrived the next morning to finish the grave. So, I went to one end of the grave and sat down to wait. Finally the midnight shift started coming home and one of them cut through the graveyard and fell in the same grave. I thought I'd just observe this man's reaction from my dark end. The man panicked, as I had. After watching the fruitless efforts of the man, I finally said, 'Give it up man, you can't get out.' And...he did!"

FAITH — O'Toole told this one. Three nuns ran out of gas driving through a desert. One walked back to a gas station miles away and the only can or container available to hold gasoline was a potty jar to carry it. Finally, while they were pouring it in the tank, an Irish bus driver stopped and saw Irish bus driver stopped and saw Baltimore Oriole manager described what happened after his team lost to a ninth inning suicide squeeze bunt: "Just before it happened, I yelled from the dugout, 'Watch (out for) the squeeze.' And then, I watched it."

WOMEN IN CLUBHOUSE

— When Terry Forster heard women reporters were trying to get baseball to let them have the same rights as their male counterparts, he said, "If they every let women in our clubhouse they'll find out all men are not created equal." They eventually did and it made some of the player's very uneasy, but not Terry nor some of the others.

REAL LOSER — This was one John Carmichael's favorite he would tell at banquets. It was about a football team that was so bad their coach told them in their pre-game huddle, "If we win the toss and receive, try to cover the fumble. If we lose the toss and kickoff, try to block their extra point."

BEATCRAPOUTAGHOST — Also, by Carmichael: A big, heavy baseball coach had been constipated for several days despite they fact he had been taking plenty of different laxatives without success. Finally, in his sleep, his stoppage broke and he messed all over his hotel sheet. Tired and disgusted, he wadded it all up and threw it out his hotel window. It billowed out and landed on a drunk walking down the sidewalk. A cop drives by and sees the drunk under the sheet punching it ferociously. The officer jerked the sheet off and asked, "What in hell are you doing?" The drunk, wiping the feces off his face slurred out his answered in all honesty, "You won't believe this, but I think I just beat the crap outa a ghost!"

CONFESSION — Another Carmichael: This Catholic ballplayer had sex with seven women one night. He went to confession the next day and asked the priest for absolution. "Take a lemon, slice it into seven parts, squeeze them into one glass, and then chug-a-lug it." "Yes sir, but I don't see how that will give me absolution of my sins light night." "It won't, but it'll get rid of that smirk on your face."

John Carmichael & Dave Nightingale

John Carmichael and his wife Kay would always come to Sarasota and stay at the same motel as the White Sox. They played gin rummy off and on the entire day. He was a Hall of Fame Sportswriter with his famous "The Barber Shop" column and eventually sports editor, all with the *Chicago Daily News*. After 43 years he retired and the White Sox hired him as a community relation representative. In the latter capacity, we worked together at many events. I was very fond of him and his style. He would spoof individuals and otherwise have fun with them in his columns, but never any serious cutting or humiliating articles.

Dave Nightingale, a regular *Daily News* baseball writer with the White Sox beat, succeeded Carmichael's column-writing. He could be vicious in some of his columns, very unlike his predecessor. He would sometimes regret something he had written the next day. According to a fellow Chicago baseball writer, Joe Goddard, Dave's wife Margo would make him send flowers of apology.

Nightingale got me in my first few weeks in my own press box. He read one of my game notes out loud to the rest of the writers and made fun of it. I don't remember what it was about, but it embarrassed me and I wanted to pop him in the mouth. However, I was new and maybe trying a little to hard to make good and I knew that I would have to control my temper. I never forgot it and even as our relationship improved, I swore to myself that I would get him back for it.

Finally, one late night in the motel bar Nightingale, a couple other sportswriters and I were drinking. We were feeling pretty good with everybody joking about the other's athletic ability. I bragged and told Dave that I could tell by the way he fast-danced that I could beat him in any sport. He laughed at me and told me he had a $100 bill that says he can beat me. We got everone involved in making the rules for the bet as I accepted the challenge immediately. This would give me my revenge for the embarrassment he had made me sustain several years ago.

The final rules we reached was that the winner of the flip of a coin would choose the first sport. After that, the loser would choose the next event until five events had be picked. The winner of three would win the $100 prize. Naturally, I lost the first flip but lucked out in his choice being 18 holes of golf. He was going to play golf the next day which was an open date in our spring training schedule, so he wanted me to join them and make that our first competition. Of course, he didn't know my extensive background in golf. To say that I was highly elated would be putting it mildly. I had extreme difficultly, with the booze in my system at the moment, keeping a huge grin from enveloping my face.

He began learning his error in selection on the first hole. It was a long par four. He hit his drive down the middle, but only about 220 yards. I blasted a 275-yarder, but pushed it all the way to the middle of another fairway. Then, with tall trees blocking my straight approach to the green, I hit a long slicing three iron upon the green. To make it an even tougher pill for him to swallow, I made the 22-foot putt for a birdie. In all, I think I beat him about 10 strokes over the 18. Aaaaaah, revenge is sweet just like they say.

Then, he chose ping pong, which I thought was going to be a easy win for me with all that experience I had playing at the USNRTC in Natchez. We didn't play until the latter part of the 1973 season after the White Sox had acquired Steve Stone as a pitcher. While a preparing Steve's biography in the press guide for that season, I learned that he was a state champion in ping pong. We got him to officiate our match at his apartment complex. I was handcuffing Dave with my wicked serve while we were warming up. However, when Stone saw it, he said it was illegal because I was hitting the ball out of my hand instead of tossing it free and then hitting it.

It devastated my serving style permitting Nightingale to even our bet one-all. I chose table shuffleboard in which I had reigned as one of the best in Natchez. He only had a little experience at that sport and was an easy second victory for me. With his back against the wall down 2-1, he had to win the next event. He chose tennis, in which he had competed in high school. I only had the experience Tex Wainscott had provided me at the NAS Miramar tennis courts. Understandably, I anticipated him winning the event.

By now the word had spread within the organization about our wager with several people showing up for the tennis competition. One of them was Roland Hemond pulling for me, I assumed.

I didn't disappoint him. Dave's serve was not too hard so I was able to return it to an area away from him. When I chopped one over the net and if he managed to hustle in enough to return it, I would then bloop it over his head to the back line. This kept him running continuously and eventually wore him to a frazzle. He was a boozer, slightly overweight, and definitely out of shape. For the match point, he had my throat. Again, I blooped it over his racket real high to bounce only a few feet inside the back line. He was so tired and disgusted; he threw returned my serve and charged the net to ram one down my throat.

Again, I blooped it over his racket real hight to bounce only a few feet inside the back line. He was so tired and disgusted; he threw his racket at the ball. Finally, he

He calmed down a little and walked up to the net offering his handshake.

"Well, you won it all," he said, but didn't pull out the loot to payoff the wager. I just shrugged it off, figuring he probably didn't bring that much money with him as I'm sure he planned to beat me.

I knew he was good for it.

It was about two weeks later at a White Sox party on the beach that I learned of what happened to my winnings. Nightingale got everyone's attention and told them of the bet we had made and how I had humiliated him in his sport to win the wager. Since I had embarrassed him so much, he called Carolyn up to the mike.

"I gave his wife, Carolyn here, the $100 prize money. She'll tell you what she did with it," he explained with a devilish look on his face.

"I'm wearing it," Gertie said pulling one side of her skirt up and making a little turn to show off the colorful light blue, with white polka dots, $100 summer dress.

I tried to appear mad, but joined how I had humiliated him in his sport to win the wager. Since I had embarrassed him so much, he called Carolyn

up to the mike.

"I gave his wife, Carolyn here, the $100 prize money. She'll tell you what she did with it," he explained with a devilish look on his face.

"I'm wearing it," Gertie said pulling one side of her skirt up and making a little turn to show off the colorful light

blue, with white polka dots, $100 summer dress.

I tried to appear mad, but joined laughing with the rest of the coaches, scouts, executives, media, and their spouses. Dave gave me a copy of the fancy signed receipt he had obtained from Carolyn. I still have it.

Dave and I became fairly

By Buck Peden

FINGER FROM SORE LOSER – Dave Nightingale, seeing that I was shooting from right field foul area with my 500MM acts as if he is brushing back his hair but he is really giving me the finger for beating him the day before that Spring Training game. Others recognizable on the bench were George Langford (left), Jerome Holtzman (leaning) and Harry Caray (next right).

good buddies after that. He even told me he had really misjudged my sports ability. We even played together in a foursome that included Ernie Harwell, Detroit's Hall of Fame play-by-play radio announcer, in the 1975 Disney World's Grapefruit Classic Golf Tournament. It was my final spring training in Sarasota, Fla.

The Sarasota Sports Committee was the city's hosting group and they did a magnificent job each spring. Ed Smith was their top honcho. He and a few others that I remember were John Schwab, Ted Morton, and Jay Rumple. The committee made things very hospitable for the White Sox staff.

My Loose Leisure Spring Training Stuff

I would treat one of the writers and his spouse, if applicable, to dinner most of the nights during spring training as all of our exhibition games were during the day. I got to know George Lanford real well and was very happy for him when he got to be sports editor of the *Chicago Tribune*. I played poker with the writers many times and usually won as I had much more experience in the game during my military time. I liked all of them, but I probably got closer to Jerome Holtzman than any of the rest.

I spent a lot of time chatting with Johnny Sain our pitching coach. I thought Steve Stone had the best curve ball of any pitcher on our staff, but Sain said Bahnsen's was best and he could put it more where he wanted it than Stone could. Bahnsen used to drive me nuts going three balls and two

strikes on the majority of his opponents. To me his games were always 30 minutes longer than other pitchers because of it.

Sain told me he was thinking of attaching an automobile inner tube to the wall and have pitchers strengthen their arm by stretch it over their shoulder in a pitching motion. I had almost completed my master's degree in kinesiology (the study of human motion) and I felt that would strengthen muscles outside one's normal range of motion in throwing a baseball, thereby inhibiting one's accuracy. However, I was afraid it would upset him as he was a very successful pitching coach and I was just a writer.

I took Johnny and Greg Gumbel to dinner the first time the rookie TV sportscaster was in camp. I got him to try my favorite dish at the local seafood restaurant, shrimp with lobster sauce. He liked it too. Sain and I liked him immediately. He was much more personable and friendly than his brother Brian, also a television announcer that made it big. Tanner liked Greg also.

Tanner, at one point in my first spring training, was not pleased with me. Holcomb had given me a hot release announcement to prepare and told me not to divulge it to anyone until he made the announcement. My military training included handling of top secret material. When I was told "not to divulge it

to <u>anyone</u>" that included the janitor all the up and through the field manager.

Tanner and some of his coaches always attended and chatted leisurely with the members of the media. The Sarasota Sports Committee always hired a good-looking female bartender for the small gathering, which only lasted about an hour and a half after the workouts. By then, the writers had filed their copy and the coaches had showered and dressed in the usual informal causal attire for the Florida nightlife.

After the media usually left, Tanner and his coaches — plus scouts if they were in the area such as Sam Hairston (his son, Jerry, would play for the WS in 1973-89), Grover Jones, and Fred Shaffer, my favorite — would discuss the talents of the rookies in camp and their potential to make the major leagues. I enjoyed these discussions immensely. Just the fact Tanner would let me sit in on the meetings showed me he had a little respect for my opinion, even though I had never played any professional baseball. After these years of watching youngsters make it to the major leagues, I know I would have never gotten above Class AA. I had the speed and fielding ability, but not a strong throwing arm for a third baseman and I couldn't hit with power.

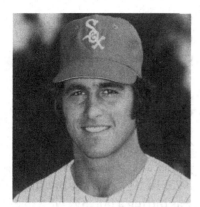

By Buck Peden

BUCKY DENT

Downing & Dent Like Night & Day

I never will forget Bucky Dent and Brian Downing being discussed. Of all the young men I saw making it to the majors, I knew every player that made it without a doubt, except Downing of Los Angeles. While Dent, the pride of Savannah, Ga., who earned everyone's acclamations with his range, fielding, throwing, and timely hitting, Downing — to me — was a lumbering ball hawk in left field that wasn't very impressive with the bat. I never thought he was major league material.

However, the powers that be, saw something I didn't and gave him a shot. Tanner used him in the outfield, behind the plate, and at third base replacing the injured Melton. At the latter position, he was so aggressive he charged in for a little pop foul that no one else would have bothered. He dove through the air the last 15 feet and made the unbelievable catch and tore up his right knee. It took him six weeks to heal. But, he proved he was not a splash in the pan, he played from 1973-92 — mostly with the California Angels — as an outfielder, catcher, and later as a designated hitter. Five of his 20 seasons he did not make a single error.

He even made the AL All-Star Team in 1979 when he batted .326. His career total however, was a much lower .267.

He started a new batting stance with his left foot in the habitual bucket position of a wide open stance to start and then stride forward with the left foot moving into a straight stance as he swung at the ball. Many other major leaguers chose to use it, most notable was Larry Walker, Colorado's outfielder. Walker led the National League in batting three times (.363 in 1998, .379 in 1999, and .350 in 2001) and doubles (44 in 1994) & home runs (49 in 1997); therefore, the stance works positively for some.

Dent only batted .247 during his 12 years mostly as a White Sox & New York Yankee player, but he was an excellent hit-and-run batter as he only struck out 349 times in 4,512 times at bat. He never hit 10 home runs in a season, but his famous three-run homer that gave the Yankees a 3-2 lead in the 1978 AL East Division Playoff Game with archrival Boston. They went on to win the game 5-4 and the division title upholding the infamous "Cruse of the Bambino."

Terry Forster's Domination Over Norm Cash

I never will forget Norm Cash's first encounter batting against Terry Forster. It was in the middle of an exhibition game between Detroit and the White Sox in Sarasota. Terry was called in relief of the starter to face Cash as his first opponent. Cash was coming off a great year for the Tigers where he had hit 32 home runs.

"Well looky here. They're bringing in a rookie left-hander to face ole Norm," he said, probably seeing Forster for the first time. Terry had pitched in only 49.2 innings in that 1971 campaign, he was probably was a little irritated when he heard Norm jeering at him.

By Buck Peden

TERRY FORESTER

Forster threw all his pitches from the three-quarter position. Therefore, his blazing fastball and wicked curve ball came from almost the same arm motion. His first pitch to Cash, who had dug in pretty tight in his left side of the batter's box, was a terrific fast ball right under Norm's chin. He just barely jerked his head back in time to avoid sustaining a "bean ball" upside his jaw.

He staggered several steps backward and almost sat down. Then he slowly made as if he was tapping the dirt off his baseball shoes while he took a few deep breaths before getting back in the box. He looked white as a sheet to me.

Then Terry threw one of his vicious hard curves that start out straight at a left-handed batter's head. Cash leaned back to dodge it. The ball broke down and towards the plate. It split the heart of it about belt high for a easy called strike. Cash was obviously embarrassed and made a late swing at a Forster's fastball and then watched another curve break over for the third strike. I made it a point to watch Cash closely every time he faced Forster during the regular season and he struck out every single time they met. Norm ticked a couple foul balls, but not one time the entire season did he hit the ball in fair territory off Terry.

Final Three Years With White Sox

Injuries hurt the Sox the next three years. Allen (.3083 & AL

By Buck Peden
RICH GOSSAGE

GOSSAGE CAREER

I felt this insert was deserving of **Rich "Goose" Gossage** *who established so many relief pitching performances for nine different major league teams during his 22 years, but has not yet been elected to the National Baseball Hall of Fame. While with the White Sox, Pirates, Yankees, Padres, Cubs, Giants, Rangers, A's, and Mariners he established a 124-107 record with a 3.01 ERA and saved 310 games. He set a NL record for most K's by a reliever in 1977 when he fanned 155 in 133 innings. Career wise he only unintentional walked 642 batters while striking out 1,502 in 1,809.1 innings. That's a strikeout in 83% of the innings pitched. He had the most saves in 1972(26), 1978(27), and 1980(33) earning The Sporting News Fireman of the Year Award in the former two and Rolaids Relief Man of Year in 1978. He was selected for the All-Star Team seven times.*

tops with 37 home runs) and Carlos May (.3078 & 17) had carried the team offense while Melton was limited to only 57 games due to a herniated disc in'74 with Dick leading the loop his back during 1972. Then Allen managed only 72 games after breaking his leg in 1973. In 1974, Buddy Bradford was hitting a hot .333 with five home runs when he sustained a broken collarbone diving for a catch in the 39 game and missed the rest of the season. Ken Henderson, the switch-hitting centerfielder, injured his leg requiring surgery and managed only 73 games in 1973.

All these major injuries and several other minor ones to others resulted in 5th place in the Western Division with a 77-85 won-lost record in 1973, a 4th place with a 80-80 in '74, and 5th with 75-86 in '75. The only highlights of those campaigns in the pitching department was Wood's four straight 20-wins-plus seasons 1971-74 of: 22-13, 24-17, 24-20, & 20-19 and Gossage's 26 saves in '75. The latter and Woods' two 24-win seasons were AL highs. Allen and Henderson rebounded again with 32 home runs and Ken 2nd with 281 total bases and 4th with 95 RBI.

My Lucky Hall Of Fame Candid

The National Baseball Hall of Fame and Museum (NBHOF&M) at Cooperstown,

N.Y., always hosted an exhibition baseball game between a ML team of each league (this was before inter-league play during the regular season was authorized) the morning prior to its induction ceremonies of that year. In l974, the Chicago White Sox and the Atlanta Braves had open dates on that year's ceremony of August 12; therefore, we were scheduled to compete so I made the trip.

Henry "Hank" Aaron tied Babe Ruth all-time home run record of 714 home runs on opening day at Cincinnati and then broke it at his hitter-friendly Fullton County Stadium in Atlanta. He did it despite the media pressure and critical fans who argued that he hit them in 3,298 games while Ruth hit his in 2,503, including 163 games as a pitcher. Some fan letters were terrible, many bringing out the fact Aaron had 3,965 more at bats. The baseball god must have been a slugger too as he has Aaron as the first player listed in the alphabetical batter register of *The Baseball Encyclopedia*.

An hour or so before Mickey Mantle and Whitey Ford were inducted in the HOF, the museum was closed to the public to allow the players, coaches, and accompanying club staffs to visit it without being hassled by the fans for autographs. I enjoyed it immensely and took many black & white photographs with high speed film so I could use available light instead of flash.

I had just looked at large photographs of Babe Ruth standing in and just outside the dugout. In between them was a wall phone that read "Babe Ruth's Voice. Naturally, I listened to the recording of Ruth made prior to his death in 1948. Then, as I was wandering down the aisle to the next display, I noticed out of the corner of my eye

had hanging around my neck and set the focus at 10 feet and cocked the shutter. I knew the aperture and shutter speed was already appropriately set as I had taken several pictures with the museum's overhead lighting.

Sure enough, he picked up the phone and I softly snapped the "Sports Candid of the Century" in my opinion. I

By Buck Peden

AARON LISTENING TO RUTH – Candid photo by author of the great Aaron listening to the recording of the late home run king, Ruth.

that "Hammerin Hank" was approaching the "Sultan of Swat" display.

The hair on the back of my neck stood on its ends as I realized that he may pick up that phone and listen to "The Bambino" himself with me only 10 feet away with a loaded camera. Quickly, I looked down to the 35MM I

had it printed and the next time the Braves played at Wrigley Field in Chicago I gave him a copy and got him to autograph one for me. The equipment manager of every team routinely gave me and the general manager an autographed ball of the team at the close of the season. This was the first time I had asked any player for an autograph. I also got his permission to publish the photograph in our Sox publications and to give one for the NBHOF&M for their use.

Interestingly, in August 2007 writing this August 1974 happening, SF's Barry Bonds hit his 756th to pass Aaron's total for a new mark.

Nolan Ryan IBM Day

On Sept. 7, 1974, the California Angels were hosting the White Sox on a Saturday afternoon game with the International Business Machines Corp. (IBM) planning to time the fast ball of MLB's strikeout king Nolan Ryan who had established an all-time season strikeout total of 383 in the 1973 season. This was several years before the manufacturing of the speed gun now used by all clubs to gauge the speed of pitchers. A huge crowd showed up to witness the promotion in which IBM was going to record Ryan's pitches with their machines recording them in the press box and then they would put it on the electronic scoreboard at Anaheim Stadium.

Everything was going smooth with Nolan throwing in the high 90's most of the game and finally hitting a high of 100.8 mph to become the first pitcher recorded to ever throw the baseball over 100 mph. I was watching it all from the next row up in the main press box. The crowd,

naturally, was ecstatic when they saw the historic figure on the scoreboard. **Then the shock happened.**

Terry Forster had been brought in relief for the Sox starting pitcher. The IBM people were recording every pitch, of course, but they weren't putting any but Ryan's on the scoreboard. Forster sizzled one in that registered 101.0 mph. The two fellows glanced quickly at each other and then one turned the hine off. They looked around, I assume to see if anyone had seen the figure. Apparently, no one else had been watching it as I had. Quickly, I looked in the other direction as if I had not seen it.

I knew what a disaster it would have been for the Angel organization's promotion to have an opposing team's relief pitcher throw a faster pill than this super man who undoubtedly was to become the greatest fastball hurler in major league history. Plus, I knew Forster, in a relief role, could throw as hard as possible for brief appearance whereas Ryan had to pace himself over the entire nine innings.

I didn't want to cause any ill feelings with my pals in California's front office, Red Patterson and Tom Seeberg. Also, their owner who had entertained me, among millions of other kids, in his career as a singing cowboy named Gene Autry. I rode many miles on my stick horses to attend the Memphis

Princess Theater at Main and Beale Streets in the early '40s to watch his Class "B" flicks. I enjoyed the few chats I had with Autry at Winter Meetings.

I started to tell Terry once or twice, but thought best not to tell anyone at that time. This is that first time anyone knows of what I saw that day. With the hard throwers nowadays, I don't think it will rattle anyone's cage or make any headlines.

Forster was named *The Sporting News* Fireman of the Year in 1974. Gossage would get the award the next season and in 1978 for the Yankees.

Appling's Uniform Number #4 Retired

I was busy preparing the materials for the retirement of Luke Appling's uniform number four during a heavy rain day. Irene Kerwin, the Sox switchboard operator for several decades, was busy answering one call after the other from fans wanting to know if that night's game was rained out. It was a sellout that night, so the number of calls were tremendous. This was before they had answering machines and computers, so all she would do was answer with only a quick short phrase, "No, the game is not rained out." One fan must have called back and asked if it was a recording. She simply answered, "No, the game is not rained out. Yes, this is a recording." My secretary, Unferth's secretary

Lillian Cortese, and I in the other end of the media office laughed out loud it was such a break in her hundreds of messages. I'm sure the caller got a chuckle out of it also.

Another crackup she gave us was when the team was in an eight-game losing streak. It had been a long day with numerous calls about the slump. It was about closing time and she had finally lost her patience. The next call she answered, "There's nothing wrong with our team. Goodbye."

The caller rang back and asked, "Why did you hang up?"

"I didn't. I said goodbye. This is a hang up," and then she hung up.

At the retirement ceremony, which was held at home plate on June 7, 1975, at a Sox-Yankee Old Timers" Game, I handed AL President Joe Cronin Appling's uniform shirt. Cronin, a Hall of Fame shortstop (elected in 1956), made an official retirement speech while handing owner John Allyn HOF (1964) Appling's #4 uniform and congratulating Luke with a handshake.

Other players I knew personally that would get their numbers retired were Nellie Fox (#2), Minnie Minoso (#9), and Billy Pierce (#19), but Appling's was the first.

Luke had been voted by the locals fans in 1969, for the second time, as the greatest player in White Sox history. He was a very successful

shortstop leading the rest of the AL players at that position in fielding for eight consecutive seasons, led in assists seven years and holds the major league record for chances accepted by a SS with 11,569.

**RETIRING #4
From left: Joe Cronin, Luke Appling, John Allyn, and me.**

He was an outstanding batter. During his 1930-50 ML career, all with the White Sox, he batted over .300 a total of 15 times and led all the league hitters with a .388 in 1936 and a .328 in 1943. The former AL batting championship was the first ever by a shortstop and the club's first by any player. He was a selection to the All-Star Game seven seasons.

His bat control was exceptional. He supposedly hit 25 foul balls on purpose while taking batting practice because the Yankee owner had denied his request for game passes. At $2 a ball, the owner reportedly gave Luke the few ducats. He frequently tipped one foul during a game when it was not of his liking but too near the plate to take

the chance it might be called a third strike.

Another "master fouler," according to the late congenial baseball writer-columnist Phil Collier of *The San Diego Union-Tribune* in one of his 1997 columns, was Hall of Famer Richie Ashburn. Collier wrote:

"(Ashburn's recent)...death brought to mind the former Philadelphia star's ability to hit foul line drives over the third base dugout on close pitches he was former Cubs teammate (Richie played 1960-61 seasons with Chicago) Jim Brewer approached him one morning about continuing arguments he was having with wife Patty. 'She'll be sitting behind our dugout this afternoon,' Brewer said. 'Take a shot at her, will ya?' Ashburn laughed and forgot all about it until he came to bat in the first inning and fouled a couple of line drives into the third-base box seats. It was then that he heard Brewer yelling: 'She's four rows back, near the end of the dugout!'"

Collier was in the sportswriters wing of MLB's HOF and one of the best in the nation while writing 40 years before dieing of cancer. He was read by millions and well liked by all of his peers.

My Only Fracas With Harry Caray

During my career with the Sox, I carried the title of publicity director and my counter part on the north side of town with the Cubs, Chuck Shriver, was called the Director of Information & Services. Virtually on all the other ML teams the position was called Public Relations Director. When we attended the MLB Winter Meetings, Chuck and I both attended those meetings and he was one of the officers. We all did the same thing, it was just titles that had evolved over the years at the two clubs.

Primarily, we all prepared pre-game notes of interest about the organization, the team, and the players. Plus, of course each team's up-to-date individual batting and pitching statistics. Monthly, most teams published a club newspaper of upcoming events. And, of course, the annual news media guides containing players and team career records were a giant production that was used by the media throughout the season. All of this was a big asset to the media and especially the radio and television crews covering both teams.

On the field, pre-game activities were usually handled by all of the PR Directors. I've already related earlier duties I had to perform during the games.

Almost all of us did community relations work and made speaking engagements. Charity work occupied some of our time and many times I went home sad from some of the things with which I

dealt. The worst one was an Indiana youngster under age 10 that was severely injured in a head-on collision with a milk truck that damaged his legs so bad he couldn't walk. The devastating thing about the unfortunate accident was the way his mother and grandmother were killed. He was seated in the middle of them in a pickup truck with his mother driving. If I remember it correctly, she was impaled by the steering wheel and his grandmother was decapitated.

He was a White Sox fan, as many Indiana lads were, so I pushed him through our home clubhouse and introduced him to some of the players there and Tanner. Then I took him out on the field and let him watch batting practice. He was very excited with it all as I had briefed some of the team members who he was and what had happened to him; therefore, many stopped and chatted with him. All were super, but if I remember correctly Third Base Coach Joe Lonnet, and the great fielding First Baseman Tony Muser were extra good.

Harry Caray was best. He must have spent five minutes talking with the youngster and all cheerful, Sox baseball items. I think one he enjoyed was when Harry told him Glenn Rosenbaum, the batting practice pitcher and coach, also lived in Indiana. "Rosie" of Union City, Ind., pitched 11 years in the minor leagues with

outstanding control so the Sox finally made him a coach and a BP pitcher. A batter having trouble hitting a curveball on the outside corner, Rosenbaum would tirelessly throw it there for him in practice. Eventually, this valuable and talented individual was made Sox traveling secretary to replace the retiring Unferth.

The youngster and his escorts were very pleased with the attention Caray and the players displayed.

Caray was extremely clever at reading notes we received from fans. This, and his colorful game comments, made him very popular in Chicago. One that I gave him that everyone liked was from a female admirer of the handsome Bucky Dent. She wrote a letter asking if Bucky made house calls. John Mahoney, the Comiskey/ White Sox Park electrician for many years, told Harry and me about having to turn the lights back on an hour after a night game to check some problem he was having with them. Lo and behold, there was a Sox player banging one of the "groupies." But, of course, Caray didn't repeat it on the air.

He got very upset with me after a long extra-inning game with the Minnesota Twins, which had caused us to miss our commercial flight in Minneapolis. We were sitting in the airport cocktail lounge drinking mixed drinks for over an hour waiting for the next flight. After about five or six cocktails, we were feeling no pain and our tongues were loose.

"Buck, why does John Allyn, Breen, and even Tanner bitch at me for 'telling it like it is?' That's my style and always has been," he asked me.

"Harry, sometimes you harp on the negative so much that it grates on them and Roland. For example, when Bill Melton missed half the season with that herniated disc and played the rest partially injured, you came up with an irritating phrase. When Bill, or any Sox player, would pop up when a home run would have won the game, you would say: 'That wouldn't be a home run in a telephone booth.' You felt bad, the Sox executives were disgusted, the team was unhappy, and the fans at home listening to you — on the edge of their seats — were so disappointed it was like a knife jammed in their heart.

"Then, the next time Melton, or whoever had popped up, would come to bat you would go over his failure in detail. Finally, in recapping the game afterwards, you would repeat it all again in a whining tone that just twisted and twisted that knife in their heart."

"That's my job," he barked, obviously offended by my reasoning.

"Yes, but it doesn't have to be so negative," I rebuked.

With that, he picked up his belongings and joined the team in the waiting room. After sleeping it off, he must have thought I was at least partially right as he was friendly to me as always. However, he continued with his "That wouldn't be a home run in a phone booth" for quite some time.

Pete Vonachen of Peoria was instrumental in informing the top brass of the White Sox about the availability of Caray following the 1970 Oakland A's season. Caray's final salary at the end of his 25 years of play-by-play with the St. Louis Cardinals was $47,500. He got $75,000 for the one-year with Charlie Finley. The Sox gave him $50,000 guaranteed, plus $10,000 for each 100,000 fans over 600,000 attending home games.

His favorite exclamatory remark field was "Holy Cow." According to a book titled *Holy Cow!* with writer Bob Verdi, Caray was hit by a car in 1968 and he heard someone holler "HOLY COW" while he was flying through the air 40 feet. Harry used it in his broadcast ever since then.

"Hot Stove League" Winter Caravan

Vonachen, who later owned a Class A franchise in Peoria, was extremely helpful in setting up our Winter Baseball Caravan stop there each year. We would take our general manager, field manager, a couple of top players, and a member of the radio or TV team. Our traveling secretary would rent a bus & driver, and arrangements, with me handling the media interviews prior to the meal attended by several hundred special guests. After the meal, a member of the Sox radio-TV team would serve as master of ceremonies at the head table to introduce Sox officials and players. The GM would usually say a few words before we opened it to questions from the audience to any of us on the dais.

We would stop at each one for the media conference and lunch and then the next city for the MC and dinner. Usually it would start in Illinois stops at Rockford, Quad Cities (Davenport, Moline, Rock Island, & Bettendorf), Galesburg, Peoria, Bloomington, Champaign, and Danville. In Indiana the stops were usually Lafayette and always South Bend.

The mid-western baseball fans called it the "Hot Stove League." At the last stop one year our MC Bill Mercer was eating his chicken lunch next to me.

"Bill, you know why the chicken breast is white meat and the thigh and leg dark?" I asked my friend.

"No, not really," he answered. "Why is it thus?"

"The breast muscles, the pectorals, are used to operate a bird's wings. As the chicken doesn't fly, those muscles receive the minimum amount of blood. Whereas they stand and walk constantly on their legs, hence plenty of blood, thereby producing dark meat.

The breasts of the pheasants and doves, for example, fly often; therefore their breasts are dark meat," I explained from my college studies.

Mercer, who had stopped eating to listen to me he was

I reluctantly stepped to the mike, thought for a few seconds, and then said, "What I explained to Bill is a little too technical and boring for this audience, so see me afterwards if you really are interested. In

SOX CARAVAN consisted of (L-R) me, Roland Hemond, Chuck Tanner, Don Unferth, J.D. Martin, C.V. Davis, Bart Johnson, Bill Mercer, and Bucky Dent.

so interested, smiled and said, "Gee Buck, that was the first time I ever heard that explained."

A few minutes later, he got up and started introducing Bucky Dent at the left end of the table and Pat Kelly at the right end, with Tanner, Hemond, Unferth, and me in the middle. Then, he shocked the hell outa me by saying, "Now, let's get Buck Peden up to the mike (microphone) and he'll explain the difference between white meat and dark meat."

the meantime, at the far end of the table to my left is Bucky Dent. That's white meat. At right end is Pat Kelly. That's dark meat"

Fortunately, they took it in the humor I had hoped and laughed as I stepped down and grabbed Mercer by the throat and acted like I was joking him for putting me on the spot. Pat and Bucky laughed about it too, so it came out alright.

Radio-TV Teams

The radio and television was very meager in those days while the Cubs across town were enjoying tremendous coverage by the super station WGN. During my five years, the master stations and announcers covering White Sox games were:

1971 & 72 - WFLD-TV & WEAW-FM Radio (Evanston): No Chicago radio. Closest AM station carrying games was **WTAQ** (LaGrange). Harry Caray & Ralph Faucher on radio, Jack Drees & Bud Kelly on TV.

1973 - WSNS-TV & WMAQ Radio: Caray (both) & Bob Waller (TV), Gene Osborn (radio).

1974 - WNSN-TV & WMAQ Radio: Caray (both) & Waller (TV), Bill Mercer (radio).

1975 - WSNS-TV & WMAQ Radio: Caray (both) & J.C. Martin (TV), Mercer (radio).

All were professional broadcasters except for Martin. He had 14 years in the major leagues with many teams, including both Chicago teams, as a catcher. He was one of few who successfully handled the fluttering knuckleballs of Hall of Famer Hoyt Wilhelm and Wilbur Wood.

Working For The Commissioner

Virtually all the MLB public relations directors from all the teams would work the All-Star and World Series games for the commissioner's office. The hosting teams of these events could never have handled the mass of news media personnel that converge to cover it. For example, one time I was assigned to assist the security people on spotting illegal media personnel on the field during the batting practice prior to that game. The field was loaded with 40-50 media individuals around the batting cage, in the dugouts, or in between grabbing players to do interviews. All of them were required to be wearing the media pass (usually a vertical card with a string to hang it from a button on one's shirt or coat button) given them on registering for the event with their company's proper credentials.

Officials, such as me, had a distinctively different colored card. The sergeant in charge of the security on the field that day, came up to me and introduced himself. I asked him if he had any problems with any of the media personnel on the field that day.

"Yes sir. That tall guy in the nice suit over there by the batting cage doesn't have a pass on him. I thought I better check with you before ejecting him 'cause he looks important," he explained with an inquisitive look on his face.

Of course I recognized him immediately.

"You were right. That's Bowie Kuhn, the Commissioner of Major League Baseball," I said smiling as he was nodding to himself. I'm sure that he was feeling he had done the right thing by checking with a baseball official first.

I ambled over later and told the commissioner of the incident and playfully chided him for not wearing a pass. I always noticed after that, although I was just kidding the famous man, he wore a baseball executive pass designed for the top brass in MLB.

While on the subject of this man, he really impressed me as an individual as well as his performance in the mind-boggling office that he held. When he would come to Chicago to attend a Pitch & Hit Club or a Chicago Baseball Writers Association function, there would be hundreds of local people with whom he would meet and socialize with his beautiful and tall wife, Luisa. They stood taller than anyone at any gathering I saw them at during my 12 years. He was 6'5" and, I bet, she was 6'3". He amazed me with his ability to remember so many of the would always speak my first name whenever they saw me from early in my MLB career. I thought they probably were punching or whispering to Bob Fishel or Wirz and asked my name, but occasionally I would show up late for some social event and approach them from their blind side. They always had the same impressive memory of this "Mr. Nobody's" first name.

There are always a few fans that make a project out of crashing these and other famous sporting events. I spotted one I have seen doing his thing at many events. As I plan to mention him again later, let's call him "Slippery Sam," probably in his 40's. At this one event, I was working the AL clubhouse at an All-Star Game, which was located next to a passage leading to the field, and had started opening the door to exit and I saw him. Keeping the door partially close so the guard and Sam couldn't see me, I learned his style.

Dressed immaculately in an expensive-looking suit and tie, he patted the guard on the back and said, "You men are doing an outstanding job at this huge event. Last year, we had several incidents we had to deal with in the commissioner's office, but so far this year we've had none. Keep up the good work," he extended his hand for a shake. The guard took it, beaming with pride. Then, with a final pat on the back, Sam walked right past him towards the field.

I stepped out and confronted the guard, "Did you see that guy's pass?"

"No, but I assumed he was from the commissioner's office from the way he talked," he answered as his face began to redden.

"He's a professional crasher. Get him," I said with him taking after Sam. I saw the guard later ejecting ole Slippery.

One time in Kansas City during an AL Championship Series between the Yankees and Royals, I spotted him again, this time trying to crash the television network's post game party. I told security who he was and they sent him on his way.

At that party, all the team executives, coaches and players are invited with great buffet food and cocktails to the delight of the network sponsor officials as honored guests. I was talking with George Brett, the great KC third baseman that would make the Hall of Fame, and his younger brother Bobby. Bobby had played on the Cal Poly Broncos team and was signed to a professional baseball contract along with team captain and shortstop Al Cappiello. We were discussing the Brett family's outstanding baseball attributes with John & Bobby playing in the minors and George and his older brother pitcher Ken (14 years with numerous clubs) starring in the majors. Suddenly, a middle-aged man and woman interrupted us.

"Excuse me Mr. Brett," the man said. "My wife wanted to kiss you. Do you mind?"

The wife was smiling, ear-to-ear. I'm sure she was expecting a little peck, but she didn't know George. He grabbed her and said, "Glad to oblige." Then he bent her over backwards and planted an open-mouth kiss for about five seconds. I looked at the husband to see his reaction,

and he was beaming as he took a picture of the two.

Bobby and I laughed for several minutes after the couple departed.

"Got to keep the fans happy," George said with a devilish grin.

Another event I will never forget was following a World Series in New York. Bob Wriz, who was in charge of assigning all the clubs PR Directors to duties for Commissioner Kuhn during the WS, had scheduled me to take notes of player's comments to the media personnel in home clubhouse. With this assignment, we would hustle up to the press box and transcribe our notes and make multiple copies for any media members who had not had time to get down to the clubhouse immediately after the game.

U.S. President Jimmy Carter had attended this particular game. I was in the clubhouse doing my chores when he came in with his entourage of bodyguards. Carter started congratulating one of the players who had been the hero of that night's game. Naturally, I had to move in fast to hear what was being said so I could reproduce it for the hundreds of writers that were in the visiting clubhouse and press box. It was so crowded that I had to push in between several media personnel to get close enough to hear good.

Wham! Suddenly I had a strong hand gripping my throat. It was a bodyguard.

He pushed me back slightly and said, "You're close enough right there."

Would you believe, I didn't argue with him.

Another shock for me one time was later on in Terry Forster's career when he was traded to the Los Angles Dodgers and they were playing the Yankees in the World Series. The female media personnel had gained to equal rights to enter the player's clubhouses, as permitted by their male counterparts, to do interviews after the games. One of them, a beautiful young chick, was waiting for her interviewee to finish his post game shower, so she sat on his stool in front of his locker.

Terry and I were chatting over old times at his locker next to her. He already had his shirt off as he elbowed me to watch him. Then he turned a little to his left and dropped his pants with his jockey strap holding his male organs right in her face. She quickly got up and walked off.

We laughed as Terry said, "That why they come in here…to see player's undress. Otherwise, why don't they just ask the player outside the door for a few quotes. The players would oblige."

Tommy Lasorda was manager then and I always liked it when I got assigned to cover the interviews in his clubhouse. He was so colorful with his comments to the media about something that happened on the field. Later in my career, when he came to Chicago he would always kid Steve Brenner, the young publicity man that always traveled with the Dodgers, that he was working on a trade involving him for me. He would do it every time without fail. I knew he was joking, of course, but it still made me feel good.

The Dodgers first baseman, Steve Garvey, was named the Most Valuable Player of the 1974 All-Star Game played in Pittsburgh that Dick Allen almost missed. The rest of the team stayed at the designated hotel and arrived at Three Rivers Stadium on the team buses, but Allen had gone to visit his mother in Wampum, Penn. His brother drove him to the stadium, but the parking attendant wouldn't let them into the players parking lot as they had no pass and apparently he was no baseball fan. He had never heard of Dick Allen and was just following orders.

Dick finally grabbed his gear out of the trunk and walked to the players entrance. There, he was refused admittance again with the"That why they come in here...to see player's undress. Otherwise, why don't they just ask the player outside the door for a few quotes. The players would oblige."

Tommy Lasorda was manager then and I always liked it when I got assigned to cover the interviews in his clubhouse. He was so colorful with his comments to the

media about something that happened on the field. Later in my career, when he came to Chicago he would always kid Steve Brenner, the young publicity man that always traveled with the Dodgers, that he was working on a trade involving him for me. He would do it every time without fail. I knew he was joking, of course, but it still made me feel good.

The Dodgers first baseman, Steve Garvey, was named the Most Valuable Player of the 1974 All-Star Game played in Pittsburgh that Dick Allen almost missed. The rest of the team stayed at the designated hotel and arrived at Three Rivers Stadium on the team buses, but Allen had gone to visit his mother in Wampum, Penn. His brother drove him to the stadium, but the parking attendant wouldn't let them into the players parking lot as they had no pass and apparently he was no baseball fan. He had never heard of Dick Allen and was just following orders.

Dick finally grabbed his gear out of the trunk and walked to the players entrance. There, he was refused admittance again with the senior guard calling me in the press box for assistance. I hopped the elevator and started chewing out the guards for keeping him from going to the AL clubhouse.

"But sir, he says he's a player but has no identification. We couldn't take a chance, so we

called you," the top officer explained.

"Couldn't you see the uniform and bats in his equipment bag that he's Allen with the Chicago White Sox," I reprimanded. And then just took Allen by the arm and started escorting him to the clubhouse. He had missed batting and infield practice, but it was still plenty of time for him to dress for the game. I showed him where I was putting his all-star personal materials from the commissioner's office in the back of his locker and took out a ticket from it for his brother.

Allen's brother Hank had played 36 games for the Sox in l972 & 73, so I knew what he looked like. But his older brother, Ron, I had never seen.

Fortunately, I stepped out the player entrance door and there he was looking for assistance. He had found a parking spot, but had no ticket. He was assuming Dick would have left him a ticket or advice at the entrance. Ron's seat was excellent and he enjoyed the few innings his brother played before giving up his first base slot to Boston's Carl Yastrzemski.

Red Sox Catcher Carlton Fisk produced the most exciting World Series that I remember working for the commissioner. It was in l975 when he hit an inches fair home run in the bottom of the 12th inning to keep Boston in the series. Then MVP of the season, Second

Baseman Joe Morgan, drove in Pete Rose in the bottom of the ninth to give Cincinnati the championship.

While mentioning Morgan, who became an excellent baseball color announcer on TV and later member of the HOF, was eating at a fancy restaurant in Chicago to which Carolyn and I coincidentally took our good friends Charlie and Cossie Kyzar visiting from visiting from Vidalia. I had gotten to know Joe so I knew he wouldn't mind me interrupting his meal to meet them. Charlie was impressed and Cossie was so thrilled she talked about it to her Natchez/Vidalia friends every time she saw Morgan on the tube.

Something One Shouldn't Do Nude

Feeling good was something I experienced every night after working one of the WS games. First I would go to the network's big bash, drink cocktails and eat until wee hours of the morning. Then I would go to my hotel bar and have a few nightcap drinks. with another club PR man, executive, or scout. After I decided to conclude the long day of toiling and partying, I would place my suitcases against the door of my huge room, just in case I walked in my sleep. The entire 20 years in the Navy and I never did it, but after I got out and had starting drinking so much, sometimes I would get up to

go to the toilet and wander in my sleep into another room. Carolyn, always a light sleeper because of the babies she raised, became cognizant of this infrequent observance and would usually catch me from going out of the house or into a non-toilet room. As I always slept in the nude, precautions such as blocking the hotel door was necessary.

Alas, in my sleep that night in this large, busy NY hotel, I walked in my slumber, removed the suitcases, and had walked down the hallway several yards before I finally woke. I was naked as a jaybird and my hotel door had automatically locked when I exited the room, so I was stranded.

I finally knocked on doors trying to get someone to call the desk for help, but, while nobody opened or talked to me, as they could use their peep viewer on the door and see I was not dressed, someone did call. A room clerk came with a master key and let me in with a suggestion that I sleep in my clothes next time.

Fortunately, Carolyn had recommended I sleep in the pajamas she packed, so I put them on after I did my job in the toilet.

Naturally, I slept like a log the rest of the morning.

I would try it again when Carolyn and Jeff were with me in NY. I got the bags removed from the door, but she caught me before I exited.

Another "hiking in my dreams" experience occurred

in Hawaii during one of MLB's Winter Meetings. I had a second floor room in this fancy hotel on Waikiki Beach. It had been a long time since my other sleep walking, so I still preferred sleeping in the nude as the night attire usually twists uncomfortably in my crotch and under my arms. However, this night it was very cool in the room and I was barely sober enough to don a pajama top. I wasn't sober enough not to sleepwalk, however.

It was about 3 a.m. when I woke and found myself standing in the elevator with the door opening on the main floor. I peeped out and couldn't see anyone in the small lobby. The desk clerk was inserting mail into the room slots and had his back to me. Quickly, I surveyed the situation and decided to try to tip-toe the short distance to permit the desk to block my nude bottom as I asked him for a key.

Fortunately, I made it. Then, I sighed with relief when I excused myself to him and asked for a key. He was a desk clerk with whom I had talked baseball several times. He knew me well so he gave me my key without questioning. I waited until he turned back to his tasks and then darted to the elevator. I added the rest of my pajama outfit and swore I would never sleep naked on the road again. My word is my bond. I have not slept naked on the road since.

Sleeping With Nukes During Navy Hitch

Mentioning sleeping reminds me of our son Bob's brave sleeping arrangements a few times while he was still in on his four-year hitch. In February 1972, he had reported on the USS CAMDEN (AOE-2) in Long Beach after boot camp and it left for Vietnam the next morning. They stopped in ports of Subic, Hong Kong, Sasebo and lots of time in the Tonkin Gulf. He learned to scuba dive from their Underwater Demolition Squad.

He went to the Nuclear Weapons Transshipment School in January 1973 so he was one of four sailors on the CAMDEN authorized to handle the nuclear weapons they hauled the next month when it made its second tour to Vietnam. The nukes had better air conditioning than thecrew's sleeping quarters. In some of the hot, humid summer nights he slept by the nukes. The ship's recreation stops this tour was Hong Kong again, Melbourne, Malaysia, and Hawaii.

Chicago White Sox Photo

COMISKEY/WHITE SOX PARK
Home of the Chicago White Sox from 1910-1990. Built by Charles Comiskey it was called Comiskey Park during most of his ownership and WSP at other times. My welcome message appeared on the left message side of this famous exploding scoreboard.

When he was discharged in '74, he worked several jobs delivering potato chips, sold water beds, furniture warehousing, and termite inspector. He also attended MSAC and took classes at Long Beach State and Cal State Los Angeles. Then in '77 he tied the knot with Virginia Kato and in the early 1980s they moved to San Diego where he sold solar heating systems and attended Mesa College; but, no more sleeping with nukes.

BGWW&P Times

1975-1982   Vol. 1, No. 16   Chicago, Illinois

The Cubs & Wrigley Field
Never Met More Devoted Fans Before Or Since

I spent an enormous time with the fans during my time with the White Sox. During the winter months I spoke at many banquets representing the Sox, some times with players Tom Bradley and later Rick Reichardt. I was interviewed several times on different radio programs and once featured on the great Chicago Bear running back Gale Sayers TV show he had after his brilliant career on the gridiron had ended due to an injury.

After the exciting 1972 season, I enjoyed telling fans about the prospects for the next season at winter banquets. Baseball fans would come up to me at the cocktail party following most of the affairs and tell me how much they enjoyed my presentation. They agreed that it sounded as if the Sox were going to go all the way with Bahnsen and Woods on the mound plus Allen, Melton, and May at the plate. The southsiders had gone from 1901, the formation of the American League, until 1971 without a home run champion.

Then posted two in a row with Melton's 33 and Allen's 37. Some of these congratulatory attendees were Cub fans which I thought would change their colors for 1973.

"You'll be coming to White Sox to see some of our games then?" I would ask.

"Oh no," they would answer. "I was born and will die a Cub fan. I'll follow them in the newspaper, but I watch my baseball at Wrigley Field."

However, apparently some of them came on May 20, 1973, during a double-header against the Twins. We had given all kids a free baseball bat with a record 55,555 fans attending. This standing room only crowd (seating capacity was 43,951) broke so many of the wooden grandstand seats cheering the Sox during rallies by banging on the seats and damaging them with the bats that we never had another "Bat Day." Chicago fans influence its sports organizations frequently.

One of the most ardent baseball fans in Chicago was Marv Samuel. He and

Jim Enright had formed the Chicago Baseball Cancer Charities (CBCC) in 1971 which raised over 11 million dollars for Northwestern & Children's Memorial Hospitals before Samuel died in 1993 of leukemia . He was a graduate of Northwester University and pitched a few years in the St. Louis Browns organization. Enright made the Basketball Hall of Fame as an official and served with several newspapers, including *Chicago Today*, as a baseball writer before he retired in 1974. He then became the public address announcer at Wrigley Field until he succumbed in 1981. I never will forget the song they played at Enright's funeral. It was an instrumental of "Take Me Out To The Ball Game" played in a very much slower speed than normal.

Billy Pierce, the greatest left-handed pitcher in White Sox history, assumed the reins of CBCC when Samuel retired. Many other former major leaguers in the area — such as Stan Hack, Don Elston, Johnny Klipstein, Moose

Skowron, and Ken Keltner — were members and later Milt "No Hitter" Papas and Ron Santo.

I was a member and participated in many golf benefits raising money for Chicago charities

MLB's youngest manager and Cleveland shortstop Lou Boudreau, who was now the WGN radio color announcer with play-by-play man Vince Lloyd, lived in the area and participated in benefit when asked, but I don't think he was a member per se of CBCC. It was quite a thrill being around Boudreau and Keltner at the same time. Joe DiMaggio had a record (still is) of 56 games in which he had hit safely playing when the Yanks arrived at Cleveland on July 17, 1941. He hit two shots just inside the third base bag that were labeled sure doubles, but Keltner stabbed both of them. Then Joe walked and his final at bat hit a hard grounder in the hole behind second base which Lou fielded and turned into a double play.

Then in late November of 1975, Samuel asked me to have lunch with him downtown. He told me Chuck Shriver, the Cubs' Director of Information and Services (another name for PR Director), had left that organization to become General Manager of a new professional basketball team being formed in San Diego. He suggested I apply for the job as the Wrigley family paid well and the Cubs had a retirement plan.

The Sox didn't and he knew it, but I told him: "Marv, the White Sox have been good to me and I have enjoyed working under Stu and now Roland. Plus, owner John Allyn is an excellent photographer himself and lets me buy any camera equipment I need. He even likes the action shots during the game that my teenage son David takes with our rapid fire

35MM magazine camera. I could certainly use more pay and the retirement availability is very appealing; however, I wouldn't have the heart to go looking for that job. Now, maybe if they approach Mr. Allyn for permission to talk to me about it, that would work."

Marv must have conveyed it to them because a few days later John informed me he had given them permission.

"For your information, and please keep it to yourself, I am in the process of selling the club to Bill Veeck. You may want to consider their offer very seriously," Allyn said. "The Wrigleys are fine people."

That threw me quite a "curve ball." I had always felt that Veeck was a promotional genius. He was probably most known for his legally sending a midget to pinch hit with the bases loaded to win a game when he owned the St. Louis Browns. However, he produced many impressive events while owning the Milwaukee Brewers, Browns,

Cleveland Indians, and the White Sox. In addition to pinch hitting the midget Eddie Gaedel, also raising (when opposition batted) and lowering the height (to 265 feet for home team)of the fences in Milwaukee, and exploding scoreboard at Comiskey Park were among the thousands of happenings this man created that had impressed me in his autobiography, "*VEECK - as in wreck.*" He used many clever gimmicks forcing MLB to make them illegal the next day.

I had received several calls from Shriver's secretary of the Cubs' Information & Services Office asking me for advice on how to handle some of the PR mail she was receiving from league and commissioner PR departments. She was so friendly and had such a cheerful personality, I ask her how she liked working for the Cubs.

"Oh, it's great," she said. "They pay well and are good to their employees."

A few days later I met with their Vice President of Park Operations, E.R. "Salty" Saltwell, for lunch in late November at a restaurant near his office at Wrigley Field. He outlined the Cubs' offer and I told him it was very adequate, but I would appreciate giving them my decision after the annual MLB Winter Meetings the first week of December. He consented.

Veeck Becomes CWS Owner For 2nd Time

The meetings were held that year ('75) at the Diplomat Hotel in Hollywood, Fla. The baseball club owners finally approved Bill Veeck, and his investors, purchase of the White Sox during the meetings and I prepared the news release of the decision and set up the most elaborate press conference I ever held in my career as a SID in college and PR Director in MLB. There were 15-20 microphones set up by radio and television stations at a table in the MLB press room. The media personnel, as usual most from New York City, Boston, Detroit, and Chicago, must have numbered near 150 hovering around Veeck shooting questions — left, right, and down the middle — at the new, colorful Sox owner.

The next morning, Hemond thought of the clever idea of setting up an open office for Veeck in the middle of the lobby. He had a coffee table set up with a telephone and had a sign made on a stand beside Bill's sofa chair that read "Open for Business." Then Veeck had me call ever 30 minutes or so as the other clubs trading executives watched inquisitively. He would fake a conversation as if he was discussing a possible trade. The scene attracted attention to non-baseball hotel occupants as well forming the audience that Veeck obviously loved.

We did it a couple days and then he asked me to meet his wife, Mary Francis, at the airport and drive her to the hotel. Which I did, of course, and she was very nice. I liked her immediately and we had a nice conversation on the way to the hotel.

The next day, I decided it was time to talk to Veeck about my situation. I found him in the dining area chatting with John Allyn after eating their lunch. I asked if I could interrupt for a moment. They welcomed me and had me sit with them. I told Veeck how the Cubs and did the proper thing and went through Mr. Allyn then made me their offer.

"Buck, I had heard nothing but good things about you so I had planned no changes in your department. Also, I am giving everyone a 10% raise, but I know I can't compete with the Wrigley family and their retirement plan financially," he said.

I thanked him and immediately called Saltwell to see if the offer was still open. He affirmed it was, so I told him I would accept with pleasure and told him I would report immediately. However, it would be for half-days until I finished the two weeks notice that I gave Veeck when I told him I had accepted the Cubs offer.

"Buck, you'll be paid for the rest of the month by the Sox, but you can move your permanent anchor now. If we need you, we'll call you and

you can come back and handle it. That's the least we can do for the many years you worked for the White Sox," Veeck was kind enough to say and it made me feel good.

I hated to miss the opportunity to work with him and Hemond as I also am very imaginative. The three of us could have made an exciting front office team. But...so be it. The decision had been made. What might have been was inessential, as it will never happen. I've always been able to eliminate thoughts of "what might have been" from my mind and not waste my time thinking of such thoughts.

"A Century of Diamond Memories" (1876-1976)

One of the first things I did after I met the owner of the pretty telephone voice, Cherie Blake, in the Information and Services Office located inside the main concourse. Then she escorted me upstairs to Salty's office. He went over some of the many duties I would have and introduced me to John Holland, the Executive Vice President and top official of the Cubs at Wrigley Field. P.K. Wrigley, the Cubs' President and Owner, operated from his office in the Wrigley Building downtown or his home in Lake Geneva, Wis. I never got to meet him before he died, but I spent many hours with his son William, who was inheriting the company and the Cubs.

When William's father died, a Vice President of the Wrigley Company, William Hagenah, would take over as President of the Cubs. I liked and respected both of them.

I asked, during my initial orientation meetings with these

history of the Chicago Cubs and would take many months to learn all of it. Therefore, first thing I did was hire Jim Enright to write the copy and assist me in my research. He had already authored a paperback book titled *Chicago*

was with the Cubs that hadn't been approved before, I would take it down town for Bill's okay.

It was finished in six weeks with 64 pages of great photographs and articles, plus a chronological listing of all players — by position — that had ever played for the Cubs as well as an alphabetical listing. Also, all the leaders in all categories were included and it sold for $2.50. On the first page, I wrote:

Chicago Cubs Photo

WRIGLEY FIELD 1979

Chicago Cubs games began playing here on April 20,1916. Prior nicknames were White Stockings (l876-89), Colts (1889-97), Orphans (1898-1902) & until final settled on Cubs (1903-present).

THE CHICAGO CUBS ARE
THE ONLY PROFESSIONAL
BASEBALL FRANCHISE
TO PLAY IN THE SAME
CITY FOR 100 YEARS.
THIS BOOK IS DEDICATED
TO CUBS FANS
THEN AND NOW, FOR
MAKING THIS RECORD
POSSIBLE.
WITHOUT THEM THERE
WOULD BE NO CHICAGO
CUBS
AND CERTAINLY, NO
BOOK.

officials, what publication was being prepared for the Cubs upcoming centennial season? Nothing they said and told me to have at it utilizing the facilities and staff members of the Meyerhoff Advertising Co. as needed. Their officials assigned the account executive Dick Lane to be at my disposal for furnishing art, layout, and design for a magazine-type souvenir edition which I named "A Century of Diamond Memories."

I knew very little of the

Cubs, so I figured that with his compilation of facts for writing that publication, his many years covering the Cubs as a baseball writer for the Chicago newspapers, and now serving as the Wrigley Field Public Address announcer would make him the perfect choice.

When I explained the reasoning of my choice to Bill Wrigley, he approved. I had been told that the Wrigley family must approve the cover of any thing to be published.

Anything I ever did while I

The cover was very colorful with a young boy in a baseball uniform holding his glove and with his Collie dog sitting beside him on the top of a hill. In the sky above him were Cub players of the past in a soft light blue ink. The only thing I told Dick that the artist had the grass on the hill yellow as if it was past summer time near the beginning of winter. He had the artist (who I never met) paint green over it and submit it to Mr. Wrigley when he finished. Dick called me a few days later that it had been approved and it was at the press. When the copies were printed and I saw the cover I was disappointed. It was painted over, but sloppily done. I just had to live with it (and still do). I'm not a perfectionist , but I do seek being as near to perfection as possible.

By Barney Sterling

MY FIRST DAY in Wrigley Field Press Box.

It was well received by everyone else, I guess, as I never heard any negative response from others in the organization when the finished products were delivered to Wrigley Field while I was at Spring Training.

Scottsdale — A Wonderful Splash In The Desert

The Cubs had their Spring Training camp in Scottsdale, Ari., until 1979. Then they returned to Mesa, Ari., both cities were among the large

mesh of small cities that surround Phoenix. I enjoyed Scottsdale the best and its wonderful restaurants. Yosh Kawano, the Cubs clubhouse and equipment manager of many decades, took me to one bar and dining spot that many of the clubs coaches and scouts frequented either for dinner, or after dinner elsewhere for a nightcap (or two, or three, or four, etc.).

I liked it immensely because I enjoyed hearing the scouts tell of funny happenings in their lifetime. Eddie Mathews was a frequent customer and we became friends, me sharing my humorous escapades in the Navy and him his while playing and scouting for the Atlanta Braves. I told him of my idea of getting him and Ernie Banks together at Wrigley Field for a "shoot-off" since they both finished their brilliant career tied with 512 home runs. He agreed to participate in such an event and gave me his phone number.

Jim Marshall, a fine gentleman, was in his second season as Field Manager of the Cubs. He thought it was a good idea so a I filed it away in my mind for future reference. Saltwell had been named VP-General Manager, but he was in Chicago so I told him of the plans later.

Marshall would compile a 75-87 record again that season. I feel a little personal comfort with myself for what I did the last game of the 1976 season. The Cubs were hosting

the Montreal Expos with Bill Madlock, who had led the NL in batting the previous season with a .354 average, currently had 170 hits in 510 at bats for a .3333 average. The mark was second in the loop to Cincinnati's Ken Griffey's .3375. They were at home against the Atlanta Braves in their season finale.

I sat down with my calculator and computed the number of consecutive hits, without an out, that Madlock would have to record before he surpassed Griffey. I put it, as well as Griffey's, all down for our pre-game notes so all the news media would know. If Griffey didn't play, and I called their PR guy Jim Ferguson to learn Manager Sparky had been talked into not starting him by teammates Pete Rose and Joe Morgan, Madlock could pass him with a four-for-four performance.

The excitement grew as Bill, with his short stroke and speed afoot, got four straight safeties. His last was a line drive to left field. The small 9,486 crowd stood and applauded heartily. They didn't know Madlock was now leading the National League with a .3385214 to Griffey's .3375. Ferguson called almost at the time Bill got his fourth single. He asked me how Madlock was doing and I had a strong urge to hang up and tell him later we got disconnected, but I knew that wasn't the ethical thing to do so I told him he was 4-for-4.

Apparently, they had done

their pre-game calculating, also, as he said, "Shit, he's ahead of Ken. I better call Sparky right away."

I waited until the Expos had made their final out in the top of the eighth inning. I knew Madlock was scheduled to bat second so I called Ferguson to see if Sparky sent Griffey into the game.

"Yeah, he pinch hit, but struck out. He's in on defense now so he may get another at bat," he said very dejectedly.

I immediately called Marshall in the dugout.

"Jim, Griffey pinch hit and struck out. Even if he gets another at bat an gets a hit he will be batting .3380782 which is shy of Bill's .3385214. I highly recommend you take him out, NOW," I said quickly.

"Buck, are you sure you're right?"

"Figures don't lie. Right now he's got another title," I said firmly.

He took Madlock out immediately and I saw Bill headed toward the Cubs clubhouse in the left field corner with his glove. I expected him to let Madlock go to the plate for his turn, then walk out and point to the clubhouse, for a dramatic effect. The way it went was the audience didn't know Madlock was out of the game until Enright announced the pinch-hitter over the public address system.

Madlock would have many more thrills and would lead the NL twice more, with Pittsburgh in 1981 (.341) &

1083 (.323), during his 15 years. But it obviously was one of the most exciting games during my 12 years in the majors.

Marshall was replaced by Herman Franks in 1977 (81-81) by Bob Kennedy, who replaced the late John Holland as executive vice president and took over the general manager duties. Saltwell then resumed the VP-park operation & secretary duties.

Kennedy's 16 playing years (1939-57) was as strong-armed third baseman/outfielder mostly with the White Sox and the Indians. After retirement he toiled at Wrigley Field in several categories. One was the head coach of the Cubs College of Coaches (1961-65) and then as special assistant to General Manager John Holland until 1965.

Bob never made the All-Star Game, but his son Terry made it as a catcher three times during his 14 years in the major leagues for St. Louis, San Diego, and San Francisco. His first three seasons over 100 games were his best with the Padres. His batting (.301, .295, & 294) and RBIs (41, 97, & 98) were commendable during those years. All our kids and grandchildren watch cheered him in '83 & '84 with us as we had settled there after my MLB career.

Pedens Trek To
To The North Side

We went to our real estate friend, Marge Lewis Fleck, to

find a house closer to Wrigley Field. She had sold us the new home in Justice and we had come to know her son, Ed Lewis, who was a season ticket holder at White Sox Park. He would marry a sweet gal named Mona, and become a veterinarian in Tinley Park. We had bought a white terrier with a light brown left ear which Jeffrey named Spooky. We kept taking Spooky to Ed on the south side even after we found a house for sale on Wolcott St. a couple blocks north of Lawrence Ave.

By David Peden
SPOOKY

Spooky was very fond of it because it had an fenced in back yard so no other males could mark it as their territory. It had an apple and pear trees to provide plenty of shade. It was three stories high with a spare bedroom, kitchen, and shower/toilet in the basement. The exit to the latter leading into the back yard had a pet swinging door which made it very convenient for Spooky on the weekends we spent in Walkerton, Ind., visiting the Huffstetters. We would leave him plenty of dry dog food and water and shut him in the warm boiler room for easy access to the backyard whenever he desired.

The two bedrooms and family room were on the top floor and it had a bathroom on each level. I bought a nice four-stool bar for the large living room where we entertained frequently and it was well covered with speakers for our stereo system and thousands of feet of taped musical albums I had been collecting during my 20 years of swapping albums to record with my teammates.

Spooky and I became very close during that time. He was my lap dog and extremely intelligent. He used to crack Carolyn up when she would peel a banana in the kitchen and he would smell it upstairs in my lap and come running down the stairs to get a treat of it.

I was gone so much of the time with all the day games at Wrigley Field, which did not yet have lights for night games, plus the many Chicagoland banquets I attended representing the Cubs. This left most of the responsibility in raising Jeffrey to Carolyn as David had finished high school and left with the Fiat for California. He wrecked it enroute, but wasn't seriously injured to make it to the San Diego area where Bobby had settled with Virginia Kato and Debra & Andy had moved. David eventually joined the Navy and spent a hitch as a hospital corpsman where he met and married Sherrie La Plant, a hospital corps woman.

Jeff not only gave the teachers problems in grammar school, but got into drugs. Carolyn kept it from me as I would get in so late attending sports benefits and banquets in nearby cities and communities she didn't want me to lose any sleep over it. We would learn to regret this lack of paternal guidance as things got worse when he reached high school level.

Chicago Cub Benefits Were Very Plentiful

The Cubs participated in many area benefits during my tenure there and I was heavily involved in most of them. The Rube Walker Benefit, which was later changed to Cubs Care Benefit, was the biggest. Its proceeds went to the Leukemia Center at Northwestern Memorial Hospital. The first one I worked the fans attended a cocktail party and a dinner attended by the Cubs colorful outfielder Jose Cardenal and a few more players who signed autographs and chatted with the attendees.

Once I got in the swing of things as a member of the committee in charge of putting on the annual dinner, we decided to move the benefit dinner to one of the major hotels. I started collecting memorabilia from the Cub players such as cracked bats, old baseball gloves, discarded old baseball spikes, stained sweatshirts, etc. We would place then on tables during the cocktail hour preceding the dinner with a sheet beside the item so that fans could bid on the item. Then during the dinner I would have the MC (master of ceremonies, usually a Chicago TV or radio announcer or one of our team announcers) announce the win of the winning bidder and present the item to the recipient.

Madlock's broken bat following one of his NL batting championship seasons ('76) and an autographed ball of one used in Rick Reuschel's final 20th victory in his brilliant 20-10 campaign ('77) brought in winning bids over $500. Eventually, scheduling the benefit during an off-day during the season, I got over half the team to attend and be host of a table of 10. One year I wrote a comedy script for the players to act out. I had a scene with mock stage of a clubhouse with lockers and a card table. None of the players knew their lines in advance. I had brief lines printed on tabs on the card table in front of each or on their locker entrance.

I had about six of the friendliest players participate. I remember Bill Buckner and

Mike Krukow were two of them. All they had to do was read their lines after the player listed at the top of the script and then say their lines. They were such trusting souls they did it perfectly as planned. Not knowing what sense their script meant until that night while performing, sometimes they would laugh at their own remarks that I had written. It went across great to the hundred of paying donors at the dinner tables in the audience. I was very pleased with it.

We also had a talented local TV announcer perform with his band and to highlight the night we brought in the Cubs Honorary Vice President Charlie Grimm and his pretty wife Marion. Grimm, nicknamed "Jolly Charlie" because of his personality, batted over .300 five years of his 20 in the majors as a excellent fielding first baseman (1916-36) mostly with the Cubs. Then he managed them 14 years of his 19 managerial years winning the pennant three times, including 1945, the last time they played in a world series. Charlie played his banjo and Marion sang a few songs.

Later I filmed comic interviews and skits of the players at Wrigley Field and showed them following the meal at the benefit dinner. It became the largest social gathering of the players, coaches, and fans. Fun was had by all and the Leukemia

Center benefited tremendously during the seven years I was with the Cubs.

When I was editing Jim Enright's copy for the *A Century of Diamond Memories* and later *day by day in Chicago Cubs history*, I became very knowledgeable of the team's great history. I had learned about Art Ahrens and Eddie Gold, two members of the Society of American Baseball Research (SABR), and their collection and research of Cubs history while attending a SABR meeting. I was fascinated with their notes and sold the Cub officers on purchasing it from them and printing it as an official publication of the Chicago National League Ball Club, Inc.

Chicago Cubs Are Biggest Winner

A couple of the items I learned among the thousands of other things was the Cubs was the **winningest franchise** in all of professional sports with over **9,000** victories. One of the most interesting season, which the true Chicago sports fans still talk about, was in 1906 when the Cubs posted a **116-36** record to win the National League with the best won-lost record **in the history of MLB**. They boasted top NL statistics in hits (1,316), doubles (181), triples (71), home runs (20, "dead ball" era), and a .262 team batting average.

Ironically enough, the White Sox (93-58) on the south side

of Chicago won the AL crown. They were the weakest hitting team in the league with a .230 team batting average enticing the baseball writers to call them the "Hitless Wonders" and ranking the Cubs as eavily favored to win the World Series. The Sox won in six games to the surprise of everyone.

The Cubs recovered and handily won their next two WS against Detroit in only five games, 4-0-1 (a tied but no losses) in 1907 and 4-1 in 1908 triumph. The latter series was the **last time the Cubs won a World Series.**

While I found tons of interesting baseball memorabilia about Cub greats in the past such as Cap Anson, Mordecai "Three Finger" Brown, the double-play combination of Tinkers to Evers to Chance, etc., but their escapades are well covered in detail by more talented baseball writers than I. Even the infamous "goof" by young Fred Merkle one will enjoy reading. Publications I highly recommend Cub and other baseball fans to read is attached at the conclusion of these memoirs.

One in particular, I used frequently at Rotary, Kiwanis, etc. and other business luncheons where after my introduction and it was sometimes tough to get the attention of the audience. Many of them had brought prospective customers with them as a guest and were busy making conversation to them. I soon learned I needed a "grabber."

"Yep, I'm with the Chicago Cubs, one of the original owners when the National League was founded in 1876. A.G. Spalding was not only manager but their ace pitcher. He toed the mound for the Cubs first game on April 25 in Louisville, Ky., and pitched a 4-0, seven-hitter and even collected a team high three hits himself. **Two months later General Custer and his troops were completely wiped out by Crazy Horse and his Indian followers at Little Big Horn,**" I said very slowly and with very much emphasis.

At first there would be complete silence as the majority of these great Chicago baseball fans were in shock as they mulled those facts over in their minds. Then there would be buzzing to one another stuff like: "That's hard to believe," "Is that true?", "I didn't know we had professional baseball before the west was settled," etc.

Spalding would win 47 games that season and later succeeded William A. Hulbert as president of the Cubs. He started, with his brother, a sporting-goods company that is one of the largest to this date.

Several later events I thought significant enough to include herein as they are applicable to some players of my seven-year era with the Cubs.

For example, George Mitterwald, a catcher for the Cubs (1974-77) was the last teammate to hit three home runs in one game. He did it at Wrigley Field in 1974 against the Pirates in a season when he played only 79 games and *only hit a grand total of seven home runs that season.*

Centerfielder Rick Monday (1972-76) did it in 1973 at Philadelphia, but his etch in Cubs history was in 1976 while playing in Los Angeles against the Dodgers and two Latino fans ran out on the outfield during the game with an American Flag and was obviously attempting to burn it in front of the large audience of baseball fans. Rick thrilled all the true Americans watching as he ran pass them and snatched the flag from their grasp and ran with it to the home plate area. Naturally, the security guards ran on the field and absconded the culprits.

Later that season, when the Dodgers were playing the Cubs in Wrigley Field, their General Manager Al Campanis came with them to present the rescued flag to Monday to keep. I already had planned to have newly crowned Miss Illinois, Betsy Jamison, introduced and throw out the first ball, but I thought it best to have Campanis presentation to Monday first. So I discussed my plans to him and explained it would be very nice to have Miss Illinois hold the flag, which was folded, in front of her with both hands. Then,

after Campanis finished with his speech, he could turn and get the flag for presentation to Monday.

"No," he said emphatically. "I brought that flag all the way from Los Angeles and I'm going to hold it until I give it to Monday."

It irritated me at first, but didn't surprise me. I had sustained several minor run-ins with him at Winter Meetings and he always had impressed me as a real anal sphincter. He proved it to the world a decade later on April 6, 1987, during a television appearance on ABC's "Nightline" with Ted Koppel. His answer to why there were no black managers, general managers, etc., he said among other things, "I truly believe they may not have some of the necessities...."

Publicity Director Steve Brener urged him not to go on the show to no avail. Fred Claire, who was made General Manager a few days later, Field Manager Tommy Lasorda, and other noted baseball executives and players denied that Campanis was prejudiced against blacks. They were friends and I believed them.

One Cub Season Mark To Last Forever

The first three-home run game hit by Cubs in its 20th century history in 1930 was by one of the most famous home run hitter to ever don a Cub pinstripe, Hack Wilson. He had led the NL in homers in three consecutive years as the "dead ball era" was waning: l926 (21), l927 (30), & l928 (31). He hit 39 the next year with teammate Rogers Hornsby, but Philadelphia's Chuck Klein blasted 43 and NY Giants' Mel Ott's 42. All four made MLB's Hall of Fame.

Then in l930 it happened, despite a record 105 bases on balls, he led the loop with 56 home runs **and 191 RBI's.** As with Joe Dimaggio's 56-game hitting streak, I don't ever expect that RBI title to ever be equaled.

In addition to publishing the century booklet, we also designed official consecutively numbered certificates of attendance for fans attending the opening home game of the second century of Chicago Cubs baseball. Barbara Sullivan, a regular attendee at Wrigley Field, was the first through the turnstiles to receive certificate #00001.

The winter months of my first year with the Cubs I spent attending many sports banquets with Ernie "Mr. Cub" Banks who had retired from play after the l971 season and was doing community relations work with me that year during the off season. He loved the many golf benefits in which we participated. We couldn't pass a big lake along the highway we were traveling without stopping and him trying to hit a golf ball over its water.

My Most Fun Of All Banquets Attended

The January New York Baseball Writers Association invited Ernie and me to attend, I think, their 1977 banquet. We were enjoying drinks at the pre-dinner cocktail party and the banquet officials threw Ernie a curve ball. He knew he was to be seated at the head table before the l,500 fans or so, but they wanted him to introduce Johnny Bench, the Cincinnati Reds' great catcher. Ernie then came to me for help. Naturally I had my briefcase with me which provided me with the accomplishments of Bench that I didn't remember. Most of them I knew, so I found a typewriter and whipped up the facts and dates on an index card for Ernie.

I ran the notes pass Johnny to make sure they were accurate, but I had to wait until he finished his story about the colorful Umpire Tom Gorman.

"Gorman had a dozen baseballs setting on a table in the Reds' clubhouse for the players to sign. A couple of games later Gorman checked the balls and found all the players had signed them except me," Bench said talking to a couple other players on the dais at the pre-banquet cocktail party. The next game I came to bat and was called out on strikes."

"Awww ump," Bench told Gorman. "That was outside."

"Gorman ignored my frowning look. He just said, 'sign the balls.'"

When I got to my table with nine paying New Yorkers, we just introduced ourselves by first names or nicknames. Suddenly, an usher came up to our table and asked which one of us was Buck Peden of the Chicago Cubs. I acknowledged it was me and he gave me a note he said was from Ernie Banks at the head table and that he was told to wait for an answer.

The guys at the table were flabbergasted.

"Buck are you with the Cubs? What did Banks write you?" was the gist of most of their comments.

I read the note and Ernie just asked if I had thought of anything else about Bench. Suddenly, I thought of a idea that would be fun for these guys. Most of the baseball fans in New York City are very knowledge about the sport and its participants.

"Yeah guys, the banquet officials have just informed him that they want him to give an introduction speech about the main awardee tonight, Johnny Bench. He wanted me to help him with some of Bench's achievements," I said very seriously. "I know he made the major leagues at age l9 and was rookie of the year... was it 1968?"

"Yeah," one excited table member added quickly, "and he won the National League's Most Valuable Player Award twice."

"You are right. That's great," I said acting like I was writing it down. "Wasn't that in 1970 and…" I hesitated and sure enough another guy came up with it.

"1972 was the other year, I'm sure of it. My son's a catcher in little league and he was the MVP the same year," another contributed.

We came up with the other items I had given Ernie earlier: led NL in homers twice, RBI thrice, and had over 100 RBI seasons six times. Ernie had all of it already so I just wrote "What you got is all I know. Go with it."

Bench, an Oklahoma City native and Choctaw Indian, was not only one of the greatest hitting catchers but he was probably the finest defensive players to ever wear the mask. But I wasn't watching him nor Ernie during the achievement material I had provided Banks was being said, I was watching the faces at our table watching them.

When Ernie would say one of the stats they thought we had given him, they would have an orgasm (not literally, of course).

"YEAH!!!!," they would yell exhilaratingly. "I gave him that one." They obviously had one of the best nights in their life and I did too. If any of them ever read this and feel offended, I am truly sorry and apologize. I only meant for them to have fun doing it and their obvious happiness was joy for me. I have always enjoyed making

people happy. And remember, I didn't mention anyone's name or the table number. Therefore, 'twas a mutual baseball happening of enjoyment shared by all of us at the time and no embarrassment was intended by me with this exposure to the public of the great night we had. I'm sure the readers will have enjoyed me sharing it with them.

Ernie Makes HOF On First Ballot

One of the reasons Banks had been included on the dignitaries list to set at the head table I think was because he had been selected for

By Barney Sterling

FIRST AUTOGRAPHED photo by Ernie Banks the day it was announced he was chosen for MLB's Hall of Fame.

———————

the National Baseball Hall of Fame on the first ballot of his eligibility and would be inducted August 8th at

Cooperstown. He was only the eighth player, since the initial balloting began, to be chosen in the first round. The others were: Ted Williams, Sandy Koufax, Mickey Mantle, Stan Musial, Warren Spahn, Bob Feller, and Jackie Robinson.

He had set or tied dozens of records and won countless honors.

For example, he was named to the NL All-Star Team 13 times and was the loop's Most Valuable Player two straight seasons (1958-59). He led the Cub career players in nine of 11 modern all-time offensive departments, including 512 home runs before he retired in 1971 after 19 years as a shortstop and finally as a first baseman with brief appearances at third base and in the outfield.

I broke out one of the official publicity photographs of Ernie the day I learned of his selection as we were having lunch at Wrigley Field and I congratulated him on the selection, which was expected by everyone. Then I asked him to give me his first autograph as a Hall of Famer. It was only the second (first was my HOF candid of Aaron) autograph I sought & acquired in my 12 years in the majors. He kindly signed it to me and added *"Thanks"* above his signature. It meant a lot to me as I knew what he meant by the appreciative word. Naturally, I had not done anything to influence his brilliant playing career, but I interpreted it as if I made some contribution to his public appearances at some of the many benefits we attended together.

Many Major Player Changes In '77 & '78

We had Banks throw the first ball for the Opening Day Game on April 7, 1977, which gave the huge crowd of 39,937 (maximum seating capacity was 37,741 at that time) a treat as six new faces took the field for the Cubs after trades made during the winter.

Bill Buckner & Ivan DeJesus came from Los Angeles, Bobby Murcer & Steve Ontiveros from San Francisco, Gene Clines from Texas, and Greg Gross from Houston. Buckner had hit .301 and stole 28 bases the year before and DeJesus, an outstanding shortstop, had hit .304 & pilfered 31 bases in Class AAA ball. Gross owned a .298 career average and hit .314 for Rookie of the Year honors in 1974. Outfielder Murcer had a .281 career batting average and had averaged 22 home runs and 90 RBI's a year in the majors. Ontiveros, a third baseman, had led the Pacific Coach League (AAA) with a .357 in l973.

Despite having to lose Monday to LA and Madlock to SF, among several other players, Kennedy and Franks were confident they had improved the overall team. When the '77 season was over and compared to the '76 campaign, they were still a fourth place team in the NL East Division but with six more victories (75-87 in '76 and 81-81 in '77). However, it was the last time the Cubs did not have a losing season while the Wrigley family still owned the club. I thought Franks' coaching staff of Mike Roark, Harry "Peanuts" Lowrey, & Octavio "Cookie" Rojas, plus the colorful batting instructor Lew Fonscea, were a good staff.

Lowrey, a 13-year major league veteran outfielder mostly with the Cubs and the Cardinals, talked with me one day about meeting my favorite slugger as a kid, Detroit's Hank Greenerg. Hank led the AL in home runs four seasons, including a 58 total in l938 before the steroids.

"His hands were so big he didn't shake hands with your hand, he shook hands with your arm," he told me laughing.

I also remember another handshaking story told to me my Charlie Grimm. He said when shaking hands with Steve O'Neill who caught in l,590 games, mostly for Cleveland.

"It was just like grabbing into a bag of peanuts," Grimm said. Charlie, as most of the old timers, was great with whom to communicate during my career.

I gave Rojas a great line of "communicating" to Willie Hernandez, a southpaw from Puerto Rica, in one of our Rube Walker benefit films. Talking in the dugout, Cookie told him, "I know you believe you understood what you think I said, but I am not sure you realize that what you heard is not what I meant." Willie then turned toward the camera with wide eyes, an open mouth, and half raised hands with open palms. The skit was well received by the audience.

Then when Franks retired and the field managerial reigns were turned over to another, Joey Amalfitano, the team faltered to an embarrassing 38-65 record during the player strike that shortened the '81 season.

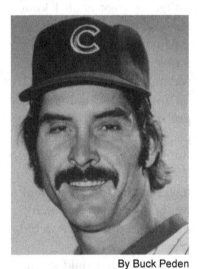

By Buck Peden
DAVE KINGMAN

I liked all these new players and got along well with all of them as well as Dave Kingman, who was acquired in the re-entry draft for the '78 season. Kingman was a slim 6'6" long ball hitter with impressive home runs totals that included 36 & 37 in '75 & '76 while with the NY Mets. Bill Wrigley told me when he and Kennedy were negotiating his salary and the powerful slugger asks them for bonuses if he broke the Cubs home run and RBI record. Kennedy, a former 16-year major league powerful throwing third basemen mostly with the Chicago White Sox, glanced at Wrigley and told him they would give him a $200,000 bonus if he broke those two marks, and Bill agreed. Obviously, Kingman did not know of Hack Wilson's 56 home runs and towering (and still unsurpassed) 191 RBI's in 1930.

While I have no knowledge of any player's salary except the $225,000 the White Sox paid Dick Allen, I know Kingman earned whatever he got for one season. During his three seasons with the Cubs (1978-80) he led the NL with 48 home runs in '79. It was his best home run season during his 16 years in the majors (1971-86) and he hit 37 for the Mets in '82 to lead the circuit one other time. He only hit over 100 RBIs once for the Cubs (115 in '79) but was far shy of Wilson's 191.

Kingman hit three home runs in a game three different times as a Cub and one of his homers was the longest I saw during my seven years at Wrigley Field. I video taped every home game in my office located in the far left corner just off the player's parking lot and across from the home club house. When I saw the ball soaring out over the left centerfield fence on my monitor and hearing announcer Jack

Brickhouse raving about the length of the blast, I ran out onto Waveland Ave. to check it out. There were always fans out on that street with gloves to catch the home runs. When they heard Vince Lloyd or Lou Boudreau on their radio saying, "There's a long hit to left center that could be out of here," they started looking up for the ball to catch it as a souvenir. One of them had been doing it for years and had his bushel basket full of balls photographed in one of the papers one year.

Anyway, I ran out to find out from them where the ball had landed. They were all amazed at the towering fourbagger and none of them could catch if as it hit halfway up the second house on Kenmore Ave. that runs into the north side of Waveland. I stepped it off and estimated it was nearly 500 feet from home plate. It was one of the highlights used by MLB on their weekend highlights.

Williams Back; Snowed-In Caravan

After Kingman's great '79 season we took him, Ontiveros, and Billy Williams on one of the Cubs Winter Caravans after the first of 1980. Williams, one of the greatest hitters in modern-day Cub history and definitely one of the Cub fans favorite players, was hired to replace Fonseca as batting instructor, Billy's achievements were many during his 16 years (1959-74).

To start the Whistler, Ala., native belted 25 home runs his first full season in the majors (1961). The most distinguished mark as a Cub was the 1,117 consecutive games he played to etch a NL record (later passed by Steve Garvey's 1,207)). The Yankees' Lou Gehrig holds the AL mark with his 2,130.

Williams 392 Cub home runs rank second to Banks on the Cubs' all-time list. He added 34 more in his final two years with the Oakland A's which gave him 426 ML roundtrippers. His best year trotting around the bases was in 1972 when he led the ML with a .333 batting average and .606 slugging percentage. He also had 122 RBI (2nd), 37 HR (tied for 3rd with WS Allen), 191 hits (3rd), and 34 doubles (4th). These impressive totals gained him NL Player of Year and ML MVP awards.

In 1970, Billy's 137 runs scored, 205 hits, and 373 total bases were also tops in the ML, but his 42 HRs and 129 RBI would only rank him second in the NL to Bench's "hot season" of 45 homers and 148 RBI. All of these, plus six selections to the All-Star Game, earned him a berth in MLB's HOF. When he was traded to Oakland and helped them win the AL West Division title in '75, Chicago got Second Baseman Manny Trillo and two pitchers. Trillo, teamed with Shortstop DeJesus gave the Cubs one of the best double play combinations in the league for four years.

Ontiveros played third base

during that period, and with Buckner at first base, the Cubs had a very competent defensive infield. With Ontiveros, Kingman, and Williams as the players on the caravan that year things were rosy until we hit Decatur in mid-east Illinois the third day. Then a snow storm hit the area and all highways were closed to traffic. I had been suffering with fever caused by a case of flu ever since we left Chicago; therefore, the mandatory lay over was genuinely welcomed by yours truly.

Billy and I were sharing a room. He knew how sick I was so when I bought a quart of vodka and two half gallons of orange juice and hit the sack, he wasn't a bit surprised. I just turned on the television and mixed me one screwdriver after the other until I went to sleep.

Williams came in later that night and woke me up asking if I was going to eat anything for supper. I was still feeling very feverish so I told him no and started mixing my screwdrivers again. We talked awhile and I learned there were many customers in the hotel stuck there as we were. He had got into a poker game with them. When I asked about Ontiveros and Kingman, he told me Steve was in his room watching TV and Dave took a dinner booth and spread out its entrails a briefcase he have brought onto the table before him. Kingman attended a junior college and

the University of Southern California. Apparently, he was utilizing our unfortunate situation to catch up on his investments.

I slept for three to four hours, wake up, drink more screwdrivers, then sleep three or four more. Finally, about noon I woke up feeling better. The fever had subsided and I had an appetite for the first time in two days, so I ordered a hamburger and French fries from room service and ate. After showering and shaving, put on some fresh clothes and went down stairs to find the poker game. During my 20 years in the military, I had played many games of poker and was usually successful using my conservative style of play.

"Mind if I join you gentlemen?" I asked noting there was an empty seat to the right of Williams with only four other players in the game.

"Sure Buck," Williams said patting the empty chair.

"Fellows this is Buck. Buck, this is Joe, Howard, Frank, and Tom," he said going around the table clockwise starting at his left. Obviously, they had only been using first names.

Fan Goes "Ape" Meeting The Cubs Great Billy Williams

We all nodded greetings and as I was sitting down I noticed Billy had most of the chips in front of him.

"Looks like Williams has been having all the luck, but then he was always lucky. When he would hit one of his home runs they would usually just barely make it to the Wrigley Field bleacher baskets," I kidded knowing how good natured he was and just trying to break the ice for my entrance.

Joe, the guy seated to the left of Williams, stared at Billy and looked him up and down.

"God! You mean I have been playing poker these two days seated next to Billy Williams? You were my favorite Cub of all time. I can't believe this is really happening," he said with extreme excitement as he grabbed Billy's hand and started shaking it vigorously.

"Please Billy," he pleaded going down to one knee. "You gotta give me your autograph or none of my Cub friends are going to believe me."

"Sure," Billy said and one player came up with a pen, but no one had any paper for him to sign. I was going to suggest to Joe that he could get paper in the lobby from the hotel clerk, but he thought of a better idea. He grabbed one of the joker cards we were not using and handed it to Williams.

"Here Billy. Just sign this 'To Joe, who donated $57 to me in a poker game,'" he said smiling ear to ear.

Williams signed it to Joe, but he wrote a more friendly message instead of the "donated" statement Joe had requested. Williams signed for the other guys and they finally returned to the game. Their conversation between hands, however, now was full of questions about something they had remembered seeing Williams do during his career when they attended games in the past at Wrigley Field.

I told them, "I learned that most home run hitting outfielders like Billy and Dave Kingman over there in the booth (pointing to Kingman) loved to fish. Williams always carried his fresh water fishing gear every where he went during off season traveling and once had spent considerable time teaching my son Jeffrey how to fish."

"That's Dave Kingman?" one of them exclaimed indicating they didn't know he also was at the hotel.

"Yep," I answered. "He has a yacht berthed in the Chicago Bay. Dave, Catcher Barry Foote, and a couple other players fish on Lake Michigan every chance they get. Kingman even has a sign hanging in his clubhouse locker that reads: 'I'd Rather Be Fishing.'"

I suggested they wait until they see him stop working out of his briefcase before they asked him for an autograph. They nodded agreement. Then I added that Ontiveros was also with us and they could get his when he came down from his room. They were nice friendly people and I kinda felt bad that Billy and I beat them out of a few bucks playing poker. But, socializing is socializing and poker is poker.

Pros & Cons Of William Buckner

They finally cleared the highways and we were able to proceed. This caravan, because of the storm, was not as successful as previous ones as we had to cancel the rest of the scheduled stops.

Buckner and his sweet wife Jody stayed over in Chicago several winters and took advantage of paid public appearances at banquets and other social gatherings in the vast Chicagoland area. We attended numerous events together and we became good friends.

I never will forget the first time he took batting practice as a Cub player in the Spring Training of the '77 season. I noticed he laced four straight line drives that would have been base hits. Then I started counting them to see how many he would get before hitting one poorly. *He laced 22 straight liners before he hit a ground ball that would have been an out in a game.*

When he stepped out of the cage, I introduced myself and told him of the number of consecutive hits I had counted.

"I gotta let the news media in camp know about that," I said.

He just shook my hand, smiled, and said, "Sure, Buck. I didn't count 'em, but it felt good up there as it should in batting practice."

A couple of times when I came out on the field during batting practice, he would throw me a glove and a ball and get me to throw him balls in the dirt so by the dugout so that h e could short hop them into his first baseman's mitt. First baseman frequently get throws like that in the dirt from the other infielders.

By Buck Peden

BILL BUCKNER

In preparing his biography for the upcoming season's news media guide, I learned of his stellar prep career at Napa High in Woodland Hills, Calif. As a wide receiver in football, he was named to the Coaches All-American teams his junior and senior year. He hit .667 as a junior and .529 as a senior.

He was doing great, hitting over .300 in every minor league in which he competed. Then in 1975 with the Dodgers, he severely sprained his ankle and had to have an operation.

He came back with a .301 in 1976, although he then had to sit in the whirlpool for a while after every game thereafter.

He was coming out of the trainers room one day and I passed him in the clubhouse.

"Buck, wait a minute," he said and I stopped and turned around to face him. Then he reached up under my nose, pinched the hairs growing there, and yanked them out of my nostrils.

As I yelped in pain, he said, "Now that looks better."

"You dirty rotten rack-a-frac," I said utilizing my usual curse word. "I'll get you for that." However, I never did and it was something I never forgot. I never let the hairs in my nose grow outside any more and, every time I saw a good-looking guy with them, I thought of Buckner and had a brief desire to pluck theirs as Bill had done mine.

He then turned to see a teammate arriving with a sour face. The player was single and loved to pick up his women at bars.

"Struck out again last night trying to score with the girls?" Buckner asked.

"More like I didn't ever get to the plate," the spurned player answered.

This was typical of the personality of Buckner. In 1978,

he led the Cubs in hitting with a .323 average and his fielding superb. In fact, lifetime among all first baseman in the history of baseball his 0.87 assists per game, which indicates the quickness and range of a first sacker, was tops in the history of baseball when he retired. That year the Chicago Pitch and Hit Club gave him the Cubs Major League Player Award and the local chapter of the Baseball Writer's Association of America presented him with the Chicago's Player of the Year. To top all that, a poll of Chicagoland area fans by Sports Phone chose him as the Most Popular Athlete in Chicago.

Then in 1980, he led all NL stickmen with a .324 average. And paced the league in doubles twice, 35 in '81 and 38 in '84. He was terrific at keeping the ball in play as he struck out only 453 times in 9,397 at bat, that's only one whiff every 20.7 trips to the plate. It's a shame, a player with all those accomplishments, especially the assists figure, would be remembered — after 22 years in the majors — only for the quirk of fate in the 18th year.

I'll only reiterate the happening that to some may define it as "that's the way the ball bounces." Buckner was

playing in the 1986 World Series for the Boston Red Sox. It was two outs in the bottom of the 10th innings of the sixth game. The Red Sox were ahead three games to two in the best-of-seven-series against the hosting New York Mets. Therefore, they needed only one out to win Boston's first WS since 1918 as Dave Henderson had hit a two-run homer in the top of the 10th for a 5-3 lead.

Things looked rosy for the visitors, but to use one of Yogi Berra's quotes, "It's not over 'til its over." Three singles and a wild pitch later and it was all tied, 5-5. Then Mookie Wilson hit a grounder straight down the first base line at Buckner, the one with the magic glove when it comes to bouncing balls. An observer of our 1,000 professional baseball games, I stunningly watched as the little horsehide sphere — whose last hop usually bounces normal and into Bill's mitt — skidded between his legs. Naturally the man on third base scored to win the game and enabled them to play and win the next game giving the World Series to New York.

BGWW&P Times

1975-82 Cont'd   *Vol. 1, No. 17*   *Chicago, Illinois*

Five Relief Masters Can't Do It All

Reminiscing about my wonderful time with the White Sox and Cubs, the fantastic relief pitchers those two club's scouts came up with was amazing. Terry Forster (1971-86) was the first one I saw and I've already mentioned him and Rich Gossage (1972-94) in the Sox chapter. They both had blazing fastballs.

Bruce Sutter (1976-88) was brought up by the Cubs with only an adequate fastball, but possessing a pitch that humiliated the batters called a "split-fingered fast ball." Coming towards

the plate it appeared to be a straight fastball and then drop two or three feet straight down. A batter swinging at a third strike, he thought was a knee high fastball down the middle the middle of the plate, would often have to trudge back to the bench after having embarrassingly swung at a pitch that bounced in the dirt to the catcher.

He really gained the nation's attention in a game in 1977. He came in relief in the 8th inning and struck out the side. **Then he strikes out the side again in the 9th, but this time with only nine pitches.**

Willie Hernandez (1977-89), a southpaw like Forster, had a good fastball and slider. He was from Puerto Rica. Louisianan Lee Smith was added in 1980 and gave the Cubs two great relievers, one from the each side of the mound as Smith was a righty.

Why did the team finish with losing seasons every

Scout **John Jordon "Buck"** O'Neil.
Smith was signed by Cub Scout O'Neil who was the most prolific and articulate scout I met in the major leagues. He impressed me with his great story telling using his eye brows and volume changes to express mood changes to enhance his tales in a most eloquent and magnificent manner.

Earlier, among the many amateurs he inked to major league pacts, two became Hall of Famers: Ernie Banks & Lou Brock. Before becoming a scout, he played in the Negro leagues as an outstanding first baseman, hitter, while managing. He was the first African-American coach in Major League Baseball before he began scouting. One of his post-retirement activities was to get former Negro league players in the MLB Hall of Fame and other important accomplishments for positive promulgation of baseball to the world.

In 1996, O'Neil with two others, published his autobiography: I Was Right On Time. Naturally, it's one of those baseball lovers should read.

In December 2006, Brock was posthumously honored with the Presidential Medal of Freedom to his brother Warren for Buck's "excellence and determination both on and off the baseball field." Other well known recipients of this award in sports are Joe DiMaggio, Jesse Owens, Muhammad Ali, and Jack Nicklaus.

---

year with such relief pitchers? The starters had trouble keeping the opposition from obtaining an early big lead and Chicago had lost most of its power. Murcer had already been traded, Kingman was sidelined half the season in 1980 with a shoulder injury and traded before the '81 season. Outfielder Leon Durham, acquired from St. Louis in that season, only hit 10 home runs and 22 the next season. He was the only power hitter the northsiders had during that era, plus six by Bobby Bonds, Barry's father, in 45 games he played in 1981.

Most relief pitchers were used anytime in games back then, not just to close out a victory for a save. Smith came up at the time managers were beginning to use their relief ace mostly in the last inning to preserve a lead. Hence, they became known as "stoppers" and would net a "save" to their pitching records. Smith, a 6'6" lad, had huge hands. One of the first publicity photographs I took of him I caught his hand at the top of his delivery and the baseball looked like a golf ball in his fingers. During his career — mostly with the Cubs, Boston, and St. Louis — he compiled 478 saves to establish the all-time MLB record.

In all, these relief masters won (387) and saved (1,363) games for a combined total of 1,750 while losing only 470 times. That's a great ratio of 3.7-to-1. They struck out 5,193

in 5,249 innings pitched (9.9 per IP) while issuing only 387 bases on balls. That's a magnificent ratio of 13.4 whiffs for every free pass.

In individual awards, Sutter (1979, 81, 82, & 84) and Smith (1983, 91, 92, & 94) both earned *The Sporting News* **Fireman/ Reliever of the Year Awards** in the years indicated. They won **Rolaids Relief Man of the Year Awards** also: Sutter (1979, 81, 82, & 84) and Smith (1991, 92, & 94) all were earned in the NL except Smith's last one which came while he was pitching for Baltimore in the AL.

By Buck Peden

BRUCE SUTTER

Only Sutter won the **BBWA**[34] **Cy Young Award** in 1979 when he paced the MLB moundmen with 37 saves and six wins. He also led the NL relievers in saves during 1980 (28), 1981 (25), 1982 (36) & 1984 (45). Smith paced the NL in 1983 (29), 1991 (47), 1992 (43), and in the AL in 1994 (33)

34 *Baseball Writers of America*

with Baltimore. Baltimore also boasted another Cy Young awardees that was well known in Chicago. RHP Steve Stone, who pitched for the White Sox (1973, 77, & 78) and Cubs (1975-78), had his best season with an impressive 25-7 W-L record in 1980 to win his coveted trophy. Stone would become a color announcer for the Cub television broadcasts by WGN for a total of 20 years (1983-2000 & 2003-4).

He was the best Chicago color announcer I ever heard.

Writing about Bruce winning the Cy Young Award gives me a sour stomach. I had called him that I had just opened my mail and received his Cy Young Award. He wanted to know if he could take it home and show it to his family during Christmas, which was the following week or so. I told him it would be officially presented to him at annual Chicago Chapter's BBWA banquet usually held in January and attended by a sellout of well over 1,000 area baseball lovers. However, I would have to get approval of Bob Kennedy, our executive VP, before letting him take it home. I told him I saw nothing wrong with him taking it as long as he returned it the first of January. Kennedy thought it was alright, so Sutter picked it up that day. It was really enjoyable watching him seeing it for the first time as my staff and I watched.

He never returned it for the presentation by BBWA

HALL OF FAMER OLD TIMERS at WF Game, June 25, 1977
L to R: Warren Spahn, Buck Leonard, Lloyd Waner, Joe Sewell, Al Lopez, Luke Appling, Joe Cronin, Monte Irvin, Fred Lindstrom, Lefty Gomez, Billy Herman, Ernie Banks, Bob Feller, & Lou Boudreau.

CUB OLD TIMERS at WF Game, June 25, 1977
L to R:*Back Row*:   Rich Nye, Gil Hasbrook, Phil Regan, Larry French, Dutch Leonard, Gene Baker, Hank Sauer, Bob Scheffing, Andy Pafko, Dick Bertell, & George Altman.

Mid Row: Riggs Stephenson, Stan Hack, Russ Meyer, Phil Cavarretta Buck Leonard, Tom Langtry, Claude Passeau, J.D. martin, Ron Santo, Dick Ellsworth, Paul Popovich, Dick Drott, Walt Moryn, Moe Drabowsky, Ernie Banks, Snipe Hanson, & Burleigh Grimes.

Front Row: Clyde McCullough, Augie Galan, Bob Will, Jerry Kindall, Johnny Klipstain, Bob Rush, Bill Hands, Glenn Beckert, Randy Hundley, & Don Elston.

---

members, who had selected him to receive it. We heard through the "grapevine" that he let some friends and/or associates present the trophy to him at their affair. Cub officials were bitter, as were the local baseball writers in charge of the program. He pitched one more season for the Cubs and was then traded to the Cardinals for Leon Durham and Ken Reitz.

P.K. Relaxes Theory On Old Timers

I would always submit my plans for promotional days for the upcoming season to P.K. Wrigley, owner; John Holland, executive manager. When Salty saw my plans for a June 1977 Old Timers VP; and Saltwell, then the general manager. When Salty saw my plans for a June 1977 Old Timers Game between the Chicago Cubs Old Timers and the Hall of Fame Old Timers, he told me P.K. would never permit it.

VP; and Saltwell, then the general manager. When Salty saw my plans for a June 1977 Old Timers Game between the Chicago Cubs Old Timers and the Hall of Fame Old Timers, he told me P.K. would never permit it.

Sure enough, I had waited outside William Wrigley's office for about three hours to go over my season proposals, but never got an audience as the Wrigley Co. officials were swamped having meetings with

heads of their international companies. I finally went back to Wrigley Field and was still in my office working at six o'clock that evening when I got a call on my private line. It was Bill Wrigley. He had called my home phone and was told I was still working by Carolyn.

First he apologized for not being able to get time to see me at the Wrigley Building, which really surprised me and made me feel extremely proud to have such a busy executive take time out after hours to phone. He said he had gone over my proposals for promotional days the upcoming season, and he was at his dad's Lake Geneva mansion as he was doubtful about P.K. approval of the Old Timers Game.

I could hear a voice in the background, so I assumed he had his speaker phone engaged so his father could hear what I was saying.

"Dad feels that the Cub fans wanted to remember their heroes as they were in their prime," Bill explained. "The fans don't want to see them with potbellies and balding heads."

I told him that the stadium would be packed at such a game with most of the fans their age possessing the same potbellies and balding heads. He thanked me and said he would get back to me with the decision.

I received a memo in a few days that all of my recommendations were approved. The preparatory

work in putting on such a day is tremendous, but I enjoyed every bit of it. Just locating the phone number of some them was quite a chore.

Charlie Grimm managed with Tom Gorman & John Rice making up the rest of the umpire crew.

Cliff Kachline, historian for the National Baseball HOF, who provided invaluable assistant to me in contacting the fame members, wrote me ater I told him the players that had excepted: "To my knowledge — except for a Hall of Fame induction ceremony at Cooperstown — there has never been so many Hall of Famers collected in one place as will be at Wrigley Field on June 25, 1977."

He sent me photographs of each fame member attending and I used photographs from our files on the Cub participants. Enright wrote the copy and I designed a scorebook we sold at the game which was attended by over 33,130 paying customers. Seating capacity was 37,741 at that time.

We gave Riggs "Old Hoss" Stephenson the honor of throwing out the first ball for the game as he was the Cubs all-time batting leader with a career .336 average which included eight seasons with .300-plus average. He was even higher than the great Cap Anson (.333), Kiki Cuyler (.325), and Hack Wilson (.322), among other well known Cub old timers.

Carolyn and I took Riggs and his wife to dinner at a nice Chicago restaurant the night before the game and I gave him a couple of his bats I had Hillerich & Bradsby make for souvenirs.

It flabbergasted me when one of the clubhouse boys brought me one of the bats signed by Stephenson for a keepsake with a note thanking me for a very enjoyable event. I'll keep it forever.

It was fun listening to some of old timers jokes or funny happenings that night at our banquet. Lefty Comez always had plenty of them that cracked me up.

One was, "Before you criticize someone, you should walk a mile in their shoes. That way, when you criticize them you're a mile away and you have their shoes." Another one was, "I'm not conceited. Conceit's a fault and I have none."

Umpire Gorman tells of attending a winter baseball banquet that had Ron Swoboda, a NY outfielder, seated next to him at the head table. Swoboda was admiring a picture of Gorman in the banquet program before either had retired.

"That's a nice picture," Ron tells Gorman. "Was it taken in high school?"

"I'll let you know how funny that was kid," the ump replied, "...during the summer on a three-and-two pitch."

Ralph Kiner told one of a customer in a country store who bought a gallon of molasses and exchanged a wad of bills for rolls of pennies. He began dropping them in the molasses one penny at a time. When queried by the attendant, he explained: "The judge made me pay alimony, but he didn't dictate me any method of payment."

John Rice, also a retired umpire, told us Phillie Pitcher Steve Carlton — who always insisted on Tim Mc Carver being his catcher when he pitched — once quipped: "When Tim and I die, we're going to be buried in the same cemetery — 60 feet, six inches apart."

Appling, who retired in Georgia, told a good one. He was noted for his great story telling. Luke said, "After many years of traveling as a ball player this middle-aged retiree moved to Georgia and bought himself what he always wanted: a pig farm. As he was inexperienced, he asked neighbors where he should breed one of his sows that he thought was in heat. Told that there was a county champion boar a mile down the road, a state champion boar two miles, and a grand champ three. He took the sow in his wheelbarrow to each on three successive days. When he woke up the fourth day, he asked his wife if the sow appeared to be pregnant. 'No, I don't think so,' she answered, 'but she's in the wheelbarrow waiting for you.'"

Charlie Grimm tells of visiting for dinner with a very old ex-ball player that competed in the late 1880s. "I was really impressed that he preceded every request to his wife with loving names like sweetstuff, honey, dearest, darling, etc. They had been married 70 years, but they still appeared very much in love. While his wife was in the kitchen, I leaned over and said to him, 'I think it's wonderful after all these years you've been married to still be calling her those pet names.' The old timer hung his head. 'To tell you the truth,' he said softly. 'I forgot her name about 10 years ago.'"

Old Jolly Charlie also told one about a rich 64-year-old woman that married a 25-year-old utility infielder. One day the game was called due to rain so he came home early and found he wife having sex with a 70-year-old man. The infielder's ego was stung. "What could he possible have that I don't?" he asked. "Patience," she said.

1945 Series Cubs & Tigers Featured

The first old timers contest at Wrigley Field, being as successful and well received as it was, made it easy three years later to bring in the 1945 World Series' Chicago Cubs (98-56) and Detroit Tigers (88-65) teams. At the time, it was the last trip the Cubs would earn to make the WS.

1945 CHICAGO CUBS

L to R: ***Front Row***: Heinz Becker, Andy Pafko, Bill Schuster, Hy Vanderberg, Dutch Leonard, Deway Williams, Charlie Crimm, Ray Prim, Don Johnson, Eddie Sauer, Payl Derrigner, & Hankd Wyse.

    Back Row: Paul Erickson, Roy Hughes, Frank Secory, Ernie Banks, Cy Block, Phil Cavarretta, Lenny Merullo, Russ Meyer, P-Nuts Lowrey, Clyde Mc Cullough, & Claude Passeau.

1945 DETROIT TIGERS

L to R: ***Front Row***: Bob Maier, Eddie Mayo, Paul Richards, Red Borom, Jimmy Outlaw, Zeb Eaton, Les Mueller, & Roy Cullenbine.

    Back Row: Eddie Mierkowcz, Art Houtteman, Billy Pierce, Virgil Trucks, Harvey Kuenn, Eddie Mathews, Doc Cramer, & Skeeter Webb.

The two teams boasted their league's Most Valuable Player Award. Phil Cavaretta, a raised as a grad of Lane Tech High just blocks west of Wrigley Field, batted an impressive .355 to lead the NL and gain his MVP Award. Other hot guns at the plate were Stan Hack (.323), Don Johnson (.302), and Andy Pafko (.298).

Detroit's Hal Newhouser was AL's MVP in 1944 (29-9), 1945 (25-9), but had to relinquish the honor in 1946 (although he was 26-9) as the great "Splendid Splinter," Ted Williams, returned from his military duty in WWII and batted .342 with 38 home runs & 123 RBI. Hank Greenberg returned from his military duty in mid-season and hit a grand slam homer in the ninth in a game in St. Louis to clinch the pennant for the Tigers. It was his 13th and final four-bagger of the season on September 30th.

Although Hank only played in nine major league games with 100 games or more to his career statistics. His other four were a one at bat "cup of coffee in 1930, 12 due to injury in 36, 19 to enter his military service in 1941, and the 78 games remaining on Detroit's schedule when he returned in 1945. He hit a total of 331 home runs and led the AL in home runs FOUR times (36 in '35, 58 in '38, 41 in '40, & 44 in '46) and RBI (170 in '35, 183 in '37, 150 in '40, 127 in '46) earning a berth in the HOF. He also drove in 146 tallies in

'38, but finished second in the majors to Jimmy Foxx of the Red Sox who recorded 175.

Unfortunately, neither of these two of my favorites with Detroit back in the '40s when the Memphis Chickasaws were the Tigers' Class AA minor league affiliate could attend the game. Greenberg, who had become famous in tennis and was referred to at one time as the greatest prominent member of the Beverly Jewish athlete in history, ran a benefit tournament annually as a Hills Tennis Club. Unfortunately, our old timers game was scheduled on the day of their big tennis tourney and he couldn't come.

When I was inviting him over the phone, he explained why it was impossible for him to attend. I could tell by his voice that he sincerely regretted it. I told him I would tell his former teammates. I know missing the opportunity to see them and the Cub players saddened him. It was quite a pleasure talking to him and Newhouser, who had personal easons he could not make it. This HOFer led the AL in games won with 29-9, 25-9, 26-9, and 21-12, respectively. His other accolades were three Cy Young Awards and the 1944 Most Valuable Player Award.

Virgil Trucks did make it. He was one of the fantastic three-man Detroit pitching staff that earned the moniker of TNT (Trucks Newhouser-Trout) by the media. I was able to spend some time with him

during the affair and found him to be a gentleman and very personable. Trout, as I wrote earlier, was deceased

Banks & Mathews HR Tie-Breaker

Eddie Mathews only played played partial seasons ('67 & '68) with Detroit during his 17 years in the majors. However, he hit his last nine home runs of his 512 total playing for the Tigers to rank 13th on the all-time home run list. Banks tied him in 1971 in his 19th season so I thought this a good day to have a shoot-off after the old timers game.

Mathews remembered me telling him of such a tie-breaking exhibition and readily sounded enthusiastic about participating in such an event. I told him we had a room reserved for him Friday and Saturday nights at a nice downtown hotel, so he could get rested up for the Saturday game.

In the meantime, we hired the famous artist of Milwaukee, George Pollard, who had painted Presidents Dwight Eisenhower and Harry Truman. He was magnificent and did charcoal drawings of the 46 old timers competing in the contest for our Official Souvenir Program given to the large crowd who attended the game. I got Illinois Bell to pay for all the expenses of drawings and printing for a full page advertisement of their new Sports Phone program on the back cover.

Everything went fine until mid-morning of the game and Eddie hadn't arrived yet. Worried, I telephoned the hotel and they rang his room with no answer. I had them check his room and it had a "Do Not Disturb" sign his hanging on the door. I immediately drove to the hotel and explained the situation to the manager. When Mathews didn't answer our knocking on the door, the manager opened it for me with his pass key.

Eddie was sound asleep, so I got the manager to send up coffee, juice, toast, and a couple of eggs immediately. I finally shook him enough to wake him. It was obvious from his odor and movements, he was hung over.

"Damn, Buck. Where were you guys? I went in every bar on Rush Street and never found anybody," he slurred indicating he still was slightly under the influence. He couldn't have made <u>every</u> bar as that famous Chicago street has several blocks of them on both sides.

While he was eating, he told me how he had a wakeup call scheduled for early this afternoon as he though it was a night game. I knew then how loaded he was when he returned to the hotel as he had played 2,322 of his career MLB games with the Braves of the NL. Therefore, all of his road games in Chicago were day games as Wrigley Field didn't have lights installed until later.

I drove him to the field after I had him get dressed with a promise that he could shower and shave in the clubhouse. I figured that Tony Garofalo, our trainer, could give him something that would sober him up enough to sign autographs on the field with the other old timers prior to the regular game.

He made it, but wasn't smiling very much signing the autographs along the low WF wall. After the official contest got underway, I went to the clubhouse to check on Eddie and he was sound asleep in the training room. I was happy to see it as he had about 3½ hours before the regular and old timers games were over. I was already dreading how he would perform in the shoot-off.

Cubs' Dennis Lamp won the regular game over Phil Niekro of all teams, the Braves, 10-5. I don't remember which team won the old timers game, but the players put on a comical and very entertaining contest. It was obvious they were there to have fun. This put the fans in a good mood for the Banks/Mathews shoot-off. We were to have an experienced batting practice pitcher lay a medium fast pitch down the middle. Banks would get six pitches, then Mathews six. This was the format twice giving each player a chance at hitting home runs off total of 12 pitches. The one with the most home runs total would hypothetically break their 512 all-time HR tie.

Ernie hits some shots, most deep in the outfield, but no home runs. Eddie surprisingly appeared dead sober as he waved to the fans before stepping into the box. Then he eradicated my illusion by hitting his first one feebly back to the pitcher. None of his other five got out of the infield. It was humiliating. Banks was going to win easily.

Once again Banks failed to hit a fourbagger during his final turn, but a couple towards the end bounced off the wall just feet below the baskets in the left centerfield bleachers. Mathews hit a few soft liners in between the grounders. With only one more pitch left in the contest, he stepped out of the batters box and asked for the towel containing the rosin batters use on the handles of their bats for a non-slip grip. I knew he very upset with himself as I could see the grim determined look on his face as he stepped back in the box.

Then, pow! He hit a high fly ball that was drifting towards right center field. All the Brave fans and players, who came back from their clubhouse to their dugout to watch the contest, were on the edge of their seats hoping the ball would make it.

It did! It was only a foot or two into the basket, but was a unofficial tie-breaking home run.

The crowd, both Braves and good-natured Cubs fans, gave them a big hand. I'm sure many of them were feeling sorry for

Mathews' performance as I. Had they seen the condition he was in that morning, they would have understood. I felt a little guilty that I hadn't planned a welcome cocktail party downtown for him and a few others that I know would have enjoyed a few toddies before retiring at their hotels. He drank me under the table many nights during Spring Training, so a little cocktail party on Rush Street wouldn't have been enough for Eddie.

Everyone will remember the day, I am sure. But the most fun was had by all the old time players that night at an exclusive banquet we held at a very nice hotel downtown. As they entered the banquet room lobby area for pre-dinner cocktails, we had put all their Pollard drawings now in handsome 21"x25" frames on A-frames in little circles of five each. To listen to the wives exclamation as they entered and saw them was very heart-warming. Particularly, when they finally found the island of drawings that contained their husband with a message in the center which contained the background of their artist and pictures of him painting the two presidents.

"Oh look honey, that's you when you were in your prime," is a typical remark they would make when they located their man. Then when our MC Jack Brickhouse closed the entertaining banquet after the post dinner remarks were over, he concluded with:

"That's it friends and we sure enjoyed seeing you guys in uniform again, even if some were a little different shaped. Have a nice trip home tomorrow, but before you leave make sure you take your portraits back there. Buck said they were yours courtesy of the Chicago Cubs and Illinois Bell," he announced and was given a standing ovation.

Not one picture was left on the stands. They either had driven there and were taking them back in their cars or they left them to be mailed. The ushers had a couple of tables set up for that purpose and to give containers to those carrying them.

Freddie Fender Singing Anthem

I had quite a few well known movie, television, and radio stars sing the National Anthem at Wrigley Field. We didn't solicit them, they (usually their agents) approached us. One I really enjoyed was James Darren, a star of teen movies in the 60s.

It was a standing room only crowd the day he sang so he was enjoying the personal tour of Wrigley Field I gave him, especially going into the dugout and meeting some of the players. Our Cub players always were very nice and went out of their way to chat with celebrities. Occasionally, such as in Darren's case, I would take them in the visitors' clubhouse if I was on good

terms with their manager. It was the Dodgers date with whom I had met and become friends with Tom Lasorda at many All-Star Games and World Series.

After James sang, I took him up to our WGN's television booth so Brickhouse could chat with him an inning or two during lulls in the game. Worming through the crowd took quite a time as young girls wanted to touch him. We made it back to my office, finally, with the able help of the Andy Frain usher escort we had. Darren was bubbling with joy as he had enoyed the whole day immensely and thanked me, many, many times before he left.

Another celebrity's agent called me one day and this one was one that I would never forget.

He telephone one day and gave me his name and then said "I'm Freddy Fender's agent. He'll be performing in Chicago next week and I understand you may have a good crowd for that day. I can get him to sing the National Anthem if you'd like to have him."

"Just a second," I said as I put his call on hold. Then I asked loudly to my staff in the office, "Who the hell is Freddy Fender? Anyone ever heard of him?"

"Oh yeah," they quickly responded. "He's had several No. 1 songs on the pop and country charts over the years. Surely you've heard him sing

Wasted Days and Wasted Nights."

Then it came to me. He was that tenor guitarist from Mexico. So I told the agent we'd be honored and explained to him to bring Freddy here an hour before the game. I explained how I always take celebrity singers to meet the players and show him the spot from where he will sing on the field.

As always, I notified the news media in my pregame notes several times the weekdays preceding his Sunday performance. Our announcers invited all Freddy Fender fans to come Sunday to see and hear him in person. It was well disseminated.

Sunday came and reached 30 minutes before game and no Freddy Fender. Man was I mad. Then, after about 10 minutes they arrive apologizing for the slow traffic. The agent introduced Fender and I shook his hand briefly saying, "Come on, we gotta go straight to the field."

"Aaah, excuse me Mr. Peden," Freddy said. "Do you have the words to the anthem?"

Shocked, I asked in an obviously unbelieving tone: "You don't know the words to the National Anthem."

"No, not by heart, senor " he said quickly noting the fear in my voice. "But don't worry. I've sung it many times, I just never took the time to memorize it."

My secretary had remained cool and was clipping the small paragraph of the NA we always printed in the scorebook. He saw her and took off his cowboy hat. Taking the clipping from her he then, getting a strip of scotch tape from the dispenser she had on her desk, he taped it on the front inside of his hat band.

He gently set it on his head, tapped it lightly, and said, "Okay, let's go sing."

I just grinned lightly shaking my head and led him to the edge of the field. I pointed to the mike stand we place near the home plate for NA singers and at the proper time I escorted him out. After I adjusted the mike for his height, I signed to the PA announcer and walked back to the sidelines to sweat it out.

Fortunately, it was not windy so when he held his hat in front of him, the words stayed stuck to the hat band. He sang it without a flaw. Of course, I noticed when he glanced at the words, but, as he was singing acappella, no one else noticed it. I breathed with relief when it was all over.

The next year the same agent called for another appearance. When I asked him if Freddy had learned the words yet and the agent didn't know, I said forget it. Freddy was a nice guy, but I wasn't going through a day like that again.

My Dealings With "Torchy" & Brock

One of the personal honors I got to perform before the Cub fans at Wrigley Field was presenting an engraved clock and our second base to Lou Brock at his last appearance there before retiring. He was signed by the Cubs in 1961 and was traded to the Cards in 1964 and finished in 1979 with them. He led the NL in stolen bases eight seasons, in runs scored twice, and in

Lou Brock's final game at Wrigley Field presented an engraved clock and our second base.

———————

doubles (46) and triples (14) in 1968. In 19 years during his 1,245 stolen base attempts, he was caught stealing only 307 times.

I got a letter from William "Torchy" Peden in 1980 saying he would succumb from cancer in a week or so. He thanked me for everything and I never heard from him again. Every since I arrived in Chicago and would be introduced to an old timer, he would usually ask me if I was any kin to "Torchy" Peden. I learned that he was a member of the Canada Sports Hall of Fame for his bicycle riding. The six-day riding competition was his specialist. He, and a partner, would compete against two opponents riding around in a bowl-like arena. One pedaling the circle while the other rested, ate, or sleep in the middle, which kept a teammate on the track continuously for the six days. It was very popular all over the world after the turn of the 20th century with "Torchy" winning an International Championship Tournament in l933. He moved to Northbrook in 1963 and was active in U.S. cycling activities, but the six-day races had lost interest in all countries but Europe.

By an unknown fan
The Famous Torchy & I

He introduced himself to me at a home game and I told him of all the Cub fans that had asked if we were kin. I told him I was honored to have the same name after what he had achieved in sports and the great reputation he had as a man. I had our picture taken together at Wrigley Field that day and told him anytime he and his family or friend wanted to come to a game to call me or my secretary. He would be the Cubs guest as long as I was with the club. He called a few times, but not many. I was very saddened when he passed away.

Unbelievable Tale Of Lost Wedding Ring

I told this story to all our kids when we flew to California to attend David's marriage to Sherrie La Plant, a shipmate hospital corps woman, on October 31, 1980. We were staying at Bob and Virginia's house in Claremont. Virginia Kato and Bob had finally made it official in September 1979 after living together a few years. Debra and Andy drove up from their home in La Mesa.

Bob was driving us to the wedding in his car with Sherrie's wedding ring, which he was to have ready as the best man, laying in an envelope on his dash. We were flying down U.S. Interstate 10 and it was a little warm, so I lowered my window on the passenger side to get some air. Bob must have thought it was a good idea and lowered his.

Then *SWOOSH*. The wind swept everything off the dash and out my window. We couldn't get over the shoulder for 2,000 or 3,000 yards as the traffic was almost bumper-to-bumper. We walked back looking for the envelope on the highway, but saw nothing. That meant it flew into the huge slope of ice plants that grew alongside the freeways from exit to exit. Finding it we figured would be impossible, so we went on to the wedding.

The bride and groom were upset, especially the bride. She didn't hide her disgust for us in the least bit. David knew Bob and I would financially make it up to him so he could buy another. It spoiled a happy wedding, but the newlyweds still left immediately afterwards for their honeymoon cabin at Big Bear Mountain.

Andy is obviously a man with a lot of determination. When he got the approximate area we lost the ring, he went there the next day, parked on the shoulder and started searching in the thick ice plant. **And, believe it or not he found it.**

We were amazed at such a lucky find. I bunched the rest of the family in a car and we drove up to the newly weds' cabin. The gals were a little dubious to barge in on them the morning after their first honeymoon night. But, I knew they'd be mad until Andy gave them the ring.

I knocked on the door and when it opened all the family behind me yelled, "Surprise!!" Sherrie was never any good at hiding her feelings and this was no exception. She had a blank look with a dropped jaw producing an open mouth.

"We thought we'd come over and have breakfast with ya'll," I said to break the ice that had come over the two newly weds. Finally, David came to life and lied like a little rascal he sometimes was during his younger days.

"Come on in and we'll rustle up something. We may have to make a run down to the village store," he said weakly.

Debra couldn't stand watching them suffer. "We're not here to eat," she said smiling broadly. "Believe it or not, Andy found your ring, Sherrie."

Andy then produced it grinning proudly. "It just jumped up out of that ice plant waving to me. I even imaged music of *'Here Comes the Bride.'*"

That broke the "ice" and Sherrie became the happiest person in the cabin. We all had a good laugh and made a little small talk and skedaddled, to their relief I'm sure.

Back to work at Wrigley Field, I reviewed the past years and was satisfied with how things had gone.

I started the first daily stats and notes sold the day of the game for $.25 cents each. Action photos I had taken were on the front cover with both league standings, day before results, and Cubs up to date statistics on page two. Visiting team's stats and media notes on page three with ticket order blank, remaining season Cubs schedule, and upcoming special events on the back page. The publication was well received by the fans.

Carolyn had been handling Bobby Murcer's fan mail for a small fee. I would take a bag full of it home for her every couple days. One day, she kidded me that she knew his salary and told me it. I asked her how she knew that and she showed me his contract he had apparently tossed it in the back of his locker with the fan mail. He thanked me when I returned it, but didn't appear surprised whatsoever.

Then he lied:

"I told her to look it over and let me know if I should ask for more money next time. She called me and I'm going to ask for more next time."

By Buck Peden

BOBBY MURCER

Carolyn was well liked by everyone and also handling the mailing of several of the Cubs publications I wrote and designed every year (i.e. News Media Guide, Cubs Calendar), plus the one time Day by Day in Chicago Cubs History I edited. I formed a Delaware corporation for her to handle it through a P.O. Box near our home on Walcott. I did it for less than $50 and named it Lance Communications,

Inc., after Jeff's middle name. He would help her with the company getting a small portion of the profit and the Cubs the rest.

Back to Murcer, he was always joking and playing tricks on teammates and employees. One time in Spring Training he saw me going through some papers out of my brief case in the dugout as they were taking batting practice.

"What are you doing there, Buck?" Bobby ask me.

"Trying to come up with a good date for a Flower Day and give all the girls attending a flower," I said.

"Why don't you give them orchids?"

"Damn Bobby, that would take too much money."

"You know a lot of people think my father owns a jewelry store, but he owns a big floral company and specializes in raising Hawaiian orchids. I bet he would be happy to donate 15,000 for a special ladies prize at Wrigley Field," he said with a serious look on his lying face.

"Well, that would be wonderful. I'll give it some thought," I added with the same deceiving straight face as I closed my briefcase to leave.

"What would be wonderful?" asked Dave Nightengale who had just walked up on the end of the conversation. As usual, he was searching for something to write about for his daily article in the *Chicago Daily News*.

"Ask Murcer. He'll tell you,"

I said and walked off. My secretary back at Wrigley Field sent me Nightingale's article about the offer for his father to provide 15,000 free orchids. He made it sound as if I fell for it hook, line, and sinker, but, of course I didn't believe one word of it. I never told Dave that I had learned long time ago not to interpret anything Bobby said as gospel. I just let Dave and his readers continue to believe it was factual.

Kennedy, our GM, made a suggestion I hire The San Diego Chicken to perform one day. He had seen the Chicken perform at a minor league park and thought he was great. I got in touch with several minor league clubs that had him perform and they all raved about him. I got his telephone number and scheduled an appearance. He was outstanding, except for one item, so we brought him back every year. Being on the Super Station WGN, that goes all over the world on satellite, got him hired later by most major league clubs.

Before his second appearance at Wrigley Field, however, I took him and Carolyn to dinner and insisted he exclude one item for which I received some negative comments from some fans. As the Chicken, Ted Giannoulas was athletically very agile and used comically movements in his custom with great skill. However, his routine with a young teenage girl on top of the visitor's dugout had The Chicken jerk a brazier out of the neck of her blouse. The young lass was obviously very embarrassed by it. Some of the fans laughed at it, but some parents empathized with the shame they thought the young girl was experiencing. I could tell he didn't completely agreed with me but agreed to exclude it. As no youngster was involved when he did other questionable things, like wiping his anal sphincter with the pitchers rosin bag, he was very entertaining to all our fans the rest of his engagements.

I always enjoyed exhibition games at Sun City, the Spring Training home base of the Milwaukee Brewers. It was full of retired seniors that had their own mechanized golf carts to drive shopping and even watch the games. They were able to drive up to the top of the sunken baseball diamond and stands. They buy their tickets to the game on entering the parking lot. Then, they would stay seated in their shaded carts to watch the game.

Bob Uecker, a MLB second string catcher for several clubs for six years in the 1960s, was the Brewers' perennial comedian and TV game announcer. It was a joy to hear his witty baseball comments and funny jokes.

One he told me I still remember: A cop spotted a male driver with no seat belt on and pulled the over car. Meanwhile the driver clicked on his seat belt. As the officer was writing the ticket, the driver pleads, "But officer I had my belt on." Looking over at the passenger, the officer asks, "Lady, is he lying to me."

"I can't say officer. I've been married to him for 30 years and I've learned never to argue with him when he's drunk."

The colorful umpire Ron Luciano told many funny stories about his career. One was my favorite and every time I heard it I thought of Uecker being the catcher. Luciano told it sounding very truthful, "Some of those major league fast balls are hard to see at dusk. I remember umpiring this kid's blazing fast ball one game and it was tough. I was doing alright until late in the game when the pitcher got into a jam and needed to reach back for his super heater. Bam! It hit the mitt and I never saw it. Sounds low, 'Ball,' I said. 'Aww ump,' said the catcher (I imaged Uecker). 'Hey,' said the batter. 'It definitely sounded low to me.' He hadn't seen it either."

I told Uecker a happening I had with another well known umpire he knew, Tom Gorman. He was retired and such an excellent speaker that MLB hired his as one of its full time speaker representative. He was riding with Randy Hundley, now a Cubs minor league manager, and me to Appleton, Wis., to speak with us at their annual baseball winter banquet. Randy was driving and yakking with Tom while I sat in the back seat working on the upcoming season publications I wrote and produced. I had *The Baseball Encyclopedia* turned to Hundley and saw where he caught 160 games and 147 were complete games.

As I told Gorman that impressive fact and said, "Man, think of all that squatting he had to do."

Tom laughed back, "That's nothing. Think of the umps in those games. They had to squat behind the opposing catcher the other half of the inning while Hundley was resting his butt on the bench."

Uecker enjoyed it and then asked me about the opening day festivities we had that previous year ('78) in which we had a Cubs record attendance of 45,777 fans. I told him of the problem I had with the pre-game ceremonies in which the U.S. Army's crack paratrooper unit was to be dropped by helicopters from Meigs Field located in south side of Chicago's bay. Our plan was for them to drop four parachutists out over the Lake Michigan beach with four flags fluttering from their chutes. The trooper with the city flag was scheduled to land at first base, the Illinois State Flag at second base, the United States Flag at third, and the final one with a Cubs Flag and the first ball to be thrown from the pitchers mound. All of this would give the grandstand fans a perfect view from the drop all the way down to their landing spot. The bleachers would only see the landing

unless they turned and looked backward as the parachutists would be sailing in over the centerfield score board.

Neat sounding performance if it was executed thusly five minutes prior to game time... **RIGHT?**

Well, the first thing happened was the wind had started gushing off the lake and they couldn't take off as scheduled. I was in hand-held radio contact with the officer in charge of the helicopter and he promised it should subside any moment. A couple of minutes passed and nothing had happened; therefore, the network that was televising the game got nervous.

"Joe Garagiola is really hot. We're on the air now. Let's get that pre-game show started," his ground foreman came yelling up to me by the home dugout. I was already high strung as one could be, so his careless attitude really pissed me off.

"You tell Garagiola if he can't adlib a few minutes of dead time then he should turn back in some of his six figure salary," I barked back at him as my contact at Meigs Field radioed that they were airborne.

Unfortunately, the wind required them to drop several blocks behind the center of the main grandstand. This meant the bleacher bums, as they called themselves, got to see that whole ceremony whereas the grandstand only saw the flag bearing troopers as they

landed at their prescribed spots.

Although every thing else went well, needless to say, I was a nervous wreck. When I got through with everything I went straight to Harley Lyons, our chef & bartender, and got me a couple double scotch on the rocks. Things were calm and rosy after that.

I usually had my lunch in our small lunch room when I wasn't out on a speaking engagement, etc. I never will forget the time I was finishing my meal with the late John Holland, our executive vice president at the time. I pulled out my cigarettes and offered one to him. I knew he had emphysema and was told not to smoke at all by his doctor, but never was able to shuck the habit.

"Thank you anyway, Buck. I have mine," and pulled out his pack.

"I'm on my final pack," I told him with sincerity. "In fact, I can see I've only got four more cigarettes and it's all over."

He grinned wryly, obviously not believing a word of it, "Sure, Buck. Sure you are."

I think he died within that year. I would pat my empty shirt and pants pockets, smiling at him, when we passed in the hall. He always smiled. He knew I was telling him I was still on the non-smokers wagon.

I can't remember if he was alive when we he had the Happy Days Softball Team at Wrigley Field playing the

Chicago Media All-Stars in an exhibition game. But I'm sure he attended an informal buffet and dance we had at a downtown hotel that night after the game. If I remember correctly all three of the Cubs Executive Committee (Chairman & Owner William Wrigley, President William Hagenah Jr., Claude Brooks, and the latter two's wives) attended the affair and seemed to enjoy chatting, and or dancing, with some of the Happy Days cast such as Tom Bosley, Henry "The Fonz" Winkler, Ron Howard, etc.

Fans also enjoyed seeing for the first time in public Media All-Stars such as Phil Donahue, Bill Frink, Rick Talley, Joe Mooshil, Bill Berg, Bob Sirott, Lorna Ozman, Johnny Kerr, Tim Weigel, etc. as well as a few of our Cubs TV & Radio team members (Brickhouse, Lloyd, & Boudreau).

Newcomers & Highlight Films

I hired Peter Mead to take over taking action shots I needed for publications after meeting him and his sweet little wife Mary several Spring Trainings. He had a much better collection of camera equipment than me or Barney Sterling, who took ceremonies at home plate in which I was involved most of the time. I later turned over the chore of writing pre-game notes for the media when our statistician Jim Davidovich took over

traveling secretary's position to relieve Dennis Beyreuther who became assistant director of park operations.

I think one of the reasons for the change was because Dennis had married his secretary, Rosemary, and didn't want to be gone from home as much as a traveling secretary. He got a very likeable replacement for Rosemary in Jeannie Jenkins.

I lost my favorite of all my past secretaries, Cherie Blake, when the management moved her to the farm department to aid two new additions, C.V. Davis and Andy MacPhail, along with long time Director of Scouting Vedie Himsl. Davis was the Farm Director of the White Sox and had the Cubs title as Director of Player Development. MacPhail, the son of AL President Lee MacPhail, was Davis' assistant.

Andrew was in the budding stage of his great baseball career. He would eventually leave the Cubs to accept a general manager post with the Minnesota Twins during which he would lead them to two World Series Championships earning the Executive of the Year Award in 1991. Then he returned to the Chicago Cubs as its President and CEO.

I would have cheerful Laurie Wojciechowski and finally classy Sue Rosberg as secretaries, plus Bill Harford as an assistant for awhile to join Regina Mezydlo, Mead, and me in our small, two-room information & services

office. Harford had played college baseball in the east and his father was a good friend of Bob Kennedy, who asked me to teach him the "ropes."

Carolyn and I both liked him. We had him for dinner many times and he taught us the board game of Risk which we played often on our picnic table in the back yard weekends the team was on the road. One Spring Training, I took him with me for a few more strands of the "rope." One time we hit each other ground balls and I could still handle them, but not near as good as he. Of course, a little of it was the middle-aged spread I was gaining nearing the age of 50. As I expected, and as he wanted, he eventually moved up the farm department with Davis and MacPhail. Just recently I learned he is a scout with the Cubs.

I was working the 1976 WS, which the Cincinnati Reds won 4 games to 0 over the shocked Yankees. When I was working the games in Cincinnati, I kept noticing this pretty young woman toting a heavy television camera on her shoulder shooting players taking batting practice, etc.

I later introduced myself to her, Marea Mannion, in the media hospitality room and found out she not only was a camera woman but a television interviewer and an artist as well. She sketched a horse running on a napkin to prove the latter. She invited me to her apartment to see her paintings and view some of her video recordings. Apparently, she was very excited when I told her I was looking for someone like her to assist me in doing Cubs highlight films. I was pleased with all that I saw, the paintings as well as the video tapes. She was single and a college grad. I spent most of 1977 talking to the Wrigley Company Vice President Claude Brooks, who — as I wrote earlier — was a member of the Chicago Cubs Executive Committee, about my idea for hiring Mannion and producing highlight films. He said he'd discuss it with the committee and let me know when I got back from my week's trip to the Catalina Island. To my surprise, they were sending me to observe and give them some promotional ideas I might have after touring the Island and viewing its many wonderful tourist opportunities.

I stayed in Avalon where their majestically impressive Catalina Casino was located on the bay and particularly enjoyed seeing the Wrigley family's ranch, the Spring Training site, and the many animals roaming free on the hills and valleys like the American Bison.

I had read how the Wrigley family had the Cubs train each spring on their beautiful island from 1921 through 1951 in Jim Vitti's *The Cubs on Catalina*. It is really enjoyable reading.

I worked often during my visit on my patio on a great promotional idea for Catalina while having my nightcaps, and submitted it to Brooks. When I never heard from him on it, although I thought it was clever, I finally figured he really didn't mean for me to go to all that work while I was there. The work I did on it, however, enabled them to write it off as a business trip.

Kennedy finally told me it was okay to hire Mannion. When I called her the news, our negotiations with her got a little testy as some agent had gotten her to raise the salary and ensure she had a title. Saltwell finally okayed a salary and we gave her the title Manager of Promotions.

She slept at our house for the first couple of weeks until she could find an apartment and purchase a vehicle to drive. I liked her very much, but she became overzealous as some television people do, I guess. For the most part, however, I enjoyed trying to teach her the ropes the few years she lasted.

She did a paintings of Kingman and Sutter for several of our newsletters and spent game days typing the play by play of the contest so I could fax it to the MLB Promotions Corporation to coincide with the video recording I would ship overnight of WGN-TV's outstanding coverage of our home games. Arne Harris was the superb producer and director of the telecasts. He loved his work as much as he loved to go to the track and watch the race horses afterwards.

She made it through the first season doing that and was helpful during our first Cubs highlight film. She was given credit for being the writer of it. I was surprised when I saw the expensive, fancy opening she had produced with a company downtown. We never lost money on any of the films as we were able to come up with well paying sponsors when they were aired on WGN-TV. In all, there were four films with Arne Harris, Jack Rosenberg, and Bill Lotzer handling most of the production work for me as Executive Producer.

In 1978, "*We Love The Cubs*" — Vince Lloyd was the narrator. It opened with the season home opener which had a Wrigley Field attendance record of 45,777 on April 14. Charlie Grimm tossed out the first ball. Larry Biittner, a great pinch hitter and my drinking pal in Spring Training, hit a home run to left centerfield to win game over Pittsburgh in the bottom of the ninth. Speedy Ivan De Jesus led NL with 104 runs in his second year with Cubs and was outstanding defensively up the middle with him and Manny Trillo. The Cubs beat rival cards an unbelievable 16 of 18 games. It had a great human interest shot by WGN of a dad catching a foul ball about 40 rows up down left field, then handing it to his 4-5 year old son who threw it back toward the field before his dad could stop him.

"**THE CHICAGO CUBS:**

Summer of '79" — Brickhouse and Boudreau narrated this one. Biittner was the opening star for his one too, but this time it was comical, not heroic. While running in trying to make a grass top catch in right field, his cap blew off onto his glove immediately after the ball touched the finer tipsof his glove. The ball slid out instantly into his cap which covered it completely. Biittner knew he had failed to make the catch and managed to cease his momentum and turn around a few steps farther, but he was totally confused because he couldn't find the ball. It could not have been executed with any more perfection for a humorous happening in baseball. Many of Kingman's ML leading 48 home runs were covered, but one by Mike Schmidt highlighted the film. It was in a game with the Cubs losing 21-9 to the Phillies with Kingman hitting three home runs and Buckner a grand slam to tie the game 22-22 in the eightth. The fans were highly elated with the exciting comeback and we were hoping for a victory as it moved into the 10th inning. That's when Schmidt pounded his 2nd homer of the game to win it. It covered Brickhouse's 5,000th game as the main TV announcer of Cub games. I had found a beautiful art piece of Wrigley Field made of stained glass that a fan had made. We bought it from him and I added gold plates engraved with every Cub player that had

played during his Hall of Fame career at WGN. It was all made into a large (approximately 40" tall & 60" wide) plaque which as given to WGN.

"THE CHICAGO CUBS: *Summer of '80"* — Milo Hamilton, new to the WGN-TV booth who would also make the Hall of Fame after announcing for the White Sox (1961-65), Braves (1966-75), and Pirates (1976-79), was narrator. It had background music that was appropriately selected for the action on the film such as Buckner winning the NL batting crown and Kingman's look when fans roared for a "cap tip" curtain call out of dugout following a four bagger with the bases full. "King Kong," as he was called, and Barry Foote were fishing buddies on Kingman's yacht on off days. Dave's had a sign in his locker that read "I'd Rather Be Fishing."

"THE CHICAGO CUBS: *Summer of '81"* — Narrated by Brickhouse, Hamilton, and Bill Frink. In addition to the action on the field and promotional events such as another great performance by Giannoulas we tabbed The Chicken Birthday Party. The film contained a press conference by William Wrigley. He had been the Cubs owner since the death of his dad P.K. Wrigley in 1977 announced the resignation of Executive Vice President Kennedy May 22 and the hiring of Herman Franks, former field manager of the club (1977-80), as

interim general manager. Then a month later, NL President Charles Feeney sent out a news release publicizing the sale of the Chicago National League Ball Club, Inc. — owned by the Wrigley Family since l916 — to the Tribune Company. Andrew Mc Kenna became Chairman of the Board. He was not very friendly and never returned my calls, instead had one of his subordinates call me as if I was a peon. This was just the opposite of Bill Wrigley and President John Hagenah.

I should have known this was the beginning of the end of my career with the Cubs. However, I was naïve and did not know my Major League Baseball vocation was subsiding. I had been a strong backer of the production of a weekly MLB highlight TV program that was now very successful; instigated photos of club officials, coaching staff and players in annual press guides; was the first PR director to serve for a club in both leagues; was one of the first PR directors to initiate annual team highlight films; originated the first Daily Stats & Notes publication for the fans to purchase; and spoke at numerous functions including many benefits representing my team.

One was when an officer of Andy Frain was escorting Bob Hope around the course meeting large donors and came all the way across a wide fairway to introduce men to him. Hope, with whom I had gained much respect for his many trips overseas to cheer military troops, had also been one of my favorite comedians. I was pleased. Then, when the charity photographer took a picture of Hope and me together and promised me a print, I was extremely pleased. Alas, I never got the photo.

Another one was a well attended (donors & celebrities) benefit on the Lake Geneva Country Club, a beautiful par 72 layout. It was played utilizing the Peoria System[35], as they called it in the Midwest. Stan Mikita, the Chicago Blackhawks all-time leading hockey scorer and hall of famer, also was an outstanding golfer. He won the low gross honors with a 73 (I think), but I had a net of 71 to win the way, ballooning on a few of the tough holes to shoot in the low tournament. I parred most of the 80s, but they subtracted several of them utilizing the Peoria System for my winning tally.

One of my favorite TV comedians, little Flip Wilson, presented me with the winning

prize, an outstanding golf bag, at the banquet following the tourney. Another benefit left me sad. It was at Cog Hill Golf & Country Club on their famous Dubsdread Course. I had hit a good drive on a par 5 hole, but skulled my second shot across a pond in 40-45 yards in front of the green. The ball came to a stop in the last few inches of water on the far edge of the pond's flat bank. I could not hit it right handed without standing in the water, so I decided to hit it the short distance with my putter.

It was a Bird's Eye putter that a fellow member of the Natchez Country Club gave me in lieu of a $20 debt he owed me for that day's round in the early 1960s when I was shooting below par frequently. He said he had paid $75 for it, but never putted well with it. I was happy to get it and, after rotating turns with it and several other putters I possessed, it became my favorite.

I never putted better in my life for the next 20 years with that putter winning mucho dollars.

Bull's Eye putters are a single blade about ½ inch in diameter with the shaft coming out the center of its heel which permitted one to putt left-handed or right-handed with it. Therefore, I thought I would blast my ball out of its half-smothered lie swinging from my southpaw side. I had to swing pretty hard, but the ball landed on he large green giving me a rather lengthy

putt for a birdie. BUT (boo-hoo) … my putter head broke and went sailing into the deep rough behind the green.

We looked for it several minutes, but had to move on without finding it. I left my name and telephone number with the golf pro there to call me it they found it cutting grass, but he never called. I bought another Bulls Eye but it was slightly heavier and I never putted as well with it.

FLIP WILSON, a star TV comedian, presents me with the golf bag I won by being the low net winner at a Lake Geneva CC golf benefit.

———

The latter tournament as sponsored by the Chicago Baseball Cancer Charities, an organization founded by Marv Samuel which I read recently had raised over $12.1 million. Salty and I were both very active members in its committee as well as our own Cubs Care Benefit.

35 No established handicaps are used. If a player records a score between *par-+3* then they get *no* handicap. If he records *par+6* stokes then his score is reduced minus *1/2* of worst hole (WH); *par+9* = minus *whole* of WH; *par+12* = minus *whole* of WH and *l/2* next WH; *par+15* = minus *whole* of two WHs; etc.

I was also very active with SABR, the Pitch & Hit Club and Old Timers Baseball Association. The latter organization was run by its enthusiastic & tireless working Executive Director Joseph Molitor, Jr. and Presdent John Rice, very popular retired ML umpire. They were very kind to me presenting me with several honors and awards: Guest of Honor Plaque presented by P&HC with OTBA humbling me with Jimmy Archer Award, Wm. C. Niesen Award, Humanatarian Award, and Honorary Life Membership Award.

I was honored in Peoria (along with Reichardt & Uecker) and Springfield (with Mantle) among other out-of-town winter "Hot Stove League" baseball banquets.

However, the most prestigious one was Man of the Year Award presented to me by the Belvidere Pitch & Hit Club. These were all positive things with the White Sox and Cubs.

They were mentioned here as the next, and last, chapter on MLB has some negative events and one real shocker to my future plans.

By Buck Peden

CUBS GAIN 1979 ORGANIZATION OF YEAR AWARD
Employees and associates of the Chicago National League Ball Club (Inc.) pose after the I970 Winter Meetings in Toronto, Canada. L-R they are: _Standing_: William Wrigley, Roger Crow, Eddie Lyons, Fred Shaffer, Dave Cross, Bill Walters, Bob Kennedy, Bill Rigney, Cliff Smith, Carl Jorgesen, William Hangenah Jr., Dwight Patterson. _Kneeling_: George Silvey, Jim Davidovich, Preston Gomez, Herman Hannah, Mrs. Carl Jorgesen, Doris Krucker, Mrs. Dave Cross, C.V. Davis, Mrs. Bill Walters, Mrs. Cliff Smith, John Cox & Buck Peden.

BGWW&P Times

1975-1982 Cont'd   *Vol. 1, No. 18*   *Chicago, Illinois*

Unforgettable Dozen Ends
Million Dollar Law Suit Survived

Jim Enright made a few of the non-golfing benefits with me before his death in 1981. He was well known in the area for his many years in sports as a basketball official, sportswriter, author, and public address announcer at Wrigley Field. After his eulogy was given at this church, he had requested that a slow, serious rendition of "Take Me Out to the Ball Game" be softly played. It was very heart warming. Attendees will never forget it.

My father also died that year. He had a stroke during his final two days and no longer felt any pain from the cancer after the strong doses of medicine, nor was he able to do anything. He just laid silent and motionlessly in his hospital bed while being fed intravenously. Mother, Carolyn, John Lee, Mary, Uncle Albert and I were in the room talking to each other as we watched him die. The doctor had told us he could go at any time. I went to his bed and started talking to his listless body about how much I loved him and appreciated everything he had done raising me as a father.

Suddenly, a thought raced through my brain that he couldn't do anything, but he may be hearing us. I leaned close to him and told him to blink his eyes twice if he could hear me. **HE DID IT!** Just to make sure I told him to do it again and he did. Crying we all said our farewells as he succumbed. It was a tremendously emotional few minutes for all of us before he passed away shortly thereafter.

Back to the majors, I have written about a few of the fans that I personally had the good fortune to assist in some way. One in 1977 I shall never forget was a lady from Downers Grove, Ill. She called that her daughter — a 21-year-old, devout Cubs fan all her life — had died. She had been cremated and had always desired that afterwards her ashes be strewn on Wrigley Field. Naturally, we couldn't allow that, but I felt sympathy for her deceased daughter's wishes. Cognizant of some men's extreme determination, I felt sure that it had been done

already without the club's approval. Admittance to the field is not that inaccessible at night for a climber.

I explained that if the public knew that we condoned such a thing that there would be many, many Cub fans expecting the same thing in the future. The Cub outfield would become known as the only cemetery outfield in history. My mind speeding for help, as usual for women, I added:

"Strange that you should call this morning about your late young lady's ashes," I told the mother. "I was in the process of preparing the publicity for next week's Camera Day. All the fans with cameras will be allowed on the outfield warning track, which is made of ashes, and take pictures of the players. They will be individually positioned on the grass outfield inside a long rope restricting the thousands of fans on the ash warning track. Maybe you can make it and bring your camera bag."

There was a moment of silence on the phone. Then:

"I will definitely be there.

Thank you very much for the information. Goodbye," she said in a very cheerful manner. August 16th she wrote me, "Mission accomplished. My heartfelt thanks to you..."

Another goodwill occurrence of mine almost cost the Cubs, ABC television announcer Keith Jackson and me a lot of money. It all started when I received a phone request from a Mrs. Gavel in Calumet, Ill. She told me that Scott, the 12-year-old son of Dwight and Mary Crull was dying of bone cancer and only had approximately four weeks to live. However, Gavel didn't think he would make it through the night.

"Scott, an avid Cubs fan, couldn't understand why he couldn't go see the Cubs play, but it was impossible as his bones were so fragile they could move him only with pillows," she said.

The Sad Crull Story

That was enough for me. I got directions to the hospital and went to see him. I took him some cubs souvenirs (e.g. helmet, cap, etc.) and met his parents. He obviously was very happy to receive them. I talked with him and his mother for quite a while. I was on the opposite side of his bed from Mrs. Crull, so when Scott asked his mother to move him as his legs were hurting, I reached to help by slipping my hands under his right femur , tibia, and fibula bones. Touching

his legs through the sheet, *my heart sunk.* The bones felt very mushy.

His favorite player was Bobby Murcer, a good man as well as an outstanding athlete with power at the plate (27 that season, tops of 33 while with the Yankees in 1972). I promised his parents as I was leaving that I would tell Bobby of him and Murcer might even telephone. I called Murcer in the clubhouse prior to the game where the Cubs were playing in Pittsburgh. I asked him to call and promise the lad that he would try to hit him a double and a home run.

Murcer not only hit a home run, he slammed two of them. I had told Davidovich to give the radio and TV crews the promise to Scott and the fact he was dying of bone cancer so they would be more apt to use it. Never did it enter my mind that anyone, much less a professional network announcer, would say that some one is dying over the airwaves. Lou Boudreau and Vince Lloyd did not, but, Keith Jackson did.

Keith has always been one of my favorites; but, as great as he is as an announcer, he's like all of us. He's not perfect. He was quoted saying afterwards: "...I don't know why I did it. It was one of those moments of judgment...I feel terrible about it for the youngster...The tragedy maybe was that the parents didn't tell the child. Or, that the person who first called the Cubs didn't tell anyone

that the boy didn't know how ill he was. I just wish to heck I never said it."

I called Mrs.Crull after the home run to find out the reaction of the family. She seemed happy, but said they had mentioned that Scott had cancer over the air. She added that fortunately Scott didn't hear it. She said she could tell he was pleased about everything by his big smile. Apparently, they mentioned the cancer again later.

I told the 30-plus news media people that called the next day that it NEVER entered my mind that ANYONE, especially a professional network announcer, would say that someone is dying over the airwaves. Many, many times over the years I had furnished the type and degree of illness to announcers. This enabled them to mention those ill in the order of seriousness as some games they have only a few minutes to cover the many received.

Virtually all of the mail Bobby and the Cubs received was regretting that Scott learned of his situation that way, but praised all of us for the contributions in making his last few days contain something other than his pain. I took him a Murcer bat and a baseball signed by the entire team. A short while after Scott succumbed, I had his parents, Dwight and Mary, and their entire family out to Wrigley Field for photographs on the field with Murcer. They seemed extremely pleased and obviously enjoyed themselves.

"Scott talked about those homers until the end," said his mother afterwards. "They meant so much. The only bright spot Scott had had for a long time."

Then — over a year later — came the shock. We were told ABC, Jackson, the Chicago Cubs and me were being sued for a million dollars, each. I was worried at first. But, after I gave our lawyers the whole story, they told me not to worry about it. They handled it with the judge who dismissed the case. It was finally officially closed after the Notice of Appeal period ended almost two years later. We always felt certain that lawyers or friends talked the family into the case.

Naturally, there was much publicity when it began, which instigated a lot of fan mail to Murcer. He shared it with me and it was all-positive.

They wouldn't have gotten that much money from me anyway. Well, maybe in 20 years with monthly payments.

Dallas Brings Talented Crew

Dallas Green won almost as many games as he lost (20-22) during his eight years as a ML pitcher and he did win more (169-136) as a field manager for the Phillies. He was a strong leader winning the World Series 4 games to 2 over Kansas City. The Cubs gave him complete control of everything when they hired him as executive vice president and general manager. Along with him he brought 10 talented "hot shots," as I called them, and four of them were given a vice president position. The VPs were:

Terry Barthelmas - *Director of Stadium Operations*, **Patty Cox Hampton** - *Director of Ticket Sales*, **Bing Hampton** - *Director of Marketing & Advertising Sales*, and **Mark Mc Guire** - *Director of Finance & Planning*.

Among the others, all non-vice presidents, were **Gordon Goldsberry**, *Director of Minor Leagues & Scouting*. I had seen him play as the Memphis Chickasaws first baseman when I was a teenager. He was a super nice guy. Others were **Frank Maloney** - *Director of Group Sales*, **Bob Ibach** - *Director of Public Relations*, **Ned Colletti** - *Assistant Director of PR*, **Mary Beth Hughes** - *Director of Speaker's Bureau & Sales Manager*, and **Valentine Judge** - *Marketing Manager*.

I first met Bing and Patty at the 1981 Winter Meetings. They were my kind of people. Green had learned of their talents at the Phillies class AAA farm club at Oklahoma City, Okla. Patty was the General Manager there for six years. She was the highest ranking woman executive in professional baseball being acclaimed 1978 National Association of Baseball's Female of the Year. She could really jitterbug as I found out dancing several times with her at our hotel cocktail lounge. I think Bing got a little irritated at us dancing so much.

We would party very much the following season. I took them to one bar to hear Ted Butterfield and his band play. Bing had an excellent ear for music. He liked Ted as much as I so we hired him to play his musical instruments while strolling through the stands at WF between innings. He was very well received by the fans and, the last time I heard about him, he was still playing. Naturally, the exposure was very helpful in him obtaining other engagements.

Bing also found a young genius piano player and bandleader named Ed Vodicka. I think he was 21 or 22 and could play by ear. Bing hired him as our organist and stayed with him in the booth with the organ during the games to teach him how to inject the type of song to fit the many different situations on the field. When off work and we were drinking somewhere, Vodicka would drink the hard stuff as if it was water. If he kept that habit the rest of his life, I'm sure it will be a short one.

He became very clever with his music as he gained more experience. The fans really liked his peppy tunes when Roy "Cotton" Bogren and has grounds crew were snappily readying the field for play. When Bogren retired to take care of his incapacitated son due to an illness, Roger "Moose" O'Connor took over eventually. He was my loveable ex-secretary Cherie Blake's favorite beau until he died in 1995.

With all the changes in personnel, I then possessed the title of Director of Promotions and Advertising. Since Bing was my direct boss, he let me schedule all the events I wanted. Two we had never had before: Baseball Card and Rag Ball Day.

Superb Rookie My Final Player Photo

I had Mead take all the action photographs of the players and a team shot. But several weeks before we went to press on the cards, Green traded DeJesus to the Philadelphia Phillies for SS Larry Bowa and a minor league infielder Dallas projected would have a great ML career. His name was Ryne Sandberg, a 22-year-old from Spokane, Wash. When Dallas told me about Sandberg's potential, I knew we had better get him in the cards. They shoved him in the lineup at third base the first day he arrived. Mead was busy in the press box during the game, so I grabbed my 35MM and took a picture of him in the ready position at the third sack.

As he was not in Spring Training with a ML club, the baseball card companies (i.e.

Topps, etc.) did not get an opportunity to photograph Sandberg for a rookie card as they usual do of every new player. These become very valuable if a rookie has a good career in the Majors. This means that the Chicago Cubs initial baseball cards that contained the photograph that I took that day was his rookie card. Now, it is worth more than a significant amount. Why?

Sandberg, after a playing the hot corner 133 games in '82, took over second base where the fans had been watching All-Star and Gold Glove keystone players the past few decades such as Manny Trillo and Glenn Beckert. Then Ryne proceeded to establish a 16-year major league career that many fans rank as the best second baseman in Cubs history. The fabulous Rogers Hornsby also played 2B for the Chicago NL club, but only for four seasons. For example, Sandberg would bat between .290 and .314 eight times in his MLB career.

On offense, he would do it all. Bunt, hit-and-run, steal bases, and score runs with the best of anyone. In fact, three times he would lead the NL in scoring runs (1984, '89, & '90 - with 114, 104, & 116, respectively). To put him in position to score all his runs, he would steal over 20 bases eight seasons peaking with 54 thefts in 1985. With the lumber, he would pace all his loop opponents not only in runs scored (**114**)

but also in triples with **19** in 1984 — while batting .314 and finishing in high in hits (200 - 2nd), doubles (36 - 3rd), and total bases (331 - 2nd) — to acquire the league's **MVP** Award. Then with **40** roundtrippers in 1990, plus by hitting 25-or-more homers in six of his seasons, he substantiated that he did possess power in his slim — 180-pound 6'2" — frame.

On defense, Sandberg would prove fabulous. He would gain a superb reputation by displaying a wide range, strong & accurate arm, and excellent double-play agilities of mental alertness, quickness, and suppleness. He would gain the top fielding record for second sackers four times (.995, .994, .993, & 986) and retire with an outstanding lifetime fielding average if .985, fourth among his position contemporaries in the history of baseball. In 1990, he would set a ML record of 123 straight errorless games to erase Joe Morgan's pervious mark of 91. He would earn the Glove Glove Award for second basemen nine consecutive seasons (1983-91).

All these accomplishments would earn him a berth in the MLB Hall of Fame. I believe this adequately explains "Why?" without a doubt. Only 15,000 of the cards were printed for the fans and distributed that day. Some non-collectors threw them away a day or so later, even though they also contained cards of Lee Smith, Willie Hernandez, Bill Buckner, and

Hall of Famers Billy Williams & Fergie Jenkins. Jenkins had been reacquired by the Cubs for his final two years of pitching with the '82 squad and Williams was the team's batting coach. With all of these, plus Sandberg's rookie card, the 1982 Chicago Cubs set, sponsored by Red Lobster, are probably very much in demand by baseball card hoarders. I would estimate less that 5,000 are still in existence among those collectors.

Ernie Banks Uniform Number 14 Retired

I got along well with the new regime, especially Dallas and the Hamptons. Bing and Patty came through my office going to the space shared by Bing, Hughes, and Judge at the far end of the building. A few weeks after all the Green group had settled with their new spaces and assignments Bing said to me, "Buck, why is it I feel warm when I go through your office?"

It made me feel good. "Maybe it's because you know there is not enough room in here for Patty and I to jitterbug," I said with Patty smiling.

They both enjoyed playing golf, which pleased me immensely. For the past few years, I had been leaving game tickets at the request of the golf professional at Cog Hill Golf & Country Club in Lemont, Ill., and he would always reciprocate with free golf and motorized carts for me and my guests. It contained several courses there, but Bing, Patty, and I played Dubsdread most of the time. It is the 7,073-yard course on which the PGA plays its annual Western Open.

Bing and I were about equal in talent, maybe he had a little edge. I used to kid him and tell him I had to let him win as he was my boss. Patty was a lot more fun on the links than most amateur women as she didn't mess around. When it was her turn to hit, she would address the ball and hit it. She didn't go through any slow pre-shot routine as many golfers.

They lived in a beautiful suite at one of the ritzy towering hotels overlooking the Chicago Bay. They would invite me up for a cocktail or two, and occasionally for dinner, following our golf. Occasionally, we would go out for dinner, Carolyn joining us, at sites containing entertainment as the Hamptons enjoyed jazz.

There were only a few things that Dallas Green and the Hamptons came up with which I did not agree. I think they were hatched in the top executive's head. One was the new road uniforms he chose. They were white pants with a royal blue pullover shirt trimmed in white on the neck and sleeves. They maintained the Cubs logo on front and bear cub on the left sleeve. I didn't like them because they looked like softball uniforms to me. I told Dallas, but it didn't change his mind.

When he told me that we were going to retire Banks' uniform number 14, I also thought the timing would be inappropriate. I definitely agreed it should be retired, but there was nothing happening in 1982 to make that the year. I thought we should wait until he turned 60 years old or some other significant time in Ernie's life. Again, my thoughts were heard, but ineffective. I must admit it was a thrill to be with clubs that retired two of baseball's greatest: Luke Appling and Ernie Banks. Years later the Cubs started flying the numbers over Wrigley Field of two more uniform numbers of the franchise's most durable and successful players, Billy Williams & Ron Santo. The flags of retired uniform numbers now are: #14 (Banks), #26 (Williams), & #10 (Santo).

A brief summary of these threesome's accomplishments:

BANKS (1953-71) — Ernie played in every game six years during the regular scheduled 154-game seasons, plus ties, by the Cubs six years from 1954-60, except 1956 when he missed 18 games. *Batting:* Of course, all baseball fans remember his career total of 512 home runs mentioned earlier herein, but only a few remember his three best seasons hitting the roundtrippers: 47 in 1958, 45 in '59, & 41 in '60. He led the NL in '58 & '60, but his 45 in '59 would be beaten one HR by Milwaukee's great third baseman, Eddie Mathews. Ernie beat him out of the RBI title that year however with l43 to Eddie's 114. Banks' 129 RBI total was tops in '58. He finished with a lifetime .274 BAVG. *Fielding:* Playing at two busy infield positions, early years at shortstop and latter at first base, he was tremendously reliable. At shortstop, he led the NL in fielding three seasons '55 (.972), '59 (.985), & '60 (.977) and 1B in '69 (.997). Overall, the brilliant baseball pro afield made only 261 errors while successfully handling 14,206 put outs and 4,355 assists for an outstanding 19-year career fielding average of .997. *Interesting notes:* The opposing managers respected Banks' HR & RBI so much that he led the loop receiving 20 ('59) & 28 ('60) intentional base on balls. He was the NL's MVP in l958 & 59. Named to the All-Star Team 13 times. First round pick for the Hall of Fame in l977.

WILLIAMS (1959-76) — Billy was one of the most invincible players to ever don a Chicago Cubs uniform. Billy played in every game they had scheduled from l964 to 1969. The consecutive games played would finally end after he compiled a total of 1,117. He was presented the Lou Gehrig Award named after the great Yankee first baseman of the 20s and 30s who possessed the Major League record of 2,130 until Baltimore's Cal Ripken passed him with 2,632 at the turn of the century. Everett

Scott, with three AL clubs in the l910-20 era, was moved down to third place and Los Angeles' Steve Garvey edged Williams out of the fourth slot when Garvey's streak was stopped with 1,207 in the 80s. *Batting:* Billy not only retired with a fine .290 career average but he also poled 462 home runs to rank second to Banks on the Cubs all time list. He led the NL in runs scored (137) and hits (205) in l970. Two years later he paced the loop hitters with a .333 BAVG and a .606 slugging mark. *Fielding:* Playing most of his career in the outfield, he made only 113 errors while handling 4,586 chances for a .976 FAVG. *Interesting notes:* Williams was NL Rookie of the Year in 1961 and MVP in 1972. He was selected for the All-Star Game six seasons joined teammate Banks in the HOF in l987.

SANTO — Ron played in 154 games, or more, in 11 of his 15 seasons as a major leaguer and all games in three years. He was highly respected as the greatest all around third baseman in Cubs history. *Batting:* Santo had a great eye at the plate. He collected over 85 base on balls seven seasons and led the NL in four of them: 86 in l964, 95 in '66, 96 in both '67, & '68. These sharp-eye performances added to his hits gave him the NL on base average records in l964 (.398) & '66 (.412). Also in '64, he led with 13 triples. He had over 100 runs batted in four seasons and 1,331 overall. He batted

.267 11 times, peaking in '64 with a .313, and etching a .277 lifetime. His RBI total with the Cubs placed him fourth in the club's all-time records behind Cap Anson (1879 in 22 seasons), Banks (1638 in 19), Williams (1353 in 18, and Santo (1,326 in only 14). Ron's 337 home runs at Wrigley Field paced him behind Banks (512) and Williams (392). Santo hit five with the White Sox his final season and Williams 34 his last two years playing for Oakland. *Fielding:* Santo led the NL hot corner players with a .97l FAVG. He won the Gold Glove Award five seasons. *Interesting notes:* He was chosen for the All-Star Game nine times. He was only one vote shy of making the Hall of Fame so I expect him to make it in 2009. It was amazing that Ron could do all that he accomplished with his diabetes. He finally had to have both legs amputated below the knees, the right one in 2001 and the left in 2002. His #10 was retired in 2003. He became a Cub broadcaster for WGN and pleased the fans many times singing the 7th inning song of "Take Me Out to the Ball Game."

Shock Of My 12-Year Career In The Majors

Toward the end of the '82 season, Bing and Dallas had attended some dinner that included Bill Veeck.

"I was talking to your former club owner, Veeck, last night.

He told me you've got to go," Hampton said with a smile on his face.

"Yeah, sure he did," I said thinking Bing was pulling one of his practical jokes he enjoyed so much. I only worked two days for Veeck before I decided to accept the Cubs' offer. He represented the White Sox at many banquets I attended for the Cubs with both of us speaking to the attendees from a dais or our table. Naturally, he was a much more experienced spokesperson than I, but he knew that. He was always friendly and would usually say something nice about what I said afterwards; therefore, I always had positive feelings about our relationship. I just ignored it as Bing being Bing.

Then the season ended with the Mets taking our 1980 & 81 position in the cellar. We finished one slot above bottom of the East Division. That's as good of a reason to celebrate as any other, so most of the employees trekked to a nearby bar on Addison Street after the final game. The owners annually held a season ending party for us. The top of our echelon (i.e. Green, Hamptons, etc.) didn't show. A few minutes later I found out why.

Dave Lamont, Manager of Group Sales, and Jerome Foran, Director of Ticket Services, were there with many other employees enjoying the free buffet meal and liquid refreshments. I was very fond of both of these lads having worked close with them for

the past seven years. Then I saw Jerry's wife, June in the corner looking at me. A warm and friendly blond working in the accounting office, she had always been — along with Cherie — my favorite females in the organization.

Then I saw she was crying. I ambled over to her to find out what was wrong. I knew how kind and softhearted she was.

"What's wrong with you baby?" I asked quietly. Then she really started bawling and hugged me a few seconds. Finally, she got it out brokenly.

"Buck honey, I typed up… your severance pay check today. They're letting you, Dave, and several other oldtimers…go tomorrow," She hugged me again, still pouring her heart out. "I'm so sorry," she said softly as she regained her composure. "I know you won't let them know I told you, but I'm afraid to tell any of the others 'cause they might."

I had sustained many negative dramas in my life, but this was **the most devastating**. As a young man, I had firmly decided what would be the zenith of my life: to be a public relations man for a professional sports organization. I observed and listened very intently to all experienced men in that area and studied well. With this consecrated effort, I had reached it. I thought I would have my position until I retired. I told Carolyn later that night that I wanted to hear it from Dallas before I believed it.

Bing, of course, was the one to give me my expiration news (he thought) when I arrived to my office the next morning. He never found out that I already knew it. I think I was able to put on a shocking front.

While telling me, he was handing me an enormous severance check and an offer to run their Oklahoma City Club. I was impressed at the amount (which June & I didn't discuss) and completely surprised at the job offer. I thanked him for the latter and told him I would think it over. Then I asked him:

"Who made the decision to give me the axe?"

"The club lost over 10 million dollars this season. The board of directors told Dallas he would have to let some of his high salaried employees go. So, there are others also released." Hampton said. I wanted to ask him if Lamont was one of them, but I thought better of it.

I knew the payroll had zoomed upward with the four vice presidents and many well paid directors/managers. But, of course, Green couldn't let them go. He had uprooted their lives elsewhere to move to Chicago. It was easily deduced; but, I wanted to hear him tell me one on one. He was noted for his abrupt, straight forward, managerial methods. If there was some other reason for my dismal, he would lay it on the line for me..

I went immediately to his office and we talked at length,

but, while no changes were made, he obviously regretted having to end my career in MLB. Patty told me he came in her adjacent office with tear filled eyes to tell her of our conversation. It obviously was not his decision to dismiss me, but his responsibility to enforce it.

I collected all my personal gear and said good bye to all my friends in the organization and luckily ran into our team physician, Dr. Jacob Suker, to thank him for his pleasant disposition dealing with me. Also, I thanked Yosh Kawano, our equipment manager, for all his aid in my dealing with the players in our clubhouse. Yosh, as well as the White Sox's counter part Charlie Saad, had always given me a baseball autographed by all the players. Those 12 balls, Ernie Banks' autographed photo after entering the HOF, and Hank Aaron's signature on the photo of him listening to Babe Ruth's voice were the only signatures I collected.

I deposited my final pay and severance check in our bank enroute home, picked up my bride, and we went to a nearby tavern. I wanted to tell her about the deflating finale of my unforgettable dozen years of photographing, writing biographies, news releases, publications, advertising copy, and as Executive Producer of highlight films. We must have drank booze for four hours trying to drown our sorrows. Unfortunately, it didn't work

Luckily we lived only a few blocks away. We pulled in our garage and BEHOLD! We finally obliterated our saddened burden, for the night anyway. How did we do it? Sex on the back seat will do it ever time. Never heard of anyone being depressed while having an organism. So what, if one is 50 years old and the other 48, it still works. Jeffrey and Spooky didn't hear a thing, which is the reason we used the garage.

Toiled In Part Time Stuff Until 1983

William J. Hagenah, Jr., former president of the Wrigley owned Cubs, wrote me a nice letter when he learned of the loss of my job. It read:

"Just wanted to tell you how very sorry I am to hear that the new management terminated your services.

"I do want to assure you the former owners thought you did a great job for the Cubs and they deeply appreciated your many years of loyalty and devotion to one of the finest organization I ever had the pleasure of working with.

"Do keep in touch.
"Sincerely yours,
/s/ Bill"

We decided to take it easy for awhile. I finally flew to Oklahoma City to examine the Hampton's Class AAA facilities and play a round of golf with the two of them on vacation there. It wasn't bad, but way below the major

league operations to which I had been accustomed. I sincerely appreciated their offer, however. So I declined and went back to Chicago.

Bill Gleason's *Chicago Sports,* a monthly magazine, hired me to take a few boxing photographs and then the Rag Ball Company hired me to take their officials to MLB's Winter Meeting in December. They wanted a booth at the banquet hall in the hotel in Honolulu, Hawaii, site of that year's event. It had been a successful promotional event at Wrigley Field that summer and they felt I could help them land a few similar with other clubs at the meetings.

I really liked the officers of the company, but I can't recall their names. At the time, I had no plans to write an autobiography; therefore, my note keeping was meager. I remember the president was a pilot and one of the owners was David Hasselhoff, the movie actor. I had an enjoyable time with them in Hawaii, especially a nice dinner they hosted at one of the big restaurants. Whether or not their company gained any more clubs, I never found out because on the way back my future plans changed.

Fortunately, Got That Second Opinion

I stopped over in San Diego, actually an adjoining city of La Mesa, to visit my daughter and her family which now included a 21-month-old son, Andrew John Lengyel II, our first grandchild. He proved to everyone early that he was going to be an exceptionally bright young lad as he started walking at nine months.

A month later his parents noticed that his left foot was turned in considerably when he walked so that took him to an orthopedic physician. The doctor told them that it was going to take operations all Andrew's life. Surprised at such a shocking prediction, Debra and Andy took him to an orthopedist at the nearby children's hospital for another opinion. After a thorough examination, this doctor gave them a brace for the little guy to wear while sleeping. Debra said she put it on him every night about a year and he was cured.

He would play shortstop in Little League and excel in the water in high school playing water polo and on the swimming team. Southern California had such good weather that many of the high schools had excellent swimmers. Andrew would become one of them winning many medals and setting records at La Mesa High School.

Debra and I were having lunch the day before I was returning home. She wanted to know what Carolyn and I planned to do to make a living. She had hoped we would move back to the San Diego area. I explained that I had no connections in Diego and was well known in Chicago. I already had several good offers for jobs there which I was going to investigate after the first of the year. Then she zinged me right in the heart.

"But dad, we're going to have at least another child in addition to little Andy and they need a grandfather," she said very softly. His paternal grandfather, John Lengyel, had died several years ago.

I remember how important my grandfather was to me before he succumbed in 1956. He was an important part of my life. I knew Carolyn and I would be thus for Deb's family. I was mulling the possibility of moving back to the SD area when she clinched it with:

"You and mom could open a business. I'm sure with all your experiences that it will be successful."

I agreed with her and made up my mind to try it. I told her so, but it wouldn't be final until I got home and talked it over with my spouse. Debra and I both knew that Gertie would move tomorrow if I wanted to do so. She always loved kids and it would give the Lengyel family two female grannies as Andy Senior's mother Sophie already had a nearby apartment.

I left the next day very happy knowing that we would be returning soon.

BGWW&P Times

1983 to 1996 | *Vol. 1, No. 19* | *La Mesa, CA*

T4U T-Shirts & Things
Back To San Diego Area One More Time

As I anticipated, my bride was all for moving back to the San Diego area. She was tired of shoveling snow off the sidewalks in front of our Wolcott house. We had really fixed the old house up with a new roof and colorful light yellow aluminum siding trimmed in white. So, when we put it on the market to sell, it went real fast. We had it sold and were on the road by February 10th.

This was the first time we had ever moved our entire household ourselves. The U.S. Navy or baseball clubs paid all those moves in the past. But with the profit we made on the house, our savings, and the severance pay, we had well over $125,000 in the bank and could afford to rent a large truck.

Of the many, many happy dealings I have had with my many puppies I raised to grown dogs, Spooky gave me one of the most exhilarating displays of all them. He had seen us pack and leave for many weekends to visit our dearest Huffstetter family in Walkerton, Indiana. Spooky was a very intelligent terrier; therefore, he had learned and filed away in his memory that when we left with a bag or two he would be put in the cellar with food, water, and a doggie door to the backyard. However, he had never seen us move all our furniture into a huge truck.

He was getting more and more nervous with every article we moved out. Then when we were finished and all the windows uncovered, he just went to the back porch and sat down beneath his leash hoping we would also take him. Then, with Jeffrey in the front seat of the truck and Carolyn behind the wheel of the brand new 1983 Mercury's Grand Marquis, everything was ready. I looked down at Spooky's pleading eyes and tilted head. Then I reached up and got his lease.

I have had dogs all my life, but I never heard one make the "Ooooooh" sound of relief he made that day. It sounded almost human. He livened up with joy as I snapped it onto his collar.

We drove to St. Louis to pick up Honora Eppert, Kevin Huffstetter's sister, at her slightly ancient abode at 8 Lenox Place. We enjoyed visiting her, hubby Frank, and kids (Victoria, Theresa, Mick, Patrick, & Brendan) there many times. She wanted to go to California and help us drive the two vehicles. Carolyn couldn't relieve me in the truck because of its straight gear shift, but Honora relieved me several times.

Everything went well until we got to Albuquerque, New Mexico. In our motel bath room, Carolyn fell and broke several ribs. That made us appreciate Honora's presence as an extra driver even more. Rest of the way was uneventful. When we arrived, the Lengyels already had us a nice two-bedroom apartment on 4th Street in La Mesa all ready for us to unload everything. The complex had a pool and we had a little balcony, but it was on the second floor which wasn't good for my bad knee.

Our sweet substitute driver stayed a few days before

leaving with our many thanks, an airline ticket, and a nice gift for her contribution. She got to spend some time with Bob and Virginia, who lived in a San Diego apartment on a bluff above the mighty Mission Valley, as well as Debra, Andy I, and Andy II.

One of the first of many things we did to get settled in our new environment was join the American Legion Post 282 in La Mesa. With its approximately 2,000 members, we could get acquainted with some local business members that could advise us on the best establishments, owners, etc. Carolyn became a member of the post's auxiliary with its about 450 members. Together, we gained many friends early. My pluses in that area was the four ships on which I had served (ORISKANY, PERKINS, CORAL SEA, & IWO JIMA) during the Korea & Viet Nam Wars and my employment with the two Chicago MLB clubs (White Sox & Cubs).

Long Search For A Business Of Our Own

We had plenty of money, but I knew we had to find some kind of business to buy or decide on one to start. I had made up my mind to license our corporation, Lance Communications Inc., in California even though it cost us around $400. Utilizing our new business cards showing our Post Office Box Address, I

started my search. That is about all I did except for a pool game or two every day at the AL Post and taking Jeffrey down the street from our apartment at a small neighborhood picnic park and tennis court. We marked off his mile run of several laps around the outer perimeters of the park which he ran every morning.

I usually went down and clocked him, giving him the same type financial rewards ever time he beat his own record. This had worked well with his two older brothers who had both broke their respective high school distance records. I did not make any of them run to break school records, but to keep them in good physical condition instead of flopping down and watching TV after school. Jeff was more fortunate then they because he had a pool only 100 feet or so from our apartment. He spent most of his leisure time swimming at first and later he spent most of his time with the local teenagers he had met as a freshman at La Mesa High, a highly regarded secondary school in California.

He stupidly rolled a marijuana cigarette in the library there one day and was expelled. His allowance wouldn't have permitted drugs purchasing. I didn't leave cash out anymore since I learned of his pilfering in Chicago; but, when I discovered some of my expensive photographic lens gone, I knew where he got some of it. He attended a

special school in El Cajon for teenagers expelled from area schools and soon learned he could just sign in and disappear to join his druggy friends. They finally caught him, of course. All this was happening while I was trying to establish a surviving income. At age 5l, all I had coming in was my Navy retirement pay which was only about $1,200 a month.

Then I found an outstanding opportunity for a small restaurant and bar that was presently shut down. It was up for bid and I adored it. It had separate booths along three walls for eating with an island bar and permanent stools. At the back end of the bar was a small kitchenette including a stove, grill top, microwave, and a large vertical refrigerator/freezer combine. Carolyn and Virginia could handle the food specializing in frozen Southern & Cajun dishes (Carolyn) and Japanese & other oriental treats (Virginia Riyoko, formerly Kato). It had a walk-in reefer at the other end of the bar for storing cases of bottle beer and kegs for the draft brew drinkers to go with the cocktail beverages mixed at the bar.

When my bid of only $15,000 was approved with a condition the owner would have two months before he turned over the keys. I reasoned it was to have my background investigated which did not bother me in the least as I had a perfect credit background and plenty of money in the bank. Also, I enrolled Bob and I into a bartender's school and we needed time to complete it. We both passed with flying colors, Bob's a little brighter hue than me. We both are hams in dealing with people, so I knew we would make a big success out of the business for the drinkers and the gals for the eaters. Gertie had tons of recipes and was now an excellent cook.

Another plus was its location. It was in a medium-sized shopping center across from a busy McDonald's Restaurant located on Miramar Road only a few blocks from the main gate of the Naval Air Station where I had served with two squadrons during the Korean War. San Diego had grown so far east on U.S. Interstate 15 that instead of open plains territory for miles it was now densely populated with businesses packed on Miramar Road and residences behind them.

Then Came Gertie's Devastating Torpedo

My bride didn't shoot down my ideas, but she knew Bob was a steady beer drinker and I was downing the hard stuff a heck of a lot more frequently. She pleaded so sincerely fearing that I would become a drunk with all that wholesale booze at my fingertips that I finally consented. I definitely did not agree with her, but I took the torpedo broadside sinking my *"Caroline's* (sic)

Bar & Grill" ideas. I even paid a professional artist to design special lettering of its would-be overhead entrance sign. It would have been beautiful.

So it was back to square one. Fortunately the owner was nice enough to let us off the hook; therefore, we lost no money in the deal. We talked when all three families would get together, usually on the beach at night while roasting hot dogs around one of Bob's wood fires. I don't know who, or which ones, came up with it, but we came up with a little sports attire shop since I knew so much about the major teams, especially baseball and golf.

Carolyn had about a year's experience at Montgomery Wards as a saleswoman before working at Mt. Santonio College and several years as a teller at the Argo (Ill.) Bank during our White Sox years so she was qualified to meet and sell to the customers as well as keep the books.

I could do all of that also and handle the advertising. Then it came to me that we could also make a customized silk-screening shop in the back if we could find a place that had a water and sink available. Preparing special T-shirts for giveaway days at Wrigley Field and working with Wrigley Company artists for seven gave me plenty of experience in preparation for a job. In fact, I designed and printed some for a friend to sell in his booth of T-shirts at

Chicago annual fair along its bay area. Of course, I would have to learn the mechanics of printing them, but I knew that would be easy with the many years dealing with printers in the composing room of *The Natchez Democrat*. Plus, I had no doubt the company selling us the printing equipment would be happy to teach me.

Carolyn and I talked about all this with our area knowledgeable friends that evening at the Legion and they were very helpful. I think it was my pool playing buddy and opponent, who possessed more one liners than any professional comedian I ever knew, that came up with Coastal Supply Company as our best bet for the silk-screening supplies and equipment we would need. His name was Jimmy Wiggins and he said the Coastal owner was Terry Willis, who was a swell guy. I found that to be true. Plus, we would become fond of his wife Marilyn and son Jason, both of whom we would deal with for years to come.

Another member said there was a two window store building available for lease on east side of La Mesa Blvd., one building south of Palm St. The next roadway south was Spring St., a main east-west thoroughfare. The Post was on the corner of University Ave. & Spring St. a block west of LMB. I was familiar with LMB cobblestones several blocks down what was affectionately called Old Town La Mesa as I drove it north to the street where we lived.

We checked it out the next morning with one of the owners of the building (his name eludes me), which was located between a photographic shop (a plus for me) and a small drug store on the corner at Palm St. It had a large carpeted front room with a good counter in front of an enclosed room. The latter opened down a wide, long hallway which also had a small office with a desk and one of the phones. The other phone was on the wall by the counter. At the end of the hallway was a small closet and toilet. It exited to the back parking lot.

The enclosed 15'x20' room was empty, but had an access to the water line in one of the front corners. It was well lit with four large, overhead, fluorescent units. It already had a 220 voltage hookup. It even had a linoleum floor, necessary with the many chemicals using in silk-screening.

We liked it for our little operation, but with two months pay (first & last) at $1,000 each, plus a security deposit of $500, I wanted to get the Coastal Supply people to approve the site before we signed the lease.

One of the others owners was the Executive Director of the La Mesa Chamber of Commerce, Gordon Austin. He understood and when I gave him my social security number to check my credit and permission to view our last bank statement showing the huge deposit we had made locally, he approved an inspection. To make it even more satisfying for him, I called Coastal, introduced myself referencing my talk with Wiggins, explained our need for his inspection, and — I'm sure anticipating many sales — he agreed to come out in the morning.

Willis kept his word and was a very impressive gentleman. I immediately decided I was going to rely on this man's advice as he explained the alterations I could make in the building to operate a silk-screening production room. I was very enthused so I went down to the LM Chamber of Commerce Office and met Gordon Austin, and gave him the $2,500 and signed a two-year lease on August 9, 1983. Then I went to Coastal Supply's store in northern San Diego (about 10 miles away) and ordered a four-color & a one-color T-shirt printing presses, a belt-driven drier, a screen burning machine, many gallons of plastisol inks, screens, squeegees, and numerous other necessary machine and other items Willis recommended. They all came to above $50,000 in cash. He came out with his delivery and began several days of not only installing the equipment but teaching me how to use it properly. I was very excited with some of the artwork ideas I already had in my mind to do on T-shirts.

New Store Named & Opening Planned

Carolyn and I were shopping for used clothes racks, wall hangers, etc. of out-of-business establishments at the auctions held weekends SD downtown when she came up with the name for our business. We could have used Lance Communications Inc., but neither of us thought that would be a good one for the telephone book and other ads to identify the type of business. We tossed ideas back and forth and bingo. **"T4U T-Shirts & Things"** was thrown to me and I caught it smiling, "That's it!"

Coastal had given us several catalogs of recommended T-shirt and clothing wholesale companies. Now that we had the racks and hangers in house, we filled them with T-shirts, sweatshirts, jackets, etc. Some of them were major professional sports orientated with their logos, etc. The excess we needed to store in a convenient place so Bob made us a long, 6' high, cabinet with triple shelves and sliding doors. Virginia was also a big help, Debra and Andy couldn't help much because both had full time day jobs, but they aided us at nite.

I bought an art table and designed our company logo and took it to a well known printing shop that had a huge camera and would make all of our negatives and positives for T4U. He made a large positive for us and I printed my first T-shirts with our logo on the

OFFICIAL OPENING OF T4U T-SHIRTS & THINGS
The La Mesa Chambers of Commerce brought out their banner used to officially welcome a store's grand opening. Carolyn & I in yellow T4U T-shirts, Debra & Antu next to Carolyn with Sophia Lengyel on the far left. Her son Andy, is the tallest with our sons Jeff & Bob to his left.

front chest. The shirts were bright yellow with the "T" and "U" in orange and the "4" in green over "T-Shirts & Things" in black inks. I was real proud of them and gave one to all our family members.

The printer also knew an artist that made the carved wooden sign I wanted to hang out over our front door. It was great and only cost us $250. I photographed it and put it in our advertisement in the La Mesa newspaper giving $1 off each shirt our grand opening week of September 22-28. Naturally, the paper did a nice article about us, including of course my career in MLB and the USN. The San Diego area is full of retired sailors.

The Chamber of Commerce sent out their usual "LM Chamber Ambassadors" with their huge red welcome sign, a long yellow ribbon with a large fake pair of scissors for us to act as if we were going to cut the ribbon to officially open for business. The newspaper got a nice photograph of it and sent us a big copy. Also in the picture were Sophie, Andy, Bob, Deb holding Antu, and Jeff. Naturally it's a keeper. Sorry Virginia wasn't there for some reason as she certainly helped us get ready for our opening.

It was about this time that Andrew II noticed that I was calling him Antu instead of Little Andy or Andrew.

"Popa," he said one day jerking on my pants leg. "My name's Andy, not Antu."

"I know," I answered laughing. "My name's Buck, not Popa. But you call me Popa, which is fine."

The little guy thought about that for a few seconds. Then, he nodded several times, agreeing that it made sense to him after all, and went on about his playing. I still call him that now. Everyone knows who I mean while they sometime have to clarify whether one is speaking about Big Andy or Andrew or Little Andy or Andrew.

The Big Week Of Natchez Oktoberfest

The shopping traffic was very meager on the three blocks of "Old Town" La Mesa on the average day. But, we had hurriedly opened so we would be ready for the big weekend festival the merchants held annually the first weekend in October. The called it Oktoberfest after the famous one held annually for two weeks in Munich, Germany. They had a box beer bar in the center of the intersection of La Mesa Blvd. and Palm Ave. This was only about 20 yards from us, which was good.

Merchants from all other for years had been reserving booths along the boulevard. It was a very popular 3-day event attended by thousands from all the nearby communities and cities. We were anticipating mucho business. I even printed several hundred Oktoberfest T-shirts featuring the official La Mesa design on the chests.

The shirts were light blue heather ringers with royal blue trim on the necks and sleeves. The design I printed in royal blue and they were great, if I do say so myself.

We also put a portable television set out front of our store hoping baseball fans would stop by to see the MLB Playoffs, which were being played.

Alas, they put the booths on each side of the boulevard facing the center of the blocked off cobblestone street. The large crowds would walk down the middle of the two rows of booths. Which was fine for the booth renters, but terrible for us and other stores along LMB as they blocked the customers view of our stores. People could still walk down the sidewalk, but all the action, games, and most of the crowd watching was in the street.

We still made a little money and sold quite a few of the Oktoberfest Shirts, but nothing like we expected to earn for the weekend. I made sure I became a member of the LM Oktoberfest Committee that runs the event. I talked at many of the meetings to individuals about how Chicago held a similar event each year, but had the booth in the middle of the street back-to-back. This way the store fronts on both sides of the boulevard would get plenty of exposure as the crowd viewing the booths would also see the store windows.

A couple of the committee officers were opposed to changing it. Therefore, we sustained the agonizing lack of exposure again in 1984, but I became one of the officers in 1985 and got it changed. As far as I know, they are still doing it my way now. Unfortunately, we heavily lost money the first three years. There was just not enough walk-in traffic of customers on those three blocks.

We moved the beer fest to a huge parking lot behind the stores on the west side of LMB. It featured draft beer among its liquid refreshments & food, long tables for eating, an island stage for entertainment and live music all three days.

With the booths back to back in the middle of the street facing out towards our stores, all the local businesses made much more during Oktoberfest.

American Legion Post 282 Mucho Fun

The two of us were spending most of our time after hours at Post 282. I enjoyed playing pool every afternoon and on the 1st and 3rd Friday of each month they had a $3 Bank Eight Ball Tournament using the drawing of numbered pills to determine one's partner. First team to make a ball determined which of the two groups (i.e. solids numbered 1-7, stripes 9-15) that team had to make for with opponents required to shoot the others. Team making all their balls could shoot to make the eight ball, and the opposition could do the same. However, if the team with the stripes made their required #15 ball in the left side pocket, the other squad must make their #1 ball in the right side only or visa versa. Made in other pockets, it would be returned, placed on the rack spot, and that team would lose its turn. First team making all their balls could start trying to bank the eight ball in any pocket.

I had played the game many, many times in Natchez and was maybe considered a little above average. I felt I was one of the top three here at the Post, but, of course, I never told anyone of my self-ranking position. The gentleman that ran it was a retired officer and always had trouble figuring out the order of shooting. I showed him one night and he asked me to help him with it every tournament.

They got to having a dinner and a dance every Friday night. Carolyn and I always tried to make them. Other than that, about all there was to do there was socialize and drink beer and booze. They had a pinball machine and a juke box, but no other fun things.

There were numerous bars & taverns in the area for whom we printed T-shirts. And of course, being a good PR man, I would return some of their money by buying a few beers or drinks. One of the first ones was Pop's Tavern owned by Dale Raymond. He was a big guy and as congenial as they come. Taking his order one day, when things were slow in his tavern, we talked about each others pasts and I got a big kick out of the happening that made his decision to purchase the business.

"I was still undecided sitting at one end of the bar drinking a glass of beer," he recalled smiling. "Then, I looked at other end of the bar counter and their was this fat girl drinking a pitcher of beer through a straw. I asked the owner trying to sell it to me if she was a regular and he said definitely, almost every day. That was it. I told him we had a deal and I bought it."

His first shirt was a commemorative one for his daughter. She had just been married and the priest kept calling her by the wrong name until she corrected him at the end. We printed the wrong name with a red circle and a slant over it and the correct name below it. It was his idea. Dale and I became such good friends we spent much of our time swapping scuttlebutt with him and his friends as the music played in the background. He once told me they wrote one of my favorites after me called "Honky Tonk Man."

Eunice and Daryl Callahan got me hooked on electronic darts at their place, Nite Hawk Inn. One day I had delivered shirts. Eunice wanted to play a game as there was only one customer in the small Inn. She didn't know my son, Bob had taught me some of the finer points of darts elsewhere. I started the game with three straight triple 20s, in darts lingo, a ton 80. As each counts 60 points, more than any spot on the board, it totaled 180 and subtracted from the starting 301 points it got my score down to 121. To make a long story short, I got down to needing only to hit the #1 to triumph, but kept hitting the #20 or #18 numbers in which the #1 is sandwiched. This bust me and she finally hit her "out" number and won the game.

Acting as if a sore loser, I said "Nice win" through my clinched teeth and fake smile. Then I prepared for the ribbing I expected from her. Instead, she told me a little truism I never forgot and passed on to the hundreds of beginners I have taught since then: "It's not how fast you get down in darts, it's who goes out first."

I enjoyed playing the game so much that I talked the local dart game distributor to put one in at the Post. Then, I started teaching the members how to play its different games. A few of the old timers had played steel darts, but very few knew how to operate the new machines. At first, I instructed them on the "count up" game which is the easiest to learn. Each player gets to throw their three darts for ten rounds and the one with the highest score wins.

As the dart board gained popularity, more and more members and family were playing it. A few active duty Navy chiefs joined and at one time six couples of them. All began playing the 301 game instead of the short lived count up contest. The former game gave one a maximum of 21 rounds if no one goes out. Both games only cost a quarter per person to play.

Eventually, the waiting line to play the board grew so numerous that we acquired another board and I started a weekly tournament of 301 blind draw partners. The twosome put in only one quarter (that's only 12.5 cents each) and took turns shooting against their foes. Playing thusly, the games didn't last too long and everyone enjoyed it. I had strict starting times (first 18 to sign up) and game rules for play & scoring. The tournament was well received by everyone and would last over 20 years.

I ran it for about 10 years and turned it over to Holly Carroll, the knowledgeable daughter of one of the bartenders, Terry Hicks, who was well liked and also played in the tournament. Later I think she turned it over to one of the Navy chiefs, who was on shore duty and lived nearby. I can't begin to remember all of their names, but the first names of some of the other regular participants I can remember were Marty & Marion; Steve & Pat; Bill, Peggy, & Bill Jr.; Rod & Mary; Bob & Tommy; Marvin; and Joe & Wilma. I can't forget the charming Gerry Cadwalader and her daughter Jeannie. Gerry did so much for the Post. Hopefully the hundreds of names I forgot will forgive this senior Señor.

Gerry The Fantastic Auxiliary Queen

I never heard of any Auxiliary member of the post that accomplished what Gerry did for veteran programs, Girls State, and raising funds for any of the Post's needy problems. The Post was chartered in 1923. She joined in March 1967 and started through the chairs in 1968 as Sergeant-At-Arms, then 2nd & 1st VP, and President working all eight major and all minor programs.

"My most rewarding was working the Department Girls State program of 548 high school girls," she said recently. "It was an educational program studying state government."

Cadwalader worked in it 29 years starting as a bus chaperone and ending the last four years as a director. However, locally Post 282 benefited most for her tremendous contributions 32 years as Mistress of Ceremonies of the **Hag Party**, the Auxiliary's Ways & Means main project. It was a risqué stage show put on by women for women. NO MEN ALLOWED. One of its highlights was a stripper who did it for 30 years until she was 80 years old.

"She really enjoyed doing the bump and grind. The audience loved her," Cadwalader told me when I inquired about the mysterious crowd of approximately 300 women I saw in line for the annual show that she said sometimes went eight nights straight for 52 years. They had many skits and dances with Gerry telling jokes in between.

"There were no reservations so women would usually start forming a line at noon for the 7:30 p.m. show. This enabled them to get the front tables. It was a good money maker and gave us money to support our Veteran programs," she said.

Chuck, her late husband, must have told fellow members she could mix a wicked martini. The Post manager hired her as the first female bartender for the clubroom.

"The men were not happy having me there, so the first year was very challenging. However, I persevered and worked a total of 25 years. I must have made them love me!" she said with a devious smile.

Gerry has been the vocalist for the Post Memorial Day Services for many years. She had three beautiful daughters: Darla, Jeannie, & Jan; and a son, Chuck II. They all possessed gifted voices and would often join Gerry delighting the area Karaoke Party attendees. My favorite was Jeannie who used to call me her number one listener because of my attention to every word she sang. I was particularly fond of the way she sang Patsy Cline's "Blue."

Naturally, Cadwalader was the one who planted and tended flowers in front of the Post building. And who makes those great taco dinners frequently on Friday nights? You guessed it I'm sure.

To me, and I am sure to many others, she is truly, without a doubt, _The Fantastic Auxiliary Queen_ of Post 282.

Our Son David Joins Our Ranks

When David and Sherrie both got out of their Navy hitch, they went to her home town, Kansas City, Missouri, and he worked for Sun Time Cookies. Their marriage finally faltered and he came and lived with us a while as he learned the silk-screening profession. Bob had pitched in some when I had a heavy load to produce, but his help was limited as he had a full time job. David became an excellent silk-screener. He seldom had a misprint or have any accidental ink transferring from his hand to the garment as he always checked both sides of his hand for ink before pulling the shirt off its platform.

Jeff helped a little but he was very undependable. He wanted to move out and live on the streets with a few of his buddies. I wouldn't hear of it. I told him we were responsible for his actions until he was 18. After that he could do what he wanted. Walked off he did too, the day he turned 18.

David's arrival gave me more

time to pound the pavement for customized silk-screening customers. Business picked up some as I got a large order from San Diego State equipment manager for football practice jerseys and shirts for the track team. I designed white long sleeved shirt featuring the Olympics that were being held in 1984 in Los Angles. I put the colorful flags of the major nations down each sleeve which took me several days of artwork, four negatives and screens. It was a tough job but well received by customers at the SDS souvenir store.

David and I had some fun in April 1984. We had all the family and a few close friends standing around a small fire one night when I came late with Carolyn. When we were about 15 yards away, they all turned around wearing white T-Shirts with "Carolyn's 50" silk-screened on it. The 50 was about a foot tall and they started singing Happy Birthday to her as I gave her a shirt with "I Love the 50s" printed on it. Obviously, it was her 50th birthday and she still talks about the affair.

While I was out selling the next day I met an artist named Nanci Wright. She was a sweet gal, but I didn't care for her pet, a large rat-looking possum. She had a beautiful and very colorful painting of an old Spanish Mission in Presidio Park, the California Tower in Balboa Park, palm and eucalyptus trees in the foreground with a large view

of SD's steel hulled Star of India sailing vessel in the bay and the new Coronado Bridge in the background.

Despite sales like those mentioned, and artwork like Nanci's, the small orders from area bars for their logo shirts, we were not making ends meet with the cost of operating the store, paying David a salary (although meager), feeding four adults, paying the huge apartment rent, the new car note, and spending most of our evenings at the Legion. I had enjoyed the 4th Street pad we had but after a visit by Pop & Mom (Virgil & Lillian) and their budding teenage grandchildren, Tom & Melissa in their camper, we were thinking of moving to a cheaper place. It would be the last good time I can remember of the apartment.

Spooky, my favorite of all my many dogs, had gotten old and was losing all his hair scratching some skin disease the vet could not cure and recommended he be put to sleep. I'm choking now just remembering it. I loved that dog as much as he obviously loved me. Carolyn was kind enough to take him for his final slumber.

Then a huge storm hit and damaged the roof causing a bad leak which soaked the carpet throughout our five-room apartment. We had to live for over a week with huge fans blowing air underneath the jacked up carpet to try to dry it. That was enough so we

moved out. I attempted to get the $400 deposit we made for any damages we made, but the manager denied it because of the knife throwing damages Jeff and his pals had done throwing at a target. Also, he had cut up his back window screen which he crawled through and shimmied down a close growing young sapling to the ground. He apparently had slipped off during our sleep to do his drugs with his friends. I didn't know how he got money until we moved and I found some of my expensive camera equipment missing.

We then rented a small two-bedroom house off University Street only a few blocks from the store at a much lower fee. David found him a place so we still had Jeffrey until he hit 18. Things were progressing more and more towards what I was fearing. We had finally run out of cash and had to sell our lot in Pinehurst and our white brick house in Vidalia that we owed only $6,000 to pay off its mortgage.

The interest we were paying on our many credit card charges we had to use in buying raw materials was eating us up. We finally missed a car payment or two on the Grand Marquis and they repossessed it while we were asleep. We had to buy an old beat up Ford station wagon for $200. It looked awful, but it ran.

Then, one day I wanted to call Carolyn or David, as the car was at the store, to come and get me. I dug in my pockets and only had one dime. I didn't have enough money to use a pay phone.

Save T4U And Adios Remains

It was decided. As an individual I would go bankrupt, but we would save the name and the silk-screening equipment. I found a good lawyer and he recommended I go into Chapter 11 Bankruptcy. That way we could pay 85% of everything we owed and be solvent again in six years. We put it into action and sold everything we could at a discount to competitors, etc., except the T4U silk-screening equipment which we stored.

Then we moved in with Debra and Andy, who had purchased a good-sized three-bedroom house. Our two twin beds practically filled the room. The day after Christmas 1985 Debra had given birth to Thomas Grant; so Antu and Thomas share one of the bedrooms. All the family would leave lights on after leaving a room and I had a bugaboo about that as it wastes electricity. Therefore, whenever I saw one on and not being used, I turned it off. Debra told other family members and a few friends I save them $20 a month on their electric bill.

After about a year of free boarding (we were able to contribute a half the food costs), I got a job as manager of a complex of 30 apartments on S. Anza St. in El Cajon from a large SD company that owned a number of them. We received a three-bedroom apartment for managing. I enjoyed it as I could paint vacant ones for $375 before new tenants arrived.

It had a nice pool and a man that comes to service it and another that kept the grass cut. All I had to do was prepare the application papers of a prospective tenant for the parent company and keep the parking lot and sidewalks swept and the small laundry room clean. It was a snap and gave me plenty of time to entertain the kids of the complex with darts in the bedroom I made into an office.

I taught them many fun games at the pool, but they made so much noise there that a couple of the senior boarders facing the pool wrote complaints to the office about it. I never did understand why until the company roving manager of all their companies told me they had mentioned I was a part of it. Other than that, my tenure as a manager was enjoyable.

Bob and Virginia were not living together enjoyably, to our surprise. The summer of 1985 they split up and a year later he loaded up his little Datsun pickup and moved to Mississippi. He called it his "geographic flight." It incongruously was a good move for his Esrey grandparents. In mid-1980s, Virgil had two strokes following an operation to relieve his heart arteries by going up through his leg. He became an invalid and was incoherent. Lillian kept him alive on a roller bed in their living room. She had to feed him, change his diapers, and bath him on it until he succumbed in 1990.

Bob was a tremendous help to her with the repairs and heavy work on the more than 14 acres while living with them. He worked at an Amoco Service Station and later for Firestone, both in Memphis, where he worked with Walter Mathis. It was the beginning of a friendship and working relation between the two that was to last for decades later as multiple Goodyear franchises of Mathis Tire and Auto Service in Shelby County, Tenn. & Desoto County, Miss.

Bob Marries Lady Met At Church

Bob, while attending Trinity Baptist Church in Southaven with his grandmother, met and fell in love with Gale Delashmit. She was an executive administrator for Smith and Nephew, an international artificial medical parts compay. She had two children from a previous marriage, Jennifer (age 9) and Timothy (5) Millican. They married in 1987 and a year later she gave him our third grandson, Scott David. They lived in Whitehaven for several years before moving into the beautiful four-bedroom brick house they had built across the road from his grandparents at the end of Esrey Road. It gave Grandmother Lillian Esrey a much safer atmosphere in the sparsely populated area as Carolyn's father, Virgil Esrey, had died less than a year earlier and she was living alone.

The next year he was 36 years old and wrote me a five-page letter in his usual hand

Bob & Gale on a desert stop enroute to Las Vegas where they would marry the next day.

printed capital letters after he had taken Timothy fishing for the first time. Obviously it triggered Bob's memory of things that happened between him and me in his youthful days. It was absolutely a gem! I saved it in a special album I had made for it and reread it occasionally. At some time in the future, with his permission, I shall share it with his son.

Meanwhile in the budding city of Santee directly north of El Cajon, we had found an

upstairs two-room suite to rent and reopen as T4U on Prospect Ave. about 150 yards east of Cuyamaca St. We used the front room as an office for Carolyn and my art table as well as a reception area. David was now our vice president and moved to Santee. He did all the silk-screening in the other adjoining room which

had an obliging huge picture window. We hung our old sign off the banister of the walkway for the upstairs traffic. Most of our original business was our old customers which resumed buying from us.

Also, Coastal Supply had moved their entire business to Santee only about five blocks west of us on Argent St. They referred a lot of local business to us.

We were finally making a profit with the low business

rental and no charge for our living quarters or utilities. However, I still was paying off my Chapter 11 Bankruptcy; therefore, we had to pay for our raw materials when received as I had bad credit. Again, we got help from our friends at the Legion in La Mesa. Member Mike Addison, and one of my pool shooting buddies, was a foreman of a fabulous home building company called Fieldstone. He introduced me to the company's administrative assistant who ordered all of their company shirts. Their main office was near Del Mar, but the drive out there was worthwhile.

She apparently liked me and our prices. They ordered two or three thousand dollars worth at a time, which was a profit of $600-$900 an order. The only problem was they didn't pay until the materials (shirts, caps, jackets, etc.) were delivered. That's when Larry Page came into the picture. Some member had told me he was a retired officer that had plenty of money and often aided fellow legionnaires. We would borrow thousands of bucks at a time and pay him back with 10% profit. It ate into our profits, but it kept us in the black now at all times.

David & Julie And Jeffrey & Anne Marry

David took a good job with Coastal Supply in 1986 and eventually became their buyer, a great job. He would finally settled down again and married Julie Lynn Dillinger in 1987. She was a super saleswoman and together they made enough money to eventually buy a very nice four-bedroom house with an excellent backyard shaded patio with a heated swimming pool in Poway, Calif. They would adopt two girls, Shelby Nicole at birth in 1992 and 2½ year old April Michelle in 1998.

They made a great family pair as Shelby is very athletic playing softball and basketball. She gave David a TV partner watching his ball games. April

By Buck Peden
DAVID & JULIE

is all girl. She loves to sing, dance, and wear pretty clothes to the delight of Julie. All members of the Peden Family adore them.

Carolyn and I also paid down on a condominium at 7819-G Rancho Fanita Drive in Santee. It had a small pool for condo complex residents that Antu and Thomas used frequently.

Jeffrey finally settled for a few years and married Anne Marie Beloit in 1988. Renting a house in Alpine and a few years later in Santee, they had male kids almost every year naming them David Lee (1989), Jesse Lance (1990), and Robert Roy III (1992).

Jeffrey, in giving David Lee his name, continued our family's fondness of the name David. My parents named their first child, that lived only a few months, Thomas David. Carolyn and I named our second boy David Thomas, Bob his son Scott David, and Jeff made it four with D.L.

Jeff had used a little of what he learned with T4U in La Mesa to get a job with a large printing company that including silk-screening with a large machine. It was a good job.

Mother Dies And T4U T-Shirts Sold

Then in June 1988 my mother died at 79. She had only part of one lung left as she smoked so much of her life. She had sold her house and moved in with John Lee after a black man broke in and raped her several years earlier. The police never found the man. If I had ever found him, I do believe I would have shot him.

She left John and me money ($38,000 to me) in her will. Gertie and I finally bought a decent station wagon, a 1984 Chevrolet Caprice Classic, to replace the old time we had.

This eased things considerably for us, but unfortunately I spent more time drinking than I should have.

Then, I met a salesgirl at a department store, Kimberly Bertalot, interested in finding her own business. After work at a local bar and we talked over the prospects of her and her husband, John, buying T4U. They came out to our business in Santee and looked it over. A few days later they met Carolyn and me at our apartment and we closed the deal. They signed an agreement for $75,000 lock, stock, and barrel. We would get $5,000 cash up front and $1,200 a month for the rest. Plus, Carolyn would stay on until Kimberly learned the business and I would stay on as vice president and production manager.

I was making it alright doing the production work, but Kimberly was not bringing in much new business. Most of the jobs we did were different American Legion & VFW Posts, Moose & Elk Clubs, and bars of which I was a member or frequented. Every lunch break I would spend at a sports bar & grill where I could play darts and drink beer while the meal was being prepared. I became good friends with the bartender named Brande Eller. She was a good looker in her 30s and had a very likeable disposition. She would buy many shirts from us and enter my life many times in the future.

It wasn't quite a full year

when Kimberly not only got behind paying my salary, but failing to make the monthly note she owed us and the rent for the business. Finally, we couldn't continue operating as we were so we repossessed the business as advised by Keith Meeker, our lawyer. We changed the locks on the doors and thought it was all over.

After midnight a week or so later, they moved an overhead vent in the hallway leading to the entrance of other suites and crawled into our space unlocking both outer doors. They dismantled all our presses and the large belt dryer and trucked it away in a rental truck. No one had seen them. We were devastated.

The police found no proof of illegal entry as they replaced the vents they used. They said it was a legal matter that would have to be settled in court. It would take us a couple of years but we finally got a $90,000 judgment against the Bertalots even though they claimed they sold the equipment for a piddling amount. We garnished Kimberly's wages for a few months. Then, they went into bankruptcy leaving us with nothing. Fortunately, our lawyer waived his costs.

The Good Ole Garage

Carolyn was working for Paul Breen, an investment broker in NE La Mesa, which kept us solvent, but just barely. My drinking was so bad that I checked in the alcohol rehabilitation program at the Veterans Hospital. It lasted a month and when I got out I started attending daily the Santee Alcohol Anonymous (AA) Meetings at 6 a.m. every morning. I didn't touch a drop of liquor for a little over a year.

Al Treadwell of Al's Sporting Goods saved us in early 1992. He not only gave me a sales clerk job in his Santee business, but gave me $2,750 in advance for all his silk-screening needs. I signed a note giving him power of attorney to sell our 1984 Chevy Caprice Classic Stationwagon as collateral to cover the remaining owed of that advance in the event of my inability to silk-screen for some reason. The transaction and job was a tremendous boost to us at the time, but it was worth much more to him in the long run as I didn't charge him for any typesetting or artwork, plus the silk-screening prices we gave him were well below the normal. I paid and worked everything off in mid-1993. It was still living payday-to-payday.

Fortunately we had a two-car garage so I built a two-color silk-screening press with a portable dryer I hung from a rail I made overhead. This way I could print a shirt, pull the dryer over it 12-or-so seconds, and it would be cured. It was slow, but I was able to put out some small jobs with it.

Then, an unfortunate accident to a fellow silk-screener in Murrieta, Calif., came to our rescue. He was the brother of Christina Boshans and, if my memory is correct, he won a big lottery. He purchased all the necessary silk-screening equipment to start a business in shed at his home and a brand new car. Not to long afterwards he died from an overdose of drugs leaving his sister and mother the business. David introduced us one day when she came to Coastal for advice and chemicals. She had no experience at silk-screening, but wanted to make a go of it.

We went to lunch together and talked. She was an intelligent woman with equipment she didn't know how to operate and I was a man with the experience, but no equipment. I took her home and show her my office and the garage I could put her belt dryer and four-color press very similar to the one I had stolen. We both liked each other so we mutually decided to set up in my garage and I would do all her artwork, typesetting, negatives, positives, and silk-screening until she felt confident to do it herself.

She named her company Kris Tees and everything worked out great after we moved it down. Chris was making money from orders she was taking in and around Murrieta and I had regained most of our former customers, who were very sympathetic with us doing it out of our garage. Brande was one of them and we would furnish her shirts for Dynamic Darts, the company she had formed to lease electronic dart machines to her customers. After a success in that, she leased a night club with cocktails, beer, wine, and dancing to live music in nearby Ramona that was very successful.

After a year or so Chris started bringing down an experienced female silk-screener who was now a friend of Chris, who never seemed to care much for doing the printing. She would get the shirts after they had dried and fold them neatly and box for delivery. She did much the same with her friend. Eventually, she ended our agreement and moved her equipment back up north.

Fortunately, I found a guy that would lend me his printer and small dryer for printing his jobs. He had gone out of business a few years ago and just had the machine stored in the corner of his garage. Antu played a mean game at shortstop during his Little League days, but as he neared his teens he and his nine-year-old brother Thomas was able to spend more and more time with us especially on the weekends. I taught them the dart game and Antu was learning the basics for silk-screening with me in the garage. We had a great time together the next decade or so silk-screening together with Thomas following in Antu's footsteps.

Hello…A Newspaper Writing Position

Suddenly, from out of nowhere, I got visit from Nancy Weingartner, the editor of *The Daily Californian's* weekly edition named *Santee Californian*. Someone from the Elks, Moose, or military retiree clubs had told her about me and my background in Major League Baseball. She wrote an interesting article about me with a full page headline and two photographs. She even included a sidebar story on the baseball game I had invented as a youngster. It appeared on page 3 of her edition of August 26, 1993.

Then, a week later after reading the article, the publisher of the paper located in El Cajon called and hired me to write a weekly column entitled "Santee Around Town." It was a piece of cake for me and I surprised them with some neat photographs of the subject(s) of my weekly piece.

One article was on a the owner of Lakeside Dog Grooming, Lois Ranger. I had taken our latest puppy, a cute little Dachshund, to them for service and Lois was so colorful and lively that I wrote about her, her employees, and her shop. Her shop was actually in the outskirts of Santee, but nearer to the center of Lakeside, thus that name.

Fortunately, her place was only a shop north of the Hi-C-Era, a beer pub owned by Olie and a regular customer of T4U. I got to know Lois quite well as I played golf with her and her beau, Mike Lyons. She became friends with Debra and Carolyn as well, and we socialized occasionally at the Legion or our house with her as guest. She would crack us up with some her remarks.

"A real handicapped golfer is one that is playing with his boss."

"I got my golf shaft shortened and the long one worked better. So my motto now is: if it feels good don't shortened it."

A guy hitting on her at a bar: "Make like the wind…blow."

Dusty Old "Down the Middle" Revived

Most of the subjects in my articles were not as colorful as Lois, but I wrote them for a couple years, plus covered much of the youth leagues and high school sports in Santee and nearby Lakeside.

Then a new publisher took over and he found out I was a golfer and an experienced columnist. When he approached me to write a weekly golf column for their main edition and shuck all the other stuff I was doing for the *Santee Californian* weekly, I felt like doing a few cartwheels despite my bad leg. However, I settled for a smile as big as the Joker in the Batman TV shows and a vigorous handshake. I knew this would get me complimentary memberships to all the golf courses in the county, which totaled over 80 at the time.

Fortunately, one of the most highest officer evolutions in U.S. Golf Association's history for San Diego County was occurring. Tom Addis III, executive golf director at Singing Hills Golf Resort on Dehesa Road in El Cajon, had worked his way all the way up the ranks to take over as President of the U.S. Golf Association. I interviewed him at his office and it was my first golf column with an eight-column headline. He had a hell of a career on the links and would continue to accomplish many more noteworthy positions in that sport.

Every time I questioned him for an article I was always impressed with his dialogue. He would discuss a subject for two or three minutes at a time without a break. Often, when I quoted him verbatim, I would have to use "..." to eliminate some of the minor information. It was always interesting to me, but I knew my articles would be much too long if I used everything.

I always enjoyed writing about him, Steele Canyon GC's Jeff Johnson, and Carlton Oaks CC's Rex Cole, among the many golf professionals I met covering tournaments at their sites and at the San Diego PGA Chapter meetings. Every once in awhile one of the clubs would host a big golf benefit and I would get a great column out of it. I would park my cart at a tee that usually would get a foursome or two backed up. This would give me an opportunity to ask some of them for their favorite golf joke. Here's a few I remember:

COW PASTURE — Golf is the game that let the cows out of the pasture but let the bull in.

DRUNKS UP — Two drunks were on the tee. One staggered up to his ball complaining he was going to have trouble hitting three balls. His partner said it wouldn't be any trouble at all since he had three clubs.

UNDER 76 — The late White Sox outfielder Al Smith boasted that his golf score never was higher then 75. He explained that he would always quit before he got to 76.

THE INTERRUPTION — This daily golfer always amazed his fellow golfers with the concentration he possessed once he addressed the ball on the tee. They claimed one could set off a firecracker on his backswing and it wouldn't distract him. Then one day he was all set to hit his tee shot and a funeral possession drove by on the road adjacent to their fairway. They were flabbergasted when he stopped, took off his cap and put it over his heart until it passed. Then he blasted one down the middle of the fairway. The guys couldn't resist asking him why he had paid his respects to a funeral possession while preparing to hit his tee shot. He said he thought he should as next month he would have been married to that woman 50 years.

GOLFING PRIEST — A priest changed out of his attire into a golfing outfit in the clubhouse. He met three shysters on #1 tee who said they shot in high 90s and invited him to join in their bets. Priest shot his normal 92, but the other three were under 80. He paid off and changed clothes. When he come out and they all tried to apologize for their wrongs. He just told them to forget it. There were no hard feelings, but if their mother ever wanted to get married, send her to him.

GOLFER & HOOKER — This guy and girl get married after a brief courting period. After the wedding, he told her he had a confession to make that he was an addicted golfer. He tees off at 6:30 every morning with his fellow golfers. She would just have to live with that. It didn't bother her at all, but she told him she also had a confession. She was a hooker. He chuckled and said that was no problem. She would just have to turn her right hand up slightly and it would correct it.

GOLF'S EASIEST SHOT — Without a doubt, the easiest shot in golf is one's fourth putt.

THE LEPRECHAUN — An American went to Ireland to play on one of their golf courses and the pro told him that if he hit in the rough where the flowers were he may see or hear the course's Leprechaun. He had a wicked slice so he was in every rough, but did not see or hear a Leprechaun until he sliced into the buttercups on the seventh hole. Then he heard, "Please kind sir, try to hit your ball out of the flowers as cleanly as possible in order not to disturb them and if you do so I'll grant you FREE butter the rest of your life." The golfer thought for a moment, then his smile changed to a frown as he asked, "Where the hell were you on the last hole when I sliced into those pussy willows?"

THREE BIBLICAL GOLFERS — This one is as old as Methuselah, but all of us ancient golfers still love to tell it: Jesus, Moses, and one other were playing golf together. Moses teed off first and the ball was headed for the lake in front of the green, but Moses parted the water and it rolled up on the green. Jesus' drive is short also and is headed into the lake. However, his ball suddenly hovers over the water and Jesus walks out on the lake and hits it on the green. Then, the third player hits his ball sinking downwards towards the lake, but a twig shot up suddenly to be a tall pine tree, which the ball hit and fell to the ground by the lake. Then a frog sucked it into its mouth on the first hop just before a hawk swooped down and grabs the frog and it flies it over the lake to the green. The frog spit out the ball which lands on the green and rolls into the hole. Moses turns to Jesus and says, "I hate playing golf with your dad."

NOT TIGER WOODS — Another time, Jesus was playing golf and Moses was caddying when they came upon a hole that had a lake in front of it. Jesus studied the shot and decided on the club to use. "Give me my nine iron, Moses," he directed. Moses handing him the club said, "Here it is, but you'll never get over that lake with a nine iron. It is a 7-iron shot." Ignoring Moses, he hit the ball and it fell in the lake. "Go get my ball, Moses." Grumblingly, he parts the water and retrieves the ball and said, "Now, hit your 7-iron, Jesus." Jesus again addressed the ball and explained, "I hit that one fat. I'll hit it square this time." Bam! In the water again. "Get the ball, Moses." Moses, now fuming fetches the ball again. "Surely, now you are going to hit your 7-iron instead of that 9-iron." Jesus analyzed, "I just didn't follow through properly on that last shot. This time I will." Moses crossed his arms and straightened his back as said, "If you hit that 9-iron again into the lake, you're going to have to get the ball yourself. I'm not getting it." Sure enough, Jesus hit it in again. Moses turned his back to Jesus and said firmly, "I told you I'm not getting it." "Take it easy, Moses. I'll get it," Jesus said walking out onto the water. While this was going on the golfers behind them came up and one poked Moses on the shoulder and asked, "Who the hell does he think he is,

Jesus Christ?" "He is Jesus Christ," answered Moses. "But, he thinks he's Tiger Woods."

Move To Spring Valley Was Successful One

In 1994, Paul died of cancer much to the sadness of Carolyn. I reached the age of 62 so I started drawing my social security, which was a good boost to our income.

Then I found a place at 3726 Bancroft Drive in Spring Valley just east of La Mesa. It was a busy thoroughfare that was marked for business or residence. It had three bedrooms and a large backyard with a lemon trees shading a 25-foot deck with an outdoor Jacuzzi. It had an eight-foot high stone wall down both sides of the yard with a tall wooden fence in rear. The backyard had a 9'x10' storage shed to house grass cutting equipment and store other items.

The front yard was completely covered by ivy vines, no grass at all. It had a two driveways and the house, with a brick front around a large picture window, was set back about 50 feet from the sidewalk and street. It had three large pepper and a mid-age willow trees. It had a beautiful patio barbeque area that was encircled with a stone wall with half wagon wheels cemented on its top layer of stone. The bottom was colorful flat stones inlaid beautifully by the original owner before he died and left the property to his daughter.

We found a real estate expert that was number one in the market the year before. He not only found us a buyer for our condo in 1995, but arranged for the owner of the Bancroft property to lend our buyer $5,000 to pay on our property as we had a note with the California Department of Veteran Affairs until June of 1999. The buyer paid us and we paid the VA without missing a single payment during those four years.

We got a loan for $116,000 to pay for the Bancroft property, including the $5,000 she had advanced our buyer, without any problem as we had paid off the Chapter 11 debt and I once again had a clean credit record.

Owning a house I was able to get several credit cards, but we still had to pay cash for our raw materials. Therefore, Larry Paige continued to keep us in business until his liver gave out on him for the heavy drinking he did near the end of the century. We settled with his daughter for what we owed him at death. It was much more, but we were able to borrow $5,000 which was a satisfactory pay off for her.

First thing we did with the new place was have a concrete parking area installed connecting both concrete driveways, which also enabled customers to drive in one and out the other. Then we had a small barn (about 12'x20')

built by a man whose company made the four sides at their Escondido, Calif., factory and then made the flooring and roof at the site. We had one window and up to 220W electrical power. He and his two-man crew put it together in two days. Naturally, I got him to receive some silk-screened shirts and jackets in lieu of half the cost of the job.

Then, we found an Australian closing his large company down town SD with some great silk-screening equipment. With what we bought from him at a wonderful price and a few items again from Coastal, we were able to open for business after I successfully tested everything. We hung an office sign outside the back bedroom door which we made into an office and a new sign on a post I built in the center of the front yard by the front sidewalk. Our original handmade sign, we hung over the barn entrance.

We had a small auto mechanic shop on the left side of us with Spring Valley Grammar School playground and building next. On the right was a nice senior lady and her daughter.

The Lemon Grove Moose Lodge #1713, which I joined after meeting its governor and his wife, Bob and Janie Oakley, was only two blocks away. We sold the Lodge many shirts and we went there many times for cocktails with Dave Schreiber, Debbie Green, Little Richard & Diane, John Walter, and many others.

Senior Softball & Fun At The Falcon Lure

The Oakleys were good friends and were well known in the area. Janie was the first one to advise me on buying my first computer and helped me learn its basics. Eventually, I would take three night courses to learn more. Bob told me of the La Mesa Senior Softball Association which I immediately joined.

John Williamson was the habitual president and he was an outstanding leader of the two-division ("A" & "B") league with very able officers such as Bill Trenkle and L.E. Young. The "B" Division had eight teams, each with 14 or 15 players of age 55 or more. They consisted of doctors, lawyers and Indian chiefs. In other words, retirees of just about any occupation could be found among its members.

John wanted me to play shortstop in the tougher "A" Division when he saw me hit and field, but after a couple of games with them I went back to the other division which had more fun win, lose or draw while the "A" guys played a more serious game. I would usually have a "bloody mary" or a "screwdriver" or two to get the rust off my pipes before going to play.

I played shortstop the first year or so, but finally went to my old "hot corner" position at third base. A couple of the guys drilled me pretty good as I usually played even with the bag to charge bunts and slow dribblers. I hadn't lost my sound glove work and could still hit those line drives. We played on the city's Little League diamond so the outfield fence was only about 250 feet from the plate. As it was slow pitch softball, even I pounded seven or eight over it a season, but due to the shortness of the fence they were only ground-rule doubles (GRD). One 80-year-old outfielder (each team had four outfielders on the field for defense) was a steady slugger among the top GRD hitters in the league.

They tried to get me to coach a team when they learned of my background in the majors, but I refused until a big, former tennis champion coached the team on which I had been placed. He was terrible, but I hung with his stupid decisions without protesting, although I had a sore mouth at the end of the season from biting my lip to keep quiet.

I volunteered the next season and we had a ball winning the championship. Jim Badami and a couple other fast runners were on the team so I came up with a hit-and-run system. When on base, the runner must not leave the bag until the ball leaves the pitcher's hand enroute to the plate. Also, there was a rule that players could not steal a base as the high lobbed pitch would take so long to reach the plate and usually bounced once before the catcher could field it. But, I had several of the players who could hit

behind the runner on first base into right field such as I have always been successful at accomplishing. If there was a runner on the initial bag, we would hold the bat in front of us before stepping into the batter's box. Our upper hand would have one, two, or three fingers separated with an upward space from the "ring" and "little" fingers. One, space, and then the three other fingers meant the batter was going to hit the first pitch; two fingers and a space he, or her, was going to hit the second pitch; etc. I used "or her" because we had one girl, Louise Williams, that played and she was very talented.

The runner would start racing for second base on the signaled pitch so he/she was halfway to second when the ball was hit. This way we never had a force play at second base and a safe hit would always send the runner all the way to third. Occasionally, he/she would score on the hit-and-run from first base. The opponents never figured out what we were doing, but we won so many games they changed the rules the next season. The runner was not allowed to leave the base until the ball crossed the plate or it was hit.

Each player in the league was required to purchase a T-shirt of the colors of all the teams and, fortunately, we had become the league's exclusive silk-screener. We also printed all their caps and I made nylon, with cotton

lining, silk-screened league jackets available. The league's business, although I gave them a cut price, was very advantageous to our income. It helped me pay Debra $200 a month for the year we had lived with them.

I was always thirsty after the game and began stopping on the way home at the Falcon's Lure, a small pub designed by Daryl Callahan. It was then owned by Cheryl, who had recently married Frank Mareno as her third husband. His humorous disposition kept all of us laughing when he came into the place. Her daughter Deena and son Iven worked there at different times and I got to meet her two adopted daughters, Lynna and Shera, but I never met her first husband and father of them, Don Hollingshead. Her second husband she stated "…is the one I don't even like to say or hear his name" so I didn't retain it. Anyway, Cheryl and I played darts after all my softball games while I drank three or four glasses of her draft beer. She was one of the most intuitive woman I had ever met and I became very fond of her. Needless to say, she bought many shirts from us.

Fun Times In Our Halloween Costumes

Carolyn and I spent many other trips to her bashes at the Lure. I liked her little shaded patio area off the back door when it was warm enough. She took Carolyn to the Sycuan Casino on the back of her motorcycle one day. I think the most fun Gertie had there was when she won the Lure's annual costume party one October. Carolyn had dressed up with a bald headed cap with a fake hair around her ears and a mustache. She wore a man's suit and tie to really look the part.

She bought me a female wig, false eyelashes, made up my face with rouge, painted my lips and put me in a dress. I really looked like a woman. Naturally, I practiced their walk and hand movements. Then, I went to all my regular stomping grounds (i.e. the bars I frequented) and had a ball. I would go up to the barmaid that knew me well and ask, in a soft girlish tone, if I could use their ladies restroom. None, not one of about 10, recognized me.

"Sure," they would say. "The ladies room is that door over there."

"Thank you very much," I would twinkle to them. Then, as I was about to enter the toilet, I would turn and, in my normal male bass voice, say, "Sis, (whatever their name was) don't you recognize me?"

They would all crack up immediately as they knew my voice. Sis, a former bar owner who now was tending bar at the La Mesa American Legion Post 282, was impressed the most. For many years after that, she would tell customers about how I had fooled her that one Halloween.

Carolyn shocked the daylights out of me at one amateur stage show they had at the Post. She won the first prize when she came strutting out on the stage dressed like an El Cajon Avenue streetwalker with the music of a stripteaser being played in the background. She had a tight black skirt, split up the side, and a sexy red blouse underneath her blond wig which contained a couple of white carnations. To go along with all that, she acted as if she was strutting down the street shaking her butt while twirling a small purse bag.

I got another shock one day when I was at the Liar's Inn, another customer that I often visited to play darts and shoot pool. I had challenged the table and won this one evening when this opposing competitor named Wes Mitchell came up and beat me soundly. I paid my losses and was sitting at the bar having a beer with him. I told him what a good shooter he was and he grinned broadly at me.

"Buck, you don't remember shooting me at the Grand Bar five years ago. You came in slightly intoxicated and challenged the bar for a pool game. Of the 15 or so men, I was the only one that accepted and you embarrassed me by winning every game. I've been waiting a long time for today. Ahhh, revenge is sweet," he said with a little chuckle.

We talked a while and I found out he was the quartermaster or manager of the American Legion Post in El Cajon, which had several other veteran organizations that used the facility. If I remember correctly, we printed a small number shirts for them. He broke me from ever challenging a bar full of customers for a pool game again.

But I kept going to bars, particularly ones with pretty bartenders. B. J. was one of those friendly ones, and a little weird: "B.J. is the initials for 'blow job,'" she told me when I asked for what the initials stood. I didn't pursue that any farther. Her bar was the Golden Keg and I did a good design for their shirts. I played a lot of pool there and gave her two pretty grandkids a lot of our slightly misprinted shirts. She was raising them, as well as a couple of pythons with live rabbits as their meals. I attended her marriage to John, one of the best pool shooters at the pub. They had been living together for several years, I think.

There were many, many others I hit trying to sell customized shirts and it was successful. However it was not doing any good for my health. Meanwhile, other members our families were having sad happenings.

More Negative Events Occur In My Life

My younger brother, John Lee, finally drank himself to death in 1996. I loved him dearly, but knew it was inevitable. His wife Mary had called me about his demeanor, although they were divorced and she had remarried a drug store owner and pharmacist next door to John's insurance office, Al Hiller. I went to Memphis and John's son Brad, now owner of a luncheon in downtown Memphis, helped me carry him to his tub and give him a good bath. He protested, but was in too bad of a physical condition to physically stop us. I did my best to talk him into changing his life style, but it was not successful.

He had sold his profitable insurance business to his associate worker and left his kids, Brad & Kelly, what he had left monetarily in his will. Brad would have a daughter in 1998, Ashley Nichole, while Kelly never found a permanent mate. She had been working on the east coast for many years in the insurance business, but returned to Memphis and witnessed some kind of fracas by a ex-convict that made her fearful of her life. She came out and started living with us.

I was always one her favorite relatives, if not "the favorite." And, she was one of mine as a cute little blond with a charming smile when she was young. Carolyn and I gave her a $300+ party in our patio so she could meet our closest friends. Then, I taught her how to help me in our T4U shop and opened her a checking account. We toured most of my usual bars playing darts and she was quite a boozer. Eventually she bought a car with the money John left for the continuation of her college education. How she talked the administrator of the will for the loot, I never found out. Finally, I introduced her to Wally Mc Cane, the golf professional at NAS North Island one night at a local bar and they clicked together. He owned a house nearby and shortly afterwards, she moved in with him.

"He's a keeper," she said.

I thought everything was cool, but I was wrong. She got a drunken driving fine for over thousand dollars, which Mc Cane paid, and a week later the same officer caught her again. Before she had to go to court she took off for Corpus Christi, Texas, and never came back to California.

We paid Mc Cane off and found out from the liquor store owner a half-block from us that she had written almost $400 in bad checks to them. He had cashed them before he was a fellow member of the local Moose Club and knew she was my niece. Naturally, we also paid him.

She called me almost daily for the following decade and had intentions, I guess, of paying us back, but she never did. She said she had been engaged to marry over 10 guys in her life, but she never married any of them. I tried every method of which I knew to help her without success. She died of alcohol poisoning later. My failure in raising Jeff and providing a substitute father for Kelly will always be a thorn in my heart.

The next shattering news came in 1999 when Cooper Mc Daniel died. With the exception of my father and Uncle Keister, he influenced my life more than any other man. I poured my feelings out to Coop's wife, JoAnn, in a three-page typewritten letter, several months after he succumbed. His attendance when Carolyn and I were married and teaching me the fine points of playing golf will always be remembered and appreciated. Golf has always been an important element in reaching my lifetime goals. JoAnn let me reread the letter I wrote almost a decade letter and I still feel every glowing personal accolade I wrote about this man.

Unfortunately, my golfing ability and softball playing ability tumbled as my knee injury sustained in combat on board the USS PERKINS (DD-877) in 1966 had finally deteriorated so much that I could hardly walk. Dr. Roman Cham operated on it in early 2000 and put in an artificial knee. I was rehabilitating pretty well four months later when I decided the vines from the backyard neighbor's bushy plants were smothering the back end roof of our silk-screening shop. I got the ladder and started removing the stiff thorny vines with my clippers when suddenly, while pulling on a stubborn section, I fell off the ladder landing feet first jamming my right knee.

Withering in pain, which was excruciating, I screamed loudly which brought Carolyn and Beauford Jackson running from the T4U office. Jackson was the Chairman of the District VFW's Ways and Means Committee and a friendly customer of ours. He always hugged and kissed my bride on the cheek when he arrived and departed. He had brought us some fresh fish, which he did frequently when he and his associates or family caught a lot. He also gave us plenty of business.

My knee pain, which was so encompassing at first, subsided while I was still laying there on the thorny branches I had cut. Then I noticed the pain in my right buttock. A ¾" thorn had rammed straight into it and took quite a yank to get it out. Unbelievably, the artificial knee was still intact. However, I never felt comfortable trotting or going down stairs any more and, of course, I have trouble getting in and out of cars, etc. I was eventually given 30% combat related disability pay, which helps tremendously.

I had another event that scared the hell out of Gertie. I had to be taken to the San Diego Naval Hospital with a heart condition. When they examined me, they diagnosed it was a "irregular-irregular heart beat." I had never heard of such a physical defect. The doctors said one's heart may beat irregular, but with a consistent irregular beat. However, mine was not consistent at all. It had to be rectified as soon as possible or I would probably have a heart attack.

Finally, three doctors and two nurses were there with two electric defibrillator paddles. They were going to inject a new drug into my veins to make my heart beat return to normal within 120 seconds. If the drug, proved successful 8-out-of-9 times they said, didn't work they would have to use the paddles. I had given them the approval to try it and was laying there watching the monitor of my heart beat still thinking that I had led a decent life. If this was the end, I thought I believed it would be satisfactory. Then, as a second ticked away, I saw my bride sitting in her chair at the foot of my bed. She was obviously very worried about the outcome. I suddenly realized my armpits were sweating. No matter how I had tried to accept the fact I didn't care if I expired from this, I guessed my ego disagreed. It wanted me to continue and try to make a few more grandchildren and a few more puppies happy.

Suddenly, the monitor stopped blinking the erratic and inconsistent heart beat. Boom, my old ticker went to a normal beat to the applause of all in attendance. Needless to say, it was a wonderful evening for Carolyn and me. I wanted to get drunk and celebrate, but of course I had to postpone it until I got released.

Our Valedictorian; Touted UCLA Next

While I was in the hospital, Antu was keeping T4U production work going. When I returned, we were knocking out the jobs fast: (1) I would load the shirts, (2) he applied the layers of ink to each as the job required, and (3) I would take each one them off the six printing platforms and put them on the belt dryer. His young hands were big and strong so his stroke of the paddle pushing the ink through the screen's design was remarkable. His many hours of swimming work on the school team had made him very strong.

Despite working for us so much, he still was making top grades in all his classes at LMHS. When he finished high school as a valedictorian, he completed UCLA with honors in a major of Electrical Engineering. We were all very proud of him. Thomas, who filled his silk-screening shoes for us at T4U, also was an LMHS grad and completed his college education at Westmont College, a Christian liberal arts school at Santa Barbara, Calif.

I had taught both of them

how to play golf and played many games with them. They were excellent young students so I always enjoyed the outings with them very much.

I never will forget the day at the crowded Singing Hills CC driving range when Antu's driver slipped out of his hands. The range monitor halted the practice shooting of all golfers to allow him to retrieve his club. It really embarrassed the young lad.

Once Thomas and I were playing early in his indoctrination of the sport and I accidentally sliced a ball near players on another fairway. I hollered "FORE" immediately.

"Why did you yell that Popa?" Thomas asked.

"It's customary to yell fore to warm them that a ball has been hit in their direction," I explained. He raised one eyebrow while digesting it, then nodded and we continued our game.

Several months later we were playing again and he hit <u>his</u> ball awry toward another player and screamed: "Fiiivvvve."

I laughed and told him the correct word and he said, "I knew it was a number, but I forgot it was 'four'."

Then I explained, "It was f-o-r-e and not the number f-o-u-r-. It probably was derived by ancient golfers of the past to '<u>fore</u>warn' other golfers they may be struck by the ball you just hit." Now that made more sense to him, I think.

Antu got very long with his drives passing the 300-yard mark often. He got a quite a charge out of beating me in 18 holes the first time as he did when he won his first game of chess. I played both of them hundreds of gin rummy games in their second decade of life. Thomas used to have a fit when he knocked in a game and I undercut him giving him a 25-point penalty. Naturally therefore, I cherished doing it.

After Andrew was entrenched in his post graduate occupation, he married Katie Grundstorm and they would come over to our house once a week for dinner and a card game of Hearts. I had a trophy made with a gold deck of cards on top and plaque reading "World's Greatest Heart Player." Whoever won the game that night would get to keep the trophy until the next week when that winner would take it home. If one won three games in a row, they would be allowed to keep it until another player won three in a row. Katie has monopolized the blooming thing. We really had fun playing those games.

BGWW&P Times

1997- 2008   *Vol. 1, No. 20*   *Spring Valley & Santee, CA; and Southaven, MS*

We Were Media Persons of the Year
My Many Golf Events At Torrey Pines GC

I played at Torrey Pines Golf Course in La Jolla many times, but always the week before the PGA's Buick Invitational was held each year in January. The Century Club, headed by Tom Wilson, ran the tournament and would always bring the previous year's winner in for a media luncheon. Peter Jacobsen was the winner in 1995 and was a great speaker at the 1996 luncheon. Kirk Triplett, who tied for runner-up, had earlier married a local girl named Cathi. A year or so later the Tripletts had twin babies. In a sub-headline in my column about the birth, I wrote "Tripletts Have Twins" which even got a chuckle out of our sports editor, Bill Dickinson.

After the luncheon, the media personnel would be presented with a Buick Invitational shirt, a cap, and some balls. Then, they were treated to 18 holes of golf on the TPGC. Very nice outings for us.

They also held a tournament there for amateurs in December preceding each tournament to determine top amateurs that would fill the two sponsor berths. In the 1995 tourney, I met the third golfer in the SD Riley family, Chris. Earlier, I had met Mike, the father, watching his older son, Kevin, play in the Century Club Matches. Chris, soon to be ranked fifth in the nation as a college golfer at Nevada-Las Vegas, won the qualifying tournament that Kevin had won in 1992. The three of them had each won the San Diego City Men's Championship: Kevin ('93), Chris ('92), and Mike ('65, '66, and tied in '67, but lost the title in a playoff to Vic Regalado). Kevin and Chris turned professional with Chris not only making it to the PGA but at this writing he had already amassed over $7 million in loot and earned a berth on the 2003 Ryder Cup Team as well.

I covered the Century Club's induction of ex-Navyman Gene Littler to their Walk of Fame where he joined golfing legends such as Arnold Palmer and Littler's boyhood friend Bill Casper. Littler and Casper were both born in San Diego. Littler won the U.S. Amateur in 1953 and became the only amateur champion the 1954 San Diego Open which was played that year at the Rancho Santa Fe Golf Course where he lives. We talked briefly about our Navy time, he was two years my senior, but we were never stationed together, so most of our conversation that day while walking through the Walk of Fame was about his golf career. He not only won 29 PGA TOUR events, including the 1961 U.S. Open; seven U.S. Ryder Cup Team appearances; and eight Senior TOUR titles. He was a pleasure with which to share a conversation.

I had met Casper while attending San Diego CC's 100th Celebration Dinner in Chula Vista and he had given me some tips on the first tee of the complimentary round of golf we played before the dinner. I was a little nervous with the great golfer standing beside me when I swung. I embarrassed myself immensely by topping a dribbler off the tee. This Hall of Famer possessing 51 PGA tour victories and only about seven months my senior, kindly said,

"Hit you a mulligan, Pal." I did and "mashed" it. Well maybe not mashed...anyway I "dented" it straight down the middle.

My Column Eagle Shoot-Off Referee

I played golf one day with a wonderful gentleman named Barry Robbins that I would get to know very well. I interviewed him thoroughly with his many accomplishments and wrote 40 inches of column type about him. When I left it on Sports Editor Bill Dickinson's desk for editing, I included a note stating "I know you'll have to break it into two or three columns." Apparently, it blew off his desk or something as he never saw it. He telephoned me at home.

"Damn Buck, we don't run 40-inch stories on the President of the United States," he said laughing and understood after I explained the missing note. He ran most of it but he, or one of the full time sportswriters, butchered what they entered into the computer for printing. I sent a complete copy to a monthly southern California sports paper and they printed the article verbatim. I appreciated that and I'm sure Robbins did.

Robbins had stout and very large forearms that reminded me of "Popeye." I had never played with an amateur golfer that consistently hit the ball well over 300 yards. I had learned about him from the pro golf staff at Mission Trails GC in SD where I played frequently and occasionally saw a coyote stalking ground squirrels on the third fairway. Barry had been a member there 14 years and won the club championship every year. He played professionally for a short time, but was more known for his amateur accomplishments.

For example, he was the first player to win the Torrey Pines Club Championship three times. Subsequently, they retired the trophy to Robbins so he has the original TPCC Trophy. I saw it at his home with well over 100 others just as he was giving almost all of them to the San Diego Junior Golf Association. He had a superintendent's position with Solar Power Corporation and settled in Tierrasanta, Calif., with his wife Pat.

However, he still managed to get in plenty of golf in the area along with the other sub-par shooters in the county. He shot his age at 64, eight-under-par, and decided then he was going to try to shoot his age the rest of his life. Some felt he would not do so when he had both knees replaced at age 66, but this man was hitting balls three weeks after the operation. Six weeks after he played 18 holes of golf and the second time he shot his age with a six-under-par 66.

I phoned him today to see how the "score-equals-age" conquests were going. He's 70 now and said he had shot his age 96 times since he started keeping up with it. A few notes he gave me about that interesting subject: (1) Casper never shot his age, (2) Littler shot his age in the high 60s, and (3) Gary Player had done it 31 times when he was 70 (that's 65 times less than Barry's). Back to when Robbins and I were playing our first few rounds together, I got this idea for an *Eagle Shoot-off* competition once a week for my *Down the Middle* column. I would find two worthy long hitting contestants and they would flip a coin for honors on the designated par four hole that was reachable with a tee shot (300-375 yards). No. 1 would hit six balls for the green, No. 2 than would hit six, and another such round giving each contestant 12 tee shots at the hole's green. The player that putted, or chipped, the most of their balls in for eagles would win the contest. If no eagles are made, the most birdies made would determine the champion of that week's contest. In the case of a tie in either case, the closest tee shot to the hole — which was always measured prior to the putting/chipping — would determine the winner. Barry was my referee and of course I would always take pictures. It was well received by our readers.

Mike Hayes, owner of Bay Sheet Metal in El Cajon, Calif., was the top winner of the contests with victories on three different San Diego County courses in 1994. He overpowered Sean Sweeney at Twin Oaks GC in San Marcos, Warren Pineo at Carlton Oaks CC in Santee, and Streeter Parker — reigning club champion & former professional reigning club champion — at Steele Canyon GC in Jamul. Daryl Dyte finally put a halt to Hayes' streak at the Mount Woodson CC in Ramona and defeated Kevin Weishan at Cottonwood GC (Rancho San Diego GC at that time in 1995) to rank second to Hayes as the only multiple winners.

The event had to be ceased when I had to have the first of my two surgeries on my left shoulder due to a severe tear of my rotator cuff. Yep, probably tore it trying to hit the ball farther while playing with these *Eagle Shoot-Off Champions.*

Christ And Peden Honored In Union

On the morning of November 11, 1997, I got one of the most pleasant surprises I ever received in reading a newspaper. The *SD Union* announced the SD PGA Chapter's annual awards. In the article it read, "...**Bob Madsen**, Singing Hills, Teacher of the Year...**Bill Christ**, Aviara, Merchandiser of the Year, Resort...**Buck Peden**, Daily Californian, Media Person of the Year...."

Naturally, I received numerous telephone calls and letters from my readers and friends. Several of my wryer ones of the latter group, particularly one or two in each of the Veteran organization of which I was a member, would come with remarks like:

"Say friend, did you read in the paper where Buck here was honored along with Christ." Some religious people didn't like that, but I took as it was meant to be: in jest.

T.R. Reinman, the *Union's* golf writer, a friend and previous winner of the award, was one of the nice ones to call. I hated to see him leave the *Union* several years later. He was an excellent writer and a good golfer.

I received the engraved plaque at the next Chapter's meeting from Mike Mathison of Warner Springs Ranch GC, an officer of the group. Afterwards, I thanked him, Cole, Addis III, Johnson, Mike Flanagan, Jim Higgins, Johnny Gonzales, and a few others who I knew were mainly responsible for me being selected for the award.

Then I was startled the next year when the organization named Jim Murray of the *Los Angeles Times* recipient of the same award. My idol, when I was a sports editor in Natchez, was to receive later on in the summer so I made up my mind to drive up to LA and congratulate him for following me in receiving the SD PGA Chapter's Media Person of the Year Award. However, I figured I better brush up on his many achievements.

He was America's Best Sportswriter 14 times; received the National Headline Award (1965 & 1977), Red Smith Award (1982), Associated Press Sports Editors Assn. Award (1984), J.G. Taylor Spink Award (1997). There were several others, such as a Pulitzer Prize (1990), and was inducted in MLB's HOF (1988).

He wrote many books, including his autobiography, and I read many of them. The first one I read I noticed he sometimes ended a sentence with a preposition. I had always been taught that the noun it modifies must follow it. So I started keeping up with them so I could kid the Pulitzer Prize winner when I visited him.

Then, I noticed he sent me to the dictionary to look up words he used on many occasions. Therefore, to also be a nice guy I would keep up with the number of times he sent me trotting to the book case with his extensive vocabulary. Both totals got so numerous in the double figures that I obliterated the idea of kidding Murray about his sentence ending prepositions. I really did admire his metaphoric style of writing as did millions other readers.

Unfortunately, he died before I got to visit him. The award had to be posthumously presented to his next of kin.

My Frequent Golf Buddy Norrie West

One of the treats of my life was getting to know Norrie West. We became friends and golfing buddies for several years in his late 70s and early 80s. While I was furnishing him with humorous and/or interesting golf, or golf-related, occurrences of my past in Mississippi and Louisiana, he would proudly share with me the many California executive positions and directorships of his past. Most noteworthy among these were: sports information director of UC at Berkeley (1946-51); news media director of Rose Bowl Games (1949-51); executive director (ED) of SD Hall of Champions (1961-68); golf columnist of *Daily Californian* (1980-82), *San Diego Tribune* (1982-83), *Times Advocate* (Escondido) (1983-87); executive vice (1965-85) & president (1985-1993) of SD County Junior Golf Association; one of founders & chief ED of Junior World Championships (1968-82 & 1986-92); and ED of Andy Williams San Diego Open (1970-79).

He listened, seemingly with much enjoyment of my stories, as he would always chuckle and smile with a twinkle in his eyes. I would display the same interest when he related some instance of sports prominence in his past, but my reaction was usually my mouth aghast and my jaw hanging somewhat.

After many renditions of this situation between shots on the golf course, I noticed the little guy (yes, he was smaller than I) would usually make his putt or hit a good ball after my comments. Then, if he had just boasted a little of some tidbit in his past, he would sometimes

By Debra Lengyel

15th ANNIVERSARY was celebrated on Aug. 9, 1998 by T4U employees: David, Antu, me, Carolyn and Thomas.

word of displeasure that his wife Jane would approve. Then immediately reasons for approving or disapproving of the new rule, which told me he was thinking of his answer while he was shooting.

miss his shot a little. It was as if he wasn't concentrating, as one must when hitting a golf ball. I think he would still be thinking of the event about which he told me, or a spinoff tale to tell me after he finished hitting.

Naturally, the tiny devil in me snuck out in me occasionally after I deduced that theory. When he could beat me on that hole with a decent shot, I would ask him a thought-provoking question about a recent rule change in golf, baseball, football, etc. Invariably, he would miss his shot, mumbled a "daggumit" or some similar

He never found out about this fun I had with him doing this or he would haven't have mentioned me along with Reinman as "both good friends" in *100 Years of Golf in San Diego County* West published in 1997. The 332-pager is a must for anyone who loves San Diego's beautiful weather and its magnificent golf courses. He personalized my copy with the message, "To Buck — A friend *and* colleague I value greatly. We are two of a kind, Norrie."

Grandson Thomas Tours 3 Continents

When Thomas was 19 and entering his junior year at Westmont, he decided he wanted to take a year off from school and travel the world. He had learned how to play the piano and guitar, but when he flew to Madrid, Spain, he naturally was able to only take the latter along with a 75-pound backpack and $3,000. He settled in Salamanca, a town west of Madrid with a contact he had and toured around Spain, Portugal, and Morocco for five months. Then he received a call from his ecstatic mother that she was marrying her boy friend Joe Corr. Afterwards he decided to fly home and surprise them with his appearance & a song he had written during the flight. As one might expect, his unexpected appearance brought tears to Debra. Several weeks later he returned to Europe and, with virtually no money left, began crossing that continent headed for Asia. While passing through a number of European countries playing his guitar & singing on the streets, he earned enough to buy a ticket through Russia on the Trans-Siberian Express. Enroute, he passed through Mongolia to China. He spent several weeks in Beijing and Shanghai and made enough money on the streets to purchase a $115 plane ticket to Singapore.

Then Thomas, although running out of money in every country, made his way back north through all of South East Asia. Receiving small sums of money from his parents, he traveled through Malaysia, Thailand, Cambodia, and Vietnam before returning to Shanghai. There he flew around the world to London arriving at 10 p.m. He had no money left and had lost his ATM card. The hostel he wanted to stay the night wouldn't take him without cash, so he went out on the streets to earn it playing for donations until 2 a.m.

For the next month and a half he traveled South visiting old European friends and singing on the streets. Eventually arriving back in Spain, he made his way back to Madrid and flew home. After eleven months of traveling over 25,000 miles making over $7,000 on the streets of 20 countries and three continents he arrived home in San Diego as a twenty year old. He still couldn't have a beer with his friends at the local pub for another year, but what a trip to talk about for years to come.

Aircraft Carrier Memorial Association

I had joined the Aircraft Carrier Memorial Association (ACMA) whose primary objective was to create a Memorial overlooking San Diego Bay on Harbor Drive two blocks south of Broadway. It was dedicated on February 17, 1993, at the site of the historic Old Fleet Landing where many hundred thousand sailors from carriers berthed at North Island before the Coronado Bridge was completed.

Two life-size bronze sculptures of a sailor holding a sea bag was added in 1995 and a naval aviator kneeling in 1996. Both appear to be looking at the 165 ships engraved on

By Buck Peden

AIRCRAFT CARRIER MEMORIAL

the Memorial's four sides from USS LANGLEY (CV-1) to USS STENNIS (CVN-74). Years later, the nine-foot, four-sided, polished black granite obelisk had USS TRUMAN (CVN-75) and USS REAGAN (CVN-76) added to it. If I remember correctly, it came from the same black granite cut for the Vietnam Veterans Memorial displayed in Washington, D.C.

Richard Roy headed the ACMA when I joined and was one of the main drummers in the unit which raised funds for the Memorial from many veteran organizations and current carrier crews. I covered all of the association's major events in the *Daily California*.

During my many events with them I met John Finn and we became friends. He had won the United States' Medal of Honor for his heroic efforts and during the attack on Pearl Harbor December 7, 1941. The Aerospace Museum made an exhibit of him with his .50-caliber machine gun. He told me all about it one night when we stopped together at AL Post 282 for a few beers.

He was aged 84 at the time we stopped but was a 32-year-old chief aviation ordnance man who was quoted as saying, "They tell me about all the planes I shot down. I can't honestly say I hit any, but I shot at every damn plane I could see."

Vacationing In Our New Travel Quest

I was still drinking and hitting all the bars close around our Spring Valley residence, plus at home with my bride. She was a very mild consumer of her favorite, scotch and water, compared to me. Then family thought it had gotten so bad with mine that they all came one night together to try to talk me into giving up the habit. I really appreciated their concern as it obviously demonstrated their love and concern for me. However, I was my own man and was enjoying my waning life. I wanted it to end doing what made me happy. I had spent many, many, years working multiple jobs, studying while toiling, and sustaining stressful situations in the Navy and Major League Baseball. I sincerely felt I deserved it.

One thing happened shortly thereafter. I had heard about Bob Smith, who had a silk-screening business called the Color Factory in El Cajon, but I was warned not to play him pool. I finally ran into him one night at a bar and he had heard about me. He invited me to his two-story house that had swimming pool and a regulation pool table, not the short bar size. I found out quickly why I was warned not to play him pool for money. He beat me handily.

I liked him immediately and was very fond of his wife, Ann. She had a 1995 Chevrolet Travel Quest Conversion Van that had less than 13,000 miles on it in 1997. It had four captain seats in the front and mid-section; with a couch that folded down electrically into a bed along with Venetian blinds on all the windows aft of the driver/navigator area; two built-in ice chests adjacent to the couch sides; a rumble seat; a separate music system from the driver and the opposite navigator seat; and a complete VCR & TV system overhead behind the two front seats. There were ear phones and plugs all around for the all sound systems. Ann just didn't feel comfortable driving it and sold it to its biggest admirer, **me**, for $20,000.

Carolyn and I decided to take it on a long trip to drive the famous U.S. Highway 101 up California, Oregon, and Washington's Pacific Coasts to enjoy our new vehicle. The views were fantastic. I had thrown my car keys to Gertie after our 50th anniversary and told her I had driven her the first 50. Now, she would have to drive me the next 50. I don't know whether she took me literally or whether she didn't trust my driving anymore. Anyway, she took the wheel on this trip so I was able to enjoy the scenery much more than her (when I was sober that is).

We stopped by several well known stops that I would recommend anyone traveling in that area to put on their **"Must See List (MSL)."** One was California's **Sequoia Trees**, which we had seen many times at Yosemite Park, and another was the Hearst Castle at San Simeon. William Randolph Hearst was a multi-billionaire I would have given my left testicle to follow around in his prime years. I made this decision after touring his Castle 1,600 feet above the Pacific Ocean. He had some tremendous artifacts from all over the world in addition to many exciting and interesting rooms with their exquisite architectural designs. It should definitely make one's **MSL.**

Headed back after making Seattle, we stopped for a couple days visit with Cousin Sandra Shaddinger in Woodland. She is the daughter of my late Aunt Mossie (Tutor) & Uncle Fred Tankersly. I used to baby sit Sandra when she was age three or four when I was a young teenager. She had married Nat, a retired officer in the U.S. Merchant Marines, and they had a lovely home with a fenced in barn area for the many, profit-making, prize Llamas they owned. We got to pet a few of them, which was interesting as it was our first time. They gave us an enjoyable tour of the area, cooked a wonderful meal, and put us up for the night. It was nice to sleep on a large bed for a change after the last two nights on the small bed in the van. Sandra prepared a unique breakfast for us which featured a big, fluffy pancake-looking dish filled with jelly. It was the icing to our visit there.

Then we headed to nearby Mount St. Helens to view the site of the last volcanic eruption on the U.S. mainland back in 1980. There is an excellent display facility near the foot of the historic mountain that shows outstanding film of the eruption and its aftermath. Included in it was a recording about an old timer that had been warned to evacuate his home to avoid the upcoming eruption and he refused. The film alone is worth driving across USA to view.

Deaths Of My Three Favorite People

By Johnny McNamara

HARRY CARAY & I in the Comiskey Park Bard's Room in 1974.

———

During this era, the waning years of the 1990 decade, three of my favorite people in the baseball world passed away. Harry "Holy Cow" Caray succumbed at age 83 on Feb. 18, 1998 leaving his wife Dutchie with their lucrative restaurant business. Then, less than six months later, Jack "Hey-hey" Brickhouse, 82, died on Aug. 6, 1998, leaving his wife Patricia. Both were great TV announcers for Chicago Cubs games over WGN for many years and both are named in MLB Hall of Fame. William Wrigley would expire the next March 8 at the young age of 66.

Bill, who was a year younger than I, always treated me with the same respect that I gave him. I was really shocked and saddened when I learned of his demise.

Harry and his "tell it like it is" style was very popular in WGN's huge international broadcast area. In my opinion, Jack had more class with his style. He was the first voice heard on WGN-TV when it went on the air in 1948.

"Brick" started when he was 18 and covered a mass of subjects during his 57 years behind the microphone before retiring in 1981 and giving the Cubs job to Caray. In addition to also announcing White Sox games, other sports he called in his career were the Chicago Bears and Notre Dame football; Bulls, Packers, and Zephyrs basketball; golf; boxing; and the colorful "sport" of professional wrestling.

A Lonnnng Vacation Back To Old Haunts

We were still having plenty of business at T4U with Thomas replacing Antu at the press when we printed shirts. Antu got us several jobs during his graduate education at UCLA, but one backfired. A girl in the Pi Beta Phi sorority had ordered over $1,000 in long sleeve T-shirts with a pocket message on the front and a messaged bottle of Vodka with golden wings and a halo with the words Absolut Pi Phi beneath it. Except for the black message in the body of the bottle, all the outline and lettering was in maroon ink. When they got the shirts and the bill, the president of PBP refused them because they were colored maroon and gold near their rival USC's colors of cardinal and gold.

We knew UCLA's colors were blue and gold, but it never occurred us that they would refuse something they had ordered. We got over $200 from them and the shirts back, so we just had to sustain the loss. We have been We knew UCLA's colors were blue and gold, but it never occurred us that they would refuse something they had ordered. We got over $200 from them and the shirts back, so we just had to sustain the loss. We have been using them for undergarments during the winter months for the next decade.

After the turn of the year, we decided to take a long vacation to Las Vegas then through Utah, Wyoming, Nebraska, Iowa, Missouri, Illinois, Indiana, Kentucky, Tennessee, Mississippi, Louisiana, Texas, New Mexico, Arizona, and back home. Naturally we saw the Huffstetters, Esreys, Manesses, Pedens, and Kyzars. I was drinking all along with Carolyn doing almost all of the driving.

In Nashville while visiting Jeff and his three sons, I got a cold and coughed up some blood. While I was in the hospital, Jeff asked forgiveness for all his misbehaviors and undesirable antics of the past. I thought seriously about it for awhile and finally told him, "I'll forgive you, but the scar tissue will always be there."

Ann and her family lived in the area, but Jeff and her were divorced. The boys were with Jeff; therefore, we enjoyed our visit with them and their cute little house dog. I had all three of the kids, then ranging 7-10 years in age, scribble a line of any shape (i.e. straight, crooked, curved, etc.) on a blank page. I would them start making figures out of them (e.g. animals, trees, cars, etc.). They first one to guess what it was would win. Surprisingly, Robbie (Robert III) won although he was the youngest. He still has that good imagination.

Cossie and Charlie threw us a nice "Return to Vidalia-Natchez Party" which was attended by many of our old friends. Celebrating with plenty of boose involved was catching up with my resistance. When we got back to California a few years later the alcohol finally surpassed my liver's ability to handle it. I almost died with cirrhosis of the liver in 2003.

On the wagon again, I began regaining my health. One of these days I'm going to write a song with that title, "On the Wagon Again."

Wonderful 50th B & C Wedding Anniversary

December 21, 2000, was certainly a day of wonderment for Buck and Carolyn. Our kids went out of their way to ensure it was a tremendous dinner/dance event at Marina Village overlooking the Pacific Coast. I have never seen a family's 50th anniversary event that surpassed this one. Kin and many friends came: Charlie & Cossie Kyzar from Natchez; Carol & Kevin Huffstetter from Valparaiso, plus his sister Honora from St. Louis; and Ray & Carmen Riale were among those from back east. These plus many of our local friends made it a nice sized party. The kids had large photographs of us all around the walls. Also, each dinner table had a centerpiece of a Ferris Wheel of snapshots of us and our kids the past 50 years, which I'm sure Bob reproduced with his mastery of the computer. Each table could determine who would get the Wheel when the party was over.

After the dinner, and before the dancing commenced, several short speeches were made with me climaxing them with a presentation of a gold, heart-shaped necklace I had made with diamonds and other jewels representing all of our kids and few significant events in our life together. I used a large white board to draw and describe them before the audience. I had too many toasts by then, so I don't think I was very entertaining.

Then, after I gave the necklace to her, I started singing as the hired disc jockey played the background music, "I'll always remember the song they were playin' the first time we danced and I knew, as we swayed to the music and held each other, I fell in love with you. *Could I have this dance* for the rest of my life..." It was the beautiful piece written by W. Holyfield and B. House and sang originally by the wonderful songstress Ann Murray.

I knew I would get emotional trying to sing it, so I had asked Gale to stand in for me at another microphone and finish it. Gale has a great soprano voice and has sung many, many specials before her church congregations and, of course, sounded much better than I did. As she continued with, "Would you be my partner every night, when we're together it feels so right. Could I have this dance for the rest of my life...etc," despite my new knee, we danced through the whole song.

With a few tears while doing so, we were happily remembering our first date at the Southside High School's

1950 Valentine's Day sock dance in the gymnasium. The words to the song fit our lives so perfectly, we thought maybe it was written for us. I think the guests gave us a standing ovation afterwards, but I was too busy planting a long smooch on my bride to notice.

After that dance was over, all the guests began dancing. Carolyn told me years later that after a dance with Charlie, probably her dance partner of all times, that he told her with a tear in his eye: "You know, this might be the last time we'll see each other again." He died a year later. We went to his funeral and it was the largest attended, other than famous celebrities or well-known U.S. officials, that we had ever seen. Many, many people in the Natchez-Vidalia area sincerely loved him.

Back to our anniversary: The kids gave us a paid trip to Hawaii and $1,000 in spending money. The condo they had for us was excellent on Kauai Island and we ate at some great restaurants the week we were there. I played several golf courses, including Poipu Bay Golf Course where the Grand Slam of Golf was being played. It was a magnificent course along the ocean front that was designed by the famous Robert Trent Jones Jr.

The surprise of the trip for Carolyn was one night after dinner when we were having a nightcap. I opened a small, separate case that I had

brought and kept locked until that night. I had found the love letters that I had written Gertie while I was in boot camp prior to our marriage. Neither of us had read them since they were originally written and received. Almost all of them had a little cartoon drawing in the upper left corner of their envelopes that she had told me her postman always viewed with pleasure. The letters were extremely mushy and we laughed all night reading the contents of a homesick 18-year-old lover stuck with only thousands of males around him.

Business & House Sold For $390,000

We got an offer for the house and property that was wonderful. We decided enough was enough. I had just turned 72 and Carolyn 70 when we found a buyer for all my artwork, files, screens, ink, and business equipment added to the little ice manufacturing company that wanted the property. We sold everything for about $390,000.

Of course, paying off all our credit cards took a healthy hunk out of it, but when we moved back to Santee in 2004 we were without any debt whatsoever. I had fun making up a golf foursome occasionally with David, and his buddies Matt Haydon and Mark Zulauf. Mark, and his wife Christy, even rented us a nice three-bedroom house on Park Avenue charging us a very fair $1,200 a month rent. It had a tall backyard fence so it wasn't long till we had us a lap dog.

We paid $100 for the little guy. The owners said he was part Chihuahua and Dachshund, but they didn't know for sure. They were members of a group of dog lovers that save ones passed over so many months in the dog pound they were to be put to sleep. He was definitely a lap dog, maybe a 150% one. Also soft and furry, but the one drawback was his fur was so thick he shed all year long. I didn't mind it though. We took to each other immediately and still do, although he is now an estimated age eight.

The street was a quiet one except for the house across from us. They had a motorcycle or two that alerted us neighbors to their coming and going. They bothered Steve De Lancy's nine cats that lived in his house. Steve was an ex-Navy pilot about my age.

Steve didn't play golf but I got to play a lot with Jay Vates, a fellow member of our VFW Post 9327 on Cuyamaca Blvd., who used to crack me up with his many witticisms and funny stories. A few of them I remember, which I think were his:

Three worst words in golf: "You're still out."

"When you get mad and throw your club, always throw it in front of you. That way, you won't have to waste time going back to pick it up."

"The tooth brush was invented in Tennessee. If it had been invented anywhere else they would have called it a teeth brush."

I think he or Dan Chase told me the one about the 6'5" lad that came into a college athletic director's office and said he wanted to play football. "I scored 232 points in high school as a QB, completed 65 of 78 passes for 1,800 yards and 25 TDs. I run 100 yards in 9.1 seconds and averaged 52.2 points per game playing basketball. I won 20 games and lost none pitching baseball, including four no-hitters. I batted .530 and hit 22 home runs," the stout young man said.

The beaming coach surveyed the fine looking prep star and asked what was the reason he had not heard about him from his scouts "...were your grades bad?"

"No sir, I was valedictorian of my school and have the highest IQ in the state," he answered.

"You must have a fault somewhere," the coach reasoned.

"Yes sir, I have one. I am prone to tell lies."

Yates had plenty of them and we would always stop by the Post when I was drinking and have a brew or two. I also played darts there every Sunday evening, drinking my O'Doul's, the non-alcoholic beer, while I was on the wagon.

Golf Pro Rex Cole & Carlton Oaks CC

Yates, Lois, Mike, my kids and grandsons played many times on the spacious links at Carlton Oaks CC. Golf Professional Rex Cole there appreciated all the articles and photographs I gave the facility as the *Daily Californian* golf columnist. I didn't pay a cent for green fees or motorized carts, nor did my guest player riding with me. He was extremely helpful to me in golf history on his course and the area links. Plus, the articles I wrote about happenings on his beautiful 18-hole layout would have been enough to fill a book in itself.

Rex, then 61, a Cleveland native, had been a golf pro for over 40 years and at Carlton Oaks over 30. He is a sincere believer in golf helping kids. "Buck, I believe its the best teaching game there is for children." Some of those we discussed were the respect for another participant, strict self-adherence to the rules, the utmost honesty, good morals, gentlemen basics, and the exemplary manners of competitive play and of losing with honor. He has been tirelessly conducting free clinics and demonstrations for kids on Saturdays and Sundays at Carlton Oaks for over 20 years. Affording adults, of course, pay for his professional instruction at other times during the week. All this, and running the golf shop, all sorts of tournaments — benefits included — and the upkeep of the terrain of the course, would be enough. However, Cole found time to also coach the girls team at the nearby West Hills High School.

Rex and his wife Karen had eight kids. Their Petra was a petite lass but top golfer of the brood. She got her golf scholarship to nearby SDSU while I was preparing notes for this publication. I first met the youngster when she was winning tournaments as a junior enroute to her attaining the SD Junior of the Year recognition several times. The many awards she has won subsequently would fill several pages of type. Just checking the scouting report on her and while at West Hills High in Grossmont League play and other Southern California competition, she won 33 tournaments, finished second 12 times and in the top 10 in eight others.

But, of all her achievements on the links, she remembers "Finishing 8th in the Junior World 10-and-under as a nine-year-old" as the most satisfying. "Someone had stole my clubs and I had to play with a borrowed set," she added. Petra hopes to play golf professionally, but, if not, she would like to be a detective in the criminal justice system such as the FBI.

I would learn later that she won the 2007 City Amateur Golf Championship while a sophomore golfer on the Aztec team.

Phil Mickelson was a youngster who played frequently at COCC. While I was researching information for this book, I asked the attendant on duty if Mickelson and Lon Hinkle still co-shared the course record with 69s from the black championship back tees. Par was 72 and the yardage was 7,225 yards from those tees.

"Strange you should ask," he answered. "Brian Dillion just shot a 64 last week to better their 69s."

Sideline notes about Hinkle: (1) he lived across the street from Carlton Oaks, (2) He was the PGA top money winner in 1979 with $247,693 (most tournaments nowadays pay more than that for first place). One of the longest hitters in the professional golf ranks, he won the 1981 World Long Driving Championship, and (3) he shot his 69 at COCC using a three-wood off the tee.

Mark Wawsczyk was not too successful as a professional golfer, but the 6'5" long ball hitter from San Diego would really add to the golf benefits played at Carlton Oaks CC and other area courses. The benefit officials would place Mark on the tee of one of the long par five holes and any of the donor golfers participating in the benefit could tribute $10 in addition to their entry fee and Mark would hit the contributing donor's tee shot on that hole. Mark's tee shot would average 290-320 yards, with some going in the 350-

400 yard range. This would give those taking advantage of the "designated-tee-hitter's" shot possessed to good change to record an eagle or a birdie. Naturally, such an entry on their scorecard would give them a better chance at winning the individual and/or team first prizes normally awarded in the benefit. Obviously, Mark was kept busy which added to the benefit's total receipts

A few other amateurs I met in their early years at Carlton Oaks and Steele Canyon were Angie Yoon, Pete Schumacher, and Joel Almquist.

Yoon, another one of Cole's protegees gave me a copy of her golf scrapbook playing from February 1987 through 1995 she won 77 tournaments before becoming the team captain at the University of Nevada.

Schumacher, an ace golfer at Valhalla High, became one of the top players on the Yale team as a freshman with team captain Ken Rizvi to win an Ivy League Championship. Pete was named on the 1997 & 1998 All-Ivy League First Teams. I got to admire his disposition and inspiration as he toiled as a golf cart attendant at Carlton Oaks during his summer months. He was well liked by all.

Almquist was named on the 1997 All-Academic First Team by the *SD Union-Tribune* after obtaining a 4.07 GPA on a 4.0 scale and a SAT score of 1200. He amazed me and his parents, Bob & Pam, by shooting a 3-under par for medalist honors in the CIF team competition of Warner Spring Ranch GC despite having a ruptured tendon in his left thumb. He was nominated to the U.S. Naval Academy by Congressman Duncan Hunter and got it. Naturally he made the golf team making the l998 All- Patriot League First Team and its All-Decade Team. He is a real gentleman and will make an outstanding officer in my old Alma Mater.

Took A Great Photo For My Dying Barber

My barber in La Mesa for over a decade was Gene Long. He was also a gentleman and a great joke teller. Naturally, I had plenty I had heard from speakers at the many baseball banquets I had attended and he had tons of those he had been told by his customers over the many years he had cut hair. So, we swapped new ones the 12 minutes or so I was in his chair. He had cancer since 1991, but the radiation treatments kept him alive.

We had played golf together many times, and we talked about the PGA tournaments, but he never was able to attend one with me. Finally, learning that the treatments were no longer taking effect; therefore, he would soon have to hang up his shears.

January of 2000, I was covering the first professional tournament of the year at La Costa Hotel & Spa GC, the

Tournament of Champions. As it has virtually all the tourney champions of the preceding year, I knew Tiger Woods (Gene and most people's favorite) would be in the event. I got him a free pass when I was collecting my photographer's arm band permitting me and my 500mm camera inside the

By Buck Peden

GENE LONG (2nd from left) watches Tiger Woods enroute to winning the Tournament of Champions in 1997. Long died a few months later.

crowd restraining cord.

Then I took him to the tee ahead of Woods and his tremendous viewers on the preceding hole. I showed him the spot to stand so I could get a shot of Tiger hitting his drive with Gene in the background. I then walked about 30 yards up the fairway sidelines and waited.

Sure enough, the crowd following Woods victory in the event rushed up beside Gene and moments later Tiger teed off. I shot it just as he reached

his follow through with Long in perfect view, although he had part of his body blocked by a little lady he allowed in front of him.

I had him a 14"x17" photograph printed and framed for his barber shop. He appreciated it immensely, but died two months later.

Farewell Round As A Californian

Bob and Scott came out for a visit, which we enjoyed very much being able to learn more about our third oldest grandson. We discussed our plans to retire at Carolyn's parents house to help take care of Mom, who was now living there alone. Lillian would reach her 90th birthday on May 17, 2005, and we wanted to get there shortly thereafter to celebrate it with an Esrey-

Peden Reunion. I told Bob I would fly there and go over the plans for adding two rooms and a carport to the house. She had already told Carolyn the house was to be hers when she died.

David, Bob, and I played my last game of golf as a Californian at Mt. Woodson CC in Ramona while we were sharing the rest of the family with Scott. I think it was the first time both of my sons had beat me in a golf game, but it definitely wouldn't be the last. Bob hits them 300 yards frequently and David occasionally, but near it all the time. I'm lucky now to reach 210, but I will swing the rusty clubs as long I can stick a tee in the ground without falling.

I talked about my final golf trek as a citizen of the state while I was having dinner with Joe Warburton on board the cruise ship he gave professional golf lessons for vacationers aboard for the winter months. During the summer months, he taught at Steele Canyon GC and was the recipient of Lifetime Membership of the Professional Golfers Association of America. Joe and his wife Bettie were also well known in the area for their country western dancing in a well known square dance group.

Unfortunately, as I wrote before, I had not planned this at Mt. Woodson CC in Ramona while we were sharing the rest of the family with Scott. I think it was the first time

both of my sons had beat me in a golf game, but it definitely wouldn't be the last. .

Bob hits them 300 yards frequently and David occasionally, but near it all the time. I'm lucky now to reach 210, but I will swing the rusty clubs as long I can stick a tee in the ground without falling on my face.

I talked about my final golf trek as a citizen of the state while I was having dinner with Joe Warburton on board the cruise ship he gave professional golf lessons for vacationers aboard for the winter months. During the summer months, he taught at Steele Canyon GC and was the recipient of Lifetime Membership of the Professional Golfers Association of America. Joe and his wife Bettie were also well known in the area for their country western dancing in a well known square dance group.

Unfortunately, as I wrote before, I had not planned this autobiography; therefore, I had no journal of notes to search for some names and dates, to my many regrets. The ship's captain was a "golf nut," according to Joe, so he seemed to enjoy my describing my two holes-in-one with the same ball as well as the brief rendition of my nautical career.

Not long after that, I thought my unique golf occurrence had been equaled when I read the headline in the **Gallery** column of the *SD Union-Tribune* of Nov. 9, 2004, that

read "**With two holes in one, hacker still shoots 101.**" I thought, damn, two in the same round with the same ball would surpass my little historical achievement. Then I read the article and learned this 31-year-old attorney, Chris Varallo, who had never broken 90 the article read, hit more than one ball as he was quoted thusly:

"I would rather have won the lottery," he said. "But, hey, I'll take this. I've got two balls and a scorecard I can keep forever."

World's Best Heart Player Marries

Antu began dating Katie Gundstrom, a senior in college studying to become a teacher. She was a tall, slim lass with brown hair and a very pretty face. I don't believe I ever saw him as happy as he was then and we saw them frequently. They would come over for dinner with us and we would play the delightful card game of Hearts.

After a couple of enjoyable months of this weekly get together, I had a trophy made with a hand holding cards and an engraving that read: "World's Best Heart Player." I told them (Carolyn, Antu, & Katie) that whoever wins that night gets to carry the trophy home with them for the next week. If a player wins it three straight times, he or she would get to keep it until someone else wins three straight games.

Of course, with all my experience playing the game, I figured I would be keeper of the trophy most of the time. But, lo and behold, Katie was the first player to win three straight weeks. I have many happy memories of those evenings with Carolyn's good cooking, the comradeship, and the Heart Game competition.

After dating her for only five months, Andrew — infatuated with Katie's wonderful personality and fun-loving attitude — decided to propose marriage to her. Brother Thomas agreed to help Antu make it a super-duper occasion to remember.

When the evening began, Anrew picked Katie up from her house. He said that he had planned a nice evening to celebrate their five-month anniversary. They drove westward to Sea Port Village, a small section of downtown San Diego, which is nestled in-between the high rises and the bay. Illuminated walking paths and small privately owned stores and restaurants make this part of downtown a perfect date setting. Arriving in the early evening, they began with a light appetizer on the grass with wine and cheese and crackers while watching people flying kites and seeing sailboats cruise by.

Katie noticed a horse drawn carriage carrying a happy couple and joked about how fun that looked and how she would like to do that some day. Little did she know,

Andy already had a private ride scheduled for later that evening. After their dinner with a beautiful view of the San Diego Bay, they casually walked along bay, laughing and enjoying the cool ocean breeze and the soft sound of water splashing against the rocks. After a few minutes they found themselves standing at the foot of a horse drawn carriage. The driver asked, "Are you Andy and Katie?" Giggling with surprise, Katie climbed aboard and snuggled in next to Andy for a comfortable and romantic ride around Sea Port Village.

On the other side of town, Thomas was frantically preparing supplies at his father's house. Antu's pre-arranged secret message was going to be a discreet phone call made from his phone hidden in his pocket. If Thomas' phone rang once he would know that Andy was on his way back to East County with Katie and that it was time to set up the final surprise. If Thomas received a second phone call, that would mean they were minutes away, and it was time for him to leave the proposal scene. Thomas had been getting the supplies ready all day long and he found himself slightly behind schedule ("As usual," Antu grinned afterwards).

Suddenly, Thomas' phone rang with the first signal! In terror, he looked around at the mess of candles, flower pedals, wine and other romantic items

which lay smattered across the living room floor. He quickly gathered the supplies, shoving them in a bag, and ran out the door. It was a race against time. He should have already been at the top of the nearby Mt. Helix thirty minutes before, staging the final scene. Instead, he was driving 100 mph on the freeway, ten minutes from the summit, thinking about how his brother was going to arrive with nothing set up! Parking at the bottom of the final hill, he had a good ¼ mile at a steep incline to go to climb the summit.

Before he reached the top of the hill he received a second call from his brother, indicating that he was only minutes from the mountain. Startled, Thomas decided to break "radio silence" to call his brother. Things were still a long way from being finished. When he answered, his brother Antu quickly explained that he was "taking Katie home after a nice date, and that he was just getting off of the freeway." Understanding his implication, Thomas quickly told him that he needed more time. Andrew replied, "Ok, have a nice evening bud. Bye." Andy hung up the phone, his mind working frantically to come up with a plan to stall, while keeping a calm expression to not alarm Katie. Thomas could only hope that Andy's statement just before hanging up the phone was a disguise to prevent Katie from being suspicious, and that

Andrew would somehow delay his arrival.

He did. Antu suggested to Katie that they go visit his childhood apartment complex which was only five minutes away. She was confused by the sudden act of nostalgia she agreed which bought a few more minutes for his rushing brother. Next, Antu claimed, "A fun idea just popped his head. It is a beautiful, clear evening. Why don't we go to the top of Mt. Helix to enjoy the view before heading home."

Probably thinking that she had found the most romantic man on the face of the planet, Katie happily agreed. Upon arrival, Andrew was careful to climb up the West side of the mountain, avoiding the East side where Thomas was still anxiously preparing the proposal site. Once they reached the peak, Antu further stalled by asking Katie to take several pictures of the two of them near the cross at the top overlooking the entire city of San Diego.

Arriving at the scene of the proposal (a dark amphitheatre at the top of the East side of the mountain), Thomas began to set up the supplies in a small stone alcove under the stars: one lit candle for every day the twosome had been together (fortunately only about 150), a blanket with their names embroidered on it, two wine glasses with their names and dates etched on them, a stereo with one of their favorite CDs,

flower pedals, boysenberry pie, and a thermos of warm water with a basin. After setting everything up Thomas began the tedious task of lighting all of the candles. Cursing at the first lighter which wasn't working properly, he switched to his only back up lighter.

Knowing that the young couple in love was now only feet away, Thomas leapt over the front of the alcove and bounded down the large stone steps of the stadium. His concentration on escaping the scene was so intense that he didn't even hear a surprised female voice exclaim, "Was that Thomas??!! What the heck is he doing here?" As the realization of what was about to happen hit Katie, Thomas reached the bottom of the stairs, out of sight, and he turned to see his brother and future sister-in-law entering the alcove. Satisfied with his work, he breathed a sigh of relief. Knowing that at this point, it was now up to his brother to get the job done.

With butterflies in his stomach, Andrew led Katie down the stone smiled broadly at the sight of Katie's astonished expression as they neared the private candle-lit alcove. After a few moments, Antu took out a piece of paper and began to read a bible passage. He then poured the warm water into the basin, and he began to repeat the act that Jesus did for his disciples: he got down on his hands and knees, and he proceeded to wash Katie's cold feet with the warm water.

KATIE & ANDREW

He said, "This is an expression of my desire to love and serve you for the rest of my life." Next, he got on one knee, and he pulled out the engagement ring. With tears of joy in both of their eyes, he asked her to be his wife. Of course, after such a romantic evening with the man she loved, Katie immediately accepted his proposal. They celebrated together with a toast using a special bottle of Hungarian dessert wine that Andrew's dad had brought back from a visit with relatives in Hungary. They also ate Katie's favorite, Boysenberry pie, and enjoyed the CD with some of their favorite songs that they had listened to together many times while dating. The newly engaged couple, bursting with love, joy, and excitement, did their best to make time stand still and enjoy every last moment of the unforgettable evening.

They were married the day after Antu's 24th birthday on March 25, 2005. The wedding was held on the Pacific Ocean beach behind the Hotel Del Coronado and the following banquet on the western porch of the magnificent hotel. When Gertie and I walked up to meet Katie's family for the first time, a pretty lady came up to me with a Hawaiian lei.

Placing it over my head she said, "I know I haven't met you yet, but if you're going to attend the wedding, I have to lei you.

I grinned and couldn't resist saying, "Howdy. I'm Buck Peden and this is my wife Carolyn, grandparents of Andrew. I must admit this is the first time I have been leid by a woman before I knew her name."

She was Sharon Gundstorm, and she laughed along with me as she introduced us to her husband Dave. They are Katie's very likeable parents and Dave is CEO & President of Marvin K. Brown Auto Center where they have those beautiful Cadillacs. We also met Katie's sisters, Stacey & Jill, and her maternal grandparents, Gene & Carol Gates. We had future dinners with both families and once visited Dave & Sharon's beautiful house on one of the small mountains overlooking El Cajon Valley.

Andrew & Katie would wisely wait over three years before having a 7 lb. 12 oz. perfect son on July 7, 2009. As close as we have been to these two, you can imagine how happy we are. We plan to see the new Carter John Lengyel in September.

It was our second great grandchild as David Lee & Jassmarie had our first, Janessa Marie, Feb. 2, 2008.

Headed For Final Resting Place

I flew to Memphis in the earlier spring of 2005 and checked the construction work of adding the two rooms, a stairway to the combined attics, bathroom, and carport on to the north end of Mom's two bedroom house she and Virgil had built in 1970. Bob had hired a contractor for us that had done good work on Walter's house recently. I made a few changes and paid him a large portion of our agreed terms. I also had him add a new roof and white aluminum siding around the entire building when finished with the construction. The entire job costs us nearly $88,000. As we invested $40,000 with Debra's company, AIG Financial Advisors Inc., in an Allianz High Five deferred variable annuity, we had to borrow over $50,000 from the local bank to which we had transferred our account.

I also made arrangements with the huge Desoto Civic Center located nearby for our reunion and birthday dinner for Mom with all her and our relatives invited. Carolyn and I paid for the entire shebang.

With all that accomplished, all I had to do when I got back to California was to send out invitations and prepare for our final move. We had a yard sale for one weekend and sold much of our miscellaneous items of which we not taking. I sold our car to one of my pool-playing friends at the Hi-C-Era pub.

Fortunately, Antu, Katie, and Thomas helped us drive to Southhaven in the van as I wanted to drive straight through without stopping to sleep. The van back couch seat was kept down in its bed position for naps after one's turn at driving. Everything went well until we ran out of gas. It happened while Thomas was driving and I hadn't checked the gauge during his long stint behind the wheel. Luckily, it was near an exit to a gas station and, with a few restarts of the remaining fumes, we were able to coast in to a pump.

It took $85 to fill the big tank with the gas prices what they were at the time. Carolyn and I related to the grandkids aboard how in 1951 we had driven from Memphis to San Diego in our '47 Frazer for only $36 of gasoline.

We got there on Friday, May 27, with all the rest of our kids and grandchildren flying or driving in Saturday for the Sunday reunion dinner. A total of 53 made the outstanding group picture which was taken by Bob using his great camera with the delayed shutter so he could also be in it. Connie left early and missed it with my sister, JoAnn, sitting in her car until ex-hubby Kenneth and his new wife Bobbie Jo left. To say that this upset Carolyn and me would be putting it mildly.

All of our kids and grandchildren were there. Mom was radiant with her only son Tommy and current wife Diane was there beside him with their son (Ilan) in front. Also, Tommy's children of an earlier marriage were there: his daughter Missy Maness (and her sons Henry & Simon) and his son Tom (& wife Lois). Lillian had many more relatives of her parents, Arthur and Annie (Holland) Bracket, in attendance.

From my mother's Tutor family there attending were brother Keister, sister Tinye, and the late brother Morris' wife Mable with her son Michael and wife Margaret.

All of Bob and Gale's youngsters made appearances and Jennifer with husband Eric Cochran, Timothy with his fiancé Lindsay Forbess, and Scott with his girl friend Laurie Fair.

Settling Down On Our Last Road

We had to sleep on inflated mattresses for a couple of days until our furniture arrived. Finally we put all of Gertie's future (bed, recliner, TV, etc.) and clothes in the large bedroom we had added. I took the large couch which folded into a bed into the other room with our entertainment center, a small reefer for my beer & Gatorade, a recliner, several desks & file cabinets, an art table, and all my electronic disc and tape players. I had been researching the notes for this autobiography for the past year at Santee and was ready to start writing.

It was always my desire to play music, if possible, when I write. I had over 5,000 songs on 7" reels of ¼ inch silicon-coated tapes 1,800 feet long that played music forward and reverse. I also had about 100 cassette tapes for my vehicles and small tape players. I used to have a lot of the 8-track cassettes, but I did away with them as soon as they came out with the thin 4½" wide compact discs. They contain the latest hits and we possess over 80 of those, each usually containing 12-18 songs. Some of the Christmas Albums contain two or three discs.

The rooms both are air conditioned with central heat and are well lit with four lights below their overhead fans. The original portion of the house has electric heat in its ceiling. Since our dog stays in my computer, entertainment, bedroom, I named the room Herman's Happy Haven (HHH) with a sign to that effect on the door leading to the hallway and bathroom. He would sleep all night with me while I slept in the couch let down into a bed, but when I decided the couch unfolded with its soft cushions, he slept in the recliner or a bed we had bought him by the carport door. I always fed him from his tray at the front door of HHH and let him out that entrance. But, no matter what exit he used (main house back door, sliding deck door, or its front door), he ALWAYS came back to the car port

doorway steps and sat or laid for admission. It was two years later before he learned a bark there would admit him almost immediately.

Our Chino Cousins Neighbors Again

Bob and I played golf at nearby North Creek and Greenbrook Golf Courses and Debra played once with us before she returned to California. Also, I played once at the former links with Jimmy and John McDaniel, both displaying the amateur game with which they had been so successful in college. Then, one day I joined Cooper McDaniel's oldest son, Michael, and Southaven's popular former Mayor Joe Cates on the nine-hole Greenbrook GC. Coop had taught all of us boys well, although I was "over the hill" with my game now.

Michael, who had married Patricia Mc Nulty, lived in the house north of us and JoAnn in a house with a huge storage building and a little pond behind our 2.3 acres. Her driveway exits on Esrey Road between Michael and us. She had always been a help to Mom. Jimmy wed Danita Newsome they lived around the corner on College Road with their two children, Kimberly & Andrew. Andrew is only a teenager, however, he already shows a tendency to becoming a good golfer like his dad.

Mary Ann, the McDaniels

only daughter, hitched with Chuck Swain and they had five kids: Chase, twins Michelle & Julia, Joshua, and Nicholas. John, the youngest of JoAnn's, played golf for Northwestern College at Senatobia, Miss., and became manager of a pizza store.

As youngsters in Chino, all three of the boys worked at nearby Los Serrano's Golf Course with Jimmy gaining an Assistant Professional status.

As a golfing prepster, Jimmy played in the state finals at Santa Barbara while attending Chino's Don Lugo High. He also attended one of my alma maters, MSAC, and later became an Air Traffic Controller in Memphis. He has been elevated now to Traffic Management Specialist at the Memphis Center, a very responsible position.

Michael acquired two BS degrees at another of my alma maters, Cal Poly (Pomona) University, and a master's degree in Engineering at the University of Mississippi (Ole Miss). He was Public Works Director of Southaven, Miss.. He now is District Manager of SW Water Co.

Added A Couple More Holes-in-One

Thirteen days after we got to Southaven I read when Louis Berratta, 78, had hit two holes-in-one at North Creek (103-yard #2 hole & 145-yard #16) in one round. I added it to my notes to call

the retired Berratta Barbeque Restaurant owner to see if he did them with the same ball. I finally called in September and the poor guy had a heart operation the week before but was kind enough to talk to me. He said he hit the first one with a Titleist and changed to a Calloway at the turn. Whew! My "two-with-same-ball" still was unequaled.

While on the HIO subject, I purchased a year's membership ($300) in the little par 33 city-operated Greenbrook GC, a nine-hole course. One of the times I was going to play alone, I was invited to join a threesome that was teeing off in front of me. I didn't like to play alone, so I joined them.

Instantly, as we introduced ourselves, the tall large one named Pete Farris asked, "Buck Peden. Are you any kin to a guy I worked with delivering mail in south Memphis named John Peden?

"Yes Pete," I said surprised. "John Lee was my close young brother who died in '96."

It was the beginning of a lot of golf between the Pete and I. A lot of it was with Bubba Ubanks, Pete's brother-in-law, and Hugh Farris, Pete's nephew. We were playing again together on the 4th hole at Greenbrook —- a minuscule 79-yard, par three — when I hit a wedge on the green and it trickled straight toward the hole.

"That's going in the hole," Bubba yelped, **and it did**. It was on July 18, 2006 and my fourth HIO.

On May 15, the next year with Bubba and Pete in attendance, I did it again for my **fifth** HIO. Werner Lang, the course manager and a 20-year Navy retired veteran himself, reported both as usual to the local newspapers. I'm sure both of them won me the beer bets for which Pete and I always played.

He invited me to Shelby's Bar & Grill near the intersection of Airways Blvd. and Shelby Dr., the latter drive running immediately south of the Memphis International Airport. That was a popular place of interesting regulars. David Wilson was the owner and chef for the weekday lunches. Some of his customers came in for the tasty, reasonably priced food he prepared, but most of them were drinkers of his ice cold beer. He probably would head the "most beers consumed per day" list himself if one would be kept.

I have been a regular at many bars in my lifetime in a number of states, but I have never seen as many regulars as he possessed. Naturally, they were all types (i.e. doctors, lawyers, Indian chiefs, etc.), including many "rednecks" and a couple of millionaire businessmen. The late Kenny Rogers, former owner of the well-known Hernando's Hideaway Night Club, was one of them. Before he died in '07 and many other regulars I enjoyed as golfing opponents as David held weekly scramble golf tournaments on Thursday afternoons and Sunday mornings at nearby courses.

One of the regulars was Oliver Jones, now called "Ollie," from my childhood days in Fort Pickering. We downed many brews and played a few games of golf together when his health permitted. Carolyn and I also got to see his brother Richard and Billie Francis at one of the quarterly Scrapper Dinners (all Southside High School graduates invited) held at the Piccadilly Restaurant in Memphis. All the Jones family have had heart problems and Ollie's wife Shirley's ticker gave way in '08.

I heard about an old Levi and Whitehaven classmate Bobby Winchester owning a SE Marketing Company in Memphis so I dropped in on him and we had lunch together. He was proud of his company being named to the Dairy Service Department's Hall of Fame in 2000. Bobby had won the 1951 Memphis Golden Gloves Heavyweight Championship by beating Tulos Meade, who later turned professional. My ole hooky-playing buddy who later became Cowboy Jack Clements also tried fighting that year, according to Winchester.

"He was knocked down four times in the first round and the referee stopped the bout," Bobby explained. "Jack kept asking why they stopped the fight."

Winchester also told me the designing company where Ernie Lee Foley worked so I stopped by and surprised her. After that, Carolyn and I got to become good friends with her and Edwina from my eighth grade year.

Debra Marries San Teacher Joe Corr

Debra fell in love again. This time it was with a nice young man named Joseph Leary Corr. He was 45-year-old eighth grade English teacher at Bell Middle School in San Diego. They sealed their relationship permanently with a marriage on Dec. 15, 2005.

**DEBRA & JOE
The newly weds in 2005.**

He is a warm, good-natured guy that our family liked immediately. His favorite hobby was water surfing and Debra learned from him. She is did sustain a broken leg once, but she is fond of the sport almost as much as Joe.

They currently live in Joe's house with a nice view and in walking distance to the Pacific Ocean. Of course, they didn't walk as they had many different surf boards which they hauled to the beach in their large camper truck.

Favorite Hitching Posts Near Esrey Rd.

My favorite places to stop and have a cool one or two, in addition to Shelby's, was Logan's Roadhouse, Lone Star Steakhouse & Saloon, Boiling Point Seafood & Oyster Bar, and the American Legion Post 1990. I also joined the VFW Post 10567, but didn't frequent it as much as the others. All were in Southaven, except the AL Post, which was in nearby Nesbit (later incorporated in Hernando).

Carl Greenwood signed my transfer to the latter and its Commander at the time, Dennis Loveland, welcomed me at the next meeting. I would find him to become one of my favorite members, as he possessed a great knowledge of MLB history providing us with mutual chatting fodder. One of the officers told me I was the oldest active member of that post.

Carolyn and I played in its dart tournament run by Joe Licci. It was a double-elimination; blind draw partners in the game of cricket. It has a $5 entry fee with the top three winners sharing the pot. The regulars were great friends and we enjoyed being with them each week.

I got to know the managers

at the non-veteran joints I found to my liking, and, of course, the regular bartenders. Most of the stops at each was returning from golf or shopping at the well planned business sections on, or just off, Goodman Road.

One of the first at Logan's was Andrea and surprisingly, she and the manager at that time were Chicago Cub fans. Desiree and Brady were our usual waiters when Carolyn and I ate.

Also at Logan's, I met for the first time a regular customer everyone called Chief, who was actually Bill Wenhold. He had wrestled professionally as Billy Blue River, a 6'4", 340-pounder. He defeated Pancho Villa for the All-Star Wrestling Heavyweight Championship in 1964 and Bob Mc Cune for the IWA Heavyweight Crown in 1977.

I asked him if he ever wrestled Lou Thez, which many consider the greatest wrestler of all time. He said twice and won once. Chief added that he, and his wife Beverly Shade (also a pro in the women's competition), promoted many of Thez's events during that era of their life

Then, about a year later, I started going to the Boiling Point for their gumbo originally, but I liked their draft beer prices and the generous side shot of Jose Cuervo Tequila that Andy & Jeremy, the bartenders, always poured me. To my surprise the sweet little Brady had started working there. I always enjoyed their hostess Katie Stallings, a student at Northwest for whom I edited a college article she turned in for one of her final historical exams.

The highlight at the Point for me was Jeanie Miller, the mother of Mel, who is the wife to owner Charlie Wiggins. Jeanie is really witty, or as some say a substitute card (a Joker, dummy). It was February 1 and I was crying in my beer to Jeanie and Lisa, the barmaid of the day, that I had forgot all about it being April Fool's Day. I had always come up with something to surprise Carolyn on this date, but I had done nothing this year.

Jeanie, as I would learn had bushel of ideas in her ingenious bag ideas, told us to wait a minute while she went to the kitchen and returned with a white container for "take home" meals.

"Give her this as her lunch for today," she said with one of the most devilish smiles I had ever seen.

I could not imagine what she had in it, so I opened it carefully. **HOLY GUACAMOLE!** It was a large crawfish, with his two large claws raised up and wide open as if he was going to lunge out and pinch me. It was a perfect idea and I thanked her. It was the largest crawfish I had seen and I had been eating them all my life. I gave Lisa an extra $10 later when I paid my tab to give to Jeanie, who was back at work in the kitchen. Whether she gave it to Jeanie or not, I never asked.

Anyway, I took it, plus another container with a real lunch in it, and phoned Gertie by phone not to eat lunch that I was bringing it home. It went over just as we had planned. After opening her lunch box, I never have seen Carolyn move so fast as she did dropping the box and leaping backward up on the kitchen counter.

A few days later, Diane and her family were visiting from Louisville and we took them to the Boiling Point to eat. Jeanie was so happy to hear Carolyn's rendition of the exciting April Fool's Day. Carolyn laughed this time telling about it, but she certainly didn't the day of the event.

Another visit we had about that time was from Robert Roy Peden III. I had sent Jeff a bus ticket for "Robbbie" and $20 for him to spend enroute from Nashville to Memphis. Robbie said later he never got the $20. I gave him $80 for helping me paint the overhead of the carport. And a few more bucks for helping us around here. He also helped Bob and I add a deck porch off the new sliding door. I took him to my new hitching post at the Lone Star. He enjoyed meeting my favorite bartender there, Jennifer May. Jenny and I got along well together as she enjoyed golf as much as I. Also, she handled my Coors beer and Cuervo shooters with a steady hand.

We also played pool at the Legion and not too many months after he finished his 10-day visit, guess who would start to work there. Yep! Brady. If she was going to keep following me around (kidding, of course), I figure I should at least learn her last name. It is Irons which is quite appropriate as old vet put it: "It's because she is a hot number."

She decorated the Post bar room with each applicable holiday trinkets, etc., and I got her to give me a copy of a cute sign posted behind the bar that read:

HIDING FROM WIFE $ Bar Phone Rates $: $1 - "Nope, not here." $2 - "Just missed him." $3 - "Just had one drink & left." $4 - "Hasn't been in all day." $5 - "Never heard of him."

Everything Was Smooth Until…

We bought a new large air conditioner for Mom's living room, plus a new stove, refrigerator, dish washer, washing machine, and dryer. She had a longtime policy on her freezer that got her a new one when it failed in 2006. We also signed up with DirecTV for our four sets, including a DVR for the entertainment center.

With the stairway we had installed off HHH, we all had easier access to the enlarged attic than the pull down steps in the hallway. We added a lot of our unused furniture and off-season clothes up there.

We got Mom to quit her job with Sam's Club as a new product sample dispensor in house and at local supermarkets, etc. We took over payment of everything groceries, house insurance, water, sewer, etc., except two items. She insisted on paying for her car maintenance & insurance and half the electric bill.

Carolyn took over 99% of the cooking and Mom loved her dishes. I never saw a 90+ year-old woman with the excellent appetite she possessed. Naturally, I took care of the outdoor chores such as cutting the 2.3 acres of grass, raking leaves, trimming trees, etc.

Debra, Antu & Katie, and Thomas made visits at different times, which we always enjoyed immensely.

Locally, we got to visit Mable Tutor's occasionally and her daughter Sue & Ken Taylor's nice home for dinner.

I visited Ronald Hall several times at his home near Hernando. This U.S. Marine cousin, had been a beautician with at mother's shop when he first got out of the service and now — to my pleasant surprise — he was the vice president of a bank in Hernando.

Like his late father Aubrey, he was always one of my favorite kin. He once told me that he thought my mother was the real backbone of the Tutors, which I agreed.

All in all, we were all happy and living well when it happened. Lillian only drove to nearby stores and to church and back in her car in the daylight hours. We drove her all the other times. Then, on Oct. 28, 2007, returning home on Elmore Road in Southaven, a drunken driver coming around the corner off Church Road glanced off an object on his lane's shoulder and rammed head-on into Lillian's oncoming car. She never gained consciousness before she was pronounced dead minutes later at the nearby Desoto Baptist Hospital.

The drunken driver, John Partain, was sentenced to 15 years in prison and to pay $48,000 in restitution to the heirs of the estate. The judge said he would order the court to garnish him $500 a month after Partain finished his sentence. Thank goodness our son, who was very distraught when he saw Mom in the casket, had been named her Executor. He and her attorney, Ben Taylor, took care of everything very effectively.

She was a devoted member of Trinity Baptist Church for 62 years, including a position as Financial Secretary. She also had been employed by IRS prior to the Sam's Club. Lillian was highly respected and well liked by all.

I always loved her dearly and could not have desired any better parents-in-law than Lillian and Virgil. They never, not once, meddled in our marital life. I was very, very thankful having them as my in-laws.

Their only children were Carolyn and Thomas Lee. Tommy went to Louisville in l996 when he partnered with Roy's of Louisville Beauty Academy until retirement in 2001 due to his Alzheimer disease. He was in a nursing home and never was cognizant of his mother's death. He succumbed himself at age 69 on June 20, 2008.

"Mr. Thomas," as he was called by most in the beauty business, was a well known guest artist, lecturer and distinguished school administrator and owner. He conducted many training seminars for various state cosmetology school associations, colleges and universities. He served on the Bluegrass; Hair Fashion Committee and was the former president of the Kentucky Association of Cosmetology Schools. Tommy was chosen to serve on the National Cosmetology Association's "Schools America" Steering Committee and was a distinguished member of Intercoiffure America. He was an award-winning hairstylist with over 20 championships and awards including the coveted Gold Trophy Award at the Midwest Beauty and Trade show in Chicago, IL in l979.

Made Long Trip To Huffstetters' 50ᵗʰ

We went through Louisville to visit Tommy's wife Diane; his daughter Melissa, and her son Henry; and Tommy's son

Tom Jr. and wife Lois enroute to-and-from Kevin & Carol Huffstetters' 50ᵗʰ wedding anniversary in Valparaiso, IN. Therefore, we were able to see Tommy before he died. He looked pitiful and really saddened my heart. Surprisingly when Carolyn bent over close to his face, he mustered a slight smile and said muttered softly, "My sister." It chokes me every time I think of that moment. I know it meant the world to Carolyn that he recognized her in his waning days of life.

The attendance of Carol and Kevin's 50ᵗʰ anniversary helped pacify our drooping hearts as we got to see all six of their kids and spouses of same, where applicable, plus their many pretty grandchildren. Father Steve, beautiful Delia, twins Mary & Annie, kind John, and — my favorite childhood shortstop — Danny, plus Kevin's brother Mickey, were all there with sparkles in their eyes and love in their hearts. Annie was sweet as ever and Mary certainly didn't act like the Florida professor she had become. She was the life of the dancers after the banquet, dancing to every song. I think the energetic lass danced with everyone in attendance that night.

It was a very successful affair for our two friends who drove all the way down to Memphis to attend Mom's farewell at Forest Hill South. Their attendance at the funeral visitation was quite a surprise as was several of the

Tutor relatives that had never met Lillian.

Tutor Reunion Held In New Albany

Among the later were Tinye, Mable, and Michael Tutor. Also, Judy Naro, Berline (Tutor) Hall's daughter, and Sandra Shaddinger, Mossie (Tutor) Tankersly's daughter, were there and told us of the Tutor Reunion planned at the latter's Baptist church on Oct. 11, 2008. We said we would definitely attend.

Four days later from that date and Keister Tutor would turn 87. So, as we had done with the 2005 Esrey-Peden Reunion I wrote about earlier, this one featured the oldest member of the Tutor Family as ours had the oldest Esrey (& Bracket) and Peden. We did attend the New Albany event, but regrettably my sister JoAnn had a racing heart and had to be hospitalized. She eventually would have a heart pacemaker inserted a few days later and recovered satisfactorily. I hated she was unable to go with us and many asked about her.

The last Tutor Reunion I put together at Keister's farm. Eighteen-year-old Bob and I tape recorded many voices, which we still have, and I took a group photograph on July 10, 1970. Many of the Tutors in that photograph enjoyed seeing themselves as youngsters as I brought a copy to the New Albany affair.

This time I did nothing but

enjoy myself as Judy, Tinye, Lynn & Fran Tankersly, and Nat & Sandy did it all. The latter twosome paid for the great food that was catered and many sent money later to the church's building fund It was great visiting with all the great Tutor bloodlines of my mother, Ruby Jane.

In closing, what does this autobiographical chronology leave?

My favorite Uncle Keister is the most senior Tutor.

Carolyn is now most senior Esrey

I am the most senior Peden.

Herman is neighborhood's senior dog.

Viva la seniors

Appendix

Approval for photographs:

I didn't identify the photographs as I took virtually all the sports ones except the one of Dick Allen hitting the ball on the Comiskey Park roof. I think that was given to me by Bob Langer or one of the other regular baseball photographers of the Chicago newspapers. Of course, all the others, such as a few U.S. Navy photographs, I identified the source. Approval of the White Sox and Cubs photos was obtained from the respective club officials.

Roland Hemond, who had regained employment with the White Sox in 2000 as Executive Adviser to the General Manager in 2000, referred me to Howard Pizer, but Scott Reifert, Vice President of Communications wrote me the approval.

Hemond's career in almost 60 years in baseball is fantastic. Three times he was named MLB's Executive of the Year. Prior to his present position, he had 24 years with the White Sox (1970-85) and Baltimore Orioles (1988-95) as general manager and five with the expansion Arizona Razorbacks as executive vice president. All this was following his minor league experience beginning in 1951.

Andy MacPhail, the successful son of Lee MacPhail who was AL President and subsequently named to MLB's Hall of Fame, wrote me the approval for my Cub photographs as he was then president of the NL club. He was in the farm department while I was there, but he went to the Minnesota Twins where he became the youngest president to win two world series (1987 & 1991). He came back to head the Cubs to two playoffs but no titles. He was a very wise president for both clubs.

Book Referrals:

The following publications I recommend to all readers:

At the top of the list is the ten volume Sports Classics, and the author of each, published by Jerome Holtzman, the late *Chicago Sun Times* baseball writer, MLB Historian, and member of MLB's HOF:

The Glory of their Time, Lawrence Ritter
The Long Season, Jim Brosnan
Veeck - as in wreck, Bill Veeck & Ed Lynn
Instant Replay, Gary Kramer & Dick Schaat
Farewell to Sports, Paul Gallico

The Boys of Summer, Roger Kahn
Babe, Robert Creamer
Eight Men Out, Eliot Asinof
The Sweet Science, A.J. Liebling
Paper Lion, George Plimpton

Other baseball ones are:

The Relief Pitcher, John Thorn
Baseball's Best, Marty Appel & Burt Goldblatt
My Prison Without Bars, Pete Rose w/Rick Hill
The Ultimate Baseball Book, multiple writers
I Was Right On Time, Buck O'Neil w/others
The October Heroes, Donald Honig
Diamond Dust Tid Bits, Ted Hamilton
Third Base Is My Home, Brooks Robinson
The Louisville Slugger Story, Spts Pub. L.L.C.

The Game & The Glory, Joe Reichler
Baseball, G.C. Ward & Ken Burns
This Great Game, multiple writers
The Last Series, Hal Higdon
Chicago Cubs, Jim Enright
Baseball's 100, Maury Allen
The Summer Game, Roger Angell
Five Seasons, Roger Angell
Hack, Robert Boone & Gerald Grunska

Three And Two! Tom Gorman w/J. Holtzman   *Holy Cow*, Harry Caray
Baseball - 100 Classic...The Game, foreword by Nolan Ryan
The History Of National League Baseball, Glenn Dickey w/introduction by Pete Rose
Some Of My Best Friends Are Crazy, Jay Johnstone w/Rick Talley
A Century Of Baseball Lore, John Thorn

Some Brief Reflections & Peden's Pet Peeves (PPP):

General

*I used to have a photographic memory but don't now as my film is past due.

*Some people are **never satisfied** with what they've got. A few examples: Straight-haired girls want curls, curly headed girls want straight hair; bald guys want hair, hairy guys shave their heads, etc.

*Some people, most of them **vegetarians**, will not eat any animal meat (cattle, pigs, sheep, turkey, chicken, etc.), but they will eat eggs. Believe it or not, some people don't know eggs are an embryo of a baby chicken. They are eating an animal.

*We used to have "one" standard dictionary of our language. Now we need many more to understand technical language as we are becoming so computerized. Example: **portrait and landscape** instead of vertical and horizontal.

*Easter Sunday 4/15/01 while all the young kids are looking for painted eggs hidden by the **Easter Bunny**, I went to the SD Zoo. I sustained a mild shock when I saw a condor eating a rabbit on a perch in his cage, a white bunny at that!!!

*I wrote about how southerners misused words such as "**fixing to go** downtown," etc. Of course there are more, but I'm sure readers will agree with me as these are often used inappropriately by all sections of the USA: know/known, to/too, up/upon, who/whom, etc.

***Sealing envelopes** by licking the glue flap was the only way I sealed envelopes if I was not in my office with a wet sponge. I didn't think of wetting finger tips with saliva to smear on envelope glue in lieu of licking them until I was in my 60s. No more bad glue taste in my mouth. I never saw anyone before or since do it.

*Another time-changed phrase I notice in the decade of 2000-2010. Response to "Thank you" was always "You're welcome." Now, especially the youngsters, the answers are **"No problem."**

*I think the only way to eliminate **terrorism** on our planet is to reverse their religious beliefs that they will be rewarded in after life when they succumb in accomplishing their suicide act of terrorism.

*A real humdinger to send to one on **Mother's Day** by a son-in-law is a note Andy Lengyel inscribed on one he sent to Carolyn: "If I had to put a special order in for a M-in-L it would have been you." .

*My advice to the fiancé: Get married on a national holiday so you won't ever forget your anniversary.

PPP - I shudder when a karaoke participant sings off key. They should put up a sign with a piggy bank below it. The sign should read: "**Current singer will stop** with a $10 donation to karaoke winner's bank below."

PPP - In some states, **cruel mass murders** only get intravenous shot of poison which puts the murder to sleep before dieing. I think that is absolutely asinine. A prospective murder knows that if he gets caught the worst thing he could get is to go to death and die. If he thought he was going to get cut up into pieces as he did his victim, he may think twice. But then, they're usually insane anyway; therefore, it probably would make no difference.

PPP - Our fads come and go in society. I usually have no problem sustaining them in my daily life. In fact, I wrote once herein where I fought on a liberty once in Yokosuka to defend a young sailor's fad of stroking his hairdo down the middle toward his face leaving a mouse tail appearance on his forehead. But this current faze many, especially actors and actresses, have of wearing their hair tangled, messy, and as if they got out of bed is ridiculous. Meg Ryan, my favorite female actress, had her hair cut jagged something like that in one movie and it looked terrible. The worst of any fad and one that has become very popular is **wearing a cap backwards**. To me it looks so stupid. They usually have a nice design on the front portion with a bill to shade the eyes and nose from the sun. To hide the design from someone you are facing and to shade the back of your neck definitely appears idiotic.

PPP - **"Land of the free"** has probably been said by all Americans at one time or the other. I did, until they passed a few laws taking away a couple of choices a person used to have: (1) Must wear seat belt and (2) All bikers must wear helmets. Double bullfeces! (1) My family always use their seat belts in our vehicles to help protect us in case of an accident. But I know the authorities use the law to stop a possible law breaker or drunk, so I guess most people like the law for that reason. (2) The helmet deal is crazy. The only one in that it protects is the biker, who may prefer to feel the air blowing through one's hair while joy riding. Therefore, if he wants to sustain the danger of not wearing it, so "free" be it. Someone in the Navy told me of a biker that was hit headon by a car and his helmet flew off his head and struck and seriously injured a kid on the side of the street.

PPP - I remember the days that television and movie films were always viewable even during a night scene. Now, if it's a night scene they sometimes make it so dark that you **cannot see the happening** only hear the audio. Maybe a flash of a pistol shot or a figure moving through a moonlights area, etc., but never clear enough for the viewer to appreciate. Also, sometimes they photo angles directly into the sun with the subject only a silhouette with no recognizable view of the individual's facial expressions. Baloney!

PPP - The worst innovation the film makers (not of unplanned happenings, events, etc.) came up with was the **hand-held camera** with its operator fast-panning the many subjects in the scene: not only the normal human's scanning preference (i.e. left to right), but up & down, right to left, jarring down & up stairs, etc. It was so upsetting to an executive producer, director, and film photographer such as me, utilizing that method throughout the whole feature was unbearable. For example, I enjoyed the writing, directing, and acting of the TV series "NYPD Blue," but finally stopped watching it because of the abrupt moving of the camera and quick cuts from one subject to the other. Obviously, it was a long-standing series; therefore, my detesting was not shared by the general public.

Golf

*Lee Trevino**, after being hit by lightning during the 1975 Western Open, is rumored to have said afterwards, "I should've held up a one iron. Not even god can hit a one-iron."

*Don't take golf so seriously. Enjoy your frolicking around the course. And, if you have the high score amongst your group, remind them you got to **hit the ball more** times than they did (price of green fee divided by number of shots, etc.)

*I thought making two holes-in-one (HIO) with the SAME BALL on two consecutive Tuesdays, was the most unique accomplishment in golf. Then I read in *Chicken Soup for the Golfer's Soul* where Margaret Waidron of Jacksonville, Fla., a legally **blind golfer** who relied on her husband to line up her shots, hit two holes-in-one in two consecutive days at Long Points 87-yard, seventh hole. I meekly dropped my HIO oddity down a notch.

*Tiger Woods** 12-stroke victory in the 1997 Masters was voted the top story of the year by the

Associated Press. "**Cool**," he was quoted as saying after learning of the selection. Runner-up, in his opinion, was the story of Mike Tyson biting off a piece of Evader Holyfield's ear in the heavyweight title fight that year

*Most duffers play once a week, all their life, and never get a hole-in-one. According to the *San Diego Union-Tribune* on 9/3/2001, Matt Lees, a 61-year-old lawyer, hit three in one round of golf. Playing on the Mission Bay Golf Course, he tallied his first one on the 11th, his second two holes later and the third on the next hole. *Golf Digest* claimed **three holes-in-one** during one round was a two-trillion-to-one chance of occurring. Therefore, Lees will probably not live long enough to see, or read, of it happening again

*One of the temperamental club-throwing golfers of my time advised me to always **throw it ahead** not behind you. That way, you don't waste time having to go back to pick it up.

*One of the reasons Palmer was so good is that he never left one on the "lip" of the cup. If it so happened, he would turn to the huge crowd of fans, that always follow the popular icon around, and holler, "**Alright army, jump.**"

***Sucking hind tit** finish in golf in the old days meant you were as the runt of a large litter of suckling pigs.

*Three **worst words** in golf: "You're still out."

***Easiest shot** in golf: "Your fourth putt."

PPP - Announcers in golf now use the term **"speed"** in lieu of **"hard"** when discussing a putt. The ball goes too far or too short depending on how hard it was hit not how much speed one puts on the stroke. For example, one could stroke the putt with a lot of speed and quickness, but if it is not hit hard enough it's not going to get there.

PPP - One of these days the networks, ESPN, and the Golf Channel will mark the outer edge of the green with a soft light green line to indicate the direction of their cameras angle registering the putts. This would give the caddies and opposing players this knowledge so **they would not block** the view of the putt from the millions of viewers watching it on television.

PPP - Replays used in any televised sports events are usually thrown in without a visual indication (there are exceptions). Viewers chatting with guests at home, or those hard of hearing, don't know when it occurs and assume it is live. One of these days, they will all ensure a **"replay visual"** is on display throughout the entire repeat.

PPP - Calling a **stroke penalty** when the wind causes the ball to move after a golfer has addressed the ball to make a putt. The golfer has nothing to do with causing it to move. Ridiculous!

Baseball

*Baseball is the only sport in which the **defense has the ball**.

*A good trivia question most people would miss is: "Who was the **first black in the Major Leagues?**" The average fan, and even some sportswriters, would say **Jackie Robinson**. However, it was Catcher Moses Fleetwood Walker in 1884 who was first and later his brother Welday with the Toledo (Ohio) Blue Stockings, then a National League Team. Virtually everyone saw Robinson in his HOF play, watched films of him, or read of all this great UCLA multiple-talented athlete. Topping his career came posthumously when his widow Rachel received his Congressional Gold Medal. The first recipient? George Washington.

*Willie Mays first safety in the majors after going **hitless in 12** at bats was a home run OUT of the New York Giants' Polo Grounds.

*Being the dog lover that I am, I really appreciated and agreed with **Joe Garigiola's** comments at the USA 1999 Westminster Dog Classic. A St. Louis native and primarily a Cardinal catcher during his MLB career, who later became a HOF sports announcer for NBC, said, "I should like to be the person my dog thinks I am."

*Whata modern thing: **Lip reading** of the pitcher on the mound talking to his catcher. Once they discovered it being done by unsportsman opponents, the pitchers started holding the glove over the television view of their mouth.

*Roger Connor's **138 career home runs** was the most by an individual in the majors until Babe Ruth arrived.

*Someone once said there has never been a revolution in the Dominican Republic during the baseball season. Baseball must be **like a religion** there.

*Giant hurler **Carl Hubbell struck out five** Hall-of-Famers-to-be in a row during the 1934 All-Star Game: Ruth, Gehrig, Foxx, Al Simmons, and Joe Cronin.

*On the subject of striking out, I checked the record books to check on five I knew personally to whom Hubbell would never have fanned in a row: Fox, Gwynn, Buckner, Appling, and Madlock. Fox had only 216 strike outs during his 9,993 trips to the plate for an amazing average of one whiff every 46.3 plate appearances, Gwynn 434-10,101: one per 23.5, Buckner 453-9,889: one per 21.8, Appling 528/10,169: one per 19.3, and Madlock 510/7,267: one per 14.2.

PPP - These, as well as most other players, would have more strike outs playing under the current check swing strike rulings. In the past, the way I remember it, if the bat on a check swing crossed the front of the plate, **with the batter's wrists broken**, then it was ruled a strike. Now, if the bat goes past the plate **without broken wrists**, it is deemed a swinging strike. With pitchers throwing 90-100 mph fast balls, a batter has to start his swing early in order to meet the ball out front of the plate, but, if he did not break his wrists, he obviously did not attempt to hit the ball. It is so asinine when the home plate umpire signals to a base ump for a check swing strike ruling and he gives the affirmative sign on an obvious negative situation, it galls me to the zenith of my anger thermometer. I have seen check swings at the shoulder level with the ball pitched in the dirt called a strike. He positively was not going for the ball and did not break his wrists, but it deemed his straight, still-cocked bat went past the front of the plate, so it will be judged a swing. I detest this ridiculous ruling on checked swings so much that, if I was young and had plenty of money, I would start a campaign urging MLB owners to ensure these particular obscure happenings in baseball be rectified. I am sure there are many millions of fans that agree with me, and certainly the players, except — of course — the pitchers.

PPP - **Advertising on outfield fences** has been in existence, I guess, ever since they have fences in MLB. I don't mind the ads although Wrigley Field vines and Fenway Park's "Green Monster" (37'2" high and 304-310' from the plate in left field) are much more pleasing to the fans. Then the batter complained about colorful ads and the crowd of colorful shirts in the background behind the pitchers that it was difficult to see the 90-100 mph fastballs. Naturally, the baseballs officials then decided to require a dark hitter's background above the centerfield fence/wall behind the pitcher's mound position. This was fine for the hitters and grandstand fans, BUT this took away advertising space in some parks. Then some of the clubs started advertising on the fences/walls behind the batters. **Holy guacamole!** This created a terrible background view of the batter, catcher, and home plate umpire. The fantastic television view of this setting to view the breaking of the ball to the plate, etc. was a very popular one for the millions of fans watching at home and in sports bars. The advertising would sometimes switch at an improper time distracting the viewer from a catcher, pitcher, or third baseman hustling to field an important bunt. To me and many of my friends, this camera view of the threesome at home plate should not have diversions at this crucial place on the field.

Football

*The innovation of allowing a few **challenges on official decisions** was a tremendous welcome by football enthusiasts such as me. It was also very much appreciated in tennis.

*Having a little experience at quarterbacking, I definitely agree with the rules they now have in roughing the passer. Just as the punter (and sometimes a pass receiver), when they are completing their job, they are in a vulnerable position and highly susceptible to serious injury due to this fact. I know football is a rough game, as it should be, but all other players have opportunity to sustain the contact and/or meet it with off-setting force of their own.

PPP - Once a QB is out of the prescribed pocket, he is allowed to **intentionally ground the ball**. An outstanding defensive player who has beaten the offensive blocker and is preparing to down the QB with a huge loss has to trot by instead. All his receivers had been diligently covered by the defenders, so he tosses it to a bare spot to eliminate an interception. Instead of a nine yard loss, the down is over and the ball goes all the way back to its previous scrimmage line. So, what does an outstanding defense unit get whose linemen forced the QB out of the pocket, have him with their grasp for a loss, and the defensive aerial unit denied open areas to the offensive receivers? A "no gain" and "loss of down." Hogwash!

PPP - Now, what if the offensive team needs to stop the clock quickly following a running play to get the field goal kicking team on the field before the end of the first half or the game. They simply rush by to a starting position and the QB takes the snap, steps back quickly and throws it to the ground for an incomplete pass to stop the clock. **Wait a minute!** This is contrary to the aforementioned **PPP** that inferred a player may not intentionally ground while still in the pocket. Tsk, tsk, tsk…pshaw, pshaw, pshaw.

About the Author

I originally planned to begin with my three trips to the Vietnam and Korean Wars, including my injury and sad losses of shipmates and friends. Then, go to my childhood, parenthood, many exciting careers, etc., etc., etc. However, it didn't take too long for me to decide the categories overlap in too many places. Hence, the chronological format of a life of a "river rat" born somewhat infamously in 1932 on the banks of Memphis. A few years later Elvis Presley arrived on the planet and eventually became internationally famous there.

Memphis, long known as the "Home of the Blues," was to become also famous as the home of the "King of Rock 'n' Roll." My first high school, Whitehaven, is only a few blocks from Elvis' Graceland. And, my Southside High "bride" and I began training our dancing shoes to the big bands of the 40s and peaked with the rocking and twisting of the 50s and 60s.

Although only a senior-to-be in high school, the Korean War found me an early enlistee. Why? Because I was a youngster almost entering teenage during World War II. Everything was thrilling about the "big one" for a boy that age. All the toys were guns, tanks, jeeps, warplanes, etc. The war movies were always exciting and, in most cases, the hero ended up with the female star. As I was a young budding teenager, females were becoming of more interest in my life. I have never met any male whose sex life began earlier than mine (older girls are great teachers). Also, the U.S. Navy aircraft pilots were my idols. Landing airplanes on a sea-going vessel was my kind of challenge. I was so "hooked" that I joined the Navy to become a fighter pilot. The recruiter was surprised at how I could identify all aircraft of nations involved in WWII. I even memorized the horsepower of power plant(s), plus the cruising and maximum speed, of each airplane. My favorite was our Corsair's F4U, a gull-winged propeller fighter. It never occurred to me until this moment, recalling this tidbit, but one of these planes almost killed me.

However, the "moonlighting" (working a civilian job at night) on shore duty between these wars helped prepare me for my career highlight era in Major League Baseball. There is no doubt about it, my "leash of life" is anchored to the sportsworld. My youth was playing or inventing sports orientated things. It gave me a second glance by people in the sportswriting and sportscasting fields. This all led to sports columnist and sports editor jobs in the newspaper business. This, along with learning the print business, was not only a challenge — which I always relished — but was mucho fun. The many hours and stress involved led to more and more alcohol. Which definitely made a "honky tonk man" out of me where there is plenty of wine, women, and song. The latter threesomes were like a personal little cloud that follows me throughout most of this autobiography.

I wasn't able to attend college fulltime until I finished my 20 years in the U.S. Navy. Finishing "With Honors" gave my mother extreme pride after her total education was a small (12 total students) high school in sticks of Mississippi. I had almost completed by Masters Degree and CA Lifetime Teachers Credential when I got into Major League Baseball and went to Chicago. It has all this covered, along with many of my photographs — including those of Chicago White Sox and Cubs personnel while heading public relations and/or promotions/marketing with them — and a little of my artwork.